WILSON:

The Road to the White House

WILSON: THE NEW FREEDOM
WILSON: THE STRUGGLE FOR NEUTRALITY, 1914-1915
WILSON: CONFUSIONS AND CRISES, 1915-1916
WILSON: CAMPAIGNS FOR PROGRESSIVISM AND PEACE

WILSON

THE ROAD TO THE
WHITE HOUSE

BY ARTHUR S. LINK

PRINCETON, NEW JERSEY

PRINCETON UNIVERSITY PRESS

FOR MARGARET

I HAVE undertaken a new study of the life of Woodrow Wilson. This volume is the first in a series that I hope eventually will constitute an historical and biographical study of Wilson and his time until his death in 1924.

I have attempted in this volume to tell one of the most amazing "success" stories that I know. Although there is an interpretive background chapter, the story begins essentially in 1902, when Woodrow Wilson takes over the presidency of Princeton University. At first there was success in great measure; but later tragedy, frustration, and despair marked the closing years of the Princeton period. And yet, Wilson's defeat at Princeton in large part made possible his subsequent political achievements. How Wilson entered public life as the godchild of a conservative political machine in New Jersey, and how he broke spiritually with the leaders of this machine and emerged from the gubernatorial campaign of 1910 one of the foremost progressive Democratic leaders is one of the miracles of modern politics. His victory over the New Jersey organization in the senatorial contest and his successful driving of the legislature of 1911 to outstanding reform accomplishments assured him a place in the coming struggle for control of the national Democratic party.

All of this would in itself constitute quite a "success" story, but it is only the beginning, the promise, of the series of events that were to follow and that conspired to catapult Wilson into the national leadership of the Democratic party and, eventually, into the White House. It is not by any means a simple story, nor an easy one to tell. It involves an account of Wilson's campaign for the presidential nomination, the subsequent struggle within the Democratic party for control of the party machinery, and the momentous conflict at Baltimore that ended in victory for the Wilson forces. It must concern itself, also, with the three-cornered presidential campaign among Wilson, Taft, and Roosevelt in the summer and fall of 1912 and, above all, with Wilson's conversion to a program that he thought would guarantee to the American people a new birth of economic freedom.

Across the pages of this book march as fascinating a series of public leaders as can be found in any period of American history: Wilson, himself the leading actor in the drama, alternately generous and sparing in his friendships, eloquent in giving expression to high ideals, yet cold, ruthless, and stubborn in personal controversies, daring and compromising in his political maneuvers, yet withal embodying a new type of leadership in American public life; George Harvey, Wilson's first political mentor, crafty, calculating, yet playing a role of major importance; James Smith, Jr. and his lieutenant, bosses of the Essex Democratic faction in New Jersey, responsible for giving Wilson the gubernatorial nomination in 1910, yet his implacable foes only six months later; the small group of men who first engineered the Wilson-for-President movement in 1911 and carried it through to victory in 1912—William F. McCombs, Walter H. Page, William G. McAdoo, and later, the unobtrusive Texan, Edward M. House; William J. Bryan, the passionate champion of rural democracy; Champ Clark, the hard-hating speaker of the House of Representatives, who almost thwarted Wilson's efforts to control the Democratic party; Henry Watterson, "Marse Henry" of Louisville, a character from the ante-bellum South; Theodore Roosevelt, the impassioned champion of social justice in 1912.

On numerous occasions I have felt compelled to disagree with most of the previous Wilson biographers. Our disagreement has often been fundamental with regard to both facts and interpretations. I have had, however, access to a great body of new materials, much of which has not before been available to scholars. Many of my findings have necessitated a radical reevaluation and reinterpretation of important events. On the other hand, I have been extremely cautious in formulating new interpretations and opinions and have come to them only after carefully weighing and sifting all the evidence.

My objectives and methods have been exceedingly simple. To give a straightforward and accurate account of Wilson's educational and political career before the White House, to explain, in so far as my capacity allows, the reasons for events that did occur, and to portray the larger setting against which these events took place—these have been my objectives. My methods have been those of an historical scholar attempting a systematic investigation of all the available sources relating to the subject.

I have tried to maintain throughout a critical and open attitude toward all the controversies with which I dealt. There was something about Woodrow Wilson that inevitably engendered controversy when he occupied positions of power and influence. Wilson was a headstrong and determined man who was usually able to rationalize his actions in terms of the moral law and to identify his position with the divine will. This combination of strong, almost imperious will and intense conviction operated to great advantage when Wilson had support among the trustees at Princeton, the legislators at Trenton, or the congressmen in Washington, because it gave him great power and an impelling drive. The time came at Princeton, Trenton, and Washington when Wilson did not command the support of the groups to whom he was responsible. Naturally, he was not able to change his character even had he wanted to change it, with the result that controversy and disastrous defeat occurred in varying degrees in all three cases.

Much of the book, therefore, concerns controversy of one kind or another. I have not come at my subject with the idea of debunking Wilson or anyone else. On the other hand, I have refrained from taking anything for granted, weighed and measured evidence against evidence, and in controversial matters have accepted no statement of fact that could not be supported by sound evidence. That has meant at times accepting the statements of Wilson's opponents instead of accepting his own.

There has been no paucity of materials in writing this volume. Although not all the manuscript collections are now available which will in the future undoubtedly come to light, I think that we now have abundant evidence upon which to construct an accurate account. With the exception of Wilson's letters to Ellen Axson Wilson and Mary Allen Hulbert (many of which have already been published), I was allowed to use in their entirety the Wilson Papers in the Library of Congress. They of course constituted my starting point of research and my most valuable source of information. The collection of Wilson materials made by the late Ray Stannard Baker was also opened to me and was an invaluable source, second in importance only to the Wilson manuscripts. Numerous other manuscript collections yielded new and important information, particularly the collections in the Princeton University Library relating to the graduate college controversy; the Edward M. House Papers at Yale University and the William Garrot Brown Papers at Duke University, which were extremely useful for the pre-nomination campaign of 1911-1912; and the papers of Jane Addams, Theodore Roosevelt, and William Howard Taft in the Library of Congress, which afforded much new information about the presidential campaign of 1912.

The great body of newspapers for this period has gone relatively untouched by Wilson scholars. For my part, I found the newspapers a source of information in many respects as important as the manuscript materials. Newspapers, for example, are the only source of all of Wilson's speeches during the period 1910-1912. For the New Jersey period I have relied heavily on the *Trenton Evening Times*, the *Trenton True American*, the *Jersey Journal* of Jersey City, the *Newark Evening News*, and the *Newark Evening Star*, as well as the New York newspapers. For the pre-nomination and presidential campaigns I have sampled newspapers representative of all shades of opinion throughout the country. My chief source of information, to be sure, has been the New York newspapers, the greatest of which was the *New York World*; but I have also relied heavily on a number of excellent southern and mid-western newspapers, chief among which were the *Raleigh News and Observer*, the *Birmingham Age-Herald*, the *Baltimore Sun*, the *Dallas Morning News*, the *Kansas City Star*, the *St. Louis Republic*, and the *Daily Oklahoman* of Oklahoma City.

Of the number of contemporary periodicals that I used the *Nation* should be mentioned first, because it afforded a partial key to the problem of the origins of Wilson's political ideas. For the Princeton period the one great periodical source is the *Princeton Alumni Weekly* —truly an indispensable storehouse of information. In so far as I know, I have examined all periodicals that are in any way relevant to the New Jersey period, 1910-1912, and the presidential campaigns of 1911-1912. Among the great variety of periodicals that I have used the following should be mentioned because of their significance in representing various groups and points of view: *Harper's Weekly*, edited by George Harvey, the first journalistic supporter of the Wilson presidential movement; *Collier's Weekly*, the leading independent progressive journal of general interest, of additional importance because Norman Hapgood, friend of Louis D. Brandeis and Wilson, was editor; *World's Work*, edited by another early Wilson supporter, Walter H. Page; the *Commoner* and *La Follette's Weekly Magazine*, spokesmen of Bryan and La Follette; the *Outlook*, the weekly editorial stump for Theodore Roosevelt; the *Crisis*, representing Negro opinion, and the *American Federationist*, organ of the American Federation of Labor; and, finally, William Randolph Hearst's *Hearst's Magazine* and the *World To-Day*, and Thomas E. Watson's *Jeffersonian*, all clearing houses of the journalistic attack on Wilson's presidential candidacy.

Memoirs and autobiographies, often so important in getting at the undercover activities of politicians, have contributed surprisingly little to my story, chiefly because most of the autobiographers of the Wilson period concentrate on the period after 1912. Tumulty's famous account, *Woodrow Wilson As I Know Him*, is not entirely reliable and must be used with great caution. Josephus Daniels' recent book, *The Wilson Era, Years of Peace*, is interesting but not very informative about the earlier period because Daniels was usually on the periphery of the scene of action. The *Intimate Papers of Colonel House* contains many valuable documents, but the student will find them all, and much additional material that is often more important, in the House Papers at Yale.

Two exceptions to the generalization about memoirs should be made, however, and heavily underscored. The first is James Kerney's *The Political Education of Woodrow Wilson*, ostensibly a biography of Wilson, but actually more an account of events about which Kerney had first-hand knowledge. The book is unmarred by any evidences of hero-worshiping and stands almost alone as one of the early and yet critical studies of Wilson. The second exception is William O. Inglis's account of Wilson's relations with George Harvey, 1906-1912. So important is this memoir that without it many things that would otherwise be inexplicable are made clear.

In the preparation of this book I have surveyed the entire field of Wilson biographies. But I have worked almost entirely from original sources and, excepting Baker's *Life and Letters*, have not had occasion to lean on any of the other Wilson biographies. Mr. Baker has done for Wilson's early personal life a job that will not have to be done again, except in so far as the origins and development of Wilson's political thought are concerned. Of the one-volume biographies, I think Herbert Bell's *Woodrow Wilson and the People* is the best. Mr. Bell and I would probably disagree on many points, but I think that he has done an excellent job and has come closer to getting at the reasons for the failures of Wilson's friendships than any other writer.

Doing the research and writing on this book has brought me into close association with many persons who have generously and freely given of their time and energies to help me. It is my pleasant duty, therefore, to recognize my deep indebtedness to them.

I owe my first interest in Woodrow Wilson to Professor Chester M. Destler, now of Connecticut College, whose lectures I attended at the University of North Carolina. For my doctoral dissertation at the same institution I prepared a thesis on the South and the Democratic campaign of 1910-1912 under the direction of Professor Fletcher

M. Green. By his patient guidance and intellectual disciplining he contributed much to my understanding of the period about which I have written in this volume, and I wish to acknowledge my lasting indebtedness to him.

From 1944 through 1946 I was engaged primarily in building the present study upon the foundation of my dissertation. Nine months were spent as a visiting student in the seminar of Professor Henry Steele Commager at Columbia University, where the first seven chapters were read in rough draft. Professor Commager subsequently read all of this study in manuscript form and made numerous stimulating comments that were helpful.

I am grateful for the wise suggestions that Professor Thomas J. Wertenbaker of Princeton University made with reference to Chapters II and III. He has influenced in a much greater way than he knows the formation of my ideas with regard to Wilson's Princeton career. Professor Joseph R. Strayer of Princeton also read these chapters and made a number of helpful suggestions; I am grateful also for his unflagging support and encouragement while I was writing this book.

To Miss Katharine E. Brand, custodian of the Wilson Papers in the Library of Congress, I want to express my thanks for reading the entire manuscript and for all her help during the period when I worked in the Manuscripts Division.

To Mr. Datus C. Smith, Jr., director of the Princeton University Press, I owe a great debt of gratitude for the support and encouragement that he has given me since the spring of 1944 when we first met. Moreover, his editing of the manuscript did a great deal to improve it.

To Professor Howard K. Beale of the University of North Carolina must go much of the credit for whatever value this book may have. He not only read the entire manuscript at a time when he was overwhelmed by other duties, but he also edited it as carefully as if it had been his own. We may still disagree on some points, but I think he will see on reading the book how deeply his ideas influenced my own.

I wish to express my gratitude to the Julius Rosenwald Fund for two research grants made in 1942 and 1944. Without the financial support of this foundation I could not have brought this study to fruition.

I wish also to express my appreciation to the following persons: to Mrs. Woodrow Wilson, for permission to use the Wilson Papers; to Messrs. St. George L. Sioussat, chief, and Thomas P. Martin, assistant chief, of the Manuscripts Division, the Library of Congress, for their help in using other manuscript collections in their department; to Mr. Julian P. Boyd, for permission to use the collections in the Princeton University Library, and to Miss Lillian Blease of the Library's Treasure Room for her assistance in using these materials; to Mr. Russell G. Pruden of the Yale University Library, for his hospitality and helpfulness when I worked through the House Papers; to Mr. Oswald Garrison Villard of New York City, who helped me to clarify the subject of Wilson's relations with the Negro leaders in 1912 and who generously opened his own private papers to me; and, finally, to Miss Nannie M. Tilley, of the Duke University Library, for her assistance in Wilson and other matters relating to my research.

To my wife, Margaret Douglas Link, I owe the greatest debt of all. She has been my own best critic in all matters relating to this book and a constant source of inspiration, encouragement, and understanding. In many respects this book is our joint enterprise.

A. S. L.

Princeton, New Jersey
October 21, 1946

CONTENTS

⟨W|ILLUSTRATIONS|W⟩

CHAPTER I

The Formative Years

By something like an historical accident, Thomas Woodrow Wilson was born a Virginian. His father, Joseph Ruggles Wilson, a youthful Ohio printer turned preacher, was the son of a Scotch-Irish immigrant; his mother, Jessie Woodrow, was born in Carlisle, England, daughter of a Presbyterian minister. Woodrow Wilson was proud of his ancestors and his Scottish, Covenanter tradition; he once declared, "The stern Covenanter tradition that is behind me sends many an echo down the years." [1] Joseph Ruggles Wilson had moved with his young wife in the early 1850's to teach at Hampden-Sydney College in Virginia. In 1855 he became minister of the First Presbyterian Church in Staunton, and it was in the Manse in that town, on December 28, 1856, that Woodrow Wilson was born.[2]

In November 1857 the Reverend Dr. Wilson moved from Staunton to Augusta, Georgia, and his family followed him shortly afterward. So it was in Augusta that Woodrow Wilson first became cognizant of his environment. "My earliest recollection is of standing at my father's gateway in Augusta, Georgia, when I was four years old, and hearing some one pass and say that Mr. Lincoln was elected and there was to be war. Catching the intense tones of his excited voice, I remember running in to ask my father what it meant." [3]

It was during the holocaust of civil war and the confusion of Reconstruction that the boy matured. Augusta was an important center of Confederate manufactures, and Joseph R. Wilson was an ardent proponent of the southern cause. His church was transformed into a hospital; the churchyard became a prison stockade for Union troops; on one occasion he even dismissed his congregation with the admoni-

---

[1] Speech at Mansion House, London, December 28, 1918.

[2] In later years Wilson was not insensible to family pride. Commenting on a news report which mistakenly described him as the scion of an old Virginia family, he declared that of course it was not true; but, he added, "I wish I could say it were." Winthrop M. Daniels, MS Memorandum in the Ray Stannard Baker Papers, Library of Congress; hereinafter cited as Baker Papers.

[3] "Abraham Lincoln: A Man of the People," Address at Chicago, February 12, 1909. R. S. Baker and William E. Dodd (eds.), *The Public Papers of Woodrow Wilson*, II, 83; hereinafter cited as *Public Papers*.

tion that they go and work in the Confederate arsenal.[4] After the disruption of the Presbyterian Church in 1861, the southern body was organized in Wilson's church in Augusta, and he became its permanent clerk. It was more the backwash of war, however, the wounded soldiers, the demoralization of southern life, and the breakdown of the economic and social order, that Woodrow Wilson saw. All of these concomitants of war made an indelible impression on him and left him with an abhorrence of bloodshed. At a later time and during a greater war he would be accused by his enemies of being a pacifist because he was "too proud to fight"!

But all was not of confusion and disorder. Life made its accustomed rounds in the South, even during war and Reconstruction, and Wilson's boyhood was notable, if for nothing else, because of his normal development. He had a remarkable family and especially an unusual father. As Wilson wrote many years later, "after all, no man comes from the people in general. We are each of us derived from some small group of persons in particular; and unless we were too poor to have any family life at all, it is the life and associations of the family that have chiefly shaped us in our youth."[5] Joseph R. Wilson was a scholarly man and a great preacher who carefully superintended the intellectual development of his son. He had a caustic wit and was his son's best critic for many years. Wilson's mother was more reserved than his father, but she was a woman of decided opinion and of stubborn conviction. Wilson, then, inherited from his family, and especially acquired from his southern environment, many of his most characteristic traits. He was always typically a southern gentleman, "too proud to fight," too proud to reply to his enemies, too proud to stoop to undignified campaign practices. He inherited the contemporary southern disdain for career women. He was always in complete accord with southern, and especially Presbyterian, orthodoxy; yet he was never bigoted or intolerant of agnostics or persons of other faiths.

In later life Wilson developed a romantic and extravagant love for the South of legend and song. His letters and addresses are full of expressions of deep feeling for the region. He was one historian, for example, who was not apologetic about the South's history. On one occasion he declared that there was "nothing to apologize for in the past of the South—absolutely nothing to apologize for."[6] Wilson, furthermore,

[4] Ray S. Baker, *Woodrow Wilson: Life and Letters*, I, 50-51; hereinafter cited as *Woodrow Wilson*.
[5] "Mr. Cleveland as President," *Atlantic Monthly*, LXXIX (March 1897), 289.
[6] *Annual Report of the American Historical Association*, 1896, p. 295.

was a Southerner who was frankly proud that the South had taken up arms against the North in 1861. Should Southerners, since they were a decided minority, have given in to the will of the majority of the North, he once asked. Not at all, he replied. Men's consciences and habits of thought lie deeper than that; the year 1861 was not a time to talk about majorities—it was a time to express convictions. Even a man who saw the end from the beginning should, as a Southerner, have voted for spending his people's blood and his own, rather than pursue the weak course of expediency. These words, it should be noted, are not the effusions of a schoolboy; they were delivered in 1909.[7] Wilson, however, never expressed a burning enthusiasm for the Lost Cause such as his father often expressed. Only fifteen years after the end of the Civil War, he frankly declared, "*because* I love the South, I rejoice in the failure of the Confederacy."[8]

Well might one ask in what ways Woodrow Wilson was a Southerner. His residence in the region for almost twenty-four years left its imprint strong upon him. As he once declared, it is all very well to talk of detachment of view and of the effort to be national in spirit, "but a boy never gets over his boyhood, and never can change those subtle influences which have become a part of him." He felt obliged to say again and again, "the only place in the country, the only place in the world, where nothing has to be explained to me is the South."[9] Wilson early espoused the southern views on the tariff, and he even followed Calhoun in doubting the constitutionality of the protective system.[10] He was characteristically a Southerner in his attitude toward the Negro. Like most Southerners of the upper class, his tolerance of and kindliness to the Negro were motivated by a strong paternalistic feeling.[11]

Woodrow Wilson's educational career began inauspiciously at a

[7] *Robert E. Lee: An Interpretation*, pp. 28-29. [8] "John Bright," *ibid.*, I, 56-57.

[9] *Robert E. Lee: An Interpretation*, p. v.

[10] See, e.g., his speech accepting the Democratic nomination in 1912, *Official Proceedings of the Democratic National Convention of 1912*, p. 404.

[11] Almost all of Wilson's biographers testify that he was essentially a Southerner. One has characterized him as a Southerner at large (James Kerney, *The Political Education of Woodrow Wilson*, p. 4); another notes the effect southern religiosity had upon him (William Allen White, *Woodrow Wilson*, pp. 63-64); an historian writes of the influence of his heritage of Virginia traditions absorbed at the law school of the University of Virginia (Matthew Josephson, *The President Makers*, p. 345). In his autobiography, Henry Watterson sardonically remarks that Wilson was born to the rather sophisticated culture of the Solid South. "Had he grown up in England a hundred years ago," Watterson added, "he would have been a follower of the Della Cruscans" (*"Marse Henry," an Autobiography*, II, p. 274).

Wilson's highly colored illusions about the South were heightened by long periods

school in Augusta conducted by a former Confederate officer, Joseph T. Derry. His boyhood friends were an unusual group and included several men who later became famous—Joseph R. Lamar,[12] Pleasant A. Stovall,[13] Thomas R. Gibson,[14] and William A. Keener.[15] In 1870 Wilson's father accepted a call to the Columbia Theological Seminary and the family moved to the South Carolina capital. Columbia had been largely destroyed by fire in 1865 after Sherman's march through the city, and in 1870 the state was completely in the hands of the Radical Reconstructionists. "Tommy" Wilson continued his education in a private school conducted by Charles N. Barnwell until his family moved to Wilmington, North Carolina, in 1874. In 1873 he had something of a religious experience and was admitted to membership in the Columbia church.[16]

Until Wilson entered college in 1873 his education had been more or less informal. Family group reading was a frequent pastime in the home and before he learned to read, Wilson heard his father read from Dickens or Sir Walter Scott; and there was always the Bible, "the 'Magna Charta' of the human soul," read daily at family prayers. Apparently the first book Wilson read was Parson Weems' famous *Life of Wash-*

of absence from the region. On one occasion he told the members of the Virginia State Bar Association that he felt the sort of exhilaration that must always come to a man "who returns from a distance to breathe his native air again and mix once more with those to whom he feels bound by a sort of intellectual consanguinity." He was proud of Virginia's traditions, for, in Virginia, among men of his "own race and breeding," he could speak his mind frankly upon any theme. "Nowhere else," thought Wilson, "has the pure strain of the nation which planted the colonies and made the independent government under which we live been kept so without taint or mixture as it has been in Virginia, and hitherto in all the South" (*Public Papers*, I, 336-337). On another occasion he declared that there had been in the South a special characteristic all its own —a strong spirit of individualism—"no doubt the jealous regard for the dignity and independence of the individual." Southern life had been formed by a singular combination of strong individuality mixed with common ideals, Wilson declared. "In the South a community produces a man, the man embodies his neighbors and their loyalty went out to him and hung to him as a matter of course" (quoted in *Norfolk Virginian-Pilot*, December 15, 1910). Wilson confessed that, after long periods of absence, he forgot how natural it was to be in the South, "and then the moment I come, and see old friends again, and discover a country full of reminiscences which connect me with my parents, and with all the old memories, I know again the region to which I naturally belong" (*Robert E. Lee*, p. vi).

[12] Appointed to the Supreme Court in 1911 by President Taft.
[13] Appointed Minister to Switzerland by President Wilson.
[14] Afterwards United States Consul at Beirut.
[15] Afterwards Dean of the Law School of Columbia University.
[16] R. S. Baker, *Woodrow Wilson*, I, 66-67.

ington. Joseph R. Wilson had for some time been a subscriber to the *Edinburgh Review* and the New York *Nation,* and before he went to college Wilson had become intensely interested in British politics. Gladstone became a hero to him, and he placed a portrait of the British "Great Commoner" above his desk.[17]

In the fall of 1873 Wilson left home for the first time and went to college. He and his family decided upon Davidson, a small but intensely Presbyterian college in Piedmont North Carolina. He was poorly prepared and the year was something of a struggle; his chief interest was in the Eumenean Society, a debating club, for which he prepared a new constitution. Wilson's health seriously deteriorated and he returned to Columbia in June 1874. The family moved to Wilmington in the fall and there he remained, a shy and timid youth, until the following year, when he decided that he was sufficiently prepared to enter Princeton.

In September 1875 Wilson journeyed to the village of Princeton to enter the College of New Jersey. He was a complete stranger in the community, but he soon fell in with southern friends and joined with them in defending the South. The academic work was hard and the first year was in many respects gruelling, but he found at Princeton the intellectual prodding and friendships that he needed for his personal development. "Wilson's second year at college was among the most important of his whole life: a turning-point," Baker writes.[18] He read *The Federalist* for the first time, Greene's *Short History of the English People,* Macaulay's *History of England,* the speeches of Burke and John Bright, and the essays of Walter Bagehot. He discovered also the *Gentleman's Magazine.* And in 1877 he published his first article; strangely enough, it was about Bismarck.[19]

Debating and oratory—the manipulation of words—had an early fascination for Wilson, and he stoutly defended the art at Princeton.[20] He was an active member of the Whig Society but also organized a debating club of his own. A prize essay on the elder Pitt was published in 1878.[21] His fellow students soon found, however, that despite appearances Wilson was no pedant and was as eager to engage in college activities as any student; but the "play of the mind," writes Robert Bridges, was exhilarating to him. It was as natural for him to talk about

[17] *ibid.,* pp. 35-37, 57.　　　　[18] *ibid.,* p. 86.
[19] "Prince Bismarck," *Nassau Literary Magazine,* XXXIII (November 1877), 118-127.
[20] See, e.g., an article in the *Princetonian,* June 7, 1877.
[21] "William Earl Chatham," *Nassau Literary Magazine,* XXXIV (October 1878), 99-105.

Burke, Brougham, or Bagehot, as for the rest of his friends to talk about Cooper or Mayne Reid.[22] He often thought of the future and what it held in store for him and formed a "solemn covenant" with a fellow-student to "school all our powers and passions for the work of establishing the principles we held in common; that we would acquire knowledge that we might have power." [23] He grew confident of his mental abilities, envisaged an active political career for himself, and even wrote out a number of cards with the inscription: "Thomas Woodrow Wilson, Senator from Virginia."

Wilson, then, as an undergraduate became absorbed in the study of politics, and while he was a senior published his first article in a national magazine. He pondered the causes for the decline of American statesmanship and oratory and concluded that the root of the trouble was to be found "in the absorption of all power by a legislature which is practically irresponsible for its acts." [24] The idea of responsible government would later be foremost in his political philosophy. In 1879 he proposed to restore responsible government in the United States by inaugurating a modified form of the parliamentary system in Congress; he would do this by giving Cabinet members seats in Congress and by holding them responsible for the passage of legislation.[25]

During the Princeton undergraduate years and the hours of his day-dreaming, the young scholar had often thought of himself as "Senator from Virginia," or even sometimes as governor of his native commonwealth. It was natural, therefore, that when he was graduated from Princeton in 1879 he should turn toward the University of Virginia for training in his chosen profession of law. The head of the Virginia law school, John B. Minor, was widely known as a scholar and professor; to the end of his life Wilson thought of him as one of the greatest men he had known and, next to his father, his greatest teacher. "The profession I chose was politics," he later wrote, "the profession I entered was the law. I entered the one because I thought it would lead to the other." [26]

Wilson engaged in student activities even more energetically at Virginia than at Princeton. He had come to study law, and study it he did

---

[22] Robert Bridges, *Woodrow Wilson, A Personal Tribute*, p. 3.
[23] W. W. to Ellen Axson, October 30, 1883, R. S. Baker, *Woodrow Wilson*, 1, 103-104.
[24] "Cabinet Government in the United States," *International Review*, VII (August 1879), 147.
[25] *ibid.*, pp. 150-163. For the origins of Wilson's ideas see *infra*, * * * pp. 15-19.
[26] W. W. to Ellen Axson, October 30, 1883, R. S. Baker, *Woodrow Wilson*, 1, 109.

in a desultory manner, only to find that he was "most terribly bored by the noble study of Law." [27] He did not, however, neglect his reading in history, political science, and literature.[28] He of course became a member of the Jefferson Society, a college debating organization, and in March 1880 he delivered a memorable address before the society in which he proclaimed his faith in American nationalism. More significant, however, was his discussion of the Manchester Liberal school of free traders and the fulsome praise he gave them.[29] A month later, in a debate with William Cabell Bruce, he endeavored to persuade the members of the society that Roman Catholicism was not a menace to American civilization.[30]

Wilson in 1880 was elected president of the Jefferson Society and soon was busy framing a new constitution for the organization. He was, however, also interested in practical politics and in the larger events that were occurring in the nation. In October 1880, for example, he wrote to a Princeton friend that the Republican party was degraded and in the throes of disintegration. But he had little more respect for the Democrats, whom he accused of allying themselves "with every damnable heresy—with Greenbackers as with protectionists," and concluded that "such a state of things is premonitory of some great change to come." [31]

At Virginia Wilson also formed one of his most intimate friendships —with Richard Heath Dabney;[32] and there he also studied with Richard E. Byrd, who, years later, led in the Wilson movement in Virginia in 1912, and with John Bassett Moore and William Cabell Bruce. But the overwhelming burden of scholastic work and college activity was too heavy for Wilson's frail physique, and he was forced to abandon his formal studies. Regretfully he left the University and went home to Wilmington, where he carried on his legal studies for an additional year and a half.

After innumerable hesitations as to a place for practice, Wilson and his father at length decided upon Atlanta, Georgia. As Wilson wrote to

[27] W. W. to Charles A. Talcott, December 31, 1879, Baker Papers.
[28] His reading included Wirt's *Life of Henry,* Jebb's *Attic Orators,* Stubb's *Constitutional England,* Shelley's poems, Lecky's *England in the Eighteenth Century,* Goodrich's *British Eloquence,* and Parson's *Contracts.* R. S. Baker, *Woodrow Wilson,* I, 117.
[29] "John Bright," *University of Virginia Magazine,* XIX (March 1880), 354-370.
[30] Abstract, printed in *ibid.,* XIX (April 1880), 448-450.
[31] W. W. to Charles A. Talcott, October 11, 1880, Baker Papers.
[32] Wilson's letters to Dabney, among the most interesting and illuminating he ever wrote, are in the Library of the University of Virginia.

an intimate friend, Atlanta, more than almost any other southern city, offered all the advantages of business activity and enterprise. There were, besides, many reasons why he should remain in the South, he thought. "I am familiar with Southern life and manners, for one thing —and of course a man's mind may be expected to grow most freely in its native air." Besides, he declared, the South had just begun to grow industrially; the region was becoming roused to a new work and waking to a new life. "There appear to be no limits to the possibilities of her development," he concluded.[33] Wilson arrived in Atlanta in June 1882, and immediately entered into a partnership with Edward Ireland Renick, whom he had known slightly at the University of Virginia. The infant firm of Renick & Wilson, however, was never besieged with clients. Many young lawyers had come to Atlanta for the same reasons that Wilson had, and, in fact, the growing city was overabundantly supplied with members of the profession. Wilson was admitted to the bar in October 1882; during the first difficult year his practice amounted to the defense of a Negro upon request of the court and the care of some legal matters for his family.

In September 1882, the United States Tariff Commission, which was then traveling about the country taking evidence, came to Atlanta. A friend of Renick's, Walter Hines Page, was in Atlanta reporting the doings of the Commission for the *New York World*. In a dingy little office on Marietta Street, Wilson and Page first met. They were both young ardent Southerners with much the same point of view. Both were weary of the outworn shibboleths of the South, and just as impatient with the new order of things; and both were intense in their hostility to the protective tariff. The trouble all along, they both agreed, had been that no one had enunciated any broad principles; there was too much concern for individual gain from the protective system; the public was unrepresented.[34] In no time at all Page discovered Wilson's deep interest in the tariff question "and considerable acquaintance with the issues involved," and persuaded Wilson to address the Commission.[35] At the hearing of the Commission the next morning, Wilson advocated the repeal of all protective laws and contended that "manufacturers are made better manufacturers whenever they are thrown

[33] W. W. to Charles A. Talcott, September 22, 1881, Baker Papers.
[34] W. W. to R. H. Dabney, January 11, 1883, Dabney Papers, Library of the University of Virginia; hereinafter cited as Dabney Papers.
[35] *ibid*.

upon their own resources and left to the natural competition of trade." [36]
In practical pursuance of this idea, he organized soon afterward in Atlanta a branch of the Free Trade Club of New York.[37]

On one occasion Wilson visited the Georgia Senate, and the proceedings of the day left a vivid impression on his mind. The lawmakers were engaged in a discussion provoked by the suggestion of Gustavus J. Orr, superintendent of education, that the state was quite able to double or treble its expenditures for schools. Only a small minority favored the proposal. The majority thrust it aside with a resolution that the representatives and senators of the state in Washington be requested to do all in their power to secure a grant from the federal treasury for support of state educational systems. The Blair bill, an early federal aid-to-education scheme, was then under discussion in Congress. Wilson heard only one speech in opposition to "this begging resolution," but he considered it a sturdy appeal to the self-respect and independence of the state. No one seemed to regard it worth while to answer this argument and the resolution was carried. "The whole proceeding impressed me as a shameless declaration of the determination, on the part of a well-to-do community, to enjoy the easy position of a beneficiary of the national govt. to the fullest possible extent," Wilson wrote indignantly several years later.[38]

The young lawyer had ample time for reading and he compensated for lack of legal business by indulging his liking for history and literature. "I allow myself my afternoons for writing—and for reading on my old and loved topics, history and political science; devouring Houghton, Mifflin, and Co's *American Statesmen* series, and Macmillan's *English Citizen* series—both altogether to my taste," he wrote.[39] He also con-

---

[36] *Public Papers*, I, 93. "I made a small beginning towards establishing a local reputation by making a half-hour speech before the Tariff Commission when it sat here," Wilson also wrote. "I did not know that notable and farcical body was to sit in Atlanta until it was actually in town, and had not had the most remote idea, of course, of going before it. But along with the Commission came that smart fellow Walter Page, the *World's* correspondent, a great friend of my partner's, and he it was who induced me to speak, promising a good notice in his letter to the *World,* and arguing that whilst I could not expect to make any impression on the asses of the Commission, I would be sure of having the stenographic report of my remarks embodied in the report to Congress, *there,* possibly, to attract some attention." W. W. to Robert Bridges, October 28, 1882, the Wilson-Bridges Correspondence, Library of Princeton University; hereinafter cited as Bridges Papers.

[37] W. W. to R. H. Dabney, January 11, 1883, Dabney Papers.

[38] W. W. to Robert Bridges, February 27, 1886, Bridges Papers.

[39] W. W. to Robert Bridges, October 28, 1882, *ibid.*

ceived a plan for a "Georgia House of Commons"—another debating club, and another opportunity to write a constitution!—but did not follow through this idea.[40] In February 1883 he wrote a short descriptive article on the Georgia convict-lease system for the *New York Evening Post* and an article on American congressional government for the New York *Nation;* both articles were rejected.

By chance Wilson happened to go to Rome, Georgia, in April 1883 on legal business for his mother. It was there that he met his future wife, Ellen Louise Axson, daughter of a Presbyterian minister, a student of art, a lover of literature and music, a kind and gentle woman. A whirlwind courtship soon was in the making, and by September they were engaged. The engagement "was in many ways the most important experience of Woodrow Wilson's life," Baker writes.[41] Certainly Ellen Axson's influence in determining the course of Wilson's life was immeasurable, for love and courtship helped him to "find himself out." As he later observed from his own experience, "A man who lives only for himself has not begun to live—has yet to learn his use, and his real pleasure too, in the world. It is not necessary he should marry to find himself out, but it is necessary he should love." [42]

Wilson's love for the South, however, was scarcely enhanced by his stay in Atlanta; actually, his liking for the region increased in direct ratio to the length of his absence from it. To an imaginative young man such as Woodrow Wilson, the barren, humdrum life of the New South was completely disillusioning. Atlanta especially was a center of the new business and industrial life of the region in the early 1880's and was filled with self-made men who had little use for a would-be political philosopher. Wilson, moreover, had earned practically nothing and was conscious of the financial burden he was causing his father. He discovered, furthermore, that the practice of law was not what he had thought. Its "practice . . . for the purposes of gain" he thought was "antagonistic to the best interests of the intellectual life." The philosophical study of the law was a very different matter from its scheming and haggling practice. His plain necessity, then, he wrote Richard H. Dabney, was some profession which would afford him a moderate income, favorable conditions for study, and considerable leisure. What better could he do, therefore, than be a professor, "a lecturer upon subjects whose study most delights me?" He had applied for a fellowship

---

[40] W. W. to R. H. Dabney, January 11, 1883, Dabney Papers.

[41] R. S. Baker, *Woodrow Wilson,* I, 164.

[42] "When a Man Comes to Himself," *Century Magazine,* LXII (June 1901), 269.

at the Johns Hopkins University, and that failing, he would go to Baltimore anyway. In Atlanta, he declared, the chief end of man was certainly to make money—"and money cannot be made except by the most vulgar methods." [43]

In going to the Johns Hopkins, Woodrow Wilson not only abandoned the practice of law; he also gave up for good, he thought, his ambition to enter politics. Professors could not participate in political affairs, he admitted, but he was now content to become "an *outside* force in politics," and was "well enough satisfied with the prospect of having whatever influence . . . [he] might be able to exercise make itself felt through literary and non-partisan agencies." [44] On September 18, 1883, two days after he became engaged to Ellen Axson, Wilson arrived in Baltimore.

At first Wilson rebelled at the schedule of courses he was required to take at the Johns Hopkins and complained of having to study "institutional history." [45] The most interesting feature of the graduate program at the University was the seminar conducted by Professor Herbert Baxter Adams. It was a remarkable group of men (including Adams, Wilson, Richard T. Ely, J. Franklin Jameson, Albert Shaw, and Davis R. Dewey) who gathered around the table in the seminar room during Wilson's day; yet after five months' residence at the University, Wilson was disappointed and dissatisfied. Adams, one of the patriarchs of American historians, he described as a "disciple of Machiavelli . . . who . . . is on the high road to preferment, even though his pupils starve, the while, on a very meagre diet of ill-served lectures." Wilson had come "to admire" and had "remained to scoff." [46]

[43] W. W. to R. H. Dabney, May 11, 1883, Dabney Papers. One is tempted to believe that had Wilson been successful in his law practice he might have had an altogether different attitude toward it. It was evident that he had been a failure as a lawyer, and for the rest of his life he tended to look with contempt upon lawyers as a class.

Wilson's attitude with regard to Georgia during the early 1880's was also colored by his unhappy experience in Atlanta. "I can never be happy unless I am enabled to lead an intellectual life," he wrote in May 1883; "and who can lead an intellectual life in ignorant Georgia? I have come deliberately into the opinion that northern Georgia is altogether a very remarkable quarter of the globe. In southern Georgia, which was settled long before this portion of the State was reclaimed from the Indians [!], there is much culture and refinement. . . . But hereabouts culture is very little esteemed; not, indeed, at all because it is a drug on the market, but because there is so little of it that its good qualities are not appreciated." W. W. to R. H. Dabney, May 11, 1883, Dabney Papers.

[44] W. W. to Ellen Axson, February 24, 1885, R. S. Baker, *Woodrow Wilson*, I, 170-171.

[45] W. W. to Ellen Axson, *ibid.*, I, 174.

[46] W. W. to R. H. Dabney, February 17, 1884, Dabney Papers.

Wilson soon, however, revised his opinion of Adams, especially when the professor freed him from the study of institutional development and gave him free rein to develop his own ideas about his dissertation. The young scholar also began, with Ely and Dewey, a history of American economic thought which was completed but never published. Wilson wrote one-third of the study and discussed the economic thought of seven "American text writers of the orthodox Ricardian school."[47] He also began work on his study of the American governmental system and, in January 1884, published a preliminary article on the subject.[48] And within a short time he had become a member of the Johns Hopkins Glee Club and the Hopkins Literary Society, for which he wrote a new constitution.[49] Under the careful tutelage of Ellen Axson, his literary interests became considerably broadened and he read in Ruskin, Swinburne's *Tristam,* Birrell's *Obiter Dicta,* Arnold, and Wordsworth.[50]

Walter Bagehot, "our most astute English critic," wrote an essay on the British Constitution in the late 1860's that so excited Wilson's admiration that he determined to write a similar treatise on the American system of government.[51] It was indeed an old interest with him, as his earlier publications testify, and the recent history of Reconstruction and the consequent post-war demoralization must have shaken his faith in the American constitutional structure. "I want to contribute to our literature," he explained, "what no American has ever contributed, studies

[47] W. W. to R. H. Dabney, February 14, 1885, *ibid.* There is a copy of the manuscript in the Baker Papers.

[48] "Committee or Cabinet Government?" *Overland Monthly,* III (January 1884), 17-33.

[49] W. W. to Ellen Axson, February 2, December 18, 1884, R. S. Baker, *Woodrow Wilson,* I, 190-191, 199.

[50] Wilson's general reading, however, was desultory, spasmodic, and his judgments on literature were usually arbitrary. He liked Swinburne's *Tristam,* for example, but never read much of Swinburne. Arnold's "Dover Beach" and "Rugby Chapel" were two of his favorite poems, yet he did not read all of Arnold's poetical works and disapproved of Arnold's literary and theological criticism. The same was true of his liking for Wordsworth: he read a few of Wordsworth's poems and liked them immensely. He had an early love for Shakespeare, Browning, and Shelley, but Keats was his favorite poet. Byron he loathed, perhaps because Byron shocked his sense of respectability. In the field of the novel Jane Austen, Scott, Mary N. Murfree, and Stanley Weyman were among his favorites. He thought *Lorna Doone* ranked "amongst our 'classics.'" R. S. Baker, "Memorandum of Conversations with Stockton Axson, February 8, 10, and 11, 1925," MS in Baker Papers; Stockton Axson, Notes on various parts of Baker's Woodrow Wilson, MS in *ibid.* (Axson was Wilson's brother-in-law and one of his most intimate friends.) See also R. S. Baker, *Woodrow Wilson,* I, 200-203.

[51] W. W. to Ellen Axson, January 1, 1884, R. S. Baker, *Woodrow Wilson,* I, 213-214.

in the philosophy of our institutions, not the abstract and occult, but the practical and suggestive, philosophy which is at the core of our governmental methods; their use, their meaning, 'the spirit that makes them workable.' " [52] By the first of January 1884, he was ready to begin work on the book, and within a few weeks read the first chapter in the seminar. During the summer he spent his vacation in Wilmington hard at work on *Congressional Government,* the title he decided to use for the book. By October the manuscript was completed and he sent it to Houghton, Mifflin & Company of Boston.

Congressional Government was Wilson's analysis of the organic functioning of the federal government and, as the title implies, asserted the absolute dominance of the legislative over the executive and judicial branches. "The balances of the Constitution are for the most part only ideal," Wilson wrote. "For all practical purposes the national government is supreme over the state governments, and Congress predominant over its so-called coordinate branches." [53]

He proceeded to judge the House of Representatives and found it wanting as an efficient representative body. He criticized the lack of unity and leadership in a body that performed its functions by means of numerous standing committees operating behind a veil of absolute secrecy. The result, he declared, was, "Both the House of Representatives and the Senate conduct their business by what may figuratively, but not inaccurately, be called an odd device of *disintegration.* The House virtually both deliberates and legislates in small sections." [54] Such a system, he charged, scattered responsibility and made it impossible for the people to hold their representatives accountable for their actions. "Power is nowhere concentrated; it is rather deliberately and of set policy scattered amongst many small chiefs," and "the more power is divided the more irresponsible it becomes." [55] The speaker of the House, Wilson declared, was an autocrat because he controlled the appointment of the standing committees and the procedure; yet he was an autocrat without responsibility.

In his discussion of the Senate, Wilson endeavored to account for the decline of leadership and ability in that once-august body and concluded that the root of the trouble could be found in the fact that national controversies had almost ceased to exist since the Civil War and that there were no longer prizes of leadership for men of great ability in the

[52] W. W. to Ellen Axson, October 30, 1883, *ibid.,* 1, 213.
[53] *Congressional Government* (first edition, 1885), p. 52.
[54] *ibid.,* pp. 66-67.   [55] *ibid.,* pp. 91-93.

Senate.[56] The Senate, he continued, could have no better men than the best leaders in the House; and because the House attracted only inferior politicians, the Senate was filled with men of the same caliber. It had the same radical defect as the House in that it, the Senate, functioned through the work of the standing committees; yet it did allow complete freedom of debate, and discussions in the Senate were often of a high order.[57] Wilson thought, moreover, that the Senate represented no class interests and that its chief usefulness was the check it applied to the democratic processes of government. "It is valuable in our democracy," wrote the young conservative, "in proportion as it is undemocratic." [58]

Probably the most notable feature of *Congressional Government,* in light of Wilson's later political career, was the treatment of the presidential office. Contrary to the history he ought to have known, even contrary to contemporary political practice, Wilson satisfied himself with writing off the president as an unimportant third wheel of the federal system, as, in short, a nonentity. The pendulum of power had swung violently in the direction of Congress after the Civil War, it is true, but Wilson, even though a student of history, failed to realize that the unbalance of power would not remain permanently *in statu quo.* Apparently the historian had forgotten Jefferson, Jackson, Polk, and Lincoln!

By way of summary, Wilson concluded, "As at present constituted, the federal government lacks strength because its powers are divided, lacks promptness because its authorities are multiplied, lacks wieldiness because its processes are roundabout, lacks efficiency because its responsibility is indistinct and its action without competent direction." [59] He contrasted the splendid concentration of responsibility and authority in the British cabinet system with the disorganization of the American system in which no person or group of persons was, as he thought, responsible for providing legislative leadership. "The British system," he concluded, "is perfected party government." [60]

Congressional Government was published in January 1885 and was at once a complete success. Most of the reviewers gave it lavish praise, but Gamaliel Bradford's comments were the most encouraging. "We have no hesitation in saying that this is one of the most important books, dealing with political subjects, which have ever issued from the Ameri-

[56] *ibid.,* pp. 196-199.
[58] *ibid.,* p. 226.
[60] *ibid.,* pp. 117-123.

[57] *ibid.,* pp. 212-218.
[59] *ibid.,* p. 318.

can press," he wrote.[61] The book was hailed by Wilson's contemporaries, and has generally been considered by more recent political scientists, as something of a landmark in the study of American politics. It was the first attempt of a scholar to examine the American political system from the pragmatic and functional point of view; and it caught the fancy of critics by subjecting to a critical analysis a political system that most Americans had for several generations declared to be the best of all possible forms of government.

As a matter of fact, however, the ideas expressed in *Congressional Government* were not original; judged by modern critical standards, the book was not profound; and it is difficult to see how one can conclude that Wilson's insight was penetrating. In the first place, the work is characterized by an amazing neglect or ignorance of economic factors in political life. It did not penetrate beneath the surface of political allegiances, nor did it lay bare the economic bases of allegiances and loyalties.[62] Wilson's assertion that "the Senate is . . . separated from class interests" [63] was a classic example of scholarly ignorance.[64] Throughout the volume one can detect a strong bias against popular democracy and in favor of government by an aristocracy of intelligence and merit.[65]

Wilson's writings on the American governmental system had begun with his essay, "Cabinet Government in the United States," in 1879 and

[61] *Nation*, XL (February 12, 1885), 142. This was a particularly generous opinion, especially in light of the fact that Wilson had derived many of his ideas from Bradford's previous writings without giving him credit for them.

[62] Wilson, of course, wrote before the day when scholars leaned toward the "economic interpretation," but one wonders whether Ely and Dewey did not make suggestions in the seminar that Wilson should give more weight to the economic factors in history and government.

[63] *Congressional Government*, p. 226.

[64] In the preface to the 1900 edition of *Congressional Government*, Wilson felt constrained to write that "It is to be doubted whether I could say quite so confidently now as I said in 1884 that the Senate of the United States faithfully represents the several elements of the nation's make-up, and furnishes us with a prudent and normally constituted moderating and revising chamber. Certainly vested interests have now got a much more formidable hold upon the Senate than they seemed to have sixteen years ago." p. viii.

[65] Wilson wrote, for example, that the House was subject to the "whims of popular constituencies" to the extent even of "servile obedience" (p. 224); that the British government was strengthened because England possessed a "reverenced aristocracy . . . [and] a stable throne" (p. 226); that the Senate was valuable in the American political system in proportion as it was undemocratic and successful in saving the country "from headlong popular tyranny" (pp. 226-227).

were continued by "Committee or Cabinet Government" in 1884 and
Congressional Government in 1885. The theme of each of these essays
is the same: that the dominance of the legislative branch which governed by committees acting in secrecy had operated to undermine and
demoralize political leadership and prevent the fixing of legislative
responsibility, and that a way out could be found in the adoption of a
modified form of ministerial government. Were these ideas Wilson's
own?

It is necessary to begin this discussion of the origin of Wilson's ideas
by taking some account, first of all, of his heavy indebtedness to Walter
Bagehot. It was the reading of Bagehot's *English Constitution* that inspired Wilson's "whole study of our government," and *Congressional
Government* was deliberately modeled after its British counterpart. The
former was, in fact, almost a replica of the latter—but in reverse. Bagehot described the dynamics of the British government and compared
the cabinet system to what he called the presidential system; Wilson, on
the other hand, analyzed the functioning of the American government
and, from this point of departure, compared the congressional system to
the cabinet system. The two authors agreed that British political practice was infinitely superior to the American practice.

Bagehot's thesis was based upon certain facts and assumptions. The
cabinet system, he declared, concentrated executive and legislative authority and responsibility in the prime minister and cabinet, who were,
in turn, directly responsible to the House of Commons. The presidential system, however, divided authority and responsibility between Congress and the president to such an extent that neither Congress nor the
president could assume leadership or be held responsible for legislation.
One result of this political vacuum was the degradation of public life in
the United States.

The prime minister, moreover, was, by the nature of the cabinet system, inevitably the leader of his party; the cabinet, consequently, was
not only the leader in the House of Commons; it was also the official
spokesman of the party in power. The result was effective party government and party responsibility. The presidential system, on the other
hand, except in unusual instances, operated to prevent the actual party
leaders from becoming president; this prevented effective, responsible
party government in the United States.

Bagehot asserted also that the cabinet's responsibility for initiating
and defending legislation before the House of Commons stimulated
exhaustive and open debate on all legislative matters; that this govern-

ment by discussion was the backbone of representative democracy; and that the American system of divided or hidden responsibility placed a heavy discount on debate in Congress. Bagehot also emphasized that the chief duty of the House of Commons, after the election of a cabinet, was to inform and teach the public.[66]

It is evident that Wilson accepted all of Bagehot's fundamental premises and made them his own; they underlie all of the discussions in *Congressional Government*. It is remarkable, also, how similar was Wilson's literary style to Bagehot's—conversational and condescending. Bagehot, however, was content for the most part to contrast the cabinet and presidential systems and to extol the one at the expense of the other; he did not suggest the adoption of a ministerial form of government in the United States. It is necessary to look elsewhere for the origins of Wilson's proposition for cabinet government in this country.

Long before Wilson began to write there had been in the public press a great amount of discussion of the decline of leadership in the government and especially of the necessity for a responsible political leadership. Much of this discussion was provoked by the publication of Bagehot's volume in this country in 1873. The *Nation,* that perennial emporium of reform ideas, in the same year scored the bungling ineffectiveness of committee government in Congress.[67] The spectacle of a Congress and cabinet indulging in the sordid corruption of Crédit Mobilier, the Whiskey Ring debauchery, or the "salary grab" act of 1873 added to the scepticism about the perfect character of the American political system. "The idea that we would impress upon the minds of all thoughtful and conscientious citizens is, that political power carries with it political responsibility," the *Nation* declared, "and that we should not grant the one without exacting the other." [68]

A realization of the maladjustment of the American political system, however, did not necessarily imply the requisite solution of the problem. To Gamaliel Bradford must go the credit for having given publicity to the plan of cabinet government which Wilson later adopted bodily in his two articles on the subject. Wilson was an inveterate reader of the *Nation* and it is inconceivable that he should not have read the report of a speech Bradford made in Boston in 1873, for there were few ideas of real significance either in "Cabinet Government in the United States," "Committee or Cabinet Government?" or *Congressional Gov-*

---

[66] Walter Bagehot, *The English Constitution* (American edition, 1873).

[67] "The Way Congress Does Business," *Nation,* xvi (February 27, 1873), 145-146.

[68] "Political Responsibility," *ibid.,* xvi (March 13, 1873), 176.

ernment that had not been set forth already either by Bradford[69] or by other advocates of reform.

In an address before the New York Historical Society in 1877, Charles O'Conor went beyond Bradford's reform proposals and suggested that responsible government could best be obtained by giving over all executive power to Congress and by inaugurating a system wherein the president would be chosen at frequent intervals by and from Congress.[70] Godkin of the *Nation* did not agree with O'Conor's proposal, but he did demand that the president and cabinet publish their deliberate opinions on "the great questions of the day." This was necessary, Godkin thought, in financial matters particularly. "There is no civilized constitutional country," he declared, "whose governmental machinery is so ill-fitted for the legislative treatment of such matters as ours."[71]

These multiform indictments of congressional government and the proposals for reform—all, incidentally, set forth before Wilson began to write—were given practical significance by Senator George H. Pendleton of Ohio who, in 1879, introduced in the Senate a bill to give cabinet members a seat in either house of Congress with the liberty of debate.

---

[69] Bradford declared that the failure of Congress to provide progressive leadership could be ascribed to the committee system of legislation in Congress. "What is the result?" he asked. "A dozen men, appointed on a committee from their acquaintance—that is to say, from their private interest in—the special subject, sitting in secret, dictate what measures shall and what shall not be passed by the National Legislature." Meanwhile, the thing is made worse by the total absence of definite responsibility. Committees are not responsible, because it is Congress, and not the committees, by which the bills are passed. Congress is not responsible because it has not time to examine into the merits of three or four thousand bills at each session, and has entrusted this work to the committees; and the President cannot be held responsible for laws which he had no part in making. "Such complete chaos and confusion are fatal to intelligent and systematic legislation," Bradford continued. "Real debate in the House has been suppressed, and in the Senate amounts to nothing."

Bradford next considered the position of the executive and concluded that it was one of "Absolute impotence. . . . To sum up the whole, we have the political power of the country lodged in the hands of an irresponsible Congress, elected by office-holders, to whom they are bound; the President who appoints these office-holders, under the thumb of the Congressional majority."

He proposed to reform this disjointed and anarchical system by giving cabinet members seats in Congress. By this means could "national representation" be secured. Continuity of legislation would also be gained by the constant presence of members of the executive branch in Congress and would afford the opposition an effective means of interrogating the leaders of the government. "Shall the Cabinet Have Seats in Congress?" *Nation*, XVI (April 3, 1873), 233-234. Compare the above with Wilson's writings.

[70] "The President and Party Responsibility," *Nation*, XXIV (May 17, 1877), 288.

[71] *ibid*. See also "The Causes of Congressional Failure," *ibid.*, XXVI (June 27, 1878), 414.

Cabinet members would not, according to the Pendleton bill, have the right to vote on measures, but would be required to be present on certain days to answer questions propounded by the members of each house.[72] Perhaps it was this suggestion that prompted Wilson to write "Cabinet Government in the United States." Bradford, whom the *Nation* in 1882 described as having "been laboring for years, with great ability as well as persistence, to convince the American public that the national salvation is to be found only, or mainly, in giving seats in Congress to members of the Cabinet," [73] returned to the fight for reform in 1882 with another scathing indictment of the congressional system.[74] It is inconceivable that Wilson did not read all or most of these editorials and articles, yet there is no mention of any of them in his writings.

The success of *Congressional Government* intensified Wilson's desire for an active political career. "I do feel a very real regret that I have been shut out from my heart's *first*—primary—ambition and purpose, which was, to take an active, if possible a leading, part in public life, and strike out for myself, if I had the ability, a *statesman's* career," he wrote in February 1885.[75] He looked about at the passing events in the political world and, although he rejoiced at Cleveland's election in 1884, distrusted the Democratic party and believed that its dismemberment was "a consummation devoutly to be wished." [76] He wished to see instead "the rise of a new party to which one could belong with self-respect and enthusiasm." [77]

Wilson was married in June 1885 to Ellen Axson, and in September they went to Bryn Mawr, where Wilson had accepted an associate professorship of history. He began his work enthusiastically, but soon

[72] "Cabinet Officers in Congress," *ibid.*, XXVIII (April 10, 1879), 243. The Pendleton bill was finally reported unanimously by a Senate committee. In its revised form the measure authorized heads of departments to occupy seats in both houses and to participate in debates relating to their respective departments. It also required them to attend sessions of the Senate on Tuesdays and Fridays of each week, and in the House on Mondays and Thursdays, and to give information in answer to resolutions or questions. "The Admission of Cabinet Officers to Seats in Congress," *ibid.*, XXXII (February 17, 1881), 107-109.
[73] "Congress and Reform," *ibid.*, XXXV (September 7, 1882), 194.
[74] G. Bradford, "The Progress of Civil Service Reform," *International Review*, XIII (September 1882), 266-267. Compare this, for example, with Wilson's *Congressional Government*, which was written two years later.
[75] W. W. to Ellen Axson, February 24, 1885, R. S. Baker, *Woodrow Wilson*, I, 229.
[76] W. W. to Ellen Axson, April 2, 1885, *ibid.*, I, 233.
[77] *ibid.*

found the teaching of women an irksome task. In April 1886 he agreed to write a textbook on comparative government for D. C. Heath & Company concerning "the origin and early history of govt viewed historically, of course, and *not à la* Rousseau, Locke, *et al;* the govts of Greece and Rome and of the Middle Ages, treated in the same spirit; comparative studies in the public law of the present, our own and the Eng. constitutions standing centrally and most prominent, of course; and, in the light of such studies, considerations on the functions and ends of govt and on law." [78] In the meantime, he prepared for his doctoral examinations and, in June 1886, was awarded his Ph.D. at the Johns Hopkins.

Even during the first year of his teaching Wilson did not cease to dream of the "covenant" he had made with Talcott and to hope for an intimate contact with the political world. He wrote, for example, of the urgent need for the right kind of political leadership and believed that a small group of intellectuals might wield great authority by agitation in the public press. The ultimate goal, Wilson thought, was the "formation of such a new political sentiment and party as the country stands in such pressing need of,—and I am ambitious that we should have a hand in forming such a group." [79] He also found time to write an article, "The Study of Administration," in which he called for a scientific study of the administration of government and a civil service responsive to popular opinion. [80]

In September 1887 Wilson began his third year at Bryn Mawr. He was becoming more and more dissatisfied with teaching women and was "hungry for a class of *men*." [81] His salary of $1,500 at Bryn Mawr was ridiculously low for a man with a wife and already two children, and he searched about for an opportunity to get away from the college. His hopes were excited when his friend Renick wrote that the first assistant secretaryship of state was vacant and advised him to apply for the position. Wilson wrote immediately to James B. Angell of the University of Michigan, "I do want—and *need*—particularly, as it seems to me, at this junction in my studies,—a seat on the inside of the government—a seat high enough to command views of the system." He dreaded becoming doctrinaire. Besides, teaching political economy and public law to women threatened to relax his "mental muscles—to exalt

[78] W. W. to R. H. Dabney, November 7, 1886, Dabney Papers.
[79] W. W. to Charles A. Talcott, November 14, 1886, Baker Papers.
[80] *Political Science Quarterly,* ii (June 1887), 197-222.
[81] W. W. to Robert Bridges, August 26, 1888, Bridges Papers.

the function of commonplace rudiments in . . . [his] treatment." [82]
Wilson actually thought that he had a good chance of success and wrote
of his "old political longings thus set throbbing again." [83] This first
venture into the business of office-seeking, however, was ill-fated and
served only to increase Wilson's dissatisfaction with the academic life.
"I love the stir of the world," he confessed.[84]

In 1888 an opportunity came to Wilson to go to Wesleyan University
in Middletown, Connecticut, at a higher salary than he had been receiving at Bryn Mawr and with the added attraction that he would
have classes of men; he seized this chance with alacrity. The family
moved from Bryn Mawr in the summer and Wilson soon was in a happier environment. At once he prompted the students to organize a
"Wesleyan House of Commons" debating society and helped to coach
a winning football team. At the same time, in addition to his regular
duties at Wesleyan, Wilson was also giving a series of twenty-five lectures a year at the Johns Hopkins University.[85]

During the period of transition from Bryn Mawr to Wesleyan, Wilson was also preoccupied with his research and writing. He finished the
page proofs of *The State* in the spring of 1889, and six months later the
book was published. It was probably Wilson's greatest scholarly achievement. For basic source material he relied chiefly upon the *Handbuch
des Oeffentlichen Rechts der Gegenwart,* edited by Heinrich Marquard-
sen of the University of Erlangen;[86] but he also used a wide variety of
secondary works on law and government. *The State* was written for
use as a textbook on comparative government in college classes; it
treated the development of political institutions from ancient times to
the latter part of the nineteenth century; and the governments of the
principal modern European states and of the United States were described in detail.

Wilson rounded out his discussion by appending to the main body
of the text a philosophical discussion of the nature and forms of government, of law and its nature and development, and of the functions
and ends of government. He saw in the eternal processes of history a
continual and progressive evolution of political institutions. "From the
dim morning hours of history when the father was king and high priest
down to this modern time of history's high noon when nations stand

[82] W. W. to James B. Angell, November 7, 1887, photostat in Baker Papers.
[83] W. W. to Robert Bridges, November 5, 1887, Bridges Papers.
[84] W. W. to James B. Angell, November 15, 1887, photostat in Baker Papers.
[85] R. S. Baker, *Woodrow Wilson,* I, 302-306.
[86] *The State* (1889 edition), p. xxxvi.

forth full-grown and self-governed," he wrote, "the law of coherence and continuity in political development has suffered no serious breach." [87]

Wilson agreed with Edmund Burke that revolution had always been followed by a fatal reaction, that "Political growth refuses to be forced." He believed with Walter Bagehot and Herbert Spencer that the evolutions of politics had been "scarcely less orderly and coherent than those of the physical world." [88] The essential characteristic of all government, Wilson thought, was force and authority. "There must in every instance be, on the one hand, governors, and, on the other, those who are governed." Government, therefore, in the last analysis was "organized force." [89] This governing authority, however, depended upon the acquiescence of the general will. Wilson believed that the true nature of government could be found hidden in the nature of society; and society, he declared, was compounded "of the common habit, an evolution of experience, an interlaced growth of tenacious relationships, a compact, living, organic whole, structural, not mechanical." [90]

The State was not yet off the press when Wilson was invited by Albert Bushnell Hart of Harvard University to prepare a volume for the "Epochs of American History Series." He accepted at once and hastened to write Hart about his political point of view. "Ever since I have had independent judgments of my own I have been a Federalist," he declared.[91] His chief interest was, of course, in American political history, and the contemporary events of the political world were disheartening. He wrote that his interest in politics had suffered a "decided collapse . . . since this reactionary [Harrison] Administration came in." [92] But this discouragement was apparently only temporary, for he proceeded to write with complete confidence in the future of democracy in the United States and in the world.[93]

Wilson believed, too, that he had "come to himself" politically, that he had already arrived at the self-complacent stage of maturity. "The *boyish* feeling that I have so long had and cherished is giving place, consciously, to another feeling," he confessed, "the feeling that I am no longer young (though not old quite!) and that I need no longer hesitate (as I have so long and sensitively done) to assert myself and my

[87] *ibid.*, p. 575.   [88] *ibid.*
[89] *ibid.*, p. 593.   [90] *ibid.*, p. 597.
[91] W. W. to A. B. Hart, June 3, 1889, copy in Baker Papers.
[92] W. W. to E. A. W., March 15, 1889, R. S. Baker, *Woodrow Wilson*, I, 308.
[93] See, for example, Wilson's review of Bryce's *American Commonwealth*, in *Political Science Quarterly*, IV (March 1889), 153-169.

opinions in the presence of and against the selves and opinions of old men, 'my elders.' " [94]

Largely through the efforts of Bridges and other Princeton friends, Wilson in 1890 was elected professor of jurisprudence and political economy at his alma mater; he accepted the appointment with joy. He was a popular lecturer, a football enthusiast, and a champion of the honor system for the students at Princeton. He continued his work at the Johns Hopkins and, in addition, began lecturing on jurisprudence at the New York Law School in 1892.[95] He had acquired considerable standing in the academic world, moreover, and within a few years was offered the presidency of several colleges and universities.[96] Three times, for example, he was invited to become the first president of the University of Virginia; three times he refused.[97]

The return to the familiar haunts at Princeton did not sufficiently satisfy Wilson to subvert his old political ambitions. He was certainly conscious of the momentous political revolution in progress in the 1890's and often longed to be a participant in the strife. The story of the agrarian revolt of the 1890's has been adequately chronicled by other historians. The Greenback movement, the National Grange, Populism, and Bryanism were successively the political phases of agrarian discontent in the latter part of the nineteenth century. In short, a complete agrarian victory would have meant the eradication of most of the gains the industrialists and capitalists had obtained by the destruction of the southern agrarian influence in Congress that resulted from the Civil War.

Wilson's reaction to the events of this period of political revolt is significant. It was of course more or less conditioned by his own en-

---

[94] W. W. to E. A. W., March 9, 1889, R. S. Baker, *Woodrow Wilson*, I, 315.

[95] *ibid.*, II, 20.

[96] Among them were the University of Alabama (James E. Webb to Wilson, March 11, 1901, Woodrow Wilson Papers, Library of Congress; hereinafter cited as Wilson Papers); Williams College (Richard A. Rice to Wilson, June 10, 1901, *ibid.*); Washington and Lee University (Lucian H. Cocke to Wilson, January 9, 1901, *ibid.*); the University of Illinois (Wilson to E. A. W., April 27, 1892, R. S. Baker, *Woodrow Wilson*, II, 21); the University of Nebraska and the University of Minnesota (*ibid.*); and the University of Virginia. He was also offered the chair of history at the Johns Hopkins to succeed H. B. Adams (D. C. Gilman to Wilson, March 16, 1901, Wilson Papers), and the headship of the history department at the University of Chicago (Albion W. Small to Wilson, April 20, 1900, *ibid.*).

[97] W. W. to R. H. Dabney, November 10, 1902, Dabney Papers. It will be recalled that the University of Virginia had been governed previously entirely by faculty committees.

vironment that was, in many respects, the proverbial "ivory tower." He had known nothing of the hard struggle for existence that was characteristic of the lives of so many of his contemporaries. He had never known economic insecurity, or poverty, or dread of the future; never had he had any intimate contact with men of the working classes. During the long period of depression and declining farm prices, which culminated in the panic of 1893, his income had risen steadily. Wilson had, it is true, arrived at a fairly definite economic and political philosophy by the end of the century, but it was a philosophy derived from historical study, not from experience in competitive struggle.

Wilson, it should be noted, was never an economist. He had an attitude almost of contempt for the "dismal science" and cared even less for the study of statistics or the "laws" of economic life. For Wilson the "economic man" hardly existed; it was, rather, the "political man" who absorbed his interest. It is significant that he thought Adam Smith, hardly an economist in the modern sense of the word, the greatest economist. Although he knew little of the science of economics, Wilson was professedly a student of political economy, and Smith, Bagehot, Cobden, and Bright—the great British free traders—were his mentors in this field. Wilson's economic thought was therefore of the brand of the Manchester Liberal School.[98] And, as has been previously noted, his writings of this period reveal no real comprehension of economic factors in history and the actions of men. As Norman Thomas later wrote of his former professor, "If he had ever heard Harrington's dictum that the distribution of power follows the distribution of property, he never discussed it with his students in the classroom."[99] Another of his students has left us with the same impression. "Mr. Wilson," wrote Frederick C. Howe, "gave us no glimpse of the economic background of the English ruling class. There was always the assumption that these public men were not moved by private gain. It was never hinted in his lecture-room that the British landed gentry, bankers, and business men enacted laws to protect their own class and group. . . . Nor that the House of Lords was in the nature of a private corporation representative of special interests even more than the United States Senate. He was not interested in economics."[100]

---

[98] See especially William Diamond's excellent discussion in his *Economic Thought of Woodrow Wilson*, pp. 50-53, and *passim*.

[99] Norman Thomas, "Mr. Wilson's Tragedy and Ours," *The World Tomorrow*, March 1921, p. 82.

[100] Frederick C. Howe, *Confessions of a Reformer*, p. 38.

Wilson's reaction to the new radicalism of the Populists and of Bryan was consequently tempered by his already decided belief in law and order, and by his conservative economic views in general. Yet he realized the existence of, if he did not fully comprehend, the new currents of national life. In one of Wilson's essays in 1897, for example, he saw that there were definite economic causes for the new radicalism and wrote that there was an "unpleasant significance in the fact that the 'East' has made no serious attempt to understand the desire for the free coinage of silver in the 'West' and the South." [101]

A realization of this fact, however, did not prevent Wilson from condemning emphatically the remedies proposed by the radicals. He wrote of "the crude and ignorant minds of the members of the Farmers' Alliance" [102] and was unsparing in his criticism of Bryan and the new departure the Democratic party had made in 1896. He thought the Nebraskan's "Cross of Gold" speech ridiculous[103] and believed, "We might have had Mr. Bryan for President, because of the impression which may be made upon an excited assembly by a good voice and a few ringing sentences flung forth. . . . The country knew absolutely nothing about Mr. Bryan before his nomination, and it would not have known anything about him afterward had he not chosen to make speeches." [104] Perhaps he at first thought of Bryan as he had thought of Andrew Jackson, whom he accused of "childish arrogance and ignorant arbitrariness";[105] but he soon came to believe the Commoner a sincere, if mistaken, man.[106] He of course voted the "Gold Democratic" ticket in 1896.[107]

The economic disturbances of the latter quarter of the nineteenth century were accompanied also by increasing labor unrest and by a general agitation for governmental control of the railroads and destruction of the trusts which threatened to destroy the American dream of equality of economic opportunity. Along with his belief in political conservatism, which he derived from Burke, Wilson at this period had an

[101] "The Making of the Nation," *Atlantic Monthly*, LXXX (July 1897), 4, 10-11; see also *History of the American People*, v, 254.

[102] *ibid.*, v, 127.

[103] R. S. Baker, Memorandum of a talk with Stockton Axson, March 15-16, 1927, MS in Baker Papers.

[104] "The Making of the Nation," *Atlantic Monthly*, LXXX (July 1897), 12.

[105] "Character of Democracy in the United States," *An Old Master*, p. 124.

[106] R. S. Baker, Memorandum of a talk with Stockton Axson, March 15-16, 1927, MS in Baker Papers.

[107] W. W. to W. J. Bryan, April 3, 1912, Wilson Papers.

abiding faith in the Smithian idea of the natural identity of interests. He believed then and for many years afterward that the activities of labor unions were inimical to the best interests of the individual laborer;[108] he revealed in his writings a hostile attitude toward the great Pullman strike of 1894.[109] Yet, as William Diamond has aptly stated, "The logical consequences of Wilson's historical conservatism and of his faith in individualism and free competition were avoided, or at least tempered, by several factors. One of the most important of these was the equalitarian tradition of American democracy." [110]

Wilson, moreover, had some conception of a positive state and in certain respects recognized the necessity of an artificial identification of interests by the state. He could write, therefore, with approval of the Interstate Commerce Act and of the general idea of railroad regulation in the public interest.[111] He looked with apprehension upon the growth of trusts and monopolies and feared that "there was risk of deeply serious consequence in these vast aggregations of capital, these combinations of all the processes of a great industry in the hands of a single 'Trust.' " He believed also that "they did give to a few men a control over the economic life of the country which they might abuse to the undoing of millions of men, it might even be to the permanent demoralization of society itself and of the government which was the instrument of society." [112]

As a consequence of this situation, Wilson was confronted with the alternative either of regulating business and industry or of seeing economic equality disappear. Yet, during this period at least, he never found his way out of the dilemma. He rejected the socialist ideal of government ownership of the means of production, on the one hand; and he also refused to accept the Populist program for control of the trusts because he thought it "smacked of the extremist purposes of experiment in the field of legislation." It would be injurious to check the economic growth of the country, he wrote; yet, on the other hand, "it would not do to leave the economic liberty of the individual or the freedom and self-respect of the workingman unprotected." [113]

On one important economic question, the tariff, Wilson was con-

---

[108] See, for example, his address to the graduating class at Princeton in 1909, published in *Trenton True American*, June 14, 1909.

[109] *History of the American People*, v, 239-240.

[110] *The Economic Thought of Woodrow Wilson*, p. 57.

[111] *History of the American People*, v, 184, 185.

[112] *ibid.*, v, 267.   [113] *ibid.*, v, 267-268.

sistent and uncompromising. In 1897 he had not changed his opinion expressed in 1882 when he advocated the repeal of all protective tariff laws and declared that protection was nothing more than a bounty to manufacturers. He does not reveal during these earlier years the penetrating insight into the alliance of big business and government—an alliance for which he would later blame the protective tariff—but the Manchester School had no more faithful representative in America than Woodrow Wilson. He was also faithful to his ideal of responsible government, earlier set forth in *Congressional Government*. Events between 1884 and 1897 had not shaken this conviction when he addressed the Virginia State Bar Association and declared, "This is not a day of revolution; but it is a day of change, and of such change as may breed revolution, should we fail to guide and moderate it." The great structural defect of the American system was still, he declared, "that Congress is the motive power in the government and yet has in it nowhere any representative of the nation as a whole." [114]

Meanwhile the closing years of the century witnessed the emergence of the United States as a colonial and world power. In 1898 Wilson made no public comment with regard to the Spanish-American War; but in 1899 he is reported as declaring his opposition to the annexation of the Philippines.[115] He was deeply concerned by the implications in America's new imperialistic venture. "Much the most important change to be noticed is the result of the war with Spain upon the lodgment and exercise of power within our federal system," he wrote in 1900. The war's most momentous consequence had been, he thought, "the greatly increased power and opportunity for constructive statesmanship given the President, by the plunge into international politics and into the administration of distant dependencies." [116]

Wilson sensed the expansionist excitement that dominated the minds of many of his contemporaries, reasoned that the "impulse of expansion is the natural and wholesome impulse which comes with a consciousness of matured strength," and concluded that "empire is an affair of strong government." [117] He certainly did not share the fear of anti-imperialists

[114] "Leaderless Government," address before the Virginia State Bar Association, August 4, 1897; *Report of the Ninth Annual Meeting of the Virginia State Bar Association*, pp. 272, 291.

[115] *Waterbury* (Conn.) *American*, December 14, 1900.

[116] Preface to the 1900 edition of *Congressional Government*, p. xi.

[117] "The Reconstruction of the Southern States," *Atlantic Monthly*, LXXXVII (January 1901), 14-15.

who believed that America's energy for reform at home would be weakened because of the new duties abroad. On the contrary, he thought that "the way to perfection lies along these new paths of struggle, of discipline, and of achievement." [118] America's emergence as a world power, moreover, could not have been prevented, and now it was the nation's chief duty to prove to the world at large the efficacy of democracy. America had now to be the champion of self-government; autonomy should be given to the Philippines and Puerto Rico as soon as the inhabitants of those islands were prepared to govern themselves.

Wilson's rationalization of American imperialism was a rather sophisticated and pseudo-religious expression of the idea of the "white man's burden." He insisted that self-government was not easily come by, and he proposed that the United States should give the Filipinos a government that would "moralize them" and "elevate and steady them" in preparation for self-government.[119] "The best guarantee of good government we can give the Filipinos is, that we shall be sensitive to the opinion of the world," he concluded. "We must learn what we can, and yet scrupulously square everything that we do with the high principles we brought into the world: that justice may be done to the lowly no less than to the great. . . . If we but keep our ideals clear, our principles steadfast, we need not fear the change." [120] The self-righteous attitude was also evident in an article Wilson wrote at the end of 1902:

"Liberty is not itself government. In the wrong hands,—in hands unpracticed, undisciplined,—it is incompatible with government. Discipline must precede it,—if necessary, the discipline of being under masters. Then will self-control make it a thing of life and not a thing of tumult, a tonic, not an insurgent madness in the blood. Shall we doubt, then, what the conditions precedent to liberty and self-government are, and what their invariable support and accompaniment must be, in the countries whose administration we have taken over in trust, particularly in those far Philippine Islands whose government is our chief anxiety? . . . They can have liberty no cheaper than we got it. They must first take the discipline of law, must first love order and instinctively yield to it. . . . We are old in this learning and must be their tutors." [121]

During the turbulent days of the 1890's life made its accustomed

---

[118] "Democracy and Efficiency," *Atlantic Monthly*, LXXXVII (March 1901), 292.

[119] *ibid.*, pp. 292, 298.

[120] *ibid.*, pp. 298-299.

[121] "The Ideals of America," *Atlantic Monthly*, XC (December 1902), 730.

rounds at Princeton. Wilson was, first of all, a professor and educator, and it was the problems of the academic world that absorbed much of his time. He began to speak forth with a new emphasis upon educational problems in 1893, when he made his first important address on academic problems at the Chicago World's Fair in July 1893. He demanded that a four-year liberal college education be required of students in law, medicine, and theology and lamented the "disease of specialization by which we are now so sorely afflicted." [122] The following year, in an address before the American Bar Association, he again demanded a general liberal education for students who planned to study law.[123] "It is the object of learning, not only to satisfy the curiosity and perfect the spirits of individual men, but also to advance civilization," he wrote soon afterward, and concluded, "Certainly we have come to the parting of the ways, and there is nothing for us to do but to choose a direction." [124]

The 1890's might well be regarded as Wilson's prolific decade. From 1893 through 1902 he published nine volumes and thirty-five articles, and made over a score of public addresses. He had been selected by Albert Bushnell Hart in 1889 to write the final volume in the "Epochs" series, largely because he was a Southerner. In March 1893 *Division and Reunion,* as it was called, came off the press and revealed what was, for the period, a remarkably dispassionate treatment of the causes of the Civil War and the aftermath of Reconstruction. Within a few months a little volume of selected essays was published under the title *An Old Master and Other Political Essays.* By sheer hard work Wilson increased the flow of publications. In 1896 *Mere Literature* and *George Washington* were completed, and in 1902 Wilson's magnum opus, his five-volume *History of the American People,* was published.

The more books Wilson wrote, however, the more his scholarship

---

[122] *Public Papers,* I, 223-230.   [123] *ibid.,* I, 232-245.

[124] "University Training and Citizenship," *The Forum,* XVIII (September 1894), 110. "The graduates of our universities no longer go forth with a common training which will enable them to hold together in a community of thought," he continued. "Some of them are trained in science, some in letters; some well and broadly trained, many ill and narrowly, with a hard technicality and mean contraction of view. Scarcely one of them has been fully inducted into the learning which deals with the common experiences, the common thoughts and struggles, the old triumphs and defeats of the men of his face in the past: their dreams and awakenings; their amibtions, humours, confidences, liberties, and follies: the intimate stuff of their minds and lives in past generations, when others were in like manner graduated from college and brought face to face with life and the unthinking mass of men." *ibid.,* pp. 110-111.

deteriorated. *Division and Reunion* was a careful and scholarly study, written in simple and concise language; but *George Washington* was a popular biography distinguished by nothing except, perhaps, Howard Pyle's illustrations and Wilson's aristocratic affectations and obviously strained literary style.[125] If Wilson wrote his *History of the American People* in order to learn history, as he later declared, the results of his efforts were neither remarkable nor encouraging. Yet the *History* apparently served one useful purpose in considerably increasing his income.

Wilson's record as a chronicler of American history has already been adequately evaluated.[126] Several of his ideas, however, are significant. First was Wilson's attempt to determine a valid measure of "Americanism" in an interpretation of American history. "Not every man born and bred in America was a great 'American,'" he thought; and he endeavored to supply an answer to Crèvecoeur's memorable question, "What, then, is this American, this new man?" There was a definite American type, Wilson insisted; and there was an American spirit distinct from the Anglo-Saxon spirit of liberty from which it sprang. The

[125] The strained literary style, most evident in *George Washington, An Old Master,* and *Mere Literature,* was characteristic of all of Wilson's writings and speeches during the period under consideration. William Bayard Hale has surveyed this whole field thoroughly in his *The Story of a Style,* and it is unnecessary here to do more than to point out the chief characteristics of Wilson's style.

In the first place, Wilson was given to the use of an extravagant number of ornamental adjectives which encumbered and pauperized his style. He used a noun rarely without a characterizing adjective in his *George Washington,* which represents the lowest point in his literary career. Estates were never simply estates—they were "broad estates" or "ancestral estates" or "broad, half-feudal estates." Times and periods in time were also appropriately labeled. Days were never merely days, but always "fateful," "terrible," "romantic," "those unhappy," "quiet," or "frosty" days. Personages were always accorded some verbal compliment or detraction. One could continue this catalogue almost *ad infinitum.*

Wilson also delighted in the use of precious words and phrases. More than one hundred sentences in *George Washington,* for example, begin with "'Twas," "'Tis," or "'Twould." Such phrases as "quaint sweetness" abound. Hale has pointed out another distinguishing feature of Wilson's style—the labored use of a few words like "counsel," "process," "essence," "handsome," "generous," "privilege," "enterprise," etc., which Wilson used indiscriminately and often improperly. An overindulgence in the use of such adverbs as "very" and "quite" was also characteristic of Wilson's style. He also persisted in affixing "Mr." to historical characters. Lincoln was always "Mr. Lincoln"; Andrew Johnson, "Mr. Johnson"; Tyler, "Mr. Tyler," and so forth.

[126] See Louis M. Sears, "Woodrow Wilson," in William T. Hutchinson (ed.), *The Marcus W. Jernegan Essays in American Historiography,* pp. 102-121; Marjorie L. Daniel, "Woodrow Wilson—Historian," *Mississippi Valley Historical Review,* XXI (December 1934), 361-374; Michael Kraus, *A History of American History,* 6. 460.

American spirit was bred in the wilderness and was consequently a "progressive, optimistically progressive," a "hopeful and confident spirit," "unpedantic, unprovincial, unspeculative, unfastidious." [127] Hamilton, therefore, was not a great American because he "rejected, if he did not despise, democratic principles." Madison failed also to meet Wilson's qualifications because he was primarily an "English constitutional statesman." John Adams and Calhoun were great provincials; Jefferson was not a thorough American because he was too much a theoretical democrat. [128] Needless to say, Wilson had by one means or another eliminated most of the great statesmen of the early national period from his calendar of great "Americans."

In an address before the New Jersey Historical Society in 1895, Wilson developed more fully the conception of a distinct American civilization. He wholeheartedly adopted Turner's frontier thesis, set forth in 1893, and gave it a twist of his own. "What in fact has been the course of American history?" Wilson asked. "How is it to be distinguished from European history?" The fact that Americans had been a frontier people, he concluded, "is, so far, the central and determining fact of our national history." The Westerner had been "the type and master of our American life." [129]

What shall we say, by way of conclusion to this chapter, of Wilson's political philosophy? It would be a relatively simple matter to gather all of Wilson's political writings before 1913 and to make up a general catalogue of his body of political beliefs. It would also be a futile and useless accomplishment, for the reason that Wilson's political thought simply cannot be studied as a whole. There are too many incongruities, too many contradictions if the scholar attempts to analyze them without reference to chronology and changing circumstances. What has to be done, rather, is to consider the periods of Wilson's political thought.

The first period, roughly speaking, lies between the publication of "Cabinet Government in the United States" in 1879 and Wilson's assumption of the presidency of Princeton University in 1902. During this period he wrote either as an historian or a political scientist concerned with the origin, nature, function, and science of government. From 1902 through 1908 he became more intimately acquainted with the economic and political problems confronting the people of the United States, and he began to speak with confidence on these problems. The

[127] "A Calendar of Great Americans," *Mere Literature*, p. 199.
[128] *ibid.*, pp. 196-197.
[129] "The Course of American History," *Mere Literature*, pp. 231-232.

fact that he published only one academic work, *Constitutional Government in the United States,* is indicative of an increasing concern with practical affairs. Whereas the first period had been characterized by an academic sort of conservatism, the second was characterized by a belligerent political and economic conservatism with regard to the important domestic issues. From 1908 through the presidential campaign of 1912 Wilson underwent a gradual transition from conservatism to militant progressivism. His political thought during this period is significant, of course; but it was so radically different from his earlier thought that it must be considered apart and as a unit in itself.

This chapter, however, is concerned only with Wilson's political thought during the academic period from 1879 to 1902. Wilson's ideas regarding the deficiencies of the American national system and his suggestion of reform by the adoption of a modified ministerial form of government have already been surveyed. What concerns us most at this point are the chief characteristics of Wilson's political philosophy.

Perhaps the most striking feature of Wilson's thought during the period was its conservatism, both with regard to the nature of government and the functions and duties of the state. His political philosophy was a compound primarily of the ideas of Edmund Burke and Walter Bagehot, with a slight touch of Herbert Spencer added for good measure. It is a significant fact that Burke, the philosopher of the British reaction against the French Revolution, should have so notably influenced Wilson's political opinions. He agreed with Burke that democracy was the result of evolutionary growth; and he believed that any democratic system was based, not upon impractical or idealistic theories, but upon sound political experience. "Nothing establishes the republican state," he wrote, "save trained capacity for self-government, practical aptitude for public affairs, habitual soberness and temperateness of action." [130] There was no communion of spirit, therefore, between American democracy and radical thought because "Our democracy, plainly, was not a body of doctrine; it was a stage of development." [131] Wilson passionately defended Burke's *Reflections on the French Revolution,* writing that Burke "hated the French revolutionary philosophy and deemed it unfit for free men." Wilson brushed aside the French ideals embodied in the Declaration of the Rights of Man and in the writings of the *Philosophes.* That, too, was all part of the French revolutionary philosophy, which Wilson declared was "radically evil and

[130] "Character of Democracy in the United States." *An Old Master,* p. 114.
[131] *ibid.,* p. 116.

corrupting. No state can ever be conducted on its principles." [132] He asserted that Jefferson was not "a thorough American" because "of the strain of French philosophy that permeated and weakened all his thought." [133] Wilson thought, instead, that Burke's definitions of a free government and liberty, rather than Jefferson's pronouncements, "might serve as a sort of motto of the practical spirit of our race in affairs of government." [134]

Richard Hofstadter has written in his *Social Darwinism in America, 1860-1915* that it was impossible for a person to be active in any field of intellectual work in the period 1865-1895 without mastering the works of Spencer. None the less it is apparent that Wilson never "mastered" Spencer; he was, however, influenced profoundly by the whole body of social Darwinist thought that was circulating during the period. He accepted the social Darwinism's conception of the state as a living thing, subject generally to the same laws of evolution as animal organisms, in contrast to the Newtonian static conception of society. It is impossible to say whether Wilson obtained his ideas from Bagehot's *Physics and Politics* or from Spencer's *Principles of Sociology,* since he quotes from neither of them in *The State.*

Wilson's reflections on liberty and the democratic state were not particularly original. The following quotation is fairly typical:

"We know that the history of politics has been the history of liberty; a history of the enlargement of the sphere of independent individual action at the expense of the sphere of dictatorial authority. It has revealed a process of differentiation. Certain freedoms of opinion and utterance, of choice of occupation and of allegiance, of fair trial and equitable condemnation, have been blocked out as inviolable territories, lying quite beyond the jurisdiction of political sovereignty. Beginning with that singular and interesting order of the classical states of the ancient world, under which the individual was merged in the community and liberty became identical with a share in the exercise of the public power, we witness something like a gradual disintegration, a resolution of the State into its constituent elements, until at length those who govern and those who are governed are no longer one and the same, but stand face to face treating with one another, agreeing upon terms of command and obedience, as at Runnymede. Conditions of submission have been contested, and, as liberty has gained upon author-

---

[132] *Mere Literature,* p. 155.
[133] *ibid.,* pp. 196-197.
[134] *ibid.,* pp. 105-106.

ity, have been jealously formulated. The procedure and the prerogatives of authority have been agreed upon; liberty has encroached upon sovereignty and set bounds to it. The process is old; only some of its results are new. What both political philosophers and political revolutionists have sought for time out of mind has been a final definition for that part of the Austinian conception which concerns the *habitual obedience* of the community. These definitions, in their practical shape as institutions, we now call constitutions. At last peoples have become conscious of their relations to the highest powers of the State, and have sought to give permanence and certainty to those relations by setting the conditions of their subordination fast in stubborn practices or in the solemn covenants of written documents." [135]

Wilson's political thought during this period was of course chiefly derived from historical study and theoretical speculation. The student will look in vain among his speeches or writings for any indication that Wilson understood even faintly the workings of the political machine, the activities of the ward heeler, or the multifarious ramifications of everyday political practice.[136]

In 1902 Woodrow Wilson rounded out the first period of his life; he had been teaching for twenty-seven years and had been speaking and writing on public questions and political policy for several more. He was then forty-five years old. His *History of the American People* was completed and out of the way and now he longed to write the book that would give immortality to his name. It would be called "The Philosophy of Politics," a *novum organum* of political study.[137] "I was forty-five three weeks ago," he wrote Frederick J. Turner in 1902, "and between forty-five and fifty-five, I take it, is when a man ought to do the work into which he expects to put most of himself. . . . I was born a

---

[135] *An Old Master,* pp. 83-84.

[136] Any discussion of Wilson's political philosophy must, almost of necessity, cover ground already traversed by other writers. The author has contented himself with discussing merely the main outlines in the evolution of Wilson's political thought in this chapter.

Good discussions of the subject may be found in William Diamond's *The Economic Thought of Woodrow Wilson,* pp. 13-60, and in Harley Notter's *The Origins of the Foreign Policy of Woodrow Wilson,* pp. 3-121. Diamond organizes his treatment topically; Notter discusses in some detail practically all of Wilson's writings and addresses. See also William Wiley Hollingsworth, *Woodrow Wilson's Political Ideals as Interpreted from His Works,* and Paul Baker, "Woodrow Wilson's Political Philosophy," *Texas Christian Quarterly,* 1 (January 1925), 6-34.

[137] There are unpublished fragments of this projected study in the Wilson Papers that make interesting reading.

politician and must be at the task for which, by means of my historical writing, I have all these years been in training. If I finish ["The Philosophy of Politics"] at fifty-five, shall I not have fifteen richly contemplative years left, if the Lord be good to me!" [138]

[138] W. W. to F. J. Turner, January 21, 1902, Baker Papers.

CHAPTER II

President of Princeton University

THE "richly contemplative years" that Wilson looked forward to with such pleasant anticipation—the years in which he would at last find time to crystallize his thoughts and write a great philosophical treatise on government—would remain a thing of hope rather than of reality. On June 9, 1902, he was elected president of Princeton University by the Board of Trustees, to succeed Francis L. Patton. The story of how Patton was persuaded to resign may some day be told; in short, his resignation was the outcome of a revolt among the faculty and trustees against his lax administration of university affairs. Wilson's election was unanimous—the trustees apparently had thought of no one else but Wilson to succeed the outgoing president—and was greeted with great enthusiasm in the faculty community. "Every one," wrote William B. Scott who was then professor of paleontology at Princeton, "felt that the right thing had been done; if there was one dissenting voice, I failed to hear it. Happily, there was no interregnum and no time for the formation of parties and the setting up of candidates, with all the accompanying bitterness and ill-feeling." [1]

To the outside world, the event was entirely unexpected; and it was a subject of some comment that Wilson was the first layman to succeed the long line of clergymen who had previously guided the University's destiny. The reaction in the country at large was enthusiastic and newspaper opinion was favorable.[2] Southerners were proud that, at last, a Southerner was president of a northern university, and many observers read in this fact the end of sectional antagonisms. "To Virginia and the South the appointment of Dr. Wilson is significant as well as important," wrote one editor. "It demonstrates the obliteration of sectionalism and the mark which men of Southern birth are making in the North." [3]

[1] W. B. Scott, *Some Memories of a Palaeontologist*, p. 255.

[2] See the *New York Times*, June 11, 1902; *New York Mail and Express*, June 10, 1902; *New York Evening Post*, June 10, 1902; *New York Daily Tribune*, June 11, 1902; *Boston Herald*, June 11, 1902; *Newark Evening News*, June 10, 1902.

[3] *Baltimore American*, June 13, 1902; on this theme see also the *Atlanta Constitution*, June 11, 1902; *Wilmington* (N. C.) *Messenger*, June 12, 1902; *Richmond Times*, June

Even with a realization of the responsibilities involved in his election as president of Princeton, Wilson was none the less supremely happy. He immediately set to the task of writing his inaugural address and confessed that he felt "like a new prime minister getting ready to address his constituents." [4] Of course he would now have to abandon his writing for several years, and that was a "heartbreaking thing for a fellow who has not yet written the particular thing for which he has been training all his life," [5] but there would be plenty of time for such things later on. His election had done at least one thing for him, he wrote: "It has settled the future for me and given me a sense of *position* and of definite, tangible tasks which takes the *flutter* and restlessness from my spirits." [6] The old political longings had given way to new visions of opportunity!

Wilson's inauguration on October 25, 1902, was a gala affair. All of the great universities in the country were represented; Grover Cleveland, Thomas B. Reed, Booker T. Washington, J. Pierpont Morgan, George Harvey, William Dean Howells, Mark Twain, Walter Hines Page, and other literary figures were among the guests of the University on the occasion.[7] It was a notable occasion, and Wilson's inaugural address, "Princeton for the Nation's Service," was an attempt to probe into the meaning of and need for higher education in America.

"In planning for Princeton . . . we are planning for the country," he began. The nation had need of efficient and enlightened men and the universities of the country "must take part in supplying them." Every great undertaking of the modern world, Wilson declared, was based "on knowledge, on thoughtfulness, on the masterful handling of men." Educated Americans, he continued, had become specialists to an unfortunate degree. "We must not lose sight of that fine conception of a general training which led our fathers," he insisted, for every mind "needs for its highest serviceability a certain preliminary orientation, that it may get its bearings and release its perception for a wide and catholic view." [8]

11, 1902; *Augusta Chronicle,* June 11, 1902; *Nashville American,* June 11, 1902; *Charlotte Daily Observer,* June 12, 1902.

[4] W. W. to E. A. W., July 19, 1902, R. S. Baker, *Woodrow Wilson,* II, 134.

[5] W. W. to Edith G. Reid, July 12, 1902, Baker Papers.

[6] W. W. to E. A. W., August 10, 1902, R. S. Baker, *Woodrow Wilson,* II, 138.

[7] For a colorful description of the inauguration, see the *Princeton Alumni Weekly,* III (November 1, 1902), 83-85.

[8] The inaugural address is printed in *ibid.,* pp. 89-98, and in the *Public Papers,* I, 443-461.

Throughout all of the eight years he was president of Princeton, it was Wilson's supreme ambition to exalt the intellectual life of the university community of faculty and students. The curriculum, new buildings, added endowment and distinguished new professors, reform of the system of classroom teaching, or reorganization of the social life of the undergraduates—all of these were means to the larger end he had constantly in view. For he did not believe that universities existed for the purpose of teaching men how to make a living. Thus, he declared in 1906: "Look, therefore, how impossible it is for him [the student] to assess any problem in a disinterested fashion, if from the first he has been taught, in college as well as elsewhere, that the chief end of man is to make a living! If the chief end of man is to make a living, why, make a living any way you can. But if it ever has been shown to him in some quiet place where he has been withdrawn from the interests of the world, that the chief end of man is to keep his soul untouched from corrupt influences, and to see to it that his fellow men hear the truth from his lips, he will never get that out of his consciousness again. There will always come up within him a great resurgence, some way or other, those lessons of his youth, and there will come a voice from the conscience which will arrest the very progress of a generation. But if you never teach him any ideal except the ideal of making a living, there will be no voice within him, he will know no other ideal." [9]

Wilson believed, therefore, that there should be some university in the country—and he would make of Princeton that university—that would undertake to teach men "the life that is in them"; that would teach students the disinterested truths of science, the truths of philosophy, and the literature that "is the permanent voice and song of the human spirit." There must sound in the halls of the true university, he thought, "this eternal voice of the human race that can never be drowned as long as men remember what the race has hoped and purposed." [10]

Wilson had written all his adult life about the need for responsible leadership in government. Now he was determined to give to Princeton that kind of leadership; in short, he would apply his political principles in the educational field. "I feel the weight of the responsibility that has come upon me, and feel it very solemnly," he wrote to David B. Jones, a

[9] Address at the seventh annual convention of the Western Association of Princeton Clubs, Cleveland, Ohio, *Princeton Alumni Weekly*, VI (June 2, 1906), 654.
[10] *ibid.*

trustee, "but I am glad to say that I do not feel it as a burden. I am glad to give all that is in me to the task now to be undertaken." [11]

Even before his inauguration, Wilson outlined in a report to the trustees the work that he thought needed to be done at Princeton. A new method of teaching undergraduates, the preceptorial system, as he called it, was foremost in his mind. He asked the trustees for $6,000,000 for immediate needs. Of this sum, $2,250,000 was needed to inaugurate the preceptorial system, $1,000,000 for a school of science, and $2,750,000 for new buildings and increases in the teaching staff. He also outlined his future objectives: $3,000,000 for a graduate school, $2,400,000 for a school of jurisprudence, $750,000 for an electrical engineering school, and $500,000 for a museum of natural history.[12]

Of all these suggested innovations, Wilson thought that the preceptorial system was the one most urgently and immediately needed. In an address at the Princeton dinner in New York on December 9, 1902, he explained this new method of teaching undergraduates. "I believe that there has to come in this country a radical change in our conception of an education," he declared, "and I believe that it must come in this way: That we shall give up the school-boy idea that men are to be examined upon lectures and upon text-books, and come to the grown-up idea that men are to be examined on subjects." It was futile, he thought, to try to instruct students in general subjects by classroom methods. "The only way to instruct them is to provide a certain number of men sufficiently qualified as instructors, as scholars, who will be the companions and coaches and guides of the men's reading." Fifty tutors were to be employed to do the job. "Gentlemen, if we could get a body of such tutors at Princeton," he continued, "we could transform the place from a place where there are youngsters doing tasks to a place where there are men doing thinking, men who are conversing about the things of thought; we know that, because we have done it on a small scale. Wherever you have a small class and they can be intimately associated with their chief in the study of an interesting subject they catch the infection of the subject; but where they are in big classes and simply hear a man lecture two or three times a week, they cannot catch the infection of anything, except it may be the voice and enthusiasm of the lecturer himself. This is the way in which to transform the place." [13]

Faculty and trustees were enthusiastic for the new idea, but the chief

---

[11] W. W. to D. B. Jones, August 11, 1902, Baker Papers.

[12] President's Report to the Board of Trustees, October 21, 1902.

[13] *Princeton Alumni Weekly,* iii (December 13, 1902), 199-203.

stumbling block was the lack of funds. Wilson immediately set to work to solicit money for endowment from wealthy philanthropists, but when this approach failed he obtained the necessary support by raising an emergency fund from the alumni that would keep the preceptorial system going for three years. The task of selecting the preceptors was arduous, for Wilson insisted not only upon scholarship, but also gentility. Thus on one occasion he explained: "The importance of the whole system lies in the character of the men who are being obtained. In the first place they are being selected along very careful lines, and only those will be taken who feel a certain love for the place, and who are in entire sympathy with its spirit, and understand the scope of the plan which is being developed. They are to be selected primarily upon their standing as gentlemen, as men who are companionable, clubable, whose personal qualities of association give them influence over the minds of younger men. If their qualities as gentlemen and as scholars conflict, the former will win them the place." [14]

Yet the work went smoothly, and in the fall of 1905 Wilson was finally able to launch the preceptorial system.

Prerequisite to the preceptorial system was reorganization of the University's curriculum and its departmental structure, which Wilson carried through in 1903 and 1904. The new plan of study, which was finally adopted in 1904, was not Wilson's handiwork in the peculiar sense that the preceptorial system was; but he did provide the driving and motivating force behind the movement for academic reform, which he regarded as preliminary to all of the University's plans for the next generation.

Wilson began work with a faculty committee on the course of study in the fall of 1903. It was a gigantic task that confronted them, involving a sweeping reorganization of the University administrative structure as well as a reform of the course program. Professors in related subjects were organized in twelve departments, which in turn were grouped in four divisions: the division of philosophy, the division of art and archeology, the division of language and literature, and the division of mathematics and science. The latter division included all the mathematical and scientific studies and was designated as the new School of Science.

On April 14, 1904, the Committee on the Course of Study completed its work. During the next week and a half the new plan of study was

[14] Address before the Undergraduate Press Club. Princeton, April 15, 1905, *ibid.,* v (April 22, 1905), 472.

presented and discussed in a series of four faculty meetings, and on April 26 the plan was adopted unanimously by the faculty. "Everyone seemed to accept the *principle* of the report and all the main features of the scheme at once and without cavil," Wilson wrote triumphantly to his wife; "and the final adoption was characterized by real cordiality. All of which makes me very happy. It is not, as it stands now, exactly the scheme I at the outset proposed, but it is much better." [15]

Wilson explained the revision of the undergraduate course of study in an address soon after the new plan was adopted. Princeton could not return to a fixed course of study, he declared, for the modern variety of courses was too great; nor would the faculty yield to the recent tendency displayed at Harvard and Yale, toward absolutely free electives. "We have never yet been able or willing to admit that experience and study counted for nothing. We believe that in study as in everything else there must be guidance by those who have had experience, and submission to guidance by those who have had none." Consequently the freshman year at Princeton would remain a year of required studies, when freshmen would be "put into the mill that enables them to do the things that have to be done after freshman year."

"In sophomore year," Wilson continued, "we try to introduce a great deal more elasticity, but with this boundary, this limitation, that the choice is among fundamental studies. A man is not to be allowed to begin at the top. He has got to go by some logical sequence in the studies of sophomore year, and prepare himself fundamentally for the studies of junior and senior year.

"At the end of sophomore year we offer the student his choice among twelve departments of study. . . . When a man reaches the end of sophomore year he can concentrate his attention upon any one of the twelve departments grouped within . . . four divisions. We limit the number of junior courses in each department, so that a man cannot take more than two. . . . And we allow him to take five courses instead of seven as at present, increasing the number of hours devoted to each course from two to three, so that on a fifteen hour schedule he has five courses of study,—two in the department of his choice, a third he is advised to take in some properly related and supporting study, a fourth he is required to take outside the department and outside the division of his chief choice. His fifth elective is free to him to select as he pleases.

[15] W. W., to E. A. W., April 26, 1904, quoted in R. S. Baker, *Woodrow Wilson*, II, 160.

"When he comes to the end of his junior year he is at liberty to re-choose his department, to all intents and purposes. He needs only two courses to qualify him for any one department in senior year; and he can so arrange his choice in junior year that he will be qualified for either of two, or, it may be, three departments in senior year. So that a man can reserve his final choice until he is about to enter senior year; and then he specializes in the department of his final choice." [16]

The adoption and inauguration of the preceptorial system and the reorganization of the departmental and divisional structure and the undergraduate curriculum constitute Wilson's greatest educational achievements. They mark him as an educational statesman of original-ity and breadth and strength. Had he resigned the presidency of the University in 1905, his educational reputation would have been secured and it could have been then said that no man, in Princeton's one hun-dred and sixty years of existence, had made a greater contribution to the University's progress and greatness.

It is difficult to say which of the two reforms, the preceptorial system or the new plan of study, contributed most to Princeton's academic ad-vancement. Actually they were both conceived by Wilson as part of one general program of reform; and both systems have, with important modifications, remained the basis of Princeton's plan of undergraduate study. One other result of the adoption of the preceptorial system should be noted in passing. Wilson succeeded in rounding up fifty of the most promising young scholars in the country to fill the new preceptorships, and many of these developed into distinguished scholars. Most of them were attracted to Princeton by Wilson's revolutionary program, because they were fired with enthusiasm for his educational ideals.[17] Never has so much new life and vigor been injected at one stroke into an estab-lished university faculty.

In collegiate circles outside Princeton, however, Wilson's plan of cur-ricular reorganization has had a profounder influence than the precep-torial system. Few colleges have had the financial resources that are necessary for the adoption of the preceptorial system,[18] but most of them have followed Princeton's leadership in requiring a coordinated plan of study with the distinguishing feature of upperclass concentra-

---

[16] Address at the Alumni Luncheon at Princeton, June 14, 1904, *Princeton Alumni Weekly,* IV (June 18, 1904), 605.

[17] See, e.g., the account of Professor Robert K. Root's speech in *ibid.,* XLVI (Novem-ber 23, 1945), 4. Professor Root was one of the original "preceptor guys."

[18] Harvard and Yale, however, soon adopted the tutorial system.

tion. Harvard followed Wilson's leadership in 1910, and Yale adopted the plan shortly afterward.

To Wilson the most encouraging sign in 1906 was the unanimity with which the faculty, students, and alumni accepted his academic reforms. "The thing which has pleased me most in regard to the Preceptorial System," he declared, "is not only the splendid fact that the alumni have given us the money to conduct the system, but have welcomed the change and have felt that it enriched their own life." At the end of the first year's trial of the new program, Wilson reviewed the progress of the University under the new dispensation. Students had been given the privilege of carrying on their studies with the advice and encouragement of older scholars; they had been transformed from dilettantes into reading and thinking men. Teachers were no longer task-masters; they were now leaders of men. "We feel," Wilson said, "that we are entitled to be full of hope in regard to the increasing intellectual life of Princeton. For, gentlemen, I am covetous for Princeton of all the glory that there is, and the chief glory of a university is always intellectual glory. The chief glory of a university is the leadership of the nation in the things that attach to the highest ambitions that nations can set themselves, those ideals which lift nations into the atmosphere of things that are permanent and do not fade from generation to generation." [19]

In the spring and summer of 1906 Wilson was at the peak of his popularity at Princeton. He seemed irresistible. The phrase, "Wilson is Princeton's most valuable asset," [20] was used by trustees, faculty, and alumni alike to describe the man who had taken a backward college with ancient traditions and transformed it almost overnight into one of the leading educational laboratories in the nation. No second-hand account can communicate the spirit of enthusiasm and confidence that pervaded the Princeton community and the alumni at this time. There was new life, new spirit, and unbounded exuberance in the Princeton atmosphere. Almost all the young preceptors were ardent followers of Wilson; many of them still declare that these were the golden years of their lives when each man felt himself an important part of a great scheme under a great leader. The biographer is being constantly reminded of the former preceptors who now quote almost automatically, "Bliss was it in that dawn to be alive," whenever writing or speaking about the period.

[19] *Princeton Alumni Weekly*, VI (June 2, 1906), 652.
[20] The phrase was apparently Cleveland H. Dodge's. See C. H. Dodge to W. W., October 15, 1906, Wilson Papers.

The following story by Edwin Grant Conklin, who was called to a professorship in biology in 1907, must have been repeated a dozen times by as many different men: "A professor from another university, who had come to Princeton about the same time that I did, said to me, 'What brought you to Princeton?' I answered, 'Woodrow Wilson. And you?' 'The same,' he said. Both of us were inspired by his ideals of a university, of education, of life, and we wanted to join with him in the great work he was doing." [21]

A prominent alumnus from Pittsburgh best summarized the feeling of the alumni in the spring of 1906 when he wrote, "It must be exceedingly gratifying to you to already realize that the splendid work you are doing for Princeton is recognized and appreciated by thousands among the alumni and undergraduates, and by hundreds of thousands of outsiders. The universal expression among the trustees, faculty, alumni and undergraduates with whom I talked during the four days I spent in Princeton was that Princeton intellectually and materially was never in such a splendid position as she is today. The credit for this was uniformly and gladly laid at your feet. It has been your genius and your spirit which has gathered together and given direction to the loyalty of the splendid men on and off the Board who are holding up your hands." [22]

Yet events had gone almost too successfully for Wilson, for the triumph that he felt in 1906 deceived him into overestimating his influence over the Board of Trustees and the alumni. Probably it would have been better for Wilson and for Princeton if Wilson had encountered stronger opposition in getting his early reforms adopted. At any rate there was one characteristic of the man that was sometimes his greatest strength, sometimes his greatest weakness. He was not able to oppose the momentum that his nervous energy had built up within himself. He was not content to capitalize upon the popularity he had won as a result of the adoption of the preceptorial system and the new plan of study. He felt a compelling urge to move ahead.

A dangerous stroke of illness halted Wilson's activity during the summer of 1906, but in the fall he was back again at Princeton, hard at work upon a scheme for the reorganization of student social life. On December 13, 1906, he presented a preliminary report to the trustees. "The questions I am about to broach," he told them, "and their proper solution have been taking form in my mind for many years, and the sugges-

[21] E. G. Conklin, "Woodrow Wilson," MS in Baker Papers.
[22] Lawrence C. Woods to W. W., June 13, 1906, Wilson Papers.

tions I am about to make, though heretical in character, are the fruit of very mature consideration." The eating clubs that the undergraduates had built were seriously undermining the "old democratic spirit" of Princeton. He recommended abolition of the clubs and the division of the University into quadrangles, or colleges, where students would live and eat together. The trustees received Wilson's proposals with apparent approval and appointed a committee, with Wilson at its head, to investigate the problems involved in the proposed reorganization of campus social life.[23]

On June 10, 1907, Wilson presented a carefully prepared report to the board at its commencement meeting. It was a lengthy exposition and went thoroughly into every aspect and implication of the problem. A new university had been created out of the old Princeton, Wilson asserted; but if Princeton would have the academic leadership she could easily win, her leaders "must study at every turn the means by which to lift her intellectual life and achievements out of mediocrity not only, but also into such an order of naturalness and energy and distinction as shall make her by reason of her way of success a conspicuous model and example." The introduction of the preceptorial system, he continued, had been the "greatest strategic move" in the direction of elevating student intellectual life that had been made "in the whole history of American universities." The new plan of study inaugurated along with and as a result of the preceptorial system now demanded a new "social coordination" that would knit the student body together in "some truly organic way which will ensure vital intellectual and academic contacts, the comradeships of a common life with common ends." This end could be achieved best by combining the undergraduates into residential groups.

Wilson next launched his attack upon the eating clubs, and it was significant that he based his indictment largely upon the ground that the club system had operated to separate the social from the intellectual interests of the students. The eating clubs were products of natural growth at Princeton, he admitted, and served a useful purpose in providing boarding facilities for upperclassmen. But the clubs could not take in all the members of the junior and senior classes—"About one-third are left out in the elections; and their lot is little less than deplorable"—and loyalty to one's club was becoming much more important to the upperclassmen than loyalty to the University itself. Freshmen and sophomores were almost completely segregated from the

Sesquicentennial Orator, 1896

Ellen Axson Wilson

upperclassmen, whose guidance they needed. The clubs, moreover, had given rise to a spirit of exclusiveness, with the result that the social ambitions of the students were encouraged and the university democracy was being discredited. There had been a notable increase in the luxury of the club houses, and the University seemed in danger of becoming, "if the present tendencies of undergraduate organization are allowed to work out their logical results, only an artistic setting and background for life on Prospect Avenue." The vital life of the University would thus be outside the University and in large part independent of it.

The only solution of this difficult problem, Wilson insisted, was the abolition of the eating clubs and the grouping of undergraduates in residential quadrangles, each with its common dining hall, its common room for conversation and amusement, and its resident master and preceptors. Students of each class would be associated in a sort of family life in the quadrangles, "the upper classes ruling and forming the lower," and all in constant association with members of the faculty who were "fitted to act in sympathetic cooperation with them in the management of their common life." The effect of the new social arrangement on the clubs would of course be either their abolition or absorption into the new quadrangles.[24]

This was the famous quadrangle plan, which has been the cause of much controversy and debate since Wilson first proposed it. After reading the lengthy report of his committee, Wilson proceeded to explain to the trustees the chief significance, as he saw it, of the plan. The object of the quadrangle plan, to begin with, was not primarily a social reconstruction of student life, he explained. It was but an indispensable part of his purpose to accomplish "the reorganization and revitalization of the University as an academic body, whose objects are not primarily social but intellectual." He would have made his proposal regardless of whether the clubs existed, he added; they simply happened to stand in the way of the full intellectual development of the university community.

"We are not seeking to form better clubs," he concluded, "but academic communities. We are making a university, not devising a method of social pleasure. The social life of the quads will be all-inclusive, and it will serve as the medium of things intellectual. . . .

"I take leave to say that Princeton is the only university in the country which has found itself, which has formulated a clear ideal and deliber-

[24] *ibid.*, pp. 606-611.

ately set about the synthesis of plan necessary to realize it. . . . She must organize her life in such a way that these contacts between the university and the student shall be stuff of daily habit, and not merely matters of formal appointment; not a thing of the class-room and conference merely, but a thing which may touch every hour, any hour, of the day, and fill seasons of leisure and enjoyment with a consciousness of what it is that vitalizes a university and makes it a force in the life of a great nation. Common counsel shall bring us to this consummation, —not without trouble, but without serious conflict of opinion or purpose, as a new exhibition of what love of Princeton can do for her regeneration when her sons set themselves to the task. The labour will be pleasant, and the abiding fame of it will belong to all of us in common." [25]

The board adopted the report and authorized Wilson to take such steps as might "seem wisest for maturing this general plan, and for seeking the cooperation and counsel of the upper-class clubs in its elaboration." Wilson was also authorized to devise detailed plans for the future consideration of the board, "so soon as such plans can be perfected by common counsel among all concerned."

The publication of Wilson's sweeping plans in the *Princeton Alumni Weekly* on June 12 set off the opposition, and by mid-summer a serious controversy was raging. At first the opponents of the "quad" proposal were puzzled and dismayed. There developed immediately a widespread feeling among the alumni and particularly among several faculty members that Wilson and the board had acted dictatorially and with improper haste in approving the proposal without first seeking their advice. Wilson had mentioned the idea to only two or three of his intimate friends among the faculty; the remainder, including most of the prominent faculty leaders, had been neither informed nor consulted in the matter. The alumni had been entirely ignored.

The publication of the quadrangle proposal came as a complete surprise, for example, to Henry van Dyke and Andrew F. West, two of the elder faculty leaders. Van Dyke wrote to Wilson on July 3, asking if the plan had been definitely adopted. When Wilson replied two days later that although the "essential idea and purpose of the plan for residential quads" had been adopted, there was to be the freest possible inquiry as to how the idea might best be implemented, van Dyke replied in distress that it was the "essential idea" that made the radical change. "I am sorry that you did not tell me, when we were walking last Spring," van

Dyke added, "of this most important plan; and still more sorry that there has been no opportunity for general consideration and discussion before the decision was announced. Of course, if the essential idea is adopted, there is little more to be said." [26]

West, dean of the graduate school, was thoroughly outraged by what he considered Wilson's high-handed action. He wrote Wilson an indignant letter in which he accused him not only of presumptuous action but also of moral wrongdoing. West pointed out that the action of the board had been taken without allowing any opportunity for faculty opinion to be heard and had now made impossible unconstrained discussion of the fundamental questions involved. "If the Spirit of Princeton is to be killed," he concluded, "I have little interest in the details of the funeral." [27]

To these serious accusations, and to similar charges made by critics among the alumni, Wilson replied over and again that he and the Board of Trustees desired full and free discussion of the question of establishing the quadrangle system at Princeton. Thus he replied to van Dyke's protest by saying that although the essential idea of the plan had been adopted by the board, there would be an unrestrained opportunity for the faculty to discuss the plan "on its merits." It went without saying, he added, that if he did not have the support of the faculty the plan could not be carried out. [28] In reply to West's charge of immoral action, Wilson retorted that if West had had any faith in his, Wilson's, character and had waited until autumn, he would have seen how "wholly gratuitous and unfounded" were his statements. [29]

Yet it should be pointed out that on the fundamental question of whether the board had adopted the essential idea of the quadrangle plan, Wilson was completely uncompromising. His attempts, therefore, to disarm his critics by replying that he sincerely wanted full debate on the question evaded the main charge that the board had already settled the question and that nothing remained to be decided but the details. Notwithstanding these rumblings of faculty protest, Wilson was confident that he would receive the support of a large majority of the professors. The preceptors, who held the official rank of assistant professor and thus voted in faculty meetings, were with him almost to a man. Moreover, Theodore W. Hunt and William B. Scott, two older faculty

[26] H. van Dyke to W. W., July 5, 1907, Wilson Papers.
[27] A. F. West to W. W., July 10, 1907, *ibid.*
[28] W. W. to H. van Dyke, July 8, 1907, Baker Papers.
[29] W. W. to A. F. West, July 11, 1907, Wilson Papers.

members, had already written of their hearty approval of the plan.[30]

The opposition of a few faculty members, however, was nothing as compared to the widespread alarm and protest of the alumni. A spokesman for the alumni members of Tiger Inn club, for example, wrote Wilson almost immediately after the publication of the report on social coordination, informing him that all the members of the club were opposed to the "quad" plan because its adoption would mean an end of the class spirit at Princeton.[31] It was just the beginning of the alumni opposition, and by July 1 Wilson could write, "The fight for the quads is on very merrily, and must now be seen through to a finish. I think that in the long run it will be taken soberly and judiciously, though now there is a great deal of wild talk, and amidst the wild talk scores of particulars come to life which show that the situation is even worse than I had supposed, and that the remedy is absolutely imperative." [32]

A great part of the opposition was based on ignorance of what Wilson had proposed, to be sure, and yet it was an impossible task that Wilson undertook during the summer of 1907 when he tried by one means and then another to counteract the rising tide of hostility to the quadrangle plan. He had opened the controversy, it will be remembered, by making several charges against the clubs that could only be interpreted as meaning that he thought the clubs were exclusive, that they stimulated social snobbishness among their members, and that they were undermining the much-boasted democracy of the Princeton student community. Had Wilson desired to make a straightforward fight against the clubs on the issue of social democracy versus snobbery and social exclusiveness, he would not have been without supporters among the Princeton group and in the country at large. Melancthon W. Jacobus and David B. Jones, two members of the board, wrote Wilson constantly during the summer and fall and endeavored to convince him that the fight against the clubs was a battle for democracy at Princeton. Both men were much more belligerent on this issue than Wilson ever was. In addition, some of the alumni and several newspapers and magazines, among them the *New York Evening Post* and the *Review of Reviews,* took up the fight and proclaimed that Wilson was battling for social democracy. Thus could the battle have been joined on this issue.

The truth is, however, that Wilson resolutely refused to make such a

---

[30] T. W. Hunt to W. W., June 26, 1907, *ibid.;* W. B. Scott to W. W., June 26, 1907, *ibid.*

[31] Franklin Murphy, Jr., to W. W., June 20, 1907, *ibid.*

[32] W. W. to M. W. Jacobus, July 1, 1907, Baker Papers.

fight. To Jacobus, who was already portraying the controversy as a struggle between the plain people and the privileged classes, Wilson wrote on July 6 that he was particularly anxious that it should be understood that he was not attacking the clubs for what they were and did. It seemed to him, he continued, that the life and spirit of the clubs was excellent; his "whole point" was that their existence led to social results that stood in the way of a simple university organization suitable for intellectual purposes.[33] And over and over he repeated in his letters this assertion—that the aim of the quadrangle plan was not primarily social, but academic and intellectual. "I should be very much distressed to have the plan regarded as an attack on the clubs," he wrote on several occasions.[34]

Instead of raising the issue of democracy, Wilson undertook to explain in detail to the alumni the purpose and meaning of the quadrangle plan. Thus to Andrew C. Imbrie, who had asked a series of questions concerning the practical operation of the "quad" plan on behalf of a group of New York alumni, Wilson wrote on July 29 a lengthy letter of explanation. Students would be assigned to the "quads" by a faculty committee, but he could see no reason why the wishes of their parents should not also be considered, or why the students themselves should not be allowed to transfer from one "quad" to another. Only juniors and seniors would be allowed to eat in the commons rooms of the "quads"; if the clubs agreed to become incorporated into the quadrangles, the sons or brothers of former club members ought to be allowed to choose their "quads"; the "quads" would be self-governing in the most extensive way possible. What he meant by saying that his object in the quadrangle plan was not primarily social, but academic, "was that the object of it was to embody the life lived by the undergraduates outside the classroom in an organization which should be a university organization and not a congeries of social organizations managed entirely by undergraduates and primarily for social purposes." [35]

Even before September it was apparent that the great majority of the alumni were definitely opposed to the quadrangle proposal. In mid-July Wilson had admitted unhappily that there had not been a "flood of commendatory letters" endorsing the idea, and certainly the opposition to it increased as the summer passed. To implement the plan would

---

[33] W. W. to M. W. Jacobus, July 6, 1907, *ibid.*

[34] W. W. to A. C. Imbrie, July 13, 1907, Wilson Papers; W. W. to A. H. Osborn, July 17, 1907, *ibid.;* W. W. to A. C. Smith, July 15, 1907, *ibid.*

[35] W. W. to A. C. Imbrie, July 29, 1907, *ibid.*

require an expenditure of some $2,000,000; Wilson had tried unsuccessfully early in the summer to obtain the money from an outside source, and it was almost certain that if the alumni did not support the idea the money would not be forthcoming. The estimate of Francis Speir, that from three-fourths to nine-tenths of the alumni were opposing the quadrangle plan by mid-September,[36] does not seem unreasonable.

The net result of the opposition of the alumni was to convince the trustees that it was now impossible to go forward with the business of "maturing" the quadrangle plan. Some of the trustees were even beginning to doubt whether they had ever approved the plan; except for Jacobus and Jones, Wilson's firmest supporters on the board had concluded by mid-summer that it was hopeless to push the matter further.

On the other hand, no member of the board and few faculty members and alumni attempted to defend the clubs as they were constituted at the time. On all sides, even from the bitterest opponents of the "quad" proposal, there was general agreement that something had to be done to broaden the clubs so as to include all the upperclassmen and to bring the clubs under university control. Bayard Henry reported on July 29 that he had discussed the situation with a number of Princeton men and that they all agreed that radical changes in the club system should be made; very few of them, on the other hand, approved the "quad" idea. Both Henry and Cleveland H. Dodge pointed out the obvious fact that although Wilson could not possibly get the quadrangle system adopted at this time, he had stimulated the thought and agitation on the subject that would make possible far-reaching reforms in the club system itself. Both men suggested strongly that Wilson follow this plan of action.[37]

The conclusion is inevitable that this is exactly what Wilson did not want to do. A reformed and non-exclusive club system might well turn out to be a permanent system and might work so successfully that he could never obtain the adoption of the quadrangle plan. At any rate, he never once came forward, in 1907 or afterward, with a proposal to reform the club system. Had he done so in 1907 or 1908 he would have probably succeeded, but he would not accept the half loaf, even if that were all it was possible to get.

Instead, he became increasingly convinced of the utter necessity of

[36] F. Speir to W. W., September 20, 1907, *ibid*.

[37] B. Henry to W. W., July 29, 1907, *ibid.;* C. H. Dodge to W. W., September 28, 1907, *ibid*.

carrying through the quadrangle plan; he now believed that the controversy at Princeton was a struggle upon which depended the future of higher education in the United States.

"As for myself," he wrote, for example, "I feel that we are here debating, not only a plan, but an opportunity to solve a question common to all the colleges and obtain a leadership which it will not be within our choice to get again within our lifetime. The colleges of the country are looking to us for leadership in this matter, as in others, and if we disappoint them it will be an opportunity irretrievably lost. I have talked this subject over with a great many men from other universities, and I feel convinced that our solution will be accepted as the general solution, if we have strength and courage to act upon it." [38]

To Bayard Henry, who had counseled him to compromise and salvage as much out of the situation as he could, Wilson responded confidently that he was absolutely certain that the alumni would support the quadrangle plan when the matter had been explained to them. It might be a long and slow process to convince them, he added, but it was absolutely necessary to make such an attempt with courage and patience. He could not too seriously assure Henry, Wilson wrote, that he deemed the whole ultimate success of what had recently been attempted and achieved at Princeton dependent on the execution either of this plan or of some other equivalent to it in object and effect. [39]

Thus Wilson, by asserting that the success or failure of his educational program for Princeton lay in the balance in the "quad" fight, had taken a position from which it would be nearly impossible to retreat. He would accept no plan for the reform of the club system because he thought the club system itself would always stand in the way of the full intellectual development of the University. At this distance, such intransigence seems suicidal. On the other hand, it should be remembered that Wilson had unbounded confidence in his own popularity and in his power to change the minds of the alumni. He had never been defeated; he had done the impossible before. Who could doubt that the idea would eventually prevail? The "quad" plan was right; it was absolutely necessary. No honest man confronted with all the facts could think otherwise. Thus did Wilson reason in the summer and early fall of 1907.

Meanwhile, the faculty had divided into two factions, one supporting, the other opposing the quadrangle plan. At a meeting of the University

[38] W. W. to A. C. Imbrie, July 29, 1907, *ibid.*
[39] W. W. to B. Henry, August 6, 1907, *ibid.*

faculty on September 26 Winthrop More Daniels presented a resolution supporting the plan; Henry van Dyke countered with a resolution for the preservation and reformation of the club system. John Grier Hibben, Wilson's most devoted friend, seconded van Dyke's motion. Four days later van Dyke's resolution was debated by the faculty and defeated on a roll call by the decisive vote of 23 to 80. Thus triumphantly Wilson went before his faculty on October 7 and made what many of his friends thought was the greatest speech of his life. In it he epitomized all the arguments in favor of the quadrangle plan that he had previously set forth.

By the time the Board of Trustees met on October 17, however, the opposition among the alumni and trustees had increased so markedly that the advantage to Wilson of the overwhelming faculty support was more than offset. The trustees felt that there was nothing left for them to do but withdraw their approval of the quadrangle plan—the approval which they had given in June. This they did; and they also voted to discharge the committee on social coordination. It was a hard blow at Wilson's leadership and, in order to ease the shock, the trustees agreed that he should have complete freedom to continue agitation for the idea.[40]

Never had Wilson known such despair and discouragement as he felt after this action of the board. The trustees, he thought, had betrayed him in his effort to revitalize the intellectual life of the University. "I have got nothing out of the transaction," he wrote indignantly on October 23, "except complete defeat and mortification."[41] He even thought of resigning and going into law practice in Virginia, and he started to write a letter of resignation to the board. He could not bring himself to do it, however, and the letter was never finished.[42]

Among Wilson's friends on the Board of Trustees, only Jacobus and Jones refused to admit defeat. Instead of confronting the situation realistically and accepting the defeat with good grace, they endeavored to goad Wilson's resentment and to force him to continue the fight. Jacobus, especially, was now more than ever convinced that the battle for democracy and righteousness must go on. "I have no hesitation as to what is your duty in this situation," he wrote to Wilson on October 25. "This is too serious a matter not to be taken seriously by the Board as well as by yourself, for it is being taken most seriously by the great

[40] *Princeton Alumni Weekly,* VIII (October 23, 1907), 67.
[41] W. W. to M. W. Jacobus, October 23, 1907, Baker Papers.
[42] The letter, which was written in shorthand, is in the Wilson Papers.

public who are interested in the matter far more deeply than the smart set of the Clubs or the sacred set of the Board at present realize. This public and the great body of the alumni of Princeton expect you to do just what the public statement said you were free to do. . . .

"Now, I would act upon this expectation; and if I had to wait for the opportunity to act, I would wait for it with the patience of Job. I would not resign now. I would fight it out. I would take my time, but I would make the scheme and the principle which it embodies so plain to every Alumni Association that the self-respecting spirit of American democracy would rise to the acceptance of them with the instinct of the preservation of our national institutions. . . . Be assured that the plain people of the great body of the alumni and of the educational world outside are with you as surely as the plain people of the nation were with Abraham Lincoln forty-five years ago, or with Theodore Roosevelt today; and in the end you have got to win out." [43]

Wilson's despair over the reversal of the board soon gave way, not to hope, but to grim determination, and in the closing months of 1907 the quadrangle question was overshadowing all other matters in his thought. He had made up his mind finally and absolutely on the question and had convinced himself that he was absolutely right. "I have never for a moment thought of giving the fight up," he wrote to Jacobus in November. "On the contrary, every indication has convinced me that it is more necessary even than I had thought. Nothing else than such reforms as we have in mind will make Princeton free of the influences which are now allowed to govern her; and if we can bring our Princeton constituency to see the necessity of the reform, it is clearly our duty to do so, no matter how long it takes or how hard the task may prove." He even contemplated sacrificing his cherished preceptorial system, if that were necessary to obtain the quadrangles. "We shall really not be free to do what we deem best at Princeton until we are relieved from the dictation of the men who subscribe to the Committee of Fifty Fund and who can withhold our living from us if we displease them," he concluded.[44]

Finally, Wilson determined upon an unusual and hitherto untried plan of action: he would carry the fight to his constituency, the alumni; he would appeal to them over the heads of his parliament, the trustees.

[43] Wilson Papers.

[44] W. W. to M. W. Jacobus, November 6, 1907, Baker Papers. The Committee of Fifty was the organization that supplied the money for the operation of the preceptorial system.

He opened his campaign in an address to the Baltimore alumni. The appeal that he made was balanced and conciliatory, and he made no reference at all to the democratic character of the "quad" fight. He was not even irrevocably committed to the quadrangle idea, he declared; he only insisted that something be done that would put the intellectual instead of the social interests at the forefront at Princeton.[45] In Chicago a few days later Wilson continued his effort to obtain the support of the alumni for the "quads." He was apparently determined to antagonize no one, and the speech was largely ineffective. On the one hand he praised the clubs; they were "as good specimens as the country can afford of clean and wholesome organizations conducted as we would wish to see young gentlemen conduct the associations they form in college and where the high standards of honor are of the spirit of the place." On the other hand, he demanded abolition of the clubs because they claimed too much of the time and energies of the students. "Intellectual matters, intellectual influences, are at a hopeless disadvantage in the competition," he declared.[46]

Wilson's appeal to the alumni was a total failure. The truth is that it was almost impossible to enlist the support of the alumni for a proposal to elevate the intellectual life of the students at a cost of $2,000,000 or more, plus disruption of the existing social life of the University. The trustees had, in January 1908, appointed a committee of Wilson's most loyal supporters to investigate the club situation. The committee made a report on April 8 that, for the most part, ended the "quad" controversy. Although recognizing and describing certain evils in the club system and advising against the establishment of additional clubs, the committee gave the clubs a clean bill of health and declared that they constituted forces for good in the lives of the students. "There are no indications that the life of these institutions tends toward dissipation," the committee declared. "On the contrary their atmosphere seems more likely to encourage morality, and in reality produces more satisfactory standards of conduct than exist among the two lower classes." The report concluded, significantly, in light of Wilson's assertion that the clubs were blocking the intellectual progress of the University, that membership in the clubs did not seem to lower academic standards, "nor to discourage study in itself." [47]

[45] *Princeton Alumni Weekly,* VIII (March 11, 1908), 370-371.

[46] *ibid.,* p. 404.

[47] "Report of Henry B. Thompson, Edward W. Sheldon, and Andrew C. Imbrie, to the Board of Trustees, April 8, 1908," *ibid.,* pp. 585-589.

With the publication of this report the ground was entirely cut out from under Wilson's feet. He was defeated on the "quads," and the defeat was final. He rarely mentioned the question again and never again broached it publicly. He was dreadfully unhappy during the year 1907-1908. Defeat comes hard to high-spirited and imperious men, and often results in a feeling of great frustration. So it was with Wilson. "I have found the past year go very hard with me," he wrote to Cleveland H. Dodge, at the end of the academic year in June 1908. "I feel, as you know, blocked in plans upon which I feel the successful administration of the University, both as a teaching body and as a wholesome society, depends, and for which I can find no substitute, and in these circumstances it has been a struggle with me all the year to keep in any sort of spirits." [48]

The conclusion is inevitable that Wilson's intransigence in the matter of social coordination, his refusal to compromise by accepting a reform of the club system, and his refusal to treat tolerantly those who opposed him were among the major mistakes of his career. He came out of the battle with bitter spirits; he broke with two of his oldest and closest friends, Hibben and M. Taylor Pyne; and he incurred the bitter enmity of Grover Cleveland, a member of the Board of Trustees. Yet it was an important crisis in Wilson's life, a crisis that revealed that he was a stubborn fighter who would not admit defeat until the odds were overwhelmingly against him. As James Kerney has written, "It was no pink-tea performance. Wilson never admitted to himself for a moment that he might be wrong. He had the true fighter's cold and merciless fury. His arrogant methods alienated many who might have otherwise helped with the reform at Princeton. But it was both his weakness and his strength to take a worthy cause and divert it into a personal quarrel." [49]

[48] W. W. to C. H. Dodge, June 18, 1908, Baker Papers.

[49] *Political Education of Woodrow Wilson*, pp. 9-10. The present writer has treated the "quad" fight in the foregoing pages only as it developed at Princeton at the time. There yet remains the question of the numerous accounts, which have arisen since 1910, showing Wilson battling the forces of aristocracy and snobbery at Princeton. Most of these accounts are *ex post facto*, for Wilson obviously made an assiduous effort to subordinate the social issues to the intellectual issues involved in the controversy.

Perhaps the most elaborate version of the "quad" fight as a battle for social democracy is William Bayard Hale's account in his semi-official campaign biography, *Woodrow Wilson, the Story of His Life*, written in 1912. See also Josephus Daniels' account in his recent *The Wilson Era*, pp. 5-6, for a later commentary on the same theme.

Wilson was not reluctant in 1912 to make political capital of the episode. The account of the controversy in the Hale biography and in the *Democratic Text-Book, 1912*, p. 57, emphasizes the social issues involved in the controversy.

CHAPTER III

"The Battle of Princeton"

HARDLY had the controversy over the eating clubs subsided than Wilson again found himself the center of an acrimonious controversy, this time over the location and control of the graduate college for which Princeton was preparing to construct a building. Andrew Fleming West, Wilson's chief opponent in the fight, was a Scotsman and was as stubborn and opinionated as Wilson himself. West had been professor of classics at Princeton since 1883; he was a world-renowned scholar. During the haphazard administration of President Patton, West had assumed a large share in the control of the University's affairs. During the sesquicentennial celebration, for example, he had been in charge of the program. He had taken the leadership in the faculty during the years 1896-1900 in the movement for the establishment and endowment of a graduate college at Princeton.

In 1900 the trustees finally yielded to the promptings of the faculty and established the graduate school of Princeton University. West was elected dean, responsible to the president and Board of Trustees, and was given control over all graduate courses, fellowships, and appointments; he was also empowered to select his own faculty committee. A trustees' committee, with Moses Taylor Pyne as chairman, was also established by the board. West took up his work with enthusiasm and soon had plans under way for the building up of an extensive graduate establishment at Princeton.

Wilson also recognized from the very first the necessity of establishing a graduate school at Princeton. In his inaugural address in 1902, for example, he had given enthusiastic approval to the idea. "We mean . . . to build a notable graduate college," he said. "We shall build it, not apart, but as nearly as may be at the very heart, the geographical heart, of the university; and its comradeship shall be for young men and old, for the novice as well as for the graduate." [1] The two fundamental ideas of a graduate school located at the approximate center of the campus and closely coordinated with undergraduate life and studies are of utmost significance. They were the things for which Wilson more or

[1] *Public Papers*, 1, 457.

less consistently fought. Wilson, moreover, understood at the time that he was faithfully representing the views of Dean West.[2]

Upon assuming the presidency of the University, Wilson asked West to continue as dean and promised him complete support for his graduate college plans. During the summer and fall of 1902 West made a trip to Europe and studied the graduate establishments of the leading European universities. He returned in December and the following month prepared a report on a proposed residential graduate college for Princeton. Wilson read the report with intense interest and made a number of revisions in the original manuscript.[3] He also wrote the following preface, which was taken largely from his report to the trustees of October 21, 1902:

"On the side of University growth, a Graduate College is undoubtedly our first and most obvious need, and the plans for such a college which Professor West has conceived seem to me in every way admirable. To carry them out would unquestionably give us a place of unique distinction among American Universities. He has conceived the idea of a Graduate School of residence, a great quadrangle in which our graduate students will be housed like a household, with their own commons and with their own rooms of conference, under a master, whose residence should stand at a corner of the quadrangle in the midst of them. This is not merely a pleasing fancy of an English college placed in the midst of our campus; but in conceiving this little community of scholars set at the heart of Princeton, Professor West has got at the gist of the matter, the real means by which a group of graduate students are most apt to stimulate and set the pace for the whole University. I hope that the privilege of building and developing such an institution may be accorded us in the near future, in order that in carrying out our plans the scope and efficiency of the University may be assured from the very outset."[4]

Because there was later considerable controversy as to the nature of Dean West's ideals for a graduate college, it is necessary to review briefly his suggestions embodied in *The Proposed Graduate College of Princeton University,* which Wilson praised so fulsomely in 1903. West's

[2] See his Report to the Board of Trustees, October 21, 1902.
[3] A. F. West to M. C. Fleming, March 21, 1910, copy in the Moses Taylor Pyne Papers, Library of Princeton University; hereinafter cited as Pyne Papers. See also A. F. West, "A Narrative of The Graduate College of Princeton University From Its Proposal In 1896 Until Its Dedication In 1913," MS in the Library of Princeton University; hereinafter cited as "A Narrative of the Graduate College."
[4] *The Proposed Graduate College of Princeton University,* p. 3.

report might be regarded as giving a classic description of an ideal graduate establishment. He realized, first of all, that no graduate school could succeed that did not have "the best professors procurable"; without them, he wrote, "architecture and gardens, even fellowships and students, will be wholly insufficient because the central inspiration will be lacking." Consequently he suggested that $1,775,000 of the $3,000,000 he hoped to obtain be devoted to the endowment of fifteen professorships. He realized, moreover, that good professors could not be had without good students, who should be carefully selected on a basis of scholarship, character, and general cultural attainments. He proposed an endowment fund, the income from which would provide for forty fellowships. Finally West proposed spending $600,000 of his general fund for buildings. He envisioned the graduate college as a thing of beauty and architectural distinction, but it would be wrong to conclude that he was primarily concerned with Gothic towers and medieval cloisters and arches. The architecture of the proposed college, on the contrary, was entirely secondary in his dynamic ideal of a graduate college (or school) that would join faculty, graduate students, and even undergraduates in one great intellectual enterprise, which he thought would stimulate scholarly achievement throughout the nation.[5]

For several years no progress was made in giving life and reality to West's proposals, because Wilson was entirely absorbed in the business of reorganizing the curriculum and securing the preceptorial system. Wilson, in fact, even vetoed West's plans to solicit gifts from the alumni for the endowment of the graduate college; he, Wilson, needed any funds that might be available for the endowment of the preceptorial system. West gave enthusiastic support to Wilson's undergraduate reform program and approved it as heartily as any member of the faculty; but he did not hesitate to point out that the preceptorial system had seriously retarded the development of a graduate school at Princeton because it had meant increased teaching loads and additional administrative duties for the professors. In 1904 Grover Cleveland, who was one of West's most intimate friends, was made chairman of the trustees' committee on the graduate school; and West soon enlisted the support of Moses Taylor Pyne, probably the outstanding trustee, in behalf of his project.

On June 10, 1905, West announced to the board that he had at last obtained a temporary residence for the graduate students at an estate

[5] *ibid.*, pp. 7-20.

named Merwick, off the campus on Bayard Lane. On September 21 Merwick was opened as a residential house for graduate students; Professor Howard Crosby Butler was master in residence. "The house is comfortable and spacious," Wilson wrote in his annual report for 1905, "stands in beautiful grounds, ornamented with delightful shade trees, and . . . has at once become an institution among us. We believe that in this graduate house we have a sure prophecy of the Graduate College for which we so eagerly hope as the crowning distinction of Princeton's later development as a University."

In March 1906, Mrs. Josephine A. Thompson Swann died, leaving to the University some $250,000 for the construction of the "John R. Thompson Graduate College." In October of the same year West was offered the presidency of the Massachusetts Institute of Technology. It was the greatest strategical mistake of Wilson's career at Princeton that he did not seize the opportunity to let the trustees know that he could not cooperate with West and that he preferred that West accept the call to M. I. T. Wilson was at the height of his power at Princeton, and had he forced a show-down fight in the board the trustees would surely have supported him. Actually, West would have gone to M. I. T. without a forcing of the issue had he had the slightest intimation that he would not be allowed to proceed with his plans for a graduate college. For it was already evident that it would be difficult, if not impossible, for Wilson and West to work together on the matter of the graduate school.

Instead of letting the trustees know where he stood, Wilson simply said nothing at all at first. At a meeting of the trustees' committee on the graduate school on October 19, West let it be known plainly upon what terms he would remain at Princeton. He declared that he had been working for ten years to secure a graduate school at Princeton and that he did not wish to be identified indefinitely with an apparently unsuccessful enterprise. When Wilson challenged him to state specifically his complaints, West replied, "The trouble, President Wilson, is that I have not hit it off with you." When Wilson demanded that he be more specific, West spent half an hour relating why he thought Wilson had not given him his support in his plans for the expansion of the graduate school. "Whether I go or stay, I should like it to be on an unmistakable basis, and I hope on a basis of friendship too," West concluded.[6]

The upshot of the meeting was that Wilson said no more. The committee, including Wilson, officially requested West to remain at Princeton and promised him wholehearted support for his graduate college

[6] A. F. West, "A Narrative of the Graduate College," pp. 25-27.

plans. On October 20 the Board of Trustees adopted a motion, written by Wilson, which declared that the board would consider West's loss "quite irreparable." "The Board has particularly counted upon him to put into operation the Graduate College which it has planned," the resolution read. "It begs to assure him that he cannot be spared."

West decided to stay and believed that he would now be given free rein in the execution of his plans. Wilson, however, did nothing at all to get the graduate project under way; and when, in 1907, he proposed instead the adoption of the "quad" system, the break between the two men was final and complete. West, Pyne, and Cleveland, and the other supporters of the graduate college project were amazed when Wilson put forward his quadrangle proposal. They objected to Wilson's injection of this new issue because they believed that he had already committed himself to undertake the building of the graduate college immediately after the inauguration of the preceptorial system. They declared that it would take several years to finance and build the quadrangles and feared that the construction of the graduate college might be postponed indefinitely should the "quad" plan be approved. In short, they felt that Wilson was guilty of a breach of faith. In the board and in the faculty West and his friends took the leadership in the fight against the "quads." The controversy that followed during 1907 and 1908 marked the divergence among the faculty and trustees that was to widen during 1909 and 1910 and result finally in an almost fatal rupture. The "quad" controversy, in short, was the beginning of the tragic dénouement of Wilson's Princeton career.

The question of the graduate college, therefore, was completely overshadowed during 1907 by the battle raging over Wilson's plan for social coordination. But when the "quad" plan was definitely rejected early in 1908, the question of the graduate college came to the front. In March the trustees' committee supported Wilson's contention that the graduate college should be built on the grounds of Prospect, the president's home, and on April 9 the board formally approved the committee's action. It was a setback for West, Cleveland, and Pyne, who had determined that the college should be off the campus, preferably at Merwick.

Wilson next proceeded to weaken West's control over the graduate school; during the early months of 1909 the president persuaded the trustees' committee and the board to adopt a reorganization measure which stripped West of most of his authority and placed control of the graduate school's curriculum and appointments in the hands of a faculty committee dominated by Wilson supporters. At the meeting of the trustees' committee when the reorganization scheme was adopted, West protested that the action of the committee was inconsistent with the declaration of confidence the board had accorded him in 1906. West asked Wilson why he supported the reorganization proposal. "I wish to say to the Dean somewhat grimly," West later quoted Wilson as having said, "that he must be digested in the processes of the University." [7]

West, however, did not resign the deanship, as Wilson had undoubtedly hoped he would do; and West refused to be so easily defeated, for he knew then that he possessed one trump card—and he was about ready to play it at this desperate moment in his academic career. On May 10, 1909, he handed to Wilson a letter from William Cooper Procter of Cincinnati, in which Procter offered to give $500,000 for a graduate college provided an equal sum were raised by the trustees. The most important part of the letter, however, was the last paragraph, in which Procter wrote that he did not approve of building the college on the campus. He objected to the Prospect site because he thought the ground space was not large enough and would prevent any future expansion of the graduate college facilities. "I feel, therefore, obliged to say," he wrote, "that this offer is made upon the further understanding that some other site be chosen, which shall be satisfactory to me." [8]

West and Procter had been friends from boyhood, and it was natural that Procter should have been influenced by West's opinions in the matter of locating the graduate college. There had been nothing particularly secret about the West-Procter negotiations that had preceded the making of the offer. West had told Wilson and the trustees' committee on April 2 that Procter's offer would probably be made soon and that Procter objected to the Prospect site; they had encouraged the dean to secure the benefaction.

Wilson was at first hopeful that some sort of amicable agreement could be reached with Procter. He declared that since the Swann bequest stipulated that the graduate college should be constructed on the University campus, the Swann money could not be legally used to construct a graduate college on any site that was not a part of the campus at the time the bequest was made. But Procter was adamant; he preferred the Merwick site, he declared, but if the president and trustees would not approve that location, he would agree to build the college on

[7] *ibid.*, p. 44.
[8] W. C. Procter to A. F. West, May 8, 1909, published in *Princeton Alumni Weekly*, **x** (February 16, 1910), 303.

the site of the golf links which had been purchased by the University in 1905 about a mile from the campus proper.[9]

It was evident by the summer of 1909 that another first-class controversy was in the making, and the lines of battle were beginning to be tightly drawn at Princeton. The faculty divided on the graduate college issue as they had divided in the "quad" fight, and a majority apparently supported Wilson. The trustees, also, were divided into Wilson and West factions. Pyne, who became chairman of the trustees' committee on the graduate school in the summer of 1909, was at first dubious as to whether the trustees should accept Procter's offer;[10] but when Procter consented to build the college on the site of the golf links, Pyne strongly urged acceptance of Procter's offer.[11]

Meanwhile, there were increasing demands from the alumni that the trustees accept Procter's offer. Wilson made one last, unsuccessful effort to persuade Procter to consent to the building of the college on the campus,[12] but Procter again refused and declared that he thought it essential that the graduate establishment have a location distinct and apart from the undergraduate college.[13] West, Pyne, and Procter, in the meantime, had combined into what amounted to an anti-Wilson bloc.[14] Pyne wrote Procter a "confidential" letter on October 5, for example, and assured him that a majority of the trustees' committee opposed Wilson in the matter of the location of the college.[15] Finally, on October 21, the board voted to accept Procter's offer and to place the graduate college on the golf links, provided "the legal right to use Mrs. Swann's money in the erection of the Graduate School upon the Golf Links be assured, and that Mr. Procter first advise us of his intention in relation to the disposition of his proposed gift." [16] It appeared that the controversy was at last settled; at least, Pyne, West, and Procter thought that it was.

Wilson was dumbfounded by the board's decision to accept the Procter offer, yet he made no protest at the meeting. In fact, the trustees were

[9] W. C. Procter to W. W., June 7, 1909, *ibid.*

[10] M. T. Pyne to R. A. Cram, May 18, 1909, copy in Pyne Papers.

[11] M. T. Pyne to R. A. Cram, June 16, 1909, *ibid.;* M. T. Pyne to W. W., July 27, 1909, *ibid.*

[12] W. W. to E. W. Sheldon, October 19, 1909, Baker Papers.

[13] W. C. Procter to M. T. Pyne, October 20, 1909, Pyne Papers.

[14] See, e.g., W. C. Procter to M. T. Pyne, October 13 and 25, 1909; M. T. Pyne to W. C. Procter, October 5 and 26, 1909, all in *ibid.*

[15] M. T. Pyne to W. C. Procter, October 5, 1909, *ibid.*

[16] Copy of resolution in *ibid.*

told soon afterward that Wilson had accepted the decision and would carry it out faithfully.[17] This, however, was a rumor without foundation; actually Wilson was greatly discouraged and felt that the control of the University had been taken out of his hands.

The truth was, however, that, as far as the general body of the trustees and alumni were concerned, the issue was not at all clear. They could not understand why there should be so much controversy over what many persons termed a "real estate proposition." Wilson's friends on the board urged him to come out frankly and tell the trustees that the real issue was not (as Wilson himself believed) the location of the graduate college, but what kind of college it would be and, more important, who should control it. As early as 1906 it had been evident that the real cause of the friction between Wilson and West was this question of control. Melancthon W. Jacobus expressed this conviction when he wrote early in 1910, "We are not discussing any further in this main issue the legality of the golf links site. . . . All these things are swept aside before the question as to whether West is to continue to have anything to do with the Graduate Department in the way of control." [18]

Henry B. Thompson, another Wilson supporter on the board, afterward wrote: "Wilson's serious mistake in the Graduate College controversy was that he permitted his opponents to make the site of the Graduate College the main issue; Wilson himself, you will see, made this most important. While it was important, it was distinctly unimportant in connection with the real issue, which was Dean West's running the Graduate College as a Dictator. . . . This was the real issue, and Jacobus, McCormick, and I, over and over again, tried to induce the President to fight it out on those lines and ignore the site." [19]

Wilson, however, refused at first to make the issue a personal quarrel. He tried to secure a compromise, and on December 18, 1909, suggested to Pyne that the Swann bequest be used to build a graduate dormitory on the campus and that a separate graduate college also be constructed on the golf links with the Procter money. Procter, Wilson added, might simply spend all his money for buildings.[20] Pyne did not think this remarkable suggestion worth consideration.

---

[17] From an untitled, undated manuscript account of the graduate college controversy by Wilson Farrand, a copy of which is in the Wilson Farrand Papers, Library of Princeton University; hereinafter cited as Farrand Papers.

[18] M. W. Jacobus to E. W. Sheldon, January 27, 1910, Edward W. Sheldon Papers, Library of Princeton University; hereinafter cited as Sheldon Papers.

[19] H. B. Thompson to R. S. Baker, March 8, 1927, Baker Papers.

[20] M. T. Pyne to J. B. Shea, December 18, 1909, Pyne Papers.

Wilson seemed to make no headway at all during those early December days; he was deeply discouraged, more discouraged than he had been by his defeat in the quadrangle controversy. Finally he wrote to Pyne on December 22 that the acceptance of the Procter offer had taken the guidance of the University out of his hands. "I seem to have come to the end," he concluded.[21] "I trust that what was evidently a hasty note pencilled by you," Pyne immediately replied, ". . . does not represent your well considered conclusions, and that you will withdraw it upon further consideration." [22]

Wilson replied in a lengthy letter, setting forth the issues, as he saw them, involved in the controversy. He had written under deep excitement, it was true, but his judgment had not been hastily formed. "The graduate establishment on the Golf Links cannot succeed," he wrote. The faculty did not approve of a graduate college which did not constitute the geographical and intellectual center of the University. West, because he had abandoned this principle, had lost completely the confidence of the faculty, "and nothing administered by him in accordance with his present ideas can succeed." "Indeed," Wilson added, "nothing administered by him can now succeed." Wilson next set forth his contention that the Swann bequest could not be used to build a graduate college on the golf links.[23] "I therefore proposed to Mr. Procter, on Wednesday last," Wilson continued, "that we carry out her will exactly by erecting Thompson College in close association with the present buildings of the University, and that as much as necessary of his proffered gift be devoted to the erection and maintenance on the Golf links of such an establishment as he favours. This suggestion meets with the hearty concurrence of my colleagues here."

The board's acceptance of the Procter offer, Wilson concluded, had reversed the policy of the faculty and repudiated his leading educational principles. "I cannot accede to the acceptance of gifts upon terms which take the educational policy of the University out of the hands of the

[21] W. W. to M. T. Pyne, December 22, 1909, *ibid.*

[22] M. T. Pyne to W. W., December 24, 1909, Wilson Papers.

[23] It is difficult to understand Wilson's adherence to this idea, upon which he based his entire argument for two separate residential colleges. Only one legal authority, W. J. Magie of the New Jersey Court of Chancery, supported Wilson's contention. The executors of Mrs. Swann's estate did not. They believed that the wording of Mrs. Swann's will requiring that the graduate college be built on "the grounds of said University," offered no legal obstacles to building the college on the golf links, since the ground had been purchased by the University and had since become University property. Pyne consulted with several leading legal authorities in New Jersey, all of whom agreed with the executors, Pyne, and West in the matter.

Trustees and the Faculty and permits it to be determined by those who give money," he concluded. Either the trustees would refuse the Procter offer, or else he would resign.[24]

It was a fighting letter and left no doubt as to Wilson's intentions. It is evident, however, that he had no idea that he would be forced to resign; on the contrary, he had just begun to fight. One is reminded of the Wilson of a later period—when he was governor of New Jersey, indefatigably rallying his forces to defeat a reactionary candidate for the Senate or to obtain the passage of a reform measure by the legislature. First, he must be sure of the support of a majority of the trustees. Consequently he sent copies of his letter to all the trustees, and added a personal note to each one. Thus, he wrote to one trustee that he had been compelled to come to an important decision—that if there was to be a university worth presiding over, gifts made on Procter's terms must be declined. Wilson added that he understood those terms now as he never did before: they meant West in the saddle, the board and faculty without choice of their own, and the whole administration in leading strings.[25]

Again, to another trustee, Wilson wrote that he had taken his stand in opposition to Procter's offer without the least personal feeling of any kind. He did not think that any man was at liberty to undertake the administration of a policy when he could not put his force and enthusiasm into executing that policy. There was involved in the question not only the principle which he stated in his letter to Pyne, Wilson added, but also a state of opinion among the leading men in the faculty which justified him in saying he could not carry out West's ideas in the administration of the graduate school.[26]

One thing, at least, Wilson had done—he had finally come out frankly and told the trustees that he could not work with Dean West in the graduate college matter; he had finally made it plain that the trustees would have to choose between him and Procter's money. On December 31, 1909, Henry B. Thompson wrote to Pyne the following letter, which explains better than anything else Wilson's feeling at the time:

"I saw the President [yesterday] at his house, by appointment, and went over the situation with regard to Dean West and the Graduate School. To boil the whole question down, we have reached a point

[24] W. W. to M. T. Pyne, December 25, 1909, Pyne Papers.

[25] W. W. to S. S. Palmer, December 27, 1909, copy in Farrand Papers.

[26] W. W. to J. B. Shea, December 31, 1909, copy in *ibid.*

which I was afraid, as far back as two years ago, we would ultimately come to, and that is, the President and Dean West cannot maintain a permanent relationship in the work of the University. I said to Cleve Dodge, at the time of the Institute of Technology offer, that it would only be a question of time when we would reach the point that we have arrived at now. The President has apparently made up his mind absolutely on the lines of the letter which he has written you. He shows no excitement, but feels that he has gone to the limit on his handling of West, and says, with entire frankness, that if the Trustees are not satisfied with his position, he is entirely willing to accept the result, but he wants it absolutely understood that this attitude is not taken as a threat or as a hold-up, but that his position is intolerable, and, unless he has relief, he cannot maintain the Presidency of the University." [27]

Thus had Wilson raised the personal issue squarely and had made it plain that the board, which was to meet on January 13, 1910, would have to choose also between him and West. During the few days before the meeting there were many conferences of little groups of trustees. One group, headed by Thompson, Jacobus, Dodge, and Edward W. Sheldon, was determined to stand by the president no matter what the odds against him. The Pyne-Procter-West group was profoundly alarmed by the recent turn of events, yet seemed not quite ready to force a show-down fight that would result in the disruption of the board and perhaps also of the University. Neither side apparently was certain of a majority.

The trustees met at Princeton on January 13 in an atmosphere tense with excitement. Wilson had prepared a resolution declaring that because of the conflict of opinion as to the site for the graduate college the trustees felt compelled to reject Procter's offer. Before the resolution could be introduced, however, Pyne startled the board by producing a letter from Procter accepting Wilson's proposal that two separate graduate colleges be built.[28] The introduction of Procter's letter threw Wilson completely off balance, and what he said subsequently amazed the board. He declared that the trustees might as well admit that they had all been arguing on a basis of false assumptions and had avoided the real, fundamental issue, which was the ideals upon which the graduate

[27] Copy in Pyne Papers.
[28] W. C. Procter to M. T. Pyne, January 12, 1910, *ibid*. Pyne and Procter used this letter intentionally for the purpose of clarifying the question of the importance of the geographical location of the graduate college. See M. T. Pyne to J. B. Shea, January 15, 1910, *ibid*.

school was to be founded. Geography and location, he declared, were not important; the faculty did not care where the college was placed. "If the Graduate School is based on proper ideals," he added, "our Faculty can make a success of it anywhere in Mercer County."

Why, then, did Wilson object to the acceptance of Procter's offer? Because, Wilson proceeded to say, Procter was attempting to carry out Dean West's ideals for the graduate college. Wilson drew a copy of West's *Proposed Graduate College of Princeton University* from under a pile of papers, held it up before him, and exclaimed, "There, gentlemen, in that book is the real reason why the Procter gift must be declined. That book contains Professor West's ideals for the Graduate School. They are his personal ideals; they are not the ideals of Princeton University, and they are radically wrong. The fundamental difficulty with Mr. Procter's offer is that it is specifically intended to carry out the ideals of that book. A graduate school based on these ideals cannot succeed." [29]

When one of the trustees asked why Wilson had written a fulsome and commendatory preface to the book, he declared that he had not seen the book when he had written the preface.[30] One contradiction, unfortunately, led to another. When one trustee reminded Wilson that Procter had explicitly accepted his proposal to construct two graduate colleges and declared that there should now be no cause for disagreement, Wilson replied that he had made a mistake. "I made my proposition to Mr. Procter in perfect good faith," he declared, "but when I told my friends in the faculty what I had suggested, they convinced me that the plan was impracticable and unwise." [31] If this statement were

[29] Wilson Farrand, MS narrative of the graduate college controversy; see also M. T. Pyne to W. C. Procter, January 15, 1910, Pyne Papers, which confirms Farrand's account in every particular.

[30] There is no point in answering in detail the Wilson apologists who contend that Wilson's preface consisted of a part of his report to the Board of Trustees of October 21, 1902, and that he had not really seen West's book when he wrote the preface for it. It is granted that this contention perhaps is correct. On the other hand, and according to West's testimony, Wilson had read and carefully edited the manuscript before the book was published (A. F. West to M. C. Fleming, March 21, 1910, Pyne Papers), and the present writer accepts West's statement as correct. If this be true, as the present writer thinks it is, then certainly Wilson had to accept full responsibility for all he had said in the preface with regard to West's ideals. This does not mean necessarily that Wilson deliberately made a false statement in order to evade an embarrassing question. He had a notoriously bad memory for details—all of his friends testify to this fact— and it is probable that in his excitement he forgot that he had ever seen the West manuscript.

[31] Wilson Farrand, MS narrative of the graduate college controversy.

true, Wilson's opponents wondered, why had he written to Pyne on December 25, 1909, to the effect that his proposal for two separate graduate colleges had the "hearty concurrence" of his colleagues at Princeton? As Pyne wrote soon afterward, "he was confused and self-contradictory, and I never saw a man more embarrassed or in a more unpleasant position where it was practically impossible for him to extricate himself from the numerous contradictory statements he has made. The result has been that practically the geographical question has been taken out of the discussion, and at present nothing more remains except the fact that your ideals and the President's differ." [32]

Nothing was settled at the meeting, and personal bitterness was greatly increased in both groups. The whole question of Procter's offer was referred to a special committee of five, appointed by Wilson, who were instructed to deal personally with Procter and to arrange some settlement that would be satisfactory to both sides.

The January 13 meeting marked the date when Pyne lost all faith in Wilson's integrity and ability to govern the University. His letters during the remainder of the controversy were exceedingly bitter, and he took no pains to conceal his disgust at Wilson's course. Pyne wrote to Wilson Farrand, a trustee, in late January, for example, and outlined an elaborate plan to discredit Wilson and drive him from the presidency of the University. Procter, he suggested, should withdraw his offer in a long letter covering the details of the controversy; West, Pyne continued, should resign the deanship of the graduate school and tell the trustees the explicit reasons for his action. These maneuvers, Pyne thought, could not fail to result in a change of administration.[33] When Pyne suggested the plan to Procter, however, Procter replied that he was reluctant to withdraw his offer because of the controversy such a move would create.[34] Pyne, nevertheless, compiled a number of Wilson's contradictory statements, printed them, and had them circulated among the trustees and alumni.

Wilson's friends on the Board of Trustees, on the other hand, were convinced that the issue was now, as one of them declared, "Pyne vs. Wilson" and began at once to prepare for a final fight in the board. "Now, while I propose to keep on good terms with everybody, in so far as possible," Thompson wrote, "I think there is only one thing to do now, and that is, take off our coats for a fight, and put Wilson

[32] M. T. Pyne to W. C. Procter, January 15, 1910, Pyne Papers.
[33] M. T. Pyne to W. Farrand, January 25, 1910, *ibid.*
[34] W. C. Procter to M. T. Pyne, January 30, 1910, *ibid.*

through." [35] Jacobus wrote: "Now I must confess that I am a believer enough in right and truth to say that any cause carried on by such despicable methods as these ["the small and sharp politics in which the opposition has indulged in trying to influence the Board and the alumni against Wilson and his ideas"] is not only inimicable to the best interests of the University, but, even if it succeeds in gaining its point for the present, must ultimately be shown up to be what it is and come to the final defeat it deserves. . . . We must do everything we can between now and the 10th of February, first of all to show that there is no legal right to the golf links site, but mostly to show that whether there is or not, the issue is the vital issue between the existence of the Graduate Department and the controlling presence in it of West." [36]

Procter, in the meantime, had apparently either seen that he and West would be defeated, or else had become disgusted with the entire business. On February 6 he withdrew his offer. In stating his reasons for withdrawing his proffered half million, Procter declared that it was still his conviction that the graduate college should be located where future expansion would be possible and where "its studious life will not be subject to interruption by undergraduates." The chief reason for his action, he declared, was the unfavorable reception Wilson and his associates had given his offer. [37]

Four days after Procter withdrew his offer, on February 10, 1910, the Board of Trustees met and discussed thoroughly the graduate college controversy. Thomas D. Jones, chairman of the special committee of five, presented the committee's report, which supported Wilson's position in the controversy. [38] The majority members of the faculty committee on the graduate school [39] also strongly supported Wilson's demand for a graduate college located on the campus and closely allied with undergraduate life and studies. [40] The minority of the faculty committee, West and Hibben, recommended that Procter's offer be accepted. [41] Debate by the board now appeared superfluous, for it was

[35] H. B. Thompson to C. H. Dodge, January 14, 1910, copy in Sheldon Papers.

[36] M. W. Jacobus to E. W. Sheldon, January 27, 1910, *ibid*.

[37] W. C. Procter to T. D. Jones, February 6, 1910, published in *Princeton Alumni Weekly*, x (February 9, 1910), 275.

[38] See the "Report of the Special Committee of Five Respecting the Offer of Mr. Procter," *ibid*., pp. 297-303.

[39] Edwin Grant Conklin, Winthrop More Daniels, Henry Burchard Fine, and Edward Capps.

[40] "Report of the Majority Members of the Faculty Committee on the Graduate School," *ibid*., pp. 304-305.

[41] "Report of the Minority Members of the Faculty Committee on the Graduate School," *ibid*., pp. 305-307.

obvious that Procter, by withdrawing his offer, had at least temporarily settled the question. The trustees consequently voted to accept the report of the special committee of five.

Wilson was overjoyed when Procter withdrew his offer; even before the trustees met on February 10 he was confident of complete success. "At last we are free to govern the University as our judgments and consciences dictate! I have an unspeakable sense of relief," he wrote.[42] He thought, of course, that the question had been settled, and he interpreted the action of the board as a vote of confidence. On the day the trustees accepted the report of the committee of five, Wilson began a movement to oust West from the deanship of the graduate school at the April meeting of the Board of Trustees. On February 10 he conferred with Professors Fine, Conklin, Capps, and Daniels and suggested that these members of the faculty committee on the graduate school tell the trustees that they could not work with West and that the trustees ought to ask him to resign. The professors, however, were not anxious to become so much involved in the controversy[43] and told Wilson that it was "questionable" whether they had the right to request the dean's resignation; they also thought it would be "almost ridiculous" for them to do so.[44] Fine, particularly, was greatly alarmed by Wilson's suggestion and wrote Sheldon soon afterward that Wilson's friends on the board should attempt to persuade him not to press the issue of West's retirement.[45] The Wilson supporters on the board were also disturbed by this display of vindictiveness in the president. Sheldon wrote Wilson on March 1 and told him as gently as he could that all of his friends on the board and in the faculty believed that it would be unwise to force the issue of West's resignation at that time.[46] The pro-Wilson trustees were convinced that they would be defeated should they force a vote on the issue at the April meeting.[47]

---

[42] W. W. to C. H. Dodge, February 7, 1910, Baker Papers.

[43] T. D. Jones wrote C. H. Dodge on February 18, 1910 (Sheldon Papers): "I had a long talk with Fine and Capps on Friday [February] the 11th at which this proposed procedure was discussed. The substance of what they had to say was that West is their official superior and that for subordinates to demand the resignation of their superior would have distinctly a mutinous aspect; and as the demand would quite certainly fail they would simply impair their influence with the Board, and would thus weaken rather than strengthen the President's case before the Board." See also M. W. Jacobus to C. H. Dodge, February 15, 1910, *ibid.*

[44] W. W. to E. W. Sheldon, February 11, 1910, *ibid.*

[45] H. B. Fine to E. W. Sheldon, February 26, 1910, *ibid.*

[46] E. W. Sheldon to W. W., March 1, 1910, *ibid.*

[47] T. D. Jones to C. H. Dodge, February 18, 1910, *ibid.*

It is an interesting and little-recognized fact that it was the graduate college controversy which, in the popular mind and in Wilson's own mind, developed into a great crusade for social democracy. At first glance it would appear that Wilson's struggle for the abolition of the eating clubs should have had greater potentialities as a democratic crusade, but, as has already been demonstrated, Wilson accepted defeat on this question without resorting to that extremity. The issue of democracy in Wilson's struggle to defeat Procter and West was first publicly set forth by Henry B. Brougham in a flaming editorial in the *New York Times* on February 3, 1910.

Brougham, who was one of the editors of the *New York Times,* wrote to Wilson on January 31, offering the editorial assistance of his newspaper in the controversy. The matter was of such great importance to the American people, he wrote, that the *Times* wanted to publish an editorial on it; he was writing to Wilson, he added, to ask for editorial guidance in the matter.[48]

It had been evident since December 1909 that Wilson was suffering from severe nervous strain. The old resentment and feeling of frustration caused by defeat in the "quad" fight had never been relieved, and during the early weeks of 1910 it had been agitated anew and greatly increased. His reply to Brougham constitutes the first reliable indication that he thought the issue of democracy was involved in his quarrel with West. Somehow all restraints gave way, and he poured out in a confidential letter the things he had secretly pondered.

Wilson answered Brougham's letter the same day he received it. He welcomed the editorial assistance of the *New York Times,* he wrote, and he was happy to furnish Brougham with the information for the editorial he had proposed writing. Princeton could not accept Procter's offer because Procter had insisted on carrying out certain ideals that the great majority of the faculty regarded as demoralizing. He thought it sufficient to say, Wilson continued, that to do what he and his friends feared Procter wished done would be to extend to the sphere of the graduate life of the University the same artificial and unsound social standards that already predominated the life of the undergraduates; to discourage serious graduate students from coming to Princeton; and to make the realization of sober ideals and of sound scholarship more difficult than ever. The question of site was important, Wilson added, because the isolation of the graduate college would contribute to the

[48] H. B. Brougham to W. W., January 31, 1910, Wilson Papers.

spirit of social exclusiveness. His own ideals for the University were those of genuine democracy and serious scholarship. The two, indeed, seemed to him to go together. Any organization which introduced elements of social exclusiveness constituted the worst possible soil for serious intellectual endeavor.

It was the idea of those who were chiefly instrumental in obtaining the offer from Procter, Wilson continued, that Princeton should have a residential college in which the graduate students should live under the eye of a master who, with a sort of advisory cabinet from the faculty, should have the right to say who should be privileged to live in the college and who should not.

There was no obscuring the fact, however, that here, as in a score of other matters of college life, the issue was now joined between a college life into which all the bad elements of social ambition and unrest intruded themselves, and a life ordered upon a simpler plan under the domination of real university influences and upon a basis of genuine democracy.

Wilson added that he was sending a copy of a special report by four faculty members, which would further explain the situation. He hoped that Brougham would find this letter a sufficient exposition of Princeton's difficulty, Wilson concluded. If not, he would be very glad, in the same confidential way, to go into any details Brougham might desire.[49]

In this manner did Wilson furnish the material for the editorial that raised the democratic standard over Princeton and brought the controversy out of the Princeton group and into full public view. The editorial was largely an elaboration on Wilson's letter. The keynote was democracy: "At Princeton, the scene of a battle fought a century and a third ago for the establishment of the American democracy, is in progress to-day a struggle not less significant for the future of American youth and of Government in the United States. It is the more significant, though pitched in academic halls, because it will decide the issue whether the American colleges shall henceforth fall short of their democratic mission." The nation is aroused against special privilege, the editorial continued. Now the exclusive and benumbing touch of special privilege is upon educational institutions, and the outcome of the controversy at Princeton will determine whether all endowed institutions are to foster "mutually exclusive social cliques, stolid groups of wealth and fashion, devoted to non-essentials and the smatterings of

[49] W. W. to H. B. Brougham, February 1, 1910, Baker Papers.

culture." The remainder of the editorial paraphrased and, in parts, literally quoted Wilson's analysis of the situation.[50]

Who can explain the reasons that led Wilson finally to propound this interpretation of the graduate college controversy? The vagaries of his mind during this period are unfathomable. It must be said in passing that there was no basis in fact for Wilson's charges. No evidence exists that West, Pyne, or any other person supporting them wanted to make the graduate college an exclusive social club. West had come to the conception of a residential dormitory set apart from the undergraduate community, it is true, but in what respect was this conception undemocratic or exclusive? How ironic it is that West's plans for a graduate college so perfectly duplicated Wilson's conception of the undergraduate quadrangle, that West was trying to do for the graduate students what Wilson had tried to do for the undergraduates!

The fact of Wilson's complicity in the writing of the editorial in the *New York Times* has heretofore been unknown. Had it been known in February 1910 that he was directly responsible for this grossly unfair attack on the West group, a fatal explosion in the Board of Trustees could not have been prevented. Pyne, Shea, Henry, and the other anti-Wilson trustees suspected that Wilson had had a hand in the writing of the editorial, but they were never able to prove that he had. It of course stirred up an immediate controversy throughout the country.

Brougham wrote to Wilson on February 4 and told him that the *Times* would print on the following day a statement by a group of alumni protesting the editorial and pointing up the inconsistencies in Wilson's own statements on the graduate college.[51] Brougham felt that it was important that someone at Princeton publish an authoritative statement explaining and defending Wilson's position in the controversy; he suggested that Wilson ask one of the older faculty members to write the statement.[52]

Wilson replied at once in a letter that was far less belligerent than his first letter to Brougham had been. In fact, he now made an effort to deemphasize the democratic issue, gave West and his friends credit for having "democratic professions," and emphasized merely the question of the graduate college as the intellectual and geographical center of the University. It is probable that he already regretted writing his analysis of the Princeton situation to Brougham, and had been alarmed by the

---

[50] "Princeton," *New York Times*, February 3, 1910.

[51] For which see the *New York Times*, February 5, 1910.

[52] H. B. Brougham to W. W., February 4, 1910, Wilson Papers.

terrific reaction the editorial had produced. At any rate, it is certain that he had no desire to press the charges any further at the time, or to become personally involved in the fight. He was willing to stand by his record, when properly understood, he wrote, and the inconsistencies with which his opponents charged him were only apparent. The "central equation" in the whole controversy, he continued, was the "personal equation." For that reason it would be extremely difficult for anyone to discuss the subject in the public press. It was still his conviction, however, that every word of Brougham's editorial was true, but to lay bare the facts that made the editorial true would be to disclose a situation in which personal elements filled a very large part and in which it would be necessary to say things distinctly detrimental to individuals.[53]

It was evident, therefore, that Wilson was not yet ready to undertake publicly any crusade for democracy in connection with the graduate college quarrel. On March 16, for example, Professor Paul van Dyke, representing the West group at Princeton, succeeded in obtaining an interview with Wilson and attempted to force him to commit himself, on record, on the issue of democracy and the graduate college. Van Dyke asked Wilson whether he accepted the *New York Times* editorial as a fair statement of the situation at Princeton. No, Wilson replied. Van Dyke understood that he, Wilson, agreed with the *Times* editorial in that he thought the plans of the West group were demoralizing to the University, but the terms of the *Times* editorial he would not accept. Van Dyke replied that it seemed that Wilson accepted the terms of the editorial, because reports were going all over the country based on the editorial to the effect that Wilson was fighting for democracy at Princeton. "Now, sir," van Dyke asked, "do you conceive that you are waging a battle in defence of these things?" No, Wilson replied; the editorial was highly exaggerated. Did Wilson think, then, that the men supporting West were endeavoring to foster stolid groups of wealth, van Dyke asked. They were not consciously endeavoring to do this, Wilson answered, but he thought this would be the effect of their plans. Van Dyke then called on Wilson to repudiate the editorial, which was "unquestionably false." He did not think this unquestionably false, Wilson retorted. In its coloring it was highly exaggerated, but the foundation of it was, in his opinion, true.[54]

[53] W. W. to H. B. Brougham, February 5, 1910, Baker Papers.
[54] "Memorandum of conversation between President Wilson and Prof. Paul van Dyke, at the President's office, March 16th," a stenographic transcription of the conversation, MS in Wilson Papers.

The most striking fact about this whole controversy was the absence of any clear-cut issue. Wilson, for his part, had done nothing to clarify the situation; on the contrary, he had shifted from one issue to another, and it was almost impossible to tell where he really stood. The situation was all the more confused when two pamphlets, "The Phantom Ship," written anonymously, and "The Princeton Ideal," by Chauncey Brown of Philadelphia, were published in early March 1910 and attempted to revive the old "quad" fight. Wilson, of course, had carefully avoided mentioning the quadrangle question in connection with the graduate college; but it was an issue his opponents were seeking to use against him.

Wilson's friends among the faculty and trustees believed strongly that he should stop talking about the undergraduate situation—which meant "quads" to his critics—and take up wholeheartedly the graduate school issue by making a great appeal for endowment for professorships and fellowships.[55] Cyrus H. McCormick, one Wilson supporter on the board who had succeeded in remaining aloof from the personal controversy, was quite insistent on this point.[56] While the Wilson men were fairly successful in preventing the injection of the "quad" issue into the graduate college fight, they could not persuade Wilson to take any constructive leadership in the matter of obtaining endowment for the graduate school. That, it is safe to assume, Wilson would never do until West had been removed from the deanship and his influence at Princeton had been destroyed.

In the meantime, Wilson made a short trip to Bermuda soon after the February meeting of the Board of Trustees. He had to get away from the turmoil of Princeton. "I did not realize until I got here how hard hit my nerves had been by the happenings of the past month," he wrote his wife. "Almost at once the *days* began to afford me relief, but the nights distressed me. The trouble latent in my mind came out in my dreams." One thought, however, consoled him, and that was that "the record of our consciences is clear in this whole trying business." [57]

Wilson was back in Princeton in early March, and was soon again embroiled in the controversy. For one thing, he was worried because of a movement among the Pyne-Procter group to elect Adrian H. Joline, an opponent of his policies, as an alumni trustee. Wilson, moreover, was also convinced that he should make another appeal to the alumni; he

[55] H. B. Fine to C. H. Dodge, March 1, 1910, Sheldon Papers.
[56] C. H. McCormick to E. W. Sheldon, March 4, 1910, *ibid.*
[57] W. W. to E. A. W., February 17, 1910, R. S. Baker, *Woodrow Wilson*, II, 330.

President of Princeton University

Thomas D. Jones

M. W. Jacobus

Moses T. Pyne

Andrew F. West

SOME OF THE PARTICIPANTS IN THE GRADUATE COLLEGE CONTROVERSY

thought that he could best overcome the opposition to his policies by going directly to his "constituents" and by explaining his position to them.

At Baltimore on March 11, he began his appeal before the Princeton Alumni Association of Maryland. It was an exceedingly conciliatory discussion of the problem, calculated to ease the tension that the controversy had generated.[58] He next spoke at Brooklyn and Jersey City. On March 26 he made an important address before the Western Association of Princeton Clubs at St. Louis. In this speech he reviewed the entire history of his administration at Princeton, defended his graduate school policy, and concluded by proposing that the whole matter be referred to the University faculty. "We all have confidence in the Faculty," he declared. "There is no finer body of men anywhere. If they should vote against my judgment, I should yield my own judgment, not because they out-voted me but because I should feel that I was wrong if they did not agree with me." The St. Louis affair, in fact, turned out to be almost a harmony meeting. McCormick and Procter were on hand, and Wilson and Procter conferred about the question. Procter told McCormick that he agreed completely with what Wilson had to say about the graduate college and that he, Procter, had no other ideals than the ideals Wilson had expressed.[59]

Wilson not only made the "swing around the circle" to defend his own position; his trip was also something of an electioneering jaunt in which he did his best to secure the defeat of Joline in the alumni trustee election. He was greatly encouraged by the reception he had received at the hands of the alumni. "My little campaign is over," he wrote to Jacobus. "I have spoken at Baltimore, Brooklyn, Jersey City, and St. Louis, and have tried in the four speeches pieced together to make as complete an impersonal statement of our case as was possible." [60]

There yet remained the New York alumni, who were the most hostile to Wilson's plans. On April 7 he laid his case before them. "The tension that evening was indescribable," writes David Lawrence, who was

---

[58] *Princeton Alumni Weekly*, x (March 16, 1910), 371-374.

[59] C. H. McCormick to E. W. Sheldon, April 5, 1910, Sheldon Papers. "The impression was unanimous at St. Louis," McCormick also wrote, "that, if any new compromise could be proposed, Procter would renew his gift, and to my mind, the way out is for the Faculty to come forward with a comprehensive suggestion and let every one else be prepared to adopt it, even tho there are some compromises in it. Personally, I should think the whole question turns upon Pyne, for if he will agree to a compromise, Procter will certainly renew the gift."

[60] W. W. to M. W. Jacobus, April 2, 1910, Baker Papers.

present at the meeting. "Never in his later career did Woodrow Wilson face an audience more hostile to him. The perfunctory cheers at the opening of the meeting were not as usual for 'Wilson' but for 'the President of Princeton'—the irony of which did not escape his notice." [61] Wilson's address that evening was his most extensive exposition of the problems involved in the graduate college controversy. "I know, of course, what your present inquiries . . . [are] reducible to," he began. "You say it is all very well and very interesting to talk about educational ideals; but it is bad business to refuse half a million dollars."

Wilson frankly admitted that the graduate school at Princeton had been successful neither in attracting students nor in making any substantial academic progress. Such a state of affairs existed, he declared, because the organization of the University had not been such as to afford success in the graduate field. The graduate school had been in the hands of a single executive officer, the dean, and the energy and enthusiasm of the faculty had not been behind it. This structural deficiency, however, had been remedied by the trustees; the control of the graduate school had been placed in the hands of the faculty, with the result that within a year's time the number of students had doubled. It was necessary, moreover, Wilson continued, that Princeton understand what graduate students wanted and what they were like. The trustees had declined to accept the Procter offer because Procter's idea was to treat graduate students "as they are not treated elsewhere in the country." The Procter offer, he asserted, was reducible to a simple business proposition: Princeton must determine whether to "Take the money at the risk of having no graduate students, or get the graduate students at the risk of having no money."

Wilson next proceeded to develop the idea that was overshadowing all others in his mind. It was that "there should be a constant, conscious, intimate action, interaction, and reaction between graduates and undergraduates in the organization of a university." The Princeton ideal was an organic ideal of the contact of mind with mind, a brotherhood of intellectual endeavor, stimulating the youth and stabilizing the mature student. Princeton, Wilson declared, had made it plain that she preferred these ideals to money. He concluded his address with the implication that a separate graduate college would be undemocratic. "Divorce the universities of this country from their teaching enthusiasm, divorce them from their undergraduate energies," he declared, "and you will have a thing which is not only un-American but utterly unserviceable

[61] *The True Story of Woodrow Wilson,* p. 29.

to the country. There is nothing private in America. Everything is public; everything belongs to the united energy of the nation." [62]

Wilson talked to the New York alumni for more than an hour—and he spoke with evident sincerity and feeling—but he was never interrupted by applause; and at the conclusion of the speech most of the audience filed out without demonstrating either enthusiasm or approval.

The period from February 10 until the meeting of the board on April 14 was an armed truce between the Wilson and the Pyne-West factions in the Board of Trustees. Wilson had spoken to five different groups of alumni in defense of his policies, yet the fact remained that the majority of the alumni, the articulate alumni, were as strongly opposed to his policies as they had been before he began his campaign. Things had come to a dangerous impasse, an impasse that could not last much longer. For one thing, the movement to elect Joline was a direct threat to the tenuous Wilson majority on the board. Henry B. Thompson, who had talked at length with Wilson about the matter, wrote to Pyne on April 5:

"If the only settlement of our difficulties is a fight to the finish between the two factions of the Board, the result—whichever way it goes —will be most unfortunate for the future interests of the University. If we expect to arrive at any definite conclusion we must forget the past discussion. This can best be dismissed by saying that both sides have shown little tact and less charity.

"As I see the situation to-day, we have now arrived at the point where Bayard Henry put it after the January meeting. The issue has now narrowed down to this,—whether you or Wilson are to control the policies of the Board.

"I do not think you ever intended or wanted to put yourself in this position, but, apparently, your friends have forced you into a position of leadership in the Board, which you cannot help but accept, and with it you accept its responsibilities and consequences. I do not for a minute question your right to take any position you want, nor do I for a minute question your good faith in your present judgment of conditions; but I do question whether it will pay to force the differences that exist in the Board to a final finish.

"The nomination of Joline was a direct challenge to the President and his supporters in the Board. The election of Joline means the immediate resignation of Wilson. This will be followed by the resignation of Cleve Dodge and Jacobus. I was told on Saturday, on entirely reliable authority, that Tom Jones and Stephen Palmer would follow them; and, I believe there is a strong probability of three more members of the Board doing the same. In addition, you are very sure to lose some of your newer and more distinguished members of the Faculty. Again, I believe you will forfeit certain subscriptions to our endowment fund, which, in the aggregate, will amount to considerably more than the Procter gift." [63]

The deadlock between the two factions was not resolved when the trustees met on April 14, 1910. The Pyne faction was this time in control and refused Wilson's request to refer the question of the graduate college to a general meeting of the faculty. Wilson had desperately wanted an official declaration on the question from the faculty, who he was certain supported him, and the refusal of the board to allow him to make an official faculty poll irritated him considerably.

Wilson went to Pittsburgh on April 16 to address the Pittsburgh alumni. He was still smarting from his recent defeat at the hands of the trustees, and there are strong indications that all the bitterness resulting from the controversy, and the repressed words he had wanted to utter and had not, created a peculiar psychological disturbance in his mind. The result was that he lost his balance and his temper completely and in this extemporaneous address—later known as "that Pittsburgh speech"—said many things he only momentarily believed and afterwards regretted saying.

Wilson began by saying that he did not know whom, but himself, he represented. A few days ago, he declared, he had thought that he would ascertain the opinion of the faculty on the graduate college question, but the trustees had refused to allow him to obtain the faculty's opinion. As a matter of fact, Wilson continued, he did not even know what the trustees thought about the matter. He, therefore, occupied a position of "splendid isolation." The trustees had simply refused to make headway in the whole matter, he added, and "It may be that the big Princeton is exposing herself to the danger of putting forth something that would be acceptable only to the little Princeton."

After this caustic introduction, Wilson let go his pent-up fury. "How does the nation judge Princeton?" he asked. Which judgment should take precedence, the Princeton family judgment or the common judgment of the country? The University was not an instrument intended for the pleasure of Princeton men, he asserted; it was intended for the

[63] Letter in the Pyne Papers.

service of the country, and it would be judged by the standards of the country.

Having thus established his right to appeal to the opinion of "the country" over the heads of the Princeton students, alumni, and trustees, Wilson then told his audience what the country expected of Princeton. "It expects of Princeton what it expects of every other college," he insisted, "the accommodation of its life to the life of the country." The colleges of America were in the same danger as the Protestant churches, which had dissociated themselves from the people and were serving the "classes" rather than the "masses" of the people. The churches had "more regard to their pew-rents than to the souls of men, and in proportion as they look to the respectability of their congregations to lift them in esteem, they are depressing the whole level of Christian endeavor." And, he continued, by the same token the colleges, or rather the privately endowed colleges, were pandering to the desires of wealthy students and alumni. What was the result? "The future is for state universities and not for the privately endowed institutions"; the state universities were seeking to serve the people, were "constantly sensitive to the movements of general opinion, to the opinion of the unknown man who can vote."

Whence came the strength of the nation? Wilson asked. From the upper classes? Not at all. "It comes from the great mass of the unknown, of the unrecognized men, whose powers are being developed by struggle." Would Lincoln have been as serviceable to the country had he been a college man? He would not have been because the process "to which the college man is subjected does not render him serviceable to the country as a whole."

Wilson's psychological intoxication increased as he spoke; he was uttering phrases he had never before uttered, saying things he probably never intended to say. "What we cry out against is that a handful of conspicuous men have thrust cruel hands among the heartstrings of the masses of men upon whose blood and energy they are subsisting." Universities, Wilson continued, would make men forget their common origins and their universal sympathies. "The great voice of America does not come from seats of learning," he continued. "It comes in a murmur from the hills and woods and the farms and factories and the mills, rolling on and gaining volume until it comes to us from the homes of common men. Do these murmurs echo in the corridors of universities? I have not heard them."

Then, rising to a great pitch of emotionalism, Wilson proclaimed his determination to democratize the colleges of the country. "I have dedicated every power that there is in me to bring the colleges that I have anything to do with to an absolutely democratic regeneration in spirit," he declared, and added that he would cease his crusade only when men in the colleges were saturated with "the same thought, the same sympathy that pulses through the whole great body politic."

The challenge of democracy, Wilson declared, forbade the construction of a graduate college on Dean West's ideals. "Will America tolerate the seclusion of graduate students? Will America tolerate the idea of having graduate students set apart?" Not at all, he replied. "Seclude a man, separate him from the rough and tumble of college life, from all the contacts of every sort and condition of men, and you have done a thing which America will brand with contemptuous disapproval," he concluded.[64]

Thus had Wilson completely abandoned caution and compromise, thrown down the gauntlet to his enemies, and said publicly the things he had written confidentially in his letter to Brougham. The graduate college controversy had been broadcast to the country, by the president of Princeton himself, as a struggle in which he was leading the forces of righteousness, who were seeking to create true democracy at the University, and opposing Dean West and his supporters, who were allied with the forces of snobbery, reaction, and darkness.

Perhaps it will never be known precisely why Wilson made the address; some of the extenuating circumstances, however, are understandable. In the first place, Wilson was suffering from an intolerable feeling of frustration, the pressure of which had been recently increased by the adverse action of the board. He was laboring under deep excitement at Pittsburgh; his nerves were on edge; he was resentful and

[64] *Princeton Alumni Weekly*, x (April 20, 1910), 470-471. It is interesting to note that the page proofs of this report of his address were corrected by Wilson before the report was published in the *Alumni Weekly*. Baker reprints in the *Public Papers*, II, 202-203, and used for his discussion in *Woodrow Wilson*, II, 340-341, a brief and very incomplete report of the address, which appeared in the *Pittsburgh Dispatch*, April 17, 1910.

It is interesting also that in the report of the speech as given in the *Pittsburgh Dispatch*, Wilson is alleged to have concluded his address with the following sentence: "If she loses her self-possession, America will stagger like France through fields of blood before she again finds peace and prosperity under the leadership of men who know her needs."

This sentence, which is Wilsonian in structure and use of words, did not appear in what was supposed to be a verbatim report of the address published in the *Alumni Weekly*. It was the subject of so much comment and criticism, however, that it is plainly evident that Wilson used it. The chances are that Wilson struck it out when he corrected the page proofs of the report that was to be published in the *Alumni Weekly*.

bitter. One observer at the dinner thought that Wilson looked very despondent and ill.[65] Wilson believed, moreover, that he was among friends who would understand what he was saying. He spoke extemporaneously, and all the bitterness in him rose at once and dictated his expression. It is doubtful that he had truly thought out the implications of his words, that he was really prepared to undertake the moral and spiritual regeneration of American democracy.

One other question remains: Did the fact that Wilson was being prominently mentioned for political office influence in any degree his new departure? It is almost unthinkable that Wilson deliberately used the graduate college controversy, even increased its fury, simply to augment his popularity with the people. Yet, as the following chapter will testify, considerable demand for his entrance into politics had already begun, and it is not unlikely that Wilson found himself being forced to take a radical position, not only in the Princeton controversy, but also on certain political issues, despite the fact that he had never believed in radical solutions.

The Pittsburgh speech stirred up excitement throughout all the country. It was reported in several eastern newspapers, and a pamphlet entitled "That Pittsburgh Speech and Some Comment" was printed anonymously and widely distributed by Wilson's opponents. His antagonists were of course infuriated. "His speech has been universally condemned by every one whom I have seen," Pyne wrote, "whether on his side or against him and I think it can only lead to one result." [66] Level-headed editors also declared that Wilson had been rash and exceedingly intemperate in his wholesale denunciations.[67] Some of the New York alumni would not believe the story of the address until they read a verbatim report of it in the *Alumni Weekly*.[68] Wilson became alarmed at the unfavorable reaction and hastened to assure his friends that he had made a "stupid blunder." He had spoken too soon after a meeting of the trustees at which the majority vote seemed to him to create an impossible situation, he wrote. "I hope—and believe—that the men who *heard* my Pittsburgh speech did not misunderstand," he wrote, "but in my deep excitement, I did not stop to think how it would sound in the newspapers. I should have done so." He promised to try to

[65] J. B. Shea to M. T. Pyne, May 16, 1910, Pyne Papers.

[66] M. T. Pyne to B. Henry, April 20, 1910, *ibid.*

[67] See, e.g., *New York Evening Post*, April 18, 1910; *Brooklyn Times*, April 18, 1910; *Independent*, April 21, 1910.

[68] *New York Times*, April 22, 1910.

remedy the mistake by giving a "more just exposition of the matter." [69]

Scarcely a month after his flaming speech at Pittsburgh, in an address before the Chicago alumni on May 12, Wilson showed considerable less fire and militancy. He spoke—and the speech was carefully prepared in advance!—at great length on the Princeton spirit and the reasons for the loyalty of Princeton men to their alma mater. Yet he came back to his theme of educational democracy. "It is a great privilege to live in such an age," he declared. It seemed to him that it was the opportunity of universities, particularly of the privately endowed universities, "to set an example which will quicken the whole thought of the age." Princeton men had the opportunity of dedicating their University to the task of "quickening . . . all thought and spiritual endeavor and all intellectual growth and enlightenment." Princeton should be, he continued, "the seat of none but generous rivalries, the place from which artificial social distinction is excluded and all men are judged upon their merits, a school of pure democracy because a school in which nothing artificial holds men apart." [70]

Meanwhile, the deadlock in the Board of Trustees had not been resolved, and in the latter part of April Pyne began finally to seek a compromise settlement that would be acceptable to the moderates in both factions. Because he had been so deeply involved in the personal controversy, however, Pyne prompted McCormick, who generally leaned toward the Wilson group, but without becoming involved in the personal bitterness of the fight, to play the role of peacemaker. McCormick conferred with Procter in Cincinnati on April 25 and learned that Procter was willing to renew his offer; that he, Procter, had no desire to interfere with the administration or curriculum of the graduate school; that Procter and Pyne did not desire to have Wilson removed as president of the University; and that Procter insisted that only two points were essential as far as he was concerned, "viz., a residential College for graduate students alone, and the Golf Links location." [71]

McCormick immediately wrote to Sheldon, who was directing the harmony conferences in New York City. Sheldon conferred with Pyne, Stephen S. Palmer, and John L. Cadwalader in New York on May 7

[69] W. W. to I. H. Lionberger, April 28, 1910, Baker Papers. See also Wilson's letter to the *New York Evening Post*, April 23, 1910. "I do not need to tell you that the reports of my recent address in Pittsburgh have, by piecemeal quotation, conveyed an entirely false impression," he wrote. "Unfortunately, my mind is a one-track affair on which I can run only one through train at a time."

[70] *Princeton Alumni Weekly*, x (May 18, 1910), 533-534.

[71] W. C. Procter to M. T. Pyne, April 26, 1910, Pyne Papers.

and 8.[72] The outcome of these conferences was the formulation of a compromise settlement that was acceptable to the leaders of both factions. The proposed settlement stipulated that the administration of the graduate school was to be left in the hands of the faculty committee on the graduate school; that West was to retire from the deanship of the graduate school and to become provost, or resident master, of the graduate college; that the Procter and Thompson buildings should be located on the golf links; and that the legality of building the Thompson college on the golf links was to be definitely settled in the New Jersey Court of Chancery.[73]

Sheldon was elated by the settlement. He wrote McCormick that the Wilson men had Pyne's "repeated assurances that it will entirely end the controversy at Princeton, and will lay the way for a peaceful administration of the affairs of the University by the President." He earnestly hoped that Wilson would accept the compromise. "If he has objections," Sheldon continued, "please use your utmost endeavors to remove them, or failing that, to defer final rejection of the plan until we can all discuss it with him on his return to the East." [74] Sheldon wrote also to Wilson: "My controlling purpose in the matter has been to save the University from the lasting injury that I apprehend would follow a break between you and a majority of the Board.[75] The proposed adjustment may insure that happy result, and at the same time relieve you of much discomfort and many obstacles." [76]

For his part, Pyne was not altogether enthusiastic about the agreement, but he accepted it reluctantly. He regretted that West should have to be retired from the deanship, but it did seem that the whole matter could now be settled and he realized that the anti-Wilson men would have to make some concessions.[77]

Sheldon's hopes that he and Pyne had found a way out of the impasse were, however, soon frustrated by Wilson's utter refusal to compromise. Wilson thought that the Pyne faction had yielded very little; a graduate college with West as resident master was as unacceptable to him as a

[72] E. W. Sheldon to C. H. McCormick, May 9, 1910, Sheldon Papers; M. T. Pyne to W. C. Procter, May 10, 1910, Pyne Papers.

[73] E. W. Sheldon to M. T. Pyne, May 9, 1910, *ibid.*

[74] E. W. Sheldon to C. H. McCormick, May 11, 1910, Sheldon Papers.

[75] This is a significant comment, which would seem to indicate that Wilson had either lost, or would lose, if he refused to accept the compromise, the support of a majority of the trustees.

[76] E. W. Sheldon to W. W., May 14, 1910, Sheldon Papers.

[77] M. T. Pyne to W. C. Procter, May 10, 1910, Pyne Papers.

graduate school with West as dean.[78] Such stubbornness is hard to understand, for Wilson must have seen that his refusal to accept the compromise, which the moderates had framed and pledged themselves to support, would lose him the support of all but the bitter-enders among his friends on the board. Palmer and Pyne, in the meantime, had informed West of the terms of the settlement. It was a hard blow for West to take, for he now saw himself stripped of all authority in graduate school affairs and established as a provost of "the still non-existent Graduate College with a vague indication, but no statement, of . . . [his] rights and duties." It was clear to him that it was not a compromise, but a surrender. Pyne and Palmer asked West to decide whether he would accept the compromise and resign the deanship; West wrestled with the problem for several days and finally decided not to resign, but to force a fight in the board.[79]

The controversy was at last settled in May 1910, but not in the manner anyone had expected. On May 18 Isaac C. Wyman died at his home in Salem, Massachusetts. His will directed that his entire estate, estimated at from $2,000,000 to $4,000,000, should be given over to the endowment and building of a graduate college at Princeton along the lines of the plans that West had proposed. West was even named by the will as one of the two executors of the estate.[80] West and Pyne were of course jubilant. "TE DEUM LAUDAMUS. NON NOBIS DOMINE," West wrote to Pyne from Salem, where he had just helped to bury Wyman.[81]

"As forecasted last week," Pyne wrote to Procter, "the Wyman gift has come to Princeton. The effect of the announcement was astounding. It is going to harmonize all differences and be the absolute defeat of the other side, which I understand today by telephone from Fine that Wilson is practically prepared to admit. Fine also says that this includes the acceptance of your offer if you will be generous enough to give us another chance to take it. It also means that West is to be undisturbed in his position and that no effort be made to change it unless it comes from West himself, (as it may very well come if he finds that the duties of the Trustee and Executorship, the administration of the Graduate School and the direction of the Graduate College overtax him,) but that is for the future and is in his hands, not in the hands of Wilson. The Board

---

[78] W. W. to E. W. Sheldon, May 16, 1910, Baker Papers.
[79] A. F. West, "A Narrative of the Graduate College," pp. 99-104.
[80] Wyman's will was published in the *Princeton Alumni Weekly*, x (May 25, 1910), 548-550.
[81] A. F. West to M. T. Pyne, May 22, 1910, Pyne Papers.

understand that West is entitled to conduct the Graduate School now. It is a complete surrender of the other side and a most gratifying victory for us." [82]

It was in every respect West's own triumph; he had been entirely responsible for securing the Wyman bequest. Wilson now had only two choices: to resign or to accept West's control of the new graduate establishment. He decided that resignation was not the proper course because it was his duty to remain at the helm at Princeton and prevent the demoralization of the University. In a remarkable letter to Thomas D. Jones, Wilson thus explained why he accepted defeat:

"On Wednesday, the 25th, I went in to New York and had a conference at Mr. Cadwalader's office with Mr. Cadwalader and Mr. Palmer. Before that, namely on Monday evening, the 23rd, I had had a long conference with Fine, Daniels, Capps, and Abbott (Conklin being away). They had all been clear as to what ought to be done in the circumstances, and therefore I went to the conference with Mr. Cadwalader and Mr. Palmer with a clear head, though not with a very light heart.

"I said to them that in my opinion (It was also, of course, the opinion of the men in the Faculty I have mentioned) West should remain in his present office as Dean of the Graduate School, because it was eminently desirable, in view of the extraordinary discretion granted in Mr. Wyman's will, that he should be included in our counsels and not excluded from them, and since it was manifestly necessary, in the circumstances, to deal with him as if of course he intended to do the right thing.

"I said also that this great gift of millions made it clear that we did not have to depend upon the attractions, or fear the repulsions, of the Graduate College in building up a graduate school, that is to say, a body of graduate students and teachers. It enables us to secure a great graduate faculty. Their presence will make a large body of serious graduate students certain. This alters the whole perspective, therefore, of the question of the graduate residential hall. I deemed it necessary in the circumstances, therefore, that I should accept defeat in the matter of the location of the college. I would no longer fight its location on the Golf Links." [83]

On June 6 Procter renewed his offer to the Board of Trustees, and it was immediately accepted. And at a special meeting of the Board on June 9 Wilson officially announced the Wyman bequest and with as

[82] M. T. Pyne to W. C. Procter, May 24, 1910, *ibid.*
[83] W. W. to T. D. Jones, May 30, 1910, Baker Papers.

good grace as was possible declared that he had withdrawn his objections to the construction of the graduate college on the golf links.[84]

Wilson's active participation in Princeton affairs came to an end with the 1910 commencement in June. During the summer he agreed to accept the Democratic gubernatorial nomination, and in September he began his first political campaign. One of Wilson's friends on the board suggested that since the trustees did not know whether Wilson would be elected, they should wait until after the election to accept his resignation, which would be forthcoming if he were elected governor. Apparently this was what Wilson hoped the board would do.[85] The anti-Wilson trustees, however, were in control and were determined not to lose this opportunity to force Wilson's resignation without creating a rupture in the board. They met in Princeton on the night before the October meeting of the trustees and sent a delegation, headed by Palmer, to tell Wilson that he must resign. According to Pyne, Wilson was reluctant to present his resignation, "and had to be told pretty positively that it had to be done." [86] One trustee, Cadwalader, had prepared a resolution calling upon Wilson to resign, and was prepared to offer it if Wilson did not do it voluntarily.[87] The following morning, on October 20, Wilson read a brief letter of resignation, asked that it be accepted at once, and then, while the trustees stood in silence, left the room and passed from his connection with the University. "With deep regret," the trustees immediately accepted the resignation.[88]

The years of the Princeton presidency were among the most important in Wilson's life. The Princeton period was the microcosm of a later macrocosm, and a political observer, had he studied carefully Wilson's career as president of Princeton University, might have forecast accurately the shape of things to come during the period when Wilson was president of the United States. What striking similarities there are between the Princeton and the national periods! During the first years of both administrations, Wilson drove forward with terrific energy and momentum to carry through a magnificent reform program, and his accomplishments both at Princeton and Washington were great and enduring. Yet in both cases he drove so hard, so flatly refused to delegate

[84] *Princeton Alumni Weekly*, x (June 15, 1910), 598-599.
[85] Farrand Memorandum, Farrand Papers.
[86] M. T. Pyne to W. C. Procter, October 25, 1910, Pyne Papers.
[87] Copy of resolution in *ibid*.
[88] *Princeton Alumni Weekly*, xi (October 26, 1910), 68.

authority, and broke with so many friends that when the inevitable re-action set in he was unable to cope with the new situation. His refusal to compromise in the graduate college controversy was almost Princeton's undoing; his refusal to compromise in the fight in the Senate over the League of Nations was the nation's undoing. Both controversies assume the character and proportions of a Greek tragedy.

It is important for our purposes, however, to remember that Wilson had changed greatly from 1902 to 1910. He had evolved from a theoreti-cian into a man of practical affairs; his experience as an administrator broke the spell that the years of teaching had cast over him. He began to travel more extensively and to speak forth with increasing emphasis on affairs political and economic. The constant turmoil at Princeton from 1907 through 1910 likewise left its mark upon Wilson. He was forced into politics of a sort—college politics—and he developed techniques that he later used with amazing results in the political field.

"I don't want you to suppose," he later told a friend, "that when I was nominated for Governor of New Jersey I emerged from academic seclu-sion, where nothing was known of politics." Politics had been seething in Princeton, he continued with an unconscious note of irony, ever since he had had any connection with the University. "I'll confide in you," he added, "as I have already confided to others—that, as compared with the college politician, the real article seems like an amateur." [89] The fre-quent councils held with friendly trustees and faculty members, the appeals over the heads of the trustees to the alumni, and the drastic and once-tried appeal to the "people" over the heads of the trustees and alumni—all were part and parcel of Woodrow Wilson's political train-ing. He left Princeton for the world of politics, therefore, not a full-grown politician, to be sure, but certainly not a novice.

[89] Henry B. Needham, "Woodrow Wilson's Views," *Outlook,* xcviii (August 26, 1911), 940.

Awakening Political Consciousness

IN 1902, even in 1905, Wilson was in certain respects a typical college president; he had been unusually successful and brilliant, it is true, but none the less he was typical of the academic executive who gets on well with trustees and wealthy patrons of his institution. By 1910 he had lost much of his old urbanity. He had been defeated in the quadrangle fight and was about to suffer a more serious defeat in the graduate college controversy. He had, however, already begun to fight; he had already demonstrated those qualities of pertinacity and doggedness that would later make him something of a glamorous political figure. He had, furthermore, revealed that he could wield a powerful verbal sword when his Scottish anger was aroused! This metamorphosis from academician to militant leader was of first-rate importance, for it had a political counterpart.

The man who stood in Alexander Hall on October 25, 1902, and took the three oaths of office as president of Princeton would scarcely have excited attention under usual circumstances. He was slender and of average height—a little short of five feet eleven. W. S. Couch writes, in one of the best contemporary descriptions of Wilson's physiognomy:

"Woodrow Wilson's face is narrow and curiously geometrical. It is a rectangle, one might say, the lines are so regular. His forehead is high and his iron gray hair retreats from it somewhat, which adds to this effect. His face is refined, a face that shows breeding and family in every line, but it is heavy boned. The cheek bones are rather high and the jaw thrusts forward in a challenging way. The mouth is small, sensitive, with full lips, a mouth almost too well shaped for a man, and a woman might envy the arched eyebrows. But the almost brutal strength of the general bony structure of the face, and that aggressive jaw promise an active, iron willed, fighting man. His eyes, blue-gray they looked in that light behind his nose glasses, are very penetrating. They have a way of narrowing when he talks that gives him a stern, almost grim expression." [1]

The quiet, academic atmosphere of the Princeton community was not

[1] *New York World*, December 18, 1910.

conducive to philosophical iconoclasm and, if anything, Wilson's habits of thought had been, during the early Princeton years, only more deeply strengthened in their orthodoxy. He was by habit extremely methodical; he liked to do things in a regular way; he had an intense admiration for order and lucidity of expression. His religious faith had never been shaken; he had, in fact, developed a strange twist of something akin to superstition.[2] His wife was sometimes troubled by religious doubt and read Hegel and Kant to reinforce her own religious ideas; but Wilson seems never to have been thus philosophically disturbed. Invariably he read a chapter of the Bible every day and was given to regular prayers. It is significant that his religious beliefs were not only orthodox—they were also Calvinistic, formal and stern. "The idea of an all merciful God," Stockton Axson writes, "was . . . to him, a piece of soft sentimentality." [3]

Wilson had an intensity of temperament that belied his outward calm. Beneath the surface he was a Puritan in ideals, a rigid Calvinist, disciplined and trained by certain habits of thought.[4] More and more he became attached to certain moral and religious beliefs. He believed that the universe was founded upon immutable moral law, and that it was man's duty to discover this law and to gauge all his actions by it. Consequently he tended to identify his own fixed opinions and prejudices with the moral law and, absolutely convinced that he was defending the right, he usually refused to compromise when he thought principle was involved in a dispute. What was often more important, he usually insisted that his associates adhere consistently to the Wilsonian line. Such a state of mind, of course, did not make for a compromising or flexible disposition, and certainly Wilson was never famous for that. The tragic break with Hibben, which brought so much sorrow to Wilson, was one of the first examples of Wilson's insistence that his friends fight for what he considered right as hard as he himself fought. There were to be several conspicuous examples in his career in later years.

Wilson was primarily interested in ideas. "It is not men that interest or disturb me primarily," he once declared; "it is ideas. Ideas live; men die." [5] Intellectual activity, the play of the mind, energetic, exhaustless

[2] Margaret Axson Elliott, *My Aunt Louisa and Woodrow Wilson,* pp. 228-230, tells of many pleasant hours Wilson spent at the Ouija board.

[3] R. S. Baker, "Memorandum of conversations with Stockton Axson, Feb. 8, 10, and 11, 1925," MS in Baker Papers.

[4] M. A. Elliott, *My Aunt Louisa and Woodrow Wilson,* p. 6.

[5] Gamaliel Bradford, "Brains Win and Lose," *Atlantic Monthly,* cxlvii (February 1931), 154.

intellectual labor seemed to him the most important thing in life, and it was this play of imagination that saved him from pedantry. His intellect was not especially profound; what characterized him as a creature of brains, as Gamaliel Bradford points out, was an enormous and constant intellectual activity. He was constantly thinking, constantly designing new mental processes leading to practical ends.[6] This intellectual alertness was characteristic of him during the presidency of the United States, at least until a paralytic stroke shattered his health in 1919. Baker wrote in 1916, for example: "I have never talked with any other public man who gave me such an impression of being at every moment in complete command of his entire intellectual equipment, such an impression of alertness, awareness. His face mirrors that eagerness. A new fact, a new aspect of an old situation, a felicitous statement of current opinion, brings to his intent eyes an expression of keen intellectual appetite." [7]

Wilson was fairly open-minded in coming to decisions and would often subject his own prejudices to argument. But once he had made up his mind upon a subject, he was usually intransigent. He was not a versatile man. He had little command of foreign languages—he learned German, for example, in order to obtain his Ph.D. and to do research on *The State,* yet he promptly forgot most of what he had learned. He was not acquainted with most of the world's great literature; he was not widely traveled; he was indifferent to science and had little use for speculative philosophy or theology. And he was definitely not a hale fellow well-met: in ordinary social relations he was shy, retiring, and diffident. To his intimate friends, however, he was unforgettably charming, warm, and lovable. This friendliness and love of life was manifested especially in his home life.[8]

Wilson came to the presidency of Princeton University at a time when the progressive movement was approaching the stage of mature development. It had ceased to be almost entirely agrarian in outlook and the leadership of the movement had passed from the hands of farmers to progressive editors, politicians, and other urban groups. The leading publicists of the movement, moreover, were no longer the "wild-eyed"

[6] *ibid.,* p. 156.

[7] R. S. Baker, "Wilson," *Collier's Weekly,* LVIII (October 7, 1916), 6.

[8] G. Bradford, "Brains Win and Lose," *loc. cit.,* pp. 158-159; see also Henry J. Ford, "Woodrow Wilson—A Character Sketch," *Review of Reviews,* XLVI (August 1912), 177-181; intimate sketches of Wilson's family life may be found in Eleanor Wilson McAdoo, *The Woodrow Wilsons,* and M. A. Elliott, *My Aunt Louisa and Woodrow Wilson.*

radical farmer-orators; they were now a group of young journalistic reformers, called muckrakers by Theodore Roosevelt, intent upon exposing the degenerate state of American political and business practices.

Wilson's intellectual reaction to the tremendous groundswell of public opinion that was rising during the early 1900's is interesting. He had been rather contemptuous, it will be remembered, of Bryan and his populist followers in 1896. By 1904, however, Wilson had become convinced that much of Bryan's diagnosis was correct. He thought that Bryan had caught the spirit and instincts of the finer aspirations of American life, yet he still mistrusted Bryan's leadership. The trouble was, Wilson thought, chiefly that Bryan had "no brains." It was a great pity, Wilson told a friend, "that a man with his power of leadership should have no mental rudder." [9]

Wilson was not reluctant to let the country know exactly what he thought of Bryan and his brand of Democracy. On November 29, 1904, he addressed the Society of the Virginians at the Waldorf-Astoria in New York. The excitement generated by the preceding election campaign was still in men's minds. Roosevelt had triumphantly defeated Alton B. Parker, the Democratic candidate, and Parker's nomination had been a repudiation of Bryan's leadership. Perhaps Wilson thought that he could help to make that repudiation complete and permanent. He proceeded, therefore, to give his southern listeners some political advice.

The opportunity of the South, Wilson declared, was to demand a rehabilitation of the Democratic party "on the only lines that can restore it to dignity and power." Since 1896, he continued, the party had been used by men who ought never to have been admitted to its councils. By themselves and under their proper designation as Populists and radical theorists, these men could never have played any role in national politics but that of a noisy minority. It was high time, Wilson declared, that the South, which had endured most by way of "humiliation" at the hands of this faction, "should demand that it be utterly and once for all thrust out of Democratic counsels." The country, he concluded indignantly, "needs and will tolerate no party of discontent or radical experiment"; but it did need and would follow a party of conservative reform, acting in the spirit of law and of ancient institutions.[10]

It was a tremendously popular declaration—as far as the wealthy ex-

Virginians seated around the sumptuous tables of the Waldorf-Astoria were concerned. Time and again they interrupted Wilson with applause, and the *Sun's* reporter observed that "President Wilson's speech was greeted with one of the most remarkable demonstrations of approval that has been manifested at a public dinner in this city for a long time." It was ironic, however, that Wilson was so ignorant of political conditions within his own party that he appealed to the South, one of the chief strongholds of Bryanism, to repudiate Bryan. As the *New York World* satirically remarked, he thought the Democratic party, though it was something like 2,000,000 votes weaker than the Republican party, was still too large.[11] The address showed conclusively that although Wilson may have been impressed by the demand of the progressives for reform, his deeply rooted sense of historical conservatism was still predominant in his mind: the solution of the problems must be conservative.[12]

Ray Stannard Baker wrote of 1906 as a "critical year" for Woodrow Wilson. It was indeed an important if not a critical year, for Wilson saw the star of his political ambition rise once again; he began to speak forth with emphasis, before audiences unconnected with university affairs, upon the important economic and political issues of the day; he had his first experiences with practical politics; he underwent, in every sense of the word, a political awakening. It is difficult to believe that his old political longings had been completely subverted during the first years of the Princeton presidency, and it is hardly possible that they should have been reawakened by a single event. The most important incident in this political reawakening, however, was Colonel George Harvey's speech before the Lotos Club in New York on February 3, 1906.

George Brinton McClellan Harvey occupied in 1906 a position pre-

[11] *New York World,* December 1, 1904.

[12] One of the most interesting comments on Wilson's address was given by the New York banker, George Foster Peabody, who wrote Wilson that he was in complete agreement with the *New York World's* scoring of the address. "My own fairly close observation as a banker in Wall Street for more than twenty years leads me to the conclusion that Mr. Bryan and other radicals are right in their contention as to the tremendously serious tendency of present conditions, particularly as regards the 'money power' as they call it," Peabody wrote. "I cannot, of course, but believe that their lack of experience and knowledge of business makes their proposed remedies lack in soundness—in justice also, in some respects; but I think no greater evil can befall the future of this country and its great mission to the world than that leaders of thought, upon whom so great responsibility is placed, should indicate a lack of sympathy with the hopes and desires of the honest minded and sincere hearted of these radical leaders." George Foster Peabody to W. W., December 1, 1904, Wilson Papers.

eminent among American journalists. Beginning his journalistic career
in Vermont in 1879, he had from 1882 to 1885 been a reporter suc-
cessively for the *Springfield Republican,* the *Chicago News,* and the
New York World. For a time, from 1885 through 1890, he edited in
Jersey City the New Jersey edition of the *World* and became active in
Democratic politics in that state. In 1890 he became managing editor of
the *New York World* and in 1892 campaigned for the renomination and
reelection of Grover Cleveland. He soon became associated with William
C. Whitney and Thomas Fortune Ryan in the public utilities business in
New York and earned enough money to buy the *North American Review* in 1899. His success as editor of the *Review* attracted the notice of
the old firm of Harper & Brothers, which was then threatened with
bankruptcy, and when the firm's directors invited Harvey to become
president of the company, J. Pierpont Morgan, the company's chief
creditor, gladly consented. In 1901 Harvey also became editor of *Harper's
Weekly.*[13]

Harvey's acquaintance with Wilson began in late 1901 or early 1902.
Albert Bushnell Hart had urged Wilson to write a volume in his
"American Nation" series, and Harvey, as chief of the firm that was
publishing the series, also wrote to urge the Princeton professor to contribute a volume to the history.[14] In October 1902 Harvey heard Wilson
deliver his inaugural address at Princeton and was so impressed by the
Princetonian's eloquence that he immediately set to work to read all that
Wilson had written. One of Harvey's close friends writes that the editor
had already, in 1902, conceived the idea that Wilson was potential presidential timber.[15] The opportunity to launch the Wilson presidential
movement, however, came much later, when the Lotos Club gave a
dinner in Wilson's honor in February 1906. The time was propitious,
Harvey thought; the company was congenial; and he lost no time in
making the startling proposal that Wilson should be nominated for
president. Wilson, Harvey began, was born in an atmosphere "sur-
charged with true statesmanship." "If one could be found who should
unite in his personality . . . ," Harvey continued, "the instinct of true
statesmanship, . . . the ideal would be at hand." Such a man was

[13] For the details of Harvey's early career I have relied mainly on Willis Fletcher
Johnson, *George Harvey, "A Passionate Patriot,"* pp. 11-78.

[14] Wilson, in a letter to A. B. Hart, January 12, 1902 (Wilson Papers), wrote that he
had had a letter from Harvey; see also W. W. to G. Harvey, January 12, 1902, and G.
Harvey to W. W., January 14, 1902, *ibid.*

[15] William O. Inglis, "Helping to Make a President," *Collier's Weekly,* LVIII (October
7, 1916), 15.

Woodrow Wilson "of Virginia and New Jersey." It was with a sense "almost of rapture" that he contemplated "even the remotest possibility" of voting for Wilson to become President of the United States.[16]

Of those at the dinner, apparently only Wilson took Harvey seriously; he was emotionally stirred by Harvey's speech and hastened to write the editor that it was "most delightful to have such thoughts uttered about me." [17] Some of Wilson's friends were delighted by Harvey's suggestion, and one South Carolinian wrote Wilson enthusiastically, "You can count on *all* of my votes in South Carolina *and* elsewhere." [18] Wilson, however, disclaimed any interest in presidential politics and replied that he was not taking "at all seriously the suggestion made by Colonel Harvey." He was afraid that the discussion would be carried so far as to become embarrassing.[19] After all, he must have feared, the affair could easily become a national joke. Harvey, on the contrary, was in dead earnest. On March 10 *Harper's Weekly* carried a full-page picture of Wilson on its front page, and Harvey reprinted his Lotos Club address and assured the *Weekly's* readers that his speech was not "a hasty or ill-considered utterance." [20] Harvey was now more than ever convinced that Wilson should some day be president.[21]

Harvey obviously was sending up trial balloons, and he must have been gratified when newspapers all over the country discussed his proposal of nominating Wilson for President and when many editors gave the idea enthusiastic endorsement. It was natural that most of the commendations of Wilson's candidacy came from conservative editors, who saw in him a man who might not only supply conservative leadership for the Democratic party, but also might overcome the progressive policies of Theodore Roosevelt. As one editor put it, "Around his banner could gather all those forces which recognize that all real progress comes by evolution rather than by revolution." [22] Or, as a midwestern editor

---

[16] John Elderkin et al, *After Dinner Speeches at the Lotos Club*, pp. 310-312.

[17] W. W. to G. Harvey, February 3, 1906, Wilson Papers.

[18] C. Meriwether to W. W., February 4, 1906, *ibid*.

[19] W. W. to A. W. Hazen, March 20, 1906, photostat in Baker Papers.

[20] *Harper's Weekly*, L (March 10, 1906), 324.

[21] A short time later one of Harvey's lieutenants came out in an article in the *North American Review* advocating Wilson's nomination by the Democratic party in 1908. It is interesting to note that the article, which certainly represented Harvey's views, emphasized primarily Wilson's southern background and the fact that the election of a Southerner would erase all vestiges of sectional antagonism. See "A Jeffersonian Democrat" (Mayo W. Hazeltine), "Whom Will the Democrats Next Nominate for President?" *North American Review*, CLXXXII (April 1906), 481-491.

[22] *Trenton True American*, quoted in *Harper's Weekly*, L (April 21, 1906), 564.

wrote, "The nomination of Mr. Wilson would be a good thing for the country as betokening a return of his party to historic party ideals and first principles, and a sobering up after the radical 'crazes.' " [23] Southern editors, moreover, were pleased by the thought, remote and unlikely though it seemed, that a Southerner should again be president. One enthusiastic Georgian expressed the opinions of many of his fellow-Southerners when he declared that Wilson "would find a solid South behind him" in the fight for the nomination.[24]

There can be no doubt that Harvey had evoked widespread discussion. Not that many observers thought there was much chance that Wilson could be nominated—he was literally outside the Democratic organization as far as the politicians were concerned; and the editors were almost unanimous in agreeing that the suggestion was impractical. Yet it was significant that so many of them approved the idea. Such widespread enthusiasm for Wilson's entrance into politics suggests that he was already, even in 1906, something of a national figure.

Harvey went ahead industriously with his publicity campaign and soon enlisted the support of St. Clair McKelway, editor of the *Brooklyn Eagle*. Wilson, however, apparently thought the matter had gone entirely too far when McKelway sent a representative to Princeton to tell Wilson that the *Brooklyn Eagle* was about to begin a systematic campaign for his nomination in 1908. The whole affair must have caused Wilson considerable disquietude; certainly it aroused his curiosity. What, he must have wondered, were the reasons for Harvey's action? He and Harvey were not intimate friends—they scarcely knew each other personally. Besides, Wilson felt strongly that Harvey's aggressive campaign might seriously interfere with his plans at Princeton. On March 11, 1906, therefore, he wrote McKelway a long letter setting forth in plain language his opposition to the Brooklyn editor's threatened plans. "Nothing could be further from my thoughts than the possibility or the desirability of holding high political office," he wrote. It would be inordinately "silly" of him to think of himself as a serious presidential possibility.[25]

Wilson's letter to McKelway sufficed to halt the campaign the Brooklyn editor was about to undertake; but if Wilson thought that his pronouncement would silence Harvey also, he was soon disappointed. Harvey kept up a vociferous publicity campaign in the *Weekly* during

[23] *Milwaukee Sentinel,* quoted in *ibid.,* L (May 19, 1906), 716.
[24] *Columbus Ledger,* quoted in *ibid.*
[25] W. W. to St. Clair McKelway, March 11, 1906, Wilson Papers.

the spring of 1906; he even went to South Carolina on a missionary journey and succeeded in obtaining a promise of support for the Wilson movement from James Calvin Hemphill, veteran editor of the *Charleston News and Courier*. Harvey began also to sound out the conservative leaders in the Democratic party.[26] By the fall of 1906 the matter had become acutely embarrassing to Wilson, who more than ever feared that Harvey's campaign would interfere with the success of the quadrangle plan he was about to propose at Princeton. Wilson finally decided that even the vociferous Colonel would have to be silenced and sent Stockton Axson to New York to tell Harvey that Wilson was distressed by his agitation. Axson returned from the mission convinced that his efforts had been unsuccessful. "I haven't much to report," he told Wilson. "I don't think that Harvey was frank with me. He was fascinating and suave and I merely got the impression that he intended to go ahead." [27]

In December Wilson conferred with Harvey in New York and shortly afterward wrote to him that he had had a great many troubled thoughts about the subject of their recent interview at the Century Association. He, Wilson, knew that the likelihood of his becoming president was a mere possibility; yet one ought to be as careful about possibilities as about probabilities, and he wished to think out his course of action as clearly and upon as definite data as possible.

He did not deem himself a suitable person to be a presidential candidate on the ticket of a party so divided and so bewildered as the Democratic party is at present, Wilson wrote. Still less did he deem himself a suitable person to be president. The party should be led at this time by a man of political experience and of extraordinary personal force and charm, particularly if he was to lead as a representative of the more conservative and less popular section of the party.

Wilson thought, therefore, that he was justified in begging Harvey to tell him what men of large political experience and of recognized political authority regarded him as an available and desirable man for the purpose. Harvey had spoken during the interview of a large number of men, whose names Wilson would be surprised to hear, who had spoken to him in support of the idea of Wilson's nomination. Do you not think that it would be wise and right to let me know who they are, Wilson concluded, and what information it was that has led you to go forward

[26] W. O. Inglis, "Helping to Make a President," *loc. cit.,* p. 15.

[27] R. S. Baker, "Memorandum of conversations with Stockton Axson, March 12, 1925," MS in Baker Papers.

with the idea you were generous enough to originate at the Lotos Club dinner? [28]

Harvey soon replied at length to Wilson's letter and described in detail the progress of the embryonic presidential movement. August Belmont, he wrote, had told him that "Mr. Wilson is the type of man to win with, if we hope to win at all." "Marse Henry" Watterson, editor of the *Louisville Courier-Journal,* had declared that Wilson was an "ideal" candidate. William F. Laffan, publisher of the *New York Sun,* perhaps the most reactionary newspaper in the United States, had told Harvey that there was a surprising amount of talk "and no little apprehension in official [Washington] circles" about the possibility of Wilson's nomination. Adolph S. Ochs, publisher of the *New York Times,* had declared that Harvey's Lotos Club speech was a "splendid suggestion"; Hemphill of Charleston wrote Harvey every week about the matter. The attitude of the "steady-going bankers . . . Democrats who have been voting the Republican ticket," Harvey continued, was just as encouraging. Dumont Clarke and J. H. Eckels, two bank presidents, were interested in Wilson's candidacy, while Thomas Fortune Ryan, notorious utilities magnate, was intensely interested and had been plying Harvey with questions about Wilson. Harvey concluded by adding a list of men who were interested in Wilson's political success. He classified his list in an interesting manner: persons interested in a general way, persons favorable to a candidate of Wilson's type, and persons favorable to Wilson personally. Among the men in the first category were Laffan and Ryan; the list of names in the second group was the longest and included Belmont, Watterson, Ochs, Clarke, and Charles R. Miller, editor of the *New York Times;* Hemphill, Eckels, and John G. Carlisle of Kentucky were favorable to Wilson personally.[29]

Here indeed was a remarkable list of men. Had Harvey deliberately attempted to enlist the support of a more typical group of political and economic conservatives, who represented better the very things against which the progressives had long been struggling, he could not have been more successful. Wall Street bankers, utilities magnates, conservative editors representing these interests, even Cleveland's secretary of the treasury, hated by the agrarian radicals for his success in maintaining the gold standard—all of these were among Wilson's early supporters. Wilson observed this singular fact, Harvey's biographer writes, and commented favorably upon it.[30]

[28] W. W. to G. Harvey, December 16, 1906, Wilson Papers.
[29] G. Harvey to W. W., December 17, 1906, *ibid.*
[30] W. F. Johnson, *George Harvey,* p. 129.

One thing, however, is obvious—that Wilson was, as Baker writes, densely ignorant of so-called practical politics. And if the Princeton president knew practically nothing about politics, the political leaders knew less about him. Although the business of publicity, of getting Wilson before the public as a potential candidate, was necessary, Harvey believed that it was also essential that Wilson become associated in some fashion with political affairs of a practical nature. In 1906 Wilson was appointed a member of the New Jersey Commission on Uniform State Laws—his first public office—but this was not what Harvey wanted. The New York editor hit upon an ingenious idea: The New Jersey legislature would elect a United States senator in 1907; if Wilson were the Democratic candidate he would most likely be defeated by a Republican legislature, but he would at least gain some national publicity and that, Harvey thought, would serve as one step toward achieving the presidential nomination in 1908 or 1912.[31]

In the early part of October 1906 a rumor began to circulate in New York and New Jersey to the effect that Wilson might become the Democratic candidate for the Senate. He had already been mentioned, one New York newspaper reported on October 2, as the candidate upon whom "the Cleveland Democrats of New Jersey would unite." [32] While Wilson was in England during the summer of 1906 Harvey had engineered a scheme to get Wilson into politics without Wilson's knowledge. Harvey had secured the support of James Smith, Jr., Democratic boss of Essex County, New Jersey, for Wilson's candidacy. On October 13 the eleven Essex Democratic candidates for the Assembly met in Newark and pledged themselves to vote for Wilson for senator if they were elected.[33]

Wilson returned to New York on October 14. "The mention of my name was without any authority from me, and was a great surprise," he told reporters. "Although I am an old-line Democrat, and would do any service to restore the party to power, I cannot see that it would be any help for me to accept such an office. . . . My duty is to Princeton, and I should be reluctant to give up my work there." [34] After the November elections, however, when it became apparent that the Republicans would easily control the legislature, the matter assumed a different complexion in Wilson's mind. And when Harvey came out in the *Weekly* in a leading editorial suggesting that the New Jersey Democrats had "a

[31] W. O. Inglis, "Helping to Make a President," *loc. cit.*, p. 15.
[32] *New York Evening Post*, October 2, 1906.
[33] *ibid.*, October 15, 1906   [34] *ibid.*

rare and glorious opportunity" to point the way for the reestablishment of the Democratic party by nominating Wilson for United States senator,[35] Wilson was convinced that there was no reason why he should not accept what would amount to an empty honor.[36]

An embarrassing complication soon arose, however, because Wilson was not the only candidate in the field. The progressive Democrats in New Jersey, long restive under the domination of the party by the two bosses, Smith and Robert Davis of Jersey City, had united in support of Edwin A. Stevens of Hoboken. Stevens and Wilson had been classmates at Princeton and were intimate friends. Stevens discussed the senatorial question with Wilson in November, urged him then to become an active candidate for the nomination, and promised to obtain the support of his friends for Wilson's candidacy. Wilson, however, declared that his name was being used against Stevens in bad faith and refused to oppose him. Stevens, consequently, redoubled his efforts to secure political support.[37]

Harvey and Wilson discussed the senatorship at the Century Association in New York early in December. Wilson asserted that he would not be a candidate in opposition to Stevens, but declared that he was willing to become a candidate if Stevens withdrew from the race. Harvey subsequently endeavored to persuade Stevens to withdraw from the contest, but the doughty progressive was now adamant. He cared nothing for the empty compliment of the nomination, he told Harvey, but he would not now abandon the progressives who were supporting him.[38]

As the time for the election of a United States senator drew near, the plain facts of the matter became increasingly evident. Harvey had enlisted the support of the bosses, Smith and Davis; the bosses were happy to use Wilson as a respectable front in order to head off the Democratic progressives. Stevens made these facts painfully clear in a letter to Wilson. The bosses who controlled the state machine, Stevens wrote, were supporting Wilson, whose candidacy was being considered by the progressive leaders not only as an act of bad faith, but also "as a sign of your willingness to allow the use of your name as a club by the very men who every good Democrat feels to have been the bane of the party and whose leadership has made the state hopelessly Republican." It was

[35] *Harper's Weekly*, L (November 24, 1906), 1662.
[36] W. W. to E. A. Stevens, January 1907, Wilson Papers.
[37] E. A. Stevens to W. W., December 29, 1906, *ibid*.
[38] W. O. Inglis, "Helping to Make a President," *loc. cit.*, p. 15.

not a personal fight he was making, Stevens insisted, it was a fight for progressive government.[39]

Wilson was apparently moved by Stevens's letter, but he was not sufficiently disturbed by the situation Stevens had disclosed to withdraw from the contest. "Possibly it is because I am such an outsider and so inexperienced in such matters," Wilson replied, "but the whole difficulty is that I cannot bring myself to see the situation as you seem to see it." If he were to withdraw from the contest and join in the fight against the bosses, Wilson continued, he would be gratuitously taking part in a factional fight. "When it was a question of actual election to the Senate," he added, "I felt bound to say that I could not accept the office; but a complimentary vote, tendered by a minority, involves no responsibility on the part of the recipient, and therefore it seems to me that it would be quite gratuitous of me to say that, if it were tendered me, I would not accept it." Such action would, he insisted, "be intervening *for the sake of settling factional differences.*" He had already declared with emphasis that he was not a candidate and, he concluded tartly, "no one, I take it, will venture to doubt my sincerity." [40]

Wilson's reply deeply disturbed Stevens and his supporters, one of whom made bold to write to Wilson, suggesting that he did not "thoroughly understand the situation here." [41] Stevens himself was deeply discouraged; above all else, however, he wanted to avoid an open controversy with Wilson. He wrote on January 5, 1907, therefore, what he must have thought was a last-ditch appeal, asking the Princeton president to withdraw publicly from the contest and to come out in support of his candidacy. If Wilson would not do this, Stevens added, he would do all that he could to withdraw from the unfortunate situation; he would ask his friends to vote for Wilson. "You will also realize," Stevens warned, "that the fight is not on the question of an empty compliment, but on one of party control, & that the Senatorial fight has its importance mainly on account of its prominence." [42]

This at last jarred Wilson's complacency; he immediately decided that the only honorable course was to abandon the contest altogether. He wrote immediately to Harvey and confessed that he had in the fall

---

[39] E. A. Stevens to W. W., December 29, 1906, Wilson Papers.

[40] W. W. to E. A. Stevens, January 2, 1907, *ibid.*

[41] E. H. Wright, Jr. to W. W., January 4, 1907, *ibid.* Wright had been asked by an unnamed person to nominate Wilson for the Senate. He wrote emphatically that the Democratic complimentary vote should go to Stevens as a sort of recognition of his long fight against political corruption.

[42] E. A. Stevens to W. W., January 5, 1907, *ibid.*

left the senatorial field open to Stevens and that it would be interpreted as an act of bad faith if he were to oppose Stevens now. He could remain passive in the matter no longer, and asked Harvey to tell him the "most courteous and convenient way" to withdraw from the fight. Wilson, however, was careful not to offend Harvey and thanked him profusely for his support in the affair.[43] Harvey replied on January 10 and enclosed the draft of a letter, which he suggested Wilson send to a Democratic leader, stating that he, Wilson, had never been a candidate for the Democratic nomination and that he wished his name withdrawn from the consideration of the Democratic caucus. Significantly, Harvey strongly advised Wilson to betray no signs of support for Stevens, "as that would involve you immediately in a faction." The Stevens faction, Harvey wrote, were "unwarrantably greedy of an empty honor, in view of a greater purpose from a party standpoint." [44]

It is interesting to speculate as to whether Wilson detected the incongruity of Harvey s statements. Harvey knew that the Democratic senatorial nomination represented a good deal more than was superficially apparent, for there were few persons in the country better informed as to the state of Democratic politics in New Jersey. Wilson might well have wondered, moreover, why Harvey had so carefully warned him not to support Stevens. It is obvious that Harvey was anxious that Wilson avoid being identified with factional politics in New Jersey—when the faction in question was the progressive wing of the party. At any rate, Wilson probably did not ponder these questions; he was too happy at his release to worry about them. Using almost literally Harvey's suggested letter, Wilson wrote to Charles C. Black, a Democratic leader in the legislature, requesting him to withhold his name from consideration in the party caucus. He carefully avoided any references to his erstwhile opponent, but he did write that "the compliment should be paid to someone of those who were active in the canvass." [45] At the same time, he wrote to Stevens and told him that he was withdrawing from the contest.[46] There was not, however, the slightest hint of support for Stevens in either the letter to Black or to Stevens, and Wilson afterward maintained a discreet silence in the affair.

The senatorial muddle was an embarrassing experience and revealed to Wilson how deeply ignorant he was of practical politics. But if he

[43] W. W. to G. Harvey, January 7, 1907, *ibid.*
[44] G. Harvey to W. W., January 10, 1907, *ibid.*
[45] W. W. to C. C. Black, January 11, 1907, *ibid.*
[46] W. W. to E. A. Stevens, January 11, 1907, *ibid.*

was now more anxious to avoid the pitfalls of the world of politics, he was also becoming acutely interested in the practical affairs of men. On April 16, 1906, two months after Harvey "nominated" him for the presidency, Wilson addressed an unofficial party gathering, the Democratic Club of New York, and for the first time endeavored to interpret the meaning of the Democratic party. He spoke about Jefferson and his meaning for the day, but it was not the unamerican Jefferson, the radical theorist of whom he had written a decade previously, of whom Wilson spoke. It was the Sage of Monticello whom he held up as the guiding spirit of American democracy. "It is the spirit . . . of the man by which he rules us from his urn," Wilson declared. The present political and economic troubles, he added, would be remedied, "not so much by wisdom as by an effectual purpose to be pure and unselfishly serviceable." If Democrats would act in the spirit of Jefferson, therefore, they would turn away from socialism. They would appeal to individual men for constructive action; they would maintain a jealous regard for the rights of the states; they would turn again to the common people of the country for inspiration.[47]

In December Wilson addressed the Southern Society of New York and again emphasized the necessity for political idealism as the motivating force in American democracy. America, perhaps, was about to lose her ancient hope, her sturdy desire to achieve what she had long since conceived to be right, he declared. It had, he continued, become the habit of the people to regard the multiform problems confronting America in sheer anger and discontent. "Indeed," he insisted, "the chief menace of our present state of mind is that there is neither patience nor prudence in our thought and action upon the matters which excite us." Wilson was thinking primarily about Theodore Roosevelt and his demand that the government regulate certain phases of business enterprise. "Governments should supply an equilibrium, not a disturbing force," Wilson insisted in good Manchesterian language. It was hard, he knew, for politicians to stand firm against the crowd, to resist the demand that the government do everything. "But the time has come," he concluded, "for such sober counsel as will relieve government of the business of providence and restore it to its normal duties of justice and of impartial regulation."[48]

[47] "Thomas Jefferson," address delivered at the dinner of the Democratic Club, New York, April 16, 1906, original MS in *ibid*.

[48] "Patriotism," address delivered before the Southern Society of New York, December 14, 1906, original MS in the Gilbert Close File of Wilson speeches, MSS in the Library of Princeton University; hereinafter cited as Close File.

Wilson had begun to lecture the American people on the problems of government, but at the same time he also began to think of his duties at Princeton in a political light. "My duties have been almost exclusively political," he told a group of alumni in 1907, "and I must say that I find myself generally thinking of a university as a political instrument . . . as an instrument for the advancement of the general intelligence and power of the country." [49] Even in his own academic field Wilson was beginning to manifest a more acute understanding of the problems inherent in the modern political structure. In April 1907 he began a series of lectures at Columbia University centered around the subject of constitutional government in the United States. The lectures, later published as Wilson's last scholarly book, provide an interesting contrast to his earlier and more immature *Congressional Government*.

Wilson had written in 1884 of the president as a powerless executive; in 1907 he described the chief executive in an entirely different light— as a powerful party leader and true national spokesman who, by appealing to the people over the heads of Congress, might exercise a very real influence over the course of legislation. The president, Wilson continued, "is . . . the political leader of the nation, or has it in his choice to be. The nation as a whole has chosen him, and is conscious that it has no other political spokesman. His is the only national voice in affairs. Let him once win the admiration and confidence of the country, and no other single force can withstand him, no combination of forces will easily overpower him. . . . If he rightly interpret the national thought and boldly insist upon it, he is irresistible." [50] Wilson had thus abandoned his former demand for cabinet government as a means of achieving responsible statesmanship in the United States and now declared that responsible government could best be attained by means of presidential leadership.[51]

Wilson also revealed in his lectures a more acute insight into the machinery of congressional government and described the House of Representatives and the speaker in a much more sympathetic manner than in his earlier writings.[52] He recognized that economic interests

---

[49] Address before the Tennessee Association of Princeton Alumni, November 9, 1907, *Princeton Alumni Weekly*, VIII (November 20, 1907), 138.

[50] *Constitutional Government in the United States*, p. 68. See also p. 110: "There is but one common solvent. The law of their [the three branches of the federal government] union is public opinion. That and that alone can draw them together. That part of the government, therefore, which has the most direct access to opinion has the best chance of leadership and mastery; and at present that part is the President."

[51] *ibid.*, pp. 80-81.   [52] *ibid.*, pp. 82-111.

were important in the business of legislation, and questioned whether newspapers, which represented "special interests," were true mirrors of public opinion.[53] He also recognized that the Senate represented fundamental economic and sectional interests, and that in many cases corporate and railroad interests had operated to secure the election of members.[54] But, he added cautiously, "In most of the states great corporations, great combinations of interest, have little to do with the choice of senators." [55] He objected to the long and costly processes of judicial litigation and declared that "our very constitutional principle has fallen into dangerous disrepair" because the cost of legal proceedings always gave a tremendous advantage to men of wealth.[56]

In his lecture on state-federal relations, Wilson demonstrated a clear understanding of the dynamic problems of the American constitutional system. He realized, he declared, that there was a widespread distrust of legislatures as law-making bodies, legislatures that were in many states under the thumbs of political bosses. He thought, however, that it would be fatal "to our political vitality really to strip the States of their powers and transfer them to the federal government." [57] The remedy lay, he asserted, in reform from within. "It may turn out," he continued, "that what our state governments need is not to be sapped of their powers and subordinated to Congress, but to be reorganized along simpler lines which will make them real organs of popular opinion." [58] Wilson concluded his lectures with a realistic analysis of practical politics in the United States—a remarkable advance over the warped and narrow discussion of politics in *Congressional Government*. Interestingly enough, although Wilson recognized the dangers inherent in the irresponsible power wielded by political bosses, he thought that bosses and secret managers were the natural fruit of the American party system.[59]

The most striking impression one gets from reading this last scholarly contribution of Wilson's—and, at that, it represented more his mature reflections covering the broad range of American politics than an original contribution to knowledge—is that two of the basic ideas that are usually associated with Wilsonism were already forcefully set forth in 1907. First of all, Wilson's conception of the tremendous potentialities of presidential leadership had supplanted his earlier desire for cabinet

[53] *ibid.*, pp. 102-107.
[55] *ibid.*, p. 128.
[57] *ibid.*, p. 191.
[59] *ibid.*, p. 210.

[54] *ibid.*, pp. 114-125.
[56] *ibid.*, pp. 153-154.
[58] *ibid.*

government. He had come to realize what his own position might be if he were ever president. Secondly, his plea for dynamic state action was significant. It ran contrary to the Herbert Croly type of progressive thought that insisted that the federal government achieve Jeffersonian ends by using Hamiltonian means. Later, as governor of New Jersey, Wilson demonstrated that the states could lead the way in reform.

Colonel Harvey, even in 1907, had not lost hope that his reluctant candidate would some day receive the political honors that he thought Wilson deserved. The wily New York editor was hard at work constructing a powerful, well-oiled organization. Early in 1907 he sent for William O. Inglis, one of his ablest writers, and commissioned him as his right-hand lieutenant, his confidential agent, in the conduct of the campaign. Inglis was to give his best energies, Harvey said, to the job of making Wilson president; as a preliminary step, however, Wilson was to be groomed for the governorship of New Jersey.[60] The 1908 Democratic national convention was more than a year in the future, but early in 1907 Harvey bestirred himself to secure the definite, unequivocal support of certain powerful conservatives in New York. At his instigation, arrangements were made by Dr. John A. Wyeth, president of the Southern Society of New York, to bring William M. Laffan of the *New York Sun,* Thomas Fortune Ryan, and Wilson together.[61] "Our little dinner is for the evening of Friday, March 15," Wyeth wrote to Wilson. "Mr. Laffan, Mr. Ryan, you and I will compose the party and the dinner is to be entirely private, at Delmonico's, at 7:30 P/M/." [62]

The meeting of the arch-conservatives was an extremely congenial affair. Apparently Laffan and Ryan were, as a contemporary writes, "a self-constituted committee of investigation and selection, acting in behalf of a conservative Democracy as against the Bryanized variety," [63] who had come to look Wilson over "to see if he came up to specifications" as a likely candidate for 1908.[64] Wilson was entirely at ease in

---

[60] W. O. Inglis, "Helping to Make a President," *loc. cit.,* p. 14. Harvey explained to Inglis that although his early support of Wilson for president had been taken lightly by most persons, he was certain that the movement could be successful. The people were alarmed at Roosevelt's radical tendencies, he continued, and they were not likely to accept Bryan's leadership. They wanted a new kind of leadership—a leadership embodying the best traditions of American statesmanship—and he was certain Wilson could furnish that leadership.

[61] J. A. Wyeth to W. W., March 9, 1907, Wilson Papers.

[62] J. A. Wyeth to W. W., ca. March 12, 1907, *ibid.*

[63] Edward P. Mitchell, *Memoirs of An Editor,* p. 387.

[64] Mitchell's account of the meeting is slightly in error. He writes, for example, that the conference took place at Wyeth's home on Lexington Avenue and that the date

the company and talked freely and conservatively, as if he were conscious of the inspection he was undergoing. He even took advantage of the meeting to approach Ryan shortly afterward for money for the endowment of the preceptorial system!

In the course of the conversation Laffan mentioned a letter he had written to Alton B. Parker in 1904, in which Laffan stated his views with regard to a platform for the Democratic party.[65] Wyeth soon afterward sent a copy of the letter to Wilson,[66] and in June Wyeth again wrote to Wilson, suggesting that he answer Laffan's letter to Parker.[67] Wilson planned to set forth his political convictions in an address before the Southern Society,[68] but for some unknown reason he was unable to make the address. Instead, in August he wrote a concise statement of his position on contemporary economic and political questions for Laffan's and Ryan's perusal.

This interesting document, entitled "Credo" by Wilson and still preserved in his papers, provides a succinct summary of the man's deep-rooted political and economic convictions at the time. It could hardly have failed to please the reactionary publisher and utilities czar, for it was conservative to the core. Taking the broad hint laid down in Laffan's letter to Parker, Wilson declared that the Constitution was the guarantee of American liberty and that it and the laws enacted under it were entirely adequate to remedy the wrongs that had corrupted modern business. On the important question of trust and business regulation, Wilson was unequivocal. Great trusts and combinations are the necessary, because the most convenient and efficient, instrumentalities of modern business, he wrote; the vast bulk of their transactions are legitimate. Some businessmen violated the law, to be sure, he added, but they should be punished under the law which they violated, not by direct regulation of business by governmental commissions. Business

was 1904. He writes that the account that he gives was given to him by Laffan shortly after the meeting occurred. *ibid.*, pp. 387-388.

[65] The letter, incidentally, "owing to circumstances," was never sent to Parker. J. A. Wyeth to W. W., March 24, 1907, Wilson Papers.

[66] E. P. Mitchell, *Memoirs of An Editor,* p. 388, quotes part of the letter addressed to Parker. "It seems to me," it reads, "as a plain citizen, that the time has come to demand a reaffirmation of the Constitution and of the Bill of Rights. We have already strayed far afield, and we are like[ly] to go further."

[67] J. A. Wyeth to W. W., June 18, 1907, Wilson Papers.

[68] J. A. Wyeth to W. W., June 21, 1907, *ibid.* Wyeth thanked Wilson for accepting an invitation to speak before the Society and added, "I shall hope between now and then to have a few minutes with you, in order to submit to you about thirty lines of my convictions of what the Southern man of to-day should represent."

practices in violation of good morals and sound business methods should be brought within the prohibitions of the civil and criminal law, he insisted; the federal government, however, should not undertake the direct supervision and regulation of business. Proceeding next to a discussion of the labor problem, Wilson set himself firmly against the union movement. The constitution guarantees to every man the right to sell his labor to whom he pleases for such price as he is willing to accept, he asserted, and added that the men who would abridge or abrogate the right of freedom of contract have neither the ideas nor the sentiments needed for the maintenance or for the enjoyment of liberty.[69]

There is every reason to believe that this remarkable pronouncement made a favorable impression upon Laffan, Ryan, and Harvey. After all, it was pretty nearly an epitomization of their own convictions; it is, therefore, erroneous to conclude that Wilson did not satisfy Laffan and Ryan in 1907 as Parker had done in 1904. It should be remembered, in the first place, that it was Harvey, not Laffan or Ryan, who was the *deus ex machina* directing the Wilson presidential movement. When Harvey decided in 1910 that the hour had arrived when Wilson should embark upon a political career, Ryan generously helped to finance his first campaign; Laffan had died in 1909, but the *New York Sun* for a time carried on his support of Wilson.

If Wilson had sincerely spurned the idea of plunging into politics in 1906—and that certainly is a controversial question—he seems to have given in to Harvey's solicitations altogether in 1907 and 1908. Perhaps he did not really believe that his nomination for president or, for that matter, for any other high political office was probable; but he certainly did his utmost to boost his own cause. He increased the tempo of his political addresses and came out more emphatically than ever against what he thought were Roosevelt's dangerous tendencies. In an address on Grover Cleveland's seventieth birthday in March 1907 Wilson made a pointed reference to Roosevelt, whom he accused of "imprudent willfulness." The American people admired boldness in their leaders, he admitted, but "they would feel much safer if boldness were tempered with good judgment and striking leadership planned along wisely calculated lines." He was unreserved in his praise of Cleveland's leadership. Cleveland had been right on the money question, Wilson declared. "In the midst of the shifting scene Mr. Cleveland personally came to seem the only fixed point," he concluded. "He alone stood firm and gave

[60] "Credo," written August 6, 1907, original MS in Wilson Papers.

definite utterance to principles intelligible to all." [70] Five years later he was to use almost these identical words in describing Bryan.

There is no doubt that Wilson did some serious thinking about the condition of the country. The immediate prospects, he thought, were not encouraging. "We are disconcerted and demoralized, beyond measure disgusted," he told the South Carolina Society of New York, "and therefore sadly in need of counsel which shall seek to restore world balances and harmonies and moderations of action." It was America's task, he declared, to save the way of life by which Americans had supposed they had set up at last a just civil order. The problems that faced contemporary America, however, could not be solved by radical action; reform must come, he admitted, but Americans "must see to it that the processes of reform are moderate and self-possessed, by putting its prosecution in the hands of those who are free from the follies of establishing a panic and radical experiment." [71] Wilson did not, however, venture to specify the men who could be trusted with the leadership of the reform movement.

No problem troubled persons concerned for the future of their country in 1907 more than the dangers inherent in the rapid growth of trusts and monopolies. Theodore Roosevelt and other progressives thought that the power of these industrial giants could be curbed only by destroying or regulating them. Wilson's first public declaration on the trust question was made in an address on July 4, 1907, at the Jamestown Exposition. As Wilson was an historian of some repute, Harry St. George Tucker, president of the Exposition, asked him to speak on the historically appropriate subject of "The Author and Signers of the Declaration of Independence." At least for the time, however, Wilson abandoned the role of scholar and assumed the more spectacular garb of the statesman; he proceeded to set forth his own remedy for the trust problem.

"There is much in our time that would cause men of the principles of Mr. Jefferson the bitterest disappointment," he declared. Individual opportunity was hampered; the chief instruments of production were at least virtually monopolized by a few men; and the people of the nation had not shared the benefits of the country's industrial development with the captains of industry. How could the situation be set aright, the nation asked. Simply by returning to the methods and ideals

---

[70] "Grover Cleveland," address at Princeton, March 17, 1907, MS in Close File.
[71] Address before the South Carolina Society of New York, March 18, 1907, from a transcription of Wilson's stenographic notes of the address, MS in the Wilson Papers.

of 1776, Wilson replied, by returning to the old ideal of law as the rule of life. The practice of punishing a corporation for misdeeds of its directors, of fining or dissolving it, was obviously futile, he insisted. Government regulation, moreover, was not the answer, for that meant "too much government." Americans had a difficult task indeed—the task of searching out with the probe of morals and law the individual malefactor in business and industry. Yet, Wilson added, "One really responsible man in jail, one real originator of the schemes and transactions which are contrary to public interest legally lodged in the penitentiary, would be worth more than one thousand corporations mulcted in fines, if reform is to be genuine and permanent." Only by adopting this approach to the problem could America escape socialism, he continued. So the answer was plain: do not attack the inanimate corporations; attack the secret and illegal manipulations of the so-called financiers; let "every corporation exactly define the obligations and powers of its directors, and then let the law fix responsibility upon them accordingly." Only by returning to these ancient democratic principles could Americans effect their emancipation and escape the burden of too much government.[72]

Wilson returned again to the trust question in an address before the Chamber of Commerce in Cleveland in November 1907. With emphasis he lamented the fact that "Our present tendency is to go almost feverishly in search of strange experimental processes by which to check the things of which we are afraid," yet he never said what those strange experimental processes were. His auditors would scarcely have learned, for example, from the following outburst of oratory:

"Nothing is more evident in our day than that the country is confused in its thinking, and needs to look its affairs over very carefully before determining what legal and constitutional changes it will make. In our haste and eagerness to reform manifest abuses, we are inclined to enter upon courses dangerous and unprecedented, I mean unprecedented in America, and quite contrary to the spirit which has hitherto ruled in her affairs. We turn more and more with a sense of individual helplessness to the government, begging that it take care of us because we have forgotten how to take care of ourselves, begging that it will regulate our industries, scrutinize our economic undertakings, supervise

---

[72] "The Author and Signers of the Declaration of Independence," original MS in Wilson Papers; the address was reprinted in *North American Review*, CLXXXVI (September 1907), 22-33.

our enterprises and keep the men who conduct them within definite bounds of law and morality. . . . In such courses we are turning directly away from all the principles which have distinguished America and made her institutions the hope of all men who believe in liberty."

Again Wilson demanded that corporations be regulated by a process of fixing individual responsibility for corporation malfeasance, yet he does not seem to have thought that corporation law could hardly be enforced by the sheer weight of public opinion, that without the vigilant supervision and regulation of the government all of his fine theories concerning liberty and freedom would be nothing but high-sounding phrases on the statute books. Viewed in this light, his eloquent denunciations of government regulation—"Government supervision . . . will in the long run enslave us and demoralize us"—sound like sheer nonsense.[73]

The horns of the dilemma were sharp indeed for Wilson! His confidence in "the operation of individual freedom," his faith in "men rather than in government" sound well enough, but he never explained how these very desirable principles could be established. The truth of the matter was that he was still too much a Manchester Liberal who trusted more the natural identification of interests and was suspicious of the positive intervention of the state in the affairs of men.

In October 1907 the business operations of the country were disturbed by a sharp panic in Wall Street and at least for a time there was a probability that the industries of the country would also be seriously affected. Wilson had gained something of a reputation as a political soothsayer, and Charles R. Miller, editor of the *New York Times,* sent one of his reporters to sound out Wilson on the general situation. The journalist apparently took the Princeton man too literally, for after the interview was printed Wilson wrote the editor a sharp letter accusing the reporter of grossly misrepresenting his ideas.[74] The headlines printed above the interview announced a "Scathing arraignment" of political and industrial conditions by the president of Princeton. That was too much for Wilson, who wrote that it was such scathing arraignments that had brought about the unfortunate state of business. The

[73] "Ideals of Public Life," address delivered at the fifty-eighth annual dinner of the Cleveland Chamber of Commerce, November 16, 1907, MS in Close File.

[74] The interview was published in the *New York Times,* November 24, 1907; for Wilson's reply see his letter to the editor, November 24, 1907, published in *ibid.,* November 27, 1907.

panic, he declared, was the result of the blundering and unintelligent activities of the government in attempting to regulate business.[75]

Wilson did not deny, however, that most of the published interview was correctly reported. He was aware, he declared, that "the abominable currency system under which we are staggering" was the chief cause for the money stringency. The proposal of a central bank made by the American Bankers' Association, the Aldrich plan, was a good one, he continued, and if put into effect would prevent financial crises. Wilson next asserted the need for an organized body of intellectuals to guide the nation's destinies—"a common council, a sort of people's forum." J. Pierpont Morgan, Wilson added, would be a good chairman for such a "common council." "I am glad to see," he added naively, "that in the midst of all this turmoil of undefined wickedness, Mr. Morgan's name has not been among the celebrities." When the reporter asked Wilson to express his opinion of Bryan, Wilson refused to say anything except that there were specific objections that he could "point out in Bryan," political propositions in his platform that he considered absurd, and could never endorse. What use, however, would it serve if he named them? [76]

Several more such interviews and Wilson would have made his nomination for the presidency at any date impossible. Harvey, however, was too shrewd a politician to have imagined that Wilson's nomination for president in 1908 by the Democrats was anything like a probability. He was looking to 1912 as Wilson's presidential year, but kept up his campaign for Wilson as the best means of securing the New Jersey governorship for him in 1910.[77]

Harvey was an intimate friend of Joseph Pulitzer, publisher of the *New York World,* and had already aroused Pulitzer's interest in Wilson's candidacy. When Harvey, therefore, suggested to the veteran publisher that the *World* should come out in support of Wilson's candidacy for the presidential nomination in 1908, Pulitzer replied that he would print an editorial, "coming out for Wilson," if Harvey wrote the article.[78] Harvey, of course, did write the leading editorial—it was a labor of love—that appeared in the *World* on January 18, 1908. "If the Democratic Party is to be saved from falling into the hands of William J. Bryan as a permanent receiver," it reads, "a Man must be found—

[75] Wilson to the editor of the *New York Times*, November 24, 1907, *ibid.*, November 27, 1907.
[76] *ibid.*, November 24, 1907.
[77] W. O. Inglis, "Helping to Make a President," *loc. cit.*, p. 14.
[78] *ibid.*, p. 15.

and soon." After cataloguing the qualifications of the candidate who could unite the party, Harvey wrote that the one Democrat "who unquestionably meets these qualifications is Woodrow Wilson," and concluded by presenting him as the southern candidate for the presidency.

The *World* editorial was a brilliant coup for Harvey; to have secured the endorsement for his candidate of the leading Democratic newspaper in the country was more than he could reasonably have expected. What was more important, the editorial set off a good deal of discussion of Wilson as a presidential possibility. W. F. Keohan, editor of the New Jersey edition of the *New York Tribune,* informed Wilson that New Jersey Democrats were opposed to Bryan's nomination and that many of them had already declared their allegiance to him.[79] Henry James Forman, managing editor of the *North American Review* was even more encouraging; "I do indeed believe that you are a possible recipient of the nomination at Denver," he wrote.[80]

The prospect of a presidential nomination, it must be admitted, was infinitely pleasing to Woodrow Wilson. He was absolutely determined, however, that he would hew to the conservative line, that under no circumstances would he allow himself to become identified with the Bryan wing of the party. The Pennsylvania progressive Democrats, for example, gave a dinner in Philadelphia for the Nebraskan—Wilson refused to break bread, or even to speak from the same platform with Bryan.[81] In the spring of 1908 Wilson was invited to speak at the important Jefferson Dinner of the National Democratic Club in New York. At first he was overjoyed at this opportunity to set forth his political faith before such a representative body of Democrats, but when he learned that Bryan would also be present he hastened to withdraw his promise to speak at the meeting. Bryan's presence, Wilson wrote, would alter entirely the character of the occasion, for he, Wilson, would be put in a very awkward position by undertaking to deliver such an address as he had planned and looked forward to. He would feel obliged to take a position extremely antagonistic to Bryan, not antagonistic to Bryan personally, but to "all the loose notions" that he put forth as a party program.[82] Finally, in order that no person might be

[79] W. F. Keohan to W. W., January 7, 1908, Wilson Papers.

[80] H. J. Forman to W. W., April 14, 1908, *ibid*.

[81] R. S. Baker, "Memorandum of an interview with Roland S. Morris, March 7 and 8, 1926," MS in Baker Papers.

[82] W. W. to J. R. Dunlap, April 1, 1908, copy in *ibid*. It should be noted, however, that Bryan could not be present at the meeting and that Wilson did make his speech after all.

ignorant of his hostility to Bryanism, Wilson publicly denounced Bryan's policies. "I have even wished at times," he told a reporter, "that every fool could be also a knave instead of being, as they often are, people who possess attractive manners and excellent intentions. Take Mr. Bryan, for example. He is the most charming and lovable of men personally, but foolish and dangerous in his theoretical beliefs." [83]

It would hardly be accurate to say that Wilson engaged in an active campaign for the Democratic nomination in 1908. He was anxious, however, that his "claims" to the nomination be presented in a vigorous manner; and it is interesting that he named Grover Cleveland as the person best fitted to describe him.[84] In March he journeyed to Chicago to set forth his views on the economic problems of the day. His speech was a wholesale condemnation of what he called the "passion for regulative legislation [that] seems to have taken possession of the country of late." The trouble was, he declared, that the reformers, who were demanding drastic governmental regulation of the complex and prodigious business enterprises of the country had neither carefully analyzed the abuses they described nor thought through the remedies they proposed. The fact that Wilson was no expert in such matters, however, did not seem to embarrass him or deter him from speaking his mind on the subject.

There was much that was wrong with current business practices, Wilson admitted—the production of many commodities had been concentrated in the hands of monopolistic corporations; unscrupulous financiers had mulcted the public by watering stock issues and misusing trust funds. "But what strikes us most about all the regulation and remedial measures adopted is that they are based upon what is for us an entirely new conception of the province alike of law and of government. Our law has hitherto dealt with individuals, with specific transactions; it now undertakes to deal directly with business itself, not upon lines of exact definition such as courts of law could act upon but with a wide range of discretion which must be entrusted to commissions and cannot be assigned to judicial tribunals."

What Wilson objected to especially was that this sort of governmental control resulted in establishing, not a reign of law, but a reign of discretion and individual judgment on the part of officials in the regulation of business. "We seem to have made almost of a sudden and without deliberation," he asserted, "a very radical and momentous choice of

[83] *Jersey City Jersey Journal,* March 10, 1908.
[84] W. W. to H. J. Forman, April 10, 1908, Wilson Papers.

practice which is also a radical departure in principle from all that we have hitherto admitted or thought tolerable in the exercise of governmental authority."

Wilson at last showed his true colors when he charged that the whole idea of governmental regulation was socialistic in principle. Once the government embarked upon a program of regulation, he asserted, government ownership would inevitably follow. He was not, however, without hope for the future; he was certain the American people would come to their senses because such "methods of regulation it may be safely predicted will sooner or later be completely discredited by experience." The only safe solution to the problem of business malpractices, he again asserted, was to ferret out the individual malefactor from among the maze of corporate organizations.[85] He seemed almost passionately eager to get this appeal across to the people. Two weeks later, for example, he delivered the same warning at Pittsburgh.[86]

In his last important address prior to the Denver convention, Wilson set forth his own platform for the Democratic party. Actually he made something of an about-face from the position he had taken at Chicago and Pittsburgh and endeavored to convince his listeners that the conservative economic program he was advocating was not really an embodiment of Smithian *laissez-faire* philosophy, that he was not opposed to governmental regulation of business, provided that the kind of regulation met his approval. He wanted the people to know that he was opposed only to executive regulation by commissions. It was the Democratic party's opportunity, he declared in summarizing his platform, to demand a return to government by law instead of by personal power; a tariff enacted for the general welfare of the people instead of for certain vested interests; a currency based upon the actual assets of the banks of issue; and the precise fixing of responsibility for illegal activities on individuals engaged in business and industrial enterprises.[87]

As the Democratic pre-convention campaign neared its culmination, it became increasingly evident that Bryan would be the master of the Democratic situation. "I do not feel that it is any longer true that I am being seriously considered as a possible recipient of the nomination at

[85] "Government and Business," address delivered before the Commercial Club of Chicago, March 14, 1908, MS in Close File.

[86] "The Government and Business," address delivered before the Traffic Club of Pittsburgh, April 3, 1908, MS in *ibid*.

[87] "Law or Personal Power," address delivered before the National Democratic Club, New York, April 13, 1908, MS in Wilson Papers.

Denver this year," Wilson wrote on April 10, "and fear that Colonel Harvey is carrying his generous loyalty to an idea and a high purpose further than the situation makes necessary." [88] There were rumors that Wilson might be nominated for vice-president as Bryan's running mate, but Wilson absolutely refused to consider the idea. He went to England before the convention met and left definite instructions with his brother-in-law, Stockton Axson, to give out, should his name be proposed at the convention, a public statement declaring that Wilson would under no circumstances accept the vice-presidential nomination.[89] In the face of the inevitable, however, Wilson continued to hope that by some chance he might be nominated for the presidency. He was in Edinburgh when the convention met and wrote his wife that he felt "a bit silly waiting on the possibility of the impossible happening." There was "not a ghost of a chance of defeating Bryan," he added, "but since Colonel H. *is* there I might as well be here." [90]

Wilson returned from England in September and refused to have anything to do with the Democratic campaign. Two Bryan campaigners, intimate friends of Wilson, went to Princeton to make arrangements for Bryan to speak in Alexander Hall on the University campus. Wilson gave his former students a lecture, criticized what he termed Bryan's "vacuity," and declared that he distrusted Bryan because he did not think clearly. He asked the two Bryan men not to embarrass him by having the meeting in Princeton; they consequently made arrangements for Bryan to speak briefly at Princeton Junction, well out of Wilson's sight.[91] Even if Wilson would have nothing to do with Bryan personally, he did at least vote for him. Perhaps the consideration that party regularity was almost a *sine qua non* among politicians helped him to overcome his aversion to the Commoner.

Although Wilson refused to join in the campaign for Bryan's election, he did have a new message of his own. In the latter days of September, when the presidential campaign was at its height, he went to Denver to address the annual convention of the American Bankers' Association. If, as William Diamond has suggested, Wilson was preaching the dogmas of a new morality in business, it was indeed a splendid opportunity he had to declare his economic program before a representative body of

[88] W. W. to H. J. Forman, April 10, 1908, *ibid.*

[89] R. S. Baker, "Memorandum of a conversation with Stockton Axson, March 12, 1925," Baker Papers.

[90] W. W. to E. A. W., July 6, 1908, R. S. Baker, *Woodrow Wilson,* II, 277.

[91] R. S. Baker, "Memorandum of a conversation with Roland S. Morris, March 7 and 8, 1926," Baker Papers.

businessmen. First, however, he sounded a note of warning and alarm to the financiers. "For the first time in the history of America," he declared, "there is a general feeling that the issue is now joined, or about to be joined, between the power of accumulated capital and the privileges and opportunities of the masses of the people." The reform movement, Wilson declared, was the natural reaction to class selfishness; socialism was taking root in progressive ranks because "the contesting forces in our modern society have broken its unity and destroyed its organic harmony—not because that was inevitable, but because men have used their power thoughtlessly and selfishly, and legitimate undertakings have been pushed to illegitimate lengths."

The striking fact about the structure of modern society, Wilson continued, was that the most formidable power was not the authority of government, but the power of capital. Men no longer feared the domination of government, but feared "capital and . . . [were] jealous of its domination." The only remedy that could save America from the extremes of socialism and monopolistic capitalism, he added, was the general acceptance of a new morality, which he defined as a "social reunion and social reintegration which every man of station and character and influence in the country can in some degree and within the scope of his own life set afoot." Capitalists, therefore, must seek first the service of society.

Most of the criticism leveled against the bankers, Wilson admitted, was based on the false premise that financiers were unwilling to serve small business enterprises. The trouble was, however, he asserted, that they "are oftentimes singularly ignorant, or at any rate singularly indifferent, about what I may call the social functions and the political functions of banking." Bankers had incurred the enmity of the people, furthermore, because they hoarded the nation's capital and refused to serve the mass of the farmers and laborers. The new morality, he concluded, dictated the obvious answer to the problem:

"It is the duty of the banker, as it is the duty of men of every other class, to see to it that there be in his calling no class spirit, no feeling of antagonism to the people, to plain men whom the bankers, to their great loss and detriment, do not know. It is their duty to be intelligent, thoughtful, patriotic intermediaries between capital and the people at large; to understand and serve the general interest; to be public men serving the country as well as private men serving their depositors and the enterprises whose securities and notes they hold. How capital is to draw near to the people and serve them at once obviously and safely is the question, the great and now pressing question, which it is the particular duty of the banker to answer. . . . The occasion and the responsibility are yours." [92]

Wilson had entered the political arena in 1906 an avowed conservative; he had denounced the "regulative passion" of Theodore Roosevelt and his followers; he had inveighed against regulation of business and industry by commissions; he had campaigned in a half-hearted manner for the Democratic nomination in 1908 on a reactionary platform. During the summer of 1908, however, he underwent a gradual, almost imperceptible, change of mind. His address to the bankers at Denver is the first clear evidence of this subtle metamorphosis.

It is difficult to say exactly when Woodrow Wilson became a progressive. Most biographers place the date of his conversion in the fall of 1910, after his nomination for governor of New Jersey, and for all practical purposes that is the time when he became a left-of-center progressive. Yet the metamorphosis from militant conservatism to radicalism was gradual; it began in 1908 and extended over a two-year period. How does one account for the change that was going on during these years? What forces were at work in Wilson's mind that caused the fundamental shift in his political and economic point of view?

It should be noted, first of all, that Wilson had, by 1907, already accepted the diagnosis of the muckrakers and progressive reformers as essentially correct. Within a short time, for example, he was telling his audiences that the trouble with American society was that economic power and ownership of property had been concentrated among a few men, who exercised political power out of all proportion to their numbers; that obviously something had to be done to restore the political balance. Wilson's new morality idea was his first step away from conservatism. In his mind the new morality was an end, not a means; he was consequently forced by the logic of his own diagnosis of the economic problems perplexing the American people to the almost inevitable conclusion that the progressives were correct to this extent: that the new morality could not be achieved by the old formulas of *laissez-faire* and legal tradition, that something more—the positive intervention of the state—was necessary to achieve the end he was seeking. "Half our present difficulties," he declared in December 1908, "arise from the fact that privileged interests have threatened to become too strong for the

---

[92] "The Banker and the Nation," address delivered before the American Bankers' Association, Denver, September 30, 1908, MS in Close File.

general interest, and that therefore the government has had to step in to restrain those who enjoyed the very privilege which it itself had granted." [93] Perhaps it was inevitable that Wilson would first discover some moral rationalization for his change of faith; at any rate it is hardly surprising that during the years from 1908 to 1911 he gradually came to accept many of the basic premises of the progressives.

In the absence of documentary evidence, any analysis of the causes for this progressive evolution must of necessity partake of the nature of speculation. First of all, it should be noted, the graduate college controversy was important in effecting Wilson's change of mind; the bitterness of the controversy was instrumental in releasing Wilson's latent idealism, in causing an outpouring of his idealistic emotions. Rightly or wrongly, he came to the conclusion that the forces of wealth were opposed to social and educational democracy. The deduction Wilson made from his Princeton experiences was obvious: the same forces that were attempting to corrupt Princeton were already at work corrupting American society. Certainly he had come consciously to this decision by the time he made his speech at Pittsburgh on April 16, 1910. In the second place, the factor of expediency cannot be ignored. Wilson wanted desperately to enter politics, to hold high office, and he must have recognized that the strength of the progressive movement, especially in New Jersey, was growing rapidly, and that a continued adherence to his conservative creed would be almost certainly fatal to his political aspirations. After his nomination for governor, Wilson was forced to make a deliberate choice between conservatism and progressivism, and he knew that the outcome of the election depended upon his decision. The choice was inevitable—he finally capitulated to the progressives.

Events during 1909 and 1910, before he entered the political field, illustrate the process of Wilson's transition from conservatism to progressivism. Probably his most startling new departure during this period was his emergence as a leader in the movement for municipal reform, a development all the more surprising when it is recalled that he had previously had no more than a passing academic interest in the question.

In March 1909 he made an important address before the Civic League of St. Louis and, for the first time, demonstrated his interest in and acquaintance with the problems of city government. "I think that as I grow older," he began, ". . . I grow more and more serious." The country had lived through a period of great excitement under the dynamic

<hr>

[93] "True and False Conservatism," address delivered before the Southern Society of New York, December 9, 1908, MS in Wilson Papers.

Roosevelt, and much heat had been generated over the necessity of reform. The Rooseveltian reformers, however, had accomplished practically nothing, Wilson continued. "We must now stop preaching sermons," he added, "and come down to those applications which will actually correct the abuses of our national life, without any more fuss, and without any more rhetoric."

The difficulties inherent in the American political system, he declared, stemmed largely from the fact that the country's political system had been constructed in the atmosphere of the eighteenth century, dominated by the Newtonian concept of mechanistic politics. The only sort of political leadership that could possibly succeed in an industrial society, he asserted, was the "leadership of one leading person," in short, a leadership made possible by a political system constructed along Darwinian lines of politics. He proceeded to analyze the difficulties that faced persons working for good city government and concluded that the remedy was "contained in one word, *Simplification,*" by reducing the number of elective officials, and by then fixing responsibility for the conduct of the government on a very few people. In other words, only by the adoption of the short ballot could Americans obtain lasting municipal reform.[94]

There is no record as to how Wilson first became interested in the short-ballot idea. Wilson, none the less, was moving fast away from the right. One of the foundations of his conservative creed—his distrust of "personal government," his insistence upon a government of law rather than of personal power—was apparently already completely undermined by the time he made his St. Louis address.

In the fall of 1909 the Short Ballot Association was organized in New York under the direction of Richard S. Childs, who became its executive secretary. From the first Wilson was associated with this organization devoted to the cause of efficient government and was a member of the first advisory board, which included also Childs, Norman Hapgood, editor of *Collier's Weekly,* Henry Jones Ford of Princeton, and Lawrence Abbott.[95] In October 1909 Wilson was elected the first president of the association; William U'Ren, a progressive political leader from Oregon, and Winston Churchill, a muckraking novelist, were elected vice-presidents.[96] In December two other prominent progressives—Wil-

[94] *Civic Problems,* address delivered before the annual meeting of the Civic League of St. Louis, March 9, 1909, pp. 1-13.

[95] Memorandum of September 28, 1909 on the organization of the Short Ballot Association, prepared by R. S. Childs, Wilson Papers.

[96] R. S. Childs to W. W., October 25, 1909, *ibid.*

liam Allen White of Kansas and Judge Ben Lindsey of Denver—entered the organization.[97] Wilson's association with these men, who were among the most aggressive progressives in the country, must have served to quicken the ferment of his mind.

During 1909 and 1910 Wilson embarked upon a crusade for the adoption of the short ballot as the means by which honest government could actually be secured. The idea became almost an obsession with him. In November 1909 he told the City Club of Philadelphia that the political machines could be put out of commission only by the widespread inauguration of the reform.[98] Wilson's appeal had broadened considerably, however, and he now believed that the fate of representative government, not only in the cities, but in the states as well, depended upon the adoption of the reform. "I believe," he declared dramatically, "that the Short Ballot is the key to the whole question of the restoration of government by the people." [99] In January 1910 he returned again to his newly found theme in an address before the Short Ballot Association in New York. Government by political machines was absolutely necessary under existing conditions, he asserted. Popular control of local and state governments was impossible because the control was nowhere concentrated. "This process of simplification [by means of the short ballot] is our only salvation," he warned.[100]

In the spring of 1910 Wilson made his final plea for the simplification of the electoral system in an article in the *North American Review*. It was written in an alarming tone and leaves the reader with the impression that Wilson was desperately concerned about the state of American politics. The "whole representative system" was in the hands of the political machines, he wrote; the people did not choose their representatives any longer; their representatives did not serve the general interest unless dragooned into so doing by extraordinary forces of agitation; the processes of government were, in short, haphazard and the processes of popular control were obscure and ineffectual. "We must," Wilson warned, ". . . at once devote ourselves again to finding means to make our governments, whether in our cities, in our States, or in the nation, representative, responsible and efficient."

[97] R. S. Childs to W. W., December 30, 1909, *ibid.*

[98] Apparently at this time Wilson had little faith in the direct primary as a means of ending boss rule. See J. M. Taylor to W. W., November 23, 1909, *ibid.* Taylor wrote that he agreed with Wilson that the direct primary would not destroy the boss system.

[99] "Political Reform," address at Philadelphia, November 18, 1909, MS in *ibid.*

[100] Address of January 21, 1910, MS in *ibid.*

Wilson proceeded to condemn the Jacksonian ideal of popularly and frequently elected minor public officials and declared that this system of rural politics was totally unfit for an urban society. He discussed the operations of the political machine and revealed a thorough comprehension of that type of political organization. He ridiculed the idea that American voters could be reasonably expected to choose wisely from among the hundreds of names that often appeared on ballots, and declared that such a system did as much as anything else to perpetuate the power of the political bosses. "The short ballot," he insisted, "is the short and open way by which we can return to representative government." Americans, therefore, were obliged to become once more thoughtful partisans of genuine democracy, he concluded. What the nation needed was nothing less than a radical reform of the electoral system; it was the duty of every lover of political liberty to become a partisan of the short ballot.[101]

Wilson's preoccupation with the short ballot was typical. Needless to say, the future of democracy in America did not hinge upon the universal acceptance of the short ballot. It was a short-lived craze with Wilson, and he soon forgot the idea when he got into politics.

Wilson's entire thought was becoming so absorbed in political and economic affairs that when he delivered the baccalaureate address at Princeton in June 1909 he seized the opportunity to restate to the members of the graduating class the principles of his new morality. His appraisal of businessmen and industrial leaders was severe; in fact he sounded much like the muckrakers when he declared that businessmen had been "unprofitable servants" who had "kept their legal obligations as well as usual and yet came near ruining the country, piled up wealth and forgot how to use it honourably, built up business and came near to debauching a nation." [102] He was also beginning to conceive of universities and colleges as fit instruments for the advancement of social democracy. Three months before he delivered his defiant address to the Pittsburgh alumni, Wilson warned, "if social impulses, social ambitions, social arrangements, which pervade the rest of the community, invade the college, . . . [the] college is going to lose its democratic feeling." When colleges ceased to be centers of democratic regeneration, "they will have ceased to be worthy of the patronage of the nation." [103]

---

[101] "Hide and Seek Politics," *North American Review*, cxci (May 1910), 585-601.
[102] "Baccalaureate Address, June 13th, 1909," MS in Close File.
[103] Address delivered at the inauguration of President H. H. Apple at Franklin and Marshall College, Lancaster, Pennsylvania, January 10, 1920. MS in Wilson Papers.

It is worthy of note that on the question of labor unions Wilson made little, if any, progress toward liberalism. In this respect his Manchester ideas prevailed over his leanings toward the left. In reply to an invitation to speak at a banquet of anti-strike and anti-boycott advocates, he wrote, for example, on January 12, 1909, "I am a fierce partizan of the Open Shop and of everything that makes for individual liberty." [104] Again, in June, he told the graduating class at Princeton that labor unions existed primarily for the purpose of keeping production standards as low as possible: "You know what the usual standard of the employee is in our day. It is to give as little as he may for his wages. Labour is standardized by the trades unions, and this is the standard to which it is made to conform. No one is suffered to do more than the average workman can do: in some trades and handicrafts no one is suffered to do more than the least skilful of his fellows can do within the hours allotted to a day's labour, and no one may work out of hours at all or volunteer anything beyond the minimum. . . . The labour of America is rapidly becoming unprofitable under its present regulation by those who have determined to reduce it to a minimum." [105]

Wilson's attack upon organized labor was based on ignorance and misinformation; it did not pass unanswered, and among those replying were many indignant laborers. When Wilson attempted to explain his position he was forced to confess that he had obtained all his information from "those who do employ labor on a great scale." He had little reply to make to the worker who severely upbraided him for his ignorance of working conditions and his unsympathetic attitude toward labor. [106]

In the meantime, Colonel Harvey and his faithful assistant, Inglis, had been quietly at work to further the progress of Wilson's political career. In May 1909, Harvey confidently wrote in the *Weekly*, "We now expect to see WOODROW WILSON elected Governor of the State of New Jersey in 1910 and nominated for President in 1912 upon a platform demanding tariff revision downward." [107] Congress had just passed the Payne-Aldrich tariff measure and Harvey was anxious that his protégé capitalize upon the popular reaction against it. "The country is red-hot over the tariff atrocity," Harvey wrote. "Why not sound a bugle blast in the N. A. Review—and take the lead?" [108]

[104] Quoted in James Kerney, *The Political Education of Woodrow Wilson*, p. 34.
[105] Baccalaureate address at Princeton, June 13, 1909, MS in Close File; also published in *Trenton True American*, June 14, 1909.
[106] J. W. Williams to W. W., July 3, 1909, Wilson Papers, quoting a letter from Wilson.
[107] *Harper's Weekly*, LIII (May 15, 1909), 4.
[108] G. Harvey to W. W., May 10, 1909, Wilson Papers.

Wilson rose to the occasion and did sound a "bugle blast" against the tariff law. In an article in the *North American Review* he minced no words in condemning the Republican system of protection. Even more significant was the fact that, for the first time, Wilson charged that the Republican party was and had been in alliance with big business and that Republican tariff laws had been used to liquidate campaign debts. "Here, in a protective tariff," he wrote, "are the entrenchments of Special Privilege, and every beneficiary will of course crowd into them on the day of battle." The chief evil was, he continued, that the tariff had ceased to be a matter of principle at all with the Republicans; it had become merely a method of granting favors to the party's business constituency.

For Wilson to say that "the tariff is the mother of trusts" was not particularly original; it was significant, however, that he did charge that high protection had given birth to the industrial giants. He was talking like a good progressive when he launched into a bitter denunciation of the trusts: "It is a very different America from the old. All the recent scandals of our business history have sprung out of the discovery of the use those who directed these great combinations were making of their power: their power to crush, their power to monopolize." Monopolies stood in a fair way of destroying the American dream of prosperous, independent business enterprises; trusts were "cruel and disastrous." And this time Wilson had a good word to say for organized laborers, whose cause he championed in their struggle with monopolies for higher wages. He proposed no radical alteration of the tariff laws; but he did insist that the protective system "must in some conservative way be altered from decade to decade, if possible from year to year, until we shall have put all customs legislation upon a safe, reasonable and permanent footing." [109]

The first six months of 1910 were exceedingly busy months for Wilson. His political addresses were demanding more and more of his energies; at the same time the graduate college controversy was becoming increasingly bitter. He took time off from the Princeton controversy in January 1910 to address the bankers of New York City. Before an audience of nabobs that included J. Pierpont Morgan and George F. Baker, Wilson declared that banking was "founded on a moral basis and not on a financial basis." The trouble was, he told the financiers, that bankers were narrow-minded men who did not know the needs of

---

[109] "The Tariff Make-Believe," *North American Review*, cxc (October 1909), 541-552.

the country because they took no interest in the small borrower and the small enterprise. Morgan, the *World's* reporter writes, looked "glum" and puffed his cigar energetically throughout Wilson's address. When Wilson sat down, Morgan proceeded to tell him that he considered that the remarks were directed at him personally. Wilson replied that he had not intended to offend anyone; he was speaking of principles.[110]

Wilson made an important address before the Democratic Dollar Dinner at Elizabeth, New Jersey, in March 1910. It was the first time he had spoken before an official party gathering in his home state, and James Smith, Jr., must have been anxiously awaiting the popular reaction to this new politico. Wilson's address constituted his last stated platform of political principles before he entered the political field.

Wilson spoke on the living principles of Democracy and declared what he thought were the principles Democrats, as a party group, should stand for. The Democratic party, he asserted, was better fitted to serve as governors of the people than the Republicans, because Democrats had an abiding faith in the people. The Republicans, on the other hand, had allied themselves with the vested interests of the country, and it was impossible for them to see the general interests of the nation in proper perspective.

The individual, not the corporation, Wilson told the Democrats, was the only single possessor of rights and privileges—and that, he continued, was a cardinal article in the Democratic creed. Wilson had a definite, if limited, platform of legislation in mind for the party's consideration. First of all, the power of the trusts must be curbed, not by direct management by the government, but by legal regulation.[111] Secondly, the government should quit the business of dispensing favors and patronage by means of the protective tariff. Finally, he continued vaguely, it was the duty of the Democrats to initiate such reforms as

[110] *New York World,* January 18, 1910.

[111] This phrase, "legal regulation," requires some elucidation. What did Wilson mean? A month later Wilson amplified this statement in an address before the New Jersey Bankers' Association. He virtually repudiated his position set forth in the Jamestown speech, opposing regulation of business and industry and relying upon legal processes to fix responsibility and punishment for corporation malfeasance. "The standard by which our great trusts and combinations and all our economic arrangements must henceforth be judged and valued," he declared, "is the public advantage, the morality of the whole procedure, *judged not by the old scale of personal honesty . . . but by the new scale of regard for the interests of others not only, but also for the interest of all. The standard, in short, is the general public interest.*" "The Banker and the Public— Big Risks and Little," address at Atlantic City, May 6, 1910, MS in Close File (italics mine).

would secure economy, responsibility in government, and fidelity to the general interests on the part of public officials.[112]

It was natural that Wilson should be thinking of the possibility that he soon might be called upon to leave the academic halls of Princeton for the more spectacular field of politics. Democrats the country over hastened to assure him that he would have their support in his battles for democracy. There was no tidal wave of popular opinion demanding Wilson's entrance into the political field, it is true; but a sufficient number of correspondents urged him to make the eventful plunge into politics to assure him that the demand was widespread. One Southerner made a passionate appeal to him to "quietly seek the Democratic nomination for Governor of New Jersey at the next State Convention." [113] More important was the encouraging letter that Warren Worth Bailey, editor of the politically influential *Johnstown Democrat,* wrote in March 1910. "In common with many others," Bailey wrote, "I had associated you with the reactionary element of the party." [114] There was, he added, a strong and growing belief in Pennsylvania that Wilson should be nominated for the presidency in 1912. Interestingly enough, most of the progressives in the state were strongly supporting the Wilson presidential movement.[115]

It was evident, also, by 1909 that Wilson was anxious to embark upon a political career. "I feel very keenly the necessity for an effective party of opposition," he wrote to a correspondent who had urged him to enter politics, "and believe with all my heart that the welfare of the country calls for an immediate change in the personnel of those who are conducting its affairs in responsible political positions." He realized, however, that he was in an embarrassing position, "because it is manifestly undesirable that the head of a university should seek a prominent part in party contests." He could not, therefore, actively campaign for

[112] "Living Principles of Democracy," address at Elizabeth, New Jersey, March 29, 1910, published in *Harper's Weekly,* LIV (April 9, 1910), 9.

[113] Adolphus Ragan to W. W., June 26, 1909, Wilson Papers.

[114] The chief reason for his suspicion of Wilson, Bailey wrote, was the character of the newspapers and magazines that were Wilson's especial champions. "Some of us have grown chronically suspicious of any man," he added, "who finds favor in the eyes of certain publications known to be affiliated [sic] in sympathy or in fact with the 'interests.'" This is the earliest criticism the present writer knows of Harvey's support of Wilson.

[115] "I was the secretary of the Bryan Democratic league in 1908 and in this way I was brought in pretty close touch with the progressive element of the party," Bailey wrote. "I am still in fairly close touch with that element and I think it is within the mark to say that the Wilson sentiment to-day is about equal to the Bryan strength three years ago." W. W. Bailey to W. W., March 28, 1910, *ibid.*

political office. If an invitation to enter the political field should come from an authoritative party source, however, he would consider it his duty to give "very careful consideration" to the question where he could be of most service.[116]

There is also some evidence that Wilson thought a third party might be organized in 1912, and that he might possibly be its presidential candidate.[117] If he had ever entertained any such ideas, however, he soon disowned them. In a letter to H. S. McClure in April 1910 he laid bare his thoughts as to the desirability of organizing a new party. "I find that a great many men have your feeling about the Democratic party," he wrote, "fearing that it is impossible to dissociate its name from errors and heresies which have recently been connected with it." Theoretically Wilson agreed that the formation of a third party was desirable, but from the practical point of view it seemed to him that this was the course of greatest difficulty and least encouragement. He did not despair of seeing the Democratic party drawn back to the conservative principles it once espoused. "I believe, from the various signs of the times," he added, "that it is quite within reasonable hope that new men will take hold of the party and draw it away from the influences which have of late years demoralized it." [118]

In the meantime, the course of events had been running disastrously against Wilson at Princeton. He had seen not only his cherished quadrangle scheme meet defeat, but his graduate college plans also. Disappointment and embitterment resulting from his defeat, combined with increasing popular demands that he enter politics, made him a receptive candidate for political honors by the spring of 1910.

It has been a devious task, this tracing of the fine threads in the development of Wilson's political thought from 1902 to 1910. The threads were sometimes subtle and his changes of mind were often gradual and imperceptible. By 1910, however, the picture is fairly clear. It is indeed a far cry from the militant conservatism of Wilson's speech in 1904, demanding Bryan's expulsion from the Democratic party, or of the reactionary "Credo" of 1907, to the rampant crusade for civic and business righteousness, flavored with progressive ideas, of 1909 and 1910. Wilson had moved from the right of center to the center;

[116] W. W. to A. Ragan, July 3, 1909, *ibid.*
[117] D. Lawrence, *The True Story of Woodrow Wilson*, p. 31.
[118] W. W. to H. S. McClure, April 9, 1910, Wilson-McClure Correspondence, Library of Princeton University.

he had generally accepted most of the basic progressive premises with regard to the nature of the political and economic organization of American society; he had rationalized the shift in his point of view by setting forth an ethical system for businessmen and industrial leaders similar to the idealistic philosophy of the progressives; and if he had accepted few of the specific progressive proposals for reform, it was more because there had been no occasion for him to think through the reforms involved than because he definitely opposed them. If not a progressive by the spring of 1910, Wilson at least had built the intellectual and emotional framework necessary for a first-class progressive leader.

CHAPTER V

The Great Decision

DURING the first twenty-one years of Woodrow Wilson's residence in New Jersey, from 1890 to 1911, the state experienced a minor political revolution. Control of the state government passed from Democratic hands in 1894-1896, and until 1911 the Republicans enjoyed almost complete political dominance. The election of 1910 marked the end of the Republican cycle, and in 1911 a Democratic administration once more assumed control of the state's affairs. Throughout the period, until 1910, Wilson's political interests were either theoretical or else they were limited almost wholly to events of national concern. He hobnobbed neither with ward heelers nor with state bosses.

It is doubtful whether Wilson had more than a passing interest in the turbulent political struggles of the two decades from 1890 to 1910; actually there is no evidence, either in his speeches or in his letters, that he concerned himself one whit about New Jersey politics before 1907. He had come as a professor to Princeton during the last years of Democratic supremacy in the state. He was a Democrat and during the post-bellum period New Jersey was perhaps the most consistently Democratic state in the Northeast. From 1869 until 1896 an unbroken line of Democratic governors guided, at least nominally, the state's political affairs. The chief cause for Democratic supremacy, it was true, was the superb political organization of the often corrupt party bosses,[1] but this was an era when revelations of corrupt machine politics did not surprise, even if they did at times shock, the average voter.

Democratic rule in New Jersey came to an end as a direct result of the debauchery and corruption of the party leaders themselves. The story of the race track scandal of 1893 is rather long and has many grimy threads, but it can be stated briefly: The election of 1892 carried into office a Democratic governor, George T. Werts, and resulted also in the election of a Democratic legislature. The legislature, however, was soon completely under the domination of corrupt race track gamblers and operators, and in 1893 the body enacted three notorious

[1] William E. Sackett, *Modern Battles of Trenton*, II, 13-14.

laws that legalized race track betting.[2] Governor Werts, who was known primarily as the author of the state's Australian ballot law, promptly vetoed the measures, but before the Anti-Race Track League and other reform leaders could get a protest movement under way, the legislature enacted the laws over the governor's veto. The fall elections of 1893 amounted to nothing less than an indignant popular repudiation of the party that had been so long in power,[3] while the election of Republican John W. Griggs as governor in 1895 gave notice that the Republicans were firmly entrenched in office. Leon Abbett, the Democratic boss who had successfully united the New Jersey Democracy, died in 1892; after his death and the race track debacle the party degenerated into several factions, the chief of which were headed by James Smith, Jr., in Newark and Robert Davis in Jersey City.

Big business was securely in the saddle and held the reins of Republican power after 1896. "Probably no part of the Union offered more impregnable defenses to the onslaughts of Progressivism than New Jersey," writes the leading authority on the period.[4] During the 1880's and 1890's the legislature had enacted a series of laws designed to encourage the incorporation within the state of holding companies and monopolies; the statutes, as revised and consolidated in 1896, allowed holding companies to engage in all the practices necessary to the stifling of competition.[5] Practically all the great holding companies in the country from that date until 1913 secured their charters under New Jersey laws, a fact which earned for the state the dubious honor of being "the mother of trusts." The interests of the railroads were equally well protected by the Republican leaders, many of whom were intimately associated with these powerful interests; as a result the railroad managers contrived, by judicious application of bribery funds and threats of intimidation, to escape equitable taxation of their property.[6] The public utilities also had a vise-like grip upon the Republican and Democratic machines in New Jersey and by virtue of this fact escaped effective regulation until after 1911. One gigantic monopoly, the Public Service

---

[2] *Laws of New Jersey,* 1893, ch. xvi, pp. 28-30; ch. xvii, pp. 30-31; ch. xviii, pp. 31-32. See also Edwin P. Conklin, "The Last Half Century in New Jersey Politics," in Irving S. Kull (ed.), *New Jersey, a History,* iii, 977.

[3] *ibid.,* p. 978.

[4] Ransome E. Noble, Jr., *New Jersey Progressivism before Wilson,* p. 3.

[5] *Laws of New Jersey, 1896,* ch. 185, pp. 277-317.

[6] R. E. Noble, Jr., *New Jersey Progressivism,* pp. 6-9.

Corporation, after 1903 controlled most of the utilities in the state; and its officials were also closely allied with the political organizations.[7]

New Jersey was thus a "state in bondage" during the early years of the twentieth century, ruled by an oligarchical alliance of corporations and politicians and completely dominated by big business and bossism. It presents to the student of American institutions the almost perfect example of "the system" in operation, one of the last strongholds of an industrial-feudal order that was the object of violent attack by progressive leaders throughout the country.

New Jersey progressivism was largely a Republican phenomenon before the advent of Woodrow Wilson on the political stage in 1910. The first major insurgent victory was Mark M. Fagan's election as mayor of Jersey City in 1901.[8] Although he made the canvass as an organization lieutenant, Fagan soon employed as his chief adviser George L. Record, an independent Republican who had only recently deserted the Democratic ranks. Record was probably the most amazing character in New Jersey politics of the period. He was the intellectual and ideological architect of the progressive movement in the state and his hand "can be seen in every major move of a progressive nature in the state from the 1890's on."[9] His economic philosophy was derived largely from Henry George; he advocated squarely and courageously equal taxation of railroad and corporate property, stringent control of public utilities, and a broad form of direct political democracy. He was, in short, the advocate par excellence in New Jersey of the doctrine of comprehensive state intervention and control.[10] Record's knowledge of progressive ideas and techniques soon made him the dominant power behind the Fagan administration in Jersey City.

It was not long, however, before Fagan and Record ran headlong into the problem of equitable railroad and utilities taxation. They envisaged a program of equal taxation for all kinds of property and, having enlisted the support of the mayors of other North Jersey towns, carried their fight against the corporations to Trenton in 1904. The legislature, however, was completely dominated by the Republican machine and turned a deaf ear to their demands for increased railroad

---

[7] *ibid.,* pp. 9-11.

[8] For the story of Fagan's career to 1906, see Lincoln Steffens, "A Servant of God and the People. The Story of Mark Fagan, Mayor of Jersey City," *McClure's Magazine,* xxvi (January 1906), 297-308.

[9] R. E. Noble, Jr., *New Jersey Progressivism,* p. 15.

[10] *ibid.,* pp. 15-17.

and utilities taxes. This, Record and Fagan thought, was conclusive proof of the corporation dominance of the Republican party and they indignantly repudiated the leaders in power, the "Board of Guardians," as Wilson was later fond of calling them. The revolt of the progressives, none the less, gained momentum throughout the state and so frightened the railroads and conservative Republican bosses that in 1905 and 1906 the legislature enacted equal taxation measures that satisfied most of the reform demands.[11]

In their fight for equal taxation of public utilities, the progressives soon ran afoul of the Public Service Corporation, with which many of the leading Democratic and Republican politicians were personally identified. The struggle between the reformers and the protectors of vested interests soon centered on the franchise question. New Jersey had no law to prevent municipalities from awarding perpetual franchises. As a result of the fight against the Public Service Corporation in Jersey City, Fagan and the local Republican boss, who had previously co-operated in city politics, became bitter enemies. But in spite of the opposition of the Republican machine, Fagan was triumphantly elected mayor for the third time in 1905.

While the progressives in Jersey City were raising the standard of revolt, a grass-roots movement of protest against the railroads and public utilities was getting under way around 1902 in nearby Newark and Essex County. It was largely a Republican movement. By 1904 Essex County was rife with discontent against the bipartisan political system; only skillful leadership was needed to coordinate and solidify the reform forces. A wealthy young lawyer of Newark, Everett Colby, had begun his political career in 1903 as a protégé of the county Republican boss.[12] When the state organization refused in 1905 to make him speaker of the Assembly, Colby hotly announced his independence of all organizations. The upshot was that the Newark legislator, who had already revealed some independent leanings, was soon converted to the cause of reform by Record and in 1905 assumed leadership of the fight in the legislature for limited franchises.

Largely at Record's suggestion, Colby and the Newark progressives[13] launched a campaign in Essex County in the summer of 1905 to capture

[11] *ibid.*, pp. 22-29; for the laws see *Laws of New Jersey*, 1905, ch. 91, pp. 189-191; *ibid.*, 1906, ch. 82, pp. 121-123; ch. 122, p. 220; ch. 280, pp. 571-572.

[12] For a description of Colby's career, see Lincoln Steffens, "The Gentleman from Essex," *McClure's Magazine*, XXVI (February 1906), 421-433.

[13] This group included William P. Martin, Frank Sommer, and Alden Freeman.

the Essex delegation to the legislature. The Colby group swept the Republican primaries in September and won a decisive victory over the Democrats in November.[14] The increasing strength of the insurgent rebels forced the Republican state machine to make several important concessions to progressive demands. In 1906 the New Idea group, as the Republican progressives had come to be called, secured the enactment of a measure designed to limit the tenure of utilities franchises,[15] while another law increased municipal taxes on franchises from 2 to 5 per cent of the gross income of trolley companies.[16] A senatorial investigation of the life insurance companies in 1906 and 1907, moreover, stimulated the enactment of several laws providing for a more careful state regulation of the activities of insurance companies.[17]

Following these preliminary victories the insurgents attempted to organize their movement on a state-wide basis; they hoped eventually to wrest control of the Republican party from the hands of the corporation-machine alliance. The movement was no longer restricted to the northern part of the state; it even invaded South Jersey as far south as Camden, the domain of David Baird, the most powerful of the Republican bosses. The New Idea platform was also broadened to include more radical demands for economic and political democracy.[18]

During the campaign of 1906 the Record-Fagan-Colby group made a hard fight to obtain the election of a New Idea legislature. In spite of the vigorous campaign the insurgents made, the Republican regulars, by skillfully injecting the liquor question and by exposing some discreditable events in Record's past, won an overwhelming victory over the New Idea candidates in the primaries in September. Both the Republicans and Democrats, however, were forced to court the progressive vote by advocating progressive measures during the pre-election canvass. In the November elections the Democrats contrived to maintain a solid front and, for the first time since 1892, elected a majority in the legislature's lower house.

The following year, 1907, saw the beginning of the disintegration of the New Idea organization. Colby refused to make a contest for the Republican gubernatorial nomination and John Franklin Fort, a Republican regular with progressive leanings, received the nomination. The Democrats nominated Mayor Frank S. Katzenbach of Trenton and

[14] R. E. Noble, Jr., *New Jersey Progressivism*, pp. 59-62.
[15] *Laws of New Jersey*, 1906, ch. 36, pp. 50-53.
[16] *ibid.*, ch. 290, pp. 644-648.
[17] *ibid.*, 1907, ch. 34, pp. 67-68; chs. 70-74, pp. 131-154; ch. 81, p. 161.
[18] R. E. Noble, Jr., *New Jersey Progressivism*, pp. 65-71.

adopted a platform that was, on the whole, more liberal than the Republican platform. Although Fort made several conspicuous overtures to the insurgents, his plurality in November was only 8,000. The most catastrophic blow to the New Idea cause was Mayor Fagan's defeat in Jersey City by H. Otto Wittpenn, a Democratic progressive. Fagan had come out squarely for an effective public utilities commission with rate-making powers and even for municipal ownership of utilities, and his defeat was all the more disheartening to the Republican insurgents for that reason.[19] In Essex County the New Idea men received another severe check when Harry V. Osborne, a young Democratic progressive who was later to play a conspicuous role in Wilson's administration, defeated Colby for the state Senate. The insurgent defeat of 1907 was simply the beginning of the end, not of progressive ideas, but of the effective power of the New Idea men in Republican politics. By 1910 there was not a single New Idea representative in the legislature!

The progressives, however, did not abandon their struggle for economic and political reform. After 1906 they shifted the emphasis in their platform from demands for equal taxation of railroad property and for limited franchises, which had already been largely achieved, to demands for the equal valuation of railroad property and effective regulation of public utilities by means of a state commission. Reform sentiment had also permeated the Democratic ranks and the bosses of Jersey City and Newark, anxious to capitalize upon the progressive discontent, sent several young progressives, notably Joseph P. Tumulty and Harry V. Osborne, to the legislature in 1907. The Democratic House in 1907 approved a bill establishing a railroad commission with rate-making powers, but the Republican Senate blocked this measure and forced the enactment of a bill establishing a commission without any real authority. It was clear that the power of the Public Service Corporation had again blocked constructive reform.[20] A concerted effort by the progressives in 1908 to amend the bill again was blocked by a combination of the utilities, the railroads, and the Republican Senate. In a final effort to placate progressive sentiment without retreating from their own position, the Republican machine leaders in 1910 extended the jurisdiction of the railroad commission to all other utilities and changed its name to the Board of Public Utilities Commissioners.[21] It was, however, a piece of farcical legislation and, since it gave the commission practically no authority, failed completely to satisfy progressive

[19] *ibid.*, pp. 91-97.   [20] *ibid.*, pp. 101-104.
[21] *Laws of New Jersey*, 1910, ch. 41, pp. 56-59.

demands. The reformers were, on the other hand, more successful in their fight for an equitable valuation of railroad property, and in 1909 an evaluation commission was established and began the task of taking serious account of railroad wealth within the state.[22]

The New Idea men also carried on a widespread agitation for reform in other fields. Under Record's leadership, for example, they began a campaign to secure the enactment of legislation for the protection of children and workingmen with the result that several notable child labor laws were enacted between 1903 and 1910.[23] The progressives made slight gains in 1909 and 1910 in their efforts to obtain effective workmen's compensation legislation,[24] although the final enactment of a thoroughgoing law was delayed until the Wilson administration. Agitation for direct primary legislation was as old as the progressive movement in New Jersey itself, and it was the amazing George L. Record who took the lead in the agitation for popular control of the election machinery. Record persuaded the legislature in 1903 to enact the first primary law, not in itself a very comprehensive measure, but certainly the entering wedge for primary reform.[25] In 1907 the legislature strengthened the primary law by extending direct nominations to candidates for the legislature and county and municipal offices[26] and provided for an expression of popular opinion on United States senatorial candidates.[27] Proposals for corrupt practices legislation were given short shrift by the Republican organization leaders, although two ineffective laws were passed in 1906.[28] The most significant political reform of the pre-Wilson period was the enactment of legislation establishing the merit system for most of the state's administrative officials. The act also permitted municipalities to adopt the system for city officers.[29]

Although the progressive movement in New Jersey before 1910 was largely a revolt within the Republican ranks, reform sentiment also spread slowly among the Democratic party members. Tumulty and Wittpenn in Jersey City, Osborne in Newark, and Stevens of Hoboken were conspicuous examples of Democratic progressives who were to come out of hiding, as it were, during Wilson's governorship. Although

[22] R. E. Noble, Jr., *New Jersey Progressivism*, pp. 114-115.
[23] *Laws of New Jersey*, 1903, ch. 201, pp. 386-387; *ibid.*, 1904, ch. 64, pp. 152-170; *ibid.*, 1907, ch. 229, pp. 552-555; *ibid.*, 1910, ch. 277, pp. 489-490.
[24] *ibid.*, 1909, ch. 83, pp. 114-117.   [25] *ibid.*, 1903, ch. 248, pp. 603-629.
[26] *ibid.*, 1907, ch. 278, pp. 697-700.   [27] *ibid.*, ch. 281, pp. 702-704.
[28] *ibid.*, 1906, ch. 206, pp. 384-386; ch. 208, pp. 388-390.
[29] *ibid.*, 1908, ch. 156, pp. 235-256.

machine leaders in both parties had kept the insurgent movement fairly successfully in check, there were many signs that a serious revolt was again brewing in 1910. The Republican regulars had made a few reluctant concessions to progressive demands, but the Old Guard leaders had hardly begun to satisfy the reformers' demands. The years of agitation carried on by the New Idea rebels were about to come to fruition. These doughty campaigners for democracy, now almost forgotten, were the forerunners of Woodrow Wilson; their courageous struggle against privilege and vested interests afforded the voters of New Jersey a veritable education in reform ideas and laid the groundwork for the sweeping reforms of the Wilson administration.

Colonel George Harvey of New York had been giving considerable thought to the general political situation at the beginning of 1910. He believed he read in the signs of the times the impending defeat of the Republican party in the fall of 1910 and concluded that the moment was propitious for the launching of Wilson's political career.[30] James Smith, Jr., one of the Democratic leaders in New Jersey, was Harvey's friend of long standing. Smith was not absolute overlord of the Democratic party and would not dictate the gubernatorial nomination in 1910, but he was the unchallenged master of the Newark-Essex County machine, and Essex was the most populous county in the state.

Smith, therefore, was the leading New Jersey Democratic politician. He was of the Beau Brummel type—six feet tall, suave, with considerable poise and dignity in his bearing. He had a striking and magnetic personality and was the perfect type of gentleman boss, portly and well-dressed.[31] During his youth he was something of an Horatio Alger character. Beginning his business career as a grocery clerk, by 1910 he had achieved prominence in New Jersey industrial and financial circles: he was president of the Federal Trust Company of Newark, head of several manufacturing companies, and publisher of a morning and afternoon newspaper in his home city. Smith was also a leader in Irish-American and Catholic affairs and neither his national origin nor his religion proved to be a handicap when he early tried his hand at

[30] William O. Inglis, "Helping to Make a President," *Collier's Weekly*, LVIII (October 7, 1916), 16.

[31] E. P. Conklin, "The Entrance of Wilson Upon the Political Stage," in I. S. Kull (ed.), *New Jersey, a History*, III, 1045; R. S. Baker, "Memorandum of an interview with Robert S. Hudspeth, November 3, 1927," Baker Papers; Burton J. Hendrick, "Woodrow Wilson: Political Leader," *McClure's Magazine*, XXXVIII (December 1911), 219.

politics. He began his political career as an alderman in Newark and his success in swinging his state into the Cleveland ranks in 1892 demonstrated aptly his political skill. As a reward, he was elected to the United States Senate in 1892 and served in that body from 1893 to 1899. His most notable action as senator was his alliance with Arthur Pue Gorman and other Democrats to defeat Cleveland's efforts at tariff reform in 1894.

There were two other Democratic leaders in New Jersey whose support would be necessary to the success of Harvey's plans to secure the gubernatorial nomination for Wilson. One was James R. Nugent, the other, Robert Davis of Jersey City. Nugent was Smith's nephew, an Irish Catholic, chairman of the state Democratic committee, a rough ward politician with a fierce temper, lacking the finesse and urbanity of the former senator. Nugent, however, generally followed Smith's political lead and Harvey could expect to receive Nugent's support if he succeeded in swinging Smith into line behind Wilson's candidacy. Davis was a humbler man than Smith. He was "one of the lower East-Side New York Tammany stripe, generous to a fault and loved by the poor."[32] He had begun adult life as a plumber and had become successively a gas-meter inspector, sheriff, and county collector of taxes. Davis, no political lackey of Smith, was a law unto himself in Jersey City and had frequently fought the Smith-Nugent organization for control of the state Democratic party.[33]

Early in January 1910, Harvey invited Smith to lunch at Delmonico's in New York and the two talked for the entire afternoon about the political situation in New Jersey. Harvey first suggested Wilson's possible gubernatorial candidacy, but Smith was definitely non-committal. He admitted that Wilson would make a strong candidate, but he declared that he was under obligation to other candidates. And, besides, he was not at all certain that the rank and file of the party workers would accept Wilson as a candidate.[34] A week later the two Warwicks met again at the same restaurant. Smith had given careful consideration to Wilson's candidacy and had, according to Harvey, "come up to the scratch in fine shape." His inquiries had convinced the Newark boss that he would have little trouble forcing the party regulars to accept

[32] James Kerney, *The Political Education of Woodrow Wilson*, p. 38.
[33] R. S. Baker, "Memorandum of an interview with Robert S. Hudspeth, November 3, 1927," Baker Papers; Charles M. Egan to A. S. Link, January 8, 1945.
[34] W. O. Inglis, "Helping to Make a President," *loc. cit.*, p. 16.

Wilson's nomination and he was ready to swing his organization into line, provided Harvey could assure him that Wilson would accept the nomination.[35]

After the decisive conference with Smith, Harvey turned next to Wilson. In many respects the Princeton man was the greatest obstacle to the editor's plans. Wilson was at the time deeply involved in the controversy over the graduate school, and he was not a man who relished the idea of running away from a fight. Several weeks after his conference with Smith, Harvey spent the night in Wilson's home in Princeton and the two men discussed the gubernatorial situation. Wilson did not show much enthusiasm at the prospect of becoming an active candidate for the nomination and declared that he would do nothing whatsoever to obtain the nomination for himself. Finally Harvey turned and said to him, "If I can handle the matter so that the nomination for governor shall be tendered to you on a silver platter, without you turning a hand to obtain it, and without any requirement or suggestion of any pledge whatsoever, what do you think would be your attitude?" Wilson paced the floor for a few minutes and finally answered slowly, "If the nomination for governor should come to me in that way, I should regard it as my duty to give the matter very serious consideration." It was an evasive enough reply, but Harvey was apparently satisfied. He related the details of the conversation to Smith and the Newark boss declared that Wilson's answer was, for the time being, at least, satisfactory to him.[36] A few weeks later Harvey went to England, but before his departure he and Smith agreed that the question of the nomination should remain *in statu quo* during Harvey's absence.[37]

During the spring Wilson was struggling desperately at Princeton to win his fight for the graduate school; Harvey was in England; and Smith was trying hard to keep his organization men in line. Several Democrats, notably H. Otto Wittpenn and Robert S. Hudspeth of Jersey City, Frank S. Katzenbach of Trenton, and George S. Silzer of New Brunswick, were being named as probable gubernatorial candidates and Smith's lieutenants were demanding that he announce his own preference.[38] Wittpenn and Silzer were outstanding progressives, but it was evident by the middle of June that the overwhelming majority of

[35] *ibid.*   [36] *ibid.*, p. 37.
[37] Willis Fletcher Johnson, *George Harvey*, p. 141.
[38] W. O. Inglis, "Helping to Make a President," *loc. cit.*, p. 37.

the party workers throughout the state were supporting Katzenbach's candidacy.[39]

Smith, in the meantime, went to Chicago in the early part of June to visit a sick daughter.[40] One of Wilson's former students in that city, John Maynard Harlan, arranged through his friend Edward N. Hurley to bring about a meeting of Smith and Roger Sullivan, head of the Illinois Democratic machine. Consequently Smith, Sullivan, Hurley, and Harlan met for a luncheon conference to discuss Wilson's gubernatorial candidacy. Smith was enthusiastic about Wilson as a possible nominee, but he was anxious to receive some assurance from the Princeton man that if he were elected governor he would cooperate with the Democratic organization.[41] The conferees agreed that Harlan should write to Wilson and endeavor to discover his attitude toward the Smith machine. Harlan subsequently wrote a careful letter in which he declared that while Smith "had not the slightest desire that you commit yourself in any way as to principles, measures or men," he "would wish only to be satisfied that you, if you were elected Governor, would not set about fighting and breaking down the existing Democratic organization and replacing it with one of your own." [42]

Two weeks later Wilson replied that he would be "perfectly willing" to assure Smith that he would not, if elected governor, "set about 'fighting and breaking down the existing Democratic organization and replacing it with one of . . . [his] own.' " The last thing he should think of would be building up a personal machine. So long as the Smith organization was willing to support such policies as would reestablish the state's reputation, Wilson continued, he should deem himself "inexcusable for antagonizing it." The arrangement would last, however, only so long as he was left "absolutely free in the matter of measures and men." [43] It was, to say the least, an open and frank declaration on Wilson's part. Hurley hastened to New Jersey with a copy of the letter, which he personally gave to Smith. Smith, Hurley writes, declared that Wilson's terms were entirely satisfactory.[44]

[39] *Trenton True American,* June 27, 1910.
[40] J. M. Harlan to W. W., June 11, 1910, Wilson Papers; also published in Edward N. Hurley, *The Bridge to France,* p. 5. Harlan wrote that Smith had been in Chicago "Within the last two or three days."
[41] *ibid.,* pp. 3-4.
[42] J. M. Harlan to W. W., June 11, 1910, Wilson Papers.
[43] W. W. to J. M. Harlan, June 23, 1910, copy in Baker Papers.
[44] E. N. Hurley, *The Bridge to France,* p. 7.

It was obvious to most observers that there was more involved in the secret scheming and manipulations than the mere governorship of New Jersey. Harvey himself had first seriously broached the suggestion that Wilson be nominated for the presidency, and by June 1910 he had convinced Smith that the Princeton man was the logical candidate for the Democratic nomination in 1912.[45] Smith, in fact, was already an enthusiastic promoter of Wilson's presidential candidacy. "Charles," he said to Charles H. Gallagher, his lieutenant in Mercer County, "we have the opportunity of electing the next President of the United States by nominating and electing Woodrow Wilson as Governor of New Jersey."[46] The Newark boss was inordinately pleased at the thought of himself as a president-maker, and during his trip to the Midwest in June took occasion to consult with the Democratic leaders of Indiana, Illinois, Minnesota, Iowa, and the Dakotas about Wilson's presidential chances in 1912. The midwestern politicians, Smith afterward declared, were greatly interested in Wilson's possible candidacy and advised him first to nominate Wilson for the governorship of New Jersey.[47]

The newspapers somehow got wind of these conferences, and a Hearst reporter visited Wilson on July 7.[48] The following day the Hearst newspapers printed stories to the effect that a combination of eastern and midwestern Democrats, led by Harvey, Smith, Sullivan, and Thomas Taggart of Indiana, had set on foot a movement to accomplish Wilson's nomination for president.[49] The Hearst newspaper in Chicago asserted: "Woodrow Wilson will be the Democratic candidate for President in 1912 if a combination of Wall Street and political interests can make him so."[50]

Regardless of the widespread discussion of Wilson as a presidential candidate in 1912, the political situation in New Jersey became extremely critical for Smith during June 1910. For once it appeared that the party workers might assert their independence and support candidates of their own choosing. The Democratic state committee met at Asbury Park on June 25 and one state committeeman after another

[45] George F. Parker, "How Woodrow Wilson Was Nominated and Elected Governor of New Jersey," photostatic copy of MS memorandum in Baker Papers.

[46] "Statement of Charles H. Gallagher, of Trenton . . . ," MS memorandum in *ibid.*

[47] G. F. Parker, "How Woodrow Wilson Was Nominated . . . ," copy of MS memorandum in *ibid.* Gallagher tells the same story in his account, cited above, and in the *Trenton Sunday Advertiser,* February 19, 1911.

[48] W. W. to G. Harvey, July 7, 1910, Wilson Papers.

[49] *New York American,* July 8, 1910; *New York Journal,* July 8, 1910.

[50] *Chicago Record-Herald,* July 8, 1910.

reported that the sentiment in his county was overwhelmingly for Katzenbach, who had been the Democratic gubernatorial candidate in 1907 and who was something of an idol to the party workers.[51] Twenty out of the twenty-one committeemen agreed that Katzenbach was entitled to and should receive the nomination.[52] Even Nugent, Smith's chief lieutenant, strongly favored Katzenbach's nomination and sent Gallagher of Trenton to ask Katzenbach to become a candidate for the governorship.[53]

Harvey returned to New York in the latter part of June. Soon after he arrived he received a telephone call from Smith, who declared that the New Jersey situation was "hot" and that he could not hold his men in line for another week without definite assurance from Wilson that he would accept the nomination if it was offered to him.[54] Harvey hastily arranged for a meeting of Wilson, Smith, and himself for the evening of June 26. Colonel Henry Watterson, veteran editor of the *Louisville Courier-Journal,* was in New York and Harvey invited him also to the conference. The stage was at last set, he thought, for the opening scene of the great political drama.

Wilson, however, had gone with his family a few days before to Lyme, Connecticut, for the summer. On June 25 he sent a telegram to Harvey, announcing nonchalantly that there was no Sunday train from Lyme before late evening and that he was sorry he could not attend the dinner.[55] Harvey was frantic; it was bad enough, he must have thought, having to persuade Smith to support Wilson's candidacy, but it was more exasperating still that Wilson was doing his best to blast his own chances for political preferment. There was nothing left to do but bring Wilson down to New Jersey, so William O. Inglis, Harvey's lieutenant, set out that evening for Lyme. After a wild ride across a rough Connecticut road on Sunday morning, June 26, Inglis found Wilson just as he was about to go to church and escorted him safely back to New Jersey. Harvey met the two men at Red Bank and the group reached Harvey's home at Deal about seven in the evening.[56]

Smith and "Marse Henry" Watterson had already arrived. It was an altogether delightful dinner; Smith, Harvey, Watterson, and Wilson

[51] *Trenton True American,* June 27, 1910.
[52] "Statement of Charles H. Gallagher of Trenton . . . ," MS memorandum in Baker Papers.
[53] *ibid.*
[54] W. O. Inglis, "Helping to Make a President," *loc. cit.,* p. 37.
[55] W. W. to G. Harvey, June 25, 1910, Wilson Papers.
[56] W. O. Inglis, "Helping to Make a President," *loc. cit.,* pp. 38-40.

were the principal actors in the little drama; Mrs. Harvey and Inglis were mere onlookers and after dinner left the four men closeted in the dining room. Harvey and Smith tried to impress upon Wilson the urgent need for him to decide soon whether or not he would accept the gubernatorial nomination. The New Jersey party leaders were willing to give him the nomination "by acclamation," Wilson was told. Harvey's and Smith's most inviting suggestion, however, was that Wilson, by becoming governor of New Jersey, would stand in a fair way of winning the presidency in 1912. "It is immediately, as you know," Wilson afterward wrote, "the question of my nomination for the governorship of New Jersey; but that is the mere preliminary of a plan to nominate me in 1912 for the presidency." [57] Smith told Wilson that "the representative politicians of Indiana, Illinois, Ohio, Minnesota, and Iowa" preferred him as a presidential candidate to Governor Judson Harmon of Ohio and had urged the party leaders in New Jersey to nominate Wilson for the governorship. "The New Jersey men are confident that I can be elected by a majority so large as to be very impressive and convincing," Wilson continued, in his account of the meeting, "and are willing to give me the nomination unanimously, without the raising of a finger on my part." [58] Colonel Watterson was very voluble during the evening. He was delighted to discover some family relationship to Wilson[59] and promised that, if New Jersey would make Wilson governor, he would "take off his coat" and work for Wilson's nomination in 1912.

Wilson was impressed by the evidence and arguments of his persuaders and was sorely tempted to give his immediate consent to his candidacy—"The opportunity really seems most unusual," he thought.[60] Yet he hesitated; he was loath to leave Princeton without first seeking

[57] W. W. to D. B. Jones, June 27, 1910, photostatic copy in Baker Papers.

[58] *ibid*. "Of course the men who are planning my nomination for the governorship look forward to putting me up for the presidential nomination later," Wilson wrote afterwards, "and there have been some rather extraordinary indications that that is what Democrats in other parts of the country want. The suggestion came from the Middle West. But I have not allowed that part of the programme to form my opinion as to my duty in the matter of the governorship." W. W. to H. B. Thompson, July 14, 1910, copy in *ibid*. See also E. N. Hurley to J. M. Harlan, July 2, 1910, published in Hurley, *The Bridge to France*, p. 11. Hurley relates in this letter an account of the conference, which Smith related to him. "The question of Dr. Wilson running for Governor of New Jersey was also mentioned," Hurley wrote, "as, of course, a preliminary step to the Presidency." Smith stated plainly "that Dr. Wilson was taking a step in running for Governor of New Jersey that would lead to his nomination for the Presidency in 1912."

[59] Mrs. Wilson and Mrs. Watterson were distant cousins.

[60] W. W. to D. B. Jones, June 27, 1910, Baker Papers.

the advice of the trustees who had stood by him so loyally in his struggles over University policies. And since Smith agreed to allow him a few days before he made the final decision, Wilson promised to give the Newark man his answer by the end of the week of June 26.[61] It was now nearly midnight. Inglis saw Smith, with a broad smile on his face, come out of the dining room and leave for Newark. Harvey, Watterson, and Wilson continued the conversation.

The following morning, June 27, Inglis, Harvey, Watterson, and Wilson went to New York. Watterson left the group at the Hudson Terminal and Harvey advised Wilson to go to Chicago and confer with his trustee friends. That would be quicker, he thought, than writing.[62] Wilson returned to Lyme, however, and wrote a long letter to David B. Jones, one of the Chicago trustees, describing the conference of the night before. "I have promised nothing," he wrote; "In order to go into this thing, I feel that I must get the free consent of yourself, your brother [Thomas D. Jones], [Cyrus H.] McCormick, [Cleveland H.] Dodge, [Edward W.] Sheldon, and the other men who have been such splendid friends of Princeton and of mine." Wilson asked Jones to discuss the problem with his brother, McCormick, and William B. McIlvaine, "asking them to give me their absolutely frank opinion and wish in the premises." If the Chicago trustees should think it necessary, he continued, he would come to that city at once for a conference.[63] Two days later, on June 29, Wilson met Sheldon and Dodge in New York and discussed the gubernatorial question with them. Both Dodge and Sheldon agreed that they knew of no reason why Wilson should not go

[61] It is interesting that Smith was so anxious to obtain Wilson's consent to the use of his name for the gubernatorial nomination that immediately after the Deal conference he, Smith, wrote to his friend, E. N. Hurley, in Chicago, "I understand our mutual friend is going to see Messrs. Cyrus H. McCormick, Thomas D. Jones and William B. McIlvaine of your City, as to the advisability of his candidacy. Wouldn't it be well to have Mr. Harlan see them before our friend meets them?" J. Smith, Jr. to E. N. Hurley, June 28, 1910, published in Hurley, *The Bridge to France,* p. 10. Harlan made a trip to New York on July 4 and impressed upon Wilson the necessity of his making an early decision. J. M. Harlan to E. N. Hurley, July 4, 1910, published in *ibid.,* p. 12.

[62] W. O. Inglis, "Helping to Make a President," *loc. cit.,* pp. 40-41.

[63] "I cannot throw off the feeling, perhaps I should say the fear, that I am in some way imposing upon your kindness and that of the other men by even suggesting that I take the liberty at this juncture of withdrawing from Princeton," Wilson concluded. "Perhaps it is the fear that this will look to you like a mere case of personal ambition. To my mind it is a question of which is the larger duty and opportunity. At any rate, I am sure that you will all judge leniently and will understand." W. W. to D. B. Jones, June 27, 1910, Baker Papers.

ahead and accept the nomination.[64] A few days later Wilson consulted another loyal supporter, Melancthon W. Jacobus, of the Hartford Theological Seminary.

On his return to Lyme on June 30 Wilson found a telegram from David B. Jones. "All four[65] concur unreservedly in opinion that no obligation whatever exists on your part," it read, "either to any individual supporters or to the University as a whole, which should deter you from following your own inclination." The Chicago trustees believed that the decision was one that only Wilson himself could make, but they promised their support should he decide to enter the political field.[66] Wilson's immediate reaction was one of relief and joy, as if he had been released from any moral obligations he might have owed to Princeton and his friends at the University. He wrote to Dodge that the support he had received from the trustees had raised his "whole estimate of the world" and he felt a richer man, he added, for having had "this experience in dealing with noble, public spirited men."[67] He expressed his appreciation in a similar manner to D. B. Jones. "I am specially privileged in having earned the friendship and confidence of such men," he wrote, "and I want to express my deep and lasting gratitude."[68]

Wilson told Harvey and Smith of his final decision sometime during the first week in July.[69] Writing soon afterwards to Dodge he declared, "I have felt obliged to say to the men who sounded me about the nomination that, if it came to me unsought and unanimously and I could take it without pledges of any kind to anybody, I would accept it and do what I could to deserve it."[70] After what he had taught his students about public duty and "the duty of the educated men to undertake just such service as this," Wilson confided to another friend, "I did not see how I could avoid it."[71]

There can certainly be no doubt that Wilson was not in any sense seeking the nomination. Although it is true that he had suffered a bitter defeat in the graduate school controversy in May 1910, he

[64] E. W. Sheldon, undated MS memorandum, photostatic copy in *ibid.;* W. W. to C. H. Dodge, July 1, 1910, *ibid.*

[65] D. B. Jones, T. D. Jones, C. H. McCormick, and W. B. McIlvaine.

[66] D. B. Jones to W. W., June 30, 1910, photostatic copy in Baker Papers.

[67] W. W. to C. H. Dodge, July 1, 1910, *ibid.*

[68] W. W. to D. B. Jones, July 1, 1910, photostatic copy in *ibid.*

[69] Inglis places the date at July 1. W. O. Inglis, "Helping to Make a President," *loc. cit.,* p. 41.

[70] W. W. to C. H. Dodge, July 11, 1910, copy in Baker Papers.

[71] W. W. to C. H. McCormick, July 14, 1910, copy in *ibid.*

evidenced no impelling desire to leave the University. "I cherish a sneaking hope," he wrote to a friend, after he had agreed to become a candidate, "that the thing may not, after all, come off." [72]

Even during the confused and hurried days of late June and early July Wilson found time to ponder certain fundamental questions that were troubling him. He must have wondered, first of all, if there was any really genuine popular demand for his nomination. It was not, to be sure, the first time he had been suggested for the governorship. Henry Eckert Alexander, editor of the *Trenton True American,* had, as early as November 1909, been an advocate of Wilson's nomination,[73] while the editor of the *Elizabeth Evening Times* had written in the spring of 1910 that a number of congressmen and senators believed Wilson's election as governor would give him a sizable claim upon the Democratic presidential nomination in 1912.[74] But the most disturbing question of all was, Why had the Democratic bosses chosen him as their candidate for 1910? Wilson searched about for an answer; he asked, he later declared, "very impertinent and direct questions of some of the gentlemen as to why they wanted me to run," but received no satisfactory answer.[75] He therefore had to evolve a theory of his own, which, incidentally, he later realized was naive and unrealistic. His conclusion was "that these gentlemen recognized the fact that a new day had come in American politics, and that they would have to conduct them[selves] henceforth after a new fashion." [76]

Actually there was nothing so very mysterious about Smith's eagerness to persuade Wilson to accept the gubernatorial nomination. Smith was, first of all, as he later admitted, enthusiastic about Wilson's presidential candidacy; he was convinced by his conversations with other Democratic leaders throughout the country that Wilson stood a good chance of winning that honor; and undoubtedly he took

---

[72] W. W. to H. B. Thompson, July 14, 1910, copy in *ibid.*

[73] H. E. Alexander to W. W., November 18, 1909, Wilson Papers.

[74] L. T. Russell to W. W., March 23, 1910, *ibid.*

[75] Address at Newark, January 14, 1911, *Newark Evening News,* January 16, 1911.

[76] *ibid.* On another occasion Wilson described his quandary. "I rather anticipated that I would be approached and asked as to my views on certain questions, and as to what I would [do] in certain contingencies, but I was not," he declared. "Everything seemed to be taken for granted. It puzzled me, and I asked a friend what it meant.

"'It means,' said my friend, 'that the Democratic State leaders, after 15 years of leading a minority, want to elect a Governor. They will gain in prestige and will gain incidental advantages, and they know that while you will only appoint fit men to office you will not discriminate against Democrats.'" Interview by S. M. Christie, in *Trenton True American,* September 29, 1910.

pleasure in the thought of himself as another Mark Hanna. Smith's motives, however, were hardly altruistic in the broader sense. He deliberately went outside the ranks of politicians and singled out a man of great reputation who he knew would be regarded as an absolutely independent person. It is not an exaggeration to say that he hoped to use Wilson as the respectable front behind which he could operate, checking the Democratic progressives, and at the same time serving his own ends. He confidently expected Wilson to carry the state in the November elections and to cooperate with the state organization in the matter of appointments. What was more important, Smith had already determined to return to the United States Senate if a Democratic legislature was elected in the fall—and he expected Wilson to carry along with him a Democratic legislature into office. At the same time that he was corralling convention votes for Wilson, Smith was making a secret campaign among the party workers for election to the Senate.[77]

In the meantime there was considerable speculation in the newspapers as to what was happening behind the scenes in New Jersey. Somehow Harry E. Alexander first got wind of the talk about Wilson's possible nomination and on July 9 his *Trenton True American* blazoned forth an editorial demanding Wilson's nomination. "To fail to enlist the services of such a man at such a time, if they can be obtained," Alexander wrote, "would be a party crime of such dimensions as would almost justify the people in repudiating a Democratic candidate of smaller stature." Other journals in like manner commended Wilson's candidacy,[78] but it was especially significant that the two leading New Idea newspapers were entirely favorable to Wilson's nomination.[79] Smith's newspapers in Newark began early in July to mention Wilson as a likely candidate.[80]

Since Wilson's intermittent conferences had brought him into contact only with the chief boss himself, Harvey believed it was now time to bring Wilson and the leading Democratic politicians together. The Colonel accordingly arranged for a luncheon conference at the Lawyers' Club in the Equitable Building in New York on July 12. Smith was not present at the meeting, but he sent as his representatives James R. Nugent, the state chairman of the party, and Robert S. Hudspeth, the

[77] Smith's campaign for the senatorial election will be discussed at length in Chapter VII.

[78] See the *Trenton State Gazette, Passaic Daily News, New Brunswick Times,* and *New Brunswick Home News,* cited in *Trenton True American,* July 16, 1910.

[79] *Jersey Journal* of Jersey City, July 15, 1910; *Newark Evening News,* July 19, 1910.

[80] See especially the *Newark Evening Star,* July 11, 1910.

Democratic national committeeman from New Jersey.[81] Harvey was master of ceremonies and he and Richard V. Lindabury, attorney for United States Steel, Standard Oil, and other trusts, represented the corporation and financial interests. Congressman Eugene F. Kinkead of Hudson County, a representative of the Davis machine, and Millard F. Ross, a lieutenant of the Smith organization in Middlesex County, completed the group.[82]

Harvey announced that he had called the Democratic leaders together in order to sound out the sentiment of the state with regard to Wilson's gubernatorial candidacy. Each of the politicians declared that Wilson was stronger than his party and would win easily in the November elections.[83] Hudspeth, representing the combined Smith-Davis forces, was the chief spokesman of the organization men. Would Wilson accept the nomination if it was offered to him by the state convention, he asked. Wilson replied that he would accept the nomination if it was offered to him without a contest. Hudspeth then turned to the liquor question. Smith's chief fear was local option. He was, Hudspeth later declared, closely allied with the brewers and represented them politically. Before the conference Smith had told Hudspeth, "Unless we can get the liquor interests behind the Doctor, we can't elect him," and Smith especially instructed Hudspeth to probe into Wilson's views on the liquor question.[84] When Hudspeth consequently asked Wilson what his attitude on the liquor question was, Wilson responded instantly that he was not a prohibitionist and that he believed the question was outside the political sphere. But, he added, "I believe in home rule, and that the issue should be settled by local option in each community." Hudspeth replied that the Democratic party had been fighting local

[81] Hudspeth, who was later to figure prominently in the pre-convention campaign in New Jersey in 1912, was born in Coburn, Canada, in 1862. He was city attorney of Jersey City, member of the legislature in 1885, speaker of the Assembly in 1888, and afterwards a member and leader of the Democratic minority in the Senate. He was a close political associate of Robert Davis in Hudson County.

[82] There have been several accounts of the Lawyers' Club conference. There were at the time incomplete accounts in the newspapers, for which see the *Trenton Evening Times*, July 15 and 18, 1910; *Newark Evening News*, July 15, 1910. James Kerney, *The Political Education of Woodrow Wilson*, pp. 44-46, has a good description of the personnel of the conference, although he is confused as to the exact date of the meeting. William E. Sackett, *Modern Battles of Trenton*, II, 299, contains an almost contemporary account.

[83] E. F. Kinkead to R. S. Baker, October 25, 1927, Baker Papers.

[84] R. S. Baker, "Memorandum of an interview with Robert S. Hudspeth, November 3, 1927," *ibid*.

option for many years, that it was "our *bête noir*." [85] "Well," Wilson replied, "that is my attitude and my conviction. I cannot change it." [86]

The conference lasted for most of the afternoon. Kinkead and Hudspeth assured Wilson that if he would only announce his candidacy the other Democratic candidates would withdraw from the contest.[87] He promised to issue a formal statement of his willingness to accept the nomination.[88]

Thus the die was cast for Wilson. On July 15 he therefore sent a letter to the *Trenton True American* and the *Newark Evening News,* formally announcing his willingness to accept the gubernatorial nomination. "There has recently been so much talk of the possibility of my being nominated by the Democrats of New Jersey for the Governorship of the State," the letter read, "and I have been asked by so many persons, whom I respect, what my attitude would be towards such a nomination, that it would be an affectation and discourtesy on my part to ignore the matter any longer." He was not, he emphasized, in any sense a candidate for the nomination and would do nothing on his part to obtain it. Nor did he wish, he continued, to be drawn away from his duties at Princeton; but his wish did not constitute his duty, and if it should turn out to be true, "as so many well informed persons have assured me they believe it will," that it was the hope and wish of "a decided majority of the thoughtful Democrats of the State" that he should consent to accept the nomination, he would deem it his duty, "as well as an honor and a privilege, to do so." [89]

Most of the Democratic, and many of the Republican newspapers greeted this declaration with real enthusiasm. One Democratic journal, for example, declared that Wilson would "sweep the State like a cyclone," [90] while another pointed out that his nomination would surely result in the election of a Democratic legislature.[91] One ebullient editor thought that his candidacy was "a compliment to the Democratic party" and that his nomination and election would inaugurate an era of statesmanlike government at Trenton.[92] With a few notable exceptions,

---

[85] Hudspeth himself was a representative of the liquor interests. He was at the time an attorney for the State Liquor Dealers' Association. *Trenton Evening Times,* July 15, 1910.

[86] R. S. Baker, "Memorandum of an interview with Robert S. Hudspeth, November 3, 1927," Baker Papers.

[87] *Trenton Evening Times,* July 16, 1910.   [88] *ibid.,* July 15, 1910.

[89] *Newark Evening News,* July 15, 1910; *Trenton True American,* July 16, 1910.

[90] *Paterson Guardian,* cited in *ibid.,* July 19, 1910.

[91] *Elizabeth Evening Times,* cited in *ibid.*

[92] *New Brunswick Times,* cited in *ibid.,* July 20, 1910.

which will be discussed later, the New Jersey press welcomed Wilson's entrance into the political field as an augury of better things to come in state politics and enthusiastically demanded his nomination at the hands of the Democratic party.[93]

Having secured the unequivocal assurance from Wilson that he was a receptive, though passive, candidate for the governorship, James Smith, Jr., set immediately to work to swing his following into line behind the Wilson movement. There was first of all the problem of what to do about the Katzenbach gubernatorial boom, since the Trenton man was undoubtedly the choice of the rank and file of the party workers. Smith was aided in his efforts to head off the Katzenbach movement by the inactivity of Katzenbach himself. Nugent, who strongly favored Katzenbach's nomination, endeavored to persuade him to come out into the open and announce his candidacy, but he refused. He even stated positively to Charles H. Gallagher, member of the state committee from Mercer County,[94] that he was not a candidate for the nomination.[95] It was not until the latter part of July that Katzenbach made his position clear. He did not want the nomination, he then declared, but if the party drafted him to lead the campaign, "being neither insensible to nor ungrateful for past honors," he would accept the nomination.[96] By the time he made this declaration, however, Smith had succeeded in swinging his lieutenants closely into line for Wilson and there was little likelihood that Katzenbach would receive much support from the organization men.[97]

Smith also succeeded in doing what most observers thought was impossible: for once he was able to come to terms with Robert Davis, head of the Jersey City-Hudson County machine. The Newark boss

[93] See the *Newark Evening News*, July 19, 1910; *Asbury Park Shore Press, Long Branch Record*, and *Passaic Daily News*, cited in the *Trenton True American*, July 20, 1910; *Hunterdon County Democrat, New Jersey Herald* of Newton, and *Plainfield Press*, cited in *ibid.*, July 22, 1910; *True Democratic Banner* of Morristown, *Warren Journal*, and *Perth Amboy Evening News*, cited in *ibid.*, July 23, 1910.

[94] Both Trenton and Princeton are in Mercer County.

[95] "Statement of Charles H. Gallagher of Trenton . . . ," MS memorandum in Baker Papers.

[96] *Trenton True American*, July 26, 1910.

[97] Nugent, for example, followed Smith's lead without hesitation. Although he favored Katzenbach for the governorship, he told James Kerney: "Of course I will do whatever the Big Fellow wants." Kerney, *The Political Education of Woodrow Wilson*, p. 38. Gallagher, who occupied a strategic position on the state committee since both Wilson and Katzenbach were residents of his county, announced on July 23, "I am . . . for Woodrow Wilson as the party candidate, thus holding to a Mercer man and bowing to the will of Democrats outside my county." *Trenton True American*, July 25, 1910.

was sure of the support of his own county, Essex, which would send 240 delegates to the state convention. Hudson County was about as populous and would send 236 delegates. If the two Democratic leaders could control their delegations and unite behind Wilson's candidacy, they would command, therefore, some 476 votes in the convention. Since 707 votes were necessary for a majority, Smith would have to find only 231 delegates elsewhere to ensure Wilson's nomination.

Before the Lawyers' Club conference of July 12, Smith and Davis had conferred and had agreed to forget past political differences and to cooperate in securing Wilson's nomination.[98] The reasons for the alliance of the two men who had for years fought each other so bitterly for control of the Democratic party in the state were most unusual. Without Davis's support, Smith could never nominate his candidate. He recognized this fact and was willing to share control of the state patronage with Davis. Davis, for his part, was faced with a major rebellion in his own domain of Hudson County on the part of Mayor H. Otto Wittpenn, who was attempting to wrest control of the party organization from him. Wittpenn was also a candidate for the gubernatorial nomination. Consequently by helping to nominate Wilson, Davis could ensure for himself a commanding voice in the new administration if Wilson was elected and at the same time could also strike a major blow at Wittpenn's political career.[99]

Smith did the job of securing support for Wilson outside of Hudson and Essex exceedingly well. There was no really enthusiastic Wilson sentiment among the party workers—few of them knew or had ever seen the Princeton president—but loyalty to the organization was stronger than any aversion some of them might have had toward the scholar in politics.[100] One by one the machine leaders began to fall into

[98] *Jersey Journal* of Jersey City, July 15, 1910; *Trenton Sunday Advertiser,* September 4, 1910.

[99] *Jersey Journal of Jersey City,* July 15, 1910. The fact that Hudspeth and Kinkead, the two chief Davis lieutenants, participated in the Lawyers' Club conference was evidence enough that Smith and Davis had united behind Wilson's candidacy. See the *Trenton Evening Times,* July 15, 1910. But when Hudspeth on July 15 declared publicly that he was certain Wilson would be the unanimous choice of the state convention for governor (*Trenton True American,* July 16, 1910), and when a weekly newspaper in Jersey City, the spokesman of Davis, came out in favor of Wilson's nomination, there was no doubt in men's minds that an alliance between the two bosses had been concluded.

[100] *Trenton Sunday Advertiser,* September 4, 1910.

line.[101] A few progressive Democratic politicians also came to Wilson's aid, but they were notably few in number.[102]

Wilson's declaration that he would accept the gubernatorial nomination and the realization that the Smith-Davis machines meant to foist him upon the party as their candidate was a crushing blow to the Democratic progressives who had for years been fighting the boss system. Wittpenn, who had been the first to announce his candidacy,[103] came out on June 21 with a platform denouncing the "corrupt State House ring" of Democratic politicians and demanding the reforms for which the New Idea Republicans and progressive Democrats had been struggling.[104] Early in July George S. Silzer, state senator from New Brunswick, announced his candidacy on an equally liberal platform.[105] Both men inaugurated their campaigns by declaring war on Smith and Davis and by demanding a public utilities commission with rate-making powers, an effective workmen's compensation law, direct primaries, equal taxation of corporation property, and an end to the alliance of political organizations and corporations.

The shadow of James Smith, Jr., and Robert Davis hung heavily over Wilson's candidacy during the summer of 1910. One thing was certain—that a little band of progressive Democrats, who were neither as numerous nor as well organized as the New Idea group, were determined to make a stubborn fight against the Princeton man. There were even vague threats that they would disrupt the Democratic party should Wilson be made the gubernatorial nominee.[106] Prominent among this group were Joseph P. Tumulty, Mark Sullivan, and John Treacy, Jersey City insurgents, who were supporting Silzer for the nomination.[107] Their chief spokesmen were two progressive newspapers, the *Hudson*

---

[101] *Trenton True American,* July 23 and 28, August 22, 1910.

[102] Dan Fellows Platt of Englewood and James E. Martine were the two progressives who supported Wilson's candidacy. *ibid.,* July 21 and 22, 1910.

[103] Wittpenn visited Wilson at Lyme, Connecticut, on July 14 and told him emphatically that the rumors that he, Wittpenn, would withdraw from the contest if Wilson agreed to accept the nomination were false. He also endeavored to explain to Wilson the true meaning of the party struggle in Jersey City that was then going on between the progressives and the Davis organization. *Trenton Evening Times,* July 16, 1910. W. W. to G. Harvey, July 14, 1910, Wilson Papers, also contains a good account of the Wilson-Wittpenn interview.

[104] *Jersey Journal* of Jersey City, June 21, 1910.

[105] *ibid.,* July 6, 1910.

[106] *Hudson Observer* of Hoboken, July 18, 1910.

[107] J. P. Tumulty, *Woodrow Wilson As I Know Him,* pp. 14-15.

Observer of Hoboken and the *Trenton Evening Times,* which launched immediately into the fight to prevent Wilson's nomination.

These men were not ignorant of most of the important steps leading up to Wilson's declaration that he would accept the nomination. "There is no denial of the fact," asserted one newspaper, "that Dr. Wilson was induced to enter the race by a combination of the very elements which the Progressives are fighting." New Jersey had for seventeen years been hopelessly Republican, it continued, largely because of the machine control of the Democratic party.[108] And now, added Kerney, when it appeared that the young reform leaders might stand a fair chance of gaining control of the party, Wilson had allowed himself "to be used as a catspaw, to serve the purposes of the bosses" in defeating the reform movement.[109]

More serious was the charge, repeatedly made by James Kerney, crusading editor of the *Trenton Evening Times,* and Matthew C. Ely, editor of the *Hudson Observer,* that Wilson's nomination was being engineered and backed by financial and corporation interests in New Jersey and New York. The Lawyers' Club conference was portrayed by his insurgent critics as simply another secret conference of the representatives of corrupt political machines and corporations, the purpose of which was patently to thwart the popular demand for reform.[110] As the *Observer* put it, "When it is remembered that the leading corporation lawyer in the state, Richard V. Lindabury . . . and George B. M. Harvey, who is closely affiliated with the Morgan Railroad interests, were active with the bosses in the exclusive conference at which Mr. Wilson's candidacy was decided upon," the voter would understand the great wave of opposition to Wilson that was sweeping the state.[111]

The few Democratic politicians who had been leaders in the progressive movement in the state were likewise up in arms. Assemblyman Edward Kenny of Jersey City announced his candidacy for the gubernatorial nomination in July and declared that the "fact that George B. McClellan Harvey is Wilson's chief sponsor should be enough to finish Wilson."[112] Wittpenn carried his fight for the nomination to the people and charged that Wilson was a tool of corporate interests,[113] while

[108] *Hudson Observer* of Hoboken, July 18, 1910.
[109] *Trenton Evening Times,* July 18, 1910.
[110] *ibid.,* July 14, 15, and 18, 1910.
[111] *Hudson Observer* of Hoboken, July 18, 1910.
[112] *Trenton Evening Times,* July 18, 1910.
[113] *ibid.,* July 25, 1910.

Assemblyman Allan B. Walsh of Trenton disposed of Wilson's candidacy by declaring, "No man wearing a Wall Street tag is intellectually great enough to be elected Governor of New Jersey." [114]

In spite of Katzenbach's seeming reluctance to make a canvass for the nomination, the majority of the progressives singled him out as the man most likely to defeat Wilson. Judge John W. Wescott of Camden, who afterward nominated Wilson for the presidency in 1912 and 1916, led the Katzenbach campaign in South Jersey,[115] while Kerney and other Mercer County Democrats took the lead in the northern part of the state. The progressives scored an initial victory early in August when Katzenbach received the unanimous endorsement of the Mercer County Democratic Committee,[116] and by the first of September it was evident that all of the county's delegates to the state convention would support the Trenton man.[117] It was, incidentally, a matter of severe embarrassment to Wilson that he could not command the support of his own county. Although the progressives asserted that a majority of Democratic voters throughout the state preferred Katzenbach to Wilson for governor, it was obvious to most impartial observers that the Katzenbach sentiment was unorganized and incoherent and that the Smith-Davis organizations had the situation well in hand.

Wilson's opponents, however, maneuvered skillfully in the fight. They endeavored, first of all, to secure his views on the important questions of the day and Kerney directed a searching inquiry at the Princeton president: What was his attitude with regard to the demand for a rate-making utilities commission, direct primaries, direct election of United States senators, workmen's compensation legislation, and corrupt practices legislation? But Wilson absolutely refused to be "smoked out" in this manner and refused to give out any statement explaining his economic and political beliefs.[118]

---

[114] See also State Senator William C. Gebhardt's statement of July 19, in *ibid.*, July 19, 1910.

[115] George Barton, "Woodrow Wilson: His Human Side," *Current History*, XXII (April 1925), 6.

[116] *Trenton Evening Times*, August 6, 1910.

[117] *ibid.*, September 8, 1910.

[118] *ibid.*, August 5, 1910. Katzenbach, Wittpenn, and Silzer answered the *Evening Times'* query in a straightforward manner and strongly endorsed the progressive measures.

At the same time these questions were put to Wilson, Dan Fellows Platt of Englewood suggested to Wilson that he should make his position known. Platt proposed that the Bergen County Democratic Committee write Wilson a letter, requesting him to state his position on the issues covered in the query of the *Trenton Evening Times*. Wilson

Wilson's refusal to commit himself on any public question afforded his opponents another powerful argument against his nomination. He had condescendingly agreed to become the gubernatorial candidate only if "a decided majority of the thoughtful Democrats" wanted him as their representative. His unwillingness, therefore, to make known his attitude toward the important issues was conclusive proof to the insurgents of his hypocrisy.[119] Who were the "thoughtful Democrats" of New Jersey, to whom Wilson had appealed, the progressives asked. "Thoughtful Democrats" had been asked to accept, on the recommendation of Smith, Davis, Harvey, and Lindabury, the candidacy of a man who refused to make known his position on public matters, who had never taken an active part in New Jersey affairs nor had the slightest experience in public life. Thoughtful Democrats were demanding to know where Wilson stood, declared one spokesman, and his refusal to commit himself on any single question was conclusive proof to the insurgents that he was "against all commissions for utilities regulation, and most of the other progressive ideas of the party." [120]

As the summer passed the charges against Wilson were multiplied by Kerney and his cohorts. Kerney first made the accusation that Wilson had not voted for Bryan in 1908,[121] a charge that was later used against him with telling effect in the pre-convention presidential campaign. Wilson's earlier conservative fulminations against Bryan and state regulation of business were resurrected and exploited by his critics, while the charge was made that Wilson's election would end in a fiasco by the election of James Smith, Jr., to the United States Senate.[122]

Wilson's opponents, however, achieved their greatest success when they succeeded in marshaling the forces of organized labor against Wilson's candidacy. His reactionary anti-union labor views were pub-

thought that there were certain manifest advantages in issuing a sort of creed on pending state issues, but he was perplexed and uncertain as to what he should do. He consequently wrote to Harvey on August 8 for advice.

Wilson wrote that he feared that if he should reply to Platt's questions it would be charged that he, Wilson, had arranged the opportunity to answer his critics, and that Platt's letter might give rise to others, from less friendly quarters, in which he would be asked questions that would be set as traps. W. W. to G. Harvey, August 8, 1910, Wilson Papers.

Harvey, it may be surmised, promptly advised Wilson to say nothing before the state convention met.

[119] *Trenton Evening Times,* August 6, 1910.

[120] *Hudson Observer* of Hoboken, cited in *ibid.,* August 19, 1910.

[121] *Trenton Evening Times,* September 6, 1910.

[122] *Hudson Observer* of Hoboken, cited in *ibid.,* August 19, 1910; *Newark Sunday Call,* cited in *ibid.*

lished widely throughout the state and generated a reaction among workingmen that appeared, at least for a time, to offer a dangerous threat to the plans of the Smith-Davis alliance. The protest movement started in Trenton, when the Central Labor Union of the capital adopted a resolution in July declaring that the laborers of Trenton were "unalterably opposed to the nomination of Woodrow Wilson for the Governorship of New Jersey." [123] The matter took an ugly turn for Wilson when the convention of the State Federation of Labor met in Newark on August 17. Smith and Nugent had sent representatives to the convention to hold the labor delegates in check, but opposition to Wilson's candidacy was overwhelming and a series of resolutions denouncing him as the "tool or agent of . . . Wall Street's interests" were adopted. [124]

In the face of the widespread and bitter opposition to his candidacy, Wilson managed to maintain a discreet silence. When Edgar R. Williamson, editor of the *American Labor Standard,* however, asked him to set forth his position with regard to labor unions, Wilson hastily seized the opportunity to tell the workingmen where he stood. In a public letter to Williamson, repudiating virtually everything he had said previously, Wilson declared that the "gross misrepresentations of my views with regard to organized labor," which were being spread by some newspapers, "were wilful and deliberate misrepresentations." "I have always been the warm friend of organized labor," he continued. It was not only legitimate that labor should organize, he added; it was absolutely necessary if labor was to secure justice from organized capital, and everything that labor did to improve the condition of workingmen ought to have the support of all public-spirited men. Wilson admitted

[123] *Trenton Evening Times,* July 30, 1910.

[124] The resolutions read: "Whereas, the financial interests of Wall Street, New York, are endeavoring to have Woodrow Wilson . . . nominated as a candidate for Governor . . . ; and

"Whereas, Woodrow Wilson has publicly shown his antagonism to organized labor. . . ." Be it "Resolved, By the New Jersey State Federation of Labor in convention assembled . . . that this Federation be placed on record as opposing the nomination of said Woodrow Wilson as a candidate for Governor, that it urges every trades unionist and wage earner in the State of New Jersey to oppose his nomination; and also urges that, should the Wall Street financial interests succeed in having Woodrow Wilson nominated to act as the tool or agent of said Wall Street's interests, if he should be elected, that every trades unionist and every wage earner . . . do their utmost to defeat him and to teach the financial interests of Wall Street, New York, that the honest voters and trades unionists of the State of New Jersey are perfectly capable of selecting their own Governor." *ibid.,* August 17, 1910.

that he had at times criticized certain activities of labor unions; "but," he added, "I have criticized them as a friend." [125]

To the New Jersey editors who had been faithfully advocating Wilson's nomination, this, his first public declaration of the campaign since July 15, was a welcome statement. "With his letter setting forth his position on organized labor," declared one Democratic journal, "Woodrow Wilson . . . stands forth stronger than ever as a candidate." [126] Practically all the Democratic newspapers approved Wilson's pronouncement[127] and the two leading New Idea journals were just as enthusiastic in their endorsement.[128] Kerney, however, was hardly satisfied with the explanation and asserted that Wilson's letter, "shifting his position towards the unions," was "ludicrous to say the least." [129] Henry F. Hilfers, secretary of the New Jersey State Federation of Labor, replied that the fact that Wilson was seeking the governorship accounted for his rapid change of heart.[130]

Throughout the long and sustained campaign of the Democratic insurgents to discredit Wilson's candidacy before the party members, Wilson was ably defended by a number of newspaper spokesmen. The Wilson editors were headed by Alexander of the *Trenton True American,* who charged time and again that Kerney and the anti-Wilson group were playing "peanut politics" and endeavoring to wreck the Democratic party and blast its chances of success in the November elections. Alexander declared that Kerney himself was not a disinterested spokesman, that he was an appointee of Republican Governor Fort, and that he was cooperating in an insidious manner with the Republican state machine to prevent Wilson's nomination.[131] More significant, perhaps, was the consistent and loyal support Wilson received from the leading progressive Republican journals that almost daily joined in the demand for Wilson's nomination and election.[132]

Wilson remained for most of the summer in Lyme, Connecticut, where

[125] W. W. to E. R. Williamson, August 23, 1910, published in the *American Labor Standard* (Orange, New Jersey), September 2, 1910; also published in *Trenton True American,* September 2, 1910.

[126] *Perth Amboy Evening News,* cited in *ibid.,* September 5, 1910.

[127] *New Brunswick Times* and *Newark Call,* cited in *ibid.*

[128] *Jersey Journal* of Jersey City, September 3, 1910; *Newark Evening News,* September 2, 1910.

[129] *Trenton Evening Times,* September 3, 1910.

[130] *Jersey Journal* of Jersey City, September 9, 1910.

[131] *Trenton True American,* August 4 and 16, September 9, 1910.

[132] See the *Jersey Journal* of Jersey City, July 22 and 29, 1910, and *Newark Evening News,* July 19, 1910, for notable editorials.

he received news of the progress of the campaign from time to time from his faithful mentor, George Harvey. This was his first real experience with the details of practical politics and he continually sought Harvey's advice and aid.[133] Wilson was measurably disturbed by the discontent and bitter feeling his candidacy had provoked. He had been persuaded by Smith and Hudspeth that his offer to accept the nomination would cause the other candidates to withdraw, and when Wittpenn and Silzer not only refused to retire from the race but also redoubled their efforts to secure the nomination, Wilson was chagrined. He was especially disturbed by the rising tide of the Katzenbach movement. He did not understand this Katzenbach business at all, Wilson wrote to Harvey; he thought that the matter of Katzenbach's candidacy had been disposed of before his willingness to be considered was announced, and he feared that he would be put in a ridiculous position.[134] Harvey, however, reminded Wilson that entire party agreement was not desirable because it would appear under such circumstances that the party was completely dominated by the bosses. Wilson was beginning to discover that political campaigns are often undignified and that candidates—even university presidents—are sometimes roughly treated by their opponents.

There were, however, encouraging signs that things were going well in New Jersey. The conviction seemed to be growing steadily among the Democratic voters that Wilson was the ablest available Democrat to lead the gubernatorial campaign, and a reaction was already setting in by the end of July against the anti-Wilson campaign.[135] Oswald Garrison Villard, editor of the *New York Evening Post,* reported late in August that "from all reports the tide in New Jersey is running very strongly in your direction." [136] It was, moreover, heartening to Wilson to receive from Villard the assurance that "nothing has so inspired and invigorated us here in the office for a long time as the prospect that we may have the pleasure and satisfaction of battling for you." [137] From Kentucky came the euphonious greetings of Henry Watterson, who wrote: "There's a speck no bigger than a man's hand—an exhalation, as it were, rising above the towers of Princeton—forming in the clouds

---

[133] See, e.g., W. W. to G. Harvey, July 16, August 3, 8, 9, 23, September 10, 1910, all in Wilson Papers.

[134] W. W. to G. Harvey, July 26, 1910, *ibid.*

[135] *Trenton Sunday Advertiser,* July 31, 1910.

[136] O. G. Villard to W. W., August 22, 1910, copy in Baker Papers.

[137] *ibid.*

that gather about the rising sun the letters, 'Woodrow Wilson.' " [138]

The Democratic primaries for the election of delegates to the state convention were held on September 13. The Davis organization in Hudson County won a sweeping victory over the Wittpenn forces and carried two-thirds of the county's delegation for Wilson. The results were even more decisive in Newark and Essex County, where the Smith-Nugent machine made a clean sweep of the primaries and elected an almost solid Wilson delegation. The anti-Smith Democrats in Newark had, at the last moment, united behind Sheriff William Harrigan for governor; they elected only six out of the county's 240 delegates. State Chairman James R. Nugent was satisfied with the results of the primaries in the remainder of the state and confidently announced that Wilson would be the choice of the state convention. [139]

During the evening of September 14, the day before the state convention met, the Democratic hosts began to gather in Trenton. Smith, as was his custom during conventions, occupied Room 100 of the Trenton House, "immemorial headquarters of the bosses of both parties." Harvey had come from New York to be on the scene of action and had a suite in the same hotel, which soon became the center of all political activity in Trenton. The progressives were just as active as their organization opponents and were even yet hopeful that some political miracle might help turn the tide against the machine coalition. At least they were vociferous enough. "Frank's entitled to it, and he's going to have it!" was a comment Inglis heard frequently that evening from the insurgents demanding Katzenbach's nomination. [140] The managers of the insurgent candidates conferred in a last-ditch effort to stave off defeat and agreed that after the first ballot, all progressives should vote for the strongest anti-Wilson candidate. There were, however, rumors that Wittpenn would desert the progressive ranks and swing into line for Wilson. [141] The situation did not look at all encouraging for the anti-Wilson men, whose chief handicap was disorganization and lack of leadership.

As far as the actual business of the convention was concerned, there

[138] *Louisville Courier-Journal*, August 14, 1910.

[139] *Trenton True American*, September 14, 1910.

[140] W. O. Inglis, "Helping to Make a President," *Collier's Weekly*, LVIII (October 14, 1916), 13.

[141] *Trenton True American*, September 15, 1910.

was first the necessity of writing a platform for the party.[142] Nugent and the state committee on September 14 appointed a platform committee, and three Democrats set to work to draft a declaration of Democratic promises. Harvey, significantly, was constantly on hand during the committee's deliberations and was supposedly representing Wilson's interests. There was little disagreement on most of the planks and Wilson's hand could be seen in the demand for thorough state administrative reorganization and corporation control. A major fight developed, however, in the committee over the declaration on direct primaries. Progressives demanded, of course, a sweeping commitment to the principle of direct nominations for all elective officers, including United States senators. Wilson was irrevocably opposed to such a thoroughgoing reform and, through Harvey, made known his views to the platform committee. Consequently a plank demanding the direct nomination of all elective officers, which had been adopted by the committee, was withdrawn and a vague and meaningless declaration was adopted instead.[143] In spite of this note of discord, however, even James Kerney agreed that the platform was, on the whole, one of the most progressive the party had ever adopted.[144]

The Trenton House, headquarters of the politicians, was jammed with delegates and politicians on the eve of the convention and reeked of the smell of cheap cigars. Harvey and Smith worked desperately all night to corral votes for their candidate. "It was the busiest night of Smith's political life," Kerney afterward wrote. "Not only did he have Nugent actively at work on the firing-line, but old-timers like William J. Thompson, 'Duke of Gloucester,' of race track notoriety, Thomas Flynn, starter at the Gloucester track, and other handy workers were

[142] Wilson and Harvey had corresponded at length during the preceding month about the platform. They met in Boston in the latter part of August and discussed it further; by September 10 they had agreed on the draft proposals.

[143] *Trenton Evening Times,* September 15, 1910.

[144] The platform pledged the Democrats to the following program: (1) a thorough administrative reorganization that would secure economy and efficiency in the state administration; (2) the equalization of the tax burden, particularly as between individuals and railroads and other corporations; (3) the preservation and wise use of the school fund; (4) conservation of the state's natural resources; (5) the establishment of a public service commission with ample power to regulate rates and services; (6) the amendment of the employers' liability act so as to satisfy the reasonable demands of labor; (7) the eight-hour day in all public works; (8) state control of corporations so as to prevent monopolistic practices; (9) an efficient corrupt practices act; (10) a general plank favoring direct nominations; (11) extension of the civil service system to all administrative departments of the state, counties, and municipalities; (12) reciprocal interstate automobile legislation. *Trenton True American,* September 16, 1910.

drafted to round up the hungry patriots." [145] At times it seemed that the progressives might actually succeed in thwarting the plans of the Harvey-Smith-Davis junto. Harvey awoke Inglis at six o'clock in the morning of convention day. His face, Inglis relates, was worn and white. "Bill," Harvey said, "we're up against it. This man Silzer from New Brunswick has got the big northern counties away from us, and the senator can't get them back." If Wilson were not nominated on the first ballot, Harvey continued, he could not be nominated at all, and at that time Smith did not have a majority of the votes.[146] By noon, however, Harvey was confident that if Smith could hold the Essex County delegates in line he could nominate Wilson.

Trenton was overrun by Democratic enthusiasts who came to the city on September 15. In the morning the marching clubs, with their inevitable brass bands, made their appearance. There were rival clubs from Hudson County: one group was headed by Davis who wore conspicuously a large Wilson emblem; the other faction was smaller but marched and shouted for Wittpenn none the less. Shortly after eleven o'clock a tremendous throng of Democrats from Essex County arrived and marched to Smith's hotel.[147]

All of this was a prelude to the more important event. At exactly 12:22 P.M. Nugent walked on the stage of the Taylor Opera House and called to order the wildest and most tumultuous state convention New Jersey Democrats had seen in twenty years.[148] The auditorium was jammed with delegates and spectators. The Mercer County delegates, unanimous for Katzenbach's nomination, were in the balcony, surrounded by delegates from Union and Passaic. The large delegations from Essex, Hudson, Ocean, Atlantic, and Monmouth were seated on the main floor.[149] Harvey occupied a prominent place in one of the boxes, while some forty Princeton students and alumni, headed by Smith's son, were seated on the stage and frequently let go with the Princeton football yell.[150]

The Reverend Otis A. Glazebrook of Elizabeth set off the political fireworks by praying so fervently for Democratic success that the convention applauded enthusiastically at the end of his prayer. John R. Hardin and William K. Devereux were elected chairman and secretary

[145] J. Kerney, *The Political Education of Woodrow Wilson*, p. 52.
[146] W. O. Inglis, "Helping to Make a President," *loc. cit.*, p. 13.
[147] *Trenton Evening Times*, September 15, 1910.
[148] *New York World*, September 16, 1910.
[149] *Trenton True American*, September 16, 1910.
[150] *Trenton Evening Times*, September 15, 1910.

of the convention, and during Hardin's keynote address Smith and Davis dramatically entered the auditorium together. This little demonstration of party unity evoked widespread applause.[151]

It was 2:30 before the platform was read and adopted and the call of the counties for gubernatorial nominations was begun. When Atlantic was called, Clarence L. Cole, who had his instructions from Smith, stepped forward to nominate Wilson. He made a rousing speech and the mention of Wilson's name was greeted with faithful applause from the Essex and Hudson delegations. The anti-machine men, however, were in an ugly mood and frequently interrupted Cole with derisive shouts and catcalls. Shortly afterward, Smith rose pompously and in a conciliatory speech seconded Wilson's nomination and pleaded for party harmony.[152]

When Josiah Ewen of Burlington nominated Katzenbach, the Mercer delegates and townspeople began an enthusiastic demonstration; but when Judge John W. Wescott of Camden seconded Katzenbach's nomination, the convention was engulfed in a storm of applause and hisses. Wescott had come to the convention determined to rouse, by one method or another, the uncontrolled delegates to vote against the machine candidate. "Bargain and sale and the double cross will not obtain in this convention," he shouted. "The sun of demoralizing politics has set." The "financial machine" that was attempting to foist Wilson on the convention was "no longer a substitute for government by the people." [153] The progressive delegates greeted Wescott's defiant charges with tremendous applause and for a time it appeared that the delegates might actually be stampeded to Katzenbach by the fire of Wescott's oratory. One Smith lieutenant rushed at the speaker, shook his fist in his face, and shouted, "Damn you, you have beaten our candidate!" [154] It was a critical time for Smith, because the progressives and regulars were so evenly divided that he was not yet certain of Wilson's nomination.[155]

Silzer and several minor candidates were subsequently nominated and, after the seconding speeches had all been made, the balloting was begun at 4:30. It was Wilson on the first ballot. Smith's own county,

[151] *Trenton True American*, September 16, 1910.

[152] *ibid.; New York World*, September 16, 1910.

[153] *Trenton True American*, September 16, 1910.

[154] G. Barton, "Woodrow Wilson: His Human Side," *Current History*, XXII (April 1925), 6.

[155] *Trenton Evening Times*, September 15, 1910; *Trenton True American*, September 16, 1910.

Essex, was an almost solid unit for Wilson, and Davis managed to swing into line 162½ of the 238 votes from Hudson. Yet it was the widespread support Wilson received from the remaining nineteen counties that brought about his nomination. The total vote on the ballot was: Wilson 747½ (forty more votes than was necessary for a nomination), Katzenbach 373, Silzer 210, Wittpenn 76½, William Harrigan 6.[156] In customary manner, the nomination was made unanimous. The delegates were about to leave the auditorium when the convention secretary announced, "We have just received word that Mr. Wilson, the candidate for the governorship, *and the next President of the United States,* has received word of his nomination; has left Princeton, and is now on his way to the Convention." [157]

Throughout the tumult and confusion of convention eve and day, Woodrow Wilson had passed the time quietly at Princeton, oblivious of the momentous struggle in Trenton, of the hurried conferences in smoke-filled rooms, of the furtive visits of the organization lieutenants to the boss' room, or of the desperate counterstruggles of the progressives. After the convention had already got under way, Harvey instructed Inglis to bring Wilson from Princeton to Trenton. "Have him here at four o'clock," Harvey said, "for they can't reach a nomination before then." If Wilson should not be nominated, he continued, Inglis was to take him back to Princeton "without letting a soul know that he has been here." [158]

Edward W. Kemble, staff cartoonist for *Harper's Weekly,* joined Inglis and the two drove to Princeton. Wilson had been playing golf during the morning and was in excellent physical condition. He greeted Inglis and Kemble cordially and said, "Gentlemen, I am ready." Inglis noted that his clothes were unpretentious: he was wearing a soft, narrow-brimmed felt hat, a dark gray sack suit, and a knitted golf jacket under his coat. The three men drove rapidly back to the Trenton House and Wilson and Inglis went to Harvey's room by way of an inconspicuous side door. Inglis found it difficult to await with patience the decision of the convention, but Wilson was perfectly at ease "and chatted on indifferent topics as casually as if he were making an ordinary afternoon call." Finally, at ten after five, Inglis heard a nervous rapping on the outer door of Harvey's apartment. It was Cole of Atlantic who had nominated Wilson and who had come to tell him that

[156] *Trenton Evening Times,* September 16, 1910.
[157] J. P. Tumulty, *Woodrow Wilson As I Know Him,* p. 19.
[158] W. O. Inglis, "Helping to Make a President," *loc. cit.,* pp. 13-14.

he was the convention's "unanimous" choice for governor. "Thanks," Wilson replied, "I am ready." [159]

Wilson had already prepared his acceptance speech and he, Inglis, and Cole made their way through a cheering mob of Democrats who had gathered outside the Taylor Opera House. As he entered the back stage door one rough ward politician was heard to say, "God! look at that jaw!" [160] Wilson went directly to the stage and his appearance was the signal for an enthusiastic demonstration; but the progressives, "feeling sullen, beaten, and hopelessly impotent against the mass attack of the machine forces," [161] viewed suspiciously the man who had been the target of their bitter attacks and who had, they thought, cooperated with the bosses to block the reform movement.

Wilson began his acceptance speech with simple thanks for the nomination and for the honor the Democrats had done him. Then he suddenly launched a bolt of political independence that astonished the insurgents: "As you know," he declared, "I did not seek this nomination. It has come to me absolutely unsolicited. With the consequence that I shall enter upon the duties of the office of Governor, if elected, with absolutely no pledge of any kind to prevent me from serving the people of the State with singleness of purpose." Not only had no pledges of any kind been given by him, Wilson continued, but none had been proposed or desired by the organization leaders. The platform, he added, was "sound, explicit and business-like," and there could be no mistaking what it meant.[162]

This straightforward declaration of independence of machine control and unequivocal promise to stand by the platform electrified the delegates, who stood on their feet and shouted at the top of their voices. Their enthusiasm increased, moreover, with each succeeding phrase. Joe Tumulty, the young insurgent from Jersey City, and his friends were converted at once. "Thank God, at last, a leader has come!" they shouted.[163] New Jersey Democrats had seen no such party enthusiasm in a generation.[164] Wilson next proceeded to outline his views on the platform. It was significant, perhaps, that although he gave hearty approval to the various progressive measures demanded by the platform,

[159] *ibid.*, pp. 14, 40.
[160] Stockton Axson, Notes on various parts of R. S. Baker's MS biography of Wilson, in Baker Papers.
[161] J. P. Tumulty, *Woodrow Wilson As I Know Him*, p. 18.
[162] *Trenton True American*, September 16, 1910.
[163] J. P. Tumulty, *Woodrow Wilson As I Know Him*, p. 21.
[164] *New York World*, September 16. 1910.

he carefully avoided mention of direct primaries; he was, however, particularly anxious that New Jersey take the lead in controlling the activities of corporations and monopolies. He concluded his address with an appeal for idealism and a spirit of sacrifice on the part of the bosses, wardheelers, and progressive politicians assembled before him. The speech was at an end, but the delegates refused to let him quit the platform and shouted, "Go on, go on." Great tasks lay before the Democratic party, he added; Americans had to reconstruct their economic order, and in so doing would reconstruct their political organization. One great burst of oratory—a peroration on the flag—and Woodrow Wilson had completed his first political speech.[165]

It was a tremendous success, for Wilson's sincerity and appearance of utter political independence had transformed a mob of sullen and curious men into a band of enthusiastic Wilson advocates. John Crandall of Atlantic County, for example, a bitter foe of Wilson before the convention, was so elated that he waved his hat and cane in the air and yelled at the top of his voice, "I am sixty-five years old, and still a damn fool." [166] As Wilson finished his last sentence the crowd stood in their seats and cheered wildly.[167] Then there was a mad rush of delegates to greet the new leader. Men tried to lift him to their shoulders and carry him along to the exit to the street. A squad of policemen formed a hollow square about him and literally carried him to an automobile where Harvey and Inglis were waiting to take him to the comparative safety of the Trenton House.[168] It was slow progress the three men made, for excited Democrats insisted upon climbing on the running board of the car and shaking hands with the nominee. As the automobile crossed State Street, Wilson turned to Harvey and said, "What was my exact majority?" "Enough," the Colonel pungently replied, and Wilson understood.[169]

There was no doubt that Wilson's nomination was the most spectacular political event of 1910. Not all progressive Democrats were mollified

---

[165] *Trenton True American*, September 16-17, 1910.

[166] J. P. Tumulty, *Woodrow Wilson As I Know Him*, p. 22.

[167] "I have heard a great many efforts of this kind," wrote Representative William Hughes, congratulating Wilson on his acceptance speech, "and have been guilty of a few myself, but I can sincerely say that I have never listened to a more effective utterance by a candidate in all my experience. There were many men in that convention who were opposed to your nomination before you commenced to speak, but there were few, if any, who would have changed candidates by the time you had finished." W. Hughes to W. W., September 20, 1910, Wilson Papers.

[168] *New York World*, September 16, 1910.

[169] W. O. Inglis, "Helping to Make a President," *loc. cit.*, p. 41.

at once by the nominee's acceptance speech, for some of them, like Wescott, refused to stay in the convention hall when Wilson entered it.[170]
Yet most of them were satisfied at the outset that Wilson's nomination
might, in spite of all the things they had said to the contrary, mean the
inauguration of a new brand of Democratic politics in New Jersey.[171]
The organization men, on the other hand, were jubilant for entirely
different reasons. Robert Davis, who usually refused to prophesy about
political events, confidently predicted that Wilson would be elected by
a majority of 25,000.[172]

To the Democratic editors of New Jersey who had been championing
their party's cause through the long years of Democratic impotency,
Wilson's nomination came as an augury of better days to come for
party and for state. Harry E. Alexander, the original "Wilson" editor in
the state, led the editorial chorus and wrote in a happy vein of the "new
era which is dawning" in New Jersey politics.[173] The Democratic newspapers repeated that Wilson was the strongest candidate the party had
offered in a generation and that he would prove a fearless and independent leader,[174] while Smith's newspapers suggested that the nominee
might easily become the Democratic presidential hope of 1912.[175]

Actually more encouraging to Wilson was the enthusiastic reaction of
the progressive Republicans, for he recognized the simple fact that without the support of thousands of these men he could never be elected
governor. George L. Record's reaction was especially significant, since
he represented the opinions of many of his followers. "I have watched
the gubernatorial contests in New Jersey since 1883," Record wrote in
his column in the *Jersey Journal,* "and it is perfectly clear that during
that time the Democratic party has put forward no man who combines
the elements of high character and ability as a thinker and power as an
orator, as does Dr. Wilson." [176] Both of the leading New Idea newspapers were just as enthusiastic as Record about Wilson's nomination.
"His nomination marks a new era in New Jersey politics," one of them

---

[170] G. Barton, "Woodrow Wilson: His Human Side," *Current History,* xxii (April
1925), 6.
[171] See the statements of Wittpenn, Hughes, Martine, and Silzer in the *Trenton
Evening Times,* September 17, 1910.
[172] *ibid.*
[173] *Trenton True American,* September 16, 1910.
[174] See editorials in *Bergen County Democrat, Perth Amboy Evening News, Dover
Index,* and *New Brunswick News,* cited in *ibid.,* September 22, 1910; also *Trenton
Sunday Advertiser,* September 18, 1910.
[175] *Newark Evening Star,* September 16, 1910.
[176] *Jersey Journal* of Jersey City, September 19, 1910.

declared, adding significantly that Wilson would be "the candidate of thousands of Jerseymen, who have never been allied with the Democracy." [177] The *Jersey Journal* began to advocate Wilson's election the day after he was nominated.

Wilson soon discovered after the eventful September 15 that he had become almost a major national political figure. Newspapers and magazines, both radical and reactionary, throughout the country hailed him as a new Democratic leader. Colonel Harvey, perhaps deservedly, assumed leadership of the bearers of good tidings and wrote, "in character, in ability, in distinction, WOODROW WILSON is such a man as every Democrat who hopes to see his party regain its share in government must rejoice to see a candidate for the leading office in a leading State." [178] But other editors were equally enthusiastic. "Intellectually he is the foremost American Democrat," asserted one leading Democratic journal. [179] One of the editors of the *New York Times* wrote to Wilson that "the Times, as you know, already warmly supports your candidacy," [180] while the reactionary *New York Sun* declared that independent voters in New Jersey would support Wilson, "on account of his high ideals, his standards of public duty and his frankness and sincerity." [181]

During the days immediately following the Trenton convention, Wilson was overwhelmed by a flood of congratulatory letters and telegrams from well-wishers. Especially heartening to him were the messages from his old and intimate friends. "Three cheers and bully for you!

---

[177] *Newark Evening News*, September 16, 1910.

[178] *Harper's Weekly*, LIV (September 24, 1910), 4.

[179] *Brooklyn Daily Eagle*, cited in *ibid.*

[180] H. B. Brougham to W. W., September 15, 1910, Wilson Papers; see also the *New York Times*, September 17, 1910.

[181] *New York Sun*, September 15, 1910; see also the *New York Evening Post*, September 16, 1910.

Many of the national magazines that interested themselves in politics were also pleasantly surprised at what they interpreted as the political revolution in New Jersey. One liberal journal declared that Wilson's victory was "one of those electrifying events which makes politics seem worth while" (*Nation*, XCI [September 22, 1910], 256-257), while the *Outlook*, Theodore Roosevelt's spokesman, welcomed Wilson into the goodly fellowship of politicians and attributed to him progressive ideas he had never thought of entertaining (*Outlook*, XCVI [September 24, 1910], 140-141. "In general," this editorial concluded, "Dr. Wilson stands for a system of social democracy with which we are in hearty agreement."). Most observers agreed, however, that the New Jersey politicians had surprised the country by doing, as one journal put it, "an ideal thing" (*Review of Reviews*, XLII [October 1910], 393).

. . . The G.O.P. is in the soup!" Heath Dabney wrote from Charlottesville.[182] A. Lawrence Lowell, president of Harvard University, however, expressed a note of chagrin that his friend might soon be taking leave of the academic world. "So you have gone and done it!" Lowell wrote. "Are not the seas of university management boisterous enough that you must seek the storms of politics?"[183] From Alabama came this cheering greeting from an old classmate: "At any rate there is one newspaperman in Alabama, with a hand at the helm of two strong dailies, who will not forget his fondness for 'Tommie' Wilson in the old days at Princeton."[184]

From all over the country, often from complete strangers, came the good wishes of influential politicians, editors, lawyers, and laymen. Charles H. Grasty, editor of the *Baltimore Sun,* promised the support of his newspaper in the ensuing campaign,[185] while Colonel Watterson wrote, "Hurrah for Wilson. Am going to do my best."[186] Nathan Straus, Herman Ridder, Edward Bok, Willis Fletcher Johnson, William G. McAdoo, George B. McClellan, Norman E. Mack, chairman of the Democratic national committee, Simeon E. Baldwin, Democratic nominee for governor in Connecticut, and a number of other men sent their congratulations.[187] A young New York lawyer, William F. McCombs, who was later to manage Wilson's pre-convention presidential campaign, wrote with a flourish, "Princeton has produced the next president of the United States."[188]

Many of Wilson's correspondents were ardent Southerners who saw in him the South's great hope for presidential preferment. One Kentuckian, for example, voiced the aspirations of many Southerners when he wrote, "I sincerely hope that this may be but the stepping stone to the Presidency . . . and that through you the South may return to its former position of leadership in the Nation."[189] Southerners were indeed proud of this product of their own region and it is interesting that

---

[182] R. H. Dabney to W. W., September 18, 1910, Wilson Papers.

[183] A. L. Lowell to W. W., September 16, 1910, *ibid.*

[184] Frank P. Glass to W. W., September 19, 1910. Glass was part-owner of the *Montgomery Advertiser* and publisher of the *Birmingham News.*

[185] C. P. Grasty to W. W., September 16, 1910, Wilson Papers.

[186] H. Watterson to G. Harvey, September 16, 1910, copy in *ibid.*

[187] Letters from the above-mentioned correspondents are dated September 15-16, 1910, and are in *ibid.*

[188] W. F. McCombs to W. W., September 16, 1910, *ibid.*

[189] W. M. Jackson to W. W., September 17, 1910, *ibid.*

a majority of the letters Wilson received from outside New Jersey were from the southern states.[190]

The battle of the summer of 1910 was over and as Woodrow Wilson stood on the threshold of the political career he had at times longed for, he seemed to realize that the academic phase of his life was at an end. He realized that it is not easy for a man who has reached his fifty-third year to change his profession, his point of view, and, to a certain degree, his friends. He confessed that he had already experienced many pangs of doubt whether he had "done the right thing or not." But he was certain that he had done the only thing he could have done under the circumstances and resolved firmly to "start out upon the new career as bravely as possible." [191]

[190] Among the southern correspondents were George L. Denny, president of Washington and Lee University; George Bryan, Hundson Cary, and Archibald W. Patterson of Richmond; Lucian H. Cocke, of Roanoke; James A. Hoyt, editor of the *Columbia* (S. C.) *Daily Record;* Albert C. Ritchie, of Baltimore; Pleasant A. Stovall, editor of the *Savannah Evening Press;* Harry St. George Tucker, of Lexington, Virginia; J. Taylor Ellyson, lieutenant-governor of Virginia; Desha H. Breckinridge, of Lexington, Kentucky; and Lewis M. Coleman, of Chattanooga. All of these men were afterwards leaders in the Wilson movement in the South.

[191] W. W. to A. L. Lowell, September 20, 1910, Wilson Papers.

CHAPTER VI

The First Campaign

WOODROW WILSON had been launched upon his political career by as strange a combination of persons and circumstances as had ever attended the inauguration of any political career in the annals of American history. His candidacy, boss-engineered and boss-supported, was now full grown and he stood forth as the unchallenged Democratic candidate for the governorship. He was, however, in no sense yet the leader of his party, for James Smith, Jr., James R. Nugent, and Robert Davis still ruled with an iron hand the party machinery, from the county committees up to the state organization, and the nominee had hardly thought, much less dared, to challenge their leadership.

It was Wilson's supreme accomplishment during the gubernatorial campaign that he succeeded in winning the support of the progressives without at the same time alienating the support of the machine leaders in the party organization. It was Smith and Nugent, in fact, who initiated him into the secrets of the political guild. Four days after the Trenton convention Wilson met Smith, Nugent, and James Kerney at a conference in Princeton to discuss the organization of the campaign. There was first of all the problem of Wilson's relation to the University; he had not yet resigned the presidency of Princeton and wished to reserve the first three days in each week for his work there. Moreover, he had his own ideas as to how a campaign should be conducted and informed Smith and Nugent that he was temperamentally unable to carry on a handshaking, baby-kissing, old-fashioned whirlwind campaign. He would prefer, he added, to make one evening speech in each county.[1] Nugent accordingly agreed to prepare an itinerary of campaign speeches for the nominee. By September 25 the itinerary had been arranged and Wilson was scheduled to deliver some twenty-seven speeches before the election in November.[2]

The Princeton conference had also another purpose: Wilson wanted to meet personally the Mercer County politicians and to endeavor to

[1] James Kerney, *The Political Education of Woodrow Wilson,* p. 63.
[2] W. W. to D. B. Jones, September 25, 1910, copy in Baker Papers.

swing them into line behind his candidacy. Mercer, Wilson's home county, had unanimously opposed his nomination in the state convention, and he was frankly worried about this. Smith, too, realized the precarious nature of the situation and, immediately after the convention, asked Kerney to prepare a list of the local party leaders. Wilson had accordingly sent letters inviting all of them to the Princeton meeting on September 19. Before the arrival of the Mercer men, Wilson discussed local politics avidly with Kerney, Smith, and Nugent. "The manner in which he grasped every suggestion was a revelation," Kerney afterward recalled. After the county leaders had been formally presented to Wilson, he launched into a discussion of local political affairs, "as if they were the one thing in all the world in which he had been taking an interest." [3]

When the issues and the practical details of campaign management were discussed, however, Wilson at first displayed an amusing naïveté and ignorance. When, for example, on September 19 he gave out his first public interview after his nomination, he seemed to be at a complete loss to know what to say about state affairs. He made a feint at discussing the tariff, conservation, and corporation control, all national issues with which he was more or less familiar. The interviewer, however, wanted to know something about his attitude with regard to state issues and asked him to amplify his views, especially with regard to direct primaries. In good professorial language Wilson contrived to make as artful a dodge of the real issue involved as one usually encounters. "The entire question of whether we shall have a representative or a delegated government," he declared, "leads back to the primary discussion of whether the legislator should be a mere deputy, going to Washington or Trenton to act as directed by his constituents . . . or whether he will be allowed to exercise his own judgment, after first hand information has been gained through exhaustive and informing debate in the legislative halls." He personally thought, Wilson added, that legislators should be allowed to do their own thinking. The reporter attempted to persuade Wilson to explain his views more definitely and Wilson countered with a statement that must have mystified him all the more. [4] The truth of the matter was that Wilson, although

[3] J. Kerney, *The Political Education of Woodrow Wilson*, p. 64.

[4] "I think the statement of the platform regarding that a very excellent one," Wilson added. "It declares for such a simplification of the electoral machinery as will make possible the effectual exercise of the right of direct nominations for all elective offices. The forms of the direct primary are so various that with my limited knowledge I cannot be specific, but it is my intention to give the entire problem careful consideration. I

he apparently opposed it, simply refused to commit himself against a measure he knew a majority of the Democratic voters supported.

Wilson also had rather naive ideas about the not inconsequential matter of financing a political campaign. His Chicago friend, David B. Jones, sent him a check of an unknown amount soon after the nomination and Wilson was deeply moved by this evidence of friendship and confidence. "I do not remember anything that ever touched me more or made me happier," Wilson wrote in returning Jones's check. "You have treated me as you would have treated your own brother." He was returning the proffered contribution, however, because he wanted to be able to say, if possible, that he had "paid every cent of . . . [his] own personal expenses in this campaign out of . . . [his] own pocket." Wilson concluded: "I do not think that . . . [the expenses] will run above a few hundred dollars; and I have arranged to deliver three addresses after the election which will net me five hundred dollars in fees. I made the engagements with the express purpose of earning the money for that object. Friends at every turn are putting their automobiles at my service; I shall have only hotel bills, the fares for short railway journeys, and the fees for extra stenographic services to pay. It will not come to much, all put together. If I get stuck, I will not hesitate to call on you for what I cannot do." [5] Later, however, when he discovered that campaigning can be an extremely expensive proposition, Wilson welcomed financial aid from his friends.

The gubernatorial campaign got under way in earnest when the Democratic state committee set up headquarters in Newark, with Jim Nugent in command, on September 26.[6] It soon promised to shape up into a real fight, for the Republicans, meeting in state convention a week after the Democrats, were fully aware of the fact that Wilson's nomination had created an unusual political situation. They nominated for the governorship Vivian M. Lewis of Paterson, who was in 1910 state commissioner of banking and insurance. Lewis was no weak antagonist. For nearly twenty years he had been active in public life as a lawyer, legislator, and administrator and, although he was not identified with the New Idea faction of his party, Lewis was no Old Guard reactionary. He was a middle-of-the-road progressive, sufficiently pro-

understand thirty States have some form of direct primary expression. The principle is certainly a most excellent one, but the method of expression, which is of first consequence, is not, by any means, settled." *Trenton True American,* September 19, 1910.

[5] W. W. to D. B. Jones, September 25, 1910, copy in Baker Papers.

[6] *Trenton True American,* September 27, 1910.

gressive, the Republican leaders hoped, to be able to hold the insurgents in line on election day. Although the Republican platform was not as liberal as the Democratic, it did give party approval to a public utilities commission with "the power to fix just and reasonable rates for service rendered." Lewis personally wanted a platform declaration promising an extension of the primary system, but the state organization prevented any such wholesale commitment to reform.[7]

On September 28 Wilson officially inaugurated his campaign for the governorship with a series of three speeches in the Democratic stronghold of Jersey City. He had dinner with State Chairman Nugent in Newark and afterwards the two men drove in the Newark boss's automobile to Jersey City. They arrived at the club house of the Robert Davis Association a few minutes before eight and Nugent escorted the nominee into the headquarters of the city machine and introduced him to the Hudson County politicians. It was Wilson's first meeting with Davis, and the two men must have made a striking contrast: Wilson, lean, intellectual, with something of the schoolmaster about him; Davis, bald and stout, the perfect example of a ward-heeling boss! "Howdy do," was Davis's simple greeting. "How do you do, Mr. Davis. I am very glad to see you, sir," was Wilson's reply.[8]

There were a score or more Democratic stalwarts in the reception room, waiting to meet the nominee. After the pleasantries were over these machine leaders formed a sort of cordon around Wilson and escorted him to the three Democratic meetings at which he spoke. They went first to St. Peter's Hall, where Wilson made his principal address. Significantly, there were no representatives of the Wittpenn organization on the platform that was crowded with Wilson's newly found friends.

It was Wilson's first appeal for political support and he was obviously ill at ease. "I never before appeared before an audience and asked for anything," he confessed to his listeners, "and now I find myself in the novel position of asking you to vote for me for Governor of New Jersey." He then proceeded to declare that he had not sought the nomination, that the organization leaders had nominated him with the understanding that he was "under no obligation to any individual or group of individuals," and that if the voters of New Jersey elected him governor he would be under obligation "to serve them and them only."

[7] *Trenton Evening Times,* September 21, 1910; the account in the *Trenton True American,* September 21, 1910, is biased in Wilson's favor.
[8] *Jersey Journal* of Jersey City, September 29, 1910.

Wilson made his chief plea, not for himself, however, but for the Democratic party, which he declared was a free agent to serve the people of the state in the matter of reform. "I wish to be your servant," he explained, "not because of any particular qualification of mine, but because I sincerely believe that the Democratic party can be of real service to the State." [9] As the speech progressed, however, Wilson's old oratorical skill seemed to fail him. He hesitated, fumbled for words, and dragged in a Negro story that had no connection with what he was saying. [10]

It was indeed an unusual sort of stump speech, and perhaps for that reason Wilson struck few responsive chords in his audience. There was not, for example, a word about "sweeping the state" or "driving the Republican hosts into the sea"; there was no mention of "the enemy," no exhortation to "stand by the party," nothing about "loyalty to the cause." In fact Wilson made it clear that he had no indictment to make of the great mass of Republican voters. "I hope sincerely that you will never hear me in the course of this campaign saying anything against that great body of our fellow citizens who have believed in the principles of the Republican party," he declared. "What I want you to understand me as doing is this: I believe that the great body of citizens is now led by persons who are not capable of realizing in a proper public spirit the great principles of the Republican party any more than they can win the acquiescence of those persons who believe in the great principles of the Democratic party."

As he was about to finish the address, Wilson stepped forward to the front of the platform and said, "And so, gentlemen, I have made my first political plea. I have endeavored . . ." This simple, artless appeal aroused an emotional response from the audience that all of his previous professions had not evoked, and the audience stood and cheered for several minutes. [11]

Wilson's progressive supporters throughout the state were disappointed in the Democratic candidate's "first political plea." It was true of course, as George L. Record pointed out, that he had completely ignored the issues in which all independent voters were interested: the relation between corrupt political bosses and big business, the fraud at primaries and general elections, and the need for state control of public utilities. "His three speeches, as they are reported in the papers," Record

[9] *ibid.; Trenton True American,* September 29, 1910.
[10] Stockton Axson, Notes on R. S. Baker's biography of Wilson, MS in Baker Papers.
[11] *Trenton True American,* September 29, 1910.

commented, "are extremely weak, and it is no wonder the independent minded hearers were disappointed." [12] It was, moreover, nothing less than farcical for Wilson to describe the New Jersey Democratic party as the only political agent free to serve the people. The party had been so thoroughly discredited by boss and corporation dominance that the less Wilson said about it during the campaign the better it would be for his chances of election. The leading Democratic journal in the state pronounced what amounted to the final, if severe, word on the Jersey City addresses: "Dr. Wilson did not discuss a living State issue. All he did was to give his hearers a revamped edition of his speech on miscellaneous corporations, which he has been delivering, with variations, for five years. . . . Aside from that he pleaded that the ins be put out and the outs be put into control of the State machinery." [13]

Perhaps Wilson was profoundly disturbed by these manifold criticisms of his Jersey City addresses, as Tumulty suggests,[14] yet he was only slightly more explicit on the campaign issues in his address at Plainfield on September 29. He even repeated the amusing, but solemn, declaration that the Democratic party, boss-ridden and boss-controlled as it obviously was, was a free agent for political reform.[15] The progressives still insisted, as the *Jersey Journal* put it on September 30, "Wilson should discuss the issues."

Events were crowding the passing days of the campaign for the Democratic candidate. On September 30, for example, he spent the afternoon conferring with Mercer County Democrats at the Inter-State Fair at Trenton; during the evening he made an important address at Newark. It was his first speech of the campaign in Smith's city and as he stood in the Krueger Auditorium he must have realized that the boss' lieutenants were carefully scrutinizing him. "You want from me, I suppose, a confession of faith," he began, "and I am ready to make it. I stand absolutely without equivocation for every plank in the platform." What was more important, he stood "for some more planks" that were not included in the platform.

Wilson proceeded to launch into a hard-hitting discussion of the problem of corporation control that lasted for half an hour. He had insisted upon a platform declaration, he declared, condemning the inordinate

[12] *Jersey Journal* of Jersey City, October 3, 1910.
[13] *Hudson Observer* of Hoboken, cited in the *Trenton Evening Times,* October 1, 1910.
[14] *Woodrow Wilson As I Know Him,* pp. 28-30.
[15] *Trenton True American,* September 30, 1910.

hospitality New Jersey had shown to "any or all corporations," but such a plank had not been included in the platform. Competition was being stifled by monopolies, he continued, yet not a single law had been enacted by the New Jersey legislature to curb the power of the trusts. He objected not to automobiles, he added by way of introducing a simile that he was to use many times, but to persons who were taking "joy rides" in automobiles. "The trouble seems to be," he pointed out, "that some men are taking joy rides in their corporations." What was needed, he asserted, was direct intervention and control by the state.

This was straightforward enough, and the audience yelled its approval. His critics were saying that Wilson was not specific, that he was evading the real issues of the campaign. Very well, he would give them a confession of faith that could not be misunderstood. "I believe that the great bodies of the people have the right of direct nomination for office," he began his new progressive credo. "I believe that the people of this State are entitled to a Public Service Commission, which has full power to regulate rates," he continued. "I believe it would be wise to . . . pass an act in favor of a constitutional amendment allowing the people to vote directly for their Senators," he added; and he proceeded to set forth a ringing declaration of his fundamental faith in democracy, in "that great voiceless multitude of men who constitute the great body and the saving force of the nation." He declared, for the first time, his conviction that the people of New Jersey were in the midst of a great political revolution, were seeking after new and better methods of conducting their political life, and that he, Woodrow Wilson, represented the cause of political regeneration.[16]

Wilson's confession of faith was his solemn pledge of fidelity to the people's cause, a declaration of his determined purpose to fight for their welfare and to do battle with malfeasant corporations. Certainly it caught the fancy of the audience. "Ye gods, but that was a great speech," cried Judge Simon Hahn, who occupied one of the boxes. James Smith, Jr., too, was measurably moved. "Wasn't that great?" he shouted amid the storm of applause that followed Wilson's speech. "The man is going to win, he's going to win." [17]

Wilson's speech at Newark was for him the watershed, the turning point of the gubernatorial campaign. It was already apparent to him, as

[16] *ibid.*, October 1, 1910.
[17] Charles Reade Bacon, *A People Awakened*, pp. 36-37. This is a compilation of Bacon's daily reports to the *Philadelphia Daily Record* and provides the most valuable single collection of Wilson's speeches during the gubernatorial campaign.

it was to all other observers in the state, that he would have to abandon
the caution and ambiguity that had characterized his first campaign utterances; that he could not possibly hope to win the governorship without the support of the progressive Republicans and independents; and
that he could not win their votes unless he committed himself wholeheartedly to the reform cause. The speech at Newark, therefore, marked
Wilson's break with his conservative past, a break that was occasioned
as much by reasons of political expediency as by any other factor. Perhaps it was a realization of his powers of leadership, of his ability to
move by simple oratory a great audience, that gave him the strength
and confidence necessary for this new role of leadership he was rapidly
assuming. At any rate, the halting phrase, the embarrassment of campaigning for votes had given way to a feeling of confidence and a new
spirit of jaunty aggressiveness; and sometimes a note of triumph crept
into his subsequent addresses. The apprenticeship was over.

Wilson followed up his Newark address with a speech at Trenton
on October 3 that was, if anything, more explicit and straightforward
on the campaign issues than his Newark speech had been.[18] It was his
first address in Trenton since his nomination on September 15, and he
began his speech by pleasantly recalling the circumstances in which he
had made his memorable address accepting the gubernatorial nomina-

[18] Wilson, it should be noted, did not strike out his new progressive course without
the prompting and tutoring of his friends. Among the most interesting letters of the
campaign are those scribbled in pencil on rough copy paper now yellow with age by
Harry E. Alexander, editor of the *Trenton True American*.

Several days before Wilson made his Trenton address, Alexander volunteered some
trenchant advice as to what he should say. "Monday night you begin your second week
in the campaign," the Trenton editor wrote. "You have given the voters of the state
ample opportunity to size you up and the scrutiny has been all to your advantage. Now
you proceed logically to *specifications*." Wilson should plant himself squarely on his own
position with regard to the right and duty of the governor "to fight *for the people* with
all the power that they have voted to him," Alexander wrote. Wilson, moreover, should
declare that he would not permit bosses or "any Board of Guardians" to rule the state.
"*The people of the whole state will be electrified by such a declaration*," Alexander
added. He proceeded to give Wilson advice on other specific details: Wilson should emphasize his approval of legislation establishing a powerful public utilities commission;
he should denounce the Republican nominee, Lewis, because he was controlled by the
Republican state machine. Lewis had stated, Alexander continued, that he would be a
"constitutional governor" and that he would not attempt to influence the legislators to
vote for reform measures. Wilson, however, should tell the people, Alexander insisted,
that "if *you* people (address them directly in second person) elect me as your Governor
and bring me to Trenton to serve you, I pledge myself to do precisely what Mr. Lewis
says that he will not do." H. E. Alexander to W. W., ca. October 1, 1910, and October
2, 1910, Wilson Papers.

Compare Alexander's suggested statements with Wilson's address at Trenton.

tion. "I now ask you," he declared, "if you approve of that nomination, and will support me." There were loud shouts of "Yes, yes" from the audience and Wilson then proceeded to tell the people of Trenton what kind of governor they might expect if he were elected. Lewis, he asserted, had told the Republican convention that if he was elected he would endeavor to be a "constitutional governor" and that he would not attempt to coerce the legislature into enacting laws it did not want to enact. "Now, I cannot be that kind of a constitutional Governor," declared the Democratic nominee. "If you elect me, you will elect a Governor, who, in the opinion of Mr. Lewis, will be an unconstitutional Governor." Of course he would bring no immoral or unconstitutional pressure to bear upon the legislature, but he was determined to be the people's spokesman before the legislators. And, he furthermore promised, if the legislature did not enact the sort of laws he thought the people were demanding, he would "take every important subject of debate in the Legislature out on the stump and discuss it with the people."

The Trenton speech was one of Wilson's greatest addresses during the entire campaign, yet it was a hodgepodge. He admitted, on the one hand, that corruption was rampant in both major parties, but corruption thrived only in darkness and for that reason he stood solidly behind the passage of a stringent corrupt practices act. He came out squarely for an effective public utilities commission and for economy and efficiency in the state administration. He made an obvious bid for the independent and New Idea vote by declaring that these progressives held the balance of power in the election and that "the beauty of the present situation, as I see it, is that the Democratic party . . . have got into an insurgent frame of mind." Finally, he concluded with a dramatic appeal for the support and confidence of the voters. "I am pleading [with you] to make me, if you trust me," he said, "a representative of these new ideas, a spokesman of these purposes, so that I may be some humble instrument." [19]

Wilson's speech-making during the first three weeks of October reveals a progressive movement toward the left, a greater determination to seize control of Democratic leadership, a burning desire on Wilson's part to be identified with the progressive movement in the state. At Woodbury on October 5, for example, he took occasion to answer Record's charges that he was not discussing the campaign issues plainly

---

[19] *Trenton True American*, October 4, 1910.

enough. "I am perfectly content," he declared, "to represent the re-organized Democratic party." He did not deign to explain, however, how and when the party had become "reorganized."[20] He also displayed an attitude of strong antagonism toward the Republican state leaders and time and again attacked the Board of Guardians, the Republican state committee, because of the alleged domination of the party by corporation and railroad interests. He even attacked the Republican candidate, not personally of course, but as the representative of an organization that no longer represented the people. Wilson did not think that he was more honest than Lewis, he declared at Burlington on October 7, but he did believe he was a freer man than his opponent.[21] He had moved so rapidly toward the progressive wing of his party that he could with apparent sincerity say by October 11, "I am and always have been an insurgent."[22]

Wilson was trying hard to avoid generalities and meaningless utterances; he realized the widespread extent of the popular demand that he speak in more definite terms—"They have accused me of indulging in glittering generalities," he declared on one occasion. After the speeches at Newark and Trenton early in October, however, he succeeded in satisfying the demands of most of his progressive critics. He reiterated his belief that public utilities should be regulated by a commission that had authority to fix rates;[23] he declared that his cause was the purification of the state's political life, and for that reason he demanded the passage of a stringent corrupt practices act;[24] he made more emphatic his former asseveration that he was in no way connected with a political machine. On October 15, when he spoke at Asbury Park, Smith and Harvey were seated together in the auditorium and heard the nominee solemnly declare, "I want to say, parenthetically, that if you find out that I have been or ever intend to be connected with a machine of any kind I hope you will vote against me."[25]

[20] *ibid.,* October 6, 1910.

[21] *Trenton Evening Times,* October 7, 1910.

[22] C. R. Bacon, *A People Awakened,* p. 95.

[23] At Paterson on October 11, for example, he singled out the powerful monopoly, the Public Service Corporation, as one utility corporation that should be regulated. *Trenton True American,* October 12, 1910. At Atlantic City on October 13, he told his audience that the price of natural gas would be half what they were accustomed to paying if an efficient commission were at work in the state. *ibid.,* October 14, 1910.

[24] "New Jersey's election laws would be ludicrous if they were not so loose and evil," Wilson told an audience at Tom's River on October 14. "Why, the very system of letting a man register by proxy and transfer his registration lends itself to fraud, and to have ballots privately distributed and marked so that the buyers of the votes can tell that they get what they pay for, is just as bad." *ibid.,* October 15, 1910.

[25] *ibid.,* October 17, 1910.

There was, however, one outstanding question that had yet to be answered by the Democratic nominee: his attitude toward organized labor. It was an ominous sign, the Democratic managers thought, that the state labor leaders had not rescinded the resolution adopted at a meeting of the State Federation of Labor in August, calling upon New Jersey workingmen to vote against Wilson should he become the gubernatorial candidate. Wilson returned to Trenton on October 18 to answer his critics among the working classes. He spoke before the Democratic League of Mercer County and proceeded to discuss the steady attacks the Republicans were making upon his formerly expressed labor opinions, attacks that "distressed" him all the more because he claimed he had been "so consistently, persistently, and malignantly" misrepresented with regard to his attitude toward organized labor.[26]

Wilson explained that his previous criticisms of labor organizations had grown out of a solicitude on his part for the interests of the workingmen themselves and that the laborers should recognize that the Republicans were proverbial false friends who neither represented them nor would legislate in their interests. A few days later he spoke again on the labor question before a large gathering of workingmen assembled at Phillipsburg. He had criticized labor organizations, Wilson further explained, because he had been afraid that labor, like capital, was developing a class consciousness all its own and identifying its own exclusive interests with the interests of the community as a whole. Thus, he continued:

"When you form a class or a caste and get into the habit of thinking in and for it alone, you are helping to make actual popular government almost an impossibility. Without popular opinion there cannot be popular government. How can there be a popular opinion representing the beliefs and desires at large when the people are divided into classes and organizations narrowing their thinking down to within their own circles?

"The trouble is that we do not think of the people in that way. Do capitalists constitute the people? Certainly not. Do the merchants constitute the people? Certainly not. When you speak of the people are you thinking of levels? Are you thinking of those who are poor, are you thinking of those who are well-to-do, . . . are you thinking of those who are very rich? The interesting thing is that the people consist of all these classes put together; it does not consist of any one, it does not con-

[26] *ibid.*, October 19, 1910.

sist of any two of them, or of any combination, except the combination that constitutes the whole." [27]

Wilson's efforts to win the votes of the workers by asserting that he had not really meant what he had said previously about labor unions in the way he had said it may have mollified many individual laborers; the officials of the state labor federation, however, were unconvinced and refused to withdraw their resolution condemning Wilson's candidacy.

It is interesting that during the period before Wilson's letter to George L. Record, definitely defining the campaign issues, was published on October 24, the Democratic nominee was gradually consolidating his position as a spokesman of all the progressive forces. The speeches of the few days preceding the publication of the letter to Record are especially indicative of this development in Wilson's thought. He was becoming more and more specific in his addresses, more and more inclined to discuss the details of progressive reform.[28] He had long since ceased to attempt to manufacture excuses for the dubious record of the New Jersey Democratic party and had changed his entire conception of the essential meaning of the campaign. "If it were my function to excuse a party," he declared, "if it were my task to seek an office for the sake of getting an office for a party, I would have nothing to do with the campaign." [29] The gubernatorial contest was in Wilson's mind no longer the concerted effort of the members of one political party to gain control of the state. It had become a crusade for political regeneration, "for free and pure politics," a movement "little short of a revolution in American politics."

One thing at least was obvious, that Wilson's campaign speeches were creating considerable stir in political circles throughout the country. The newspapers of New York and Philadelphia gave more space in their columns to his canvass than had been given to any other New Jersey campaign within a generation. Oswald G. Villard was true to his promise to campaign for Wilson's election, and his *New York Evening Post* carried frequent accounts of Wilson's speeches. Charles Reade Bacon, ace reporter for the *Philadelphia Record,* wrote daily reports for his newspapers, while the *New York Times,* the *New York Sun,* and the *New York World* sent special reporters into the field to gather news of the campaign.

It was not simply that another gubernatorial contest was in progress

[27] *ibid.,* October 22, 1910.

[28] See, for example, his speech at Somerville on October 19, *ibid.,* October 20, 1910.

[29] Address at Somerville, October 19, *loc. cit.*

in New Jersey that caused this widespread interest. It was the nature of the contest and the character of the Democratic candidate that were chiefly responsible. As most observers had predicted, Wilson was turning out to be a fascinating character, an unusual campaigner, so unique a personality in Democratic politics that his utterances often commanded a priority on front-page newspaper space. As one astute observer put it, "The one thing that is new is a personality, and upon that personality is focused just now the attention of the whole country." [30] It was significant, too, that the *New York Times,* certainly no idolizer of persons, declared as early as October 5, "There is not much risk in saying that Dr. WILSON has the makings of a statesman. He certainly has the statesman's point of view and breadth of sympathy and comprehension. He is an extremely good specimen of a leader in these times when a cool head, a trained intellect, and sound moral sense are particularly needed." [31]

Wilson's cause was of course heartily championed by all the Democratic editors in the state, for most of them had since early summer seen the great possibilities inherent in his candidacy. Alexander realized early in the contest the necessity of presenting the Democratic nominee to the people as a rampant progressive. "Woodrow Wilson is UNITING THE INSURGENT FORCES of New Jersey," the Trenton editor wrote in mid-October. "He is fast becoming the very embodiment of the insurgent idea." [32] In addition to the support of the Democratic press, Wilson also had the powerful aid of the two leading independent newspapers, the *Jersey Journal* and the *Newark Evening News,* both of which never once wavered in their advocacy of Wilson's election.

It should not, however, be assumed that the campaign was entirely a one-sided affair, for Wilson had serious opposition from his Republican rival. Perhaps it was because he believed sincerely in the righteousness of the progressive cause, or perhaps it was the constant hammering by the Democratic candidate that forced Lewis gradually to move toward the left as the campaign progressed. He came out strongly in favor of equipping the public utilities commission with rate-making authority; he asserted his belief that the direct primary law should be extended so as to include candidates for Congress and for the governorship; he

[30] "Woodrow Wilson and the New Jersey Governorship," *Review of Reviews,* XLII (November 1910), 556.
[31] *New York Times,* October 5, 1910; also the *New York Sun,* October 6, 1910; *New York World,* October 23, 1910.
[32] *Trenton True American,* October 13, 1910.

avowed his belief in the popular election of United States senators; he urged the passage of a stringent corrupt practices law. In fact, Lewis heartily endorsed all the measures the adoption of which Wilson was advocating. As if to prove to the people of the state the genuine character of his progressivism, furthermore, Lewis declared that "if the Republican party turns down progressivism it will cease to be a party," and again, "I believe the people of this State demand what we term progressive legislation."[33] Lewis occupied a position similar to Wilson's precarious position as the new leader of the Democratic party. Both men were candidates of parties that were largely boss-controlled; both were obviously far more progressive than their party leaders. Although it was true that the Republicans could present a record of more solid progressive achievement, the gubernatorial campaign in New Jersey was essentially a contest of personalities. Wilson's professions were no more progressive than Lewis's; if he won the governorship he would win by some dramatic act or utterance that caught the fancy and won the approval of the independent voters.

If Lewis rapidly abandoned the heights of Republican stalwartism, the mounting fury of Wilson's attacks did not budge the leaders of the Republican machine from their conservative position. They at first pretended to regard Wilson's candidacy as of little importance. "He is running for Governor," commented Senator John Kean, a member of the Board of Guardians, "with the idea of reforming the whole State, although he never considered it worth while to give the people the benefit of his advice until he became a candidate for Governor." "Now don't you people worry about South Jersey on election-day," remarked David Baird, Republican czar of Camden, "for we propose to lick this man."[34]

It did not, however, take the Republican managers long to discover that Wilson was a dangerous opponent, and during the latter weeks of the contest they inaugurated a campaign of calumny against the Democratic nominee that betrayed their growing alarm. They circulated numerous circulars and pamphlets that charged that Wilson was an enemy of labor unions, that he was antagonistic toward the Catholic Church, that he had spoken in a disparaging manner of the American flag, and that he was politically insincere.[35] What the *True American*

[33] *ibid.*, October 19, 1910.

[34] Both quotations are taken from *Harper's Weekly*, LIV (October 22, 1910), 4.

[35] The anti-Wilson campaign is described in the *Trenton True American*, November 7, 1910.

termed the "pinnacle" of the Republican state committee's "campaign of falsehood" was a paid political advertisement, published in Hebrew in the *New York Jewish Daily News* shortly before the election, which charged that Wilson was an enemy of unrestricted immigration and that he "prefers Chinese as workingmen and citizens to the immigrants that arrive in eastern ports." [36]

The Democratic organization, on the other hand, was extremely well coordinated and united behind the leadership of Smith and Nugent, while Davis and his Hudson County machine for once cooperated wholeheartedly with the Newark bosses. Never before had the Democratic machines been so well oiled and run so smoothly. Speakers by the score toured the state and aroused enthusiasm for the Democratic ticket, while Wilson clubs were organized in most of the cities and towns by loyal Democrats. A spirit of confidence and optimism seemed to pervade the ranks of the party workers.

Effective political organization is an expensive proposition and the funds with which to finance the campaign had, for the most part, to be raised by the Democratic state committee. Some of Wilson's friends added their contributions to the party's campaign coffers. Colonel Harvey, for example, canvassed the list of his friends for donations and succeeded in collecting almost $10,000 from an astounding array of the financial and industrial leaders of the country, many of whom were the so-called "malefactors of great wealth." [37] It is impossible to calculate with any degree of certainty the amount the organization leaders expended during the campaign. Smith afterward declared that the state committee obtained $3,500 from certain Princeton friends of Wilson,

---

[36] This refers to a famous passage in the fifth volume of Wilson's *History of the American People,* which was later exploited by his opponents during the presidential pre-convention campaign. This will be discussed in a subsequent chapter; the above incident is interesting as the first example of this specific anti-Wilson attack.

[37] Harvey wrote soon after the November election, describing in detail his list of contributors, a number of whom were Republicans and Union Leaguers. Harvey's list of contributors included Thomas F. Ryan, notorious financier and utilities czar, whom Harvey described as "'a Virginia Democrat,' who always responds generously to anything in which I am personally interested"; Frederick H. Eaton, president of the American Car and Foundry Company; George W. Young, Jersey City banker; Francis L. Stetson, president of the Northern Pacific Railroad and general counsel for several great corporations; Wayne MacVeagh, attorney-general in Garfield's cabinet; Patrick Calhoun, utilities magnate; Clarence Hill Kelsey, president of the Title Guarantee and Trust Company of New York; Benjamin F. Yoakum, railroad magnate of the Southwest; John D. Crimmins, New York banker and real estate dealer; and J. Hampden Robb, retired banker of New York. G. Harvey to W. W., November 14, 1910, Wilson Papers.

that he personally contributed $50,000 to the campaign fund, and that all in all the Democratic managers collected and spent some $119,000 during the course of the campaign.[38] The sum does not seem unreasonable.

There is absolutely no doubt, therefore, that in spite of Wilson's frequent protestations of independence of and antagonism toward the political machines of both parties, the Democratic state organization fought loyally and skillfully for his election in November. Smith had been profoundly moved by Wilson's campaign appeals; he could applaud just as vigorously as any progressive when Wilson launched a general attack on political organizations. Yet the growing political independence of his candidate secretly worried the Newark boss and on one occasion he is reputed to have declared that Wilson was "a Presbyterian priest and the devil of a fellow to handle on the liquor question." [39] Smith at first consoled himself with the thought that Wilson's condemnation of party machines was a mere campaign gesture,[40] but he must have realized the irreconcilable nature of the rift that was already developing between himself and Wilson even before Wilson came out and openly attacked the Smith machine.

Yet in spite of his condemnation of political bosses, Wilson's continued and conspicuous fraternal relations with the Democratic machine leaders was becoming more irritating to the progressive leaders every day the campaign progressed. They were willing to take Wilson at his word and believe that he was under no obligation to the organization, but what they demanded from him was more than a mere profession of political independence. They insisted that he repudiate the organization's support of his candidacy. Even by the latter part of October, Kerney had not been converted to the Wilson cause and his newspaper had not once advocated Wilson's election, largely because the Trenton editor believed that the organization would dominate Wilson's administration if he were elected. "Thus far," Kerney wrote in his *Trenton Evening Times* on October 22, ". . . Dr. Wilson has given no particular indications that, in the event of his election, the state will not be managed by the Democratic machine that nominated him."

It was, to say the least, an incongruous situation. Wilson was traveling

[38] G. F. Parker, "How Woodrow Wilson Was Nominated and Elected Governor of New Jersey," photostatic copy of MS memorandum in the Baker Papers.

[39] R. S. Baker, "Memorandum of an interview with Robert S. Hudspeth, November 3, 1927," MS in *ibid.*

[40] J. Kerney, *The Political Education of Woodrow Wilson*, p. 71.

about the state blandly telling the voters that the Republican organization was "dilapidated" and "misguiding the Republican voters," while at the same time his constant traveling companion was James R. Nugent, representative of an organization whose record was every bit as notorious as that of the Republican machine. Still another serious problem arose to perplex the Democratic nominee. It was the disturbing question as to whether Smith was using Wilson's candidacy as a lever by means of which he would attempt to return to the United States Senate. The attitude of Wallace M. Scudder, editor of the faithful *Newark Evening News,* was significant in this regard. The *Newark News* had been consistently a Wilson paper, but in the latter part of October Scudder told a friend that "the spectre of Senator Smith had loomed up so ominously as to put nearly everyone [in the *News* office] on the fence." The independent voters, the Newark editor added, feared that if Wilson was elected governor, Smith would also return to the Senate; and they preferred Wilson's defeat to Smith's election to the seat he formerly held.[41] "There is no doubt whatever, I think," wrote Richard V. Lindabury, certainly no radical himself, "that the issue at this end of the State [North Jersey] is becoming to be Smith, Nugent and Davis."[42]

The opportunity for Wilson to state once and for all his solemn adherence to the progressive program and, at the same time, to state in language that could not be misunderstood his attitude toward the Democratic bosses, came in an unexpected manner. During his Trenton speech of October 3, Wilson had in an offhand manner thrown out a challenge to public debate to his Republican opponents. "I welcome any politician in the State," he had declared, "to a debate upon the public platform."[43] It was probably a slip of the tongue on Wilson's part, but it was just the sort of opportunity George L. Record, Republican candidate for Congress in the ninth congressional district, was looking for and he hastened to reply to Wilson's challenge. "I am keenly interested in public questions, and I hope I am enough of a politician to qualify under your challenge," the doughty insurgent leader wrote. "At all events I accept your challenge, and am willing to meet you in public discussion at any of your meetings or at such other time and place as you may suggest."[44]

[41] R. V. Lindabury to W. W., October 21, 1910, Wilson Papers.

[42] *ibid.*

[43] *Trenton True American,* October 4, 1910.

[44] G. L. Record to W. W., October 5, 1910, Wilson Papers; also published in the *Trenton True American,* October 7, 1910.

Record's letter created something of a panic in the Democratic camp, for Record was completely unpredictable and might ask Wilson some particularly embarrassing questions about the Democratic state machine. Job H. Lippincott, chairman of the state auxiliary committee, hastened to advise Wilson not to walk into the trap Record had set for him.[45] Nugent, too, was alarmed and held a hurried conference at Burlington with the Democratic candidate; Wilson was reluctant to cross swords with Record and he and Nugent decided to parry the thrust. On the day that Record's letter appeared in the newspapers, Wilson's reply, made through Nugent, was given to the public. Wilson had asked him, Nugent declared, to write to Senator Frank O. Briggs, chairman of the Republican state committee, in order to "ascertain officially if Mr. Record has been or will be designated by the Republican State Committee and the Republican candidate for Governor as their representative and spokesman." If Record should be selected by the Republicans as their spokesman, Nugent would arrange with Briggs "for such joint meetings, as may be agreed upon." [46]

Would Wilson refuse to seize the unusual opportunity Record had offered him? Record, at least, thought that he would. "The great Dr. Wilson," he commented scornfully, "who is to lift the politics of New Jersey to a new and a higher plane, at the first test has gone down to the Jim Nugent plane and commences to dodge and pettifog." [47] The Republican leaders, on the other hand, were delighted at Wilson's discomfiture. Briggs announced gleefully that Wilson should either debate with Record or else withdraw his previous challenge.[48]

It is evident that Wilson had decided that he should not take public notice of Record's challenge. During the few days following the publication of Nugent's statement, however, Wilson was warned directly by several of his advisers in the New Idea camp that should he fail to answer Record he would probably lose the votes of the progressive Republicans. Joseph and Walter Dear, publishers of the *Jersey Journal*, went to Princeton, reiterated this warning, and finally obtained from Wilson a promise that he would answer Record's challenge. There was certainly nothing that he need wish to avoid in a mere expression of opinion, Wilson wrote to Harvey, who had probably advised him to re-

---

[45] J. H. Lippincott to W. W., October 7, 1910, Wilson Papers.

[46] Nugent's statement of October 6, published in *Trenton True American,* October 7, 1910.

[47] G. L. Record, in the *Jersey Journal* of Jersey City, October 7 1910.

[48] *ibid.*, October 8, 1910.

main silent. He had found, Wilson added significantly, that it would make a very bad impression in Hudson County if he seemed to try to dodge Record's onset, because of course he, Wilson, was trying to secure the votes of the New Idea Republicans, and Record was their leader.[49]

On October 11 Wilson accordingly cut loose from the guidance of the Democratic managers and wrote an honest and straightforward public letter to Record. He was convinced, Wilson wrote, that he and Record would have to deal with each other "as individuals and not as representatives of any organization of any kind." The Democratic state committee had so arranged his speaking program, Wilson continued, that it would be impossible for him to debate with Record publicly. "I am very anxious, however, to meet you with absolute candor upon the matters regarding which you are in doubt as to my position," he added, and ". . . would esteem it a favor, therefore, if you would be kind enough to state the matters . . . in a letter, to which I would take pleasure in replying in a letter which you would be at full liberty to publish." [50]

Record's letter to Wilson, which propounded a series of searching questions that covered in detail every aspect of progressive reform then in vogue in New Jersey, was published in the state press on October 19. Wilson obviously realized the tremendous importance of the nature of his reply; moreover, he was aware that his political future lay in the balance, that it was the progressive Republicans and independent voters who would elect him governor, if he was elected, and that these insurgents wanted specific assurances from him that a group of Democratic bosses would not be substituted for the Board of Guardians as the result of a Democratic victory.[51] In one of the boldest strokes of his political career, Wilson rose dramatically to the occasion and on October 25 gave his answers to the newspapers. He did not dodge or attempt to run away from Record's attack, but met it squarely and with complete candor.[52]

Record first of all sought to ascertain Wilson's position with regard to the specific reform measures the progressives were demanding. Did Wilson, he asked, favor a public utilities commission with power "to fix

[49] W. W. to G. Harvey, October 11, 1910, Wilson Papers.

[50] W. W. to G. L. Record, October 11, 1910, published in the *Trenton Evening Times,* October 12, 1910.

[51] For forceful statements of this viewpoint see A. S. Alexander to W. W., October 20, 1910, and R. V. Lindabury to W. W., October 20, 1910, both in Wilson Papers.

[52] Record's letter to Wilson is dated October 17; Wilson's reply is dated October 24; both letters are in *ibid*. The complete correspondence was published in the *Trenton True American,* October 26, 1910, and in most of the newspapers in the state on the same date.

just and reasonable rates"? Did he believe that the property of all public utility corporations should be evaluated by the state, and that such physical valuation should serve as the basis for local tax assessments? Did he believe that the physical valuation of utilities property should serve as the basis for rate-fixing by the utilities commission? Did Wilson agree that the primary law should be extended so as to include candidates for governor, congress, and delegates to national conventions, and did he favor the popular election of United States senators? Would the Democratic candidate support a law compelling legislative candidates to file a pledge to vote for the party candidate for the Senate who had received the greatest number of votes at a senatorial preferential primary? Would Wilson agree to support election reform laws and a stringent corrupt practices act that forbade "all political expenditures except for the objects named in the act, with drastic penalties for the violation of the act; prohibiting the employment of more than two workers or watchers at the polls . . .; prohibiting the hiring of vehicles for transporting voters; limiting the amount to be expended by candidates; prohibiting political contributions by corporations"?

Did Wilson approve the principle of workingmen's compensation legislation and would he, as governor, endeavor to obtain the enactment of such legislation? Did he agree with Record that the County Board of Elections law and the Hillery maximum tax law should be repealed? Did the Democratic platform "declare for the choice of candidates for all elective offices by the direct vote system"?

Wilson made direct and simple reply to this first list of questions. He was in complete agreement with Record on most points and, as if to emphasize the completeness of his agreement, answered most of them with a single word, "Yes." On only one question did he reveal any essential divergence from Record's views: it was the question regarding physical valuation of utilities property as the sole basis for rate-making. "I think that such valuation should form a very important part of the basis upon which rates should be fixed," Wilson wrote, "but not the whole basis. All the financial, physical and economic circumstances of the business should be taken into consideration."

Wilson had stated many times during the campaign his position on these details of reform; these questions, however, constituted a prelude to the greater issue: the position of the political machines in New Jersey and, specifically, Wilson's own relation to the Democratic organization. Record proceeded to set forth his conception of what the boss system was: a virtual partnership between the public utilities corporations, the railroads, and the leaders of both party organizations. The terms of this partnership, Record continued, were "the corporations in question to receive from public officials franchises, privileges and advantages . . . , that candidates are nominated by the bosses in both parties who can be trusted to do nothing if elected to interfere with these privileges, when granted, and who will help to grant new ones when needed . . .; that these privileges enable these favored corporations to exact huge sums from the public in excessive rates and exemptions from taxation; that in return for these privileges the corporation managers grant certain favors to the party leaders or bosses; that these favors take the form of either direct money payments, or heavy contributions for campaign expenses, or opportunities for safe and profitable business ventures, according to the standard of morality of the particular boss or leader." The system was by necessity bi-partisan, Record continued. "I do not hesitate to call it the most dangerous condition in the public life of our State and nation today—an evil that has destroyed representative government . . . and in its place set up a government of privilege."

With this by way of introduction, Record proceeded to ask Wilson some blunt questions. Did he admit that the system existed in New Jersey as Record had described it? "Of course, I admit it," Wilson replied. "Its existence is notorious." He had made it his business for many years to observe and understand the system, he added, and he hated it as thoroughly as he understood it. How would Wilson propose to abolish the system of political organization-corporation control? Record asked. "I would propose to abolish it by the above reforms," Wilson replied, and "by the election to office of men who will refuse to submit to it and bend all their energies to break it up, and by pitiless publicity."

Record's remaining five questions were the most significant of his list, and Wilson's replies answered finally the demand that he repudiate the Democratic leaders and assume personal leadership of the party:

Record's Question No. 15:
"In referring to the 'Board of Guardians,' do you mean such Republican leaders as [David] Baird, [Franklin] Murphy, [John] Kean and [Edward] Stokes? Wherein do the relations to the special interests of such leaders differ from the relations to the same interests of such Democratic leaders as Smith, Nugent and Davis?"

Wilson's Answer: "I refer to the men you name. They differ from the others in this, that they are in control of the government of the State, while the others are not and cannot be if the present Democratic ticket is elected."

RECORD'S QUESTION No. 16: "I join you in condemning the Republican 'Board of Guardians.' I have been fighting them for years, and shall continue to fight them. Will you join me in denouncing the Democratic 'Overlords,' as parties to the same political system? If not, why not?"

WILSON'S ANSWER: "Certainly; I will join you or anyone else in denouncing and fighting any and every one, of either party, who attempts such outrages against the government and public morality."

RECORD'S QUESTION No. 17: "You say the Democratic party has been reorganized, and the Republican party has not. Can a political party be reorganized without changing either its leaders, or its old leaders changing their point of view and their political character? Will you claim that either of these events has taken place in the Democratic party? If yes, upon what do you base that conclusion?"

WILSON'S ANSWER: "I do remember saying that it was seeking reorganization, and was therefore at the threshold of a new era. I said this because it is seeking to change its leaders, and will obviously change them if successful in this election. If I am elected I shall understand that I am chosen leader of my party and the direct representative of the whole people in the conduct of the government. . . ."

RECORD'S QUESTION No. 18: "Is there any organized movement in the Democratic party in this State, which corresponds to the Progressive Republican movement, of which you have favorably spoken?"

WILSON'S ANSWER: "I understand the present platform and the present principal nominations of the Democratic party in this State to be such an organized movement. It will be more fully organized if those nominees are elected. This is, as I interpret it, the spirit of the whole remarkable Revival which we are witnessing, not only in New Jersey, but in many other States.

"Before I pass to my next question, will you not permit me to frame one which you have not asked, but which I am sure lies implied in those I have just answered? You wish to know what my relations would be with the Democrats whose power and influence you fear, should I be elected Governor, particularly in such important matters as appointments and the signing of bills, and I am very glad to tell you. If elected I shall not, either in the matter of appointments to office or assent to legislation, or in shaping any part of the policy of my administration, submit to the dictation of any person or persons, special interest or organization. I will always welcome advice and suggestions from any citizen, whether boss, leader, organization man or plain citizen, and I shall constantly seek the advice of influential and disinterested men, representative of their communities and disconnected from political 'organizations' entirely; but all suggestions and all advice will be considered on their merits, and no additional weight will be given to any man's advice or suggestion because of his exercising, or supposing that he exercises, some sort of political influence or control. I should deem myself forever disgraced should I in even the slightest degree cooperate in any such system or any such transactions as you describe in your characterization of the 'boss' system. I regard myself as pledged to the regeneration of the Democratic party which I have forecast above."

RECORD'S QUESTION No. 19: "Will you agree to publicly call upon the Republican and Democratic candidates for the legislature to pledge themselves in writing prior to the election in favor of such of the foregoing reforms as you personally favor? If not, why not?"

WILSON'S ANSWER: "I will not. Because I think it would be most unbecoming in me to do so. That is the function of the voters in the several counties. Let them test and judge the men, and choose those who are sincere."

Woodrow Wilson had finally arrived, baggage and all, in the progressive camp; he had cut loose from every vestige of boss connection that once encumbered him and had scaled the most formidable heights of progressivism. Historical parallels are often deceptive, but it seems reasonable to assume that Wilson's letter to Record had about the same decisive effect upon his subsequent political career as Lincoln's question at Freeport and Douglas's reply had upon the political futures of the two famous Illinoisans. Certainly it is true that the Record-Wilson correspondence was the decisive factor in assuring the Democratic nominee's election, for its publication won him the support of an overwhelming majority of the progressive Republicans. The reply to Record was the first great milestone in Wilson's career as a liberal statesman. One is reminded at this point of the statement of Francis Place, one of the wisest labor leaders in British history: "There are times and circumstances, and both were now combined, when quiescent men, who take the most moderate views of public matters, and are willing to let political movements take their own course, shake off their usual apathy, assume a new character, and become the resolute promoters of the greatest changes. This was now about to become the case here." [53]

Wilson's reply, at any rate, left Record dumbfounded, and he was reported to have admitted, "That letter will elect Wilson governor." [54] To Record the most encouraging result of the entire affair was that Wilson had surrendered unconditionally to the demands of the New Idea men. "Thus the principles for which we stand are slowly coming

[53] Quoted in Graham Wallas, *The Life of Francis Place*, p. 275.
[54] *Trenton True American*, October 26, 1910.

into a full triumph," he declared.[55] James Kerney, the progressive curmudgeon of Trenton, was also at last converted. "To those who have been fighting the pernicious boss system," he wrote, ". . . the letter of Woodrow Wilson to George L. Record, will come as the brightest ray of hope that New Jersey has yet seen." [56] Strong words, these, from the pen of Wilson's severest New Jersey critic!

The most significant result of the correspondence was the sudden change in the thought of the independent and progressive Republican voters. They had been slowly coming over into the Democratic camp before the letter was published, it is true, but Wilson's dramatic declaration provided the impelling force that converted most of them into enthusiastic Wilson supporters. The upshot was that a week after the Record-Wilson correspondence was published there were few progressives still in the Republican ranks. The hundreds of letters in the Wilson Papers written by New Idea men and the joyous editorials of the New Idea newspapers testify to this.[57] Scudder of the *Newark Evening News* thought Wilson's reply to Record was "the greatest political document he had ever read." There was no longer any lukewarmness of Wilson sentiment in the *News* office! [58]

Of course most Democratic progressives were already ardent Wilson supporters and needed no further persuasion to support the Democratic ticket. Wilson's reply, however, meant perhaps more to them than to any other single political group, for he had definitely promised to be their leader and their spokesman. Tumulty was speaking only for the small progressive faction of the party when he wrote, "The New Jersey Democracy gladly accepts your virile leadership," [59] but his letter was none the less prophetic of things to come. Were the hopeless years of political impotency at an end for these men who had so long been leaderless, disunited, and without any real program?

On the other hand, what did the chief Democratic boss think of this truancy of his political godchild? One thing is certain, that Smith was no fool and surely could not have mistaken the intent of Wilson's declaration. Smith, however, now found himself on the horns of a dilemma: his candidate was now more popular with the voters than he

[55] *Jersey Journal* of Jersey City, October 27, 1910.

[56] *Trenton Evening Times,* October 25, 1910.

[57] See, e.g., *Jersey Journal* of Jersey City, October 26, 1910; *Newark Evening News,* October 25, 1910.

[58] R. V. Lindabury to W. W., October 27, 1910, Wilson Papers.

[59] J. P. Tumulty to W. W., October 25, 1910, *ibid.*

had been at any time during the campaign; the election was but two weeks in the future; and Smith knew that he probably could not under any circumstances prevent Wilson's election. He consequently must have decided to go down the line for Wilson and trusted that he, Wilson, would turn out to be manageable after all. Consequently Smith's editorial spokesman unctuously remarked that Wilson stood "toweringly alone among the public men in New Jersey." [60]

The Record-Wilson correspondence was published two weeks before the general state elections. It was the culmination point of the campaign for Wilson, but he still had work to do and refused to halt for a moment his hammering at the Republican state machine and its misrule in the state. On the day that he finished writing his answer to Record, for example, Wilson went to Camden and launched a spirited attack upon David Baird, the Republican czar of South Jersey. Wilson was even in a jocular mood. "I . . . have no disturbed thoughts about the Democratic candidate," he declared. "I know what his intentions are, but I cannot tell you what his performances are going to be. You have got to take a sportsman's chance and risk it; but I can promise you this, that it will not be dull; it will be interesting." [61]

Wilson's defiance of the Smith-Nugent machine also became more and more straightforward. At Salem on October 25 he explained again the terms upon which he had accepted the nomination and added with significant bluntness that it might yet develop that the machine leaders would find that they had "picked out the wrong man, after all." [62] During the last ten days of the campaign he made a whirlwind tour of the northern half of New Jersey. On October 27 he spoke before audiences at Rutherford, Englewood, and Hackensack; the following evening he addressed a sizable audience at Elizabeth. On October 31 he spoke before large audiences of workingmen at Elizabethport and Bayonne and discussed in specific detail the kind of workmen's compensation legislation he would support if he were governor.[63] The last week of the campaign was hurried and hectic; Wilson seemed to feel that time was growing short and he apparently wanted to state over and again his progressive credo and explain his new position of leadership within the party. There followed in rapid succession during the early days of November speeches in Passaic, Carlstadt, Montclair, Madi-

[60] *Newark Evening Star*, October 25, 1910.
[61] *Trenton True American*, October 25, 1910.
[62] *ibid.*, October 26, 1910.
[63] *ibid.*, October 28, November 1, 1910.

son, Dover, Morristown, Perth Amboy, Carteret, and, finally, Newark.[64]

It was ironic that Jim Nugent had singled out Newark as the scene of Wilson's last appeal to the people of New Jersey before the election. The candidate went straight into the heart of Smith's reservation and proceeded audaciously to throw out his final ultimatum to the Essex County machine leaders. There is no doubt that he understood the tremendous import of the declaration: "I want to say therefore that I understand the present campaign to mean this—that if I am elected Governor I shall have been elected leader of my party." More remarkable still was Wilson's statement, "When I was approached with regard to the nomination for the Governorship, I understood it to be distinctly represented to me that the purpose of those who asked my leave to use my name for that purpose was that I should be invited to take the leadership of the Democratic party." If the organization leaders did not understand the agreement as he did, Wilson added, "they ought to withdraw the invitation on the eighth day of November." In the audience was Smith, who wept as Wilson made his final appeal: "I am not claiming that I am qualified for leadership—that is not the point; but I am claiming that I did not seek the leadership and that I was asked to take it, but that I was asked to take it with the understanding that I was absolutely free from pledges and obligations of any kind. Now, I have been asked if I have said that the Democratic party has been reorganized. No, I have not said that; I have said that the Democratic party is seeking reorganization. It depends on the voters on the eighth day of November whether it gets it or not. That is the issue. If you think I am a suitable leader and that my leadership will produce a reorganization and that I can put that party upon a new footing and give it new objects, then it is clearly your duty to support me, but if you do not think so, then I must just as frankly say that it is clearly your duty not to support me. . . . I regard myself as pledged to the regeneration of the Democratic party." [65]

This final declaration was a display of incredible audacity, to be sure; but it was also a serious distortion of Wilson's original agreement with Smith made at the time he agreed to accept the gubernatorial nomination. Nothing outright had been said then about party leadership, but Wilson had declared that he would not attempt to destroy the Smith-Nugent organization and replace it with an organization of his own. The implication of this promise was plain enough, for at the time the

[64] *ibid.*, November 2, 3, 4, 5, 1910.
[65] *Trenton Evening Times*, November 7, 1910.

Smith-Nugent organization constituted the leadership of the Democratic party in the state. Wilson had either already forgotten his earlier promises to Smith or, more likely, he had felt compelled by the necessities of political expediency to strike out on an independent course, the pursuance of which would violate the spirit of the pre-nomination understanding and lead to an inevitable conflict with the Smith organization.

As the gubernatorial contest came to a not altogether unexpected climax, there were increasing signs that Wilson would win the election by an overwhelming majority. All of the Democratic and independent journals in early November predicted Wilson's election, while Harvey confidently prophesied that he would be elected by a 40,000 majority.[66] Numerous unknown supporters, many of them New Idea Republicans, wrote and pledged their support. From Walter H. Page, editor of *World's Work,* came this cheering greeting: "And now my thanks— we all owe you hearty thanks—for a campaign done with meaning & sincerity & eloquence—the good old times of politics come again." [67] On election day there came from Wilmington, North Carolina, the most unusual message of all: "I am praying for your election as Governor of New Jersey. David Bryant (Your Fathers old Servant)." [68]

During the last week of the campaign eastern newspapers and magazines reviewed the progress of Wilson's canvass for the governorship and, almost without exception, pronounced it brilliant and invigorating. "Of all the candidates for any office in any State the man who has done most to raise the political, moral and intellectual level of the campaign is Woodrow Wilson," declared the authoritative *New York World* on November 8. Theodore Roosevelt's editorial spokesman readily acknowledged that Wilson had become the leader of the progressive movement in New Jersey and for that reason deserved to be elected.[69] It was the general consensus in the East, therefore, that Wilson had served his political apprenticeship well and that he had developed into one of the outstanding Democratic leaders in the country. As one editor put it, "If Dr. Wilson should triumph at the polls next Tuesday, not only will the State of New Jersey have a new Governor, but the Democracy of the country will have a new leader." [70]

[66] *Harper's Weekly,* LIV (November 5, 1910), 4.
[67] W. H. Page to W. W., November 5, 1910, Wilson Papers.
[68] D. Bryant to W. W., November 8, 1910, *ibid*.
[69] *Outlook,* XCVI (November 5, 1910), 521.
[70] *Baltimore Sun,* November 4, 1910. The *Philadelphia North American,* October 27, 1910, had the following comment to make upon the New Jersey campaign: "Woodrow

The November elections in the several states proved that 1910 was what political observers call a "Democratic year." For a number of reasons—a popular reaction against the Payne-Aldrich tariff of 1909, perhaps, or, as many Democrats said, a popular desire to repudiate Theodore Roosevelt, who had played a prominent role in the campaign in New York; or the rising tide of progressive feeling, dissatisfied with the conservatism of the national Republican leadership—the voters of the United States on November 8 elected for the first time since 1892 a Democratic House of Representatives. Democratic governors were also elected in the normally Republican states of New York, New Jersey, Massachusetts, Connecticut, Ohio, Indiana, North Dakota, and Colorado.

The results in New Jersey were almost a foregone conclusion by election day. What surprised most observers was the sweeping character of the victory that Wilson and his party achieved. By official count the Democratic candidate won New Jersey by a plurality of 49,056 and carried along with him into office a Democratic Assembly. Wilson received a total vote of 233,933; Lewis, 184,573; Killingbeck, Socialist candidate, 10,166; Repp, Prohibitionist, 2,822; and Butterworth, Socialist Labor nominee, 2,070.[71] Wilson's majorities in Essex and Hudson counties were unexpectedly large. He carried the former by 14,269 and the latter by 26,865 votes. Lewis won Atlantic, Camden, Cape May, Cumberland, Passaic, and Salem counties by slight majorities, but Wilson won the remaining fifteen. He even carried his home county of Mercer by a majority of 139.[72] All in all it was a gratifying victory, and the extent of Wilson's accomplishment is better understood when it is recalled that Taft had carried New Jersey in 1908 by a majority of over 80,000.

During election day Wilson remained quietly at home in Princeton. The incoming returns revealed early in the evening that he had carried the state by a sweeping majority, and a throng of jubilant Democrats from the town and a thousand Princeton students joined in a parade in his honor. Red lights and fireworks were set off as the line of

Wilson is little short of a revelation. He would not be so unusual in Wisconsin or Iowa or Georgia or Oregon. But the appearance of a scholar, gentleman and patriot, running by grace of machine bosses, and yet facing the people as one of them and without the concession of a quibble or an utterance of double meaning, declaring a code of action of broad, nonpartisan, pure Americanism, in 'straight-flung words and few,' is a spectacle inspiring almost without precedent."

[71] *Trenton True American,* November 30, 1910.

[72] *ibid.,* November 11, 1910.

marchers made their way through the streets leading to the Wilson home at "Prospect." Wilson was visibly moved by this spontaneous expression of confidence and affection from his fellow townsmen and former students. "I am certainly gratified at this celebration in my honor," he said, "but think that I have said nearly all I know in my speeches during the campaign." He also made a statement to newspaper reporters on the outcome of the election, in which he expressed his deeply felt appreciation of the great honor the people of the state had done him. "I regard the result of the election as a splendid vindication of the conviction of the Democrats of the State," he declared, "that the people desired to turn away from personal attack and party maneuvers and base their political choices upon great questions of public policy and just administration." [73]

There was no doubt now that Wilson was a figure of national importance, and congratulatory letters and telegrams from all parts of the country, from personal friends, from leading Democrats, from editors, and from complete strangers, poured in upon the governor-elect. William J. Bryan of Nebraska at last took notice of this rising Democratic leader in the East and wrote, "Congratulations on your election. May your administration be crowned with signal success." [74] "I welcome you," wrote Thomas R. Marshall of Indiana, who was to be Wilson's running mate in 1912, "into the company of governors who think that principles are worth maintaining." [75] Wilson's friends, too, were jubilant over his great victory. "Hip Hip Hurrah Your Va. friends are shouting with joy," Dabney wrote from Charlottesville,[76] while Henry B. Thompson gave voice to the feeling of the Wilson men among the Princeton trustees when he wrote, "Glory Glory hallelujah and you go marching on." [77]

It remained for the gentlemen of the Fourth Estate to pass final judgment upon the meaning of the "political revolution" in New

[73] *ibid.,* November 10, 1910.

[74] W. J. Bryan to W. W., November 9, 1910, Wilson Papers.

[75] T. R. Marshall to W. W., November 9, 1910, *ibid.* For letters from other national Democratic leaders, see R. C. Sullivan to W. W., November 8, 1910; C. A. Culberson to W. W., November 9, 1910; R. S. Hudspeth to W. W., November 9, 1910; E. N. Foss to W. W., November 9, 1910; N. E. Mack to W. W., November 9, 1910; A. B. Parker to W. W., November 9, 1910, all in *ibid.*

[76] R. H. Dabney to W. W., November 9, 1910, *ibid.*

[77] H. B. Thompson to W. W., November 9, 1910, *ibid.;* see also H. H. Wayt to W. W., November 8; C. H. Dodge to W. W., November 9; D. B. and T. D. Jones to W. W., November 9; W. M. Rice and E. O. Lovett to W. W., November 9; E. W. Sheldon to W. W., November 9; James Bryce to W. W., November 12, 1910, all in *ibid.*

Jersey. Perhaps not all editors were as happy over the Democratic victory as was Villard, editor of the *New York Evening Post,* who wrote, "I cannot resist the tempation to tell you of the great happiness in this office over your tremendous victory. Not in my recollection has the entire staff so enjoyed taking part in a campaign as it has in yours." [78] There was, of course, a good deal of rejoicing in the Democratic newspapers in New Jersey on the morning after the election.[79]

The independent progressive spokesmen of the state, however, injected one sober note of warning into the excited atmosphere and bluntly informed Wilson that he owed his election to the thousands of independent voters who had supported him, and not to the Democratic machines that had nominated him. This was a fact of first-rate importance and they did not want Wilson to forget it. This was the warning and advice that Scudder wished especially to convey to Wilson when he wrote what was the soundest and most thoughtful analysis of the election results:

"New Jersey has recorded its political insurgency. The election of Woodrow Wilson is nominally a Democratic victory, but it is of larger significance than mere party success.

"The insurgency-progressivism of New Jersey, long repressed, burst out into nominal Democracy, but it is Democratic only in name. Insurgency has been active in New Jersey for years. It has grown and spread, starting from the Colby revolt, until the great majority of the independent voters favored it in principle.

"But the 'regulars' had been able to suppress it and keep it from gaining control by conceding enough to it to save their own necks. They were aided by the lack among the Progressives of some man who was generally regarded as a sane, constructive leader. . . .

"Progressivism languished for its leader, a man who by his sane, constructive ideas could command general confidence—a man who did not want to sweep things away, but to work them out.

"The leader was found, and he was found in the ranks of the Democrats. He was tested, proved a real Progressive, and was made Governor. . . .

"Governor Wilson has been given the commission by the people of the state to redeem the political reputation of New Jersey and to re-

[78] O. G. Villard to W. W., November 11, 1910, *ibid.*

[79] See, e.g., *Trenton True American,* November 9, 1910; *Newark Morning Star,* November 9, 1910; *Newark Evening Star,* November 9, 1910.

construct the character of the controlling forces in the State House at Trenton." [80]

[80] *Newark Evening News,* November 9, 1910; see also the *Trenton Evening Times,* November 9 and the *Jersey Journal* of Jersey City, November 9, 1910, for further expressions of this idea.

CHAPTER VII

The First Battle

THE climax of the gubernatorial campaign had left Woodrow Wilson in an embarrassing impasse. Many times during the course of the canvass he had asserted his leadership of the Democratic party, but there is a difference between oratory and political control. Wilson had achieved the leadership of the progressive minority of Democratic voters, as well as of the New Idea and independent factions; but these liberal groups, no matter how vociferous they might be, did not constitute the Democratic party. In 1910 that party was a vested interest, a stagnant institution representing not the people of the state or even the mass of Democratic voters, but a small group of men within the party organization. The state committee, the county committees, the ward organizations in the cities—all the organs of party machinery— were controlled largely by Smith, Nugent, and Davis.

Wilson apparently had no idea what his relationship to the Smith-Nugent machine would be after the election. He had certainly done his best to make cooperation with the organization forces difficult. Before he agreed to accept the nomination, he had been assured by Smith that he would be left free by the organization in the matter of "measures and men"; on the other hand, Wilson had promised not to set out to destroy the Smith organization and had tacitly accepted its leadership in party affairs. With no provocation either from Smith or Nugent, but simply because the progressives had forced him to take the advanced position, Wilson had repudiated the Smith organization during the campaign and had given notice that he would set about building up a party following of his own. By the time Wilson was elected governor, therefore, the stage was set for a far-reaching struggle for party leadership.

As fate would have it, the crucial battle between Wilson and Smith, the battle that decided the question of party leadership, developed even before Wilson was inaugurated as governor. It was the contest that grew out of the election of a United States senator to succeed John Kean. This provided the issue, and Wilson used it to rouse the party members against the Essex boss and to seize control of party leadership himself.

In order to pick up the first threads of the senatorial fight it is necessary to review the events of the early summer of 1910, as they related to the senatorial question. When Wilson was mentioned in June and July, 1910, as a probable Democratic gubernatorial candidate, progressive spokesmen immediately charged that Smith was scheming to use Wilson's candidacy as a means of obtaining the election of a Democratic legislature and his own subsequent election to the Senate. Wilson read these charges, but they did not seem to disturb him measurably during the pre-convention period.

Before Wilson agreed in July to accept the nomination, Harvey had assured him that Smith would not be a candidate for election to the Senate. "Before I consented to allow my name to be used before the State Democratic convention for the nomination as Governor," Wilson later explained, "I asked the gentleman who was acting as Mr. Smith's spokesman if Mr. Smith would desire to return to the Senate in case the Democrats should win a majority in the State legislature. I was assured that he would not. I was told that the state of his health would not permit it, and that he did not desire it." [1] Smith later vehemently denied that he had ever authorized anyone to make such a statement,[2] and Wilson never adduced proof.

The evidence in the controversy as to whether Smith promised Wilson that he would not run for the Senate is not sufficiently complete to warrant a final judgment on the matter. Kerney has written, "Not once, but a dozen times, . . . [Smith declared] that under no circumstances would he be a candidate for the United States Senate";[3] Assemblyman Frank A. Boettner of Newark asserted that Nugent had told him before the gubernatorial election that Smith would not be a candidate.[4] Neither statement implies that Smith had given a definite promise that he would not be a candidate.

One fact, however, is certain, that Smith was willing to subordinate any senatorial ambitions he might have had in order to assure the success of Wilson's candidacy. Before the Trenton convention met, Smith told Harvey that if he thought at any time the ambiguity of the senatorial question was injuring Wilson's chances for the nomination, Harvey should promptly announce that under no circumstances would the

[1] *Trenton True American*, December 24, 1910.
[2] *ibid.*, December 27, 1910.
[3] *The Political Education of Woodrow Wilson*, p. 26.
[4] Statement quoted in *Newark Evening News*, January 20, 1911.

James Smith, Jr.

James R. Nugent

Governor of New Jersey

Newark man be a candidate for the office.[5] During the gubernatorial campaign, Smith repeated the offer; he later declared that "assurance was given to Dr. Wilson during the campaign that if he thought the prominence given to my candidacy through[out] the State was hurting his chances I would announce that I was not in the field." [6]

Wilson made his first strategical error when he followed Harvey's advice[7] and failed to take advantage of Smith's offer to make a public renouncement of senatorial ambitions. Harvey apparently was afraid that such action on Wilson's part would weaken the support of Wilson by the Smith organization men. The upshot was that Smith naturally concluded that Wilson had no objection to his candidacy and began quietly to negotiate for support in the event that he did decide to run. He sought, first of all, an understanding with his erstwhile enemy in Jersey City, Robert Davis. After an open break between Wilson and Smith had occurred, Davis unwittingly, it appears, made public the fact that Smith had asked for his support in the senatorial election. "My promise was to support Mr. Smith *should he become a candidate,*" Davis declared. "It dates back into the early summer." [8] However, few politicians in New Jersey, probably not even Smith himself, thought the Democrats would elect a majority of the legislators and consequently the senatorial question was not an important issue during the gubernatorial campaign.

The legislature of New Jersey had enacted in 1907 a law providing that senatorial candidates might submit their candidacies to a popular referendum in a senatorial primary. In 1910 several prominent Democrats were requested by progressive leaders to enter the primary contest, but either because of the slight prospect of the election of a Democratic legislature or else because these men were anxious to avoid offending Smith (who was regarded as a likely candidate, in spite of his declarations to the contrary), none would enter the senatorial primary.[9] When it became evident that no other Democrat would submit his candidacy to the suffrage of the voters, William W. St. John, a Trenton newspaperman, and Martin P. Devlin, a progressive veteran from the capital, called on James E. Martine of Plainfield and urged him to become a candidate for the Senate.

[5] W. O. Inglis, "Helping to Make a President," *Collier's Weekly*, LVIII (October 7, 1916), 16.

[6] Smith's statement in the *New York Evening World*, December 19, 1910.

[7] W. O. Inglis, "Helping to Make a President," *loc. cit.*, p. 16.

[8] *Trenton True American*, December 22, 1910. Italics mine.

[9] J. Kerney, *The Political Education of Woodrow Wilson*, pp. 77-78.

Martine was the leading Bryan Democrat of New Jersey. Lovable, enthusiastic, liberal, always anxious to serve his party, Martine was nevertheless the laughing-stock of the state Democracy. He delighted in the sobriquet "Farmer Orator," but he was a farmer only by a strange distortion of the word. His two chief diversions were speech-making and running for office. Twice he was a candidate for a congressional nomination; three times he ran for the state Senate; four times he was a candidate for the lower house of the legislature; and twice he was a candidate at state conventions for the gubernatorial nomination.[10] On every occasion he had been defeated, although his supporters attributed this dismal political record to the fact that he lived in Plainfield, a stanchly Republican town.

No politician took Martine seriously before 1910, and when St. John and Devlin urged him to become a senatorial candidate, he at first categorically refused. Kerney describes a ridiculous scene in which Martine is alleged to have fallen on his knees and declared, "For God's sake, Mart and Saint, don't humiliate me any further. I am now married to a good woman, and it isn't fair to her for me to permit myself to be regarded as a political buffoon." [11]

In spite of Martine's protests, St. John and Devlin affixed the "Farmer Orator's" name to the primary petition and placed it on file in the office of the secretary of state. With remarkable grace Martine accepted the *fait accompli* and on August 20 announced his candidacy for the senatorship. At the same time he set forth a declaration of progressive principles that he promised to follow should he be elected to the Senate.[12] Martine's only rival in the senatorial primary was Frank M. McDermit, a Newark lawyer of unsavory reputation; on September 13 the Democratic voters gave 48,449 votes to Martine and 15,573 to McDermit.[13] The primary results were given scant notice by the newspapers and there was apparently no inclination on the part of the party leaders to regard Martine as the official Democratic nominee for the senatorship. Even Martine himself was strangely quiet about the affair until it became apparent after the November elections that a Democratic majority in the legislature had been elected. Then he hastened to declare, "The next session of the New Jersey legislature will elect me United States Senator to succeed John Kean." Were the results other-

---

[10] "The Farmer Orator," *Saturday Evening Post*, CLXXXIII (April 8, 1911), 27.
[11] J. Kerney, *The Political Education of Woodrow Wilson*, p. 78.
[12] *Jersey Journal* of Jersey City, August 20, 1910.
[13] Figures given in the *New York Times*, December 18, 1910.

wise, Martine added, "the Democratic party would be plunged into a sea of political infidelity, chicanery and double dealing." [14]

Although the election of a Democratic legislature[15] had apparently come as a surprise to Smith, he lost no time in deciding definitely that he wanted to return to the seat he once held in the United States Senate. Immediately after the election, therefore, he began to line up support for his candidacy. He used every means at his disposal to obtain pledges of support from Democratic legislators-elect; in dealing with them, Wilson later charged, he assumed that his organization would control the forthcoming legislature, that its offices would be distributed as he should direct, and that members would be assigned to committee posts as he directed.[16]

Shortly after the election Smith paid a personal visit to Wilson at Princeton. The Newark boss was in good spirits and informed Wilson that he had decided to enter the senatorial race; his health, he declared, was much better than it had been before the election and he now hoped the legislature would offer him the senatorship. "I pointed out to him," Wilson afterward stated, "that this action on his part would confirm all the ugliest suspicions of the campaign concerning him, and urged him very strongly not to allow his name to be used at all." [17] Smith, however, was adamant, Wilson further related, and declared that he was determined to enter the contest.[18] Wilson next resorted to cajoling tactics and attempted to coax Smith into abandoning his ambition. He asserted that Smith's candidacy would meet with opposition from many Democrats and that the people "wanted a man who had not previously appeared in the political arena, some untried man." [19] Wilson admitted that the senatorial primary was a farce and that it would be a disgrace to send Martine to the Senate. Finally he suggested that Smith propose a compromise candidate who would be acceptable to all Democratic factions.[20]

[14] *Trenton True American,* November 12, 1910.

[15] That is, a legislature with a Democratic majority in a joint session of the two houses. Although the Democrats had an overwhelming majority in the Assembly, there was a slight Republican majority in the upper house.

[16] See Wilson's statement of December 23, 1910, in *Trenton True American,* December 24, 1910.

[17] *ibid.*

[18] cf. Smith's statement: "I called upon Dr. Wilson shortly after [the] election. The Senatorial matter was discussed. I told him that I had not reached a decision as to my candidacy." *ibid.,* December 27, 1910.

[19] *ibid.*

[20] It is a most important point, which should be borne in mind throughout the controversy, that Wilson was opposed to Martine's election and did attempt to find a

Smith left Princeton apparently just as ignorant of what Wilson would do in the senatorial contest as Wilson was himself. Wilson certainly wanted to avoid an open break with the Smith-Nugent organization; he was grateful to Smith for his great aid in the pre-nomination and gubernatorial campaigns; and he decided to give the matter careful thought before committing himself to either side. As late as November 20, however, Wilson declared that he did not think Martine should be elected. It was obvious to Kerney, who conferred with him on that day, that the popular expression at the senatorial primary had made little impression on Wilson. "He gave voice to the thought that the Democrats should pick a man of the exceptional type of John R. Hardin, a Princeton '80 man," Kerney writes, "who had first-class ability and would represent New Jersey with both intelligence and credit. . . . To our suggestion that the Democrats had already definitely decided on Martine he gave little weight." [21]

Wilson's position of neutrality soon became untenable, however, because soon after the November elections the progressive leaders in New Jersey began a tremendous pressure campaign to force Martine's election and, at the same time, to compel Wilson to take up the fight for the "Farmer Orator." These liberal spokesmen argued that Martine had polled a majority of the votes in the senatorial primary and, as a matter of simple justice, should be elected senator. As one New Idea newspaper put it, "If Martine should be robbed of his rights by the Democratic machine, the people will realize that they have been betrayed." [22] The progressive leaders also asserted that a good deal more than Martine's rights were involved in the fight, that a principle, the direct election of senators, was at stake, and that they were battling for this principle chiefly, not for Martine personally. Here was an opportunity, the progressives claimed, to smash once and for all the corrupt system of bargain and sale in senatorial offices, to force the Democrats

compromise candidate. Wilson later admitted in a public statement that he had suggested that Smith retire in favor of a compromise candidate. "I told him that feeling as he did," Wilson declared, "the only honorable course open to him was to come out and say that he was not himself a candidate, and would co-operate in the choice of any man whom general opinion might agree upon as representing not special interests, but the opinion and the character of the State." Wilson's justification for his action was: "I hope that I need not say again that I proposed no compromise candidate and no compromise of any kind for myself. I was foolishly trying to advise him. I was not making a choice for myself." *ibid.*, December 29, 1910. This explanation reveals that Wilson regretted later that he had counseled compromise.

[21] *The Political Education of Woodrow Wilson*, p. 81.
[22] *Jersey Journal* of Jersey City, November 11, 1910.

to remain true to their campaign pledges, and to test the character of Wilson's progressivism. One after another, the progressive Democratic and independent journals joined in the demand that Martine be elected and that Wilson abandon his position of neutrality and join in the battle for the vindication of the senatorial primary principle.[23]

During the early days of November the pressure on Wilson to adopt such a course was terrific; scores of voters from all over the state wrote, reminding him of his duties to the people and above all of his campaign promises that he would be their spokesman. Typical of the many letters written by "average" Democrats and independents was George L. Hoxie's admonition: "You are reported as having said that if elected you would regard yourself as elected leader of the Democratic Party in the State. It is therefore fair to ask you, as such leader, to take a hand in selecting for member of the United States Senate a progressive man . . . and also to ask you to lead the party in fighting any attempt to elect to the United States Senate any man whose past record is notoriously reactionary. I now make these requests of you." [24]

The warnings that leading progressive Democrats freely gave must have made even a deeper impression upon the governor-elect. Wescott, Charles O'Connor Hennessy, and Frederick W. Kelsey, for example, all agreed that the senatorial election would provide the acid test of Wilson's leadership. Wescott stated the situation most succinctly when he wrote: "My duty to you, to good government and Democratic achievement require me to say that the United States Senatorship presents grave possibilities. From scores of people I have gathered an argument that runs this wise: if Mr. Smith is chosen, these results are certain: (1) his election will prove a bargain and sale, the office going to the highest bidder; (2) Doctor Wilson is controlled by the same interests and methods that control Mr. Smith; (3) Dr. Wilson, so far as his usefulness in American regeneration is concerned, would be a negative quality and quantity; (4) the Democratic party in New Jersey would be put out of power at the next election and its restoration thereto would be postponed another twenty years." [25]

This, be it noted, was not only a warning, but also a threat. Unquestionably the belligerent attitude of the insurgent leaders disturbed

[23] See *ibid.*, November 14; *Newark Evening News*, November 16; *Hudson Observer* of Hoboken, *Paterson Guardian*, and *Elizabeth Evening Times*, all cited in the *Trenton True American*, November 19; *Trenton Evening Times*, November 21, 1910.

[24] November 21, 1910, Wilson Papers.

[25] J. W. Wescott to W. W., November 14, 1910, *ibid.*; see also, F. W. Kelsey to W. W., November 24, 1910, *ibid.*; C. O'C. Hennessy to R. S. Baker, July 1, 1926, Baker Papers.

Wilson profoundly;[26] yet he still refused to come out for Martine. He seems to have concluded after his conference with Smith that the Newark leader would not be a candidate for the senatorial post.[27] Wilson acted swiftly, however, when in mid-November Smith publicly declared, "If I find that my friends think I should make the fight, I will enter the race and I will win it." [28] On November 15 Wilson wrote to George Harvey and expressed with remarkable candor his foreboding of the dangers inherent in Smith's candidacy. The letter is of such great importance that the parts relating to the senatorship are given in full:

"I am very anxious about the question of the senatorship. If not handled right, it will destroy every fortunate impression of the campaign and open my administration with a split party. I have learned to have a very high opinion of Senator Smith. I have very little doubt that, if he were sent to the Senate he would acquit himself with honour and do a great deal to correct the impressions of his former term. But his election would be intolerable to the very people who elected me and gave us a majority in the legislature. They would never give it to us again: that I think I can say I know, from what has been said to me in every quarter during the campaign. They count upon me to prevent it. I shall forfeit their confidence if I do not. All their ugliest suspicions, dispelled by my campaign assurances, will be confirmed.

"It was no Democratic victory. It was a victory of the 'progressives' of both parties, who are determined to live no longer under either of the political organizations that have controlled the two parties of the State." The Democrats who left the party in 1896 came back with enthusiasm,

---

[26] By November 18, Congressman William Hughes of Paterson, State Senator Harry V. Osborne of Newark, State Senator William C. Gebhardt of Hunterdon County, and Assemblyman Allan B. Walsh of Trenton also had come out strongly for Martine and were demanding that Wilson commit himself. *Trenton Evening Times*, November 18, 1910.

[27] On November 20, Kerney and Matthew C. Ely, editor of the *Hudson Observer* of Hoboken, went to Princeton to confer with Wilson about the senatorial situation. Even at this late date Wilson believed that Smith would not become a candidate. J. Kerney, *The Political Education of Woodrow Wilson*, p. 81.

[28] "The majority of the caucus would give me the nomination," Smith added, "and there would be no further question of the results. During the last fifteen years of Democratic losses and struggles in this State, I have worked constantly, sometimes quite alone among the leaders, to maintain the party organization and keep it in condition to grasp the opportunity when it came. I think this is appreciated by the Democracy of the State. I understand there will be some bitter opposition to me in case I am a candidate, and this would be unpleasant, but it would not alter my decision." *Newark Sunday Call*, November 13, 1910.

but would again draw off in disgust if their expectations were disappointed. For himself, he could not do this. "It is grossly unjust that they should regard Senator Smith as the impersonation of all that they hate and fear; but they do, and there's an end of the matter. If he should become a candidate, I would have to fight him; and there is nothing I would more sincerely deplore. It would offend every instinct in me,—except the instinct as to what was right and necessary from the point of view of the public service. I have had to do similar things in the University.

"By the same token,—ridiculous though it undoubtedly is,—I think we shall have to stand by Mr. Martine." After all that had been said and done, he continued, they would be stultified if they did not. There was no one who stood out conspicuously as the one whom the entire body of public opinion would accept as the man to send. Moreover, if they did not send Martine, apparently it might be Katzenbach, and in Wilson's opinion a worse choice could not be made. Through sheer weakness and lack of virile intelligence and principle, he would serve the vested interests much more effectively than would Smith, who was a keen politician and knew what he was doing. Wilson had had several talks with men who were closely associated with Katzenbach during the gubernatorial campaign of 1907, and they thanked God that he was not elected. They believed that his administration would have ruined the party.

"I have stripped my whole thought, and my whole resolution, naked for you to see just as it is. Senator Smith can make himself the biggest man in the State by a dignified refusal to let his name be considered. I hope, as I hope for the rejuvenation of our party, that he may see it and may be persuaded to do so.

"It is a national as well as a State question. If the independent Republicans who in this State voted for me are not to be attracted to us they will assuredly turn again, in desperation, to Mr. Roosevelt, and the chance of a generation will be lost to the Democracy: the chance to draw all the liberal elements of the country to it, through new leaders, the chance that Mr. Roosevelt missed in his folly, and to constitute the ruling party of the country for the next generation." [29]

This was the only occasion on which Wilson frankly unburdened his thoughts on the senatorial question. Wilson implied that Harvey should show the letter to Smith, and it was probably written for the purpose of persuading Smith not to become a candidate.

[29] The original of this letter is now in the Wilson Papers.

Wilson's letter reveals, first of all, that he had deliberately come to the decision to support Martine because it was expedient to do so, because he was convinced that any other course would be disastrous to his future political career. If he really believed that Smith was an honest man, a clear-headed politician who was being persecuted by the "grossly unjust" progressives, then he could not honorably have done otherwise than support Smith, to whom he owed his nomination for governor. If Wilson thought, as he undoubtedly did, that Martine was a "ridiculous" candidate, the tremendous battle he later waged for Martine's election loses most of its idealistic glamor. How does one account for Wilson's failure to mention in his letter to Harvey the holy cause of direct election of senators, which he stressed so greatly during the senatorial campaign? In the second place, it is significant that Wilson realized that the senatorial contest was a national issue, or at least might be made just that, and that his chances for seizing leadership of the progressive forces in the country at large might be completely wrecked should he fail to support the progressive cause in New Jersey.

In justice to Wilson, however, it should be pointed out that he had come to the point where it was impossible for him to do anything but support Martine. The progressives constituted the balance of power in the legislature; their support was absolutely essential for the success of Wilson's legislative program. And they had given notice that if Wilson refused to assume the leadership of the anti-Smith forces he would never receive their support. They drove Wilson, therefore, against his will, into a position of progressive leadership.

Smith was not only unmoved by Wilson's admonition that he retire from the senatorial contest; he was also infuriated by the opposition of the man he had nominated for governor. Shortly after his meeting with Wilson, Smith sought out Harvey in New York; both men agreed that in an out-and-out fight Wilson would probably win, but, Smith added tartly, "Well, by God, I guess I'll let him beat me." [30] By November 18 he had apparently decided finally to make the fight;[31] there was no doubt as to his intentions when on November 19 Essex County's eleven Democratic assemblymen-elect addressed a public letter to their leader, requesting that he "permit the use of . . . [his] name as a candidate for United States Senator." [32] Political observers realized at once that the Newark legislators were merely doing the bidding of the Smith-

[30] W. O. Inglis, "Helping to Make a President," *loc. cit.,* p. 14.

[31] See C. H. Dodge to W. W., November 18, 1910, Wilson Papers.

[32] Letter published in the *Trenton True American,* November 22, 1910.

Nugent machine. A few days later James R. Nugent, chief lieutenant of the Smith organization, announced bombastically that Smith
would receive the support of the Hudson County delegation in the
legislature, and this, Nugent added frankly, because Davis had agreed
to "deliver" the votes of the Hudson men to Smith in the senatorial
election.[33] It would have been ironical indeed had the same tactics, the
combining of the Smith and Davis forces, which had been successfully
employed to nominate Wilson at Trenton, been used to defeat him in
this first struggle for party leadership. That was Smith's strategy, none
the less, and to all outward appearances it would again succeed.

The news that the Smith and Davis organizations had allied for the
purpose of electing Smith to the Senate goaded Wilson into immediate
action. On November 25 he made an unannounced visit to Jersey City
and first sought out Joe Tumulty. The two men discussed the senatorial
crisis for an hour, and then Tumulty led Wilson to Davis's modest
brick home at 230 Grove Street, among the plain people of the city.
Davis, who had recently returned from a sanatorium in New York, was
slowly dying of cancer; his face was pinched and white. Wilson quietly
reviewed the senatorial question and asserted that the Democratic party
had for many years advocated the direct election of senators and that it
was consequently the duty of New Jersey Democrats to vote now for
Martine. It was the first time Wilson had stressed the party's obligations
to stand by the results of the primary for the sake of the primary
principle. Davis explained that he had given a solemn promise to Smith
to deliver Hudson County's thirteen legislative votes and he could not
break his promise.[34] The dying Jersey City leader, however, was anxious
to avoid giving offense to Wilson. He suggested that Wilson keep his
hands off the senatorial powder-keg. "If you do, Governor, we'll support
you in your whole legislative program," he said. "How do I know you
will?" Wilson replied. "If you beat me in this the first fight, how do I
know you won't be able to beat me in everything?" Davis laid his hand
affectionately upon Wilson's shoulder. "I've given my word to Smith,
Governor," he said. "Nothing now can induce me to go back on
him."[35]

Wilson's visit to Davis was a capital stroke, not because he was able
to persuade Davis to abandon his support of Smith, but because of the

[33] *Trenton Evening Times,* November 23, 1910.

[34] *Trenton Evening Times,* November 26, 1910; *Trenton True American,* November
28, 1910.

[35] Burton J. Hendrick, "Woodrow Wilson: Political Leader," *McClure's Magazine,*
xxxviii (December 1911), 225.

impression the meeting made upon the loyal party workers in the Davis organization, who were delighted that the new Democratic leader should have paid deference to their old chieftain.[36] After his meeting with Davis, Wilson discussed the senatorial affair with Mark A. Sullivan, a progressive leader in Jersey City, Senator-elect James A. C. Johnson, Assemblymen-elect Garrabrant R. Alyea and William H. Hinners of Bergen County, and with Assemblymen-elect James A. Hendrickson and Elmer H. Geran of Monmouth.[37] A few days later Mayor H. Otto Wittpenn gave out a public statement demanding Martine's election.[38]

There were encouraging signs that Wilson's efforts to capture Smith's main fortress were securing good results. By November 26, for example, it was reported that nine out of the thirteen legislators-elect from Hudson had agreed to join in the fight against Smith.[39] More important, it was also apparent that Davis himself was weakening in his support of Smith. Shortly after Wilson's visit to Jersey City, Davis asked Tumulty to confer with Hudspeth and to request Hudspeth, *"in his* [Davis's] *name,"* to confer with Smith and to suggest to him the "advisability of declining longer to remain a candidate." [40] Davis was frankly worried by the prospect of an open fight with Wilson, and it is evident that he was determined to avoid at all costs such a test of strength. "My impression of the situation here is that Davis is very sorry that he finds himself in his present predicament," wrote Assemblyman-elect Joseph M. Noonan of Jersey City to Wilson, "that he is anxious to please you in all things, but that he will adhere formally, perfunctorily, to his promise to Smith. I am quite convinced that he will not attempt to exert any 'pressure' on any of our legislative delegation." [41] Most important of all, Davis, in the latter part of November, let it be known that he would "not feel hurt" if the Hudson County legislators refused to follow his orders to vote for Smith in the senatorial election.[42]

[36] J. P. Tumulty, *Woodrow Wilson As I Know Him,* pp. 56-57.

[37] *Trenton Evening Times,* November 26; *Trenton True American,* November 28, 1910.

[38] *Trenton Evening Times,* November 29, 1910.

[39] *ibid.,* November 26, 1910.

[40] J. P. Tumulty to W. W., November 30, 1910, Wilson Papers. Hudspeth had requested, Tumulty added, that Wilson not make a public statement until he, Hudspeth, had talked to Smith.

[41] J. M. Noonan to W. W., December 4, 1910, *ibid.*

[42] J. P. Tumulty to W. W., November 30, 1910, *ibid.* Davis gave out an amusing, if mendacious, statement on the senatorial question: "I had a pleasant chat with the Governor-elect and we parted good friends. I have said to no one that I am for Martine

Wilson realized at the outset of the controversy that if he were to succeed in wrecking Smith's plans he would have to confer personally with the legislators-elect; in short, he would have to go over the heads of the local county bosses in his fight to obtain Martine's election. In early December, therefore, he began a series of conferences with the members of the legislature that lasted for several weeks; during this period he appealed for personal support to almost every Democratic member of the legislature that would convene in January, 1911. He first invited the Hudson delegation to his home in Princeton, and on December 5 the entire group, with the exception of Edward Kenny and Thomas M. Donnelly,[43] arrived at "Prospect." Wilson was in dead earnest when he made his plea to the Jersey City men. He had now taken up the popular election of senators and had already made it into a holy cause. He was pleading for Martine's election not because of any particular qualifications of the "Farmer Orator" but because he believed that should the Democrats refuse to stand by the verdict of the senatorial primary, their betrayal of the popular will would ruin the party in the state.[44] The results of the conference were encouraging both to Wilson and to Tumulty,[45] for State Senator James F. Fielder and the ten assemblymen-elect who were present at the meeting agreed to stand by Wilson and vote for Martine.[46]

It amazed veteran politicians to see the deftness and skill with which Wilson was handling the senatorial fight and moving to line up his forces for the coming battle. Of course, he was not fighting the battle alone, and that was important. He had the enthusiastic support of every Democratic and independent newspaper in the state, with the exception of Smith's two journals in Newark and the *Long Branch Record,* while the progressive politicians in the state were giving him hearty support.

Wilson's success in marshaling the Hudson men into an almost solid bloc for Martine probably decided the senatorial fight, for Hudson County was the key to victory in the struggle. "It looks as if we had Smith safely beaten for the Senatorship," Wilson confidently wrote to

or against him, or for Smith or against him. I say, 'let the legislators get together at the proper time and decide on the Senatorship.' The Hudson members will loyally support the choice of the majority of the legislators. The fuss over the Senatorship is being kicked up by the Republicans. The Democrats will be able to settle the thing without trouble." *Baltimore Sun,* November 28, 1910.

[43] Kenny and Donnelly were already publicly committed to vote for Martine.

[44] *Trenton Evening Times,* December 7, 1910.

[45] J. P. Tumulty to W. W., December 7, 1910, Wilson Papers.

[46] *Trenton Evening Times,* December 6-7; *Trenton True American,* December 6, 1910.

Villard early in December. "It is equally clear that we have sufficient majority to elect Mr. Martine." Wilson, however, was anxious to have a show-down conference with Smith. "I hope tomorrow to see Senator Smith," he added, "and tell him very plainly what my position is in order to induce him, if possible, to decline the candidacy. If he will not do that I will come out openly against him." [47]

The final conference between Wilson and Smith was held on December 6; Wilson came to Newark from Princeton and Smith and his son drove him from the railroad station to their home on Washington Place.[48] In a meeting that lasted more than an hour, Wilson pleaded with the Newark man and begged him, for the sake of party unity and fidelity to campaign pledges, to withdraw from the senatorial contest. "You have a chance to be the biggest man in the state by not running for the Senate," he told Smith.[49] Smith replied at length that he had been faithful to the Democratic party in New Jersey; that he had stood by it and, at great expense to himself, had preserved the party organization at times when it would have gone to pieces without his support; and that he desired an opportunity to vindicate his record in the Senate.[50] One newspaper reported that Smith had boasted that he controlled thirty-four out of the fifty Democratic votes in the legislature and that under no circumstances would he withdraw from the race.[51]

After the Newark conference there was no doubt in Wilson's mind that he would be forced to make an open break with the Smith-Nugent organization. "Ex-Senator Smith proves to be the tough customer he is reputed to be," he wrote two days after his conference with Smith, "and there is nothing for it but to fight him openly and to a finish. It is a hard necessity but I think that the public opinion of the State is eager for an opportunity to express itself openly, and with emphasis on my part." [52] Accordingly, on December 8 he gave the newspapers the following statement:

"The question, Who should be chosen by the incoming Legislature of the State to occupy the seat in the Senate of the United States, which will presently be made vacant by the expiration of the term of Mr. Kean, is of such vital importance to the people of the State, both as a

[47] W. W. to O. G. Villard, December 5, 1910, copy in Baker Papers.
[48] *Trenton Evening Times*, December 7, 1910.
[49] S. Axson to R. S. Baker, August 29, 1928, Baker Papers.
[50] B. J. Hendrick, "Woodrow Wilson: Political Leader," *loc. cit.*, p. 225.
[51] *Trenton Evening Times*, December 7, 1910; also, *Trenton True American*, December 8, 1910.
[52] W. W. to T. D. Jones, December 8, 1910, photostatic copy in Baker Papers.

question of political good faith and as a question of genuine representation in the Senate, that I feel constrained to express my own opinion with regard to it in terms which cannot be misunderstood. I had hoped that it would not be necessary for me to speak, but it is.

"I realize the delicacy of taking any part in the discussion of the matter. As Governor of New Jersey I shall have no part in the choice of a Senator. Legally speaking, it is not my duty even to give advice with regard to the choice. But there are other duties besides legal duties. The recent campaign has put me in an unusual position. I offered, if elected, to be the political spokesman and adviser of the people. I even asked those who did not care to make their choice of Governor upon that understanding not to vote for me. I believe that the choice was made upon that understanding; and I cannot escape the responsibility involved. I have no desire to escape it. It is my duty to say, with a full sense of the peculiar responsibility of my position, what I deem it to be the obligation of the Legislature to do in this gravely important matter.

"I know that the people of New Jersey do not desire Mr. James Smith, Jr., to be sent again to the Senate. If he should be, he will not go as their representative. The only means I have of knowing whom they do desire to represent them is the vote at the recent primaries, where forty-eight thousand Democratic voters, a majority of the whole number who voted at the primaries, declared their preference for Mr. Martine of Union County. For me, that vote is conclusive. I think it should be for every member of the Legislature. Absolute good faith in dealing with the people, an unhesitating fidelity to every principle avowed, is the highest law of political morality under a constitutional government. The Democratic party has been given a majority in the Legislature; the Democratic voters of the State have expressed their preference under a law advocated and supported by the opinion of their party, declared alike in platforms and in enacted law. It is clearly the duty of every Democratic legislator, who would keep faith with the law of the State and with the avowed principles of his party, to vote for Mr. Martine. It is my duty to advocate his election—to urge it by every honorable means at my command." [53]

It should be remembered that Smith had not yet announced his candidacy. He was surprised and hurt, and charged that Wilson was lacking in "that fine courtesy which should control not only southern gentle-

[53] *Trenton True American*, December 9, 1910.

men, but the conduct of all gentlemen." Wilson's assault, he declared, was "a gratuitous attack upon one who has befriended him, but whose candidacy has not been announced." It was also "an unwarranted attempt to coerce the Legislature." [54]

The arguments set forth by the Smith spokesmen were not without some validity and reasonableness. Both the federal and state constitutions, they asserted, guarded carefully against encroachment by the governor on the prerogatives of the legislature in the election of United States senators. "The present act by the Governor-elect has no parallel in State history," one Smith newspaper added, "and it will be recalled that no governor in the past has attempted to dictate to the Legislature in matters outside of his authority without rebuke by the Legislature." [55]

The Smith spokesmen, moreover, ridiculed Wilson's contention that the 48,449 votes cast for Martine in the senatorial primary bound the Democratic legislators; 213,272 voters elected the Democratic legislators and it required a wild imagination, they declared, to assert that one-fourth of the voters spoke for the remaining three-fourths. To make matters worse, the Smith men contended, Martine was a confessed free-trader and free silver advocate, who would in no sense represent his party or his state.

Smith's editorial spokesmen also met squarely the question of party leadership in the state. During the last few days of the campaign Wilson had asserted his leadership of the party, they admitted, but they pointed out that he had done nothing during the long years of Democratic weakness to aid the party, that party leadership consisted of control of an organization and the ability to deliver votes and swing elections. It did not, they claimed, consist of the type of leadership Wilson was demonstrating. [56]

But to the progressive Democrats who had been struggling for years against machine leadership, Wilson's declaration was the outward sign that he had, as Kerney put it, "the courage and ability to lead a political revolution." [57] The progressive editors saw with remarkable perspicacity the fundamental character of the test of strength between the old leader and the new statesman. They realized that if the immediate issue at stake was the election of a United States senator, the essential issue was: who would control the Democratic party in New Jersey? Had Wilson

[54] *ibid.*, December 10, 1910.
[55] *Newark Evening Star*, December 9, 1910.
[56] *ibid.*, December 27, 1910.
[57] *Trenton Evening Times*, December 9, 1910.

decided not to interfere in the controversy, they declared, the question of party control would have been decided *ipso facto*. The progressive spokesmen realized, furthermore, that the stakes in the fight were high. On the one hand, Wilson would not only lose the tenuous control of the state party he then had, but he would almost certainly forfeit any claim he might have for the presidential nomination if he did not defeat Smith.[58] On the other hand, Smith would not only lose a seat in the Senate, he would also be forced to surrender the party into other hands if he did not defeat Wilson. George L. Record, by all odds the ablest political commentator in the state, expressed this idea when he wrote that Wilson would be "the unquestioned leader of his party" if he succeeded in securing Martine's election. And Wilson could not help to elect Martine, Record added, "without smashing the Davis machine here, and the Smith-Nugent machine in Essex." [59]

Insurgent Democrats in the state, therefore, were entirely satisfied that Wilson was a genuine progressive who had great capacity for leadership. "The people of New Jersey and of the country generally, while reposing confidence in you heretofore," wrote Wescott after the publication of Wilson's statement, "have to-day, by reason of the senatorial situation in our state and your attitude thereto, . . . vastly more confidence in you and your future work as a public man." [60] It was evident also by the early part of December that Wilson was rapidly being catapulted into national fame because of his energetic defense of the principle of direct election of senators. Members of Congress were interested in the New Jersey scene and Representative William Hughes reported on December 9 that Wilson was the presidential favorite for 1912 of a majority of the House Democrats.[61] "The issue has, indeed, assumed national proportions," declared an Indiana editor; ". . . the choice of Smith would discredit the party throughout the country." [62] Few newspapers in the nation rose to defend Smith's senatorial ambitions;[63] most editors thought that the issue of the fight was plain and that Wilson was fighting for democratic principles and for the overthrow of corrupt boss politics and consequently gave him their hearty

---

[58] The *Jersey Journal* of Jersey City, November 26, 1910, aptly expresses this idea.

[59] *ibid.*, November 29, 1910.

[60] J. W. Wescott to W. W., December 10, 1910, Wilson Papers.

[61] W. Hughes to W. W., December 9, 1910, *ibid.*

[62] *Indianapolis News*, December 27, 1910.

[63] See, however, the *New York Sun*, November 30, 1910, for a violent attack upon Martine's candidacy; also the *Chicago Inter-Ocean*, January 9, 1911, for a criticism of Wilson's position.

support.[64] Even from the progressive Olympus of Lincoln, Nebraska, came Bryan's benediction upon Wilson's course: "Governor Wilson has taken the proper position." [65] John Sharp Williams's verdict on Wilson's decision to fight Smith openly, "You did exactly right," [66] was a terse expression of the general opinion of the Democrats in every part of the country.[67] In strange contrast to the vociferous publicity newspapers and magazines throughout the country were giving the senatorial controversy, Harvey simply ignored the fight. Not one word about Wilson's most important battle before 1911 appeared in *Harper's Weekly*.

All sorts of rumors were taken up and given credence by news-hungry readers; the most sensational was a report emanating from Chicago to the effect that Roger Sullivan, boss of the Illinois Democratic organization, had conferred with Wilson and had declared that if Wilson would abandon his fight against Smith, he, Sullivan, would agree to swing the Illinois delegation in the national convention in 1912 into line behind Wilson's presidential candidacy. "That does not appeal to me at all," Wilson is reputed to have replied, adding that if New Jersey, Ohio, and New York elected conservative senators there would be no Democratic party in 1912.[68] Sullivan of course later denied categorically the report and declared that he was not at all interested in the New Jersey matter,[69] but the story is illustrative, none the less, of the tremendous popular interest the struggle evoked.

It seemed a bit anticlimactic when Smith, on December 15, formally announced his candidacy for election to the Senate. He made his announcement in the conventional manner by replying to the Essex assemblymen-elect who had requested him to enter the field. "I have received so many assurances of like nature from other members-elect," Smith wrote, "that I am convinced the majority view of the Democratic

[64] "The people of the country are interested in the election of a Senator from New Jersey not only because they want to see that body free of the reactionary influence that now dominates it," wrote Charles P. Grasty in the *Baltimore Sun*, December 11, 1910, ". . . but because they are interested also in seeing the Democrats of New Jersey redeem the promises they made before the election to break up the domination of the bosses in their State."

[65] *The Commoner*, December 23, 1910.

[66] J. S. Williams to W. W., December 14, 1910, Wilson Papers.

[67] See, e.g., the *New York World*, December 10 and 17; *New York Times*, December 11; *The Nation*, XCI (December 15), 571; *Louisville Courier-Journal*, December 28; *Birmingham Age-Herald*, December 10; *Columbia* (S. C.) *State*, December 27; *Chattanooga Daily Times*, December 10; *Daily Oklahoman* of Oklahoma City, December 20; *New Orleans Times-Democrat*, December 14 and 21, 1910.

[68] *Chicago Daily Tribune*, December 15, 1910.

[69] *New York Evening World*, December 19, 1910.

members who will comprise the next legislature coincides with your view." [70] Except, however, for his own newspapers, Smith's announcement was greeted by a cold silence on the part of the Democratic editors in the state. Davis remained loyal to his Newark friend and boasted that Smith had "the necessary votes in the . . . fight," [71] but Smith's pronouncement goaded Alexander of the *Trenton True American,* who had previously refused to take sides in the contest, into making a repudiation of Smith's candidacy.[72]

During the latter part of December the senatorial situation became increasingly tense and Wilson, who had been cautiously polite, soon realized that he would have to adopt stern, even harsh, methods in the controversy. "The fight is a tough one," he wrote to a friend on December 21, "and I must say some rough things before it is over but it is positively the right thing to do." [73] Wilson wrote to another friend the day after Smith announced his candidacy: "Smith has at last come openly out and defied me to defeat him: and defeated he must be if it takes every ounce of strength out of me. I feel pretty confident it can be done; but a nasty enough fight is ahead, and I shall have to do some rather heartless things which I had hoped might be avoided. They are against all the instincts of kindliness in me. But you cannot fight the unscrupulous without using very brutal weapons." [74]

There was first of all, Wilson realized, an urgent necessity for unity among the progressive forces, and early in December he set about uniting the men who were fighting for Martine's election. On December 19 Wilson met with a group of progressive leaders in Trenton to discuss the senatorial campaign. Tumulty and Sullivan, who were the Wilson leaders in Hudson County, and Harry V. Osborne, who was leading the Wilson-Martine forces in Essex County, argued that Wilson

[70] *Newark Evening Star,* December 16, 1910. Smith also set forth the sort of program he would support were he elected senator. It included tariff reduction, national economy and conservation of natural resources, the fortification of the Panama Canal, and—of all things—an amendment for the popular election of United States senators.

[71] *Trenton True American,* December 15, 1910. Davis later explained at greater length his reasons for supporting Smith. "I am sorry that Governor-elect Wilson and myself are not in accord on the Senatorial question," he declared. ". . . I am moved by loyalty to my party and to my friend. I favor Mr. James Smith, Jr., for the office of United States Senator. I take this stand for two reasons: Because he is far better equipped for the office than the only other candidate named, and because he holds my promise to aid his selection by all honorable means." *ibid.,* December 22, 1910.

[72] *ibid.,* December 17, 1910.

[73] W. W. to C. H. Dodge, December 21, 1910, copy in Baker Papers.

[74] W. W. to Mary A. Hulbert, December 16, 1910, published in R. S. Baker, *Woodrow Wilson,* III, 120-121.

should go on the stump and carry the fight to the people. Tumulty, it appeared, had already arranged for a mass meeting in Jersey City. Wilson consequently agreed to make speeches in Jersey City and Newark, at least, and even in Morris, Middlesex, and Monmouth counties if the progressive leaders thought the latter addresses were necessary for the success of Martine's cause.[75]

At the Trenton conference Wilson also decided to assault the very citadel of bossism itself, to carry the war into Smith's own domain of Essex. On December 20 he invited the eleven assemblymen-elect from Essex to a conference at "Prospect": "I think that it is imperative in the common interest that we should fully understand each other with regard to the question of the United States Senatorship," he wrote.[76] The following day a little band of five assemblymen[77] from Newark—Edward D. Balentine, Frank A. Boettner, Charles W. Brown, William P. Macksey, and James P. Mylod—went to Princeton late in the afternoon for a momentous three hours' conference with the governor-elect. Wilson must have realized the difficulty of the task he had undertaken in attempting to alienate from Smith's support the very men who had publicly requested Smith to become a senatorial candidate; yet he was determined to tell the entire story of the senatorial affair to the Newark men.

Here was a strange party leader, the Essex men must have thought. He did not order them to vote for Martine; he did not attempt to force them to agree with him; he offered no patronage as payment for their votes. He simply told in detail the story of the senatorial matter from start to finish and appealed to the Essex men to vindicate the honor of the Democratic party by standing by the results of the senatorial primary.[78] The following day, on December 22, Wilson met the other

[75] *Trenton Evening Times*, December 19; *Trenton True American*, December 20, 1910; J. P. Tumulty, *Woodrow Wilson As I Know Him*, p. 60.

[76] Letter published in *Trenton Evening Times*, December 20, 1910.

[77] Wilson divided the Essex delegation into two groups. The first group consisted of five assemblymen-elect who he thought might be won over to Martine's cause. The remaining six Wilson apparently thought were unredeemable. W. P. Macksey to R. S. Baker, December —, 1927, Baker Papers.

[78] Wilson told the Essex men that they had been tricked into pledging their support to Smith and that, as a means of maintaining their honor as men and of performing their duty as representatives, they would be justified in withdrawing their pledges of support. He further declared that Smith's defeat was an absolute certainty and that they would be wasting their votes and jeopardizing their reputations and political futures in voting for Smith. Wilson explained in detail his relations with Smith and declared that the Newark boss had given him absolute assurance before the Trenton convention that he would not be a candidate for the Senate. *Newark Evening News,*

Essex assemblymen-elect in New York and presented again his argument for Martine's election.[79]

Wilson's efforts to alienate from Smith the support of his own organization men in Newark seemed to be at least partially successful, for the five legislators who conferred with Wilson at Princeton on December 21 were weakening in their support of Smith soon afterward. Wilson had impressed them as a virile and forthright leader, they admitted. "He is a great man," declared one of the Essex men, "and he talked to us as a father would."[80] At Princeton on December 23 Wilson again presented his plea to five more assemblymen-elect from Union, Hunterdon, Middlesex, and Bergen counties.[81] He also sought to supplement his arguments for Smith's defeat by writing personal letters to the legislators who he thought might support the progressive cause. Most of these letters have been destroyed, but fortunately one remains that illustrates his method.[82]

By the end of the third week in December Wilson had presented personally his case for Martine's election to almost every Democratic legislator-elect, and by that date he was confident of victory over the Smith-Nugent forces. On December 23 he gave to the newspapers a detailed review of the progress of the senatorial battle. "In view of Mr. James Smith, Jr.'s, public avowal of his candidacy . . . ," he began, "it becomes my duty to lay before the voters of the State, the facts, as I know them, and the reasons why it seems to me imperative that Mr. Martine and not Mr. Smith should be sent to the Senate." Wilson related Smith's alleged pre-convention declaration that he would not be a senatorial candidate, recounted the episode of Smith's visit to "Prospect" shortly after the election, and told the story of Davis's agreement to support Smith's candidacy. Wilson charged, furthermore, that Smith had been

December 22; *Trenton True American*, December 22-23, 1910. There are no records, it should be reiterated, to prove that Smith gave anyone "absolute assurances" that he would not be a candidate.

[79] *Trenton Evening Times*, December 23, 1910. Wilson conferred with five Essex assemblymen-elect—Harry F. Backus, Michael Leveen, John J. Bracken, M. F. Phillips, and Frank P. Shalvoy. M. J. McGowan, Jr., the other Newark legislator, refused to attend the meeting. None of this second group agreed to support Martine.

On December 22, Wilson also discussed the senatorial question in New York with two other legislators-elect, Charles H. Meyer of Sussex and Eugene Burke of Morris counties.

[80] *Trenton True American*, December 23, 1910.

[81] *ibid.*, December 24, 1910.

[82] For which see W. W. to William P. Macksey of Newark, January 13, 1911, Wilson Papers.

dealing with the legislators-elect in a highhanded manner and that he had assumed that he would control the Wilson administration. "In brief," Wilson added, "he has assumed that he and other gentlemen not elected to the legislature by the people would have the same control over the action of the houses that is understood to have been exercised by the so-called Board of Guardians of the Republican party in recent years."

GOOD LORD! HE REALLY MEANT IT!
Newark Evening News

If Smith were sent again to the Senate, Wilson reiterated, he would represent the same industrial and railroad interests that Kean represented; as proof of the community of interests among the bosses, Wilson pointed to the significant fact that Baird's newspaper, the *Camden Courier,* was supporting Smith's candidacy. The people, therefore, should let their legislators know in unmistakable terms that they would

not tolerate Smith's election. "Confirm the vote of Mr. Martine and
the principle of the people's choice is established—will live vitally in
practice," Wilson concluded by emphasizing the party's obligation
firmly to establish the direct primary system; "ignore it and the people
will distrust both primaries and parties." If the members of the legislature turn away from the people in this crisis, he finally warned, "they
will never again have or deserve another opportunity to enjoy their
support and confidence." [83]

The reverberations caused by this ringing declaration had hardly
ceased to echo in political circles in New Jersey before Smith struck
back hard at Wilson in a public statement that deserved much more
attention than it received. Smith bluntly endeavored to give the lie to
Wilson's oft-repeated statement that he had promised, before the Trenton convention, not to enter the senatorial contest.[84] The voters, however, were in an angry mood and applauded Wilson all the more when
he replied indignantly, "I am quite willing to go with Mr. Smith before
the court of public opinion on the charge of attempted trickery and
deceit." [85] Record had by now awakened to the exciting fact that Wil-

[83] *Trenton True American,* December 24, 1910.

[84] There were three main charges in Wilson's statement that demanded rebuttals,
Smith wrote. First was Wilson's charge that he was the candidate of Wall Street. "Dr.
Wilson should have been the last of men" to make this statement. Second, "Dr. Wilson
says that he was assured by my spokesman before his nomination that I would not be
a candidate for the senatorial office. I never made such a statement. No one was ever
authorized by me to make such a statement, and no one representing me made such a
statement to Dr. Wilson. Furthermore, here is a challenge which I submit for his
acceptance. Let him name the man or men coming from me who so informed him."
Third, "No agreement was ever made by me nor by any one in my behalf, with the
leader of the Hudson county organization that the votes of that county would be cast
for me as senator." Smith next proceeded to tell his version of the Smith-Wilson conference at Princeton and asserted that Wilson had suggested that Smith propose a
compromise candidate for the Senate. Smith repeated his assertion that the senatorial
primary, in which only 48,445 Democrats voted, was not binding on the Democratic
legislators who had been elected by 213,273 voters. *Trenton True American,* December
27, 1910.

[85] But was he? Wilson was unwilling to accept Smith's challenge to reveal the name of
the person who had allegedly represented Smith in the pre-nomination negotiations.
Obviously the man was Harvey. "I certainly would not have allowed my name to go
before the convention that nominated me if I had not thought that the gentleman who
told me that Mr. Smith would not be a candidate for the Senate spoke for Mr. Smith,"
Wilson added. This entire statement must be regarded as an *ex post facto* judgment; it
is doubtful whether the senatorial question loomed so large in Wilson's mind before the
Trenton convention. Wilson explained that he would not reveal the name of the liaison
man "because he is a man whom I very highly esteem and upon whom I do not care to
bring the mortification of being drawn into this now very public matter." *ibid.,* December 29, 1910.

son had met the acid test of progressive leadership. His appeal for Martine's election, Record wrote, was "without exception the most powerful, far reaching and epoch-making utterance ever made by a public man in New Jersey. It fairly makes one rub his eyes to make sure that it is true." [86] Other editors were just as enthusiastic as Record over the progress of the senatorial campaign and would certainly have agreed with his assertion, "This is a revolution, the end of which no man can see." [87]

There were numerous indications that Wilson's fight against the Smith-Nugent-Davis combine was stirring the Democrats of New Jersey as no other political controversy within a generation had stirred them. The overwhelming majority of the Democratic and independent newspapers kept hammering steadily away at the Newark boss, but it was also significant that the Democratic voters themselves were at last aroused to action. A group of progressives in Essex County, headed by Julian A. Gregory, Alexander R. Fordyce, J. C. Sprigg, and Samuel Kalisch, organized a Democratic Direct Primary League to fight Smith in Newark,[88] while Democratic voters in other counties organized in a similar manner to present the progressive cause before their legislators.[89] State Senator William C. Gebhardt of Hunterdon County also joined in the struggle for Martine's election and declared, "I am glad that the Democratic party . . . has at last a leader who is not controlled by the corporations and special interests." [90]

Wilson's decision in early January 1911 to make Tumulty his private secretary was a direct outgrowth of the senatorial fight. He had seriously considered naming the New Jersey reporter for the *New York Evening Post* to the position; he realized, however, that the Smith forces were "trying to coil . . . [him] about with plans of their own," and that he needed the advice of a man who had been active in state politics. "I am therefore going to ask one of the ablest of the young Democratic politicians of the State," he wrote Villard, "if he will not act as my secretary in order that I may have a guide at my elbow in matters of which I

---

[86] *Jersey Journal* of Jersey City, December 24, 1910.
[87] See, e.g., *Trenton True American*, December 23, 1910, January 6, 1911; *Newark Evening News,* December 20, 1910, January 3, 4, and 11, 1911; *Baltimore Sun,* December 28, 1910.
[88] *Trenton Evening Times,* December 13, 1910.
[89] See, e.g., the *Trenton True American*, December 26, 1910.
[90] *ibid.,* December 31, 1910.

know almost nothing." [91] Tumulty, after some prompting from his progressive friends, agreed to accept the position.

Wilson's campaign for Martine had been so encouraging that by the first week in January 1911 it was apparent that unless some untoward accident changed the course of events the "Farmer Orator" would win the senatorship. Wilson, on the other hand, was still determined to carry the fight over the heads of bosses and legislators to his constituents, the people. It was at St. Patrick's Hall in Jersey City on January 5, where he had made his first "political plea" of the gubernatorial campaign, that he began his post-election series of discussions of state issues before the voters of New Jersey.

It was a tumultuous affair; the auditorium was crowded with men and women who had come to witness the rare spectacle of a governor-elect making war on the organization that had nominated and helped to elect him. Mark A. Sullivan presided and introduced State Senator George S. Silzer, who spoke on Martine's behalf until the arrival of Wilson, Tumulty, and Martine evoked a storm of applause and ended the speech. In a characteristically flowery and sentimental speech Tumulty introduced Wilson: "I know you are awaiting with impatience the coming of a great man with a great soul," he dilated. "How we have yearned, how we have longed through all these weary years for just such leadership as this." The multitude rose to their feet and shouted; there was a crash of brass, a flash of color as a thousand flags waved over the heads of the throng.

Wilson had never been in better oratorical form and quickly revealed that he was complete master of the rough-and-tumble variety of stump-speaking. He declared that he had come to Jersey City again to fulfill his promise that he would offer himself as the people's spokesman. He had been told, he said, that the Democratic party was divided. That was not true; the party did not consist of a little group of men in Essex County; it consisted of the rank and file of the Democratic voters. The Smith-Nugent machine was a wart growing on the body politic, that was all, and it was not a serious operation to "cut off a wart." ". . . it can be done while you wait, and it is being done; the clinic is open, and every man can witness the operation."

Smith, Wilson declared, represented "not a party but a system," which was a covert alliance between businessmen and politicians. He pointed to a recent conference, which he declared was attended by

[91] W. W. to O. G. Villard, January 2, 1911, copy in Baker Papers.

Smith and two leading Republican bosses, Baird of Camden and Louis Kuehnle of Atlantic City, as proof of the bi-partisan character of the "system." The whole thing had been "smoked out," Wilson asserted; the people had "thrashed" the bosses at the recent elections, and they were "going to stay thrashed."

He and his progressive cohorts were fighting for a great principle, Wilson pleaded. Reactionaries might sneer at the senatorial primary results as having no meaning, but all true Democrats were "morally bound" by the tremendous opportunity to establish the direct election of United States senators firmly in New Jersey political practice. Wilson deliberately avoided a discussion of Martine's political record and qualifications for public service—the less said about that the better; but the crowd greeted the mention of Martine's name with tremendous applause. It was the cue Wilson had been waiting for and he turned dramatically to Martine, who was sitting directly behind him on the stage, and said:

"I have heard a great many men hope for compromise. God defend us against compromise! All weak men want compromise. Every man who is afraid to stand to his guns wants compromise. . . . I appeal to Mr. Martine never, under any circumstance, to withdraw. We are not in this fight to find the easy way, the complacent way. We are in it to find and pursue the right way, and any man who turns away from the right way will be marked, labeled, and remembered. . . . There are some weak hearts, and I feel sorry for them. . . . I'd rather be a knave than a coward."

There was certainly no danger that the perennial candidate, Martine, would withdraw from the fight, now that he scented victory, but the crowd went wild.

Wilson usually concluded his political addresses with a burst of high-sounding oratory. His speech at Jersey City was no exception to this rule and he declaimed about old mists being rolled away and the hosts of free men marching onward. He added, however, a final ultimatum to the machine forces that had a real sting to it:

"These are our terms: War, if you are allied with the enemy. Peace if you are on the other side of justice. It is not a truce, but it is honest, fair, equitable peace, but implacable war if an alliance, though ever so slender, remains with the men who are our enemies, and who do not know their welfare." [92]

---

[92] The address is printed in full in the *Trenton True American*, January 7, 1911.

The effect of Wilson's flaming declaration of war was electric. He had fallen easily into the habit of defying the bosses, it is true, but never had he so dramatically asserted his leadership of the Democratic party and of all the progressive forces in the state. He usually had a careful regard for the truth, even in campaign speeches, but he had been badly informed in certain respects before he made his speech at Jersey City. Smith was goaded by Wilson's accusations into making an emphatic reply to Wilson's indictment. Gone was the suavity and air of calm detachment that usually characterized the Newark leader's public pronouncements. He was embittered, sarcastic, and immeasurably agitated as he branded as absolutely false Wilson's charge that he had conferred with Baird and Kuehnle about the senatorial election.[93] He further pointed out that Wilson had refused to name the person who had informed him that Smith would not be a candidate for the Senate.

"He has had 10 days in which to answer that challenge. Having failed to do so, I now regretfully charge him publicly with resorting to the trick of attempting to deceive the people that he might strike down one who had befriended him and upbuild an ambition that has mastered him. . . .

"What a spectacle for public contemplation! Here is a man chosen by the people as the chief executive of the State. His duties, if they are conscientiously performed, will keep him well engaged. But meanwhile he must have relaxation as he rushes into the senatorial affray. He talks of principle to some and of his power to others. Now his conscience is at work; later he puts aside conscience and tries the arts of untruthfulness and deceit. In private he laughs at the primary law and scowls at its 'preference.' In public he treats both as holy. In theory he is swayed by lofty impulses. In practice he is using the baser emotions to accomplish his purpose.

"In the annals of political history there is no such example of insincerity as is here presented."[94]

Smith's periodic answers to Wilson, however, did not impress the people of the state. They were stirred by Wilson's call to arms and were, on the whole, solidly behind his campaign to smash the Smith-Nugent machine. Smith, too, was stirred into increased activity in his own behalf by the rising tide of Martine sentiment, but he was still the old-time boss type politician: Wilson's swashbuckling campaign tactics had

[93] Wilson was evidently mistaken with regard to this matter. He never mentioned it again.
[94] *Trenton True American*, January 7, 1911.

completely baffled him. In order to check the growing spirit of independence among the Hudson County legislators, Smith and Nugent held a series of conferences on January 6 with Davis and his numerous lieutenants.[95] It was a last-ditch measure, this effort of Smith to prevent Davis's political influence in Hudson from disintegrating. But Davis's political power was waning rapidly, just as his hold on life was weakening. The veteran campaigner died on January 9, and his death released his followers from any commitment in the senatorial matter that once had burdened them; it was the death-knell of Smith's hopes to return to the United States Senate.

One more speech, one more great heave, Wilson thought, and victory for Martine was assured. On January 14, therefore, only eleven days before the legislature was to elect a senator, Wilson went to Newark to make his final appeal to the people. Samuel Kalisch, the leading Wilson spokesman in the city, presented Wilson to a tremendous crowd that had gathered in the New Auditorium. According to friendly newspaper reporters, the meeting was even more successful than the earlier rally in Jersey City.

Wilson confessed to his listeners that he was sorry it was necessary for him to come to Essex and give the reasons why he thought "an eminent citizen of Essex" should not be sent to the Senate. He had not begun the fight, he added, but the fight was on and his Scotch-Irish blood was aroused. The controversy had begun when Smith refused to acknowledge the verdict of the senatorial primary as binding; it had become a battle for the reestablishment of popular government in New Jersey. Wilson then promptly proceeded to employ the effective device of elevating the local issue to universal importance, of identifying his own cause with the cause of God and liberty. Viewed in this light, therefore, he and his allies were battling not merely for Martine's election, nor even for the principle of direct election of senators only.

"Gentlemen, what is it that we are fighting for? Does not your blood jump quicker in your veins when you think that this is part of the age-long struggle for human liberty? What do men feel curtails and destroys their liberty? Matters in which they have no voice. The control of little groups and cliques and bodies of special interests, the things that are managed without regard to the public welfare or general opinion— the things that are contrived without any referendum to the great mass of feelings and opinions and purposes that are abroad among free men

[95] *Jersey Journal* of Jersey City, January 7, 1911.

in a free country. Whenever things go to cover, then men stand up and know and say that liberty is in jeopardy, and so every time a fight of this sort occurs, we are simply setting up the standard again. One can almost see the field of battle. On the one hand a fort that looks strong but that is made of pasteboard. Behind it stand men apparently armed with deadly weapons, but having only playthings in their hands. And off cowering in the distance for a little while is the great mass of fearful, free men. Presently they take heart; they look up; they begin to move slowly. You can see the dust of the plain gather, and then as they take heart and realize that whether the fort is hard to take or not life is not worth living unless it is taken. And they go on, and, as in the old Bible stories, the first shout of victorious and irresistible free men causes the stronghold to collapse.

"The reign of terror is over. There is nothing in the fort, and the gentlemen who once stood behind this eminent fortification are seen to kow-tow and say: 'It was a long struggle to do the will of the suffering people.' " [96]

Wilson was later to discover that the organization that had for years controlled his party could not be so easily dislodged from power, even by a blast from Gideon's trumpet. It was, however, great speechmaking, just the sort of oratory men like to hear. The campaign was at an end for Wilson, but Smith had the last word in the battle of words. In a futile attempt to answer Wilson's Newark speech, he issued a long and final statement.[97]

The legislature of New Jersey convened in mid-January and Wilson was inaugurated governor on the 17th. On January 23 a Democratic caucus was held by party leaders to determine the official party position with regard to the senatorial election. Each of the nine Democratic senators and twenty-four of the forty-one assemblymen voted for Martine; Smith received fourteen votes, William Hughes two, and Frank S. Katzenbach one vote. Forty-one votes were necessary for election, and since Martine was already assured of thirty-three votes, Smith's defeat was almost a certainty. Nugent, however, issued a bombastic statement after the caucus and declared that Martine had reached his peak strength and could not possibly be elected.[98]

Trenton on January 23, the eve of the day on which the legislature was to elect a senator, was a place of feverish activity. Smith and his en-

---

[96] *Newark Evening News,* January 16; *Trenton True American,* January 16, 1911.

[97] *Newark Evening Star,* January 16, 1911.

[98] *Trenton True American,* January 24, 1911.

tourage came up to the capital and opened headquarters in the boss's old Room 100 at the Trenton House, while Wilson and his supporters were making final preparations for the fight in the executive offices at the State House.[99] At about eleven o'clock in the evening a great throng of Smith supporters from Newark, headed by a brass band, marched from the Pennsylvania station to the Trenton House and loudly greeted their leader. It was a futile demonstration; even Smith seemed to realize this when he made a short, but touching speech to his followers. "My dear friends," he said, "I wish I could tell you how much I appreciate this evidence of friendship and loyalty, but I cannot. I can only say that it cheers me mightily to see so many friends at my side." [100]

The legislature balloted at noon on January 24. On the first ballot Martine received forty votes, thirty-one in the House and nine in the Senate—one less than was necessary for his election. Smith had the support of only ten assemblymen—Harry F. Backus, John J. Bracken, Charles W. Brown, Michael Leveen, William P. Macksey, Mark F. Phillips, Michael J. McGowan, Jr., and Frank P. Shalvoy from his own county, and James H. Christie and Thomas F. Martin of Hudson. Four assemblymen who had voted for Smith in the Democratic caucus on January 23 supported Martine the following day,[101] while Leon R. Taylor changed from Katzenbach to Martine and Cornelius Ford shifted from Hughes to Martine.[102]

Now that it was inevitable that Martine would be elected, Smith issued a statement releasing his delegates. "In view of the preponderance of legislative favor for Governor Wilson's candidate for the United States Senate," he announced sorrowfully, "I feel that I should no longer stay the consummation of the Executive's purpose." He would like to believe that the party would retain the people's confidence under Wilson's guidance, Smith concluded, but his mind was "not free from foreboding." Immediately after giving out the statement, Smith quietly left Trenton for Newark. Wilson of course was elated by the turn of events. "I can say with sincerity that it is what I expected," he declared, commenting on the results of the first ballot, "for I hadn't the slightest doubt that the Legislators would act in the spirit of responsibility to

[99] Tumulty tells us that Wilson and he worked until four or five o'clock in the morning of January 24, "keeping in close contact with our friends both by telephone and personal conference." J. P. Tumulty, *Woodrow Wilson As I Know Him*, pp. 67-68.

[100] *Trenton True American*, January 25, 1911.

[101] They were John V. L. Booraem and William E. Ramsay of Middlesex, John J. Matthews of Hunterdon, and Charles A. Meyer of Sussex.

[102] *Trenton True American*, January 25, 1911.

their constituents. . . . The people will know that henceforth they will make free choice of Senators on their own responsibility." [103]

The last scene in the senatorial drama was enacted the following day, January 25, when the legislature voted for a second time. Martine had 47 votes, Smith 3, Edward C. Stokes, leading Republican nominee, 21, and there was a small scattering of votes for other Republican candidates. Only three Democratic assemblymen, McGowan, Phillips, and Shalvoy, remained loyal to their old leader from Newark.[104] Wilson afterward wrote: "I pitied Smith at the last. It was so plain that he had few real friends,—that he held men by fear and power and the benefits he could bestow, not by love or loyalty or any genuine devotion. The minute it was seen that he was defeated his adherents began to desert him like rats leaving a sinking ship. He left Trenton (where his headquarters had at first been crowded) attended, I am told, only by his sons, and looking old and broken. He wept, they say, as he admitted himself utterly beaten." [105]

It was just the sort of victory Wilson needed most at this juncture in his career to establish himself as one of the chief progressive leaders in the country. He had a great many things to "live down," but he was doing exactly that, and doing it with a speed that startled his friends. Henry Watterson, always either very much in favor of a cause or very much opposed to it, was jubilant over Wilson's triumph. "First blood for Wilson!" he wrote; ". . . Smith is a fool—an old fool—and deserves what he has got." [106] "You poor scholar & amateur in politics!" wrote Dodge; "Why don't you get an expert like Smith to advise you?" [107]

Progressive leaders all over the country hastened to welcome Wilson into the brotherhood of liberals. Typical was the following letter from Judge Ben B. Lindsey of Denver: "I am just delighted over your victory and so proud of you. I wish sometime I had a chance to tell you of some of the things that I had heard before you came out for Martine and took the stand that you have taken—that has lined you up with the Progressives—I hope[d] for all the time, for there is certainly a big fight ahead, and it is so good to know *you* are on the right side." [108]

---

[103] *Trenton True American,* January 25, 1911.

[104] *ibid.,* January 26, 1911.

[105] W. W. to M. A. Hulbert, January 29, 1911, published in R. S. Baker, *Woodrow Wilson,* III, 126-127.

[106] H. Watterson to ———, January [?] 29, 1911, Wilson Papers.

[107] C. H. Dodge to W. W., January 26, 1911, *ibid.*

[108] January 28, 1911, *ibid.;* also, T. P. Gore to W. W., January 28, 1911, *ibid.*

The New Jersey insurgents, however, thought they had the most to be grateful for as a result of Smith's defeat. Now surely the day had come, they believed, when a courageous leader had dethroned the bosses, smashed their machines, and made possible the achievement of the reform program. "It requires no gift of prophecy to reveal the meaning of the people's victory," Kerney wrote. "It means the passing of the boss system, which received its death-blow when the roll was called at noon yesterday." [109] Record's cup of joy almost ran over; Martine's election, he asserted, was "the most remarkable event in the political history of the State." [110]

It was immeasurably fortunate for Wilson that the senatorial controversy occurred at the outset of his political career, for it threw him out upon the foremost waves of insurgency in the nation.[111] The news of his campaign against Smith had spread like wildfire throughout the country and responsible Democrats began to mention him frequently as the probable Democratic presidential nominee in 1912. Progressive Democrats in New York were fighting to prevent the election of William F. Sheehan, a Tammany leader, to the Senate at the same time the controversy was raging in New Jersey, and the *New York World* was daily giving them courage and inspiration by pointing to Wilson's stand in New Jersey. "New York needs a Woodrow Wilson," was the *World's* slogan.[112]

After the furor and the name-calling of the campaign had given way to a sober consideration of the true meaning of Smith's defeat, it was evident that the most significant outcome of Martine's election was Wilson's success in establishing himself as the leader of the Democratic party in the state. Smith and Nugent had not been defeated in their own populous county, it should be remembered, nor had bossism in New Jersey been crushed forever; the rank and file of the party workers outside Essex, however, were willing to follow Wilson's lead now, not so much because of what he stood for, but because of what he might be

[109] *Trenton Evening Times,* January 25, 1911.

[110] *Jersey Journal* of Jersey City, January 27, 1911.

[111] For Bryan's comment, see *The Commoner,* February 3, 1911; for La Follette's comment, see *La Follette's Weekly Magazine,* iii (February 18, 1911), 3.

[112] *New York World,* January 28, 1911. Practically every newspaper of any size in the country gave full publicity to the senatorial controversy, and there are hundreds of editorials supporting Wilson's position in the press. See, for example, the *New York Times,* January 26; *Chicago Evening Post,* January 25; *Chicago Record-Herald,* January 26; *Atlanta Georgian,* January 25; *Nashville Banner,* January 25; *Richmond Virginian,* January 25; *Raleigh News and Observer,* January 29; *Houston Post,* January 27; *Dallas Morning News,* January 27, 1911.

in a position to give them by way of patronage. Without victory in the senatorial fight, it is safe to assume, Wilson could not have secured the passage of the reform laws that he persuaded the legislature to enact in the spring of 1911; without these reform accomplishments behind him he would not have won the presidential nomination in 1912. One other important result of the controversy, hardly noticed at the time, was that Wilson's war on the New Jersey machine caused Harvey's presidential schemes for Wilson to tumble like a house of cards. Harvey had erected an elaborate presidential structure, the chief foundation stone of which was the support of moneyed conservatives and machine politicians in other parts of the country. After Wilson had shown his true colors with regard to politicians who had the temerity to oppose him, the veteran bosses quickly turned away from his support. The reform program of the 1911 New Jersey legislature and Wilson's subsequent progressive development gave the *coup de grace* to Harvey's plans. In January 1911, however, the presidency seemed far in the future for the New Jersey governor. There was work to be done in the state, plenty of it, and, as Wilson wrote, "it has only begun." [113]

[113] W. W. to M. A. Hulbert, January 29, 1911, published in R. S. Baker, *Woodrow Wilson*, III, 127.

In the Governor's Office with W. B. Hale and J. P. Tumulty

Commander-in-Chief of the New Jersey National Guard at Camp Wilson
Sea Girt, New Jersey

With the Officers of the State Guard at Sea Girt
(Dennis F. Collins on Wilson's right)

CHAPTER VIII

The New Jersey Legislature of 1911

It was fortunate for Woodrow Wilson that he had virtually won his battle for Martine several weeks before the senatorial election occurred, for during the first half of January 1911, he found himself confronted with the necessity of planning a reform program for the legislature that was to convene on January 10. It was obvious from the beginning that he could not expect to receive the advice and support of Smith and Nugent, and since Wilson had identified himself so completely with the progressives there was nothing left for him to do but take the next logical step and seek their aid in constructing a legislative program.

First, he sought Record's advice; at a conference at Princeton Record suggested that Wilson should gather around him a group of trusted counselors, representatives of both parties, who might give him advice on administrative policies and programs. Wilson agreed to call a conference of insurgent leaders to frame a legislative program before his inauguration; however, he also insisted upon inviting the official Democratic leaders in the legislature, although there was at least one Smith lieutenant in the group.[1]

As New York was a more convenient meeting place than Princeton for most of the men he had planned to invite, Wilson decided to have the conference at the Hotel Martinique on January 16, the day before he was to be inaugurated governor. "I think it would be to the common advantage," he wrote on January 11, to the leading progressive editors and politicians of the state, "to have a little conference of a few gentlemen particularly interested in formulating bills for consideration of the Legislature before my actual entrance upon my office as Governor."[2] Wilson presided at the meeting,[3] but it was at once apparent that Rec-

---

[1] J. Kerney, *The Political Education of Woodrow Wilson,* pp. 100-101; also, R. S. Baker, "Memorandum of an interview with George L. Record, April 6, 1926," MS in Baker Papers.

[2] Quoted in Kerney, *The Political Education of Woodrow Wilson,* p. 101.

[3] Present were Wilson, Record, State Senators William C. Gebhardt, James F. Fielder, and Harry V. Osborne; John J. Matthews, leader of the Democratic majority in the Assembly; Matthew Ely of the *Hudson Observer;* James Kerney of the *Trenton Evening Times;* Walter A. and Joseph M. Dear, publishers of the *Jersey Journal;*

ord was the intellectual sparkplug of the group. He had come armed with a sheaf of materials on direct primary and election reform, corrupt practices, public utilities, and employers' liability legislation; although there were some few protests that the state was not yet ready for such thoroughgoing reforms, Wilson and a majority of the conferees agreed to adopt all four measures as the official administration program. To Record Wilson assigned the task of writing the direct primary and corrupt practices bills; he also requested various members of the conference to prepare the other measures.[4]

Wilson actually seems to have thought, as he told Kerney, that everyone would "respect the fact that it was purely a private and confidential gathering." [5] Contrary to Record's emphatic warning, however, he had invited John J. Matthews of Hunterdon County, Democratic assembly floor leader and a Smith follower, and had thus precluded any chance of keeping the details of the meeting secret. Matthews hastened from New York to Newark to tell Smith the details of the conference; the result was that on January 19 Smith's newspapers proclaimed in flaming headlines the story of the "secret conference" in New York, the news of which had "stunned the Democrats." [6]

Most of what the Smith newspapers said was true. It was certainly evident, as they asserted, that Record was rapidly becoming the dominant figure in the Wilson circle; on the other hand, it was doubtful that the new administration would be "bossed" by Record, as the *Evening Star* lamented. Smith was of course trying any way he knew to discredit Wilson; perhaps he thought the voters would resent this secret conclave, this strange mixture of Republicans, Democrats, and insurgents, meeting outside the state to draw up a program that Wilson intended to force upon an unwilling legislature. More important, the senatorial fight was still in progress and Smith thought he saw an opportunity to discredit Wilson before the Democratic party workers. Record, the Smith editors asserted, now controlled Wilson completely,

---

Tumulty; a Mr. Rider; John J. Treacy of Jersey City. The speaker of the Assembly, Edward Kenny, State Senator George S. Silzer, Judge Mark A. Sullivan, and Wallace M. Scudder of the *Newark Evening News* were also invited, but for one reason or another could not attend. From Wilson's statement in the *Trenton Evening Times,* January 19, 1911.

[4] The best account of the Martinique conference is in Kerney, *The Political Education of Woodrow Wilson,* pp. 103-104; see also, R. S. Baker, "Memorandum of an interview with George L. Record . . . ," MS in Baker Papers.

[5] Kerney, *The Political Education of Woodrow Wilson,* p. 104.

[6] *Newark Morning Star, Newark Evening Star,* January 19, 1911.

and that control was "assuming a sinister aspect" because Wilson had allegedly agreed to deliver all the patronage over to Record and the progressive Republicans.[7] If that were true, the regulars must have thought, what would be left for "good Democrats"?

Wilson was considerably agitated by these gad-fly attacks and immediately struck back at his opponents. "There was absolutely nothing secret about the conference held in the Hotel Martinique, New York," he retorted. "It was simply a continuation of the policy I have followed ever since my election of consulting everyone who was interested in the reforms which concern the whole state." He named the men present at the meeting and answered the charges made by Smith's newspapers that he was "controlled" by Record. He had no apologies whatever to make for having sought the New Idea leader's advice and help, he declared. "Mr. Record is well known to be one of the best informed men in this State with regard to the details involved in most of the reforms proposed. . . . He generously consented to put his unusual store of information at the service of the conference, which was non-partisan in its purpose and meant in the public interest." [8]

Meanwhile, Wilson was inaugurated as the forty-third governor of New Jersey on January 17.[9] The people of Trenton were astir early for the ceremonies and the streets of the capital were crowded with spectators who had come from all the counties of the state to witness the first inauguration of a Democratic governor since 1893. At 11:30 in the morning the members of the legislature assembled in the State House and marched together to the Taylor Opera House, where they convened in joint session. Meantime, Wilson and Governor Fort were driven from the State House to the auditorium, through streets lined with cheering crowds.

The inaugural ceremonies were completed in less than an hour. After the invocation, Chief Justice William S. Gummere administered the oath of office and Wilson swore with his hand upon the Bible that he would "diligently, faithfully and to the best of his knowledge, execute the office of governor in conformity to the powers delegated to him." [10] Fort then handed over the official seal of the state to Wilson. "You have commenced right," Fort said. "The people already acclaim you as their tribune for civic advance, and as the foe of every baneful and corrupt

[7] *Newark Evening Star,* January 21, 1911.
[8] *Trenton Evening Times,* January 19, 1911.
[9] That is, since the adoption of the state constitution of 1776.
[10] *Trenton True American,* January 18, 1911.

influence in our public life." [11] The band in the pit struck up "Hail to the Chief," a battery of cannon nearby began the governor's salute of seventeen guns, and the audience arose and cheered wildly. Fort next introduced Wilson to Ernest R. Ackerman, president of the Senate, who in turn presented him to the members of the legislature.

"I assume the great office of Governor of the State with unaffected diffidence," Wilson began his inaugural address. ". . . A long tradition of honorable public service connects each incumbent of it with the generation of men who set up our governments here in free America, to give men perpetual assurance of liberty and justice and opportunity." At once he launched into a discussion of the necessity for economic and political reform. It was obvious, first, that New Jersey's laws defining the relations of employer and employee were "wholly antiquated and impossible"; the state, therefore, must have a workmen's compensation law that would not place upon the worker the burden of fighting powerful composite employer groups to obtain his rights. Effective state regulation of corporations Wilson thought a "much more fundamental" problem; the most urgent need was a thorough overhauling of the state's corporation code so as to prevent industrial and corporate abuses and malpractices. "In order to do this it will be necessary to regulate and restrict the issue of securities, to enforce regulations with regard to bona fide capital, examining very rigorously the basis of capitalization, and to prescribe methods by which the public shall be safeguarded against fraud, deception, extortion, and every abuse of its confidence."

State control of corporations was particularly imperative for public service corporations. The public utilities commission, impotent because it had no authority to begin with, must have "complete regulative powers: the power to regulate rates, the power to learn and make public everything that should furnish a basis for the public judgment . . . , the power, in brief, to adjust such service at every point and in every respect, whether of equipment or charges or methods of financing or means of service."

After endorsing the movement for the equalization of taxation as between corporations and individuals and that perennial reform topic, conservation, Wilson came to the question of primary and election reform. "I earnestly commend to your careful consideration in this connection the laws in recent years adopted in the State of Oregon," he told the legislators, "whose effect has been to bring government back to the

[11] *Journal of the Sixty-Seventh Senate of the State of New Jersey,* p. 57; hereinafter cited as *Senate Journal,* 1911.

people and to protect it from the control of the representatives of selfish and special interests." New Jersey's primary laws should be extended to every elective office and to the election of every party committee or official as well. Systematic ballot reform and stringent laws against corrupt practices in elections were other primary necessities of legislation, Wilson continued. "Here, again," he suggested, "Oregon may be our guide." [12]

"We are servants of the people, of the whole people. Their interest should be our constant study. . . . It is not the foolish ardor of too sanguine or too radical reform that I urge upon you, but merely the tasks that are evident and pressing, the things we have knowledge and guidance enough to do; and to do with confidence and energy. I merely point out the present business of progressive and serviceable government, the next stage on the journey of duty. The path is as inviting as it is plain. Shall we hesitate to tread it? I look forward with genuine pleasure to the prospect of being your comrade upon it." [13]

After the inaugural, Wilson went directly to the State House, where he reviewed the marching columns of Democrats who had come to Trenton to celebrate the return of their party to power. The most remarkable thing about the celebration, Record afterward recalled, was the "subdued, not to say sad, behaviour of the crowd of important and would-be important politicians who attended." [14] After the parade had filed past the governor's stand, Wilson entertained the former governor, members of the legislature, the justices of the Supreme Court, and other state officials at the traditional governor's luncheon at the Hotel Sterling. In the afternoon he went to the executive offices in the State House for a mass reception of New Jersey citizens. [15]

Wilson's comment upon the inaugural ceremonies gives us an illuminating insight into his thought about this, the most important political event in his life before 1912, and reveals something of the deep seriousness with which he undertook the governorship. To Mary A. Hulbert he wrote on January 22:

"I got into harness last Tuesday. The ceremony was simple enough:

[12] John E. Lathrop, editor of the *Washington News*, had strongly advised Wilson to mention the Oregon system favorably in his address. "On this fundamental issue of popular government," Lathrop wrote, "your attitude will be defined nationally by that recommendation beyond all hope of correcting false impressions later." J. E. Lathrop to W. W., January 6, 1911, Wilson Papers.

[13] The inaugural address is printed in the *Senate Journal*, 1911, pp. 58-68.

[14] *Jersey Journal* of Jersey City, January 19, 1911.

[15] *Trenton True American*, January 18, 1911.

the exercises of the inauguration were over in an hour. Only the all-afternoon and all-evening receptions were fatiguing; and even in them there was variety enough to take at least monotony away and afford constant amusement, and, better than amusement, constant human interest. All sorts and conditions of people came, men, women, and children, and I felt very close to all of them, and very much touched by the thought that I was their representative and spokesman, and in a very real sense their help and hope, after year upon year of selfish machine domination when nothing at all had been done for them that could possibly be withheld! Since Tuesday I have been in Trenton every day, except yesterday, getting into harness and learning the daily routine of the office; and all the while deeply moved by the thought of my new responsibilities as the representative and champion of the common people against those who have been preying upon them. I have felt a sort of solemnity in it all that I feel sure will not wear off. I do not see how a man in such a position could possibly be afraid of anything except failing to do his honourable duty and set all temptations (if they be disguised enough to be temptations) contemptuously on one side. I shall make mistakes, but I do not think I shall sin against my knowledge of duty." [16]

There had been no magical rainbow in the skies above Trenton to herald the inauguration of the Wilson regime, no outward sign of the change of government, save, of course, the milling throngs of people that crowded the capital on January 17. New Jersey progressives were certain, none the less, that the years of boss domination would now give way to an era of political righteousness. "I have attended many inauguration ceremonies at Trenton in years past," wrote the astute Record, "but that of Governor Wilson . . . was different from all of them. . . . That such a man at such a juncture should be Governor of New Jersey is a political miracle, and nothing else." [17] A Passaic editor summarized the opinions of most progressives in the state when he wrote of Wilson's inaugural address: "It is a great utterance—great in its thought, great in its simplicity, great in its vision. It may indeed be that our hope has been realized and that a great leader has arisen from among us." [18]

The legislature, meanwhile, had convened on January 10 in its one hundred and thirty-fifth session. The Assembly, with 42 Democrats and

[16] Published in R. S. Baker, *Woodrow Wilson*, III, 134-135.
[17] *Jersey Journal* of Jersey City, January 19, 1911.
[18] *Passaic Daily News,* January 17, 1911.

18 Republicans, elected Edward Kenny, a progressive Democrat from Jersey City, speaker.[19] John J. Matthews, a farmer from High Bridge, was elected majority leader in the lower house by the party caucus.[20] The Senate, Republican by a majority of 12 to 9, elected Ernest R. Ackerman of Plainfield president.[21]

The legislature of 1911 was not unlike most other state legislative bodies of the same period in so far as the caliber of its members was concerned. The average legislator, Democratic or Republican, could boast of little political ability. Most of them were mediocre transients in the legislature; few of them succeeded in avoiding the limbo that is the fate of most local politicians. Democratic leadership in the legislature of 1911, therefore, was limited; however, there were four able senators—James F. Fielder of Jersey City, Harry V. Osborne of Newark, George S. Silzer of New Brunswick, and William C. Gebhardt of Clinton[22]—who Wilson at once named as his spokesmen in the upper house. In the Assembly the paucity of able Democrats was painfully apparent. Practically all the eleven Essex assemblymen, who constituted one-fourth of the Democrats in the lower house, were dutiful lieutenants of their political master, and Wilson could not expect to receive their support. The Hudson delegation, on the other hand, included a few men of ability, notably Edward Kenny, Cornelius Ford, Charles M. Egan, and Thomas F. Martin. Allan B. Walsh, an electrician from Trenton, and Elmer H. Geran, a Princeton graduate of the class of 1899 from Monmouth County, were two other young progressive Democrats who were soon to become Wilson leaders in the lower house.[23]

Wilson was enough of a politician to realize that the great majority of laws, both public and private, enacted by the legislature of any state during any single session were of slight consequence to the public. He knew, too, that his own legislature, even in the momentous year of 1911, would demand its share of petty legislation, and he resolved from the outset of the session to insist only upon the passage of four sweeping reform measures. Their enactment, he believed, would redeem Democratic pre-election campaign pledges. "I am not backing up by my pub-

[19] *Minutes of Votes and Proceedings of the One Hundred and Thirty-Fifth General Assembly of the State of New Jersey*, pp. 1-3; hereinafter cited as *House Journal*, 1911.

[20] *Trenton True American*, January 11, 1911.

[21] *Senate Journal*, 1911, pp. 1-7.

[22] Osborne, Silzer, and Gebhardt were prominently identified with the progressive wing of the party.

[23] Personal information concerning the legislators has been gathered from the *Manual of the Legislature of New Jersey*, 1911, pp. 286-339.

lic utterances," he later declared, "any bill in Trenton except the four bills which are the explicit redemption of our promises made in the platform of the Democratic party, and, for that matter, in the platform of the Republican party too." [24] On February 4 he conferred for several hours at Trenton with Tumulty, former Assemblyman John J. Treacy, Fielder, Silzer, Osborne, and Gebhardt. This group, already designated as the governor's legislative steering committee, agreed that the administration should sponsor and support bills providing for direct primaries and election reform, corrupt practices legislation, workmen's compensation legislation, and public utilities regulation. [25]

Record, meanwhile, had been hard at work preparing primary and election and corrupt practices bills. [26] He left voluminous drafts of these two measures at Wilson's office some time near the end of January. "I have been handed copies of the bills you drew up and shall read them with greatest attention," Wilson informed him on January 27. "My hope will be to get them introduced and to get them out as Committee reports, if that is possible." Wilson next sought out his former student, Geran, and entrusted to him the task of introducing the primary and election reform measure into the Assembly. [27]

Geran introduced the bill in the lower house on February 6; the disclosure of its provisions, which deliberately aimed a body blow at the traditional type of party organization, at once evoked a storm of protest from the Smith-Nugent spokesmen, who were dumbfounded by the sweeping character of the changes the measure envisaged. They charged that it was Record who was primarily responsible for this alarming threat to their organization and lamented that Wilson was now so completely under the domination of the New Idea leader. The Smith leaders, however, quickly recovered from their initial shock, and soon were accusing Wilson, too, of base motives. The chief reason for the introduction of the Geran bill, the *Evening Star* asserted, was Wilson's inordinate lust for power, his ambition to be the absolute master of the Democratic party in the state, and his desire to become the presidential candidate of his party in 1912. [28]

Only a few days passed before the machine leaders in the Assembly began their attack upon the chief article of Wilsonian reform. The

[24] Speech at Harrison, February 28, 1911.
[25] *Jersey Journal* of Jersey City, February 4, 1911.
[26] R. S. Baker, "Memorandum of an interview with George L. Record, April 6, 1926," MS in Baker Papers.
[27] See the *Trenton Evening Times*, February 15, 1911.
[28] *Newark Evening Star*, February 7, 1911.

bill had been referred to the judiciary committee of the Assembly, which was supposedly favorable to it; soon, however, rumors were circulating that Martin and a clique of conservative assemblymen were scheming to have the measure taken from the judiciary committee and referred instead to the hostile committee on elections. Wilson struck back immediately; the bill, he reminded the lawmakers in a public statement on February 15, embodied an attempt to redeem one of the most important campaign pledges made by the Democrats the year before; its purpose was to place the entire election process in the hands of the voters, "to make the government in every part the people's government." Opposition to the Geran bill, he further warned, would not come from within the legislature, but from without, and the names of the persons who opposed it would constitute "an excellent list of the persons who oppose popular government, or who have some private purpose to serve in perpetuating the present system." The bill was in the hands of the judiciary committee, he concluded tartly, and, as far as he was concerned, there it would remain.[29] There were no further attempts to remove the bill from the judiciary committee! However, Wilson was not intractable in his demand that the original Geran bill be adopted exactly as Record had written it; he conferred with a group of Democratic leaders[30] on February 17 and admitted that the measure might have to be amended in order to meet the valid criticism of its opponents.[31]

"Things are getting intense and interesting again," Wilson wrote two weeks later. "The bills for which we are pledged and on whose passage the success and prestige of my administration as governor largely depend are ready for report to the legislature, and the question is, Can we pass them? I think we can, and my spirits rise as the crisis approaches: It is like the senatorial contest all over again,— the same forces arrayed against me; and no doubt the same sort of fight will enable me to win."[32] What was needed more than anything else to make his legislative program successful, Wilson realized, was for the great weight of public opinion to become aroused behind the cause of reform. He had successfully awakened the voters to the dangers implicit in Smith's senatorial candidacy; he would employ the same barnstorming tactics in his fight for legislative reform.

[29] *Trenton True American,* February 16, 1911.
[30] Osborne, Fielder, Silzer, and Geran.
[31] *Trenton Evening Times,* February 18, 1911.
[32] W. W. to M. A. Hulbert, March 5, 1911, published in R. S. Baker, *Woodrow Wilson,* III, 138.

He began the spade work early, long before the reform bills were reported out of committee. First, in an address before the New Jersey Editorial Association at Trenton on February 27, he demanded the enactment of the Geran bill, a public utilities law, a corrupt practices act, and a workmen's compensation law.[33] The following evening, in an address before the West Hudson Board of Trade in the town hall at Harrison, he proclaimed his determination to do battle with the bosses who were scheming to defeat his program. He explained in detail the provisions of the Geran bill and declared that there had been enough talk about the measure. "Very well, then, let us insist, after one reasonably good method is suggested, that the talking shall stop and to go to work and try that method and see whether it will work out or not." He was immeasurably irritated by the numerous petty criticisms that had been made of the bill and shot this defiance at its detractors: "I am for that with every ounce of force there is in me; and the challenge that I issue is this: Let no man oppose this thing unless he is willing to oppose it in public and for reasons." He disclaimed, however, any desire to dominate the legislature: "I want you to understand, gentlemen, that, as your representative, as the only representative of the whole State, for such is the Governor, I am not trying to run the Legislature at Trenton. It might be an amusing thing to try to run it, but I couldn't if I tried. I know a majority of the members of that Legislature pretty well and I respect them thoroughly, and let me tell you that those men are going to act upon their consciences and cannot be run by anybody." [34]

Two days later he returned to Hudson County, the storm center of the state Democracy, to strengthen the courage of the Hudson legislators who were being subjected to great pressure from the local bosses to vote against the Geran bill. In an address before the annual banquet of the Hoboken Board of Trade he declared that political considerations were not involved in the discussions at Trenton centering around the four great measures of the session. He then proceeded to define the issues involved, as he saw them:

"Now the business of politics at this moment is to reconstitute our government by putting it upon its right basis again, which is the basis of the popular will and not the basis of private arrangement. The partnership is about to be dissolved by public process; the partnership is about to be made impossible by pitiless publicity; pitiless not to-

[33] *Trenton True American*, February 28, 1911.
[34] *Jersey Journal* of Jersey City, March 1, 1911.

ward those who are honest; pitiless not toward those who are seeking, even in some partial and blind and groping way, to serve the general interests, but pitiless toward those who are trying to follow the lines which serve only themselves who are afraid that changes will be made, because of the effect the changes may have upon their bank account.

"Now the object of the Geran bill is to restore the government to the people; and the Geran bill is going to be adopted. I know that it is going to be adopted. I know that it is going to be adopted because I know that the people of New Jersey want it. . . .

"I am going to stand for this thing through thick and thin." [35]

Governors in the United States are not usually prime ministers within their states; more often they are leaders neither in an official nor a party sense. Although Wilson was not the first American governor to recognize the vast potentialities inherent in the executive's position as a party leader, no governor in our history has ever made better use of his political opportunities and potentialities than did Wilson in his relations with the Democratic majority in the New Jersey legislature in 1911.

He was truly a prime minister in the state, in an unofficial, a party sense, at least. He prepared the legislative program; he argued the cause of reform before the Democratic legislators; he endeavored to whip recalcitrant lawmakers into line by using the party caucus to determine party policies; as a last resort, he threatened when cajoling did not succeed.

On March 6 he met for the first time with the full Democratic caucus. It was a lengthy meeting of over four hours, and Wilson was on his feet, discussing various measures and answering questions for two hours and ten minutes. The Geran bill was the pivot of the discussion, but Wilson also outlined in detail his complete legislative program. Dissatisfied assemblymen voiced objections to certain features of the Geran bill, it is true, but there was little friction and disagreement and Wilson was entirely gratified with the results of the conference, chiefly because the Democrats agreed to support as party policy the four chief cornerstones of the Wilson program. [36] Wilson's meeting with the Democratic majority in the Assembly was something unusual in New Jersey politics, and political observers noted that it was the first time in the state's history that a governor had undertaken

---

[35] *ibid.*, March 3, 1911. See also Wilson's speech before the Trenton Chamber of Commerce, March 7, *Trenton True American*, March 8, 1911.

[36] *Trenton Evening Times*, March 7, 1911; *Trenton True American*, March 7, 1911.

to assume personal leadership of the members of his party in the legislature.[37]

It was inevitable that the Geran bill would arouse the fiercest opposition the Democratic organization leaders, both in Newark and in Jersey City, could muster. It was a natural reaction because the bosses saw in the primary provisions of the bill a serious threat to their control, not only of party nominations, but also of the actual party machinery. In Jersey City, after Davis's death in early January, the party situation had become chaotic. No single leader had yet emerged as the boss of Hudson County, and the remnants of control of the old Davis organization were tenuously held by a group of bosses known as the "Big Five." [38] On March 10 the "Big Five" summoned the Hudson legislators to a stormy conference at the clubhouse of the Robert Davis Association in Jersey City and ordered them to vote against the Geran bill. That the power of the Hudson organization had deteriorated tremendously since the heyday of Davis's power was demonstrated by the fact that eight of the eleven assemblymen at the meeting absolutely defied the local bosses and avowed their determination to stand by Wilson and the "popular cause." [39]

Smith and Nugent had also been profoundly disturbed by the apparent certainty that Wilson would succeed in pushing the Geran bill through the legislature, and were doing everything they knew to defeat the measure. One of the best expressions of the Smith-Nugent attitude toward the bill comes from the editorial page of the *Newark Evening Star,* March 20, 1911: "Everything at Trenton tonight at the beginning of the eleventh week of the session will be overshadowed and put out of sight by the Geran bill, a personal partisan measure that has almost exclusively occupied attention at the State house since the session began ten weeks ago. It goes without saying that all the vitality that is given to the bill that George L. Record is known to have drafted comes from the feverish desire of the Governor to get it on the statute book regardless of any consequences to the Democratic

[37] *Trenton Evening Times,* March 7, 1911.

[38] The members of the group were Democratic County Chairman James Hennessey, Patrick R. Griffin of Hoboken, John McMahon of North Hudson, Sheriff James J. Kelly and City Clerk Michael J. Fagan of Jersey City.

[39] *Jersey Journal* of Jersey City, March 9 and 11, 1911. The assemblymen who declared they would support the Geran bill were T. M. Donnelly, Edward Kenny, Charles M. Egan, Charles E. S. Simpson, Thomas Griffin, James Agnew, William S. Davidson, and Peter James. Thomas F. Martin, James McGrath, and James H. Christy agreed to vote against the measure. Cornelius Ford was not present at the meeting.

party. But for this unreasoning attitude and the powerful appeal to self-interest represented in the executive appointments, so long withheld, the Geran bill would not have blocked legislation for ten weeks. It would have been reported and quickly disposed of by an unfettered Legislature."

It was Nugent, however, not Smith, who dealt with the legislators; Smith was far too sophisticated for work of that kind. On the very day the legislature convened, Nugent made his appearance at the State House, neither moved nor intimidated by the defeat his organization had suffered in the senatorial controversy. Perhaps he thought the "good old days" of 1907, when the Democrats once before had a majority in the Assembly, had returned, the time when he, as Smith's own personal representative, was the master-politician at Trenton who manipulated the strings and directed Democratic voting. At any rate, in 1910 he still held an office of great power, the state chairmanship, and proceeded to carry on his activities, which were exceedingly obnoxious to Wilson and the progressives.

It was inevitable that Wilson and Nugent, each of them strong-willed and determined to be leader or master of his party, should come to blows. Nugent's continued presence in the legislative chambers and lobbies of the State House evoked such a storm of protest from progressive legislators that Wilson finally decided to take the matter in hand. It was a courteous enough conference the two men had on February 17, despite the absurd rumors that were circulated soon afterward to the effect that Wilson had threatened to "lick" Nugent; Wilson, on the other hand, informed Nugent that his presence about the Assembly and committee rooms was irritating a number of legislators and that he should go back to Newark.[40] Nugent did not leave, but for several days he did his work a little more quietly and unobtrusively. Soon, however, he was back at his work of open obstruction; during the last week of February, for example, he was active on the floor of the Assembly, and one newspaper asserted that he was cooperating with the Republican minority leader in the lower house, Thomas F. McCran, to block progressive legislation.[41]

Nugent devoted most of his time during the following month to the task of defeating the Geran bill. He discovered, however, much to his chagrin, that he had hardly any influence among the men outside Essex County; only a half dozen or so loyal friends remained of

[40] *Trenton True American,* February 18, 1911.
[41] *ibid.,* February 27, 1911.

what was once a powerful political machine. As a last-ditch measure, therefore, Nugent resorted to a familiar trick: he tried to confuse the assemblymen by having Michael J. McGowan, Jr., of Newark introduce a substitute primary bill on March 14. Nugent was in the Assembly chamber when McGowan introduced the measure; the speaker, a stanch Wilson man, immediately referred the bill to the judiciary committee, which was packed with Wilson supporters. Nugent angrily protested and demanded that the bill be referred to the committee on elections, headed by his lieutenant, Mark F. Phillips of Newark. After a hot exchange of words, in which Nugent and the speaker almost came to blows and Nugent warned the legislators who were supporting the administration that they would not be reelected, Nugent left the Assembly room. "I won't stand for any attempt to queer that bill," Kenny, the speaker, retorted as Nugent was leaving. "The Geran bill will pass, and don't you forget it." [42] Thus was business transacted in the august Assembly of the State of New Jersey!

The decisive break between Wilson and Nugent came on March 20, at the end of an extremely short conference. Wilson was determined to have one show-down conference with Nugent on the Geran bill and summoned him to the governor's office. Wilson asked Nugent if he intended to persist in his efforts to defeat the bill; Nugent replied that he intended to fight the measure with every resource he could muster; that he was opposing it because all genuine organization Democrats in the state were opposing it; and that it was supported chiefly by the progressive Republicans and "traitorous" Democrats. Wilson replied that the Assembly would pass the measure, none the less, and Nugent countered by suggesting that Wilson was using patronage to persuade assemblymen to vote for the bill. Wilson's temper had slowly been rising, but the imputation that he was using the club of his patronage power to obtain the adoption of the Geran bill infuriated him, or at least gave him an excuse for losing his temper. "Good afternoon, Mr. Nugent," he said, motioning toward the door. Nugent stammered and shuffled toward the door, shouting that the governor was no gentleman and that he had always thought he was no gentleman. "Good afternoon, Mr. Nugent," Wilson shot back. [43]

The report of the interview of course spread rapidly, and soon Wil-

[42] *ibid.,* March 15, 1911.

[43] This account is a combination of both Wilson's and Nugent's statements, printed in the *Trenton Evening Times,* March 21, 1911, on the set-to. Both agreed substantially as to the facts of the meeting.

son's office was filled with excited Democrats anxious to congratulate him for having expelled a state chairman from his office.

He wrote to Mrs. Hulbert on March 26: "It was a most unpleasant incident, which I did not at all enjoy; but apparently it did a lot of good. It has been spoken of with glee all over the country, and editorials written about it, of which the enclosed is a specimen. One paper had a cartoon entitled 'Good afternoon,' in wh. Nugent was to be seen flying head foremost from a door out of which protruded a foot marked 'Wilson.' In the distance, nursing his bruises, sat Smith. It is all very well to get applause and credit for such things, but I need not tell you that they are not at all to my taste. I cannot help feeling a bit vulgar after them. They commend me to the rank and file, and particularly to the politicians themselves, I believe, but they do not leave me pleased with myself. I feel debased to the level of the men whom I feel obliged to snub. But it all comes in the day's work." [44]

The Wilson-Nugent clash was spectacular, to be sure, but it had little effect upon the fate of the Geran bill. The fate of that measure was decided at a memorable caucus meeting of the governor and the Democratic assemblymen on March 13. The caucus had been called by the Democratic leaders in the house and Wilson announced that he, as the Democratic leader of the state, would attend. There were emphatic protests against this alleged intrusion by the governor upon the prerogatives of the legislative branch, and there was a good deal of talk about preserving the separation of powers.

When the caucus met in the Supreme Court room in the State House, however, Wilson quickly and finally disposed of these charges. What constitutional right had he to interfere in legislative matters, one assemblyman, Martin, asked. Wilson paused for a moment, then took out of his pocket a copy of the state constitution and proceeded to read from section 6, article 5: ". . . he [the governor] shall communicate by message to the legislature at the opening of each session, and at such other times as he may deem necessary, the condition of the State, and *recommend such measures as he may deem expedient.*" He said, "I stand upon that provision of the Constitution." [45]

---

[44] Published in R. S. Baker, *Woodrow Wilson*, III, 143-144.

[45] C. M. Egan to A. S. Link, January 8, 1945; *Trenton True American*, March 14, 1911. Wilson further declared that it was clearly within the meaning of the constitution that his suggestions might be in the form of regularly formulated bills. He said that it would have been his choice, therefore, to send to the Assembly the primary and election bill and to ask the legislators to vote upon it directly. Rather than play the role of a prime minister openly, however, he had preferred to cooperate with his "colleagues in

For three hours Wilson stood before the Democratic assemblymen, explaining in detail the provisions of the Geran bill. He discussed the measure section by section and recounted the experience of other states in similar legislative experiments.[46] He asserted that it was absolutely necessary, if the Democrats were to keep faith with the voters of the state, that the bill should substitute for the existing system of choosing party nominees and election officers a method that would be a closer approach to what was impartial and open and without taint of machine management. The Democratic party, he continued, had for sixteen years been a minority party because it would not open its nominating processes to popular choice and to the free control of public opinion; because, in short, the people had not believed that the party was their servant.

The Democrats had carried the recent November elections, Wilson continued, because they had challenged and obtained the support of the independent voters. The Geran bill was a means of keeping faith with those voters. He was confident, he added, that any appeal of his to public opinion would arouse an overwhelming endorsement of the bill, but he wished to make that appeal unnecessary. He wanted the members of the caucus to relieve the party of the suspicion that they were unwilling, without pressure from the outside, to carry out the pledges of the gubernatorial campaign. As far as he was concerned, Wilson added, he would relish going to the people on the issue of the Geran bill. Such a campaign, however, he pointed out, would probably bring him into collision with, and force him to criticize, the action of certain members of the legislature. Then, turning to the legislators, he made a dramatic appeal for support: "You can turn aside from the measure if you choose; you can decline to follow me; you can deprive me of office, and turn away from me, but you cannot deprive me of power so long as I steadfastly stand for what I believe to be the interests and legitimate demands of the people themselves. I beg you to remember, in this which promises to be an historic conference in the annals of the party of the State, you are settling the question of the power or importance, the distinction or the ignominy of the party to

the legislature"; he had taken advantage of the kindness of individual members to introduce the Geran bill and other measures that he felt it was his duty to urge, so that the bills might go out in the regular order of legislative procedure. He had done this, he concluded, so that he might not seem to be forcing upon the legislators the choice of whether they would follow him or not.

[46] B. J. Hendrick, "Woodrow Wilson: Political Leader," *McClure's Magazine*, xxxviii (December 1911), 230.

which the people with a singular generosity offered the control of their affairs." [47]

Wilson's plea for the Geran bill, in addition to his more persuasive threat to carry the fight to the people should the assemblymen refuse to adopt the measure, was completely successful. Thirty-eight assemblymen attended the caucus; twenty-seven of them voted to support the Geran bill as a party measure. The progressives had of course been greatly impressed by Wilson's plea for election reform,[48] while all but eleven of the conservatives were either converted by Wilson's eloquence—or, more likely, were frightened by his threats—into supporting the radical reform measure.

Events moved rapidly after the decision of the Democratic majority was made. The measure, considerably revised and reworked, was reported to the Assembly on March 15 by the judiciary committee. When the bill reached its second reading on March 21 it was evident that the supreme test of strength between the Wilson supporters and the organization men had come. The legislators had returned to Trenton, after a short recess, on March 20, and with them came a horde of lobbyists from the Republican and Democratic machines. Whereas the power of every political boss was being thrown against the bill, the people of the state were also considerably agitated and were demanding the bill's enactment. Popular excitement was as fully aroused as it had been during the senatorial controversy.

The battle for the Geran bill was won on the night of March 20, won by a narrow majority, it is true, but won irrevocably none the less. Just before the opening of the legislative session that evening, the speaker announced that a Democratic caucus would convene immediately in his office. Nugent, who was in the Assembly room at the time, stepped forward and forbade his followers to attend the

---

[47] *Trenton True American*, March 14, 1911.

[48] "I have never known anything like that speech," one legislator afterward told Hendrick. "The Governor talked for at least an hour. . . . And the whole thing was merely an appeal to our better unselfish natures. The State had trusted us, as Democrats, with great duties and responsibilities. Would we betray the people or would we seize this splendid opportunity? But it is useless to attempt to describe the speech or the effect that it produced. We all came out of that room with one conviction; that we had heard the most wonderful speech of our lives, and that Governor Wilson was a great man. Even the most hardened of the old-time legislative hacks said that. . . . When we went into that caucus we had no assurance as to what the result would be. But opposition melted away under the Governor's influence. That caucus settled the fate of the Geran bill, as well as the whole Democratic program." "Woodrow Wilson: Political Leader," *loc. cit.*, p. 230.

meeting. Eleven men,[49] cowed by the specter of machine vengeance, remained in their seats, but thirty Democrats filed into the speaker's office.[50] Twenty-nine assemblymen, one less than was necessary for a majority in the house, pledged themselves to vote for the Geran bill.[51]

The machine Democrats, in alliance with the Republican minority, might have succeeded in defeating the bill if they could have maintained a solid bloc of opposition to it; the redoubtable Record, however, had foreseen such a development and had quietly persuaded Thomas R. Layden and Arthur Phelps Jackson, both of Passaic County, to support the measure.[52] When these two Republican assemblymen announced that they would join with the Democratic majority, the backbone of the opposition was broken.[53] At the end of a five-hour session the following day the Assembly passed the Geran bill by a majority of 34 to 25.[54] Thirty-one Democrats and three Republicans voted for it; ten Democrats and fifteen Republicans opposed it.[55]

It was another magnificent victory for Wilson personally; unfortunately, however, the election bill that the Assembly had adopted was lamentably constructed and was full of minor errors that made it, as Kerney writes, "an absolutely unworkable document." Sent up from the Assembly to the Senate on March 21, it was referred to the committee on elections consisting of Joseph S. Frelinghuysen, William J. Bradley, and James F. Fielder. As the Senate was predominantly Republican, Wilson was at first afraid that the opposition in the upper house might, for purely partisan reasons, wreck his reform program by refusing to accept the primary reform bill.[56] But there was no likelihood at any time that the Republican senators would adopt a policy

[49] Harry F. Backus, John J. Bracken, Charles W. Brown, Michael Leveen, Michael J. McGowan, Jr., Mark F. Phillips, and Frank P. Shalvoy, all of Newark; James C. Agnew, James H. Christie, and Thomas F. Martin of Jersey City; and George B. Cole of Warren County. *Trenton True American,* March 21, 1911.

[50] There were of course forty-two Democrats in the House. Cornelius Ford of Jersey City refused to attend the caucus, not because he opposed the bill, but because he refused to be bound by the party caucus.

[51] *Trenton True American,* March 21, 1911.

[52] J. Kerney, *The Political Education of Woodrow Wilson,* p. 109, gives an account of Record's work in support of the Geran bill.

[53] *Trenton True American,* March 21, 1911.

[54] There were no less than ten important amendments and substitute bills proposed by assemblymen. McGowan offered a complete bill, twenty-one printed pages in length, as a substitute. All of these measures were rejected. *House Journal,* 1911, pp. 623-663.

[55] *ibid.,* p. 664.

[56] W. W. to M. A. Hulbert, March 5, 1911, published in R. S. Baker, *Woodrow Wilson,* III, 138-139.

of obstruction; unlike their Republican colleagues in the Assembly they were not controlled by the Republican state machine, and they realized that they might easily wreck their own party by refusing to accept a measure that an overwhelming majority of the people demanded. From the very beginning of the session, therefore, they seem to have decided to follow Wilson's lead in legislative matters and to attempt to secure for their own party as much credit as was possible for the reforms they helped to enact.[57]

When the Senate committee on elections held public hearings on the Geran bill, opponents of the measure severely criticized it from all sides. Record, who had remained notably quiet during the fight in the Assembly, hastened to defend the bill before the committee and bluntly warned the Republicans that if they defeated the measure they would only afford Wilson a splendid platform for the 1911 legislative campaign. At Wilson's instigation, the Senate committee asked Record to suggest amendments to the Geran bill that would correct its numerous flaws.

The measure that the Senate finally adopted on April 13, therefore, represented a systematic revision of the Assembly version;[58] none of the essential provisions upon which Wilson had insisted was fundamentally altered, however. Most encouraging of all, it was adopted by a unanimous vote in the upper house. Wilson was in Indianapolis, attending a Democratic dinner rally, when a messenger brought the news that the Senate had unanimously adopted the revised Geran bill. "The passage of the direct primary bill by the Republican senate of the New Jersey legislature," he told the reporters, "is the result of a popular uprising in which the voices of the people made their demands so clear that there was no escape." [59.]

The Assembly quickly adopted the Senate amendments[60] and the bill was sent to Wilson for his signature in the latter part of April. In brief, the Geran law required direct party primary nominations of all elected officials and delegates to national conventions. Candidates for the legislature were required to declare, before the primaries were

[57] For editorial discussions of this question, see the *Trenton Evening Times,* April 14, 1911; *Trenton True American,* April 14, 1911.

[58] The amendments adopted by the Senate are printed in the *Senate Journal,* 1911, pp. 853-854.

[59] *Trenton True American,* April 15, 1911.

[60] The revised Geran bill was sent back to the Assembly on April 19 and was adopted, without a dissenting vote, by the lower house on the same day. *House Journal,* 1911, pp. 1243, 1246.

held, whether they would support the senatorial candidate endorsed by the voters at the party primary. Officials of the district election boards were to be chosen by the Civil Service Commission on a basis of examination, while the election and appointment of local election officials was to be made under the supervision of the courts. The state convention was also reconstituted by the law as a convention of party nominees and the governor only, which should meet for the single purpose of writing the party platform. The Geran law, moreover, incorporated the following provisions, which one would normally expect to find in a corrupt practices act, aimed at election reform: personal registration was required of voters in general elections in cities over 5,000; sample ballots were to be mailed to all voters before a general election; an official ballot was to be substituted for the old party ballot, which had previously been used and had been the source of much corruption.[61]

The final chapter in the story of the struggle for primary and election reform in New Jersey occurred in Wilson's office in the State House on April 19. Geran had brought the bill over from the Senate, and Tumulty and former Assemblyman James G. Blauvelt, one of the original New Idea leaders, stood nearby as Wilson signed the act. "This is certainly a grand consummation," Wilson declared as he wrote his signature in a firm hand.[62]

There were few political commentators who were not enthusiastic when relating the story of Wilson's fight for the Geran law. The *New York Sun,* oracle of all reactionary opinion in the country, had by April 1911 repudiated Wilson and naturally regarded the measure with contempt. The Geran law, the newspaper declared, represented "the individual opinions and ambitions of the original draughtsman and is filled with crudities and absurdities which justly excite the ridicule of the merest amateur in actual political administration."[63] The overwhelming majority of editorial spokesmen, however, seemed to recognize that the passage of the law presaged a fundamental change in the character of New Jersey politics. "The enacting of the election law," declared one progressive midwestern newspaper, "is a victory as important as the defeat of Smith . . . for senator."[64]

Once Wilson had obtained the acceptance of the Geran bill by the

---

[61] *Laws of New Jersey,* 1911, chapter 183, pp. 276-325.
[62] *Jersey Journal* of Jersey City, April 20, 1911.
[63] *New York Sun,* April 15, 1911.
[64] *Kansas City Star,* April 17, 1911.

Assembly his hardest fight was over and his greatest victory had been accomplished. Not that the opposition of the party bosses would completely crumble once the Geran bill had become law, but Wilson's victory for election reform made almost certain the success of the remainder of his legislative program. At the very time Wilson signed the Geran bill, Record was in the Senate chamber, lobbying for the adoption of a corrupt practices act.[65]

Corrupt practices legislation, like primary and election reform, had been one of the chief cornerstones of the New Idea and progressive Democratic program. Corruption and the fraudulent and extravagant use of money in elections was an ancient theme in Jersey politics. Corruption was bi-partisan, the tool of the bosses of both parties, and just as prevalent in the election of 1910 as in earlier years. When sample ballots were sent to the registered voters in Newark in the fall of 1911, for example, 11,000 were returned. Many had been addressed to vacant lots, and in many instances scores of persons were credited with residence in houses where only one or two registered voters lived. Corruption in Newark, however, was on an amateur scale compared to the methods of Republican Boss Louis Kuehnle and his lieutenants in Atlantic City, which was at that time the hell-hole of New Jersey politics. A legislative committee investigating election frauds in that city discovered in 1911 that the registration rolls were padded with the names of 4,000 phantom voters. The agents of the committee traced one band of 106 repeaters from Philadelphia and interviewed their leader, who was then in prison. He testified that many of his men had voted in every precinct in Atlantic City in the election of 1910, at $2 a vote. There were districts where the vote was four-fifths fraud. Kuehnle's lieutenants, moreover, had stood out in the streets buying votes openly, and a clerk in the auditor's office paid 200 voters in a room back of a store. Among the city and county officials—all members of the Kuehnle machine—involved in the corruption were the city building inspector, a city assessor, a postmaster, various councilmen, members of the board of freeholders, the sheriff, a city clerk, a county engineer, a city electrician, health inspectors, and a variety of lesser politicos.[66]

Corruption was not an incidental by-product of the boss-corporation system: it was the oil that kept the machinery of the system

---

[65] *Jersey Journal* of Jersey City, April 20, 1911.

[66] See the *Trenton True American,* December 30, 1911, for a review of the findings of the Macksey investigating committee.

running, as Lincoln Steffens has so vividly demonstrated. Record was the undisputed expert on corrupt practices and election reform in New Jersey before 1911,[67] and Wilson, it will be recalled, had asked him at the Martinique conference to draft a corrupt practices bill. Record wrote a tentative draft early in the legislative session, but the fight for the Geran bill had so engrossed the legislators' attention that it was not until almost at the end of the session that they began serious work on the bill. From the beginning of the session, Wilson had demanded the passage of a stringent law and had declared that such a measure was an integral part of his reform program. It is, therefore, interesting that it was the Republican Senate that took the lead in this reform measure.

Various corrupt practices bills had at one time or another been introduced during the session by Assemblymen Allan B. Walsh of Trenton and John J. Bracken of Newark and Senators Harry D. Leavitt of Trenton and John D. Prince of Ringwood. Prince, a professor at Columbia University in 1911, was chairman of the judiciary committee and Republican majority leader in the Senate.[68] He had personally introduced three corrupt practices bills modeled after the British statutes and, as majority leader, insisted that his bills be adopted by the upper house. Since Prince's measures did not meet Wilson's specifications, an impasse resulted, which was not broken until two Republican leaders in the Senate, Ackerman and Bradley, persuaded Prince to accept a measure considerably broader than his own. Ackerman, Bradley, Prince, Record, and Assistant Attorney-General Nelson B. Gaskill conferred during the evening of April 17 and agreed that Record and Gaskill should draft a measure that would meet completely the demands of the governor and the progressive leaders.[69]

Record had already framed a corrupt practices act very much like the Oregon statute. After the conference with the Senate majority leaders, he and Gaskill worked all night and, "with paste-pot and shears, hastily put together a new corrupt practices act, containing all the drastic provisions of both the English and the Oregon statutes." [70] The Senate then moved with incredible speed. Record handed his draft of the bill over to Prince on either April 18 or April 19, and on April 20 the upper house, again by unanimous vote, adopted the

[67] The background of election reform in New Jersey is discussed in Chapter Four.
[68] *Manual of the Legislature of New Jersey,* 1912, pp. 304-305.
[69] *Jersey Journal* of Jersey City, April 18, 1911.
[70] J. Kerney, *The Political Education of Woodrow Wilson,* p. 111.

bill.[71] There was simply no opportunity for discussion and debate on the Prince bill in the Assembly, for the lower house was anxious to adjourn and was in the midst of a wrangle over a bill to provide for commission government for New Jersey cities. On April 20, therefore, without a dissenting vote it hastily enacted the Senate measure into law.[72]

The corrupt practices law required all candidates to select committees that would be responsible for their campaign. The committees were required to file a detailed sworn statement of campaign contributions and expenditures after primaries and elections. Each candidate, also, had to file a statement of his personal contributions to the campaign fund, and certain definite limits were placed upon the amounts candidates for office could expend. During campaigns no money could be expended by candidates or their committees for the hiring of vehicles or watchers at the polls, or for the colonizing of voters, which was specifically prohibited. Candidates were also forbidden to solicit funds for a church during a campaign, or to make unusual gifts to clubs, churches, etc. Corporations, or persons owning majority stock in a corporation, were forbidden to contribute to campaign funds. The bill further listed a number of specific expenditures that were unlawful: false registration, fraudulent voting, stuffing of ballot boxes, and betting on election results. Any candidate who violated the law should not only suffer the regular penalties prescribed by the statute, but should also forfeit his office.[73]

Legislation designed to regulate effectively the rates and services of public utilities and public service corporations had long been perhaps the chief demand of the New Idea and progressive Democratic agitators. The movement for legislation to implement this demand and its accomplishments have already been discussed. It will be recalled, also, that Wilson had set himself squarely behind the movement for effective regulation and at the beginning of the session of 1911 had made it clear that he would be satisfied with nothing short of a thoroughgoing measure to take the place of the ineffective law the Republican legislature had enacted in 1910.

Harry V. Osborne, Democratic minority leader in the Senate, took the lead in the upper house; he and Frank H. Sommer, one of Record's associates in the New Idea movement, wrote a public utilities bill modeled closely after the New York statute of 1906, the so-called

---

[71] *Senate Journal,* 1911, pp. 983-985.   [72] *House Journal,* 1911, p. 1308.
[73] *Laws of New Jersey,* 1911, chapter 188, pp. 329-349.

Hughes law. It was introduced into the Senate by Osborne on January 23, while a similar bill was introduced into the Assembly by Charles M. Egan, a Democrat of Jersey City, on February 6. The Osborne-Egan bill, as the utilities act soon was called, was given the full weight of administration approval and was immediately designated as another of the "governor's bills." [74]

Backed by the force of the administration, the bill encountered few obstacles in either house. What open opposition there was to the measure was directed chiefly against the provisions of the bill endowing the commission with authority, subject to review by the state supreme court, to fix rates, but even this opposition was desultory. The Assembly and Senate versions of the bill were finally written as one act by a legislative conference committee and adopted by the legislature on the last day of the session. [75]

The Osborne-Egan law, one of the most thoroughgoing public utilities statutes in the country at the time, incorporated all of the provisions for which progressives in the state had been struggling for the past decade. The act created a board of three public utility commissioners, to be appointed by the governor with the consent of the Senate, which should publish its findings and decisions from time to time in a series of reports. A "public utility" was defined by the statute as any individual, partnership, association, or joint-stock corporation that owned or operated in New Jersey any steam railroad, street railway, traction railway, canal, express company, subway system, pipe line, gas, electric light, heat, power, water, oil, sewer, telephone, or telegraph system, plant, or equipment for public use. The commission was empowered to appraise and evaluate the property of any public utility; to fix just and reasonable rates upon a basis of physical valuation; to require all public utilities to file schedules of their rates; to set standards of service for electric companies; to require any railroad or street railway company to establish and maintain junction points and connections with other lines and private sidings; to require any public utility to comply with the terms of its charter and to render safe and proper

[74] *Jersey Journal* of Jersey City, February 21, 1911.

[75] The Senate passed the Osborne bill on April 5; the Assembly passed the Egan bill on March 13. For several weeks something of a deadlock occurred because apparently both houses wished to have the honor of sponsoring the bill. Finally the two houses agreed to appoint a joint committee to draw up a bill that would be the property, so to speak, of both houses. On April 21, the last day of the session, a conference bill, which was a combination of the Osborne and Egan measures was adopted by the Assembly and the Senate. *House Journal,* 1911, *passim; Senate Journal,* 1911, *passim.*

service; and to order suspension of announced increases in rates. A series of prohibitions against the activities of public utilities virtually gave the commission control over the financial transactions of all companies. The orders of the commission might be reviewed by the state supreme court by writ of certiorari and this court was empowered to set aside rulings of the commission when the rulings were deemed unreasonable.[76]

The last of the four chief administration measures was the workmen's compensation law. In spite of the continued agitation by the New Idea reformers during the early years of the century, New Jersey, as late as 1908, continued to be "shamed by having the most ancient and unjust of any employers' liability laws in the country," as one editor put it.[77] Employer-employee liability relations were still regulated solely by the principles of the common law, and an employee who was injured found it almost impossible to recover damages because of the operation of the ancient rules of "assumption of risk," "contributory negligence," and "fellow-servant negligence." The burden of industrial accidents, therefore, fell entirely upon the injured employee and his family, or upon private charity. Agitation by the progressives and also by the forces of organized labor forced the Republican Old Guard to modify in slight measure in 1909 the operation of the common law principles, but the statute was so half-hearted that it satisfied the demands neither of the laborers nor of the progressives. Their struggle for labor reform forced the Republican leaders in 1910 to concede the appointment by Governor Fort of a commission of inquiry, headed by Senator Walter E. Edge of Atlantic County, to investigate the problem.

Soon after his inauguration, Wilson conferred with Edge on the question of an employers' liability law that would meet the reasonable demands of organized labor. Although the commission was predominantly Republican in composition, Edge assured Wilson that the members would cooperate wholeheartedly with him in carrying out this primary article of his program. Early in the session, on January 16, Edge introduced into the Senate an employers' liability bill, which was reworked in committee and passed by the Senate on March 15.[78]

[76] *Laws of New Jersey*, 1911, chapter 195, pp. 374-389. For the subsequent development of public regulation in New Jersey, see M. C. Waltersdorf, *Regulation of Public Utilities in New Jersey*, especially pp. 178-204.

[77] *Newark Evening News*, April 6, 1908, quoted in R. E. Noble, Jr., *New Jersey Insurgency*, p. 181.

[78] *Senate Journal*, 1911, pp. 45, 374-375.

When the measure was sent to the lower house, however, it encountered the opposition of Cornelius Ford, assemblyman from Jersey City and chairman of the committee on labor and industries. As president of the New Jersey State Federation of Labor, Ford was recognized as the leading spokesman of organized labor in the state. He had already introduced two bills of his own on January 16 and now insisted that his measures be adopted by the Assembly, chiefly because they provided for greater compensation for workers in industrial accidents. Consequently, he succeeded in holding the Edge bill in his committee for two weeks without reporting it to the lower house.

Fearful lest the disagreement between the two houses result in no liability legislation at all, Wilson conferred with Ford and endeavored to persuade him to accept the Edge bill. "Don't you think it would be the part of wisdom to accept the Edge bill and make sure of getting something?" Wilson asked.[79] Impressed by the logic of Wilson's argument, Ford soon afterward conferred with labor leaders in the state and decided to accept the Edge bill as a compromise measure. On April 3, therefore, the Assembly by unanimous vote enacted into law New Jersey's first workmen's compensation statute; on the following day it received Wilson's signature.[80]

The Edge act was divided into three parts. Section 1 applied to suits brought by employees for compensation by action at law and abolished the "fellow-servant negligence" and "assumption of risk" common law rules in such cases. Section 2 laid down a definite schedule of payments to be made in case of injury or death and provided that during the first two weeks after injury the employer should furnish reasonable medical and hospital services and medicines to the injured employee. These provisions were to become effective when the employee and employer had by agreement accepted them; such agreement was to be deemed implied in the contract at the time of employment unless either party made known his refusal to be bound by it. The last section defined willful negligence on the part of the employee, in case of which the act was not to apply, and set forth the general provisions of the law.[81]

Although Wilson had at first declared that he was interested only in the four leading measures of the legislative session, he soon found himself involved in a struggle for the enactment of a number of other

---

[79] This story is best told in the *New York World,* June 5, 1912.

[80] *Trenton True American,* April 4-5, 1911.

[81] *Laws of New Jersey,* 1911, chapter 95, pp. 134-145.

bills. An interesting case in point was a bill that had been prepared by a committee of the Trenton Chamber of Commerce, enabling the cities and towns of New Jersey to adopt the commission form of government. The measure was introduced simultaneously into the Assembly and Senate by Allan B. Walsh and Harry D. Leavitt on February 20.[82] Kerney tells us that Wilson at first manifested little interest in the measure; when his friends, however, pointed out that the commission form of government was popular in the West and that its adoption by New Jersey would give a boost to his presidential candidacy, Wilson readily threw the weight of his support to the bill.[83]

It was not until the early part of April, however, that Wilson found time to give attention to the Walsh-Leavitt bill. On April 10, at a conference of the representatives of New Jersey cities who were supporting the measure, he first made public an emphatic declaration that the legislature should adopt the commission government bill.[84] The following day he sent a message to the legislature, urging that the measure be enacted into law.[85]

Soon it became evident that the battle for municipal reform could not be won without another hard fight with the bosses; the bill threatened to undermine the city organizations, the strongholds of machine politics, and the bosses marshaled their forces for one last battle against Wilsonian reform. Nugent, in spite of the rebuffs he had received at Wilson's hands, was still ubiquitous in the State House; he and the Republican minority leader in the Assembly, McCran, succeeded in seriously impairing the effectiveness of the Walsh-Leavitt bill by obtaining the adoption of an amendment[86] stipulating that before commission government could be adopted by any municipality, there should be cast in its favor at least 40 per cent of the number of votes cast for members of the General Assembly at the most recent election. The amendment was so obscurely worded that the progressive leaders in the lower house did not perceive its damaging import and it was adopted by an overwhelming majority.[87]

On Wilson's return from Indianapolis in mid-April, he was amazed to discover that the machine politicians were still at work and had

---

[82] *House Journal*, 1911, p. 235; *Senate Journal*, 1911, p. 139. The background of the Walsh-Leavitt bill is discussed in the *Trenton True American*, February 21, 1911.

[83] See J. Kerney, *The Political Education of Woodrow Wilson*, p. 112.

[84] *Trenton True American*, April 11, 1911.

[85] The message is printed in the *Senate Journal*, 1911, pp. 768-770.

[86] The amendment was introduced on April 11 by Thomas F. A. Griffin of Jersey City.

[87] *House Journal*, 1911, p. 1066.

succeeded in this underhanded manner in crippling the commission government bill. He at once announced that he would not accept the Griffin amendment and began a movement among the legislative leaders to obtain the adoption of the original bill, which required approval by only 26 per cent of the voters in the most recent general election.[88]

The final show-down between the supporters of municipal reform and the old-line party bosses occurred on the last day of the legislative session. The progressive leaders in the Assembly were certain that they had sufficient strength to pass the original bill, but an unexpected event wrecked their calculations. The Democratic majority leader, Matthews, who had faithfully cooperated with the Wilson reformers throughout the session, finally reverted to the organization type and announced that he would support the Griffin amendment. Frightened by the defection of their party leader in the lower house, the progressives compromised with their opponents.[89] The statute, as finally adopted by the legislature, required approval by 30 per cent of the number of voters in the most recent general election for the adoption of commission government by a municipality. The law also stipulated that any city that adopted the commission form would also adopt the initiative, referendum, and recall, which might be used by the voters for the adoption or repeal of city ordinances or the recall of city officials. The commission form of government and the initiative, referendum, and recall were integral parts of the same act and could not be adopted separately.[90]

The progressive leaders in the legislature had, in addition to the commission government bill, a reform program of their own that in many respects went far beyond the bounds of Wilson's four-cornered platform. A year later, during the presidential pre-nomination campaign, Wilson received the credit for the enactment of these measures. He gave his support to these other reform ideas, to be sure, and his victory over Smith and Nugent in the fight for the Geran bill had made their achievement possible; yet he was in no sense the dynamic force behind them. A number of these less spectacular laws completed the general reform program: certain important school reforms,[91] storage

[88] *Trenton True American,* April 18, 1911.
[89] *ibid.,* April 22, 1911; *House Journal,* 1911, pp. 1470-1471.
[90] *Laws of New Jersey,* 1911, chapter 221, pp. 462-483.
[91] *ibid.,* chapter 346, p. 727; chapter 276, p. 588.

and food inspection laws,[92] and laws that required stringent factory inspection and regulated the hours and the kind of labor of women and children.[93]

The legislative session of 1911 came to a sudden end in the early morning of April 22—officially, however, on April 21. Wilson was on hand to witness the concluding hours of the greatest reform legislature in the history of the state and has left the following account of the eventful night:

"The newspaper men seem dazed. They do not understand how such things *could* happen. They were impressed, too, with the orderly and dignified way in which the session ended, despite the long strain of the closing night, when the houses sat from eight until three. Generally there is wild horseplay, like that on the stock exchange, but this time everything was done decently and with an air of self-respect. I took several naps in my office during the long hours of the session, coming out into the outer office in the intervals to talk and swap stories with the men who were sitting there, my secretary, the reporters who were coming and going, and interested friends who had come down to see how things ended. Then a committee from each House called on me to ask if there was anything more I had to lay before them before adjournment,—and the session was over. Most of the members dropped in to say good bye, and by four o'clock your tired and happy friend was in bed in the noisy little Hotel Sterling, with the strong odours of late suppers in his nostrils, floating in at the open window. It's a great game, thoroughly worth playing!"[94]

There were other matters of state that Wilson had to deal with during the session. One was the question of the ratification of the Sixteenth Amendment, authorizing Congress to levy income taxes. By the end of March thirty states had ratified the amendment and Wilson was anxious that New Jersey identify itself with this national reform movement. "I take the liberty of calling your attention to a very important matter awaiting your decision—," he wrote to the legislature on March 20, "the question of the ratification of the proposed amendment to the Constitution. . . . Liberal opinion throughout the country clearly expects and demands the ratification of this amendment."[95] The Assembly, with-

---

[92] *ibid.*, chapter 221, pp. 462-483; chapter 189, pp. 349-353.

[93] *ibid.*, chapter 136, pp. 194-200; chapter 210, p. 442; chapter 327, pp. 698-699.

[94] W. W. to M. A. Hulbert, April 23, 1911, published in R. S. Baker, *Woodrow Wilson*, III, 171.

[95] Wilson to the legislature, March 20, 1911, *House Journal*, 1911, pp. 601-602; *Senate Journal*, 1911, p. 401.

out a dissenting vote, quickly ratified, but the Senate adamantly refused to give its approval to the amendment.[96]

On April 4 Wilson addressed a special message to the upper house and again urged the ratification of the amendment. Since the Senate was predominantly Republican he emphasized that the amendment had no partisan color, that it had been proposed by a Republican Congress and endorsed by a Republican president. In enumerating the arguments for ratification, Wilson made one interesting statement: "One decision of the Supreme Court of the United States, based upon erroneous economic reasoning, has made this amendment necessary." [97] In spite of Wilson's plea, however, the Senate refused to ratify, and when the amendment became a part of the Constitution it was without New Jersey's consent.

So harmonious were the relations between Wilson and the legislature during the 1911 session that his vetoes were infrequent and, on the whole, inconsequential. He returned, without his approval, ten Assembly and three Senate bills, and in every instance his veto was upheld by the legislators.[98] Most of the measures Wilson vetoed were petty bills relating to the cities of the state. Thus, for example, he vetoed Assembly bill No. 163, an act designed to raise the salaries of employees in the fire departments of the various cities, because the bill was a violation of the principle of home rule and was a measure of extravagance.[99] Most of the veto messages were extremely short and Wilson indulged in few attempts at rhetoric and satire. However, when on March 30 he vetoed Assembly bill No. 245—an act authorizing any borough to appropriate money for the celebration of the fiftieth anniversary of the founding of the borough—he commented tersely, "It seems to me very unwise to authorize any community to saddle itself with debt in order to enjoy the pleasure of a celebration." Such expenditures, he asserted, should be provided for by private subscription.[100]

In his veto messages Wilson seems to have been mainly concerned with preventing extravagance on the part of the legislature and in preserving the integrity and right of self-government of the cities of the state. Thus, when he vetoed Senate bill No. 184, "An act for the better regulation and control of the taking, planting and propagating of oys-

[96] *Trenton True American*, March 31, 1911.

[97] Wilson to the Senate, April 4, 1911, *Senate Journal*, 1911, 639-640.

[98] Only a simple majority was necessary to override the governor's veto. See the state constitution, Article 5, Section 7.

[99] *House Journal*, 1911, pp. 602-603.

[100] *ibid.*, 1911, pp. 877-878.

ters on lands lying under the tidal waters of the county of Burlington," he pointed up the issue of extravagance. "No real necessity seems to exist for the addition of another Oyster Commission," he asserted. "It is generally felt by students of the political organization of the State that the number of commissions is already excessive and that the better source of legislation would be retrenchment and the consolidation of the various commissions now dealing in separate places with practically the same subject matter." [101]

In striking contrast to the great antagonism his veto messages provoked in 1912, Wilson's vetoes during the session of 1911 attracted little public attention. The question of appointments, of disbursing the patronage, was an entirely different matter. Few governors in the country possessed the sweeping range of patronage that the governor of New Jersey had at his disposal in 1911; he appointed practically all high-ranking judicial and administrative officials.[102]

If Wilson was something of a political newcomer with regard to the details of administration when he came into the governorship, the fact was never better illustrated than by his treatment of appointments. In the first place, he had no sense of obligation to men who had done him political favors in the past, especially if they now opposed his policies; secondly, he simply was not interested in doling out state jobs. After the November 1910 election, he had been deluged with applications for petty jobs and with recommendations of various candidates for the more important offices. Early in the legislative session he delegated to Tumulty and Kerney the task of selecting the mass of minor officials.[103] "Wilson was not interested in dealing with office patronage," writes Fielder, one of the administration leaders in the Senate. "He was not acquainted with the men of his party who, in the several counties, felt they were entitled to recognition when it came to appointments to office. He did not know whom to trust and very largely he left to Kerney and

---

[101] *Senate Journal,* 1911, pp. 796-797.

[102] He appointed, for example, the chancellor of the Court of Chancery, the justices of the state Supreme Court, the judges of the Court of Errors and Appeals, the justices of the state Circuit Court, the judges of the District Courts, the secretary of state, the attorney-general, the officers of the state branch of the National Guard, the commissioner of education, the state warden, the state librarian, the commissioner of banking and insurance, the chief of the Bureau of Labor and Statistics, the members of the State Board of Assessors, the public utility commissioners, the members of the state Civil Service Commission, the commissioner of public roads, the commissioner of charities and corrections, and a host of minor officials.

[103] J. Kerney, *The Political Education of Woodrow Wilson,* pp. 115-116.

Tumulty the selection of his appointees." [104] There were a few important exceptions to this rule, however, and occasionally Wilson insisted upon appointing personal friends to high-ranking offices.

On February 6 Wilson sent his first group of nominations to the Senate. It was a remarkable list: Mark A. Sullivan, a progressive from Jersey City, to be judge of the Court of Errors and Appeals of Hudson County; Clarence L. Cole of Atlantic County, who had nominated him for governor, to be judge of the Circuit Court of southern New Jersey; and Frank Smathers, a young ex-North Carolinian, to be judge of the District Court of Atlantic County. [105] A few days later Wilson appointed his classmate Edwin A. Stevens of Hoboken to the important position of commissioner of public roads. [106]

There were a few intermittent appointments during the remainder of the session, the most notable of which was the appointment of William P. Martin, a prominent New Idea man, to be judge of the Court of Common Pleas for Essex County; [107] it was not, however, until the last day of the session that the governor sent to the Senate the main body of appointments. If, as the Smith newspapers asserted, Wilson waited until the legislature had accomplished its work in order to persuade doubtful assemblymen to support his reform program, none but the Smith spokesmen were disturbed. It is reasonable to assume that Wilson was persuaded by Tumulty and Kerney to wait until the end of the session, and for this very reason.

On April 21, at any rate, he named ninety men and women to fill positions of varying importance in the state government. Samuel Kalisch, the Wilson leader in Newark, he named associate justice of the Supreme Court; Kalisch was the first Jew in the history of the state to sit upon that court. Winthrop M. Daniels, an intimate friend at Princeton, was appointed to the Public Utility Commission; Record was given an appointment, reluctantly made on Wilson's part, to the State Board of Assessors; Edward E. Grosscup, soon to be Nugent's successor as state chairman of the Democratic party, was appointed to the State Board for the Equalization of Taxes. [108] Without a murmur of protest the Senate confirmed these appointments; however, it acted strangely with regard to Record's appointment. It confirmed the entire

[104] J. F. Fielder to A. S. Link, December 6, 1944.
[105] "Journal of the Executive Sessions of the Sixty-Seventh Senate," *Senate Journal*, 1911, pp. 1260-1262.
[106] *ibid.*, pp. 1262-1263.
[107] *ibid.*, p. 1276.
[108] *ibid.*, pp. 1284-1289.

batch of appointments, with the exception of Record; a few minutes later the senators unanimously confirmed his nomination.[109]

The general consensus in New Jersey with regard to Wilson's appointments was that he, or rather Tumulty and Kerney, had done an excellent job. Progressives of both parties were pleased that not a single member of the Smith-Nugent organization had been given office, while the New Idea men were especially gratified by Wilson's recognition of Record, Martin, and Mark M. Fagan; the latter was appointed to the Hudson County Board for the Equalization of Taxes. Wilson's appointment of Kalisch to the Supreme Court was especially pleasing to the progressives. "Kalisch is a new type of man for this job," commented Record. "He is a Hebrew, he got his living at the bar by serving individual clients as against the corporations, he had no political pull, he was not 'safe and sane,' and he did not belong to 'our set.' " [110] Wilson's insistence, furthermore, that corporation lawyers should not be named as prosecuting attorneys also endeared him to the progressives.

At the end of the legislative session, when he paused to contemplate the results of his labors during the past three months that had just passed, Wilson was filled with understandable pride and gratification. "I think . . . [the time] will always be remembered as extraordinary in this," he declared in a public statement, reviewing the accomplishments of the recent legislature, "that it witnessed the fulfillment by the Legislature of every important campaign pledge." There was still much reform legislation that needed to be enacted, he admitted; no single legislature, however, "could possibly be expected to accomplish more than this one has accomplished." [111] The glowing pride of victory was still evident when he spoke a few days later before the members of the Free Synagogue in New York. "I have come out of a contest," he told his audience. "I have gone through six months of ceaseless vigilance for fear things that ought to be done will be left undone, and things that ought not to be done will be done." [112]

But not only Wilson was jubilant over the work of the session of 1911; progressive editors in New Jersey and the rest of the country hailed the avalanche of reform laws as the crowning political achievement in the state's history. These progressive spokesmen knew that Wilson was no pioneer of reform, either in the state or in the nation. Many of them

[109] *ibid.*, p. 1286.
[110] *Jersey Journal* of Jersey City, July 15, 1911.
[111] *Trenton True American,* April 22, 1911.
[112] *ibid.*, April 25, 1911.

had personally helped Hoke Smith in Georgia, Bob La Follette in Wisconsin, Hiram Johnson in California, or Charles Evans Hughes in New York to push through similar reform programs years before. These all paved the way for Wilson's success. New Jersey had been one of the last strongholds of the boss-corporation system and most people had thought the fortress of privilege in that state was impregnable. That, however, only made Wilson's victory all the more spectacular.

Recent events had occurred in so kaleidoscopic a fashion since December 1910, that the New Jersey editors were literally dumbfounded. It all seemed a miracle, this unbelievable series of events: Wilson's translation from Princeton into politics, his campaign for the governorship, his defeat of the Smith-Nugent organization in the senatorial controversy, and now the passage of reform laws for which progressives in the state had been crusading for a decade. Even the legislature had behaved in a singular manner; there had been a notable absence of partisanship, and Democrats and Republicans in the Senate had cooperated with good will in achieving the same reform goals. Moreover, while the specter of boss domination had at first hovered over the assemblymen, Wilson had cleared the air of bossism and made the legislators feel that they were free men—free, at least, to do the popular will as he interpreted it.[113] "The present Legislature ends its session with the most remarkable record of progressive legislation ever known in the political history of this or any other State," was Record's boast.

Progressive spokesmen in the state, moreover, freely acknowledged that Wilson was primarily responsible for the victory. Every single item of reform that the legislature of 1911 enacted into law had, at one time or another, been the object of agitation by reform leaders long before he had given thought to the problems of political and economic regeneration. Yet he had succeeded where the pioneer propagandists had failed. He succeeded because he marshaled into a coherent unit the force of public opinion, because he was a competent party leader, but above all because the necessary fundamental agitation had already been accomplished by other men.[114] In short, he was the catalytic agent of

---

[113] For a discussion of these ideas, see the *Newark Evening News,* April 22, 1911.

[114] In a speech at Wilmington, Delaware, October 17, 1912, Wilson made the following statement: "I love these lonely figures climbing this ugly mountain of privilege, but they are not so lonely now. I am sorry, for my part, that I didn't come in when they were fewer and there was no credit to come in when I came in. The whole nation had awakened. All of New Jersey, at any rate, was tired of the game and was willing to try an unsophisticated schoolmaster, because it was in search of somebody that didn't know how to play the old game."

reform. After the work of earlier progressives was taken into account
by reform leaders in 1911, however, they did not hesitate to declare, as
Record put it, "Without him nothing of substantial importance would
have been passed." [115] The *Jersey Journal* expressed best the seasoned
opinion of New Jersey insurgent thought with regard to Wilson's role
in the drama of 1911 when it declared:

"On the Governor's side, the fight for progressive legislation in redemption of platform promises was perhaps the most scientific political
battle ever waged in New Jersey. Wilson was the man skulkers and
reactionaries were afraid of. His methods were open and sincere, and
his insistence that party promises be kept literally and fully overcame
the wavering and drove opposition to the wall. The victory Governor
Wilson has won is a revelation of the man's character and leadership
and a marvel to the country. No Governor has ever achieved so much
in so short a time. In less than four months he has turned New Jersey
from one of the most conservative and machine-dominated States into
a leader in the forefront of progressive commonwealths." [116]

The significance of Wilson's reform administration as far as the country at large was concerned can hardly be overestimated. The spirit and
meaning of his victory was even more important than the success of his
program. He demonstrated to the people that by electing responsible
leaders they could obtain responsible government. His administration
was an open rebuke to bosses and meddling corporations. Furthermore,
as one North Carolina editor wrote, his demonstration that a state under
responsible leadership could fulfill its proper place within the federal
framework was an answer to the arguments of Roosevelt's New Nationalism.[117]

More important for the success of Wilson's political career, the accomplishments of his reform program in New Jersey provided a powerful impetus to the movement that had already got under way to make
him the Democratic presidential nominee in 1912. There is abundant
evidence that Democratic progressives throughout the country were
beginning to look upon him, as one Texas editor later declared, as the
"most hopeful figure in American politics." [118] In an excellent summary
of editorial opinion, the *New York Times* asserted on April 23:

"The whole country has watched with interest the first session of

[115] *Jersey Journal* of Jersey City, April 22, 1911.
[116] *ibid.;* also, *Trenton True American,* April 24, 1911.
[117] *Raleigh News and Observer,* May 10, 1911.
[118] *Galveston Daily News,* January 11, 1912.

New Jersey's Legislature under Gov. Wilson. It meant the beginning of the combat between him and the old system, between the interests of the people as he represented them and the other 'interests' intrenched and emboldened by long years of dominance at Trenton. It was a critical time for the new Governor. If he had failed, he would have been much less heard of, much less thought of, in the future, than will now be the case. He has succeeded, and the measure of his success is really very great. What his triumph implies and portends for the future is sufficiently obvious."

Wilson himself has written the most fitting epilogue to this chapter when to Mrs. Hulbert he wrote on April 23: "The Legislature adjourned yesterday morning at three o'clock, with its work done. I got absolutely everything I strove for,—and more besides. . . . Everyone, the papers included, are saying that none of it could have been done, if it had not been for my influence and tact and hold upon the people. Be that as it may, the thing was done, and the result was as complete a victory as has ever been won, I venture to say, in the history of the country. I wrote the platform, I had the measures formulated to my mind, I kept the pressure of opinion constantly on the legislature, and the programme was carried out to its last detail. This with the senatorial business seems, in the minds of the people looking on a little less than a miracle, in the light of what has been the history of reform hitherto in this State. As a matter of fact, it is just a bit of natural history. I came to the office in the fulness of time, when opinion was ripe on all these matters, when both parties were committed to these reforms, and by merely standing fast, and by never losing sight of the business for an hour, but keeping up all sorts of (legitimate) pressure *all the time,* kept the mighty forces from being diverted or blocked at any point. The strain has been immense, but the reward is great. I feel a great reaction to-day, for I am, of course, exceedingly tired, but I am quietly and deeply happy that I should have been of just the kind of service I wished to be to those who elected and trusted me. I can look them in the face, like a servant who has kept faith and done all that was in him, given every power he possessed, to them and their affairs. There could be no deeper source of satisfaction and contentment! . . .

"But I have not felt that I could relax my attention for a moment while the session lasted,—and it had already begun when I was inaugurated, you know, and plunged into the first fight, the fight for the senatorship. Winning that, by the way, made all the rest easier; but it also made the session some two weeks longer than usual. What a vigil it has been! I am certainly in training for almost anything that may come to me by way of public tasks. There are serious times ahead. It daunts me to think of the possibility of my playing an influential part in them. There is no telling what deep waters may be ahead of me. The forces of greed and the forces of justice and humanity are about to grapple for a bout in which men will spend all the life that is in them. God grant I may have strength enough to count, to tip the balance in the unequal and tremendous struggle!" [119]

[119] Published in R. S. Baker, *Woodrow Wilson*, III, 169-171.

CHAPTER IX

New Jersey Politics, 1911–1912

THE great national acclaim that came to Wilson as a consequence of the achievements of the legislature of 1911 made him one of the leading contenders for the presidency and naturally stimulated his political ambitions. Already an organized movement was under way to make him the Democratic presidential nominee in 1912. Shortly after the legislature adjourned, Wilson left New Jersey and made a speaking tour of the West; it was his first outright bid for the Democratic presidential nomination, and he returned to the East a month later imbued with a desire to become president of the United States.

During the remainder of the year, however, Wilson did not allow his rapidly growing interest in national politics to obscure the importance of political affairs within his own state. For one thing, he realized that most reformers ultimately fail because they cease agitating once they have obtained the immediate objectives for which they have been fighting. He knew also that the machine politicians in the cities and counties of New Jersey had only been driven under cover, that they were biding their time, awaiting the day when they might once again secure control of the Democratic party.

Therefore Wilson welcomed the opportunity to "go to the people" of the state when the issue of municipal reform arose in the early summer of 1911. The Walsh-Leavitt act, recently passed by the legislature, had provided a legal means whereby the voters might, by accepting the commission form of government for their cities, turn out the local city bosses. The adoption of the new system simply meant that the existing government of the city in question would cease to exist a few weeks later and that a government administered by five commissioners would take its place.

Wilson threw himself wholeheartedly into this movement for city government reform; by the early part of June he had returned from trips to the West and the South and was back at Princeton, planning a systematic state-wide campaign for commission government. Bayonne was the first city in the state to vote upon the question, and Wilson hastened to go there to throw the weight of his prestige behind the fight the Government by Commission Association was making. "I have come here tonight," he told the people of Bayonne on June 7, "because I believe in government by the people." It was a rousing speech that he made and there were frequent references to "machines," "Providence," "the devil," "cowards," and "sidesteppers." The city machines were the backbone of the boss system in the state, he asserted; the existing system of divided responsibility and control allowed corrupt officials to hide in the secret passageways of a complicated governmental system. On the other hand, commission government centered responsibility upon a few men and placed the processes of city management in the open so that every man might judge if the governing officials were honest and efficient.[1]

A week later he spoke at a rally held by the Commission Government League of Trenton and proceeded to explain why American cities were the worst governed in the area of western civilization. Most of what he said was a rehash of his earlier arguments for the short ballot, but he used his favorite device of elevating the local issue and expanding its importance into universal proportions. Concluding, he said:

"Do you recognize the significance of this meeting? We are here to discuss a matter of principle that concerns the city of Trenton, but we are really here discussing a transaction that concerns mankind. If America fails in the making of city government, if she does not know how [to solve] the problem so that her people will be free, happy and comfortable, then . . . to whom shall the men of the nations look? When I see an earnest body of men like this gathered together to discuss a serious business-like proposition, such as you have before you tonight, I think I feel some of that great spirit of mankind which is abroad, whither we know, a bit of its wings has started, always beating upward. . . . And a great meeting like this is one of the items in the great combined struggle of mankind toward the political light America is finding, for America is again taking on the armor of her indomitable perseverance and hope, and we shall again say to her enemies: 'We hold you in contempt; our light is bright and the day is ours to possess.'"[2]

Wilson returned to Hudson County and pleaded for the cause of municipal reform at Hoboken on June 21 and at Jersey City on July 14.[3] At Passaic on July 20 he concluded his whirlwind campaign with another rousing speech before a crowd of local reformers.[4]

[1] *Trenton True American,* June 8, 1911.
[2] *ibid.,* June 14, 1911.
[3] *ibid.,* June 22, July 15, 1911.
[4] *Trenton Evening Times,* July 21, 1911.

By mid-summer it was evident that the fight for commission government had become a virtual campaign to overthrow the power of the city bosses; Wilson, progressive politicians, and vociferous editors had succeeded fairly well in stirring up public opinion in behalf of the cause. But the organization politicians were also united in their resistance and the campaign got off to a bad start when the voters of Bayonne, by the suspicious majority of two votes, rejected commission government. On June 20, however, Trenton voted 6,792 to 4,890 to accept the reform and it appeared momentarily that Wilson's campaign might succeed after all.[5] That, however, was not to be the case, for, one after another, the larger cities of the state refused to follow Trenton's lead: Bayonne, Hoboken, New Brunswick, Jersey City, Paterson, Orange, Cape May, East Rutherford, Garfield, Metuchen, Rahway, and Elizabeth all rejected the measure. Only Trenton, Passaic, Atlantic City, Long Beach, Hawthorne, Irvington, Margate City, Ocean City, and Ridgewood supported the reform movement.

On July 7 Wilson left Princeton with his family to go for a few days to their summer retreat in Lyme, Connecticut. His departure from the state provoked some comment in political circles because he had not yet named the new state commissioner of education; on his return a week later, however, he announced the appointment of Calvin N. Kendall to the position.[6] Kendall, the superintendent of schools in Indianapolis, was of course an "outsider," and there was some criticism of Wilson for selecting him to fill the much-coveted $10,000-a-year position.[7]

It was such petty criticism that troubled Wilson most at times, that caused him to pause and wonder if his political career was really affording him the deeper sort of satisfaction he was seeking. He was extremely busy, to be sure, and he enjoyed at moments a sort of transient satisfaction in victories won or bosses overthrown. Perhaps he was driving too hard, expecting too much from his political associates. At any rate, he wrote a strange letter to Mrs. Hulbert in mid-summer, confessing his longing for the time when he was simply Woodrow Wilson, private citizen:

"Truly, I know what 'public life' is now! I have no private life at all. It is entertaining to see the whole world surge about you,—particularly the whole summer world,—but when a fellow is like me,—

[5] *Trenton True American*, June 21, 1911.
[6] *Trenton Evening Times*, July 13, 1911.
[7] J. Kerney, *The Political Education of Woodrow Wilson*, p. 121.

when, i.e., he *loves* his own privacy, loves the liberty to think of his friends . . . and to dream his own dreams—to conceive a life which he cannot share with the crowd, can share, indeed, with only one or two, who seem part of him, rebellion comes into his heart and he flings about like a wild bird in a cage,—denied his sweet haunts and his freedom." [8]

But these moments of depression were only fleeting during which Wilson's thought went "back for refreshment to those days when all the world seemed . . . a place of heroic adventure, in which one's heart must keep its own counsel while one's hands worked at big things." The truth was that he had little time to think about matters outside the political field.

One anomaly, in particular, must have disturbed him immeasurably: the fact that although he, Wilson, was now the real leader of the Democratic voters in the state, Nugent continued to be the official party head, the chairman of the state Democratic committee. There had been numerous protests against Nugent's holding the post when he was so completely at odds with the governor and the progressive majority. Wilson, however, steadfastly refused to join in any open movement to oust the Newark man; he preferred to wait for Nugent to make some fatal misstep that would cost him the chairmanship.

Nugent finally made the blunder the progressives had been hoping for. On the night of July 25 he was enjoying a party with some friends at Scotty's Cafe in Neptune Heights. Probably intoxicated, he rose and proposed a toast as several New Jersey National Guard officers nearby looked on. "I propose a toast to the Governor of New Jersey, the commander-in-chief of the Militia," he declared, "an ingrate and a liar. I mean Woodrow Wilson. I repeat, he's an ingrate and a liar. Do I drink alone?" [9] Legend has it that he did drink alone and that the officers smashed their glasses and left the restaurant.

It was just the sort of "break" the anti-Nugent Democrats had been waiting for and they united at once in a loud demand for Nugent's resignation. "Nugent must get out, or he must be kicked out," the *Jersey Journal* demanded on August 7. With obvious relish, the progressive editors charged that Nugent represented the "vulgar" and "booze-fighter" type of Democratic politician;[10] that he was, as one editor put it, "simply a fragment of the old, discredited machine—a

[8] W. W. to M. A. Hulbert, July 30, 1911, published in R. S. Baker, *Woodrow Wilson*, III, 155.

[9] *Trenton Evening Times*, July 26, 1911.

[10] *ibid.*, July 27, 1911.

fragment that has not been dislodged merely because red tape and anti-quated customs have made it inconvenient to dislodge him." [11]

Shortly after Nugent proposed his toast, Wilson and a number of the state committeemen were at Sea Girt, the governor's summer home, to witness the annual review of the state National Guard, which was then camping nearby at "Camp Wilson." Committeemen representing eight counties met in the headquarters of Brigadier-General Dennis F. Collins, Union County member of the state committee, on July 27 and unanimously agreed that Nugent should be immediately relieved of his position. They drafted, therefore, a pointed letter to the state chairman suggesting that he resign at once.[12] There was not much Nugent could say in reply; on July 27 he admitted in a public statement that he had proposed the famous toast and the following day endeavored to make some sort of explanation. "The affair was purely social in character," he declared, "and the remarks I made were intended for the ears of only those who were of the social party, it being a sort of birthday party." He had been goaded into proposing the toast, he further explained, by the jibes of his friends.[13]

The ousting of Nugent was finally accomplished amidst one of the most disgraceful scenes in the history of the Democratic party in the state. Nugent refused to call a special meeting of the state committee; none the less, a majority of the committee met at the Hotel Coleman in Asbury Park on August 10 to consider the matter of the state chairmanship. Much to the surprise of the members present, Nugent attended the meeting, accompanied by a strong-arm mob of petty gangsters from New York. During the meeting Nugent's henchmen kidnapped W. H. Kraft, who was representing by proxy William H. Davis of Camden; in this way they succeeded for a time in preventing a quorum. With his back to the wall, his jaw thrust forward, and his face flushed with anger, Nugent confronted the remaining committeemen. He made a short speech defending his action and then left the room, accompanied by Charles H. Gallagher of Trenton. Just when the meeting was about to break up, George C. Low, Ocean County member, arrived; a quorum was once again established, and Nugent was quickly voted out of office.[14]

[11] *Trenton True American*, August 9, 1911.
[12] Published in *ibid.*, July 28, 1911.
[13] *Trenton Evening Times*, July 29, 1911.
[14] The story of the Asbury Park meeting is best told in the *Trenton True American*, August 11, 1911.

The following day Nugent charged that the Asbury Park meeting was "neither formally called nor legally held" [15] and later asserted that he was the victim of a plot engineered by General Collins, who he declared had started the movement to oust Nugent in order that he, Collins, might be elected the new state chairman.[16] Nugent's protestations, however, sounded more ridiculous each time he repeated them. The *dénouement* of the struggle was actually more important than the event of Nugent's dethronement, for the upshot of the affair was the formal reorganization, along progressive lines, of the machinery of the Democratic party in the state. The state committee, meeting in Trenton on August 24, unanimously elected Edward E. Grosscup of Gloucester County state chairman; neither Nugent nor Gallagher nor Katzenbach was at the meeting.[17] Grosscup's election was satisfactory both to the progressives and to the organization men who had thrown in their lot with Wilson. A loyal party worker who had done service in the Smith organization, Grosscup was nevertheless a faithful disciple of the governor and an experienced and astute politician.[18]

The ousting of Nugent was the outward sign of a fundamental reorganization of the Democratic party that was taking place in New Jersey during the summer and fall of 1911. The process began early in 1911 with the defeat of Smith's candidacy for the Senate; it received a tremendous impetus when Wilson established his dominance over the Democratic legislators; it would culminate in 1912 with the certain establishment of Wilson as the popular leader of his party and the final retirement of Smith from the political field.

If the state party machinery had at last come under the control of the Democratic progressives by August 1911, certainly Wilson realized that the most necessary kind of reorganization would have to come from within the ranks of the voters themselves. Such a movement had already got under way in Newark by the summer of 1911. With Wilson's support and blessing, the progressive Democrats of Essex County began as early as March to form a political organization to wrest control of the local Democracy from the last stronghold of the Smith-Nugent machine. Led by John J. Gifford and Samuel Kalisch, the anti-Smith Democrats of Newark on March 10 organized the Woodrow Wilson

[15] *ibid.*, August 12, 1911.

[16] *ibid.*, August 16, 1911.

[17] *ibid.*, August 25, 1911.

[18] It will be recalled that Grosscup was appointed by Wilson to the State Board of Equalization of Taxes on April 20, 1911. He was later named state treasurer by Wilson.

Democratic League of Essex County;[19] it soon included most of the progressive Democrats of the county. Wilson of course welcomed this sign of Democratic regeneration; perhaps he thought there was a likelihood that the League would capture the Democratic primaries in Essex in September. At any rate, he went to Newark in the latter part of June to give official sanction to the reform movement.[20]

In mid-July the governor also carried his message of Democratic regeneration to the party workers of Monmouth County. In a speech at Asbury Park on July 18 he clearly intimated what had already become an obvious fact: that Democratic progressivism in New Jersey had become Wilson's peculiar domain, that his principles were progressive principles and his program the progressive program. "I have no challenge but this," he told the Democrats of Monmouth, "if you agree with me, stand by me. That's all I ask. If you don't agree with me and your opinions are honestly formed, I'll grasp your hand. But if you cut under and try to stab the truth in the back I'm your enemy and I'll tell any man anywhere that I believe you to be a scoundrel." [21] The personal pronoun was becoming ever more conspicuous in Wilson's addresses!

The Wilson organization that finally emerged from the political jockeying during the summer and fall of 1911 represented a curious mixture of political groups. The progressive Democrats naturally constituted the heart of the coalition and furnished many of the leaders; however, there was also a large number of old-line politicians, particularly from Hudson County, in the mixture. The Wilson organization evolved in a peculiar manner: it started in 1911 as an organization to assure Wilson of New Jersey's support in the Democratic national convention in 1912; before 1911 had passed, however, the pre-convention presidential organization had become synonymous with the new progressive state organization. It was altogether natural that the two movements—the campaigns to make Wilson the presidential nominee and to establish a state-wide progressive organization—should have coincided and merged into one, for New Jersey Democrats who supported the Wilson policies in the state would most likely support him for the presidency.[22]

[19] *Newark Evening News,* March 11, 1911.
[20] For Wilson's speech, see the *Trenton True American,* June 29, 1911.
[21] *Trenton Evening Times,* July 19, 1911.
[22] The myth, which is still current in New Jersey and elsewhere, that the organization politicians, particularly the Smith-Nugent men, supported Wilson for the presidential nomination in order to get him out of state politics is absolutely without basis in fact. As will be demonstrated later in this study, the Smith-Nugent machine and certain

A number of Wilson-for-President clubs were organized in the state during the summer, and by October Wilson was assured of the support of the New Jersey Federation of Democratic Clubs, an organization of Bryan Democrats. It was more necessary, however, for Wilson to obtain the cooperation in the new state coalition of as many veteran organization politicians as was possible. Wilson had seen from the beginning that there were two kinds of organization men, and the success of his victories in the senatorial and legislative battles can be largely gauged by the success of his efforts to win the support of the organization men who were sincerely concerned about the welfare of the people.

There still remained by the summer of 1911, however, a group of influential politicians, including the former lieutenants of Davis in Hudson County, who had not yet been brought into the Wilson ranks. They had been sorely offended by Wilson's courtship of the New Idea voters and especially by his alliance with Record. Hudspeth, perhaps the most important member of the faction, expressed their resentment when he was asked to join the movement to make Wilson president. To William C. Liller, chairman of the National Democratic League of Clubs, he wrote: "Regarding the effort of friends of Gov. Wilson to make him a Presidential candidate, and your kind suggestion that I co-operate, I would say that I appear to be persona non grata so far as this movement is concerned in New Jersey. For some reason best known to the Governor and his friends, all those who appear to have been identified with active politics heretofore in this State have been relegated to the rear and are not invited to participate in any movement or action affecting the Governor or his political future." [23]

If the organization men in Hudson County thought they had been snubbed by Wilson during the period of the 1911 legislative session, there was at least evidence on all sides that they were anxious to get back, full-fledged, into the Democratic fold. Representative Eugene F. Kinkead, who had been a dutiful lieutenant in the Davis organization, flamboyantly announced on August 24 the determination of the Hudson leaders to stand by Wilson. "Until 'Bob' Davis's death I was with him," Kinkead told the state committee. "I was with him frequently when he was wrong, because I owed everything I was to him. Now 'Bob' has gone to glory and I owe nothing to any man." [24]

Jersey City politicians did everything in their power to defeat Wilson's endorsement at the presidential preferential primary in May 1912.

[23] Published in the *New York Times,* August 7, 1911.
[24] *Trenton True American,* August 25, 1911.

Was Kinkead endeavoring to establish himself as Davis's successor in Hudson by striking this new role of a Wilson leader? Many observers thought that he was, for Kinkead carried on a systematic campaign during August and the early part of September to obtain for Wilson the support of the "Big Five," the leading county bosses. On September 8, much to the surprise of everyone in the state, Kinkead met with the Hudson leaders and obtained a unanimous endorsement of Wilson's program and presidential candidacy from the Hudson County Democratic committee.[25] To add one miracle to another, Hudspeth, who had just returned from a long vacation in Canada, announced his reconciliation with the governor. Hudspeth declared that he would support wholeheartedly the Wilson program.[26]

By the end of the first week in September, therefore, the formal reorganization of the state-wide party machinery had been completed. It was accomplished, it would seem, voluntarily on the part of the party leaders who had not been integral cogs in the Smith-Nugent machine; it was, moreover, an almost inevitable result of the course of party politics since Wilson's accession to power. There was to be much wavering and indecision, particularly on the part of the Hudson County politicians, and during the spring of 1912 it would appear that this coalition of organization men and Wilsonian progressives would be wrecked by the vagaries of a few Jersey City leaders. But in the summer of 1911 the new organization—if such it can be called—appeared to offer the hope of establishing progressive Democracy in the state on a solid political foundation. The alliance had been effected none too early, for the Democrats were to hold their first primary election under the Geran law in September, and certainly the Wilson men had need of a solid front during this important campaign.

In a ringing declaration at Belvidere on August 16, Wilson gave warning of his intention to lead the fight for the nomination of legislative candidates who had supported the progressive policies. "I serve notice on all the constituencies of the State," he told an estimated audience of 20,000 farmers at a county fair, "that I intend to stand by the men who stood by me. If there is going to be a fight I want to help do

---

[25] *Jersey Journal* of Jersey City, September 9, 1911.

[26] *ibid.*, September 12, 1911. Hudspeth had a long conference with Wilson on September 28 at Trenton. After the meeting a reporter asked Hudspeth "if a flag of truce had been displayed." "There was never any need for a flag of truce," he replied. "Like all good Democrats we have had our little differences, but I am not of the political temperament to harbor any ill feeling toward anyone." *Trenton Evening Times*, September 28, 1911.

the fighting." He was in perfect rough-and-tumble form, full of jaunty confidence, and leveled a sizzling barrage against machine politicians who still dared to oppose reform. He had, he declared, attempted to convert the unreformed machine leaders.

"There are men in the various counties I could name who have had the chance of their lives. I have asked them whom they serve—the organization or the people? I serve notice on them that the game for them is up. They have preferred burial with dishonor to life with honor.

"I have held conferences with these men and talked matters over with them, and I have left them with the idea that they realized their duties and opportunities, but they went away like hogs to wallow in their own dishonor." [27]

Wilson continued his campaign in South Jersey for progressive Democratic nominees in another turbulent attack upon the Smith-Nugent machine at Camden on August 17. "When I was here ten months ago I was appealing for your suffrage," he told an audience of farmers; "now in a way I am accounting for my stewardship, and I think you will admit there has been something doing in New Jersey. I want you to understand that I am not particularly interested in running for office, but I also want you to understand that I will make it as hot as I can for those who do not represent the people, whether I am in office or out of it." [28]

Wilson's opening speeches in South Jersey were fiery enough, but they were only a prelude to a whirlwind campaign he made in the northern part of the state. He spoke first in Newark on September 18 and made two speeches there under the auspices of the Woodrow Wilson League. "It is something unusual for a governor to campaign for candidates prior to a primary," he admitted. ". . . But I made a promise to come back and tell you what your legislators from Essex had done, and I am here." The Wilson League had endorsed for renomination State Senator Osborne and Assemblymen Boettner, Balentine, and Macksey and had offered besides a slate of progressive Democrats for nomination to the remaining legislative seats. Opposing these men were the Democratic regulars supported by Smith and Nugent. Wilson pleaded especially for the renomination of the men who had stood by him in his fight for reform during the session of 1911 and also heartily endorsed the League's other candidates. [29]

[27] *Trenton True American*, August 17, 1911.
[28] *ibid.*, August 18, 1911.
[29] *ibid.*, September 19, 1911.

In striking contrast to the rampaging campaign he had been making during the primary fight, Wilson went to Jersey City on September 21 and made a speech so compromising that it jolted his progressive followers there. With great gusto he began the address:

"I came down here in response to what I believe to be a solemn obligation. I made many promises during the last campaign, not on the impulse of the moment, but always with deliberation. I promised that if you honored me with your votes and made me Governor, I'd come back and tell you not only what I had done, but what my associates had done. It is not pleasant to discriminate, but I shall speak with candor—justice is not a sentimental thing, it does not discriminate between friend and enemy. Justice speaks of facts as they are. No man who didn't stand by the leader of his party in carrying out its pledges can explain away his conduct."

With this belligerent introduction, and with the memory of his famous speech of January 5, 1911, at Jersey City, in which he promised that the enemies of reform would be "marked, labeled, and remembered" still in the memory of his listeners, Wilson proceeded to make an about-face by publicly endorsing for renomination Thomas F. Martin, one of his most implacable enemies in the 1911 session,[30] and Cornelius Ford, who had certainly only reluctantly supported the Wilson program. Only James J. McGrath, an unregenerate machine assemblyman, felt the weight of Wilson's condemnation. Of course Wilson endorsed the remainder of the Hudson legislators who were running for renomination; they, after all, had been among his most loyal supporters.

Wilson concluded his primary campaign with speeches in Orange and Newark; in both cities he discussed chiefly the election frauds that had recently been uncovered when over 11,000 sample ballots, which had been sent to "registered Democrats" in Newark, were returned unclaimed. "That thing has been going on all over the State," Wilson declared. ". . . I blush to think that I may have been elected last year by fraudulent votes. If I could I would go back and set it right." [31] He was determined, however, to prevent a repetition of such corrupt practices in the 1911 primary election; on the day before the primary was held he issued a proclamation to the voters of the state, warning them that "those who planned and executed those frauds last year will endeavor

---

[30] "I have something to say about Mr. Martin," he declared. "He never made any pretense. He always stated in and out of my presence what he thought and what he was going to do. . . . I have this to say about Mr. Martin. He fought me and fought me like a man. I have nothing to say against him." *ibid.,* September 22, 1911.

[31] *ibid.,* September 23, 1911; also *Trenton Evening Times,* September 23, 1911.

to repeat them this year," and instructing election officials and county prosecutors to prevent illegal voting. "False voting at primaries goes to the foundation of free government," he concluded, "and I give public notice that I will use the utmost power of my office to bring the full penalty of the law upon any person who fraudulently votes at tomorrow's primaries and upon any election officer and other public official who neglects any duty imposed upon him by law in this regard." [32]

If the primaries of September 26 provided the first measurable test of Wilson's new leadership of the Democratic masses, the results must have greatly encouraged him and the progressives; in every county in the state, with the important exception of Essex, Wilson Democrats were victorious at the polls. Even in Essex, moreover, Osborne, one of Wilson's most loyal supporters in the Senate, was renominated. [33] The primary fight was especially bitter in Hudson County, where the entire slate of Wilson legislative candidates was nominated, in spite of the opposition of the "Big Five," and McGrath, whom Wilson had singled out for defeat, was narrowly defeated for renomination. [34] Essex County was the scene of a clear-cut battle between the Smith-Nugent machine and the newly organized Wilson League. The result was catastrophic— a smashing victory for the Smith-Nugent candidates: every ward in Newark, for example, gave a majority to the Democratic regulars. [35] Progressives accounted for the victory of the machine by pointing to the fact that only 20,000 of the 80,000 registered Democrats went to the primary polls. [36]

The outcome of the Republican primary campaign was a victory, all along the line, for the regulars. The organization candidates in Essex, for example, defeated progressive Republican candidates, while Boss Louis Kuehnle's nominees routed the liberal candidates in the primaries in Atlantic County. "Czar" Baird, Republican boss of South Jersey, defeated the renomination of Senator William J. Bradley, who had been a loyal supporter of the Wilson reform program. Bergen County's progressive Republican candidates were likewise defeated. [37]

[32] *ibid.*, September 26, 1911.

[33] It should be pointed out, however, that Osborne had been endorsed for renomination by the Smith-Nugent organization. He therefore had no real opposition in the primary campaign.

[34] *Jersey Journal* of Jersey City, September 28, 1911.

[35] *Newark Evening News*, September 27, 1911; *Newark Evening Star*, September 27, 1911.

[36] *Trenton True American*, September 28, 1911.

[37] *ibid.*

In spite of the disaster in Essex, Wilson was gratified with the over-all results of his first primary campaign. "The returns, except in Essex County, are entirely satisfactory to the friends of progressive legislation among the Democrats," he declared. "The defeat of the progressive candidates in Essex County was expected and discounted beforehand, and represents a final effort from the Smith-Nugent machine to discredit the new regime in New Jersey." [38]

The first Democratic state convention under the new dispensation met in Trenton on October 3. It was a Wilson affair, pure and simple, and the new leadership of the party was emphasized when State Chairman Grosscup called the convention to order and Osborne presided. It was also remarkable in that hardly any of the old-line bosses attended: Nugent came down from Newark with the Essex delegation, but he refused to be a part of what turned out to be a Wilson celebration and left early for Newark. [39] Under the provisions of the Geran law the business of the convention was strictly limited to writing the party platform. The Democrats at Trenton, however, wanted to do more than that; they wanted to endorse Wilson's presidential candidacy and his administration as governor. Wilson succeeded in tabling a resolution that had been introduced by Charles M. Egan, endorsing him for the Democratic presidential nomination; he did not, however, succeed in defeating a resolution heartily approving his reform administration. [40] After adopting a platform for the coming legislative campaign, the shortest and the freest Democratic state convention held within many years adjourned. [41]

The primary campaign of 1911 had provided the first real test of Wilson's leadership of the Democratic rank and file; the election in November was to offer the first opportunity since his accession to power of gauging his popularity with the people of the state as a whole. The fall election was crucial in many respects, but especially because the fate of Wilson's presidential movement depended to a degree, at least,

[38] *ibid.*

[39] *Trenton Evening Times,* October 4, 1911.

[40] Wilson explained that he opposed the resolutions, not out of a sense of modesty, "but because I have a strong conviction, sir, that this action would be inconsistent with our recent legislation." *Trenton True American,* October 4, 1911.

[41] The platform promised the following legislation should a Democratic legislature for 1912 be elected: a revision of the jury system, an equalization of taxes, reform in the methods of chartering corporations, a reorganization of the charitable institutions of the state, conservation of the state's water supply, the elimination of dangerous grade crossings over railroad tracks, and a revision of the legislative rules so as to prevent slip-shod lawmaking.

upon his ability to prove to Democrats throughout the country that he could carry New Jersey, a Republican stronghold normally, in a straight Republican-Democratic fight. Consequently Wilson labored just as mightily for the election of a Democratic legislature in 1911 as he had fought for his own election in 1910. Again he went to the people, confident that they would approve what he fondly called "the new regime."

Wilson chose South Jersey, the source of regular Republican strength, to open the legislative campaign. He was in high spirits when he began his attack upon the Republican organization at Woodbury on October 5. "So many of our platform pledges were carried out," he remarked sarcastically, "that the poor, breathless representatives of the Republican party admitted that they were out of breath. They held up their hands in protest and said, 'In God's name, let us go slow a while.'" His chief appeal, however, was directed at the independent and progressive Republican voters, whose support had been instrumental in electing him governor and in carrying through his progressive program in 1911. Thus he declared:

"I believe that both parties have been singularly slow in waking up to the meaning of a new age, and what I want to call your attention to is that a large proportion of the men now active in leading the Democratic party have waked up to the meaning of the new time and have waked up, too, to those who are leading the Republican party. . . .

"It is . . . true that the progressive element of the Democratic party now dominates that party. Does not every man know that if the circumstances should change and the retrogressive element should get in control of the Democratic party that it would lose all possibility of success? That it would lose all the chances it apparently now has to lead the nation? The Democratic party realizes that, and the nation realizes it." [42]

The following day Wilson went to Camden and during the course of two speeches there leveled a terrific attack against the local Republican machine. "I should feel very proud if I might lead Camden out of her bondage," he declared. "You know that when there is a movement in all the rest of the State to reclaim it from its political servitude, everybody says that Camden is hopeless." Moreover, he ridiculed the Republican platform with sarcastic scorn:

"The Republican platform is one of these old-fashioned, smooth-bore, brass-mounted affairs, that goes off like a blunderbuss. I do not

[42] *Trenton True American*, October 7, 1911.

see the slightest difference between this platform that was adopted by the Republican convention Wednesday and the Republican platforms that preceded it; it has the same boasting about things that never existed; it has the same claiming of credit for everything good that was done; it has the same promises put in such phrases that they can be read backward or forward and mean the same thing; just the kind of thing you have been familiar with and never did know the meaning of." [43]

October was an incredibly busy month for Wilson: he went up and down the state, reporting to the people on his stewardship, giving an account of what his party had accomplished, courting the independent vote, lampooning the Republican platform and leadership. "The whole future of the Democratic party depends on its remaining under the control and guidance of its independent section," he declared at Flemington on October 8. The following night he spoke at Trenton and pleaded for the election of Democratic assemblymen from Mercer County. "You know that the character of the government of the State has been altered," he told the citizens of the capital. "Do you want to go back to the old style, you men of Mercer? You men of Trenton, who year after year have cast votes that promoted the old style?" [44] Wilson spoke also at New Brunswick and Perth Amboy on October 10,[45] at Red Bank, Asbury Park, Long Branch, and Freehold on October 11,[46] and at Princeton on October 12.[47]

What was lacking, more than anything else, in Wilson's speeches was some definite commitment as to what the Democrats would do were they again given control of the legislature. His denunciations of machine politicians, his appeals for progressive candidates, his increasingly partisan attacks upon his Republican opponents sounded spectacular enough at first, but his constant repetition of these themes day in and day out must have become monotonous indeed. What the voters obviously wanted from him was some assurance that the reform program of 1911 would be supplemented by other reforms in 1912.

During the latter half of October Wilson redoubled his efforts to win the approval of the voters for the Democratic legislative candidates. The burden of his appeal, however, was still almost entirely negative; his campaign was still a supreme effort to convince the Republican voters that their own party was dominated by conservatives and bosses and

[43] *ibid.*
[45] *ibid.*, October 11, 1911.
[47] *ibid.*, October 13, 1911.
[44] *ibid.*, October 10, 1911.
[46] *ibid.*, October 12, 1911.

that the only hope for progressive reform lay in the Wilson-Democratic party. He spoke to tremendous audiences at Paterson on October 16, and at Newton and Sussex the next day repeated his plea for independent support.[48] On October 18 Wilson for the first time got down to particulars; in a speech at Phillipsburg he promised his audience that a Democratic legislature would enact "full crew" legislation for the protection of travelers on the railroads.[49] At Elizabeth the following evening he launched a lengthy criticism against the plank in the Republican platform relating to the abolition of grade crossings, but was forced to admit several days later that his criticism had been founded entirely upon an erroneous impression of the Republican platform's declaration on the subject.[50] In Somerset County on October 20 Wilson paused briefly in his attack upon the Republican bosses and directed his fire against the Smith-Nugent machine.[51]

Unfortunately for his own cause, Wilson did not have the opportunity to write another letter to Record, to epitomize in one dramatic summary the issues of the legislative campaign. He did, however, endeavor to capitalize politically upon the disclosure by an Assembly investigating committee several months earlier of an incredibly corrupt political ring in Atlantic City, one of the Republican strongholds in the state.

Louis Kuehnle, the Republican boss of Atlantic County, it was revealed, had mulcted the county by a series of fraudulent and corrupt transactions; he was the political overlord of the county and under his direction thieves and crooks regularly stuffed ballot boxes and stole elections.[52] Such flagrant rascality had been possible only because under New Jersey law the sheriffs selected the grand juries—and Kuehnle of course controlled the sheriffs of Atlantic County. The existence of wholesale corruption in the county was generally known by the state authorities; but they were powerless and could not bring Kuehnle and his petty gangsters to justice.

One of Wilson's appointees, Justice Samuel Kalisch, who was assigned to the Atlantic circuit soon after his appointment to the Supreme Court, at last found a way to apprehend the criminals. Faced with the problem of dealing with a sheriff controlled by Kuehnle, Kalisch

[48] *ibid.*, October 17-18, 1911.
[49] *ibid.*, October 19, 1911.
[50] W. W. to C. B. Pierce, published in *Trenton Evening Times*, October 24, 1911.
[51] *Trenton True American*, October 21, 1911.
[52] The story of the Atlantic City imbroglio is related in an article in *ibid.*, December 30, 1911.

adroitly introduced the British practice of having the judge appoint elisors to draw grand juries when he did not trust the sheriff. Within a few weeks after Kalisch began his work, the details of the operation of as corrupt a political machine as existed in the country were made known. Thus a contemporary chronicler of the Wilson era writes:

"Only those who were participating in the movements of the day can fully appreciate the decisive and far-reaching effects of these procedures. The discovery by the Court of a way of stripping the boss-named Sheriffs of the prerogative of drawing the grand juries that had been protecting the looters of both parties all those years shook the boss system to its very foundations. It was Governor Wilson's last masterly blow at the white sepulchre of boss power he had set out to shake down. It gave him a new prestige among the people as one who knew how to make good his pledges to free them from their oppressors and despoilers. . . .

"It frightened the fattened bosses from their prey. If elisors were to draw grand juries they could no longer protect themselves and their fellow-looters from suffering the consequences of their crimes. . . . Fear drove them to the woods. They were not apt to be on hand in effective numbers to queer Governor Wilson's primary laws, or on election day to cheat him out of his vote." [53]

Kuehnle and his mayoralty candidate, Harry Bacharach, were under indictment for fraud and violations of the corrupt practices act when Wilson went to Atlantic City on November 1 to rally the citizens of the city to overthrow their corrupt leaders.

The situation there was made to order for Wilson: the thieving politicians were Republicans, and he had been making great efforts to convince the Republican voters that their party was boss-dominated. The result was that Wilson made one of the most swashbuckling speeches in his career. "As I have stood here tonight and looked into your faces I have wondered how it feels to live under a reign of terror," he began. "How does it feel? How does your self-respect fare in the circumstance?" The people of Atlantic City had submitted to the terror; they had stood by, cowed and submissive; they had seen the things done that had marked the city as the center of corruption in New Jersey. "You are my fellow-countrymen; you are men like myself. . . . Why is it that here, and here only, men like yourselves have permitted such things to exist for a single twelve months? I have come to challenge you to self-consciousness. Have you been asleep?" The Republican bosses and their Democratic allies in the city, Wilson continued, were

[53] W. E. Sackett, *Modern Battles of Trenton,* ii, 355.

neither Republicans nor Democrats: they were common thieves. "There are policemen at the door, and they would lay their hands on me if they dared, because I have come here and told you what you know, but perhaps you would not like to stand upon this stage and say it."

There was a way out of this shame; Atlantic City voters could redeem the honor of their town; they could become politically free men again by turning Kuehnle's subordinates out of office and by voting the Democratic ticket. He assured his listeners, moreover, that the election and corrupt practices laws would be rigidly enforced. He could not personally enforce the law, he admitted, but he could find out about things and proclaim them from the housetops. "Any gentleman who is a candidate to have his name gibbetted knows how to apply." He concluded with this final admonition: "Do not leave this hall thinking the issues of Atlantic county are merely the issues of Atlantic county. Do not forget that you are Americans. Do not forget that the American character is in your keeping. Do not forget that the vindication of American institutions is in your keeping. . . . Let these things fill your minds as with a sort of divine affection, so that you may go out transformed from the image of those who slink about in fear to keep out of trouble, in the image of those who carry themselves erect, and, come what may, men will die facing their God and honest men." [54]

Wilson concluded his campaign in southern New Jersey with four speeches in Atlantic and Cumberland counties on November 2. The following day he returned to the northern part of the state and spoke in St. Patrick's Hall in Jersey City. "A year ago South Jersey was lethargic," he declared. ". . . Now they come out as if it had suddenly dawned upon their consciences that perhaps even they might change their opinions, and with their opinions, change their votes." [55] At Bound Brook and North Plainfield on November 6 he concluded his campaign for a Democratic legislature.[56]

Because Wilson had made such an inordinately confident campaign for personal endorsement by the voters, the results of the election on November 7 were particularly discouraging: the Republicans had majorities in both houses of the legislature. At first glance the election results revealed a crushing popular repudiation of Wilson's leadership and of his reform program, for the opposition won 37 of the 60 Assembly seats and five of the eight Senate seats contested.[57]

[54] *Trenton True American*, November 2, 1911.
[55] *ibid.*, November 4, 1911.   [56] *ibid.*, November 7, 1911.
[57] *ibid.*, November 9, 1911.

The chief cause of the Republican victory, it was soon apparent, was the rejection by the voters of Essex County of the entire Smith-Nugent slate of legislative nominees. Smith and Nugent, it seems, had deliberately undertaken, even at the cost of causing the defeat of their own candidates, to assure the election of a Republican legislature in order to discredit Wilson and head off his presidential movement.[58] Especially discouraging was Osborne's defeat in Newark, for his election would have guaranteed a Democratic majority in the Senate. Smith and Nugent had got considerable revenge, but at the cost of the betrayal of their party. Had Essex County elected the Democratic ticket, the General Assembly would have had, for the first time in two decades, Democratic majorities in both houses.

After they had recovered from the initial shock of disappointment, Wilson spokesmen reached some startling conclusions about the election results. They declared that the election had been an endorsement, not a repudiation of the Wilson administration and that Wilson had succeeded in converting New Jersey into a solid Democratic state.[59] Huge inroads had been made by the Democratic candidates in South Jersey: in Salem County a Democratic senator, assemblyman, and sheriff were elected; in Camden County a Democratic sheriff was elected and the Democratic legislative candidates came within a narrow margin of defeating their Republican opponents. The best indication of the widespread protest against Republican boss control of the several counties was revealed in the fact that fourteen out of the seventeen sheriffs elected in 1911 were Democrats.[60] A total of 160,184 votes were cast for Democratic legislative candidates, while Republican candidates had polled only 157,084—a striking contrast to the Republican legislative majorities of 61,586 in 1908 and 41,502 in 1909.[61] During the 1911 campaign Wilson had spoken in twenty out of the twenty-one counties in

[58] The two organs of the Essex machine, the *Newark Morning Star* and the *Newark Evening Star,* for example, had refused absolutely to join in the campaign, even for the election of the Smith-Nugent candidates. See the *Newark Evening Star,* November 7, 1911, for an explanation of the apathy of the Essex organization. Wilson spokesmen pointed to the election figures in Essex as proof that the local organization had refused to get out the vote. In 1910 there were cast in the county 35,577 Republican and 40,516 Democratic votes; in 1911, on the other hand, the Republicans cast 30,646 and the Democrats 23,360 votes.

[59] See especially the *Trenton True American,* November 18, 1911, for a final analysis of the election figures.

[60] *Legislative Manual, State of New Jersey, 1912, passim.*

[61] *Trenton True American,* November 18, 1911.

the state;[62] in the counties in which he campaigned, Democratic legislative candidates increased their majorities from 9,531 in 1910 to 10,188 in 1911.[63]

But the manipulation of election figures by progressive editors to prove that the election of 1911 had been, after all, a Democratic victory, certainly could not change the obvious results of the contest. The fact remained that the legislature would have an overwhelming Republican majority and that Wilson had not succeeded in overthrowing the Smith-Nugent machine in Essex. "I, of course, deeply regret the loss of the house by my party through the loss of Essex and the failure to gain in the Senate," Wilson declared on the day after the election, "but I look forward with great interest to the next session as affording an opportunity to the Republican leaders to fulfill the very explicit pledges of their platform." [64] It was the treachery of Smith and Nugent that was responsible for the Democratic failure, Wilson thought. To Charles H. Grasty, editor of the *Baltimore Sun,* he wrote on November 10: "I think the results in New Jersey mean simply this, (indeed upon an analysis I am sure that they do) that wherever the influence of James Smith, Jr., could be made effective, it was exercised to defeat the Democratic Assembly candidates." [65]

The Democratic pre-convention presidential contest had got under way in earnest by the fall of 1911 and since Wilson was then the leading candidate for the Democratic nomination it was inevitable that he should find it necessary to divide his energies between New Jersey af-

---

[62] Wilson had been invited by the Democratic campaign committee in Essex County to speak in Newark, but he had refused to speak there.

[63] *Trenton True American,* November 25, 1911.

[64] *ibid.,* November 9, 1911.

[65] Baker Papers. The Essex leaders, on the other hand, were not at all disposed to accept the guilt for the defeat of their party in the campaign. Nugent replied to Wilson's accusation in a sarcastic statement and charged, "If there is any responsibility to be placed upon persons who call themselves Democrats for the failure to elect Senator Harry V. Osborne and his associates, that responsibility is upon Governor Wilson and upon Mr. Grosscup and the other supporters of the Governor. The only Democrats in Essex County who did not vote for the legislative candidates were the so called Wilson Democrats." *Jersey Journal* of Jersey City, November 11, 1911.

All of the progressive editors in the state, however, agreed that Smith and Nugent were the chief villains of the affair, but there was considerable disagreement as to the consequences the election results would have upon Wilson's political future. Perhaps the sanest judgment was that pronounced by the *Jersey Journal* on November 9: "The probability is that the election in this State on Tuesday will not have much effect one way or the other on the Wilson [presidential] candidacy. Wilson appears to be as strong as he was before with the people, and it is to the people and not to the old-time party machines that he must look for a nomination."

fairs and the greater national movement. One fact, however, has been overlooked by Wilson's critics who have charged that he neglected state affairs to pursue the presidential goal: he had given his best energies to the reorganization of his party and to the legislative campaign during the summer and fall of 1911. After the November election, on the other hand, Wilson's attention was increasingly absorbed by the bitter struggle for the leadership of the national Democratic party.

His first annual message to the new legislature on January 9, 1912, however, gave no hint of this important change in Wilson's attitude with regard to the legislative body. It was a cautious document, it is true, and the sense of impelling urgency and force that had characterized his inaugural address, the words "must" and "reform," which had been so conspicuous the year before, were noticeably absent. Wilson none the less made plain to the Republican majority his willingness to cooperate with them in carrying through "every program that is judged to be for the common benefit." He was the leader of his party, he acknowledged, but he was certainly not "a partisan or strategist for mere party benefit."

Wilson gave over the greater part of the message to a detailed discussion of the need for a reorganization of the administrative agencies of the state government. He envisaged, however, also a broad program of supplemental reform legislation that would provide for a greatly expanded system of state intervention and regulation in order to insure the health, happiness, and general welfare of the people of the state: a thorough overhauling of the system of tax assessment and even of the tax structure itself, a greatly expanded program of public health, supplemental labor legislation, and legislation requiring the abolition of dangerous grade crossings over railroad lines. "These are all matters of serious business," he concluded, "and it will be a great pleasure to me to be associated with you in trying to fulfill our obligations in regard to them in a manner that will satisfy the just expectation of those who have intrusted to our care the interests and the welfare of this great State." [66]

In spite of his assurance of willingness to cooperate in close association with the legislators during the session of 1912, the fact is that Wilson simply refused to provide leadership for the Republican majority; and, more important, at no time did he give any indication that he consid-

[66] The message is printed in the *Minutes of Votes and Proceedings of the One Hundred and Thirty-Sixth General Assembly of the State of New Jersey*, pp. 11-19; hereinafter cited as *House Journal*, 1912.

ered himself the leader even of the Democratic minority. It is startling, this contrast between Wilson in 1911, a vigorous, driving party leader, and Wilson in 1912, content for the most part to carry on the routine business of state. Not once did he meet in caucus session with the Democrats; not once did he attempt to determine party policy or coerce the legislature into enacting reform legislation by going to the people to rouse public opinion in support of some specific measure.

The causes underlying this fundamental shift in Wilson's conception of his duties as governor and popular leader are obvious. First of all, he was faced in 1912 with a legislature dominated completely by the opposition, and this Republican majority consisted for the most part of conservative organization men. He would approve with entire good will every measure of reform the legislature might enact, but he believed that he had neither the right nor the obligation actively to lead his opponents. Moreover, the Republicans were not anxious to give further impetus to the Wilson presidential movement by adopting legislation that would again boost the governor's political stock. The "political honeymoon" of 1911 was over; by 1912, one contemporary writes, "the Republicans had recovered somewhat from the political charm he had exerted over them as a result of his popularity with the people . . . and his ability by speeches to convey to the legislative mind his idea of the people's wishes." [67] "The Republicans were bitterly hostile to Mr. Wilson," observes another Wilson spokesman in the legislature, ". . . because of his official successes which received nation wide publicity and his evident growing strength as a presidential contender." [68]

Wilson later attempted to explain his failure to provide leadership for the legislature of 1912 by declaring, "I did not deem it wise or courteous to avow, as the session advanced, by repeated messages that the great matters were to be ignored and that the whole force of the session was to be spent upon questions of another sort and of questionable expedience." [69] It seems reasonable to suppose, however, that had not Wilson's energies been so overwhelmingly absorbed in the fight for the presidential nomination he might have been, as he was in 1911, the tribune of the people before the lawmakers. Instead, he campaigned in a dozen different states from Massachusetts to Iowa and made at least forty speeches in his fight for delegates to the Democratic national convention. It was the period of his greatest activity before the convention met,

[67] J. F. Fielder to A. S. Link, December 6, 1944.
[68] C. M. Egan to A. S. Link, January 8, 1945.
[69] *Trenton True American*, April 12, 1912.

and it is inconceivable that he did not neglect his duties as governor and party leader to seek after the larger goal.

In spite of the lure of national politics, Wilson could not avoid dealing with one vexing problem in New Jersey, the state patronage. The appointments he made in 1912 were perhaps not so numerous as in 1911, but from the political point of view they were more important.[70] One thing was especially evident in 1912, that Wilson deliberately used the appointing power for the purpose of rewarding his friends, strengthening his own progressive organization, and adding further recruits to his presidential movement in the state.

It was a delicate matter for Wilson, this business of rewarding his friends and strengthening his influence among the rank and file of the party workers by means of the patronage, for there were always more candidates than jobs. In Essex County, the Wilson leaders who had sacrificed their political careers trying to overthrow the Smith-Nugent machine there, were generously provided for. Osborne was made judge of the Court of Common Pleas in Essex; Alexander R. Fordyce was given a berth on the Civil Service Commission; William P. Macksey, one of the defeated assemblymen from Newark, was appointed the Essex member of the County Tax Boards; James P. Mylod, another former assemblyman, was named judge of the District Court in Essex.[71] On January 15 Wilson sent to the Senate a list of Camden appointments, and of course they were all leading Wilsonian progressives.[72]

A serious rift threatened to develop within the ranks of the Wilson followers over the appointment of a new secretary of state in 1912. David S. Crater, state committeeman from Monmouth County, and State Senator George S. Silzer of Middlesex were both candidates for

---

[70] One important appointment Wilson made, however, was not political in character and deserves only brief mention. In March 1912, President Taft appointed Chancellor Mahlon Pitney to fill the vacancy on the national Supreme Court caused by the death of John M. Harlan, and the task of appointing a new head of the state Court of Chancery fell to Wilson. At first he was apparently willing to follow the lead of the judges of the state who had suggested that Charles G. Garrison, an associate justice of the state supreme court, be named chancellor. Wilson, however, was persuaded by his insurgent adviser, Martin P. Devlin, that Garrison's appointment would be politically inexpedient and he named Edwin C. Walker, a lawyer with no corporation connections, instead. See "Journal of the Executive Sessions," *Journal of the Sixty-Eighth Senate of the State of New Jersey,* p. 1350; hereinafter cited as *Senate Journal,* 1912.

[71] *ibid.,* pp. 1328, 1352, 1356, 1357.

[72] They were Howard Carrow, member-at-large of the Democratic state committee, to be judge of the Court of Common Pleas of Camden County; William T. Boyle, to be the county prosecutor; and William C. French, to be the judge of the District Court. *ibid.,* pp. 1323-1324.

the appointment and each stubbornly insisted that the governor had promised the coveted position to him. Apparently for reasons of pure political expediency, Wilson appointed Crater, and by so doing angered the members of the Senate who had demanded Silzer's appointment.[73] Silzer, however, was placated by an appointment as county prosecutor of Middlesex.[74] Wilson's appointment of his former colleague at Princeton, Henry Jones Ford, as commissioner of banking and insurance, in March 1912 also provoked a minor revolt among the Democratic party workers. The rank and file of the organization men protested that Ford had been a resident of New Jersey for only three years and that he was a conservative Democrat who had been formerly an anti-Bryan man;[75] the Senate delayed confirmation of Ford's appointment until an investigating committee had made inquiry into his qualifications for holding the position.[76]

In spite of the petty rivalry over the spoils of office that muddied Democratic waters during the session of 1912, it should be emphasized that the over-all effect of Wilson's appointments was to strengthen greatly his power among the Democratic politicians and to lay the foundations for a strong Wilson-for-president coalition in the state.[77] As one contemporary historian of the period writes: "It must be known that the Smith machine was all this time engaged in efforts to disarrange the Governor's plans to secure delegates from the State to the coming National Convention. . . . It was necessary that he be adroit in the dispensation of the patronage, lest a mistake in its bestowal, or in

[73] *ibid.*, p. 1351; *Trenton Evening Times*, March 21, 1912.

[74] "Journal of the Executive Sessions," *Senate Journal*, 1912, p. 1360.

[75] *Trenton Evening Times*, March 21, 1912.

[76] "Journal of the Executive Sessions," *Senate Journal*, 1912, pp. 1351-1352; 1367-1368.

[77] Wilson, for example, placated Mayor Wittpenn of Jersey City by naming his president of the city police board, Job H. Lippincott, as assistant secretary of state. Peter N. Wedin, the sheriff of Hudson County and Wittpenn's rival, on the other hand, was placated by the appointment of J. M. Hannan, a former saloon keeper of Weehawken, to the deputy clerkship in the Chancery office. W. E. Sackett, *Modern Battles of Trenton*, II, 338-339.

Wilson added further recruits to his state organization by appointing John J. White of Atlantic County and John J. Treacy of Hudson to be judges of the Court of Errors and Appeals; Walter L. Hetfield to be judge of the district court of Plainfield; Thomas B. Madden of Trenton to be warden of the state penitentiary; Harry E. Newman to be prosecuting attorney of Ocean County; William A. Dolan to be prosecuting attorney of Sussex County; and Isaac W. Carmichael to be prosecutor of Ocean County. Another deft appointment was Wilson's naming of William Hughes, popular congressman of Paterson, to be judge of the Court of Common Pleas in Passaic County. See the "Journal of the Executive Sessions," *Senate Journal*, 1912, pp. 1328, 1331, 1349, 1351, 1354.

the conditions that surrounded the bestowal, put a weapon in the hands of his enemies. By the moves that have been detailed, he had made peace with the dominant factors in all the Counties, Essex excepted, in which the Smith influence was felt." [78]

The preeminent question before the legislature of 1912 was the abolition of dangerous grade crossings across railroad tracks. Agitation for the abolition of grade crossings had been carried on for a number of years by mayors' leagues and other municipal organizations, particularly in the North Jersey towns of Paterson and Passaic where, as Kerney writes, "railroads ran through the middle of the streets in the business center." [79] Both the Republican and Democratic platforms of 1911 had specifically demanded legislation to abolish grade crossings and Wilson, in his message to the legislature on January 9, had emphatically urged that the legislators enact a statute to implement these platform declarations.[80]

Early in the session the Republican leaders in the Senate and Assembly undertook to write a law that would satisfy even the most drastic demands of the agitators for reform. The railroad companies sent a horde of expert lobbyists to Trenton to argue against the enactment of a harsh measure, but the organization of mayors had its own special lobbyists, too. The result was a free-for-all fight in which the reformers and the Republican leaders stood firm. Finally a substitute bill evolved that combined the best features of bills that had been introduced earlier by Thomas F. McCran in the Assembly and Jacob C. Pierce in the Senate. The measure, as enacted by the legislature, required railroads to remove, entirely at their own expense, at least one grade crossing a year for every thirty miles of track they operated in the state. The Public Utilities Commission, the law further stipulated, was to determine specifically which grade crossings were to be eliminated.[81]

There was little doubt among political observers in the state that Wilson would sign the measure. Had not the Democratic party been demanding, year after year, such legislation? Moreover, the Democratic presidential pre-nomination campaign had reached its most crucial stage and few persons thought Wilson would veto a measure that progressives were supporting and the railroad interests were frantically opposing. Yet he refused to sign the bill. Perhaps he was influenced

---

[78] W. E. Sackett, *Modern Battles of Trenton*, ii, 344.
[79] J. Kerney, *The Political Education of Woodrow Wilson*, p. 197.
[80] *Senate Journal*, 1912, p. 16.
[81] The measure is summarized in Wilson's veto message, *ibid.*, pp. 998-1000.

by the voluminous briefs the railroad attorneys had drawn up for his perusal or by the arguments presented personally to him by railroad presidents and lawyers. Even the heads of the Pennsylvania and the Delaware, Lackawanna, & Western systems, which had already begun voluntarily to abolish grade crossings, were opposed to the bill. The Mc-Cran-Pierce bill, it was pointed out to Wilson, was so absolute and mandatory that its operation would almost inevitably bankrupt several of the smaller and financially less secure railroads. Tumulty, always the cautious politician, reminded Wilson that his veto of the bill might have an adverse effect upon his campaign for the presidency.[82] To this, Tumulty tells us, Wilson replied: "I realize the unjust and unfortunate inference that will be drawn by my political enemies from a veto of this bill, but the bill, as drawn, is unjust and unfair to the railroads and I ought not to be afraid to say so publicly. I cannot consider the effect of a veto upon my own political fortunes. If I should sign this bill it would mean practically a confiscation of railroad property and I would not be worthy of the trust of a single man in the state or in the country were I afraid to do my duty and to protect private property by my act." [83]

On April 2 Wilson sent his veto message to the Senate. "I know the seriousness and great consequence of the question affected by this important measure," he declared. There was an imperative popular demand that grade crossings be dealt with, but there was no demand for "unjust and impracticable" legislation. The mandatory provisions of the McCran-Pierce measure sought to accomplish "an impossible thing," because they took no account of the varying capacities of the railroads to build the underpasses. What was needed, he asserted, was an entirely different approach to the subject: the Board of Public Utilities Commissioners should be empowered "to push the elimination of such crossings as fast as it is possible to push it without bringing hopeless embarrassment upon the railways." "I do not believe," he concluded, "that the people . . . are in such haste as to be willing to work a gross injustice, either to the railroads or to private owners of property or to the several communities affected." [84]

In vetoing the grade crossing bill, it will be remembered, Wilson had sent the veto message to the Senate; this was a careless error, for the bill had originated in the lower house and the fact of its origin had been

[82] As a matter of fact, it was used extensively against Wilson by the Hearst press in the pre-convention campaign.

[83] J. P. Tumulty, *Woodrow Wilson As I Know Him*, p. 79.

[84] *Senate Journal*, 1912, pp. 998-1000.

plainly written on the outside of the printed copy. Republican leaders, therefore, immediately charged that the bill had become law, notwithstanding the governor's veto, because the time allowed by the constitution during which the governor might veto a measure had already elapsed before the error had become apparent. The attorney-general, however, ruled that because the legislature had adjourned for several days, the governor still had time to get the veto message to the proper house.[85] Wilson then hastily withdrew the message from the Senate and sent it to the Assembly.[86] The lower house, after avowing its belief that the measure was already law, overrode Wilson's veto by a straight party vote of 33 to 18; the senators, on the other hand, by a vote of nine to six upheld the veto.

Wilson's indignant veto of the most important measure of the session was little calculated to improve relations, already exceedingly strained, between the executive and the legislature in New Jersey. To say that relations between the governor and the Republican majority were exceedingly strained is perhaps an understatement, for the veto of the grade crossing bill was the climax of an unprecedented number of vetoes, fifty-seven in all, on Wilson's part. There could be no doubt that the Republican leaders had intended to attack during the session some of the more stringent provisions of the 1911 reform laws, particularly of the election reform and corrupt practices acts; Wilson, on the other hand, was determined to stand guard over and to protect his entire 1911 program. The result was a discouraging illustration of what often happens when the executive and legislators are at odds.

Almost half of Wilson's fifty-seven vetoes were directed against inconsequential and careless legislation.[87] Wilson also set himself squarely against all legislation designed to raise the salaries of state, city, and county officials and became increasingly irritated as the legislature, the Assembly particularly, insisted upon passing such bills and upon passing them again over his veto.[88] The climactic blow at legislative extrava-

---

[85] The attorney-general was Edmund Wilson; his opinion is printed in *ibid.*, pp. 1022-1025.

[86] The message is printed again in the *House Journal*, 1912, pp. 1518-1520.

[87] See the *Senate Journal*, 1912, pp. 814, 1001, 1001-1002, 1002-1003, 1003-1004, 1006-1008; *House Journal*, 1912, pp. 1099-1100, 1288-1290, 1291, 1331, 1384, 1472, 1472-1473, 1473-1474, 1475-1476, 1477-1478, 1479, 1481, 1482.

[88] See Wilson veto of Senate bill 156, *Senate Journal*, 1912, p. 1002; Senate bill 276 (passed over his veto), *ibid.*, pp. 1006-1007; also his veto of Assembly bill 76 (passed over his veto), *House Journal*, 1912, pp. 1098-1099; Assembly bill 283 (passed over his veto), *ibid.*, pp. 1288-1289; Assembly bill 346, *ibid.*, p. 1384; Assembly bill 574, *ibid.*, p. 1476; Assembly bill 582, *ibid.*, pp. 1476-1477; Assembly bill 648, *ibid.*, pp. 1479-1480.

gance came with Wilson's veto of the bill to defray the incidental expenses of the 1912 session.[89] Wilson vetoed about an even tenth of the measures adopted by the legislature. It was a tremendous job analyzing all the bills that came from the General Assembly, and Wilson relied to a considerable extent upon the advice of Tumulty and other progressive leaders. Judge William P. Martin of Newark, Kerney tells us, wrote many of the veto messages.[90]

Although most of the veto messages were brief and were directed against a class of unimportant legislation, it should also be remembered that Wilson felt compelled to veto most of the important bills of the session.[91] He had to meet, first, a concerted attack by the Republican majority upon the election reform and corrupt practices laws. He vetoed Senate bill No. 8, for example, which provided that neighbors might transport each other to the polls on election day because it seemed to "open the way to many corrupt practices which the Legislature cannot have had in mind when the bill was passed." [92] Again, he unsuccessfully vetoed an amendment to the corrupt practices act relating to the filing of campaign expenditure accounts.[93] The Assembly twice endeavored to amend the election reform and corrupt practices acts, but for some reason Wilson's vetoes were not overridden.[94]

Wilson sent forty-two stinging veto messages, in which he accused the Senate and Assembly of passing "scandalous," "whimsical," "arbitrary," and "dangerous and objectionable" legislation, to the legislature on April 2. The lawmakers, in the meantime, had adjourned temporarily on March 29 and did not consider the veto messages until they met again in session on April 10. The forty-two vetoes at one blow, coupled with the veto of the grade crossing bill, upset the equanimity of the Republican legislators. The legislature had hardly got under way on April 11 before a bitter partisan quarrel broke out in the lower house between Republicans and Democrats. The factional fireworks were set off by the presentation of a petition from the Paterson Board of Trade, scoring Wilson's veto of the grade crossing bill and his frequent ab-

[89] *ibid.*, pp. 1480-1481.
[90] *Political Education of Woodrow Wilson*, p. 203.
[91] It should also be borne in mind that the veto of the governor of New Jersey was in the nature of an advisory veto, which could be overridden by a simple majority of both houses.
[92] *Senate Journal*, 1912, pp. 940-941. The measure was passed over his veto.
[93] *ibid.*, pp. 1005-1006.
[94] *House Journal*, 1912, pp. 1468, 1475.

sences from the state.[95] An actual fracas was narrowly averted by the sergeant-at-arms.[96]

Republican tempers were at the breaking point and the majority members in both houses issued a joint statement that constituted one of the severest rebukes ever given a New Jersey governor by the opposition members of the legislature. The Republicans bitterly arraigned Wilson for a "deplorable lack of study" of many of the measures he had vetoed; they further asserted that although Wilson had had at his disposal ten days in which carefully to study the bills, he had given them only two days' consideration and then had hurried from the state to campaign for the presidency. The statement, curiously enough, also condemned Wilson for his failure to provide leadership for the session and asserted that, aside from a few messages that he had sent to the legislature, Wilson had not submitted a single policy or made a single suggestion with regard to legislation that should be enacted. The Republican manifesto concluded by criticizing what it termed the "crudity" of many of Wilson's vetoes and by pointing to numerous errors of detail, which proved that Wilson had not been concerned with the details of many of the laws he vetoed.[97]

It was a dismal ending for the second legislature of Wilson's gubernatorial career. He had just returned from a campaign tour in Illinois and was outraged by the attack from his opponents. "Ordinarily I would remain entirely silent under partisan attacks of this kind," he retorted, "but feel that it is due to the people of the State that I should speak my very emphatic protest against an uncalled for grossly discourteous attack upon my official career, proceeding as a manifesto from a conference of Republican members of the legislature." He would say nothing as to the merits of his vetoes. "But," he continued, "the statement that I have by my frequent absences from the State in any degree neglected my duties as Governor, is absolutely false. No important matter of business has been allowed to fall in arrears in my office. . . . I have been absent from the State only two of the session days of the legislature."[98] He blamed the legislature itself for playing fast and loose

[95] The petition is printed in *ibid.*, p. 1486.
[96] *Trenton Evening Times,* April 11, 1912.
[97] *Trenton True American,* April 12, 1912.
[98] In view of the frequent trips, some of them for as much as a week at a time, this is a remarkable statement. I have carefully examined Wilson's itinerary during the period of the legislative session and have checked it against the legislative journals. Wilson was correct.

with the business of lawmaking and pointed out that he was allowed by the constitution five, not ten, days during which to veto bills. The legislators, by piling 150 bills on his desk on the last day of the session,[99] had made it impossible for him to consider the measures as carefully as he would have liked.[100] If the session had been barren and disappointing, as it had been, the people of the state would know where to bestow the blame. However, he concluded with a parting shot that was typically Wilsonian, there was still plenty of time to get things done if the legislature was desirous of reform, and he was "at their service." [101]

Wilson, therefore, had the final word in the bickering that accompanied the closing days of the session, the last few days of which the Republicans spent passing bills wholesale over his veto. Wilson must have given considerable thought to the failure of the session of 1912. He rarely mentioned it, however, in his letters to his friends. In one of his few comments on the session, he revealed the extreme bitterness and revulsion that he felt. To Mrs. Hulbert he wrote on April 1: "This has been a petty and barren legislature. It has done nothing worth mentioning except try to amend and mar the wonderful things we accomplished last year. Small men have ignorantly striven to put *me* in a hole by discrediting themselves! It is a merry world—for a cynic to live in. For a normal man it is not a little sad and disheartening. And what shall we say when we find the leader of the petty partisan band a learned and distinguished Professor in a great University[102]. . . with plenty of independent means and plenty of brains, of a kind, but without a single moral principle to his name! I have never despised any other man quite so heartily,—tho. there are others whom I have found worthier of hate and utter reprobation—in *another* university!" [103]

The difficulty was that Wilson had run headlong into the vagaries of partisan politics. In large measure, however, the debacle of the session

---

[99] He refers here to March 29. Actually the last day of the session was April 16.

[100] Wilson, however, was begging the question. The 150 bills were passed by the legislature on March 29 and were probably sent to him either on that day or the next. Between March 29 or 30 and April 2 he studied the bills and vetoed forty-two of them on April 2. He left the next day to begin a campaign for the presidential nomination in Illinois. After March 29 the legislature did not meet again until April 10, presumably in order to give Wilson ample time to review the bills. There was, unfortunately for Wilson, much basis of fact in the Republican assertion that he had had ample time to study the bills.

[101] *Trenton True American*, April 12, 1912.

[102] Wilson evidently refers here to Senator John D. Prince, Republican majority leader in the Senate and a professor at Columbia University.

[103] Published in R. S. Baker, *Woodrow Wilson*, III, 292.

of 1912 was the result of his own failures and personal limitations. First, his absences from the state deprived the legislature of the vital personal leadership which had been the chief factor in the success of the legislature of 1911. Second, Wilson had revealed his temperamental inability to cooperate with men who were not willing to follow his lead completely; he had not lost his habit, long since demonstrated at Princeton, of making his political opponents also his personal enemies, whom he despised and loathed. He had to hold the reins and do the driving alone; it was the only kind of leadership he knew.

The period of the session of 1912 marks the lowest point in Wilson's career as governor of New Jersey, both with regard to his effectiveness as a political leader and his popularity with the people. Momentous days were ahead, however; the time was close at hand when the supreme test of his popularity with the Democratic masses would reveal whether he was still the acknowledged leader of his party in the state.

CHAPTER X

The Presidential Movement
Gets Under Way

IT WAS Woodrow Wilson's great good fortune that he entered upon the national political stage at a time when party politics was being convulsed by the broadening humanitarian crusade of the early 1900's. The agrarian revolt of the 1890's had smashed existing party lines as no other movement had done since the slavery controversy; and before any satisfactory realignment could take place following the campaign of 1896, the progressive upsurge of the first decade of the new century upset the party organizations again. From 1900 to 1910 reform was the keynote in politics: Theodore Roosevelt gave presidential approval to the movement; a number of reform governors and mayors—Joseph W. Folk of Missouri, Hiram Johnson of California, Hoke Smith of Georgia, Tom Johnson of Cleveland, and Sam Jones of Toledo, to mention a few of the leaders—set out to clean up state and city governments. A host of muckrakers, the publicizers of the reform movement, flooded the country with reform literature.

With Roosevelt's blessing, William Howard Taft undertook to carry on the reform tradition in the White House. Unfortunately for the Republican party, however, Taft did not possess his predecessor's skill in carrying the leadership of the reform movement at the same time that he worked hand in glove with his party's reactionary leaders. Roosevelt had somehow managed to play both ends against the middle and crowned with a halo of righteousness almost everything that he did. Taft, however, lacked Roosevelt's skill at holding together the insurgent and conservative Republicans in Congress. The inevitable debacle came when administration leaders in Congress wrote a new tariff law in 1909 and the mid-western insurgents were finally convinced that the party of Taft, Cannon, and Aldrich was the party of big business and reaction.

With the rift between the insurgents and the Old Guard leaders widening at a rapid rate after 1909, Democratic hopes of profiting from the division in the enemy's ranks were realized in the congressional and gubernatorial campaign in the fall of 1910. The November election of that year was a virtual Democratic landslide throughout the country. Moreover, there emerged from the campaign almost a new Democratic party, with new leaders and new issues. Bryan was still the titular head of the party, to be sure, but the Democratic success in the congressional and gubernatorial elections was not a Bryan victory. Bryan, actually, had bolted the Democratic ticket in Nebraska and had come out against the Democratic gubernatorial candidate there.[1]

New Democratic leaders, among them Woodrow Wilson, Governor Judson Harmon of Ohio, Governor-elect John A. Dix of New York, and Champ Clark of Missouri, who would be the next speaker of the House of Representatives, had carried the Democratic banner during the campaign and were now challenging Bryan's domination of the party. Practically every Democratic newspaper in the country believed that the reorganization of the party was at hand and would culminate in the nomination of a new candidate at the national convention in 1912.[2] "For the first time since Jackson's administration the Democratic party is emancipated and master of its own destiny," asserted the *New York World,* the leading Democratic newspaper, on November 19, 1910. "All the shackles have been struck off. There is no load of sectional issues or dead issues or economic fallacies for . . . [the party] to struggle under. As secession followed slavery to the grave . . . , so the Bryan socialism has followed silver, and the Democratic slate is wiped clean. The party is back to first principles again, under leadership that is fit to lead."

It was inevitable that Wilson's election as governor of New Jersey, his defeat of the Smith machine in the senatorial contest, and his success in obtaining the enactment of a reform program by the New Jersey legislature in 1911 should have made him, by the spring of 1911, one of the leading contenders for the Democratic presidential nomination in 1912. At that time there was only one other candidate who was seriously considered as being in the race; and he was Judson Harmon, the stolid, conservative governor of Ohio, a not too formidable opponent at that.[3]

George Harvey and Henry Watterson, the two chief architects of the early Wilson presidential movement, had been watching intently the fortunes of their protege. Harvey had worked industriously during

[1] Bryan refused to support Mayor James Dahlman of Omaha, the gubernatorial nominee, because Dahlman was opposed to prohibition, in which Bryan fervently believed. For Bryan's statement see the *New York Times,* September 21, 1910.

[2] See *ibid.,* March 9, 1911, for a trenchant discussion of the "new" Democratic party and leadership.

[3] For a description of Harmon, see B. J. Hendrick, "Judson Harmon: Progressive Candidate," *McClure's Magazine,* xxxviii (April 1912), 619-624.

the fall of 1910 to add recruits to his organization and in October was able to report that Clark Howell, publisher of the *Atlanta Constitution,* had "declared himself in";[4] a few months later he wrote that he had been attempting to swing Joe Bailey, erratic senator from Texas, into line.[5] Harvey and Watterson together approached Thomas F. Ryan, traction and tobacco multimillionaire, in an effort to persuade him to join the Wilson ranks. In December 1910, the three men who were later to figure prominently in the controversy following Harvey's break with Wilson, held their first conference at Ryan's estate in Virginia. Watterson, writing to Wilson about the meeting, was in high spirits; he had not played so prominent a role in national politics since 1876, when he fathered Tilden's candidacy. "If we are to organize a movement for 1912, we must start right," he wrote in his almost illegible script, "must understand precisely one another and where we are 'at,' and *what* we expect and *how*."[6]

Yet within three months the entire presidential organization that Harvey had so painstakingly constructed collapsed completely. Wilson's attack upon the Smith-Nugent machine in the senatorial contest was the chief factor in ruining Harvey's plans. Harvey had gathered about him practically every Democrat identified with anti-Bryanism, boss rule, and Wall Street. The bosses in New York, Illinois, and Indiana, who had expressed a keen interest in Wilson's candidacy in the summer of 1910, were no longer interested in supporting a man so adept in smashing political machines. After his first few months as governor, furthermore, the reactionary, Wall Street-dominated wing of the Democracy thought little better of Wilson than of Bryan. Harvey, it is interesting to note, cooled noticeably in his personal relations with Wilson. Watterson, on the other hand, did his best to preserve unity within the small group of early supporters,[7] but he labored without success. Of the original group of powerful supporters, only Harvey, Watterson, and Hemphill remained even outwardly faithful to the Wilson cause; even these men soon became the chief conspirators in a scheme to wreck the Wilson movement. The Wilson presidential campaign, abandoned by the veteran politicians, was by January 1911 left unfathered and unguided.

Wilson was never interested in organizing a realistic nation-wide

[4] G. Harvey to W. W., October 14, 1910, Wilson Papers.
[5] G. Harvey to W. W., March 1, 1911, *ibid.*
[6] H. Watterson to W. W., December 9, 1910, *ibid.*
[7] H. Watterson to W. W., January 29, 1911, *ibid.*

campaign before 1912, but it was impossible for him to ignore the considerable groundswell of popular opinion that did not wait for a signal from the professional president-makers to be heard. Wilson was rapidly becoming a serious presidential probability in spite of the desertion of the bosses and the conservatives. Wilson-for-President clubs were being organized spontaneously throughout the country—the first at Staunton and Norfolk, Virginia, on November 26, 1910.[8] Immediately after Wilson's election as governor, the leading progressive Democrats in Texas hastened to proclaim him their standard-bearer for 1912.[9] These examples could be multiplied many times; an overwhelming majority of the Democratic spokesmen, aside from the politicians, who had expressed an opinion on the matter in early 1911 favored Wilson for the presidential nomination. When William Gibbs McAdoo, Hudson tunnel-builder, at a banquet of the Southern Society of New York, toasted Wilson as a "future President of the United States," he was simply taking cognizance of what seemed to be the dominant political sentiment.[10]

Indicative also of the apparent trend toward Wilson was the haste with which progressive Democrats assured him of their support in the pre-convention campaign. "I give you good cheer and renew my expression of faith," wrote the editor of the *Washington News,* "that your position on the pending popular government issues . . . will instantly constitute you the inevitable leader for 1912." [11] William C. Liller, president of the National Democratic League of Clubs wrote to Wilson: "I believe that the party in order to win next year must be PROGRESSIVE and not reactionary and that it must select as its standard bearers men who can command the united Democratic support and that of thousands of voters of independence and courage. That is to say I want to see the convention name you for President." [12] Former Governor John Lind of Minnesota let it be known in January, 1911, that he was an enthusiastic Wilson man,[13] while from the South came the reassuring promise from Clarence Poe, editor of the *Progressive Farmer,* "I am not a politician, . . . but I have a paper of 100,000 cir-

[8] *Richmond Times-Dispatch,* November 30, 1910; *Norfolk Virginian-Pilot,* July 3, 1912.

[9] A. S. Link, "The Wilson Movement in Texas, 1910-1912," *Southwestern Historical Quarterly,* XLVIII (October 1944), 171.

[10] *Baltimore Sun,* December 15, 1910.

[11] J. E. Lathrop to W. W., December 22, 1910, Wilson Papers.

[12] January 12, 1911, *ibid.*

[13] Allan Benny to W. W., January 30, 1911, *ibid.*

culation among the foremost planters and farmers in the South, and I think I shall be able to help along the Wilson boom." [14]

By the early part of 1911, therefore, there already existed a great body of unorganized Wilson sentiment; only a push was needed to get the campaign under way. The first move came from Baltimore, in December 1910, when Henry S. Breckinridge proposed to Wilson the organization of a national association to boost his candidacy. Wilson had by no means yet made himself the master of the Democratic party in New Jersey and so discouraged Breckinridge that he dropped the suggestion altogether. [15]

By February 1911, however, Wilson was decidedly more hospitable to the idea of an organized presidential movement; when James C. Sprigg of New Jersey, Walter McCorkle of New York, and southern friends of Wilson in New York decided to organize a movement to boost his claims to the presidency, Wilson was at least interested. But Wilson did not think that Sprigg was "a very wise person," and he was "a little uneasy" about any movement that Sprigg might start. Wilson had, therefore, sent McCorkle to Walter Hines Page, editor of *World's Work* and a friend of long standing, for "hard headed advice." [16]

Early in March 1911, Page arranged for a conference to discuss the strategy of campaign organization and invited Wilson, McCorkle, and William F. McCombs. Nothing definite was settled with regard to the selection of a campaign manager or the establishment of a formal organization, but the members of the "provisional" committee agreed that the most important job on hand was to get Wilson before the people of the West. Wilson was easily convinced that the support of the western delegations would be necessary for his nomination in 1912 and promised to make a tour through the West after the New Jersey legislature had adjourned. A fund of $3,000 to finance the jaunt was raised among Page, McCombs, and McCorkle, and Frank Parker Stockbridge, a newspaper reporter, was hired to make arrangements for the tour and to act as Wilson's publicity agent. [17]

This, then, was the beginning. The little group of "original" Wilson organizers was a fascinating lot. Page, a "refugee" North Caro-

---

[14] C. Poe to W. W., February 17, 1911, *ibid.*

[15] J. E. Lathrop to H. S. Breckinridge, April 1, 1911, copy in *ibid.*

[16] W. W. to W. H. Page, February 10, 1911, photostat in Baker Papers.

[17] F. P. Stockbridge, "How Woodrow Wilson Won His Nomination," *Current History*, xx (July 1924), 561.

linian, had labored for almost a quarter of a century to improve the educational system of the southern states and to raise the lot of the small farmer in his native region; in 1911 he was a distinguished author and editor of *World's Work*.[18] McCorkle, born near Lexington, Virginia, was the newly elected president of the Southern Society of New York; in 1911 he was a "corporation lawyer" in the City.[19] McCombs was the most intriguing character of all. Born in Hamburg, Arkansas, a cripple since his youth, he had been graduated from Princeton as one of Wilson's honor students, had studied law at Harvard, and had subsequently settled in New York.[20] Suave, well-bred, and ambitious, McCombs had not yet displayed the maladjustment that later warped his mind. "He has something of the pleasant Southern drawl," one reporter noted in 1912, "a broad, full forehead and 'a wide, disarming smile.'"[21]

Soon after the New York conference, Stockbridge set out to organize a publicity campaign for Wilson. He hired an assistant, Maurice F. Lyons, and the two set to work arranging the itinerary of Wilson's western tour, preparing the advance sheets of his first speeches, and sending out newspaper cuts and biographies of Wilson.[22] Later in the month Wilson conferred with Stockbridge and outlined the policy the "information bureau" was to follow. "I am not to be put forward as a candidate for the Presidency," he told Stockbridge. "No man is big enough to seek that high office. I should not refuse it if it were offered to me, but only if the offer came from the people themselves; no man is big enough to refuse that. You must not ask any one to say a word or print a line in my behalf. Confine your activities to answering requests for information."[23]

Wilson's protestations that he was not to be put forward as a presidential candidate can be taken for what they are worth; most men desperately interested in the presidency would say about the same thing. Perhaps he really believed what he said then; at any rate, he soon overcame his reluctance and before many months had passed was

[18] For biographical data on Page, see B. J. Hendrick, *The Training of An American*, and *The Life and Letters of Walter H. Page*, 3 vols.

[19] For a biographical description of McCorkle, see the *Raleigh News and Observer*, March 10, 1912.

[20] For biographical data on McCombs, see M. F. Lyons, *William F. McCombs, the President Maker*, and McCombs's own story, *Making Woodrow Wilson President*.

[21] *Current Literature*, LIII (December 1912), 638.

[22] F. P. Stockbridge to R. S. Baker, August 7, 1928, Baker Papers.

[23] F. P. Stockbridge, "How Woodrow Wilson Won His Nomination," *loc. cit.*, p. 562.

engaged in an energetic campaign for national support for his candidacy.

Wilson went to Atlanta in March, at the invitation of the Southern Commercial Congress, to begin his campaign for the presidency. "I am not going because I want to go," he confessed, "or because I have something in particular that I want to say, but, I am half ashamed to say, because I thought it wise (which, being translated, means politic) to go." [24] Arriving in Atlanta on March 9, he met the leading progressive Democrats of Georgia at a dinner given in his honor that evening. The aging Judge George Hillyer, who had years before given Wilson his license to practice law, declared felicitously, "we have with us . . . a man who is going to be President of the United States." [25]

On March 10 Wilson delivered his opening address in the prenomination campaign; it was an idealistic appeal to the South to rise and "take its place in the councils of the Nation." The fullness of the welcome he received in Atlanta and the enthusiasm of the people could scarcely have failed to impress Wilson, on this, his first campaign junket. "It has been a long time since there has been a more popular speaker in Atlanta than the Governor of New Jersey," wrote the editor of the *Savannah Evening Press* on March 11. The editors of the two leading progressive newspapers in Georgia, James R. Gray of the *Atlanta Journal* and Fred Seeley of the *Atlanta Georgian,* were converted at once to the Wilson cause and soon afterward began an editorial campaign for Wilson's nomination.[26] During his stay in Atlanta, Wilson also executed plans for initiating his campaign in the state. He had long conferences with Hoke Smith, and Smith declared three weeks later that he would support Wilson for the presidency.[27] This, incidentally, was the first public announcement of an important political figure in behalf of Wilson's candidacy.

In April Wilson went again to the South, this time to Norfolk to speak before the Pewter Platter Club. Because he thought he had something in particular to say to his southern friends who were advocating his nomination, he welcomed this opportunity to go to Virginia. "The South is a very conservative region—just now probably

[24] W. W. to M. A. Hulbert, March —, 1911, published in R. S. Baker, *Woodrow Wilson,* iii, 196.

[25] *Atlanta Journal,* March 10, 1911.

[26] See A. S. Link, "The Democratic Pre-Convention Campaign of 1912 in Georgia," *Georgia Historical Quarterly,* xxix (September 1945), 143-158, for the subsequent development of the campaign in that state.

[27] *Nashville Banner,* April 6, 1911.

the most (possibly the only) conservative section of the country," he wrote soon after his return to Trenton. ". . . I am *not* conservative. I am a radical. I wanted a chance to tell my friends in the South just what I thought, just what my programme is, before they went further and committed themselves to me as a 'favourite son.' I do not want them to make a mistake and repent it too late." [28]

Wilson's idea of himself as a radical was amusing, and if he thought the South was the most conservative section in the country it was an indication that he had not even yet understood the political convulsion that had rocked southern politics during the years of the agrarian revolt. At any rate, his belligerent intentions faded once he got to Norfolk among "men of his own breeding." Perhaps it was the fulsome and sentimental tribute Edwin A. Alderman, president of the University of Virginia, delivered that took the sting out of what Wilson had intended to say. He did not, however, hesitate to tell his southern friends that he was a progressive, in the respectable sense of the word: he arraigned machine politics, political bosses, and reactionary business-men, upheld free and open criticism of public institutions, and advocated publicity as a remedy for many of the ills affecting the country's politics.[29]

Besides these halting attempts at getting his campaign started, Wilson accomplished a much more important objective before he began his western tour in May: he met personally and won the public approval of the Democratic leader, William J. Bryan. Probably because of his status as a fledgling presidential aspirant, Wilson's earlier contemptuous attitude toward Bryan's program had mellowed gradually into positive approval of the Commoner's diagnosis of the ills, economic and political, allegedly plaguing American society. He had concluded, apparently, that although Bryan did not have a logical brain, he at least had logical sympathies.

Wilson's spectacular entrance into politics in the fall of 1910 caught Bryan's attention, and Bryan hastened to welcome the former Princeton president into the fellowship of Democratic politicians.[30] For once, however, Bryan was puzzled. He had been told that Wilson was a progressive, yet he could not understand why newspapers that were "generally accredited as more or less friendly to the big interests,"

[28] W. W. to M. A. Hulbert, April 30, 1911, published in R. S. Baker, *Woodrow Wilson*, III, 198-199.

[29] *Norfolk Virginian-Pilot*, April 30, 1911.

[30] W. J. Bryan to W. W., November 9, 1910, Wilson Papers.

Harper's Weekly, the *New York Sun*, the *New York World*, and the *New York Evening Post*, were praising Wilson.[31] "Where does Governor Wilson stand?" the Nebraskan demanded.[32] When such journals, Bryan asserted two weeks later, gave enthusiastic support to any man's candidacy for the presidency, public interest required some investigation as to the reason for their enthusiasm.[33]

Wilson's fight for Martine, however, finally convinced Bryan that Wilson was after all a progressive, and not an agent of Wall Street. "The fact that you were against us in 1896 raised a question in my mind in regard to your views on public questions," he wrote to Wilson early in January, "but your attitude in the Senatorial case has tended to reassure me." He enclosed in the letter a worn copy of the Democratic platform of 1908, with the request that Wilson explain his position with regard to the respective planks.[34]

It is amusing to observe the manner in which Bryan endeavored to take Wilson in hand and lead him into the paths of progressive Democracy. When Wilson unequivocally endorsed the Denver platform, Bryan replied that he was "greatly gratified." But, he cautioned, "I notice that you do not recommend the income tax. . . . I hope that you will see your way clear to send a message to the legislature on that subject, for one state may be important." [35] When Wilson, three weeks later, complied by sending a strong message to the legislature urging the adoption of the income tax amendment, Bryan avowed that Wilson was a governor who recognized "the responsibilities of his position." [36]

It was Mrs. Wilson who was responsible for bringing her husband and Bryan together personally. Wilson was in Atlanta when an announcement was made that Bryan would speak at the Princeton Theological Seminary on March 12, 1911. Mrs. Wilson invited Bryan and his New Jersey host, Thomas H. Birch, to dinner and telegraphed an urgent message to her husband to return to Princeton at once.[37] Wilson, who in 1908 had refused to speak from the same platform with Bryan, now hurried home and arrived in time to hear his address. After the meeting Bryan and Birch dined with the Wilsons at the Princeton Inn.

---

[31] *The Commoner*, December 23, 1910.   [32] *ibid.*, December 16, 1910.
[33] *ibid.*, December 30, 1910.
[34] W. J. Bryan to W. W., January 5, 1911, Wilson Papers.
[35] W. J. Bryan to W. W., March 1, 1911, *ibid*.
[36] *The Commoner*, April 14, 1911.
[37] J. Kerney, *The Political Education of Woodrow Wilson*, pp. 162-163.

"I feel that I can now say that I know him, and have a very different impression of him from that I had before seeing him thus close at hand," Wilson wrote of Bryan the following day. "He has extraordinary force of personality, and it seems the force of sincerity and conviction. . . . A truly captivating man, I must admit." [38]

Three weeks later the two men met again, and this time they spoke from the same platform at a Democratic rally at Burlington, New Jersey. Wilson delivered a militantly progressive broadside at the "great interests" that must have delighted Bryan, and discussed at length the reform legislation he was endeavoring to push through the legislature. He was more than cordial to Bryan, whom he welcomed with open arms and unstinting approval. His first public commendation of the Nebraskan was as undiscriminating as his numerous former excoriations had been: "Mr. Bryan has borne the heat and burden of a long day; we have come in at a very much later time to reap the reward of the things that he has done. Mr. Bryan has shown that stout heart which, in spite of the long years of repeated disappointments, has always followed in the star of hope, and it is because he has cried America awake that some other men have been able to translate into action the doctrines that he has so diligently preached." [39]

Bryan, too, was in an expansive mood. "No citizen of New Jersey was more happy than I when the news came of the splendid victory of Governor Wilson at the polls," he declared. ". . . Our hopes in the west are raised by Governor Wilson's record. I am glad to stand on this platform with him and, of his constituents here, there is none more anxious to do him honor than I." [40]

Less than a month after the second meeting with Bryan, Wilson embarked upon his first great national campaign tour. Conditions could not have been more propitious; newspapers and magazines were reviewing with high commendation the achievements of the legislative session of 1911. Wilson was riding the crest of the wave of popularity; editors throughout the country were proclaiming him the new progressive Democratic leader. In May, for example, Page issued a Wilson edition of *World's Work;* it carried Wilson's picture on the cover, a laudatory article by William Bayard Hale, and a leading editorial praising his New Jersey accomplishments. James Kerney summarized Wilson's reform achievements in an article in the *Independent*

[38] W. W. to M. A. Hulbert, March 13, 1911, published in R. S. Baker, *Woodrow Wilson,* III, 210.
[39] *Newark Evening News,* April 6, 1911. [40] *Trenton True American,* April 6, 1911.

that was every bit as laudatory as Hale's.[41] The stage was now set for the opening of the great campaign, and political observers anxiously awaited the results of Wilson's first bid for national support.

Wilson left Princeton on May 3 and met Stockbridge in Philadelphia; Stockbridge, of course, had already obtained invitations from community organizations and colleges in the leading cities of the West. Wilson and Stockbridge were met by McKee Barclay, who Charles H. Grasty, publisher of the *Baltimore Sun,* had sent along to report Wilson's speeches for his newspaper.[42]

They went first to Missouri, arriving on May 5 in Kansas City, where Wilson delivered his keynote appeal to the West before the Knife and Fork Club. He lost no time in getting straight to the point of certain progressive issues; he wanted the West and, incidentally, the East also to understand his position. He proceeded, therefore, to avow his faith in the efficacy of direct legislation, in government by the initiative, referendum, and recall, as one means by which the people might work out their own political salvation.[43] These reform measures, he admitted, were allegedly "characteristic of the most radical programs" and were "supposed to be meant to change the very character of our government." In an age when legislatures were easily controlled by political machines, however, they had no such purpose; they were designed to enable the people to restore representative government in those states where it did not exist. He announced his opposition, on the other hand, to the recall of judges, a measure that was then popular in the West; he opposed the recall of judges because he thought that the independence and sense of dignity and freedom of the judiciary was "of the first consequence to the stability of the state." [44]

From this distant view, Wilson's Kansas City speech appears innocuous enough to satisfy sensible conservative opinion; it was cautious and temperate in tone, an appeal to the moderate opinion of the West. There was nothing fundamental or penetrating about it, and perhaps for that reason it was a great success. "Everybody is talking about Woodrow Wilson," wrote the enthusiastic editor of the *Kansas*

[41] J. Kerney, "Woodrow Wilson, Governor," *Independent,* LXX (May 11, 1911), 986-989.

[42] F. P. Stockbridge, "How Woodrow Wilson Won His Nomination," *loc. cit.,* p. 564.

[43] Wilson had already been carefully tutored on these reform measures by Record and the inscrutable William S. U'Ren, Democratic leader of Oregon, and had been willing to admit even before he began his western trip that his former denunciation of the reforms was based on false reasoning.

[44] *Kansas City Journal,* May 6, 1911.

City Star. ". . . If he keeps on as well as he has been doing I don't see how he could fight The Star off and keep it from supporting him for President." [45]

Wilson, Stockbridge, and Barclay arrived in Denver, the next leg in their journey, on Sunday, May 7. Wilson had promised to speak before the Presbyterian congregation of the Reverend J. H. Houghton; the year 1911 was the tercentenary of the King James translation of the Bible, and Wilson expected to address a small gathering at Houghton's church on the general subject of the Bible and progress. Consequently, he had not given much thought to the subject. When they reached Denver, however, he was horrified to discover that the morning newspapers had announced that he would address a mass meeting at the municipal auditorium and that all the Protestant churches in the city had canceled their evening services! "I wonder what I have let myself in for!" Wilson told Stockbridge. ". . . I must have a little time today to think over what I shall say."

Somehow Stockbridge miraculously managed to arrange for Wilson to have one hour, just before the meeting, in which to prepare his address. Fearing lest the speech be inaccurately reported—"Nothing is more dangerous to a public man's career than to be misquoted on a religious subject, and nothing is more likely to happen"—Stockbridge had hired a court stenographer to make a verbatim copy of the speech.[46] It seemed as if the entire Protestant community was present in the auditorium: most of the colleges and universities in Colorado had sent their presidents; Protestant ministers of all denominations filled the stage; and the auditorium was jammed with over 12,000 people. Governor John F. Shafroth was on hand to present the New Jersey governor to the citizens of Denver.

For once in his life, Woodrow Wilson was "utterly abashed" by

[45] W. R. Nelson to Henry Watterson, May 20, 1911, Henry Watterson Papers, Library of Congress; hereinafter cited as Watterson Papers.

[46] T. M. Patterson, publisher of the *Rocky Mountain News* of Denver, promised to print the address in full in his newspaper. "As soon as the speech was finished," Stockbridge relates, "the stenographer and I went to The Associated Press office, where he dictated from his notes to me at the typewriter, making a dozen or more carbon copies, to supply all the papers and press associations. The next day four hundred copies of The Rocky Mountain News were purchased and mailed to as many religious publications, of all denominations, with a form letter giving them permission to reprint the address. All printed some part of it; many used it entire. . . . During the following year more than a million reprints of this address were printed and circulated as the result of this publicity." F. P. Stockbridge, "How Woodrow Wilson Won His Nomination," *loc. cit.,* p. 566.

his audience. He was a master of impromptu speechmaking, however, and had little need of preparation to speak on a religious subject, for his religious beliefs were deeply rooted in his fiber. He had a supreme faith in an unalterable moral law: "We know that there is a standard set for us in the heavens, a standard revealed to us in this book which is the fixed and eternal standard by which we judge ourselves"; he believed in the ultimate triumph of the inexorable will and purpose of God; he believed that the individual has a direct, personal responsibility to God: "everyman . . . [is] a distinct moral agent, responsible not to men, not even to those men whom he put over him in authority, but responsible through his own conscience to his Lord and Maker"; he thought of the Bible as the supreme revelation of God to man.[47]

Wilson succeeded at Denver in accomplishing the ultimate in political addresses by identifying Christianity with progressive democracy and by revealing himself as the champion of Christian-social democracy. The Bible, he asserted, was "the people's book of revelation," the textbook of social and economic reform, and reform consisted in "trying to square actual laws with the right judgments of human conduct and human liberty." As a result, there was constant warfare in the world against passion, exploitation, and greed; it was "that untiring and unending process of reform." Then, in one unexampled emotional outburst of words, "I will not cry 'Peace' so long as there is sin and wrong in the world," he placed himself in the leadership of the movement for moral regeneration.

Wilson's address, which was rambling and disjointed enough, ended on a familiar note, the inevitability of progress: "And the man whose faith is rooted in the Bible knows that reform cannot be stayed, that the finger of God that moves upon the face of the nations is against every man that plots the nation's downfall or the people's deceit; that these men are simply groping and staggering in their ignorance to a fearful day of judgment and that whether one generation witnesses it or not, the glad day of revelation and of freedom will come in which men will sing by the host of the coming of the Lord in His Glory." [48]

Neither a millenarian nor a social gospel preacher, as this sentence might imply, Wilson was simply attempting to find moral authority for the progressive movement in orthodox Protestantism. It is extremely

[47] All quotations are from the Denver address.
[48] *Rocky Mountain News* of Denver, May 8, 1911; the Denver address is also printed in the *Public Papers*, ii, 291-302.

doubtful whether Wilson had thought through the implications of his words. The address was another of his "prose poems," and if Wilson assumed the role of prophet it is more than likely that he fell prey to the sound of his voice. But it was an immensely popular address, "one of the most notable ever heard in this city," the *Rocky Mountain News* declared the following day. After all, Wilson was telling middle-class property-minded Protestants what they were most anxious to hear.

On May 8 Wilson spoke before the Denver Chamber of Commerce, and his leading editorial advocate in the city observed that never before in the history of Denver had one man been accorded "so enthusiastic a reception as that [given] to Governor Wilson last night." [49] The following day, in a speech before the Mile High Club, he wound up his Denver visit by denouncing the secret machinations of corrupt political bosses and their private alliances with anti-social businessmen. [50] There was never any doubt as to Wilson's popularity with the people of Denver. "Why is Governor Woodrow Wilson the national figure which he is today? Why is he the most frequently mentioned Democratic candidate for the presidency? . . ." the *Rocky Mountain News* asked. "We think the answer is to be found in two words: progressiveness and courage." [51] ". . . the town is wild over Woodrow Wilson and is booming him for President," declared one Denverite to a New York reporter. [52]

Leaving Denver, Wilson reached Los Angeles on May 21. It was the first time he had been west of Denver, and he was fascinated by the desert and the wild scenery on the way. The fact that he was getting deeper into "progressive country" was embarrassingly evident soon after his train had crossed the Colorado River. Newspaper reporters boarded his train and demanded to know Wilson's position with regard to woman suffrage. It was a delicate question, one that Wilson was especially anxious to avoid answering, because woman suffrage was an issue in the impending state election in California. He was, besides, opposed to the idea; woman's place, he thought, was "in the home," and in his conversations with Stockbridge he expressed his disgust for the "unsexed, masculinized woman." The issue had been

[49] *Rocky Mountain News* of Denver, May 9, 1911.
[50] *ibid.*, May 10, 1911.
[51] *ibid.*, May 9, 1911.
[52] E. A. W. to W. W., May 11, 1911, published in R. S. Baker, *Woodrow Wilson*, III, 220-221.

bothersome in Denver, but somehow Wilson had avoided taking a stand; he soon discovered, however, that it would be impossible to avoid giving out some sort of statement in California. Consequently he decided that the only way he could honestly dodge the issue would be to declare, "Suffrage is not a national issue, so far; it is a local issue for each State to settle for itself." [53] That was positively all he would say on the matter!

Wilson made his first address in California on May 12, before the Jefferson Club of Los Angeles, and once again discussed the threat to democracy inherent in machine politics and corporation dominance of the nation's political life.[54] At the Los Angeles City Club the following day, he discussed specific weapons of reform, the short ballot, commission city government, the direct primary, and the initiative, referendum, and recall.[55] On May 13 he spoke also at Pasadena, and the popular reaction was enthusiastic. "No citizen of the United States," commented the local newspaper, "has ever been given a heartier or more sincere greeting than that accorded the great reformer of the east." [56]

In San Francisco, Wilson encountered an acutely embarrassing situation. He had agreed to speak before the combined Princeton, Yale, and Harvard clubs, but when he arrived in the city he discovered that the arrangements for the meeting had been made by the so-called reactionary businessmen of San Francisco. Governor Hiram Johnson, a rampant Republican insurgent, who was supposed to introduce Wilson, had refused to attend the meeting.[57] Discarding the speech he had already prepared for the occasion, Wilson proceeded to tell the masters of the wealth of the West Coast area that he was disgusted with the political machinations of financial and industrial leaders. Thus he declared: "Money is at the botton of all misrepresentation of the people. Not money put into hands—not bribes, that's old-fashioned and crude. The present plan is to convince men that, if they do not do as they are told to do in politics, they can't get money for their business— they can't get accommodations at the bank." Needless to say, Wilson's broadside evoked vigorous denials from his listeners and loud praise from the progressive newspapers of California.[58]

[53] F. P. Stockbridge, "How Woodrow Wilson Won His Nomination," *loc. cit.*, p. 567.
[54] From MS stenographic report in the Wilson Papers.
[55] *Los Angeles Times*, May 14, 1911.   [56] *Pasadena Star*, May 13, 1911.
[57] R. S. Baker, *Woodrow Wilson*, III, 222.
[58] *San Francisco Bulletin*, May 16, 1911; see also the *Sacramento Bee*, May 20, 1911, for a description of the affair.

On May 16 Wilson, Stockbridge, and Barclay left California and began their journey to Oregon, home of the arch-progressive, William S. U'Ren. Oregon greeted Wilson with open arms. "Woodrow Wilson is the unexpected," declared the leading newspaper in the state. "He is a national surprise. . . . Wilsonism is today one of the largest facts in American life." [59]

Soon after his arrival in Portland on May 18, Wilson set to work to study at first hand the working parts of the famous "Oregon system" of direct government. [60] There was a long meeting with U'Ren; he conferred with judges of the state supreme and circuit courts, with political leaders of both parties, with city officials in Portland, with state legislators, and with business and professional leaders. "I am going at the matter from the standpoint of the student," he told reporters. [61] On May 18 he delivered a ringing defense of the "Oregon system" in a speech before the Portland Commercial Club. "You have broken the machine," was his salutation to the citizens of Oregon, [62] and from his point of view it was about the most complimentary thing he could say. [63] The next day he spoke at a luncheon at the YMCA; U'Ren himself was toastmaster. [64]

After a hurried visit to Seattle, [65] Wilson went next to Minnesota. During the long trip across the Northwest he at last had an opportunity to ponder the results thus far of his western speeches and to take account of his own political future. At the outset of the western tour he had determined that he would not decide whether to enter the presidential contest until he could weigh the results of the swing around the circle. It had been a successful tour, he thought; he had been immensely encouraged by the spontaneity of the reception that Westerners had given him. At Portland he had admitted that "no man is too big to refuse" the presidential nomination, [66] and during the journey east-

[59] *Oregon Daily Journal* of Portland, May 18, 1911.

[60] For a detailed description of the progressive movement in Oregon, see Allen H. Eaton, *The Oregon System.*

[61] *Portland Evening Telegram,* May 19, 1911.

[62] *Oregon Daily Journal* of Portland, May 19, 1911.

[63] "I most heartily indorse the principles of the Oregon system," Wilson told a New York reporter, "but I do not go so far as to say that it will work out with the same satisfactory results as it seems to have here. Its application generally throughout the country in States where conditions are different, it seems to me, would be a matter of expediency rather than of the principle involved." *New York World,* May 19, 1911.

[64] *Portland Evening Telegram,* May 19, 1911.

[65] See the *Seattle Times,* May 21, 1911, for an account of Wilson's trip to Seattle.

[66] *New York World,* May 19, 1911.

ward he at last confessed that he did want to be president. "While there is no certainty of my being nominated," he told Barclay, "on the other hand, if I am nominated, I shall be elected." He wanted to be president because he wanted the country to have a leader who would do "certain things." There were other men who could accomplish these reforms better than he, Wilson modestly admitted, but he could not be sure that they would stand firm and carry them through. "I am sure that I will at least try to the utmost to do them." [67]

Arriving in Minneapolis on May 24, Wilson had his first introduction to the city's leaders at a luncheon at the Publicity Club. In the afternoon the booming governor's salute of seventeen guns greeted his arrival at the state capitol, where he conferred with the heads of the state departments, the governor's staff, and newspaper reporters from St. Paul. [68] At a banquet in St. Paul during the evening, he spoke before the political and industrial leaders of Minnesota. It was a festive occasion, his most important address in the state during the pre-nomination campaign, and he met the approval of the leaders of the Minnesota Democracy, Fred B. Lynch, Thomas D. O'Brien, and Pierce Butler. "I am not attempting on this trip to form public opinion," he told his audience, "but to educate myself in what is public opinion." The following morning he concluded his campaign in Minnesota with an appeal to the students of the University of Minnesota to enter politics. [69]

Wilson's trip to Minnesota paid huge political dividends. In the first place, he won the hearty approval of most of the old-line Bryan Democrats; but, more important, he succeeded in gaining the support of Lynch and O'Brien, the two chief leaders of the progressive wing of the state Democracy, in the pre-convention campaign. These two Democrats, in fact, took no pains to conceal their enthusiasm for Wilson. More and more, they declared, he reminded them of the late Governor John A. Johnson, [70] and that was the highest praise a Minnesota Democrat could bestow upon any public leader.

The last leg of Wilson's journey took him to Nebraska; arriving in Lincoln on May 26, Wilson was met by a committee of the Lincoln

[67] Notes made by McKee Barclay, published in R. S. Baker, *Woodrow Wilson*, III, 225-226.
[68] *St. Paul Pioneer Press*, May 25, 1911.
[69] *St. Paul Dispatch*, May 25, 1911; *Minneapolis Evening Tribune*, May 25, 1911.
[70] *Minneapolis Journal*, May 25, 1911.

Commercial Club headed by Charles W. Bryan, W. J. Bryan's brother
and editor of *The Commoner*. W. J. Bryan was in the East at the time,
but he sent a cordial telegram welcoming Wilson to Lincoln. Wilson's address before the Commercial Club on May 26 was the last
speech of the western tour. Of course he did not forget that he was in
Bryan's home town and bestowed lavish praise upon the "great Nebraskan." The main burden of his speech, however, was a discussion
of the vital role the states were playing in the matter of initiating
and experimenting with reform legislation.[71]

As he turned eastward again, Wilson must have thought that his
tour had been a great success. His speeches had been widely reprinted
in newspapers throughout the country; some ardent Wilson journals
had even published all of them in full, and for the first time his new
progressive creed was broadcast on a national scale. It made little difference to the people who heard him or who read his addresses in
the newspaper that much of what Wilson said was either meaningless, trite, or a mixture of sentimental and religious optimism, unfounded in historical experience; that the burden of his western appeal
could be summarized briefly in the statement, "I believe in popular
government." He made this first bid for national support, be it noted,
at a time when Bryan's leadership was rapidly declining, when progressive Democrats were searching about anxiously for a new leader
who would preserve the best features of the progressive-Bryan tradition without burdening the party with the stigma of free silver,
populism, and government ownership of the railroads. Whether Wilson could steer a middle course between Bryanism and conservatism
would determine the future of his political career.

The western tour, therefore, had given a tremendous boost to Wilson's presidential candidacy. He was progressive enough without being
radical, and it seemed that he had won the support of the masses of
the people. Although Wilson would later discover that political campaigns are not won by speeches alone, that people often shout one
way and vote another, that most of the western state Democratic organizations were controlled by politicians unfriendly to his cause, he
did succeed in generating the popular enthusiasm for his candidacy
that carried Oregon and Minnesota into his ranks at the national convention in 1912. Political observers generally agreed, as the *Springfield
Republican* put it, "With the conclusion of his successful Western

---

[71] *Nebraska State Journal* of Lincoln, May 27, 1911.

tour, Governor Wilson . . . may be said to be a candidate in the fullest sense." [72]

Wilson did not go directly to Trenton after his return from the West. He had promised to make addresses in North Carolina and South Carolina in the latter part of May and early June, and he hurried from Lincoln to Chapel Hill, where he made the commencement address at the University of North Carolina on May 30. The following day he went to Raleigh, where he was greeted with open arms by Josephus Daniels, editor of the powerful *Raleigh News and Observer* and one of the leaders of the progressive faction in North Carolina. Daniels had already come out in support of the governor's candidacy, but he took Wilson's visit to the state as an opportunity to get a full-fledged publicity campaign started.[73] Other editors and politicians were also at work in behalf of the Wilson cause and within less than nine months Wilson's North Carolina managers could confidently announce that they had carried the state for him. "When a man is in North Carolina he is in the Wilson country," one editor accurately observed.[74]

Wilson went from Raleigh to Columbia, South Carolina, where he was the guest of William E. Gonzales, editor of the *Columbia State* and editorial spokesman of the middle-of-the-road progressive Democrats in the state. Gonzales introduced Wilson to practically all the leading editors and progressive politicians in South Carolina, most of whom had already espoused his candidacy.[75] Wilson's address to the members of the South Carolina State Press Association, however, was

---

[72] May 28, 1911. Nor was the rising tide of Wilson sentiment ignored by Democratic politicians who had their ears to the ground throughout the country. The reception Wilson had received in the West and his popularity in the East convinced Governor Shafroth of Colorado that Wilson was "getting a remarkable hold on the people" (*New York Times,* May 23, 1911). William C. Liller of Indianapolis assured Wilson that the movement to make Governor Thomas R. Marshall Indiana's "favorite son" in the presidential contest would soon be quashed; that he, Liller, was leading a strong movement to obtain the Indiana delegation for Wilson (W. C. Liller to W. W., April 22, 1911, Wilson Papers). Blind Senator Thomas P. Gore of Oklahoma, a political gamester of the first order, sensing the mounting wave of Wilson sentiment, announced in the latter part of May that he had "concluded to support Mr. Wilson for the nomination" (T. P. Gore to H. S. Breckinridge, May —, 1911, published in *Raleigh News and Observer,* May 27, 1911).

[73] See the *Raleigh News and Observer,* May 31, June 1 and 2, 1911.

[74] *Wilmington* (N. C.) *Morning Star,* September 16, 1911.

[75] Wilson met the editors at a luncheon given by August Kohn for the members of the South Carolina State Press Association during the afternoon of June 2; he met the politicians and educational leaders at a dinner given by Gonzales that evening.

the notable event of his Columbia visit. Once again he was in Bryan country and, tempering his address in the best agrarian tradition, struck out at the "money power," which he called the most dangerous combination in the country.[76] It was easily the most "radical" speech that Wilson had yet made in the campaign and it completely captured most of the South Carolina editors for the Wilson movement. True it was that Governor Cole L. Blease, demagogic leader of the tenant farmers and mill workers, would have nothing to do with Wilson because he had stayed at the home of Gonzales, his mortal enemy;[77] but for once Blease was at odds with the dominant political sentiment in the state.[78]

Leaving Columbia on June 3, Wilson arrived in Washington the following day. He wanted, first of all, to meet personally the prominent Democratic congressional leaders, whose work in rewriting the tariff laws had impressed him favorably. To the newspaper reporters he made known his emphatic approval of the House's recent action in voting a 20 per cent duty on raw wool.[79] It was a dangerous statement, however, for Bryan had nearly disrupted Democratic unity in Congress by loudly demanding free wool and then by attacking the leadership of Oscar W. Underwood, chairman of the Ways and Means Committee, who had thwarted Bryan's demand for free wool. Underwood's success in thwarting Bryan's demands, in fact, gave the first impetus to the Alabaman's own presidential movement.[80]

Wilson was particularly pleased by Underwood's skillful leadership in the House. Several times on the western tour, according to Stockbridge, Wilson had discussed presidential possibilities, and of all the leaders in the party he thought most highly of Underwood. Once he allegedly said that if he were sure Underwood was devoted to the fundamental principles of democracy, he would cancel the rest of his tour, tell his friends that he could not possibly be a candidate, and give

[76] *Columbia State,* June 3, 1911.

[77] *Charleston News and Courier,* June 4, 1911.

[78] There was almost complete unanimity among South Carolina Democrats in favor of Wilson's candidacy. For example, every single newspaper of any importance, with the exception of the *Charleston Evening Post,* Blease's personal organ, supported the Wilson movement. With the exception of Blease, who was certainly in a class by himself, all the leading politicians were in the Wilson ranks. South Carolina is unique in that it was the only state in which there was no organized opposition whatsoever to Wilson. See A. S. Link, "The South and the Democratic Campaign of 1910-1912," chapter XIII (Ph.D. dissertation, Library of the University of North Carolina).

[79] *New York Times,* June 5, 1911.

[80] For the details of this controversy, see A. S. Link, "The Underwood Presidential Movement of 1912," *Journal of Southern History,* XI (May 1945), 232-234.

his support to the Alabaman. After an hour's conference with Underwood on June 4, however, Wilson made it plain that he was not impressed by Underwood's "fundamental democracy." [81] Champ Clark,
speaker of the House and afterward the leading contender for the
Democratic presidential nomination, called on Wilson. Wilson's opinion of Clark had never been very complimentary, and the meeting did
not change his previously expressed opinion that the Missourian was
"a sort of elephantine 'smart Aleck.' " [82]

On his arrival in Washington, Wilson also found a little band of
faithful supporters—Page, McCombs, McCorkle, Representative Frank
Page of North Carolina, Vance McCormick, Democratic leader in Pennsylvania, Stockbridge, and Tumulty—who were anxious to begin the
formation of a full-scale campaign organization and to undertake immediately the campaign on a nation-wide basis. Wilson, however, was
hesitant about beginning the organizational work so early in the campaign. "I am willing to let you gentlemen go this far," he told them.
"I am getting heavy mail from people throughout the country who are
asking me to make speeches or suggesting organization. I haven't time
or strength to deal with them. If you gentlemen want to take the responsibility of answering these letters, it would be a great relief to me."
On the other hand, since some sort of organization for publicity purposes was obviously necessary, Wilson appointed Stockbridge to take
charge of the information bureau and delegated to McCombs the task
of raising the money for the support of Stockbridge's office. [83]

A few days later Wilson explained to Page his conception of the
kind of campaign his supporters ought to undertake: "I have been
thinking a good deal about the matter we discussed the other day with
regard to a manager. I find in so many quarters the feeling that in
some sense the movement in my favor ought to be allowed to 'take care
of itself'; that my present judgment, at any rate provisionally, is, the
further we keep away from the usual methods, the better. Of course
I am far too well acquainted with practical considerations to think that
the matter can be allowed to take care of itself. But if we were to secure
the services of a man of large caliber who would direct attention to
himself inevitably and who would stand in the same category as in the
case of the one who is managing for Harmon, I think we would seem

[81] F. P. Stockbridge, "How Woodrow Wilson Won His Nomination," *loc. cit.,* p. 568.
[82] W. W. to M. A. Hulbert, March —, 1911, published in R. S. Baker, *Woodrow Wilson,* III, 196.
[83] F. P. Stockbridge to R. S. Baker, undated interview, MS in Baker Papers.

to have descended into the arena and would create some very unfavorable impressions."

He would like soon, Wilson continued, to get hold of Page and talk along this line: would it not be well for the present to maintain merely a bureau of information that a man like Stockbridge could manage until he obviously came to the end of his capacity, at which time they could alter the organization. "My idea is that we could refer everybody who wanted such information as co-operation must depend upon, to Stockbridge. He could constitute the necessary clearing house and by mere diligence in keeping track of everything, prevent matters from getting into confusion, or persons in different parts of the country working at cross purposes. He could be supplied with the necessary judgment in important matters by counsel with ourselves." [84]

Shortly after the Washington conference Stockbridge set up an office in some vacant rooms, which he had obtained rent free in the American Press Association building on West 39th Street. McCombs soon raised an initial campaign fund of $1,000 from Cleveland H. Dodge, and Stockbridge moved his office to 42 Broadway around the first of July. By the middle of September the publicity campaign was in full swing. To the editors and politicians who wanted information about Wilson, Stockbridge sent reprints of speeches, photographs, or summaries of favorable editorial opinions. Harry E. Alexander of the *Trenton True American* was eager to help and offered to issue a weekly Woodrow Wilson edition of his newspaper. Stockbridge furnished the materials for the edition and filled the pages of the *True American* with Wilson's speeches, reports of the activities of Wilson-for-President organizations, and editorial opinion favorable to his candidacy. Copies of the weekly edition were sent to almost every editor in the country and to "everybody whom we could learn of who had ever been active in Democratic politics." By November some 40,000 names were on the mailing list! [85]

During the summer a new recruit, William Gibbs McAdoo, joined the company of Wilson managers. Born in Georgia and reared in Tennessee, McAdoo had come to New York as a young lawyer in the early 1890's. With a genius for organization and handling large business operations, he had become the leader in the enterprise of tunneling the Hudson River. In 1911 he was president of the Hudson and Manhattan

[84] June 7, 1911, photostat in *ibid*.

[85] F. P. Stockbridge, "How Woodrow Wilson Won His Nomination," *loc. cit.*, pp. 568-569; F. P. Stockbridge to R. S. Baker, undated interview, MS in Baker Papers.

Railroad Company, a prominent businessman yet not identified with "Big Business," a leading financier yet not allied with "Wall Street." [86] Wilson and McAdoo had first met in Princeton in 1909. McAdoo had supported Wilson in the gubernatorial campaign of 1910 and was an enthusiastic admirer of Wilson's subsequent reform accomplishments in New Jersey. Although McAdoo's exact status in the Wilson organization was never exactly defined before the national convention, he was more an assistant campaign manager than anything else. As the months passed and the campaign became increasingly hectic, Wilson leaned more and more on McAdoo for support and guidance.

Meanwhile, countless invitations were coming to Wilson from all over the country, urging him to speak before this chamber of commerce or that local Democratic club. He could not go everywhere, of course, but when the leaders in the progressive faction of the Democratic party in Pennsylvania invited him to speak at the organizational meeting of the Pennsylvania Federation of Democratic Clubs at Harrisburg on June 15, he hastened to accept. Champ Clark, too, was on hand and proudly recounted the accomplishments of the Democratic House of Representatives. Colonel William C. Liller, president of the National League of Democratic Clubs, who had secretly undertaken to use his organization to further the Wilson movement, was also present to give his blessing to the progressive revolt in Pennsylvania.

In an address that covered the entire field of progressive reform, Wilson proclaimed his faith in the Democratic party as the party of progress and outlined in sweeping fashion the Democratic program. Then, almost without warning, he launched into an attack upon the "money trust," an attack which was later to cause him much concern: "The great monopoly in this country is the money monopoly. So long as that exists our old variety and freedom and individual energy of development are out of the question. A great industrial nation is controlled by its system of credit. Our system of credit is concentrated. The growth of the nation, therefore, and all our activities are in the hands of a few men, who, even if their action be honest and intended for the public interest, are necessarily concentrated upon the great undertakings in which their own money is involved and who necessarily, by every reason of their own limitations, chill and check and destroy genuine economic freedom. This is the greatest question of all and to this statesmen must

[86] For biographical data on McAdoo, see his *Crowded Years, Reminiscences of William G. McAdoo,* and Mary Synon, *McAdoo.*

address themselves with an earnest determination to serve the long future and the true liberties of men." [87]

There could be no doubt that Pennsylvania Democrats overwhelmingly approved of Wilson's leadership. So strong was the Wilson sentiment in the state that when the two factions of the party, the old-line conservatives and the progressives,[88] met at Harrisburg in July to reconcile their differences and reorganize the party machinery, they both hastened to endorse Wilson for the presidential nomination. The opposing groups were unable to compromise their differences, and consequently there were two Democratic state committees in Pennsylvania; each, however, stoutly contended that it was the genuine Wilson organization.[89] Wilson was elated by the turn of events in Pennsylvania and immediately recognized the progressive state committee as the legitimate party organ in the state. The support of the Pennsylvania delegation at the national convention would mean a great deal, he wrote to A. Mitchell Palmer, but what meant more was the character of the men from whom he had received this endorsement.[90]

In July Wilson yielded to the importunings of his Kentucky friends and went to Lexington to address the Kentucky Bar Association.[91] The following October he made an important campaign tour in Wisconsin and Texas. The trip to Wisconsin was to have a profound influence on Wilson's future political career, chiefly because it brought him into personal contact with practically all the Democratic politicians and editors in the state and was a decisive factor in obtaining the support of Wisconsin's delegates at the Baltimore convention. There were, however, encouraging signs that Wisconsin Democrats had already committed themselves to Wilson's candidacy by the time he arrived in the state.

Arriving in Madison on October 25, Wilson proceeded to give strong impetus to the Wilson-for-President movement already under way in Wisconsin. In an address before some seven hundred leaders of the state Democratic party the following day, he praised Wisconsin as "one of the states that has led the way in the sort of reform which the whole country desires," and declaimed at length upon the sort of "people's

---

[87] *Harrisburg Patriot*, June 16, 1911.

[88] The conservatives were headed by Joseph M. Guffey of Pittsburgh, national committeeman; the newly organized progressives were led by Vance McCormick, A. Mitchell Palmer, Representative William B. Wilson, Roland S. Morris, George W. Guthrie, and Francis F. Kane.

[89] *Jersey Journal* of Jersey City, July 20, 1911.

[90] W. W. to A. M. Palmer, July 20, 1911, photostat in Wilson Papers.

[91] *Louisville Courier-Journal*, July 13, 1911.

government" the Democrats were determined to establish in Washington. The kind of "people's government" Wilson was talking about, it should be noted, was a government representative not only of the workers and farmers, but also of the middle and upper classes, and even of the "special interests"; an ideal commonwealth, a classless society in the sense that economic freedom would insure unlimited opportunity for persons in the lower classes.[92]

Three days later, on October 28, Wilson arrived in Dallas, Texas, and proceeded to deliver several decisive blows in his own behalf.[93] At the Baptist church in Dallas bishops, preachers, politicians, and laymen made up the motley crowd of five thousand men and women who heard Wilson speak again on the celebration of the three-hundredth anniversary of the translation of the Bible into English. A few hours later he was the guest of honor at a luncheon of representatives of every faction in the Texas Democracy—Bourbons and progressives, prohibitionists and wets. In the afternoon he spoke before a tremendous crowd at the state fair grounds; Senator Charles A. Culberson, one leader of the Texas progressives, introduced Wilson and publicly declared his support of Wilson's candidacy. During the evening Wilson went to Fort Worth and repeated his Dallas address.[94]

In Texas, Wilson saw at first hand the results of the remarkable campaign the state Wilson-for-President organization was making. At about the same time that the New Jersey governor made his Texas tour, an unobtrusive Texan whom he did not know and had never seen joined the Wilson ranks. Edward M. House, called "Colonel" against his own wishes, a veteran of several political campaigns in his native state, a man of progressive ideas,[95] was later to become Wilson's chief confidant and aide.

House's chief desire was to help "make" a president, and at first he espoused the candidacy of Mayor James F. Gaynor of New York. When Gaynor's presidential stock went down precipitously in 1911, however, House yielded to the promptings of his Austin friend, Thomas Watts

---

[92] *Madison Democrat,* October 27, 1911.

[93] As early as April, 1911, Thomas B. Love and his colleagues in the state Wilson organization had urged Wilson to come to Texas. See T. B. Love to W. W., April 18, August 5, 1911; W. W. to T. B. Love, April 24, July 31, August 8, 1911, all in Baker Papers.

[94] *Dallas Morning News,* October 29, 1911.

[95] The best summary of House's political ideas may be found in his anonymous *Philip Dru: Administrator,* published in 1912. It reveals that House was acquainted with all the reform nostrums on the market.

Gregory, and joined the movement for Wilson's nomination.[96] Disquieting rumors that Wilson had never voted for Bryan, and that he had even voted against Parker in 1904, were being circulated in Texas during the summer of 1911;[97] as Wilson was to speak in Dallas in October, House set to work to silence the rumor-spreaders. In his first letter to House, Wilson assured the colonel that he had voted for Bryan in 1900 and 1908 and for Parker in 1904.[98] Consequently House informed Culberson and, through him, Texas, of Wilson's regularity.[99]

Wilson first heard of House through the ubiquitous Harvey, who commended the Texan to Wilson for his "sound" political views. The two men finally met on November 24, 1911, in House's apartment in New York. It was a delightful meeting; House, however, was impressed more by Wilson's personal amiability than by his intellect. Wilson, he wrote, was not the ablest man in public life he had met, but he would rather "play with him" than with any prospective candidate he had seen.[100]

House had a sizable independent income, and with nothing better to do than to dabble in politics he soon ingratiated himself into the inner circle of Wilson managers. House disliked the hurly-burly of practical politics, however, and his activities in the national Wilson organization were entirely advisory. Occasionally he conferred with state and national Wilson leaders, and often he advised McCombs on the management of the campaign.[101] On one occasion he brought David F. Houston, chancellor of Washington University in St. Louis, to New York to advise Wilson on the tariff question.[102] In December, 1911, House returned to Austin; during most of the winter of 1912 he was seriously ill, but as his strength returned in the early spring he now and then gave advice to the leaders of the Texas Wilson organization.

So much of legend and myth has grown up as a result of House's subsequent mysterious relations with President Wilson that many writers have assumed that House was the "president-maker" in 1911 and

[96] E. M. House to T. W. Gregory, August 29, 1911, Edward M. House Papers, Library of Yale University; hereinafter cited as House Papers.

[97] C. A. Culberson to E. M. House, quoted in letter of E. M. House to W. W., October 16, 1911, *ibid.* "There is a good deal of talk now," Culberson wrote, "as to Governor Wilson's attitude to the Party in the past and it is not doing him any good."

[98] W. W. to E. M. House, October 18, 1911, *ibid.*

[99] E. M. House to C. A. Culberson, October 20, 1911, *ibid.*

[100] E. M. House to S. E. Mezes, November 25, 1911, *ibid.*

[101] See, e.g., E. M. House to W. F. McCombs, February 12 and 23, March 6, 1912, *ibid.*

[102] D. F. Houston, *Eight Years in Wilson's Cabinet*, 2 vols., I, 18-20.

Joseph P. Tumulty

Edward M. House

George Harvey

William F. McCombs

SOME LEADERS IN THE PRE-CONVENTION CAMPAIGN

Campaigning for the Presidency

1912. Nothing could be farther from the truth. House endeavored to cement the already friendly relations that existed between Wilson and Bryan, and the House biographers have made much of this point; but it is extremely doubtful whether House's promptings had any measurable influence on the inscrutable Nebraskan. Moreover, in fairness to the tremendous work done by the Texas Wilson leaders, it should be stated once and for all that House did not "carry" Texas for Wilson in 1912.[103] In so far as his activities in the national organization itself are concerned, it is difficult to imagine that House played a decisive, or even an important role in deciding the strategy of the campaign.

As will be demonstrated in a following chapter, the really important work in the Wilson pre-convention movement was done by his advocates in the several states, most of whom are now forgotten. Theirs was the important task of organizing the state campaigns and winning the delegates to the national convention; and to them must go most of the credit for the success the Wilson movement enjoyed. In so far as the national organization is concerned, however, it is McCombs, and not House or Page, who stands out as the most resourceful and energetic general of the campaign.

Actually, it was not until October that McCombs was definitely designated by Wilson as his campaign manager. Finally given a free hand in the matter of organization, McCombs took up the work enthusiastically. First, he sought to establish personal contact with editors and public leaders, and by the end of the year had at least put in motion the business of establishing the nuclei of Wilson organizations in the states.[104] By the end of November he could report that he had conferred with Charles G. Heifner of Washington State; J. O. Davis of Berkeley, California; G. E. Hosmer of Denver; Lawrence B. Stringer and Irving

[103] See my amplification of this point in "The Wilson Movement in Texas, 1910-1912," *loc. cit.*, pp. 178-179.

[104] The following letter, addressed to the publisher of the *Charlotte Daily Observer,* is typical of many that McCombs was writing during this period: "As you are aware, I am deeply interested in furthering the Presidential candidacy of Governor Woodrow Wilson and realizing that the time has arrived when a definite move must be made in the direction of state organization, I am writing to ask if you would be willing to join in the work in your state.

"There is no question whatever about the popular sentiment in support of Governor Wilson everywhere, and the great problem now is the crystallization of that sentiment, so that it may be effective in the next national convention.

"I shall be very glad to hear from you with any suggestions that you may be pleased to offer and trust that you will find it possible to take an active part in this work in North Carolina." W. F. McCombs to Daniel A. Tompkins, October 26, 1911, Tompkins Papers, Library of Congress.

Shuman of Illinois; Thomas A. Anketell and Aldrich Blake of Michigan, "and perhaps a dozen others." [105] McCombs also toyed with the idea of a national organization, which would include Senator John Sharp Williams of Mississippi, E. M. House, and a senator or two from the West, and even suggested the idea to House. However, McCombs was apparently so pleased when House intimated that McCombs himself could direct the campaign more effectively alone that he dropped the idea altogether.[106] The burden of raising funds to keep the Wilson campaign going also fell almost entirely upon McCombs's shoulders. The bureau at 42 Broadway was constantly expanding its operations, and the demands for more money increased proportionately. By December McCombs had succeeded in raising $35,000, half of which was contributed by Cleveland H. Dodge.[107] It was only the beginning, however; McCombs had troubles to come.

By December, moreover, it was obvious to McCombs that the exigencies of the campaign required a different sort of publicity campaign from that which the New York bureau had been carrying on. What was needed was some official spokesman for the Wilson organization, some agency that would represent Wilson's interests before the public. Consequently a branch office of the organization was established in Washington in December, and Thomas J. Pence of Raleigh[108] was appointed director. Pence at once organized a comprehensive publicity campaign for the Wilson movement. While the New York headquarters was still sending out second-hand accounts and editorials, Pence distributed only original material for the eight hundred daily and six thousand weekly newspapers he soon had on his mailing list.[109] Within a few weeks the Washington bureau had become the official and public spokesman for the Wilson movement.

McCombs has become the chief whipping boy of the eulogistic Wilson biographers, who have singled him out as the source of all the defects of the pre-convention campaign. It is true that by the fall of 1911 he was already beginning to reveal the erratic temperament and dom-

[105] W. F. McCombs to W. H. Page, November 27, 1911, Walter H. Page Papers, Library of Harvard University.

[106] E. M. House to T. W. Gregory, October 30, 1911, House Papers.

[107] From McCombs's testimony before the Clapp investigating committee, *Campaign Contributions* (United States Senate document, 1912), p. 877.

[108] Pence had for ten years been the Washington correspondent of the *Raleigh News and Observer*.

[109] For a description of the work of the Washington bureau, see the *Raleigh News and Observer*, September 1, 1912.

ineering personality that often impaired the efficient operation of the campaign organization. Crippled from his youth and given to much introversion, he was jealous of his co-workers in the Wilson circle. Determined that he alone should be the Warwick of the movement, McCombs regarded with increasing bitterness the fast-growing friendship between Wilson and McAdoo. Moreover, McCombs had extreme difficulty in getting along with most of his subordinates because he feared that they, too, were endeavoring to gain a special position in Wilson's favor. The friction between Stockbridge and McCombs became so intense, for example, that Stockbridge quit the organization, but not before he was able to install Byron R. Newton, head of McAdoo's railroad publicity staff and a "better scrapper" than Stockbridge, as head of the "information bureau." [110] Newton, however, like Stockbridge, was a protege of McAdoo and he and McCombs could not make it together. When Newton left the organization early in 1912 he was succeeded by Walker W. Vick, a young North Carolinian living in New Jersey. Fortunately for Wilson, Vick was able to cooperate with McCombs and carried on the work in New York until the Baltimore convention met in June 1912.[111]

In spite of his faults of personality, on the other hand, it should be emphasized that McCombs was a loyal and indefatigable laborer in the Wilson cause and the chief source of strength of the Wilson campaign. In contrast to most other men close to Wilson at the time, he was at least a realistic campaign manager. He was no parlor politician like Page or House; he knew from his slight experience in Tammany politics that political campaigns are not won merely by eloquent appeals to the people, as Wilson seemed to think, and he saw the fallacy of depending upon propaganda alone to obtain the support of the state organizations. He realized that it was organization and alliances with state leaders that produced results, and what realistic direction there was about the Wilson pre-nomination campaign came largely from him. He sought and welcomed the support of the old-line politicians and came to lean heavily upon such veterans as Senator Thomas P. Gore of Oklahoma and Willard Saulsbury of Delaware for support and advice. He also sought, for the most part unsuccessfully, to let the pol-

[110] F. P. Stockbridge to R. S. Baker, March 10, 1927, Baker Papers.

[111] McCombs has left an account of this early period of the pre-convention campaign in his *Making Woodrow Wilson President* that is, for the most part accurate; see also M. F. Lyons, *William F. McCombs*, pp. 13-25; W. G. McAdoo, *Crowded Years*, pp. 114-120; F. P. Stockbridge, "How Woodrow Wilson Won His Nomination," *loc. cit.*, pp. 570-571.

iticians know that Wilson was a good "organization" man who would not forget his friends should he reach the White House.[112]

The Democratic pre-convention battle got under way in earnest late in the fall of 1911. Two other candidates, Oscar W. Underwood and Champ Clark, had emerged in the meantime as powerful contenders for the nomination. For his part, Wilson redoubled his efforts at speech-making and made several bids for popular support during December 1911 and the early part of January 1912. On December 5 he went to Baltimore and spoke in behalf of commission government and on the problems of southern agriculture.[113] The following night he addressed an audience that had gathered in Carnegie Hall in New York to protest the discrimination practiced by the Russian government against American Jews. "We are not here to express our sympathy with our Jewish fellow-citizens," he declared, making a bold bid for Jewish support, "but to make evident our sense of identity with them. This is not their cause; it is America's." [114] Jacob H. Schiff of the banking firm of Kuhn, Loeb, & Company was so deeply impressed by Wilson's address that he shortly afterward gave McAdoo $2,500 for the campaign treasury and promised to support Wilson's candidacy;[115] Henry Morgenthau, another prominent Jewish leader, at once enlisted in the Wilson ranks and promised to contribute $4,000 a month to the campaign fund.[116]

By December 1911 Wilson had spoken in a general way with regard to most of the economic and political questions then troubling Democratic voters. By scattering his attacks in so many different directions, however, he had confused the average voter, while his vacillation on certain issues was not calculated to clarify his position with regard to them. In this connection, let us consider Wilson's treatment of the issues of the initiative, referendum, and recall and the "money trust." His Knife and Fork Club address, in which he gave ungrudging approval to the initiative, referendum, and recall, and his Harrisburg address on the "money trust" constituted his two most important public declarations during the early pre-convention campaign. They were especially important because they served to identify Wilsonism with Bryanism and evoked a spirited campaign against Wilson by the conservative Democratic leaders.

[112] W. F. McCombs to E. M. House, December 22, 1911, House Papers.
[113] *Baltimore Sun*, December 6, 1911.
[114] *New York Times*, December 7, 1911.
[115] W. G. McAdoo, *Crowded Years*, p. 122.
[116] J. Kerney, *The Political Education of Woodrow Wilson*, p. 155.

It is difficult in this latter day to comprehend the intensity of the bitterness and the overwhelming dread with which conservatives during this period looked upon the initiative, referendum, and recall. The opposition of those persons who profited directly or indirectly from corruptly awarded franchises or other special privileges in the cities and states can be easily understood, for the measures were allegedly weapons the people could use to cut through the wall of "invisible government" separating them from their legislatures and city councils. Yet conservative members of the middle and upper classes, who had no connection with the system of special privileges, also shrank back in dread from the initiative, referendum, and recall. Somehow the reforms became identified in their minds with socialism, with a general frontal attack upon property rights.[117]

The fact that Wilson had been, during his professorial years, an outstanding opponent of the initiative, referendum, and recall[118] only served to intensify the bitterness of the attack that the conservatives made upon his new progressive doctrines. "A year ago we followed you with enthusiasm," one of his friends in St. Louis wrote; "today many of us are perplexed, and hesitate. The doctrines and measures which are now associated with your name have aroused a vague fear of your future conduct." [119] The countless tirades in the newspapers were loud and prolonged. The *New York Sun,* which had originally been in the vanguard of the Wilson movement, turned on Wilson during the western tour and at once assumed command of the anti-Wilson campaign. Following the *Sun's* lead, the entire conservative anti-Bryan press turned its guns against Wilson. The reaction of the old-line Democrats was particularly violent in the South, where James C. Hemphill of the

[117] This reaction was best expressed by Methodist Bishop Warren A. Candler of Georgia, who wrote a thinly veiled attack upon Wilson that was published in the *Macon Telegraph.* "Certain politicians," Candler declared, "have within recent months put forward the most preposterous schemes of government and named them progressive policies." The agitation for the adoption of the initiative, referendum, and recall was agitation for class warfare. The "radicals" intended to mulct the upper classes of their property under the cloak of progressive reform. The adoption of the measures would result in the establishment of a "turbulent Greek democracy" in the United States, in which "an irresponsible and passionate majority may trample upon the most sacred rights of minorities." The initiative, referendum, and recall, Candler concluded, were nothing less than proposals to "lynch representative government." See W. A. Candler, "Progress and Pi," reprinted in the *Houston Post,* April 5, 1912.

[118] See Wilson's criticism of the measures in *The State,* p. 489 (1895 edition), and especially in his letter to James Callaway, October 30, 1907, Baker Papers.

[119] I. H. Lionberger to W. W., October 16, 1911, Wilson Papers.

Richmond Times-Dispatch and later editor of the *Charlotte Daily Observer* led the attack upon Wilson's candidacy.[120]

The belief that Wilson had departed from the paths of "safe and sane" Democracy, that his views were socialistic and populistic, that he was a "quick-change artist" who had abandoned the convictions of a lifetime in order to obtain the support of the radicals, became especially prevalent in Virginia during the summer of 1911—so dangerously prevalent, in fact, that there was no longer any certainty that Wilson would receive the votes of his native state at the Baltimore convention. John Stewart Bryan, publisher of the *Richmond News-Leader,* voiced the opinion of conservative Virginia Democrats when he wrote that Wilson had "broken away after false gods" and that Wilson's approval of the initiative, referendum, and recall had created in the minds of his Virginia friends the belief that he was either vacillating in purpose or unsound in judgment. "He has said enough," Bryan asserted, "to make people in this part of the world feel that he is probably an unsafe man." [121] The leader of the conservative faction in the Virginia Democratic party, Senator Thomas S. Martin, campaigned against Virginia's endorsement of Wilson's candidacy on the ground, in part at least, that Wilson's advocacy of the western reforms had made him unfit as a presidential nominee.[122]

So alarming did the situation in Virginia become that Wilson attempted personally to intervene in his own behalf. In a letter to Dabney, which was subsequently published in the state press, Wilson sought to rationalize his position on the initiative, referendum, and recall with the conservative political beliefs of his "fellow Virginians." He declared that the reforms were simply effective means to an end, the restoration of popular control of the state governments. In states in which genuine representative government existed, "as I believe there is in Virginia and in the South in general," the measures were not needed. Wilson further significantly asserted that the innovations should under no circumstances be made national issues, that the states individually should be

---

[120] See, e. g., *New York Sun,* June 6, 1911; *Richmond Times-Dispatch,* May 3, September 16, 1911; *Florida Times-Union* of Jacksonville, September 15, 1911; *Birmingham Age-Herald,* March 17, 1912, quoting *Macon Telegraph; Houston Post,* January 28, 1911, April 5, 1912.

[121] J. S. Bryan to William G. Brown, December 29, 1911, William Garrot Brown Papers, Library of Duke University; hereinafter cited as Brown Papers.

[122] T. S. Martin to R. W. Perkins, March 19, 1912, original letter in the Albert Sidney Burleson Papers, Library of Congress; hereinafter cited as Burleson Papers.

the judges of their needs in the matter.[123] Of course "genuine representative government" did not then exist in Virginia, which was controlled
absolutely by the Martin machine, and Wilson knew that it did not
because he was in communication with the progressives in the state. At
any rate, it was his last word on the subject for a time; we can be sure
that he had had enough of initiative, referendum, and recall!

Wilson's advocacy of direct legislation evoked little criticism in the
North and the West, except among extremely hostile critics like the
New York Sun. It was his statement that a money trust existed and
was the most dangerous monopoly of all that alarmed conservative
Northern Democrats. No sooner had he made his Harrisburg address
than a chorus of conservative and moderately progressive northern
newspapers, the *New York Sun*, the *New York Times*, the *New York
World*, and the *Springfield Republican* among them, rushed to attack
his "radical" and "dangerous" financial views. The charges of "money
power," "Wall Street," and "money monopoly" were familiar enough,
to be sure, but had they not been made by Bryan and his agrarian
followers in the South and West? Was Wilson making a deliberate bid
for the support of these groups? [124] Was he "Bryanizing," the *New
York World* asked. "How like Mr. Bryan's language of sixteen years
ago!" it declared. Thus the *World* continued: "Gov. Wilson misrepresented the money situation. He has painted a vivid picture of misused
concentrated power not warranted by facts. Why has he done this?
Surely so able and intelligent a man would not presume to teach the
people on a subject of which he is ignorant. . . .

"Thinking men must deplore such unjustified statements on the part
of Gov. Wilson. . . . The responsibility of wise, honest guidance rests
upon gifted leaders like Gov. Wilson. The trend toward irrational leadership makes it imperative that he disdain the appeal to the unthinking
and prejudiced, and adhere rigidly to conscientious thought and truthful speech. . . .

"Does Gov. Wilson think that playing to the gallery will promote

---

[123] W. W. to R. H. Dabney, November 16, 1911, original in the Dabney Papers; published in the *Richmond Times-Dispatch*, December 18, 1911.

[124] *New York Times*, June 16, 1911. Interestingly enough, Wilson's attack upon the
"money trust" was immensely popular in the South, where it was regarded as the
recognition of a fact southern progressives had been proclaiming for a generation. See
the *Columbia State*, August 2, September 9, 1911; *Charleston News and Courier*,
September 25, 1911; *Spartanburg* (S. C.) *Herald*, quoted in *Nashville Tennessean and
American*, January 1, 1912.

his Presidential candidacy? Does he believe that the efforts to win Mr. Bryan's approval and to capture his following will increase his political strength? Is he Bryanizing himself? Is he preparing with his initiative, referendum and recall programme and his money-trust bugaboo to swallow Mr. Bryan's entire Confession of Faith?" [125]

Two months later Wilson again incurred the criticism of the conservative eastern press by denouncing the Aldrich plan for a centralized banking system. "I am afraid that any measure of that character bearing Mr. Aldrich's name," he told a reporter, "must have been drawn in the offices of the few men who, through the present system of concentrated capital, control the banking and industrial activities of the country." [126] Yet, almost in the same breath, he admitted that he was completely ignorant of the details of the Aldrich proposals! "It is disappointing, it is discouraging," lamented the *New York Times* on September 1, 1911, "to get from him so trivial and so shallow an opinion upon a great question, or to get any opinion at all so long as he confesses his lack of qualifying preparation to express an opinion worth giving."

The truth was that Wilson had broached the most explosive question of the day. The old fear of 1896, of free silver and cheap money, still plagued the minds of conservative Democrats who believed that their party had been once before wrecked by the same issue. William Garrot Brown, editorial writer for *Harper's Weekly,* voiced the apprehension conservatives felt when he wrote to the Assistant Secretary of the Treasury, "I think a little thought will convince you and Senator Aldrich that Wilson could help or harm your movement more than any other Democrat. He has the ear of the Democrats most likely to make trouble." [127] Brown was so deeply disturbed that he "risked a snubbing" by appealing to Wilson for a soberer consideration of the money question. He wrote:

"I fear I cannot make clear to you how much concern I really feel about the relation of this question to your leadership. I give you my word that from the very start of your political career I have been troubled with precisely this anxiety, and I believe I now speak for thousands of sincere men to whom your rise and your party renascence has seemed to offer their first chance in many years—their first opportunity to take the aggressive for their political faith and ideals. In Cleve-

[125] July 31, 1911.

[126] Quoted in H. B. Needham, "Woodrow Wilson's Views," *Outlook,* xcviii (August 26, 1911), 946.

[127] W. G. Brown to A. Piatt Andrew, November 2, 1911, Brown Papers.

land's day our hopes were wrecked by the free silver blunder, and we feel that the party's greatest weakness and danger is still its proneness to go wrong on questions of finance. There is not a democrat in Congress of *proved* competence to deal with such questions, and the country is full of men ready to appeal to ignorance, to class and section, when such questions come up. . . .

"It is my deliberate judgment that you can at this moment do more in this matter for sound ideas and wise action than any other American —more than Taft or any other Republican. . . . You are in a position to keep your party from going wrong—or to set it wrong hopelessly, irretrievably. As a leader of the Democratic Progressives, you can speak for caution and fairness. . . . But I urge it rather as a duty. . . . It is your *courage,* Governor, that has made you really our leader." [128]

These warnings from the nation's leading newspapers and his friends caused Wilson to abandon, at least for a time, the one really penetrating and significant attack upon the system of privilege and monopoly he had made. Was it fear that he would lose the confidence of "men of his class," as Brown had so subtly suggested, that caused Wilson to shift entirely away from the money question? He admitted that he was sorry he had attacked the Aldrich plan. He wanted to begin by saying that he knew perfectly well that he went off half cocked about the Aldrich matter, Wilson wrote to Brown. He so thoroughly distrusted Aldrich that it was incredible to Wilson that anything bearing Aldrich's signature could be other than a scheme to put the country more completely "in the hands from whose domination we are trying to escape." The demands of public life, Wilson further explained, had prevented him from studying the banking proposals as he should have studied them.[129]

Wilson's confession of his ignorance of the money and banking question, his promise to give the matter "sincere study," and his avowal that the question "must be approached with caution and fairness and receive dispassionate and open minded treatment" quieted the fears of most of his conservative supporters.[130] Colonel House, it is interesting to note, industriously circulated a copy of the letter among financial and business circles.[131]

[128] W. G. Brown to W. W., October 30, 1911, *ibid*.

[129] W. W. to W. G. Brown, November 7, 1911, *ibid*.

[130] See W. G. Brown to A. P. Andrew, November 10, 1911; W. G. Brown to E. S. Martin, November 10, 1911, both in *ibid*.

[131] The author found a well-used copy of the letter in the House Papers.

It was such shilly-shallying on Wilson's part that most disturbed McCombs and House, who believed that Wilson needed to become wholeheartedly identified with at least one reform cause that was safe. House was insistent that he should emphasize the question of tariff reform, for here was sure Democratic ground. "I want the people," House wrote in November, "to forget the initiative, referendum, recall, the short ballot and some other things that they have connected him with." [132] There was no doubt, as House pointed out, that Clark and Underwood were reaping the benefits of the tariff agitation almost exclusively because Wilson had refused to make an important straightforward declaration on the subject.

Wilson's managers finally acted to identify him with the tariff reform movement by obtaining for him an interview in the *New York World,* which was certain to be read by most Democratic editors. Much to the delight of the old-line Democrats who were supporting him, Wilson announced that the tariff was to be the "greatest" issue of the presidential campaign of 1912. "It must be so by its very nature," he added. "No frank mind can doubt that the great systems of special privileges and monopolistic advantage that have been built up have been built up upon the foundation of the tariff. The tariff question is at the heart of every other economic question we have to deal with, and until we have dealt with that properly we can deal with nothing in a way that will be satisfactory and lasting." [133] A short time later Wilson told a group of Democratic politicians in New York that the chief problem confronting their party was the divorcing of big business from the government in the matter of tariff legislation. It was a hard-hitting address, his best tariff speech in the entire pre-convention campaign, and at times he revealed a deep sense of moral indignation at Republican collusion with businessmen in writing tariff schedules.[134]

Historians generally agree that the Jackson Day Dinner in Washington on January 8, 1912, marked the real beginning of the intensive scramble for delegates to the national convention. By the same token, it also marked the conclusion of the first phase of Wilson's national campaign, the formative, provisional phase, to get his message of progressive reform across to the people.

For a person who declared that he did not intend to seek the Dem-

[132] E. M. House to T. W. Gregory, November 19, 1911, House Papers.
[133] *New York World,* December 24, 1911.
[134] *New York Times,* January 4, 1912.

ocratic presidential nomination,[135] Wilson was taking extraordinary measures to get his appeal before the American public. Within the space of eight months he had made a spectacular 9,000-mile transcontinental tour and had campaigned besides in Georgia, South Carolina, North Carolina, Virginia, Pennsylvania, Wisconsin, Texas, and New York. There was no orderly scheme of development in his addresses during this period. He had espoused almost every idea that progressives were then advocating and it seemed for a while, at least, that he had succeeded in placing himself at the head of the Democratic progressive movement. He had struck out boldly in support of several reforms and shortly afterward hedged on his position when he discovered the strong current of opposition to them. He had with great gusto endorsed popular government, but these were meaningless words. He had espoused the cause of direct legislation, and then attempted to sidetrack the question by declaring that it was not a national issue. He had attacked the money trust, and then admitted that he knew nothing about the subject. He had denounced monopolistic practices of great corporations, but he never defined the practices that should be suppressed. Finally, he had endeavored to seize the leadership of the tariff reform movement, but Underwood and Clark were firmly entrenched in their positions as the official Democratic tariff reformers. In short, Wilson's appeal had been moralistic and idealistically earnest, but it rarely touched upon the fundamental economic problems then demanding solution—an effective means for federal control of combinations in industry and finance, the income tax, the question of collective bargaining and strikes and lockouts, the problem of agricultural credit, the exhaustion of the land, or the ominous increase in the tenancy rate.

Wherein, then, lay Wilson's strength as a campaigner for liberalism? Simply in the fact that he, more than any other Democrat, personified and epitomized the things for which progressives had been fighting for over a generation. He did not attack property rights; but neither did the progressives. He came forward with an appeal calculated to end the warfare between the middle and the upper classes, to reconcile the interests of big business with the small producer, to pacify the workers by ameliorative legislation. It was often a vague, idealistic, and meaningless appeal that he made; yet by his facile eloquence and forthright honesty and integrity he had by the end of 1911 convinced a good portion of the voters that he was the leader of progressive Democracy.

[135] W. W. to J. M. Gordon, September 20, 1911, Wilson-Gordon Correspondence, Library of Princeton University.

CHAPTER XI

The Campaign Against Wilson

THE rumblings of conservative protest that greeted Wilson's new progressivism in the summer and fall of 1911 were ominous enough, but they were mere spluttering criticisms, scarcely audible, when compared to the aggregation of whispering campaigns, organized misrepresentations, and outright conspiracies to defeat Wilson's nomination for president that were set on foot during the period from December 1911, through May 1912. It was a vast network of schemes, intrigues, and propaganda attacks. Its axis was in New York and Washington; its leaders included a curious mixture of editors, reactionary politicians and Wall Street financiers, demagogues and former Populists, and self-styled radicals.

Curious conglomeration though it was, the anti-Wilson coalition waged a campaign so deadly that the Wilson movement was almost wrecked. Few candidates for the presidential nomination have been the object of an attack so overwhelming, so well-concerted, so effective. The campaign against Wilson was essentially three-cornered; it consisted of a series of exposures published by the *New York Sun* and designed to discredit Wilson before the progressives; the Harvey affair, engineered by George Harvey, Henry Watterson, and James C. Hemphill, calculated to ruin Wilson's candidacy by convicting Wilson of "ingratitude"; and the campaign of abuse and vilification carried on by William R. Hearst, Tom Watson, and other Clark and Underwood publicists.

There was something so secret and malign about the attacks upon Wilson that his managers and editorial spokesmen often charged that some Wall Street master-mind, undoubtedly Thomas F. Ryan, was directing the activities of the anti-Wilson movement.[1] Arthur Krock, on the other hand, declared that Senator Clarence W. Watson of West Virginia was the leader of the attack and that Senator Thomas S. Martin of Virginia was his chief lieutenant.[2] The truth is that there was no central direction; the diversity of the persons involved and the different directions of their assault testify to this.

[1] See, e.g., *Arkansas Democrat* of Little Rock, February 8, 1912.
[2] *Louisville Courier-Journal*, January 1, 1912.

Edward P. Mitchell, petulant editor of the *New York Sun,* had been the chief antagonist of Wilson's new progressive course since the spring of 1911. He was, after all, the spokesman par excellence of the Wall Street, big business, Old Guard Republican line, and that was reason enough for his opposition to the candidate he had once ardently supported.[3] The first of the anti-Wilson incidents was the disclosure by the *Sun,* in a front-page story on December 5, 1911, that Wilson, soon after his resignation from Princeton in October 1910, had applied for an annuity retirement grant from the Carnegie Foundation for the Advancement of Teaching.[4] Ellen Wilson, in a letter to Richard H. Dabney, told the story of Wilson's application:

". . . before the recent change of rule [by the trustees of the Foundation] there were in effect *two* sorts of Carnegie pensions,—one an *old age* pension given to all who were sixty-five years old and otherwise eligible,—and the other a *distinguished service* pension, given after twenty-five years of teaching in specially selected cases.

"At first the 25 year pension was given very freely by the board, but when the number of colleges under the foundation was so greatly increased, it became clear that the money would not suffice to make that so general a rule. Then it was decided (Woodrow being on the committee and largely instrumental in . . . reaching the decision,) to make the 25 year pension *exclusively* and *conspicuously* a question of distinguished service, and in *no* sense one of superannuation. It was thought that to have such pensioners on the list would not only benefit scholarship in America but give to the 'Foundation' a dignity and prestige which it has not secured so far. . . .

"That it should be considered disgraceful or humiliating to receive it is a monstrous perversion of the idea. Woodrow himself being not only on the board but on the [pension] *committee* from the first can speak with authority of all this. There would have been no question of concealing the matter if he had received it, and indeed he made no secret of his application. His friends here were merely amazed and indignant that there should have been any question about granting it. . . .

"Of course, though honorable to receive it, it is more or less humili-

---

[3] Perhaps there were other, even personal, reasons for Mitchell's opposition. The answer is not to be found either in Mitchell's *Memoirs of An Editor* or Frank M. O'Brien's *The Story of the Sun.* When one considers the *Sun's* general editorial policy at the time, however, it is difficult to imagine Mitchell in any other role than that of a chief anti-Wilson editor.

[4] The Foundation was chartered by an act of Congress on March 10, 1906, and was subsequently endowed by Andrew Carnegie with $15,000,000.

ating to anyone to be refused, and hence it was regarded as a point of honour (or rather of *decency!*) to keep all applications secret,—a rule invariably observed except in Woodrow's case. . . .

"Such as I have described them were the rules when Woodrow resigned from Princeton and from the Carnegie Board. But when he sent in his application to the committee he was told that they had just come to the conclusion that no more 25 year pensions should be granted for any cause,—that they should in the future be exclusively old age pensions; and that such a change of rule was to be proposed at the next meeting of the Board." [5]

How the *Sun's* reporters got wind of Wilson's application is still a mystery. Mrs. Wilson was convinced that a certain trustee of the Foundation had given the story to the *Sun* and even suggested that Dabney should let his name leak out in this connection. There was, however, apparently no evidence to substantiate this accusation. [6] As Wilson made no secret of his application, it is more probable that the fact became known by his own admission.

Wilson was in Baltimore on December 5, the day the *Sun* published the pension story, and immediately issued a public statement admitting that he had applied for a "retiring allowance" the year before. "I have no private means to depend on," he explained. "A man who goes into politics bound by the principles of honor puts his family and all who may be dependent upon him for support at the mercy of any incalculable turn of the wheel of fortune, and I feel entirely justified in seeking to provide against such risks, particularly when I was applying for what I supposed myself to be entitled to by right of long service as a teacher." Then, with a typically Wilsonian phrase—"I have not renewed the application"—he dismissed the matter. [7]

The Carnegie pension affair, however, was an unfortunate reality that could not be dismissed so blandly. Here was the first real "break" Wilson had made and the anti-Wilson editors hastened to make political capital of it. With undisguised delight they pointed out that Wilson was fifty-three at the time he had made his application; that, as Hemphill observed, "The Carnegie Foundation was created for indigent teachers

---

[5] E. A. W. to R. H. Dabney, February 9, 1912, Dabney Papers. The remainder of the letter, describing Wilson's financial straits, is published in R. S. Baker, *Woodrow Wilson*, III, 244-245.

[6] See Alec C. Humphreys (secretary of the Carnegie Foundation) to W. W., June 27, 1912, Wilson Papers.

[7] *Baltimore Sun*, December 6, 1911.

and not for indigent politicians." [8] "Woody Wilson," declared the *Washington Post*, "finds that the Carnegie pension fund is no campaign bar'l." [9] A pension application, another editor jibed, presupposed past work and present need. "What are Prof. Wilson's reasons for claiming a Carnegie pension? What want-wolf howls at his door? What work has he done?" [10]

"I cannot understand how a real Democrat could touch such money," declared an ex-Populist leader from Massachusetts. "It is steeped in the human blood of Carnegie's workers, shot down by his hired Pinkertons, while struggling for a decent wage out of the hundreds of millions which their labor was rolling into the Carnegie coffers." [11] This was the line of attack that the Hearst newspapers and magazines emphasized most repeatedly. [12] Several comparatively sane Democratic journals thought that Wilson's application had ruined any hopes he might have had for the Democratic presidential nomination. A man who applied for a pension from the Carnegie fortune would never be accepted as a leader by the Democratic party, one editor thought, for Carnegie was "a Trust man from beginning to end, and the author of the Homestead trouble, which forever bars him and his pensioners from the public crib." [13]

It was a difficult task indeed that the Wilson spokesmen undertook in attempting to counteract the unfavorable impression Wilson's Carnegie application had made. Most of them let the incident pass without comment, but several loyal Wilson editors declared that since Wilson was

[8] *Charlotte Daily Observer*, December 7, 1911.

[9] Quoted in *Wilmington* (N. C.) *Morning Star*, December 8, 1911.

[10] *Pensacola Evening News*, January 16, 1912.

[11] George Fred Williams, in the *New York American*, February 3, 1912.

[12] Alfred H. Lewis, Hearst's ace writer, best expressed the Hearst point of view in "The Real Woodrow Wilson," *Hearst's Magazine*, xxi (May 1912), 2269-2271. "Mr. Andrew Carnegie was worth $500,000,000," Lewis wrote. ". . . They were gathered in the blood and tears of such upheavals as the Homestead strike, when children starved, women wept, and workmen were shot to death on their own poor doorsteps. . . . For myself, I do not question the purity of Mr. Wilson's motives, as he stretched out an eager hand for that Carnegie pension. And yet, remembering his White House aspirations, I confess that I cannot see how he brought himself to do it. Mr. Carnegie's gold had come to him through that system of protection that Mr. Wilson condemned as a crime against the people. . . .

"And there occurs a further thought. Gratitude is among the most graceful of emotions. . . . Could Mr. Wilson, without feeling grateful, become Mr. Carnegie's pensioner? . . . It is evident that Mr. Wilson believed he could take a pension from an arch-protectionist, a pension whereof every dollar bore the unclean mark of the beast, and still do his most and best to destroy protection."

[13] *Natchez Daily Democrat*, December 7, 1911.

entitled to a Carnegie pension, there was no reason why he should not have applied for it.[14] They pointed to the fact that the disclosure had come from the *New York Sun,* a reactionary journal, and that the pretended indignation at Wilson's action had come from his conservative enemies, not his progressive friends.[15] For his part, Wilson did not re-

"What Jefferson Would Do."—*Gov. Wilson*
An anti-Wilson cartoon from the *New York Sun*

gard the matter so lightly. The publicity given to the affair by his enemies had convinced him that it was much more dangerous than he had thought. Five days after he had made his curt public statement in Baltimore, he wrote: "Everywhere it is beginning to be perceived that the

[14] The *New York World,* which was not particularly supporting Wilson's candidacy at the time, declared that "if one use of the Carnegie Foundation is to bar retired educators from public life, it needs reform." *New York World,* December 7, 1911.

[15] See, e.g., *Collier's Weekly,* XLVIII (December 30, 1911), 8; *Columbia* (S. C.) *State,* December 8, 1911; *Nashville Tennessean and American,* December 11, 1911.

likelihood of my being nominated is very great and must be taken seriously,—and it *is* beginning to be taken very seriously, by certain big business interests in N. Y., who know that I could not be managed to their mind, and by everybody who, like Hearst, for personal reasons, wants to see me beaten. They are looking high and low for some means by which to discredit me personally if not politically. Just at this moment (in spite of a perfectly frank statement by me of all the facts) they are trying to make me seem ridiculous and discredited because I applied to the Carnegie Foundation for a retiring allowance,—and may, by lying misrepresentations, partially succeed—with the people who always want an honourable man brought down to their level." [16]

The second anti-Wilson exposure emanating from the *New York Sun* threatened to have far worse consequences than the first. At the very time when Wilson's managers believed they were bringing Bryan and Wilson together politically, Mitchell published a letter Wilson had written to Adrian H. Joline in 1907 expressing a highly uncomplimentary opinion of the Nebraskan. The move was well-timed, for the letter was published in part the day before and in full the day of the Jackson Day Dinner in Washington, when both Bryan and Wilson were to speak before the leaders of the Democratic party.

Adrian F. Joline, president of the Missouri, Kansas, & Texas Railroad and a trustee of Princeton University, spoke before the directors of his railroad at Parsons, Kansas, on April 4, 1907, and attacked Bryan's proposal for government ownership of the railroads. "You and I know who are responsible for this socialistic, populistic, anti-property crusade," he asserted. "It is the cry of the envious against the well-to-do—the old story." [17] Joline and Wilson at the time were on friendly terms,[18] and when Joline sent Wilson a copy of the address, the Princeton president replied enthusiastically, on April 29:

[16] W. W. to M. A. Hulbert, December 10, 1911, published in R. S. Baker, *Woodrow Wilson*, III, 243-244.

[17] Joline further defended overcapitalization on the ground of *caveat emptor* and declared that it would be the policy of his railroad to resist by all legitimate means the enactment of laws inimical to the railroad's interest. If the laws were enacted, he promised to carry the fight to the courts. He would, however, "obey them honestly and faithfully, if they are ultimately declared to be valid, even if it leads to insolvency and a receiver." The address is given in full in John F. Joline, Jr., "A Footnote to the Campaign of 1912, The Joline Letter," unpublished MS in the Library of Princeton University.

[18] They soon parted company, however. Joline was a supporter of Dean West in the Graduate School controversy and Wilson succeeded in defeating him for reelection to the Board of Trustees in 1910.

"Thank you very much for sending me your address at Parsons, Kan., before the board of directors of the Missouri, Kansas and Texas Railway. I have read it with relish and entire agreement. Would that we could do something at once dignified and effective to knock Mr. Bryan once for all into a cocked hat!" [19]

By a very devious route the letter found its way into the hands of the editor of the *New York Sun*,[20] who published a garbled copy in the *Sun* on January 7, 1912; on the following day, with Joline's permission,[21] he printed the accurate copy. Here indeed was an amazing spectacle—one of the bitterest anti-Bryan and anti-Wilson newspapers in the country endeavoring to drive a wedge between the Nebraskan and the New Jersey governor! Mitchell's object was immediately apparent to most observers. He "had two designs, both sinister," commented Senator Gore. "First—to put Wilson and Bryan asunder, to divide progressive Democrats and conquer them. Second—to inflame the animosity and resentment of Mr. Bryan's faithful friends and followers and cause them to desert Wilson." [22]

The anti-Wilson editors were in high glee over the incident and gloated over Wilson's embarrassment; many of them rushed to their dictionaries to find the meaning of "cocked hat." Letter-writing was a dangerous pastime for a candidate, they declared, and reminded Wilson of Henry Clay's unhappy experience in 1844. "The sentiment expressed in . . . WILSON's private letter to . . . JOLINE, which has now been made public, will strike a responsive chord in the hearts of all sound-minded, clear-sighted members of the Democratic Party," chuckled the editor of the *New York Times*. "That BRYAN and Bryanism should be 'knocked into a cocked hat,' . . . is the earnest desire of every voter who upholds the principles of true Democracy." [23] "We should say," Hemphill added, "that in this case, the Schoolteacher was

---

[19] As published in the *New York Sun*, January 8, 1912.

[20] Joline afterward declared that in the spring of 1911 he had given a copy of the letter to Otto T. Bannard, Representative Martin Littleton, and another prominent reactionary, "on their solemn promise not to let it get into the newspapers." One of these men gave a copy to Edward P. Mitchell of the *Sun*. See J. F. Joline, Jr., "A Footnote to the Campaign of 1912."

[21] "It must not be inferred from this, or from my giving out this letter," Joline declared, "that I have any ill-feeling toward Dr. Wilson. . . . I am giving you the original to copy, because from two sources I learn that Dr. Wilson would like to have its full text published, to avoid misquotation or garbling." A. F. Joline to E. P. Mitchell, January —, 1912, published in *St. Louis Republic*, January 8, 1912.

[22] T. P. Gore in *Daily Oklahoman* of Oklahoma City, January 16, 1912.

[23] *New York Times*, January 8, 1912.

not guilty . . . of anything more criminal than 'animated moderation.' " [24]

The publication of the letter broke like a bombshell in the Wilson camp. McCombs was frantic and charged, "The attacks on Gov. Wilson and the furnishing of letters emanate from Wall Street. Mr. Joline has been employed as attorney by Thomas F. Ryan, and we are willing to let that fact stand for itself." [25] "Wall Street" was to become McCombs's stock-in-trade answer to any charge against his candidate! Wilson was in Washington, preparing for the Jackson Day Dinner, when the letter was published. [26] He was embarrassed and at a loss to know what to do. "Even if a man has written letters it ought not to embarrass him if they are published," he told the members of the National Press Club on the afternoon of January 8. "Even if a man changes his mind it ought not to embarrass him." [27] It was as if Wilson were whistling in the graveyard. He sent a telegram to his secretary, Joseph P. Tumulty, urging him to come at once to Washington. When Tumulty reached the capital he found Wilson, McCombs, Thomas J. Pence, Senator James A. O'Gorman, and Dudley Field Malone [28] in Wilson's room at the new Willard, trying to think of some way to counteract the effects of the publication of the Joline letter. [29] The Governor's advisers urged him to publish a statement, and he wrote out a hastily written, clumsily worded justification of his "cocked hat" sentiments. [30]

It was fortunate for Wilson that Bryan was in Raleigh, visiting at the home of Josephus Daniels, when the Joline letter appeared in the news-

---

[24] *Charlotte Daily Observer,* January 10, 1912.

[25] *Louisville Courier-Journal,* January 8, 1912.

[26] "I am on my way down to Washington," he wrote on January 7, "where I am to speak to-morrow evening. The Democratic National Committee is to meet there to-morrow (which is Jackson's birthday) [Jackson's birthday was March 15; January 8 was the anniversary of Jackson's victory over the British at New Orleans.] and the banquet in the evening is to be a grand dress parade of candidates for the presidential nomination on the Democratic ticket. I hate the whole thing, but it is something 'expected' of me by my friends and backers, and, after all, an honest and sincere man need not be embarrassed by being put on exhibition." W. W. to M. A. Hulbert, January 7, 1912, published in R. S. Baker, *Woodrow Wilson,* III, 257.

[27] *New York World,* January 9, 1912.

[28] O'Gorman and his son-in-law, Malone, were both progressive Democrats from New York who had, by January, already joined the ranks of the Wilson organization.

[29] J. P. Tumulty, *Woodrow Wilson As I Know Him,* p. 96.

[30] The statement was never published; Wilson decided instead to deliver a tribute to Bryan at the Jackson Day Dinner. The original draft of the statement, in the possession of Dudley Field Malone, is published in part in R. S. Baker, *Woodrow Wilson,* III, 260-261.

papers. Daniels, a loyal friend of Bryan and Wilson, tried desperately to soften the impact of the blow. Bryan, however, was visibly irritated by Wilson's indiscretion. ". . . you may just say that if Mr. Wilson wanted to knock me into a cocked hat," he told a reporter for the *New York Sun,* "he and the *Sun* are on the same platform. That's what the *Sun* has been trying to do to me since 1896." [31] By the time he and Daniels reached Washington, however, the Nebraskan's anger had disappeared entirely. When reporters asked him to comment on the Joline letter, he shrewdly refused to commit himself;[32] and when O'Gorman and Malone went to Bryan's room to sound him out on the Joline letter, they found him altogether generous about the affair. Bryan was a man who bore few grudges, and, after all, too good a politician not to perceive the obvious purpose of the *Sun's* editor in publishing the letter. "I believe that when Mr. Wilson wrote that letter to Joline, he believed it," Bryan told O'Gorman and Malone. It did not, however, follow that Wilson held the same convictions in 1912. "If the big financial interests think that they are going to make a rift in the Progressive ranks of the Democratic party by such tactics," he added curtly, "they are mistaken." [33]

During the evening of January 8 the Democratic leaders gathered in the ballroom of the Raleigh Hotel for the festive Jackson Day Dinner; it was the quadrennial party reunion and the presidential hopefuls and their supporters, members of the national committee, and local Democratic worthies from every state in the Union gathered to see the parade of presidential candidates and to witness the formal inauguration of the pre-convention campaign.[34] Senator O'Gorman was toastmaster; Bryan, wreathed in smiles, was at the speaker's table, along with at least five candidates for the Democratic nomination and the entire Democratic national committee. Wilson sat between Senator Francis G. Newlands of Nevada and former Governor Joseph W. Folk of Missouri.[35]

[31] Josephus Daniels, *The Wilson Era, Years of Peace, 1910-1917,* p. 32.

[32] *Louisville Courier-Journal,* January 8, 1912.

[33] R. S. Baker, "Memorandum of an interview with Dudley Field Malone, November 1, 1927," MS in Baker Papers.

[34] One hundred ardent Wilson men had come from New Jersey to boost their governor's candidacy, but they could not find tickets to the dinner. Jim Nugent, by hook or crook, had bought all of the dinner tickets assigned to New Jersey and he and his Newark followers did their best to discredit Wilson before the Democratic organization politicians. State Chairman Edward E. Grosscup and his band of Wilson Jerseymen, however, did effective work for Wilson. See the *Trenton Evening Times,* January 8-9, 1912.

[35] *New York Herald,* January 9, 1912.

Even the anti-Wilson newspapers admitted that the Jackson Day Dinner was virtually a complete triumph for Wilson. There were numerous other speakers—Bryan, Champ Clark, Newlands, Folk, Hearst, and Senator John W. Kern of Indiana among them—but none received the tumultuous reception that was given Wilson. The affair was a Wilson victory, moreover, because Bryan took careful pains to demonstrate his unstinting approval of the author of the "cocked hat" letter.

Shortly before midnight Wilson spoke briefly in reply to a toast. After a cursory discussion of the Democratic progressive program he turned dramatically to Bryan and said: "We have differed as to measures; it has taken us sixteen years and more to come to any comprehension of our community of thought in regard to what we ought to do. What I want to say is that one of the most striking things in recent years is that with all the rise and fall of particular ideas, with all the ebb and flow of particular proposals, there has been one interesting fixed point in the history of the Democratic party, and that fixed point has been the character and the devotion and the preachings of William Jennings Bryan.

"I, for my part, never want to forget this: That while we have differed with Mr. Bryan upon this occasion and upon that in regard to the specific things to be done, he has gone serenely on pointing out to a more and more convinced people what it was that was the matter. He has had the steadfast vision all along of what it was that was the matter and he has, not any more than Andrew Jackson did, not based his career upon calculation, but has based it upon principle."

The finishing touch was one of Wilson's triumphs of eloquence: "Let us apologize to each other that we ever suspected or antagonized one another; let us join hands once more all around the great circle of community of counsel and of interest which will show us at last to have been indeed the friends of our country and the friends of mankind." [36]

The speech was spectacular, the applause tremendous! Bryan rose from his seat, put his hand affectionately on Wilson's shoulder, and murmured, "That was splendid, splendid." "I am indeed fortunate that you think it so," Wilson replied.[37] Some of Wilson's friends thought that the affair was the turning point in the Wilson presidential movement, so excited were they by the events of the evening. Bryan's address, which followed Wilson's, was regarded by some optimistic Wilson and Clark men as the Nebraskan's abdication of party leadership. "No

[36] *Washington Post,* January 9, 1912.
[37] *New York World,* January 10, 1912.

friend of mine," Bryan declared, "need be told that I am so much more interested in the things for which we are struggling than I am in office, that I shall give more valiant service to he who bears the standard of our party than I could ever render to myself." [38]

Most observers agreed that Mitchell had failed completely in his object in publishing the Joline letter. Indeed, the affair actually ended by strengthening the friendly relations between Bryan and Wilson. A correspondent for the *Sun* admitted as much, but declared none the less that Bryan would oppose Wilson's nomination because he had applied for a Carnegie pension! [39] Joline's final word on the matter provides an appropriate epitaph for the affair: "This little tempest in a very small teapot should teach an old man like me to keep his mouth shut about practically everything." [40]

In spite of the failure of this most serious effort to divide Bryan and Wilson, the Bryan issue was raised frequently during the early months of 1912 by Wilson's enemies. The charge most often made was that the governor was a party bolter, that he had never voted for Bryan and had even voted against Parker in 1904. Of course it was true that Wilson had voted the "Gold" Democratic ticket in 1896, and he frankly admitted it;[41] but he was forced to declare time and again that he had voted for Bryan in 1900 and 1908, and for Parker in 1904. The charges of party irregularity, however, were not made by Wilson's opponents with the object of dividing Wilson and Bryan, but for the purpose of drawing away from Wilson's candidacy the support of the Bryan progressives and the old-line Democrats who treasured party regularity above all things political. In the South, especially, the Bryan issue was frequently invoked to discredit Wilson by the very editors who hated Bryan most intensely. The *Pensacola Evening News,* for example, obtained a letter from Charles H. Gallagher of Trenton, allegedly proving that Wilson did not vote at all in 1908,[42] and Wilson's written denials of the accusation were completely ignored by the editor of this, the most violent anti-Wilson newspaper in the South.[43] The case in point was not an iso-

---

[38] Bryan's speech is printed in *The Commoner,* January 12, 1912.

[39] *New York Sun,* January 9, 1912.

[40] *St. Louis Republic,* January 8, 1912.

[41] W. W. to W. J. Bryan, April 3, 1912, Wilson Papers.

[42] *Pensacola Evening News,* March 18, 1912.

[43] "It is extraordinary how persistent long lived lies are," Wilson wrote to Frank L. Mayes, editor of the *Pensacola Journal.* "I did, of course, vote the Democratic ticket in 1908. There has been so much question of the matter that I have had the records looked up and one of our local papers will presently publish the whole thing, though I must

lated incident; it was typical of the general anti-Wilson attack in several states.[44]

With the failure of the Joline affair, Mitchell left the ranks of the active anti-Wilson conspirators and was content to carry on a desultory editorial campaign against Wilson. There had been rumors, however, even before the publication of the Joline letter, that the *New York Sun* was about to publish a letter written by Grover Cleveland to Henry van Dyke severely castigating Wilson.[45] Perhaps the boomerang effect of the Joline incident was the chief reason Mitchell did not again indulge in the sport of publishing personal letters; a more probable reason, as David Lawrence suggests, was Van Dyke's absolute refusal to give a copy of the Cleveland letter to the New York editor.[46] The existence of the letter is still something of a mystery, although the evidence indicates very strongly that it did exist and that Cleveland had characterized the former Princeton president in unpleasant terms—as a man of "an ungovernable temper," who lacked "intellectual integrity." [47]

Wilson and his wife were considerably alarmed by this threatened attack. "I would much prefer to have the letter printed rather than hinted at in this nasty way," Mrs. Wilson wrote in the fall of 1912. "I think it does exist & that they meant to print it but were frightened off by Joline's experience." [48] Wilson was so worried by the threatened publication of the letter that in December he wrote to Thomas D. Jones, suggesting that Jones and the other Wilson supporters on the Princeton Board of Trustees "might be ready in a joint statement which would effectively meet all the counts of the indictment they evidently intend to bring against me." [49] Jones's reply was completely reassuring. "You can, of course, safely count upon your old friends on the Board," he wrote, "to do anything which may be found to be possible to contradict

admit that it is a little mortifying to me to have my word backed up by legal proof." Published in *Pensacola Journal,* March 26, 1912.

[44] See, e.g., *Houston Post,* February 4, 1912; *Atlanta Constitution,* April 12, 1912; *Florida Times-Union* of Jacksonville, March 15, 1912.

[45] *Baltimore Sun,* January 5, 1912.

[46] David Lawrence, *The True Story of Woodrow Wilson,* p. 27.

[47] As quoted in *ibid.*

[48] E. A. W. to Mrs. Crawford H. Toy, September 23, 1912, copy in Baker Papers. Mrs. Wilson thought that the fine Italian hand of Dean West was at the bottom of the Cleveland letter affair. West, she declared, had Cleveland, who had failed miserably toward the end, mentally as well as physically, completely in his power.

[49] W. W. to T. D. Jones, December 15, 1911, copy in *ibid.* Wilson was also afraid that the Graduate School controversy would be dragged into the political arena by his enemies and this seemed to worry him about as much as the threatened publication of the Cleveland letter.

any false statements that may be made with regard to your conduct as president of the University." [50] He refused, however, to take the matter seriously and advised Wilson to wait until the attacks were made in the open before he endeavored to answer them.

One week after the publication of the Joline letter, Wilson's candidacy was given a jolt that for a time threatened to wreck it altogether. It was the revelation of Wilson's break with George Harvey. The affair, which has become something of a *cause célèbre* in American history, eventually involved Wilson, Harvey, Watterson, McCombs, Ryan, Hemphill, Tillman, and a host of other participants. It has perplexed many historians and biographers. Judged apart from the setting of the general anti-Wilson campaign, it is an incongruous mystery; placed in its context of the anti-Wilson movement, it fits into the picture like the largest and most important piece in a difficult jig-saw puzzle. It marked the culmination of the Wall Street, reactionary phase of the attack upon Wilson.

Colonel George Harvey, editor of *Harper's Weekly* and the *North American Review,* occupied an anomalous position in the Wilson movement. He had been perhaps the "original" Wilson man; he had been at least indirectly responsible for Wilson's nomination as governor of New Jersey in 1910. More than any other single individual, he was responsible for Wilson's political career. Through the medium of his two journals, Harvey poured forth a barrage of Wilson propaganda during 1910 and 1911. On November 11, 1911, he flung forth the Wilson banner in *Harper's Weekly* and printed at the masthead of the editorial page: "For President: Woodrow Wilson."

On the other hand, Harvey's position in the Wilson presidential campaign was exceedingly awkward. He saw the presidential organization he had painstakingly built collapse following Wilson's break with the New Jersey machine. Although he was one of the original Wilson supporters, he never became associated in any way with the New York organization. On the contrary, he saw a group of young, inexperienced, would-be politicians seize control of the Wilson movement and displace him as the "president-maker." Even more important, he saw his conservative candidate become a leader of the progressive Democrats, a new Bryan, as it were. Like many other conservatives, Harvey was alarmed by Wilson's attack upon the "Money Trust" and remonstrated against

---

[50] T. D. Jones to W. W., December 19, 1911, published in full in James Kerney, *The Political Education of Woodrow Wilson*, pp. 181-182.

it.[51] Harvey and the interests he represented were unalterably opposed to anything that smacked of Bryanism, and it was one of Harvey's proudest boasts that he had never voted for Bryan![52] Harvey's support, on the other hand, naturally laid Wilson open to suspicion among the Bryan Democrats. "The best thing that could happen to Mr. Wilson at this time," Bryan's organ declared on one occasion, "would be his open repudiation by these publications [like *Harper's Weekly*] that are now speaking kindly of him, but whose masters mean no good to the Democratic party and no service to the American people." [53]

By December 1911, Harvey was wavering in his support of Wilson. On December 5 he told Colonel House that "everybody south of Canal Street was in a frenzy against Wilson," and that they were bringing pressure to bear upon him to oppose the governor. Harvey declared that he had an open mind and that if his friends convinced him that Wilson was a "dangerous man," he would come out in opposition to his candidacy.[54]

From among all the "original" Wilson men Harvey had recruited in 1910, "Marse Henry" Watterson, petulant editor of the *Louisville Courier-Journal,* alone had remained loyal to the Wilson cause. He was an old man, in the early stages of senility, and his increasing years had in no wise abated his violent temper, his exaggerated notion of the obligations of friendship, and his complete inability to view a public question impartially. Yet Wilson's relations with Watterson had been extremely cordial during 1911[55] and the old Kentuckian had bestowed gracious praise upon the governor in his editorial columns. On one occasion he declared that Wilson was "the intellectual and moral light of the Democratic situation";[56] again, he asserted that Wilson stood before the people as "that rarest of phenomena, a public man who, elevated to office, faithfully keeps his pre-election promises." [57]

In spite of his seventy-one years, Watterson wanted to do more than cheer from the sidelines; he wanted to make some practical contribution to the Wilson campaign. Consequently, in the fall of 1911 he set to work to secure a campaign contribution from his friend Thomas F.

[51] W. G. Brown to A. P. Andrew, November 2, 1911, Brown Papers.

[52] Willis Fletcher Johnson, *George Harvey, "Passionate Patriot,"* p. 177.

[53] *The Commoner,* May 19, 1911.

[54] E. M. House to W. J. Bryan, December 6, 1911, House Papers.

[55] See, e.g., Wilson's over-friendly letters to Watterson of December 31, 1910; June 15 and 29 and July 14 and 24, 1911, all in Watterson Papers.

[56] *Louisville Courier-Journal,* October 11, 1911.

[57] *ibid.,* July 13, 1911.

Ryan.[58] Harvey followed Watterson's effort and visited Ryan at his country estate in Nelson County, Virginia. The utilities czar declared that he was anxious to participate in the pre-convention campaign and stated that he would support Wilson because he was a native Virginian. On December 2, 1911, Harvey visited Washington and boldly announced to several congressmen that Ryan was ready to support the Wilson movement with his fortune.[59]

On December 7 Watterson, Harvey, and Wilson met in Watterson's apartment in the Manhattan Club in New York for the purpose of considering "certain practical matters relating to Governor Wilson's candidacy." [60] As the conversation veered toward the "practical details," Watterson suggested that the Princeton alumni who had been financing the campaign could not be expected to bear the full burden of expenses. Wilson agreed. "Marse Henry" then declared that Ryan would be happy to contribute to the campaign fund and suggested that Wilson meet with him and discuss the matter. Wilson, however, definitely did not like the idea. He said some "uncivil things" about Ryan and declared that if the knowledge of such a contribution became noised about it would do his candidacy immeasurable harm.[61] Nothing, however, of a discourteous, even of an unfriendly nature occurred during the conversation.[62]

As the three men were walking out, Harvey put his hand on Wilson's shoulder and said, "I want to ask you a frank question and I want a frank answer." Wilson promised to speak frankly. "I want to know," Harvey continued, "if the support of *Harper's* is embarrassing your campaign." "I am sorry you asked me that!" Wilson replied. "Let's have the answer anyway," Harvey urged. "Some of my friends tell me it is not doing me any good in the West," Wilson admitted. Harvey declared that he feared Wilson might "feel that way about it" and that he would "have to put on the soft pedal." For a few minutes they discussed means to counteract the impression that Harvey was controlled by J. P. Morgan and Wall Street; but they could think of no method

---

[58] See H. Watterson to G. Harvey, September —, 1911, published in W. F. Johnson, *George Harvey*, pp. 181-182. It will be recalled that as early as December 1910 Watterson and Harvey had conferred with Ryan with regard to the financing of the Wilson campaign.

[59] *New York World*, January 23, 1912.

[60] Henry Watterson, statement to the press, January 17, 1912; see *Louisville Courier-Journal*, January 18, 1912.

[61] Watterson, "To the Democrats of the United States," *ibid.*, January 30, 1912.

[62] Watterson, statement to the press, January 17, 1912, *ibid.*, January 18, 1912.

to get the fact of Harvey's editorial independence before the people. They parted, Wilson thought, in perfect friendship.[63]

Wilson thought Harvey and Watterson understood the reason for his answer. Obviously they did, for as early as October, Watterson had suggested to Wilson that it would be wise for Harvey, in view of his alleged reactionary environment, to moderate his aggressive campaign. He probably suggested the same thing to Harvey.[64] Colonel House, too, had discussed the desirability of less enthusiastic support of Wilson from the *Weekly* with his friend Edward S. Martin, an associate editor of the journal.[65]

Soon after the Manhattan conference, Harvey took Wilson's name off the masthead of the editorial page of *Harper's Weekly*. Stockton Axson, Wilson's brother-in-law, scented the danger of the situation and told Wilson that he was afraid he had offended Harvey and that a serious

[63] R. S. Baker, "Memorandum of a conversation with Stockton Axson, March 12, 1925," MS in Baker Papers. This is the report Axson heard Wilson tell his wife the day following the Manhattan conference.

A month later, when rumors of the Wilson-Harvey break were being circulated, Mrs. Wilson wrote her cousin, Judge Robert Ewing of Nashville, Watterson's brother-in-law, and related the details of the incident as Wilson had told them to her. "This is the simple story of the interview in question," Mrs. Wilson wrote. "For two hours they talked over the whole 'situation,' in the most intimately friendly and harmonious fashion, Woodrow in his usual absolutely open, frank manner. Then, as they rose to go, Col. Harvey said he wanted from Woodrow 'a perfectly frank answer' to one question, viz. : Whether the 'Weekly's' constant booming of him seemed to him unwise or embarrassing (in view, of course, of Harper's alleged connection with Wall Street). Now, as it happened, Col. Watterson himself had brought up that very subject with Woodrow a few weeks before; had declared that it *was* having an unfavorable effect, and that he meant to suggest to Harvey a more politic course for the time being. There had also been the same comment at the 'Wilson Headquarters' in New York. So when Col. Harvey begged him to be frank, Woodrow unwillingly, for it was at best, an ungracious thing to do, told him what the general impression was. Col. Harvey took it in perfect humor and said that he would have to 'put on the soft pedal.' There was not for one moment the slightest sign of excitement or irritation on the part of any one of the three. They stood discussing for some time longer how best to make the public understand the *real* independence of Col. Harvey and The Weekly, and then parted in the most cordial manner. Woodrow never for a moment dreamed that they had misunderstood him, or been 'hurt.'" E. A. W. to R. Ewing, January 12, 1912, copy in Wilson Papers.

Ewing promptly sent a copy of the letter to Watterson who replied, "The narrative given by Mrs. Wilson is substantially as I recall the episode." H. Watterson to R. Ewing, January 16, 1912, published in W. F. Johnson, *George Harvey*, p. 199.

Harvey's account of the famous conference differs only slightly from Wilson's and Watterson's accounts. See *ibid.*, p. 186, for Harvey's memorandum on the interview.

[64] Watterson, statement to the press, January 17, 1912, *Louisville Courier-Journal*, January 18, 1912.

[65] Charles Seymour, *The Intimate Papers of Colonel House*, I, 53.

break in their relations might result.[66] Wilson was completely surprised and immediately wrote to Harvey in an effort to restore the old friendly relations. So important were the letters that they are given in full:[67]

Personal.

MY DEAR COLONEL: 21 December, 1911.

Every day I am confirmed in the judgement that my mind is a one-track road, and can run only one train of thought at a time! A long time after that interview with you and Marse Henry at the Manhattan Club it came over me that when (at the close of the interview) you asked me that question about the *Weekly,* I answered it simply as a matter of fact, and of business, and said never a word of my sincere gratitude to you for all your generous support, or of my hope that it might be continued. Forgive me, and forget my manners!

Faithfully yours,
WOODROW WILSON.

Personal. Franklin Square, New York.

MY DEAR GOV. WILSON: January 4, 1912.

Replying to your note from the University Club, I think it should go without saying that no purely personal issue could arise between you and me. Whatever anybody else may surmise, you surely must know that, in trying to arouse and further your political aspirations during the past few years, I have been actuated solely by the belief that I was rendering a distinct public service.

The real point at the time of our interview was, as you aptly put it, one simply "of fact and of business," and when you stated the fact to be that my support was hurting your candidacy, and that you were experiencing difficulty in finding a way to counteract its harmful effect, the only thing possible for me to do, in simple fairness to you no less than in consideration of my own self-respect, was to relieve you of your embarrassment, so far as it lay within my power to do so, by ceasing to advocate your nomination.

That, I think, was fully understood between us at the time, and, acting accordingly, I took down your name from the head of the *Weekly's* editorial page some days before your letter was written. That seems to be all there is of it.

---

[66] S. Axson to R. S. Baker, August 29, 1928, Baker Papers. It was Axson, not Tumulty, who first called attention to the matter.

[67] The Wilson-Harvey correspondence was published in the *New York Evening Post,* January 30, 1912, and in the general press on the following day. The originals of Wilson's letters to Harvey are now in the Wilson Papers.

> *Whatever little hurt I may have felt as a consequence of the unexpected peremptoriness of your attitude toward me is, of course, wholly eliminated by your gracious words.*[68]

Very truly yours,
GEORGE HARVEY.

MY DEAR COLONEL HARVEY: 11 January, 1912

Generous and cordial as was your letter written in reply to my note from the University Club, it has left me uneasy,—because, in its perfect frankness, it shows that I *did* hurt you by what I so tactlessly said at the Knickerbocker [*sic*] Club. I am very ashamed of myself,—for there is nothing I am more ashamed of than hurting a true friend, however unintentional the hurt may have been. I wanted very much to see you in Washington [at the Jackson Day Dinner], but was absolutely captured by callers every minute I was in my rooms, and when I was not there was fulfilling public engagements. I saw you at the dinner, but could not get at you, and after the dinner was surrounded and prevented from getting at you. I am in town to-day, to speak this evening, and came in early in the hope of catching you at your office.

For I owe it to you and to my own thought and feeling to tell you how grateful I am for all your generous praise and support of me (no one has described me more nearly as I would like to believe myself to be than you have!), how I have admired you for the independence and unhesitating courage and individuality of your course, and how far I was from desiring that you should cease your support of me in the *Weekly*. You will think me very stupid,—but I did not think of that as the result of my blunt answer to your question. I thought only of the means of convincing people of the real independence of the *Weekly's* position. You will remember that that was what we *discussed*. And now that I have unintentionally put you in a false and embarrassing position you heap coals of fire on my head by continuing to give out interviews favourable to my candidacy! All that I can say is, that you have proved yourself very big and that I wish I might have an early opportunity to *tell* you face to face how I really feel about it all.

With warm regard,

Cordially and faithfully yours,
WOODROW WILSON.

MY DEAR GOV. WILSON—   January 16, 1912.

Thank you sincerely for your most handsome letter. I can only repeat what I said before—that there is no particle of personal rancor or resentment left in me. And I beg of you to believe that I have not said one word to anybody of criticism of you.

[68] Italics mine.

I *have* to print a word of explanation to the *Weekly's* readers, but it will be the briefest possible.

Very truly yours,
GEORGE HARVEY.

If Wilson was possibly guilty of begging, Harvey stands convicted of utter and complete hypocrisy. His thinly veiled sarcasm belies his hypocrisy; his action at the time convicts him of it. For by the time the correspondence had ended, Harvey had laid careful plans for what he thought would be Wilson's political destruction. He would wreck Wilson's candidacy by exposing him as an "ingrate," insensible to all feelings of friendship and obligation. It was too splendid an opportunity to let escape. Wily politician that he was, Harvey was unwilling to be drawn personally into the controversy that would inevitably follow the revelation of Wilson's "ingratitude." Could he not use Colonel Watterson, perhaps, as the medium for the attack?

Unfortunately for his own reputation, Watterson proved to be the perfect tool for Harvey's scheme.[69] Two weeks after the Manhattan Club conference, Watterson made a lecture tour through the Southeast (speaking, of all things, on world peace!). He went first to Atlanta where he told Clark Howell, publisher of the *Atlanta Constitution,* that he and Harvey were planning to expose Wilson before the Democratic voters as a gross ingrate. However, he had not yet decided upon the most effective method to use. From Howell's office in Atlanta he wrote to Harvey, cautioning him to say nothing about the affair: *"On no account* make the first move. Don't doubt the thing will keep at least the next ten or twelve days. You hold a full and a winning hand. . . . I have a perfectly definite plan and have thought it out in every detail. . . . I am an old hand at the bellows at this sort of business, and *know I am right."* [70]

---

[69] With his ante-bellum sense of honor and friendship, Watterson had been genuinely outraged at Wilson's answer to Harvey; for the old Kentucky editor had a very intimate, almost a fatherly, affection for Harvey. He later remarked that Wilson's manner at the Manhattan Club had been "autocratic, if not tyrannous." Furthermore he could not rid himself of "the *impression* that Governor Wilson had been receiving letters from Kentucky written by enemies of mine who seek to use his name and fame to get in some ends of their own." Statement to the press, January 17, 1912 (italics mine). One of the Kentucky "enemies" referred to was former Governor John C. W. Beckham, Watterson's bitterest opponent in the state, who had come out in support of Wilson. Perhaps Wilson, moreover, did not pay the old man sufficient deference. Watterson, we know, felt that there were not the qualities of cordiality and *bonhomie* in Wilson that made for effective party leadership. H. Watterson to R. Ewing, January 16, 1912, published in W. F. Johnson, *George Harvey,* p. 199.

[70] H. Watterson to G. Harvey, December —, 1911, published in *ibid.,* p. 193.

Harvey's biographer has endeavored to prove that it was Watterson who engineered the conspiracy to destroy Wilson's candidacy. The Kentuckian, he writes, was "wholly and inexorably intransigent," and nothing less than the defeat of the Wilson movement would satisfy him.[71] The evidence reveals, on the contrary, that it was Harvey, not Watterson, who was impatient of delay. He sent his friend Wayne MacVeagh to Atlanta on December 24 to urge Watterson to take the initiative in disclosing the Manhattan Club incident,[72] and it was this prompting that moved Watterson to write the letter cited above. By the next mail Watterson wrote more fully, disclosing his plans:

"Your messenger came to me as I was starting for my audience and I had time only to say a word or two to him and to scribble a few lines to you. The burthen of these was, 'wait.' In my judgment it would spoil all to give it out prematurely or in the loose form of an interview. My plan is to treat it much more seriously. I propose immediately on reaching home to write to Governor Wilson a letter fully and frankly explaining why I can go no further in the support of his candidacy. In this I shall give as my pivotal point his treatment of you, making common cause with you. This cannot fail to result in a correspondence in which we have everything to gain, he everything to lose. In the meantime if you feel that they are pressing you—though in your place I would let them press and 'chaw' on it a lick or two!—you can say, or intimate, that I know something about it. Your original idea of saying that no one but Governor Wilson himself could take down his name from the top of your columns, still seems to me wise. It would entirely belittle the case and might put us in the vocative for me to butt in, as it were, without any rhyme or reason known to the public. In all this I am sure of my ground and yours, for our opportunity will not get away from us. . . . Whatever I do must emanate from Louisville."[73]

Watterson went next to Charlotte, North Carolina, where he spoke on December 29. He told the story of the Manhattan Club affair to James C. Hemphill, who had already become an outstanding critic of Wilson. Hemphill and Watterson attempted to reach Harvey by telephone, but were unsuccessful. Watterson wrote instead: "Hemphill thinks with me that we have everything to gain by playing a waiting game; not too long a wait, only to draw the public fire and focus."[74]

[71] *ibid.*, p. 195.

[72] Watterson, statement to the press, January 31, 1912.

[73] H. Watterson to G. Harvey, December 26, 1911, published in W. F. Johnson, *George Harvey*, pp. 193-194.

[74] H. Watterson to G. Harvey, December 29, 1911, published in *ibid.*, p. 194.

Keystone

Oscar W. Underwood

Harris & Ewing

William R. Hearst

Harris & Ewing

Champ Clark

LEADERS IN THE CAMPAIGN AGAINST WILSON

At the home on Cleveland Lane

Hemphill also wrote Harvey a violent letter, declaring that both Harvey and Watterson had been "most damnably treated." [75]

At Richmond, on December 31, Watterson was again accosted by MacVeagh, who brought from New York Harvey's urgent suggestion that Watterson make public the Manhattan Club affair.[76] Watterson, however, was still reluctant to take the fateful step. "We must not undervalue either Wilson's craft or his nerve," he added. "This will surely beat him, as it ought, but it must be handled with prudence, tact, and dignity. I feel entirely sure of my ground." [77]

Soon rumors were circulated to the effect that there had been a personal break between Harvey and Wilson, a natural development since it was quite obvious that something was wrong. Hemphill first gave credence to the rumors. On January 5, 1912, he printed a dispatch written by Watterson and sent it on to Washington. "All sorts of rumors are flying about. One has it that Col. Henry Watterson was a party to the breach between the two eminent Easterners, or at least that he knows a great deal about it and has been seriously affected by it," the dispatch read. "The other has it that Wilson found Harvey's support a handicap with the Democratic Radicals and rudely demanded of Harvey that he stop it." [78]

Wilson countered with a statement to the newspapers denying that there had been "any breach of any kind" between Harvey and himself.[79] He was profoundly disturbed, however, and as a desperate, last-ditch measure Mrs. Wilson wrote her cousin and Watterson's brother-in-law,

[75] J. C. Hemphill to G. Harvey, December 29, 1911, *ibid.* Hemphill carried on an extensive correspondence with President Taft during the development of the controversy, and his letters to the President are among the most interesting the author has found. "I wish I could see you," he wrote on January 1, 1912, "as I could a tale unfold about the pension grabbing Governor of New Jersey and his treatment of George Harvey and Watterson. It is the most remarkable thing I have ever known in politics and I hope that I shall be able to bring it out in *The Observer* a little later, but just at this time I do not care to say anything about it or have anything said about it. For cold blooded selfishness and utter disregard of all political common sense, it is the worst I have ever heard of." William Howard Taft Papers, Library of Congress; hereinafter cited as Taft Papers.

[76] Watterson, statement to the press, January 31, 1912.

[77] H. Watterson to G. Harvey, December 31, 1911, published in W. F. Johnson, *George Harvey*, p. 195.

[78] *Charlotte Daily Observer*, January 5, 1912. "I think I have fired a shot this morning that will be heard around the country," Hemphill wrote to Taft. "It is the most remarkable story of political ingratitude and personal infidelity I have ever known. When I see you the next time I can tell you some very interesting things about it, in which I am sure you would rejoice." J. C. Hemphill to W. H. Taft, January 5, 1912, Taft Papers.

[79] *New York World*, January 6, 1912.

Robert Ewing of Nashville, and asked him to write to Watterson and to intercede for Wilson. She and Wilson had been told, Mrs. Wilson wrote, that Watterson had turned violently against Wilson because of his alleged ill-treatment of Harvey. She related the details of the Manhattan Club conference[80] and declared that Wilson was greatly disturbed by the matter. "Imagine how dazed we are to hear of Colonel Watterson's 'rage,'" she continued. It was part of the general irony of things that Wilson was not convinced that Watterson and the men at 42 Broadway were right in their contentions that Harvey should cease supporting his candidacy. "Col. Harvey was *by far* his ablest advocate," and even had harm been done Wilson's candidacy by his support, it had been more than counterbalanced by the support Wilson had gained elsewhere. Mrs. Wilson believed that Ewing could make everything clear to Watterson.[81]

Ewing hastily sent a copy of the letter to his brother-in-law and expressed his confidence in Watterson's sense of justice and in Wilson's integrity. Had not Hemphill misquoted him about the Manhattan Club meeting? The entire business was inconceivable to him.[82] Mrs. Wilson's letter gave the old editor a severe jolt.[83] He immediately replied to Ewing and explained the reason for the estrangement, but declared that he was sending Harvey the letters from Mrs. Wilson and Ewing "as the most direct and fitting method of reaching some kind of an understanding."[84]

Watterson knew that Harvey had already written a statement for publication in *Harper's Weekly,* explaining why he had ceased advocating Wilson's nomination. He therefore hastily telegraphed Harvey to hold the statement. "Have received most important communication from the other side," he wrote. "It may put entirely different face on the matter and compel different treatment."[85] Harvey replied that Watterson's telegram was too late, that the statement had already been sent to more than a score of important newspapers and to Wilson himself.

[80] See *supra,* p. 362, n. 63.

[81] E. A. W. to R. Ewing, January 12, 1912, Wilson Papers.

[82] R. Ewing to H. Watterson, January —, 1912, published in W. F. Johnson, *George Harvey,* p. 198.

[83] There can be no doubt that Harvey had not shown Watterson the apologetic letters Wilson had written him. It is extremely unlikely that Watterson would have joined in the attack if he had known that Wilson had done his best to make amends for his indiscretion.

[84] H. Watterson to R. Ewing, January 16, 1912, published in W. F. Johnson, *George Harvey,* p. 199.

[85] H. Watterson to G. Harvey, January —, 1912, published in *ibid.*

Harvey afterwards declared that had he seen the letters before sending out the statement, he would not have changed a word of it.[86]

This much, then, is clear: Harvey had failed to persuade Watterson to take the initiative in disclosing the conversation at the Manhattan Club and, fearing lest Ewing and Wilson might pacify Watterson, he resolved to force Watterson's hand before he had become reconciled to Wilson. Harvey therefore dispatched a statement, which had previously been approved by Watterson, to the newspapers on January 16. The statement also appeared in *Harper's Weekly* in the issue of January 20:

TO OUR READERS:

We make the following reply to many inquiries from the readers of *Harper's Weekly*:

The name of Woodrow Wilson as our candidate for President was taken down from the head of these columns in response to a statement made directly to us by Governor Wilson, to the effect that our support was affecting his candidacy injuriously.

The only course left open to us, in simple fairness to Mr. Wilson, no less in consideration of our own self-respect, was to cease to advocate his nomination.

We make this explanation with great reluctance and the deepest regret. But we cannot escape the conclusion that the very considerable number of our readers who have cooperated earnestly and loyally in advancing a movement which was inaugurated solely in the hope of rendering a high public service are clearly entitled to this information.

The statement was dishonest in that it left out far more than it explained; it told nothing about Harvey's direct question to Wilson, but implied, rather, that Wilson had gratuitously demanded that Harvey cease advocating his nomination, that Wilson was nothing less than an ingrate who had abandoned his best friend and most loyal supporter for reasons of sheer political expediency.

The announcement struck like a thunderbolt. Wilson's enemies throughout the country fairly overdid themselves in their rejoicing. It was as if the chorus were directed by a single baton, for at one prearranged signal all of the anti-Wilson leaders moved in to give the death blow to the Wilson movement.

The *New York Sun* was appropriately first in the field and printed Harvey's statement on January 17, one day before the other newspapers

[86] *ibid.*, pp. 199-200.

made it public. "We hope it is no rash effusion to say," Mitchell wrote, "that, in memory of this beautiful episode in the history of gratitude, Colonel HARVEY is now wearing a brass serpent's tooth on his watch chain." [87] The Hearst newspapers carried a sensational account of the Manhattan Club conference. Without a word of warning, the account ran, Wilson had turned to Harvey and said, "Harvey, the time has now come when your open advocacy of my candidacy for President is doing me more harm than good, and I want you to stop it." [88] Surely, exulted Wilson's opponents, the Harvey affair would mean the end of the Wilson presidential movement. "It is to me a really painful thing that the school teacher should have been so greedy and was willing to desert his best friend for the sake of making political capital with the mob," Hemphill confided to President Taft. "If the people of this country were what they used to be, this exposure of the school teacher's treachery to his friends would be sufficient to make him impossible as a Presidential candidate." [89] Taft, too, was confident that the affair would injure the Wilson movement. "The Harvey-Wilson episode," he wrote, "is going to stir up the Democratic politics for some time. It shows Wilson in a perfectly bloodless chase for the White House and willing to sacrifice friendship." [90]

Hemphill, the "long suffering and devoted Presbyterian . . . , now residing, temporarily he hopes, in the town of Charlotte," led the anti-Wilson chorus in the South. "In the cold, gray dawn of the morning after," he wrote, "this falling of the mask from one who had been hailed with high hopes as a statesman . . . will come with peculiarly painful force to some." [91] Wilson had dropped the pilot "who had brought him from the shores of political obscurity" a trifle too early, declared a former Richmond supporter;[92] another editor asserted that Wilson had "swapped the simple, dignified garments of pure Democracy for the Joseph's-coat of Bryanism and buncombe." [93] "He who abandons a friend will abandon a principle," moralized one of Hearst's editors, "and what a man does to an individual he will do to a people." [94]

Harvey's statement took Wilson's supporters completely by surprise.

[87] *New York Sun*, January 17, 1912.
[88] *New York American*, January 17, 1912.
[89] J. C. Hemphill to W. H. Taft, January 18, 1912, Taft Papers.
[90] W. H. Taft to J. C. Hemphill, January 17, 1912, *ibid.*
[91] *Charlotte Daily Observer*, January 19, 1912.
[92] *Richmond News-Leader*, January 18, 1912.
[93] *Augusta* (Ga.) *Chronicle*, January 18, 1912.
[94] *New York American*, January 18, 1912.

Most of them made no immediate attempt to justify what appeared at first glance to be outrageous ingratitude and ambition, and had Harvey's pronouncement represented the whole truth of the matter there is little doubt that Wilson would have lost the support of many of his most ardent advocates.[95] Most loyal Wilson editors let the attack of the anti-Wilson crowd go unanswered;[96] they were waiting for subsequent developments in the affair.

Harvey's statement was published on January 17 and 18. On January 17 Watterson abandoned the caution which had characterized his previous course and gave to the Associated Press his famous account of the Manhattan Club conference. He told the story "regretfully." Nothing of a discourteous, even of an unfriendly nature had passed during the interview, he declared; Wilson's statement that Harvey's support was injuring his candidacy had been made in answer to a direct question from Harvey himself. Watterson's chief grievance, therefore, was Wilson's "autocratic" and "tyrannous" manner, which had convinced Watterson that Wilson was not a man who made "common cause with his political associates." [97]

It is difficult to imagine a weaker pronouncement from the Harvey-Watterson point of view. It was, after all, too truthful to have any other result than to exonerate Wilson completely from charges of ingratitude and, for that reason, it broke the spell that Harvey's announcement had cast. The Wilson spokesmen were up in arms immediately in praise of Wilson's conduct. How else, they asked, could Wilson have answered Harvey? "It passes our understanding," one editor observed, "that a candidate for President . . . can be assailed for having the conscience to speak the God's truth." [98] As for the charge of ingratitude, the *New York World* promptly disposed of it in a classic editorial that was reprinted in most Wilson newspapers:

" 'Ingratitude!' arises the chorus of Gov. Wilson's shocked oppo-

---

[95] A good example of the immediate unfavorable reaction among many pro-Wilson journals is revealed by the declarations in the *Galveston Daily News,* January 18, 1912, and the *Dallas Morning News,* January 18, 1912. These two newspapers were almost the official Wilson spokesmen in Texas.

[96] The present writer has not made any effort to catalogue here the several hundred severely unfavorable editorials on the Harvey affair that he has in his files. Suffice it to say that there was hardly an anti-Wilson journal in the country that did not try to make political capital out of the episode.

[97] Watterson, statement to the press, January 17, 1912, published in *Louisville Courier-Journal* and throughout the country on January 18, 1912.

[98] *Wilmington* (N. C.) *Morning Star,* January 23, 1912.

nents. We should be far from shocked even if we could discover ingratitude in Gov. Wilson's position.

"Ingratitude is one of the rarest virtues of public life. 'Gratitude' is responsible for many of our worst political abuses. Upon 'gratitude' is built every corrupt political machine; upon 'gratitude' is founded the power of every ignorant and unscrupulous boss; in 'gratitude' is rooted the system of spoils, of log-rolling, of lobbying. Lorimer was elected by 'gratitude,' Payne-Aldrich bills are passed for 'gratitude,' Harriman campaign funds are raised for 'gratitude.' The great majority of the voices which are denouncing Wilson's ingratitude are the voices of machine politicians, chief among whose stock in trade is this 'gratitude.'

"No, what we need in public life is a great deal more of discriminating ingratitude. . . . Gov. Wilson may or may not be the wisest choice for the Presidential nomination. But his gratitude or ingratitude to Col. Harvey will not be the paramount issue in the Baltimore Convention." [99]

The publication of the Watterson letter literally knocked the foundations from under the anti-Wilson men; for the most part they remained silent and the initiative was taken up by the Wilson spokesmen.[100] On January 19 William F. McCombs gave out the official statement on the Harvey affair. McCombs's statement was short and to the point; Watterson, he declared, had said all that needed to be said on the matter.[101] Wilson was in Detroit on a speaking tour when the Watterson letter was published. He wrote out a long statement on the Harvey affair, expressing his embarrassment over the misunderstanding and his high regard for Harvey's editorial independence; but, for reasons of expediency, the statement was never published.[102]

Nothing indicated better the marked trend of popular opinion in Wilson's favor than Bryan's sweeping endorsement of Wilson's conduct at the Manhattan Club. In a public letter from Lincoln, Bryan called the controversy an "Irrepressible Conflict" which illustrated "the im-

---

[99] *New York World*, January 19, 1912.

[100] The *New York World, New York Globe, Boston Evening Transcript, Indianapolis News, Baltimore Sun, Raleigh News and Observer*—the entire Wilson press and many independent newspapers, in fact, pressed the attack to vindicate the honor of their candidate. See the review of editorial opinion in A. S. Link, "The South and the Democratic Campaign of 1910-1912," pp. 124-125, and in the *Literary Digest*, XLIV (January 27, 1912), 144-145.

[101] *Birmingham Age-Herald*, January 20, 1912.

[102] The original MS is in the Baker Papers and is published in facsimile in R. S. Baker, *Woodrow Wilson*, III, opposite p. 254.

possibility of co-operation between men who look at public questions from different points of view." Harvey's support had been a distinct disadvantage to the Wilson movement, Bryan continued. "Col. Harvey should recognize the situation and face it like a man." Wilson had begun his political career as a conservative; he had rapidly become a militant reformer. "As soon as it became apparent that he was a progressive Democrat the predatory interests were shocked. . . . The masses, on the other hand, were attracted and his political strength today is in exact proportion to the confidence that they have in the completeness of the change he has undergone. His former friends are now his bitter enemies and they are proving the sincerity of his present position by the violence of their attacks upon him. They are publishing his former utterances in the hope of alienating his new found friends, but they forget the EXTENT of the change while the venom of his adversaries removes all doubt as to the REALITY of the change." [103] A week later Bryan declared that Wilson's break with Harvey was a "shining illustration that Mr. Wilson is the best modern example of Saul of Tarsus." [104]

Bryan's blessing proved to be a valuable asset to the Wilson managers in their general counterattack; but the unhesitating support Wilson received from several other important Democratic leaders was just as effective in rehabilitating his political fortunes. Senator Gore, who jauntily declared that the controversy was "a bubble, not a billow," [105] succeeded in persuading Senator Francis G. Newlands of Nevada, who had himself been mentioned for the presidential nomination, to declare his support of Wilson's candidacy. [106] Thomas W. Gregory, in an address to the Democrats of Texas, declared that *Harper's Weekly* was financed and controlled by J. P. Morgan and that Harvey's support had been injurious to Wilson's candidacy. [107] Judge Robert Ewing of Nashville

[103] "An Irrepressible Conflict," published in the newspapers January 24, 1912, and in *The Commoner*, January 26, 1912.

[104] *Dallas Morning News,* January 31, 1912.

[105] *Raleigh News and Observer,* January 20, 1912. Senator Gore, however, told the author (August 15, 1942) that the Wilson managers thought the affair was not only a billow, "but a cyclone and hurricane all rolled into one." When Harvey's statement was published, Gore was in Washington with McCombs and Thomas J. Pence. They spent three days "trying to steady the boat."

[106] *Raleigh News and Observer,* January 19, 1912.

[107] In his letter to the Texas Democrats, Gregory emphasized Watterson's characterization of Wilson as a "schoolmaster." "If giving a candid answer to a candid question is (as suggested by Col. Watterson) characteristic of a schoolmaster, and not of a statesman, then so much the better for the schoolmaster and so much the worse for the

wrote an account of the Manhattan Club conference that was based on Ellen Axson Wilson's letter of January 12;[108] it was reprinted widely throughout the country and was another important factor in getting the facts of the Harvey affair before the people. Because the Harvey-Wilson controversy had convinced him that Wilson was in no way connected with Wall Street, Representative Albert S. Burleson of Texas announced his support of Wilson's candidacy on January 26. "It looks as if there is a whole lot of truth in the saying," Burleson commented, "that every time one of these anti-Wilson explosions is pulled off you are sure to find the remnants of a Wall Street alarm clock in the wreck." [109]

The course of events had taken an ugly turn for Watterson and Harvey. It would have been fortunate for them if the affair had ended with the publication of Watterson's statement. But the end was not yet for "Marse Henry." The day after his statement was published, Ralph Smith sent a dispatch to the *Atlanta Journal* that announced that Wilson had broken with Harvey because Harvey attempted to persuade him to accept financial aid from Ryan.[110] The report spread rapidly and was immediately taken up by all of the Wilson journals.[111]

At a dinner given in his honor at Charlotte on December 29, 1911, Watterson had talked in his garrulous manner to Senator Lee S. Overman; he told Overman that an effort had been made at the Manhattan Club conference to persuade Wilson to meet Ryan. When Watterson's statement was published on January 18, Overman confided to his friend Senator Ben Tillman of South Carolina that "Marse Henry" had omitted an important part of the conversation in his account. Overman, moreover, told Tillman the story about Ryan that Watterson had related to him.[112] The secret was too good to keep; on January 24 "Pitchfork Ben" relayed the story to newspaper correspondents in Washington. "I had given Henry Watterson credit for more sense than to try to foist off a story like this with the material facts concealed," Tillman

statesman," he declared. *Dallas Morning News,* January 28, 1912. Gregory later claimed that his statement had been an important factor in gaining the support of the 40,000 rural school teachers in Texas for the Wilson movement. T. W. Gregory to R. S. Baker, May 29, 1928, Baker Papers.

[108] *Nashville Banner,* January 19, 1912.

[109] *Dallas Morning News,* January 27, 1912.

[110] *Atlanta Journal,* January 19, 1912.

[111] See Thomas J. Pence in the *Raleigh News and Observer,* January 25, 1912, for the "official" Wilson version of the story; also the *New York World,* January 23, 1912; *Nashville Tennessean and American,* January 25, 1912.

[112] Pence in *Raleigh News and Observer,* January 25, 1912.

declared, "though I now recall he went back on free silver and Bryan." Wilson, he added, "saw through the scheme, measured Harvey and Watterson correctly and refused to be lassoed and tied by Thomas F. Ryan." [113]

Tillman's statement infuriated Watterson, who sent a second to the South Carolinian and demanded to know the authority for his "serious accusation." [114] Tillman blandly replied that all the newspapers seemed to know the reason for the Wilson-Harvey break; yet Watterson, in his detailed statement, had said nothing about the actual reason for the rupture.[115] Watterson's reply was bitter; he had been aware, he wrote, that spokesmen for Wilson had industriously circulated the rumor that the Ryan issue was the cause of the break between Harvey and Wilson. "Now, Senator," he continued, "I know of my own knowledge that the story is a lie, made out of the whole cloth." It was "dastardly," too, yet Watterson concluded by admitting that it was he, not Harvey, who had suggested that Wilson discuss the finances of his campaign with Ryan. At Wilson's suggestion, Watterson declared, he had undertaken to assist his managers to raise the considerable sums of money necessary for the campaign. The name of Thomas F. Ryan came to his mind. "He is a Democrat. He is a Virginian. He is my friend. *Knowing him to be a disinterested man, having no axe to grind,* I hoped that I might induce him to help out what I believed to be a worthy cause." Wilson's managers had been delighted by the suggestion, Watterson concluded, but Wilson had vetoed the proposal.[116]

During the controversy Wilson had consistently refused to become a party to an affair that was growing increasingly acrimonious. When he read the correspondence between the two old Democratic veterans, however, he felt compelled to issue a statement. "Insofar as I am concerned," he declared, "the statement that Colonel Watterson was requested to assist in raising money in my behalf is absolutely without foundation." Neither he, nor anyone authorized to speak for him, had made such a request of Watterson.[117]

It was more than Watterson would tolerate, this attack by the governor of New Jersey upon his integrity. He not only declared that he

[113] *Atlanta Journal,* January 24, 1912.
[114] H. Watterson to B. R. Tillman, January 25, 1912, published in *Louisville Courier-Journal,* January 27, 1912.
[115] B. R. Tillman to H. Watterson, January 26, 1912, *ibid.*
[116] H. Watterson to B. R. Tillman, January 26, 1912, *ibid.;* italics mine.
[117] *ibid.*

had definite proof that Wilson's statement was untrue; he also proposed that a "court of gentlemen" be established to decide the issue of veracity![118] When it became apparent that Wilson would ignore this challenge, moreover, Watterson gave to the press what he declared was his "final statement" on the matter; it was, needless to say, a bitter excoriation of Wilson.[119]

Watterson emerged a very poor second-best in the controversy over the question of the Ryan contribution. Few editors defended his attempt to place Wilson under financial obligation to Ryan who, one editor wrote, was associated in the public mind "with the very rottenest and foulest transactions of rotten high finance, trust building and extortions."[120] It had truly been ludicrous for the Kentuckian to bluster so mightily in defense of Harvey and then, in a second breath, to admit that he himself had been the agent in the Ryan negotiations. Watterson had been so deadly in earnest about the entire controversy that it had become ridiculous. His long, verbose letters to the Democrats of the United States, the imminent "duel" between Watterson and Tillman, Watterson's suggestion that a "court of gentlemen" be established to judge whether he or Wilson had lied all seemed highly amusing to a good many observers who enjoyed Watterson's capers as much as they enjoyed a good burlesque. "Out of the Harvey-Watterson-Wilson controversy," one editor sardonically remarked, "the Kentucky Colonel emerges with ruffled plumage, which is almost always the result when a high-combed rooster is chased with a pitchfork."[121]

Throughout the controversy, Wilson said little, even in letters to his intimate friends. He wrote Dabney on January 25 that he was sorry to

[118] "I propose," Watterson explained, "that Governor Wilson name two confidentials, I naming two, the four to name a fifth, and this court of gentlemen be established to determine the issue between us." *ibid.,* January 28, 1912.

[119] H. Watterson, "Address to the Democrats of the United States," *ibid.,* January 30, 1912. He had not published the evidence in his possession, Watterson declared, because such an act would have been "reckless disregard of . . . party prudence and private rights." Two weeks before the Manhattan Club conference he had been approached by a "gentleman of distinction closely associated with, if not actually directing, the Wilson organization," who told of the organization's urgent need of campaign contributions. (This was probably McCombs. See M. F. Lyons, *William F. McCombs,* pp. 20-21.) In answer to this appeal, Watterson had secured at once a considerable sum of money. Wilson's managers, moreover, had been delighted by Watterson's suggestion that Ryan be brought into the Wilson organization; but when Wilson refused to deal with Ryan, Watterson had dropped the matter entirely.

Watterson's account is undoubtedly the truth of the matter. See *ibid.,* pp. 61-63.

[120] *Roanoke* (Va.) *Times,* January 27, 1912.

[121] *Richmond Times-Dispatch,* January 28, 1912.

hear what Dabney had reported of the effect of the affair on the opinion of some of his friends in Virginia. But, he added, he could not but hope that this was only temporary, because surely Virginians were not going to be the only people in the country who did not understand.[122] Harvey's suggestion that the Wilson-Harvey correspondence be published in the *New York Evening Post* evoked a letter from Wilson that revealed his bitterness. Thus he wrote to Oswald G. Villard, publisher of the *New York Evening Post,* that he found himself in a position in which it was difficult for him to judge what was right. Wilson did not think that Harvey had entitled himself to the "justice" of having the letters published, because his initiative statement in the *Weekly* had been so incomplete as to be virtually untrue and unjust to Wilson. Only Watterson's statement had enabled the public to see the affair in some of its true aspects, but the action of both Watterson and Harvey had been unjust and ungenerous. He, Wilson, did not feel that he owed them anything whatsoever in the matter.[123]

The publication of the Wilson-Harvey correspondence by the newspapers on January 30 and 31 put Watterson in a ridiculous position. While he had been carrying on single-handedly a bitter campaign for his friend Harvey, whom he had portrayed as having been grievously wounded, the letters revealed that Harvey, at least to all surface appearances, had forgiven Wilson of his indiscretion long before the great fight was made. Watterson well understood his embarrassing position. The publication of the letters, he wrote Harvey, put him "in the false position of making a quarrel with Wilson about nothing—of calling him down on your account when you had forgiven him—exposing me to every manner of misrepresentation and abuse." [124] Watterson, however, got in a parting shot—this time at Harvey. From first to last, he declared, he had acted not only with Harvey's full knowledge and approval, but always at his *insistence.*[125]

The publication of the Wilson-Harvey letters brought to a sudden end this cyclonic episode. The letters of course absolved Wilson of the charge of ingratitude, but they did not square Watterson's industrious activity on Harvey's behalf, or Harvey's behind-the-scenes machinations. It was Watterson's great misfortune that he was so impulsive, so un-

[122] W. W. to R. H. Dabney, January 25, 1912, Dabney Papers.

[123] W. W. to O. G. Villard, January 26, 1912, original in the private papers of Oswald Garrison Villard, New York City; hereinafter cited as Villard Papers.

[124] H. Watterson to G. Harvey, February 28, 1912, published in W. F. Johnson, *George Harvey,* pp. 208-209.

[125] *Louisville Courier-Journal,* February 1, 1912.

thinking as to allow himself to be used as a tool by Harvey. The Harvey affair, as engineered by Harvey and Watterson, was patently a miserable failure. No single editor or Democratic politician of any importance who had sincerely supported Wilson's candidacy deserted the governor as a result of the incident, while he undoubtedly gained many new supporters in the rural West and South. Ironical though it indeed was, therefore, Wilson's candidacy received a perceptible boost as a result of the attack. One little-noticed outcome of the affair occurred in Charlotte. There the "long suffering and devoted Presbyterian," Hemphill, was ousted from the editorship of the *Charlotte Daily Observer* by its publisher, Daniel A. Tompkins.[126] What was begun as a movement to destroy the candidacy of the most prominent Democrat had degenerated into a comic dog-fight.[127]

Even if the opposition of powerful financiers, politicians, and editors was not enough to disturb the Wilson managers there was another threat that worried them. They became convinced early in 1912 that there existed an agreement among Clark, Underwood, and Harmon by which these three candidates had united in a "presidential trust" or "combine" to defeat Wilson. Albert S. Burleson first gave publicity to the charge when he asserted in March that the "nice understanding," which seemed to exist among Harmon, Underwood, and Clark, had "all the earmarks of those old-time trust fights against a competitor." The Clark, Underwood, and Harmon managers, Burleson charged, had agreed to a "suspicious division of territory."[128] McCombs took up Burleson's accusation with alacrity, published it in all the Wilson journals in the country, and sent copies of it to some 100,000 persons.[129]

On March 27 the Wilson headquarters in New York gave official sanction to Burleson's charge by declaring that it had "conclusive proof

[126] Tompkins had had numerous complaints against Hemphill's anti-Wilson editorials from subscribers who were Wilson supporters. See, e.g., J. M. Archer to Circulation Manager of the *Observer*, April 3, 1912; Howard Banks to D. A. Tompkins, February 2, 1912; A. S. Tompkins to D. A. Tompkins, February 5, 1912, all in the Daniel A. Tompkins Papers, Library of the University of North Carolina.

[127] Watterson, nevertheless, was determined to have the last word in the controversy. See his "To the Democrats of Kentucky," *Louisville Courier-Journal*, February 21, 1912, for the bitterest of his attacks upon Wilson.

[128] *Raleigh News and Observer*, March 5, 1912. "I get from the Dallas News your full statement regarding the 'Presidential Trust,'" House wrote to Burleson, "and I do not hesitate to proclaim it the most effective campaign document that has yet been issued in behalf of Governor Wilson." E. M. House to A. S. Burleson, March 6, 1912, Burleson Papers.

[129] W. F. McCombs to E. M. House, March 20, 1912, House Papers.

of the existence of a presidential candidate combine having for its object the prevention of Governor Wilson's nomination." The "conclusive proof" was Harmon's and Clark's withdrawal, in Underwood's favor, from the presidential primary contest in Florida.[130] "There is not the slightest doubt that Clark, Harmon and Underwood are being financed by the same source," McCombs had written a few days earlier. ". . . It is a question with us as to whether the people in Wall Street shall be

Splitting Up the Country
Brewerton in *Atlanta Journal*

able to get away with the nomination by the use of money." [131] Wilson himself was convinced of the existence of the conspiracy. "Signs multiply," he wrote, "that there is a combination of Clark, Underwood, and Harmon (with a division of territory quite after the manner of the industrial combinations), and the evidence that the combination is being financed from Wall Street falls short only of legal proof." [132]

[130] *Raleigh News and Observer,* March 28, 1912.
[131] W. F. McCombs to E. M. House, March 20, 1912, House Papers.
[132] W. W. to E. M. House, March 15, 1912, *ibid.*

Although the headquarters of the three candidates charged with conspiracy gave out vigorous denials of the existence of an agreement among their candidates,[133] and although Clark termed the accusation a "malicious lie," [134] the Wilson supporters kept up the hue and cry of "presidential combination." "Has Woodrow Wilson had a square deal in this race?" asked one commentator. "Where is the honest man to say so? Where is the intelligent man who does not know that he is opposed by a scurvy combination?" [135] Bryan, too, made the accusation, although he included only Harmon and Underwood, the "reactionary" candidates whom he had already outlawed, in his indictment.[136]

The publication of the Joline letter and the Harvey-Watterson attack had only served to strengthen friendly relations between Wilson and Bryan and to secure more firmly Wilson's hold upon the progressive Democrats. The near-failure of the Wilson movement, therefore, was not caused by these badly aimed attacks that nearly always ended by operating in Wilson's favor; it was, rather, a result of the unprecedented campaign of misrepresentation, abuse, and slander waged by the chief spokesmen for Clark and Underwood. After the failure of the Harvey-Watterson attack in late January 1912, the leadership of the anti-Wilson campaign passed from "Wall Street" to the four chief self-proclaimed radicals in the Democratic party. George Fred Williams, former Populist leader in Massachusetts; Richard F. Pettigrew, former Populist senator from South Dakota; and William Randolph Hearst, leading American "yellow" journalist, were the chief publicists of the Clark prenomination campaign. The fourth member of the group, Tom Watson

---

[133] There was, indeed, much circumstantial evidence to substantiate the charges of the Wilson managers. Underwood, for example, made the campaign in the Lower South, with the exception of Louisiana, unmolested by competition from Clark or Harmon. In Oklahoma the Harmon and Clark supporters united in an attempt to defeat Wilson. Clark had absolutely no opposition from Harmon or Underwood in the Western states. Perhaps it was true, as one Wilson editor declared, that Clark, Underwood, and Harmon displayed wise judgment in refusing to attack one another. They recognized that it was Wilson against the field, but they denied that this meant that he was the first choice of a majority of all the Democrats. *Charleston News and Courier*, April 5, 1912. Two anti-Wilson leaders, Clark Howell, publisher of the *Atlanta Constitution*, and Senator Joseph W. Bailey of Texas, frankly admitted that this was true. In some states, Bailey declared, Clark had been given the field against Wilson; in others, Harmon; while in the Lower South Underwood represented the combination. *Raleigh News and Observer*, May 12, 1912. See also the *Atlanta Constitution*, March 17, 1912, for a significant editorial.

[134] *Birmingham Age-Herald*, March 29, 1912.

[135] "Savoyard" (E. W. Newman) in *Birmingham News*, quoted in *Pensacola Journal*, April 25, 1912.

[136] *The Commoner*, May 12, 1912.

of Georgia, Populist candidate for President in 1908, was Underwood's leading spokesman in the Southeast.[137]

Interestingly enough, Wilson's own *History of the American People* furnished nine-tenths of the ammunition for these men. Williams opened the Clark-Hearst phase of the attack in February 1912 by writing a public letter to Pettigrew, explaining the reasons why he could not support Wilson's candidacy. He had thoroughly combed the fifth volume of Wilson's *History* and emerged with sufficient evidence to damn almost any candidate. "It is Toryism of the blackest type," Williams wrote. "It is not a history of the American people, but a history of Woodrow Wilson's admiration for everything which the radical democracy now seeks to change, and a series of sneers and insults to every class of men who have sought to alleviate the injustices of capitalism. The worst is that there is no note of sympathy for any suffering and protesting class, but he seems to search for phrases to show his contempt for them." Then, by methodically quoting from page after page of the most damaging evidence in Wilson's own writings, Williams pretty conclusively proved that Wilson, in 1902 at least, "had a profound contempt for the Farmers' Alliance, the Populists, greenbackers, bi-metallists, trades unionists, small office seekers, Italians, Poles, Hungarians, pensioners, strikers, armies of unemployed." [138]

Unfortunately for Wilson, the attack of the Clark-Hearst campaigners was all the more devastating because most of what they said was true. Wilson had written American history from the conservative point of view; he had castigated the agrarian radicals, praised Cleveland's attack upon Debs and the railway strikers in 1894, ridiculed Coxey's Army, in short, had written history he would not have written if he had known he was some day to become a presidential candidate. Most unfortunate of all, he had written about as uncomplimentary an opinion of the Poles, Hungarians, and Italians as it is possible to conceive:

". . . but now there came multitudes of men of the lowest class from the south of Italy and men of the meaner sort out of Hungary and Poland, men out of the ranks where there was neither skill nor energy nor any initiative of quick intelligence; and they came in numbers which increased from year to year, as if the countries of the south of Europe were disburdening themselves of the more sordid and hapless elements of their population, the men whose standards of life and of

---

[137] C. Vann Woodward's *Tom Watson: Agrarian Rebel,* is an excellent study of Watson's life.

[138] The letter is published in full in the *New York Times,* February 2, 1912.

work were such as American workmen had never dreamed of hitherto." [139] Then, as if to perfect the characterization, Wilson compared the Chinese to the "new" immigrants in the following terms: ". . . yet the Chinese were more to be desired, as workmen if not as citizens, than most of the coarse crew that came crowding in every year at the eastern ports." [140]

It was Hearst, however, who soon assumed leadership of the anti-Wilson campaign after the failure of the Harvey affair. Hearst's opposition was all the more bitter because Wilson, during the summer and fall of 1911, had unceremoniously rebuffed several offers of support Hearst had made. Wilson refused to have anything to do with the yellow journalist; he had nothing but contempt and scorn for him. [141] "Tell Mr. Hearst to go to hell," was his remark on one occasion; [142] on another he declared, "God knows I want the Democratic presidential nomination and I am going to do everything legitimately to get it, but if I am to grovel at Hearst's feet, I will never have it." [143]

Early in the fall of 1911, Hearst intimated that he would probably support Clark in the presidential contest, [144] but it was not until January 29, 1912, that he opened his tremendous campaign for Clark's nomination and Wilson's defeat. Then, day after day, his newspapers in New York, Boston, Atlanta, Chicago, San Francisco, and Los Angeles emblazoned on their front pages Wilson's uncomplimentary opinion of southern and eastern Europeans. The irate protests of various Polish-, Italian-, and Hungarian-American societies throughout the country were glorified and made front-page headline stories. [145]

On March 14 Hearst gave to the newspapers a long statement explaining why he was opposing Wilson's nomination. "Professor" Wilson (he delighted in calling Wilson "Professor"), he declared, was a Federalist who distrusted the people, a Tory, a modern Judas. "To my mind," he concluded, "he is a perfect jackrabbit of politics, perched upon his little hillock of expediency, with ears erect and nostrils dis-

---

[139] *History of the American People*, v, 212-213.

[140] *ibid.*, v, 213.

[141] Undated MS memorandum of Frank P. Glass in Baker Papers; F. P. Stockbridge, "How Woodrow Wilson Won His Nomination," *Current History*, xx (July 1924), 570.

[142] S. Axson to R. S. Baker, August 29, 1928, Baker Papers.

[143] Undated MS memorandum of F. P. Glass, *ibid.*

[144] *Chicago Examiner*, September 26, 1911.

[145] See, e.g., *New York American*, January 29, February 2 and 10, March 4, 13, and 25, 1912.

tended, keenly alert to every scent or sound and ready to run and double in any direction." [146]

So the Hearst attack of ridicule, scorn, and contempt went merrily on during the spring of 1912.[147] It mattered little to the readers of the Hearst newspapers and magazines that practically all of the so-called respectable press recoiled in disgust at Hearst's "yellow" attacks,[148] that the mayor of New York publicly denounced him as a "hog" who wanted to "get the hobnails of his shoes" into Wilson's flesh.[149] The men who read Hearst editorials in New York, Boston, Atlanta,[150] Chicago, Los Angeles, and San Francisco[151] voted—and, for the most part, voted against Wilson in the presidential primaries.

The practical results of the Hearst campaign against Wilson will be discussed in the following chapter. Perhaps it is sufficient to conclude this discussion of Hearst's anti-Wilson campaign by quoting the following typical editorial:

"Governor Wilson, of New Jersey—he is at home in his own State just now, for a change—asks the citizens [of New Jersey] to give him

[146] *Washington Post,* March 14, 1912.

[147] The most abusive attack to come out of the Hearst press was Alfred Henry Lewis' "The Real Woodrow Wilson," *Hearst's Magazine,* xxi (May 1912), 2265-2274, which every student of campaign literature should examine.

[148] "There is no dirtier owner of power in the world than Hearst," declared the publisher's chief editorial antagonist. "He loves the word 'Judas'—he of the Hughes overnight change, the Harriman deal in California, the sale of editorials, the poisoning and defrauding of the poor, the tricky and dishonorable methods of the Star Corporation. . . . Hearst is a snob for money, a defamer for profit. His mere wealth, enabling him to purchase numberless newspapers and magazines, gives him a mighty power, which he uses every year more relentlessly for his personal ambition. Now Clark is his beneficiary, Wilson his obstacle and therefore the target of his dirt." *Collier's Weekly,* xlix (May 25, 1912), 8.

[149] William J. Gaynor to W. W., March 6, 1912, published in *New York World,* March 13, 1912.

[150] Early in 1912 Hearst bought the *Atlanta Georgian* from Fred L. Seeley, an ardent Wilson supporter, and sent one of his editors, John Temple Graves, to Atlanta to carry on the fight against Wilson. Graves effectively executed the will of his master. Within a few days after taking charge of the *Georgian,* Graves had convicted "the Professor" of being a Federalist, anti-Jeffersonian and anti-Jacksonian, an enemy of Jews and foreigners, a party traitor, and an ingrate to his friends. See, e.g., *Atlanta Georgian,* March 27, 1912.

[151] In 1912 Hearst owned the following newspapers: the *New York American, New York Evening Journal, Das Morgen Journal* of New York, *Boston American, Chicago American, Chicago Examiner, Atlanta Georgian, San Francisco Examiner,* and *Los Angeles Examiner.* See Oliver Carlson and Ernest Sutherland Bates, *Hearst, Lord of San Simeon,* pp. 284-285.

their votes tomorrow at the primaries and declares that he ought to be President of the United States.

"Woodrow Wilson will not be nominated by the Democrats. It is safe to predict that.

"And it is safe to predict that Woodrow Wilson will not get many votes in New Jersey tomorrow—excepting votes whose owners favor Chinese labor.

"Professor Wilson is on record as an advocate of Chinese labor. He has declared over his own signature that he considers the Chinaman, with all his vices, preferable to white immigrants from Southern Europe —Italians, Hungarians, Poles, et cetera. . . .

"Railroads are backing Wilson—naturally.

"Professor Wilson vetoed the bill that would have compelled the railroads to do away with grade crossings. . . .

"The railroads want Governor Wilson for President, of course; they also want Chinese labor.

"If the railroads could have Woodrow Wilson in the White House and a million Chinese laborers, as a starter, to work for them, it would be a very fine combination.

"Woodrow Wilson would, as President, protect them against legislation in favor of the people." [152]

Nothing disturbed Wilson during the pre-convention campaign as greatly as did Hearst's attacks. Several times he was goaded into replying to the New York demagogue,[153] but for the most part he was concerned with halting the overwhelming tide of opposition to his candidacy that developed among the foreign-born voters as a result of Hearst's campaign.

The Polish, Italian, and Hungarian groups in New York and Chicago, particularly, were up in arms in protest against Wilson's candidacy. "As Mr. Wilson has shown that he is narrow and unjust in his attitude toward the Poles . . . ," reads a resolution adopted by the United Polish Societies of Manhattan, "we, Polish American citizens of the United Polish Societies, strongly and unanimously oppose his possible nomination." [154] Polish priests, one account declared, were admonishing their parishioners in New York to vote against Wilson. "What he says is an insult to the white race," declared the Reverend John H. Strzelecki of St. Stanislaw's Church.[155] Italian- and Hungarian-American organizations were just as vociferous in their opposition to Wilson as were the Polish-American groups. The Italian-American Civic Union of New York, for example, on February 6 adopted a resolution opposing Wilson's nomination because his writings had revealed "a prejudiced and narrow mind of very limited intelligence," [156] while the Italian-Americans in Chicago were even more outspoken in their protests.[157] Wilson's opinion of Hungarian immigrants, declared one leader of that nationality in New York, was "not only a gross libel on our people, but an insult, wanton and gratuitous." [158] These examples of mass protest, provoked by the foreign-language press, demagogic politicians, and by the Hearst press could be multiplied a hundredfold. A few editors of foreign-language newspapers—Joseph A. Di Silvestro of *La Voce del Popolo* of Philadelphia and Alphonse Chrostowski of the *Jutrzenka* of New York, for example—supported Wilson, but they were rare exceptions.

Wilson made desperate attempts to explain away his derogatory comments upon southern and eastern Europeans, to overcome the opposition of these groups to his candidacy. Day in and day out he wrote letters to Polish-, Italian-, and Hungarian-American leaders professing his great admiration of and love for the "new" immigrants. To an Italian-American editor he wrote:

"I beg that you will judge the passage in Volume v, of my 'History of the American People,' to which you allude, in connection with its full context, and not by itself.[159] I yield to no one in my ardent admiration for the great people of Italy, and certainly no one who loves the history of liberty should fail to accord to Italians a great place in the history of political freedom.

"I should be very much pained if I thought I had been guilty of an injustice. I was, in the passage alluded to, only deploring the coming to this country of certain lawless elements which I had supposed all thoughtful Italians themselves deplored. I was thinking only of the men who have once and again threatened to give to that whole, fine body of Italians, who have enriched American life, a reputation which they did not deserve. Certainly, the Italians I have known and honored have con-

---

[155] *New York American*, January 29, 1912.
[156] *ibid.*, February 10, 1912.   [157] *ibid.*, March 4, 13, 1912.
[158] *ibid.*, February 2, 1912.
[159] This was one of Wilson's stock-in-trade answers. Reading the derogatory passages in their "full context" does not change their meaning.

stituted one of the most interesting and admirable elements in our American life." [160]

To the Poles and Hungarians Wilson wrote in a similar vein. "I yield to no one in my admiration of the Polish character," he wrote on one occasion. "I have received the greatest stimulation from my reading of Polish history.[!] If my terms were too sweeping they must be attributed to my clumsiness in expressing myself." [161] In a letter to another Polish-American leader, Wilson declared that he had referred in his *History* only to laborers who were brought to America under contract.[162]

It is difficult to believe that Wilson was really sincere in these fawning letters. Had he straightforwardly admitted that he was mistaken when he wrote the passages in 1902 and that subsequent events and experience had convinced him of his error, he might have convinced more persons of his sincerity. Instead he endeavored to prove that he had not meant what he had written in 1902, with the result that he satisfied the complaints of few of the organizations of foreign-born voters.

The climax in Wilson's great apology came when a Polish-American group in New York suggested that he have an "erratum slip," retracting his derogatory remarks, inserted in the unsold copies of his *History;* that he rewrite the passages in the next edition of the work; and that he make a public apology to Americans of Polish, Italian, and Hungarian birth and descent.[163] There was a time when Wilson would have hastened to rebuke such "impudence"; now, however, he was a politician and quaffed the bitter draught. Ignoring two of the requests, he replied, "I think with you that it would be best for me at the earliest possible moment to rewrite the passage referred to in my history. I shall get into communication with my publishers and ascertain the feasibility of doing this at an early date." [164] He was as good as his word and wrote at once to Harper & Brothers, asking if a new printing of the fifth volume of his *History* was to be made soon. If so, he added, there were one or two passages in the volume that he would like to reconsider and rewrite

[160] W. W. to Joseph A. Di Silvestro, published in *Trenton True American*, April 5, 1912.

[161] W. W. to F. Ignatius Drobinski, February 7, 1912, published in *New York Sun*, February 10, 1912.

[162] W. W. to N. L. Piotrowski, March 13, 1912, published in A. S. Bacon, *The Enemies of Woodrow Wilson* (pamphlet, 1912), pp. 9-10.

[163] F. I. Drobinski to W. W., February 29, 1912, published in *New York American*, March 25, 1912.

[164] W. W. to F. I. Drobinski, March —, 1912, published in *ibid.*

in order to remove the false impressions which they seemed to have made.[165]

The most important cause of the opposition of the foreign-born voters to Wilson's candidacy was their fear that should Wilson be president he would encourage legislation to restrict immigration. Wilson said nothing about his immigration views, but his managers endeavored to convince the foreign-born voters that he was, from their point of view, sound on the issue. Fortunately for his cause, Wilson had joined the movement against immigration restriction in 1906, and the testimony of the president of the National Liberal Immigration League of New York in Wilson's favor was spread among the foreign-born groups by the Wilson supporters.[166]

Hearst's attack was deadly enough, to be sure, but in one respect it failed utterly. He and the other campaigners for Clark agitated to swing the forces of organized labor against the Wilson movement, but for once they were checkmated. As soon as the anti-Wilson forces began their attack upon Wilson's labor views, the executive committee of the New Jersey State Federation of Labor adopted a ringing declaration approving Wilson's gubernatorial administration and declaring, "Organized labor would be derelict in its duty if it allowed to pass this opportunity to show appreciation for services rendered the workers of New Jersey." [167] Copies of the resolution were sent to every labor organization in the country, we may be sure.[168]

Notwithstanding Hearst's vagaries and the skill of his attack, there was one other editor who surpassed him in the art of abusing, vilifying,

---

[165] W. W. to Harper & Brothers, March 4, 1912, copy in Baker Papers.

[166] "In 1906," Edward Lauterbach, president of the League, wrote, "when the Senate voted unanimously for the anti-immigration bill, . . . and when in the House the overwhelming majority was for restriction, and throughout the land a great agitation was going on against immigration, Governor Wilson consented to be one of the directors of the National Liberal Immigration League, lending to our cause his aid and influence. . . . As a member of the General and Educational Committees, his Excellency has stood with us through all our fights against numerous anti-immigration bills, and in our efforts at proper distribution of immigrants and labor, and certainly the League owes much of its uninterrupted success to the influence of Governor Wilson." E. Lauterbach to I. L. Bril, April 23, 1912, printed copy in Burleson Papers.

It should be pointed out, however, that Wilson's action here described was not necessarily a sign of liberalism on his part. The American Federation of Labor had demanded immigration restriction, and Wilson's desire for unlimited entry might well have been motivated by his then pro-manufacturer, anti-labor sentiments.

[167] *Trenton True American*, February 14, 1912.

[168] There is a printed copy of the resolution, issued in pamphlet form by the Wilson headquarters, in the Wilson Papers.

and misrepresenting Wilson. He was Thomas E. Watson of Georgia, one of the original Underwood men, an old-time Populist and ex-radical who had grown increasingly bitter as the years passed. By 1912 the special objects of his hatred were Negroes, Catholics, Jews, Hoke Smith, and Woodrow Wilson. It seems that he, too, first conceived his hatred of Wilson after reading his *History of the American People.* "His own books are responsible for my deep-seated dislike of him," Watson wrote to a friend.[169] "JUDGED BY HIS BOOK, THE NORTH WAS HIS LOVE, NOT THE SOUTH," Watson wrote in his weekly magazine.[170] "He neglected and spat upon the South." [171]

Another cause of Watson's anti-Wilson ardor was his dread that should Wilson be President, the Roman Catholic Church would control the federal government. Tumulty, after all, was a Catholic, and that proved "what a tool of Rome . . . [Wilson] would be in the White House." [172] Wilson's treatment of Negroes as human beings also aroused Watson's intense wrath. Watson fulminated because Wilson addressed Negroes "in the same way he would address you or any other distinguished white man," [173] because he had allegedly sent Booker T. Washington a message of condolence "WHEN THAT COON WAS CAUGHT AT A WHITE WOMAN'S BED-ROOM DOOR, AND WAS DESERVEDLY BEATEN FOR IT." [174] Watson charged, moreover, that Wilson was a Hamiltonian, an enemy of the farmers and workingmen,[175] a confirmed Wall Street candidate, *"backed by Wall Street money,"* [176] an "arrant liar," and a "hide-bound Tory." [177] "Can any of these statements be disputed?" he asked. The answer, obviously, was: "Not one." [178]

[169] T. E. Watson to W. J. Jelks, December 21, 1912, Thomas E. Watson Papers, Library of the University of North Carolina; hereinafter cited as Watson Papers.

[170] *Jeffersonian* (Thomson, Georgia), April 18, 1912.

[171] *ibid.,* April 25, 1912.   [172] *ibid.,* April 4, 1912.

[173] T. E. Watson to W. J. Jelks, December 21, 1912, Watson Papers.

[174] *Jeffersonian,* April 11, 1912.   [175] *ibid.,* April 4, 1912.

[176] *ibid.,* April 11, 1912.   [177] *ibid.,* February 8, 1912.

[178] *ibid.,* April 11, 1912. Watson's line of attack was used against Wilson in Texas. During the pre-convention campaign in that state, E. A. Glenn of Bowling Green, Missouri, head of the Clark central office at Fort Worth, had a printer strike off 15,000 copies of a circular entitled "The Nigger and the Governor of New Jersey." T. B. Love to E. M. House, May 5, 1912, House Papers. Love gave conclusive evidence that it was the Clark manager who had the pamphlet printed and distributed. One quotation reveals the offensiveness of the malicious sheet: "When that arrogant nigger, Booker Washington," was caught at a white woman's door and was beaten by a white man, "Woodrow Wilson was one of four asinine celebrities to telegraph consolation and confidence to the nigger." Published in *Dallas Morning News,* May 2, 1912. The Wilson managers in Texas scotched the rumor by securing a telegram from Wilson which declared that he had sent no such message to Washington.

It is impossible to survey the extent of the widespread whispering campaign that was carried on against Wilson by his opponents. Perhaps a few examples of this line of attack will suffice. In the primary campaign in Wisconsin, the German-Americans of Milwaukee were told that Wilson was a prohibitionist; Wilson's shilly-shallying evasion on this issue, however, was largely responsible for these rumors.[179] Suffragettes were against him because he refused to commit himself on the question of woman suffrage.[180] In Irish-American communities like Boston, it was whispered that Wilson was "narrow and bigoted" in religious matters. During the pre-convention campaign in Illinois the report was spread about that Wilson could not enter a restaurant without quarreling with the waiter, and seldom got on a streetcar without reprimanding the conductor![181]

Wilson's reaction to these multiform attacks was one of disappointment and chagrin. Thus he wrote to Gaynor on March 11, 1912: "Misrepresentation is the penalty which men in public life must expect in the course of their effort to render service. The unfortunate fact is that there are probably hundreds of men in America of first rate intellectual

[179] Wilson had written a letter to the Reverend Thomas B. Shannon of New Jersey on May 1, 1911 (mimeographed copy in the Wilson Papers), declaring that he was wholeheartedly in favor of local option, but that he believed the liquor question was entirely social and moral and should never be made a political question. This doctrine was tolerable to northern Democrats and undoubtedly represented Wilson's view of the matter.

When, however, a Texas correspondent demanded to know what he thought of prohibition as a political question, he responded in a different fashion entirely. After all, his supporters in Texas were for the most part ardent prohibitionists, and it would not be politic to offend them. "You mistook me, if you thought that I was treating your first letter as the communication of a politician," he wrote to E. W. Grogan of Byars, Texas on June 6, 1911, "or if you supposed that I was trying in any way to avoid the important question you put to me.

"The reply I made, was made in all sincerity. I believe that for some states, state wide prohibition is possible and desirable, because of their relative homogeneity, while for others, I think that state wide prohibition is not practicable.

"I have no reason to doubt from what I know of the circumstances, that state wide prohibition is both practicable and desirable in Texas."

Unfortunately for Wilson, his letter fell into the hands of the newspapermen and his opponents used it against him in northern cities like Milwaukee. McCombs's reply when the letter was published was that it was a "trick of Wall Street." See *New York Times,* January 8, 1912, for a copy of the letter and a detailed account of the unfortunate repercussions of the letter.

[180] See, e.g., the exchange of correspondence between Wilson and Edith M. Whitmore, published in *New York Sun,* February 10, 1912.

[181] Dudley Field Malone, "Woodrow Wilson—the Man," *National Monthly,* IV (September 1912), 91.

force, of genuine public spirit and broad patriotism, who would be of immeasurable value to public service, but who are deterred from entering it because they shrink from this particular penalty. They prefer to pursue private careers, rather than expose themselves and their families to unfounded criticism and attack, and the country is thereby impoverished. Such attacks, moreover, create personal feeling and party factions, which render the task of government infinitely difficult for anyone who undertakes it. It is the more necessary, however, as I look at it, that these things should be borne with fortitude, if not indifference, in order that our duty may be rendered without regard to our personal feeling." [182]

In a letter to Edith Gittings Reid he revealed more intimately his feelings about the anti-Wilson campaign: "Everybody over here seems to agree that there has never been a Campaign in which there was such a systematic and malevolent attempt to destroy a man's reputation for character and intellectual integrity as has been made by my opponents all over the country, including the representatives of the other Candidates for the Democratic nomination, and in such circumstances one *needs* to hear the voice of true and loyal friends to keep him in heart.

"Not that I actually lose heart. I find I am of too firm a fibre, and of too firm a faith, for that; but the world grows sometimes to seem so brutal, so naked of beauty, so devoid of chivalrous sentiment and all sense of fair play, that one's own spirit hardens and is in danger of losing its fineness. I fight on, in the spirit of Kipling's 'If', but that is oftentimes a very arid air." [183]

[182] Published in the *New York World*, March 13, 1912.
[183] May 26, 1912, published in R. S. Baker, *Woodrow Wilson*, III, 316.

Collapse of the Wilson Movement

"IT BEGINS now to 'look like business.' I like it less than I did before," wrote Woodrow Wilson six days after the inauguration of the Democratic pre-convention campaign at the Jackson Day Dinner.[1] His managers, however, were filled with high hopes and optimism on the eve of the epic battle. To all appearances, Wilson was far and away the strongest contender for the Democratic presidential nomination. There seemed, in fact, to be slight doubt that he would enter the Baltimore convention with a majority of the delegates, and it was a matter of some speculation among political observers whether Clark, Underwood, and Harmon could prevent Wilson's nomination by a two-thirds majority on the first ballot.[2]

The results of the nine months' campaign ending January 8, 1912, had been altogether gratifying. Wilson had won the support of a number of the most influential magazines and newspapers in the country:

---

[1] W. W. to M. A. Hulbert, January 14, 1912, published in R. S. Baker, *Woodrow Wilson*, III, 267.

[2] In the fall of 1911 Colonel House began a quiet campaign to obtain the abrogation of the two-thirds rule at the Baltimore convention. The conservatives, he wrote to Bryan, meant to use the rule to block the nomination of a progressive, presumably Wilson. E. M. House to W. J. Bryan, October 25, 1911, House Papers. McCombs thought House's suggestion was splendid, and promised that the Wilson organization would push the idea of abrogating the rule vigorously. E. M. House to T. W. Gregory, October 31, 1911, *ibid*. House and McCombs thought that if the two-thirds rule were abrogated Wilson would easily be nominated on the first ballot, and a long convention fight might thereby be forestalled. Wilson, too, was convinced that the two-thirds rule was "a most undemocratic regulation," and expressed these sentiments to House. W. W. to E. M. House, October 24, 1911, *ibid*.

The Washington correspondent of the *New York Times* wrote on January 5 that the Wilson managers were carrying on a quiet campaign to obtain the abrogation of the two-thirds rule. McCombs, the report continued, would present the matter before the national committee; and if he was defeated in his attempt to obtain the endorsement of the national committeemen for the abrogation of the rule, he would carry the fight to the floor of the convention. *New York Times*, January 6, 1912.

Needless to say, the movement was immediately abandoned when it became apparent that Wilson would not control a majority of the delegates at Baltimore. Had House and McCombs been successful in obtaining the abrogation of the two-thirds rule, they would have made Champ Clark's nomination inevitable!

World's Work, Outlook, Independent, the *Nation, Review of Reviews,* for example, among the magazines; or, among the newspapers, the *New York Evening Post, Philadelphia Record, Cleveland Plain Dealer, Baltimore Sun, Kansas City Star, Raleigh News and Observer,* and the entire Scripps chain of thirty-four newspapers in sixteen states.

Just as encouraging, especially from Wilson's point of view, had been the support that church magazines and religious leaders had given his candidacy. Not only Presbyterian leaders, but Methodists, Episcopalians, and Baptists as well were behind the Wilson movement.[3] Wilson, it should be remembered, had succeeded in identifying the progressive movement with Christian righteousness and in providing a solid moral foundation for reform. It was not surprising, therefore, that religious journals described him as "the Christian in politics," whose life was patterned "after the Perfect Man," [4] or that preachers over the country declared that the Almighty had chosen him to lead the American people.

Moreover, the enthusiasm for Wilson's candidacy that swept through educational circles had been little short of phenomenal. Educational leaders, from universities and country schools, were playing an important role in the movement, while the caustic remarks of anti-Wilson editors, which reflected on Wilson's political availability because he had been a teacher, drove thousands of teachers into the Wilson ranks. "We resent," declared the president of the University of North Carolina in a typical statement, "the sneering use of . . . [the term 'school teacher'] with the implication that because we are teachers we are unfit for other service." [5] The important part that teachers played in the presidential campaign should not be underrated. As a general rule, teachers are inclined to eschew the hurly-burly of political campaigns; often they contemn the sordidness of "practical politics" or feel themselves intellectually superior to the politician; more often teachers are very discreet politicians themselves and carefully avoid offending the dominant local or state organizations. At all events, the pre-convention campaign brought the nation's teachers forward to lend their support to the candidacy of the "scholar in politics," and from Maine to California they took up the cudgels for Wilson.[6]

[3] See, e.g., the Rev. Dr. George Chalmers Richmond of Philadelphia, quoted in *St. Louis Republic,* December 25, 1911; the Rev. Dr. Len G. Broughton of Atlanta, quoted in *Raleigh News and Observer,* April 2, 1912; also *Presbyterian Standard* (Charlotte, N. C.), March 24, 1911, April 24 and July 17, 1912; *Presbyterian of the South* (Richmond, Va.), February 8, 1911.

[4] *Christian Advocate* (Nashville, Tenn.), March 8, 1912.

[5] Francis P. Venable, statement in the *Raleigh News and Observer,* March 23, 1912.

[6] In the pre-convention fight in Oklahoma, for example, Senator Thomas P. Gore, Wilson's manager in that state, found his strongest allies among the country school-

College students, too, were up in arms for Wilson. Clean-cut, moralistic, a courageous leader of men, Wilson appealed to the youthful idealism of college students at a time when the Y.M.C.A. movement was at its height and its motto was "The evangelization of the world in our generation." An upsurge of enthusiasm prompted students at the University of South Carolina and the University of Virginia to organize the Woodrow Wilson League of College Men in November 1911.[7] By the following January, the League had affiliated clubs throughout the country at Harvard, Yale, Columbia, Wisconsin, Chicago, North Carolina, and other universities; by June, 1912, the League counted over 100 branch organizations that enrolled some 10,000 students. Campus polls at Oberlin, the University of North Carolina, and other colleges revealed that Wilson was practically the unanimous choice of students and faculty for the presidency.

Democratic politicians had their ears to the ground and could scarcely ignore the groundswell of pro-Wilson sentiment. To be sure, few conservative Democratic leaders had aligned themselves with the Wilson movement, but most Democratic progressives in the East and the South had already done so, and the Wilson managers did not doubt that public opinion would quickly force the recalcitrants into line. It was all invigorating and refreshing to Wilson and his supporters.

At the time the Harvey affair was exploding in the newspapers, Wilson opened the second phase of his pre-nomination campaign by making a tour through Michigan. He spoke three times in Detroit and twice in Grand Rapids, and for the most part his speeches consisted of commonplace homilies addressed to chambers of commerce and ladies' literary clubs. However, at Detroit on January 18 he deviated from his usual campaign appeal and broached for the first time the economic philosophy that was later to be symbolized by the title of the "New Freedom." The Detroit address was a faint indication of that radical shift from political to economic issues that was to come later in the course of the presidential campaign.[8] During the remainder of the pre-convention campaign, however, Wilson did not further pursue the will-o'-the-wisp New Freedom appeal.

---

teachers who, he later declared, "won the fight for me." T. P. Gore to A. S. Link, August 15, 1942. The reader will recall T. W. Gregory's statement that the support of the 40,000 rural school teachers in Texas was instrumental in carrying that state for Wilson.

[7] For an account of the organization of the Woodrow Wilson League of College Men, see the *Columbia State*, November 16, 1911.

[8] *Detroit Free Press*, January 19, 1912.

By January 21 Wilson was back in Trenton, where the legislature was now in session. New Jersey politics and problems of state, however, were now receiving scant attention from the governor. On January 27 he opened his New England campaign with speeches in Boston and Cambridge.[9] A few days later Wilson made a full scale invasion of Virginia, taking with him McCombs, Stuart Gibboney, a Virginian working in the Wilson headquarters, Dudley Field Malone, and Walter Measday, his press agent.[10] Wilson's visit to Richmond[11] was the occasion for the organization of the Wilson movement in Virginia on a state-wide basis. Everyone knew that the dominant Martin-Swanson organization had already undertaken to defeat the Wilson movement in Virginia, but Wilson's friends were optimistic, and Richard E. Byrd, speaker of the House of Delegates and formerly one of Martin's chief lieutenants, agreed to lead the Wilson forces.[12] It would be a supreme tragedy, Wilson's friends thought, should his native state refuse to support his candidacy at Baltimore.

The following day Wilson hurried to Philadelphia to speak before the annual banquet of the Periodical Publishers' Association. Arriving in the city late in the afternoon, he had only a few minutes in which to write out the bare outlines of his speech. An imposing array of publishers, writers, and public leaders gathered at the Bellevue-Stratford Hotel for the affair; Senator Robert M. La Follette, Mayor Rudolph Blankenburg of Philadelphia, Cyrus H. K. Curtis, publisher of the *Saturday Evening Post* and president of the association, and William J. Burns, the famous detective, had also been invited to speak.

Wilson was in rare oratorical form. "He spoke with flawless art," one of the listeners afterward wrote; "his dignity and upstanding presence commanded attention, while his voice made every symmetrical sentence melodious. The whole company, easily eight hundred men, sat under the spell."[13] Wilson's address was a brief, but fairly inclusive summary of the objectives progressives were fighting for.[14] It was another of his prose poems that were by now becoming hackneyed; but

---

[9] *Boston Post*, January 28, 1912.

[10] *Richmond Times-Dispatch*, February 2, 1912.

[11] For a colorful description of the affair see the *Staunton News-Dispatch*, February 2, 1912. Wilson's address, which was the most notable of his southern pre-convention campaign, is printed in the *Public Papers*, II, 367-388.

[12] *Norfolk Virginian-Pilot*, February 2, 1912; *Richmond Times-Dispatch*, February 2, 1912; *Staunton Dispatch News*, February 3, 1912.

[13] Owen Wister, *Roosevelt, the Story of a Friendship*, p. 299.

[14] The address is printed in the *Philadelphia North American*, February 3, 1912.

he received a great ovation from the audience, and the newspapers the following morning agreed that the affair had been a Wilson triumph.[15]

After his Philadelphia speech of February 2, Wilson increased the tempo of his campaign addresses to an unusual degree. He spoke in Allentown, Pennsylvania, on February 7; two days later he was in Frankfort, Kentucky, to speak before the General Assembly of that state.[16] A week later, on February 15, Wilson traveled to Concord, New Hampshire, where he was lionized by the leading Democratic politicians in the state.[17] On February 17 he returned to Philadelphia and spoke at a peace rally held by the Universal Peace Union.[18]

In the latter part of February, Wilson set out upon a long tour that took him by a circuitous route to Kansas, Tennessee, and Iowa. In answer to an urgent call for help from his Kansas managers and at McCombs's prompting, he went first to Topeka, where he spoke before a gathering of more than 1,000 Democratic leaders at the Masonic Hall on February 22.[19] It was truly an ovation that he received at the hands of the Kansas Democrats.[20] Wilson left Kansas and arrived next in

[15] See, e.g., the *Philadelphia Record,* February 3, 1912. What was, at least temporarily, Wilson's apotheosis turned out to be La Follette's nemesis. La Follette was exhausted by labor and by anxiety for the life of a daughter who was desperately ill; given the last place on the speaker's list, he launched into a long and bitter tirade against the money trust and the newspapers and magazine publishers. La Follette's performance immediately gave rise to rumors that he had suffered a breakdown; these rumors were the excuse that Theodore Roosevelt used for discarding La Follette's candidacy and announcing his own. La Follette, it should be noted, had generously boosted Wilson's candidacy at the Philadelphia banquet. "If a Democrat is to be elected the next president of the United States," he declared, "I hope it will be Woodrow Wilson." *Philadelphia North American,* February 3, 1912.

[16] *Louisville Courier-Journal,* February 10, 1912. In Kentucky Wilson found a discouraging political situation; the Wilson movement had made practically no headway there because the Democratic party was split wide open over the liquor question.

[17] *Boston Post,* February 16, 1912.

[18] *Philadelphia North American,* February 19, 1912.

[19] Kansas had been one of the early strongholds of Wilson enthusiasm. When a group of Democratic leaders, for example, gathered in Topeka in September 1911 to discuss state and national politics, every man at the conference reported that the Democrats in his county were unanimously behind Wilson's candidacy. *Kansas City Star,* September 13, 1911. The rise of Clark's candidacy had of course drawn away from Wilson the support of a number of Kansas Democrats, yet a competent observer declared on February 22, 1912, that Wilson would find the Democratic party in the state almost solidly united in his support. The progressive Democratic leaders in Kansas, Fred Robertson, T. M. Anderson, J. J. Parker, J. W. Howe, and C. F. Foley, outnumbered the Clark leaders three to one. Henderson Martin, the chairman of the state Democratic committee, was leading the Wilson campaign in the state. *ibid.,* February 22, 1912.

[20] For Wilson's speech and an account of the affair see the *Topeka State Journal,* February 23, 1912.

Nashville, Tennessee, on February 24.[21] Five days later he was in Des Moines, Iowa, the guest of the Iowa Wilson League, to make his only speech in the state during the pre-convention campaign. Over 4,000 persons crowded the Des Moines Coliseum on March 1 to hear the eastern candidate for the presidency.

It was a straightforward, progressive speech that Wilson made at Des Moines, one of the best of his winter campaign, and the knowledge that many of his listeners were insurgent Republicans caused him to direct his appeal chiefly to them. "We are brothers in principle," he told them, declaring that the only difference between progressive Republicans and himself was that "You speak of a protective policy with a certain air of piety and I don't." He again professed his confidence in the initiative, referendum, and recall as useful tools of democracy and proclaimed his belief in the principle of direct election of United States senators. "We recognize in the Senate of the United States," he added acidly, "a seat of privilege." In perhaps his clearest pronouncement on the progressive movement during the pre-nomination campaign, he thus continued:

"We have come to a point in our affairs as a nation at which we should speak as citizens rather than as partisans, on real thoughts about things as they are and about the way in which they should be dealt with. In November we shall . . . make a choice of parties, but let us determine that we will make that choice upon the facts and not upon prejudice or upon ancient prepossessions.

"The country is not astir over anything. The agitation of its thought is not due to busy demagogues, but to the circumstances of its life which it is coming more and more fully to realize and for which it is bound to hold somebody in particular responsible.

"The fact is, however you may explain it, that special interests have

[21] He found the pre-convention outlook in Tennessee exceedingly gloomy. The Democratic party in the state had been completely disrupted by the prohibition issue. So bitter was the conflict within the party that in 1910 the prohibition-progressives, led by Luke Lea and R. M. Barton, had seceded *en masse* from the party, had organized the Independent Democratic party, and had helped to elect Ben W. Hooper, a progressive Republican, governor. In spite of its promising beginning, the Wilson movement had made no appreciable headway in Tennessee because of factional politics. Wilson's candidacy had been espoused wholeheartedly by the Independent Democrats and their spokesmen, the *Nashville Tennessean and American, Nashville Banner,* and *Knoxville Sentinel;* and the old-line Democrats who controlled the regular party machinery, suspicious of any candidate who had the support of their mortal enemies, had come out in support of Clark, Underwood, or Harmon. For a discussion of the Tennessee situation, see A. S. Link, "Tennessee Politics and the Presidential Campaign of 1912," *East Tennessee Historical Society's Proceedings,* 1946.

been built up and fortified and that the common interest has suffered; that monopoly has been established among us; that monopoly has been buttressed by law and that those who have created the monopolies have been more influential at our state capitols and at Washington than the people have been at the polls. . . .

"It is plain how special interests got their control; they got it by determining which party they should support. The Republican party, ever since the Civil War, has had a great ascendancy in this country, but its ascendancy was established at an earlier time and upon services which had nothing to do with the questions which confront us now. No man can claim that its greatness has arisen out of the actions or traditions of the last sixteen years. It is during these years that the real control at its command has been made manifest. Iowa was one of the first states in which Republicans themselves began to perceive what had happened and to assert themselves, as men of free minds and unpurchased purpose, to swing their party round to another course.

"But have they succeeded? . . . Look at the tariff question! . . . The question of monopoly and special privilege undoubtedly centers in the tariff. That is the nest where the brood is hatched. That is the great and inexhaustible source of special advantage. Competition has been checked, discouraged and, in some cases, actually shut out. The masters of American industry are the masters of the country. . . .

"There are other affirmative things to do. . . . Who shall do these things? I ask you candidly, can you expect the Republican organization even under new leadership to do these things within our immediate decade? Can you expect them to pull up roots that are a generation deep? Can you expect them to cut every thread of intimate connection that has bound them to the financial world where the great plans have been made that have bound us as with cords? For my own part, I do not think it is reasonable to expect it, and I do not." [22]

Wilson returned to Trenton from Iowa on March 3; five days later he went to Annapolis to speak before the Maryland legislature.[23] The following evening he concluded his winter campaign tour with a powerful speech before the Brooklyn League. His address was a hodgepodge of what he had been saying during the past six months, but he seemed now more than ever concerned with the problems of social welfare and human happiness. He was afraid that the end of the frontier era had meant that America's "seething millions" would turn upon

[22] *Des Moines Register and Leader*, March 2, 1912.
[23] *Baltimore Sun*, March 9, 1912.

themselves and the cauldron of society would grow "hotter and hotter." "We have got to get a *modus vivendi* in America for happiness," he asserted dramatically, "and that is our new problem." [24]

If, as Wilson asserted in his Brooklyn address, the people were to be "absolutely trusted" in political matters, he was about to witness the un-folding of an interesting experiment in political democracy. The sover-eign voters of the Democratic party, either directly in presidential pref-erential primaries, or indirectly through their elected representatives in district and state conventions, were about to decide the fate of the pre-nomination contest and to determine the question of the leadership of the national party. The scramble for delegates was already under way in several states.

Missouri was the first state in which Democrats voted upon the presi-dential candidates. The story of the struggle in that state between former Governor Joseph W. Folk and Champ Clark for control of the Missouri delegation is somewhat complicated; but it is significant be-cause it decided the fate of the Clark presidential movement. In Septem-ber 1910, many months before the pre-convention battle had begun, a Democratic state convention, meeting at Jefferson City, had pledged the support of the Missouri Democracy to the presidential candidacy of reform Governor Joseph W. Folk.[25] Champ Clark, statesman from Pike County and representative from the ninth congressional district, was chairman of the convention that endorsed Folk's candidacy. There was little discussion of the presidential question in Missouri until the fall of 1911. Meanwhile, Clark had become speaker of the House; his ambi-tion had expanded enormously; and by the fall of 1911 he was an avowed candidate for the Democratic presidential nomination. Senator William J. Stone, affectionately known as "Gum Shoe Bill," first set off the Clark presidential boom by coming out in favor of Clark's nomina-tion.[26] A month later, in December, Clark supporters opened St. Louis and state headquarters for a campaign to win the support of the Mis-souri delegation for Clark's candidacy.[27]

As unexpected as it was unheralded, the rise of Champ Clark's can-didacy was the major political phenomenon of 1912. James Beauchamp Clark, born near Lawrenceburg, Kentucky, early dropped his baptismal name and adopted the abbreviated "Champ" by which he was known the rest of his life. Educated at the University of Kentucky and at Bethany College in West Virginia, he was subsequently a college presi-

[24] *Brooklyn Daily Eagle*, March 10, 1912.   [25] *St. Louis Republic*, September 15, 1910.
[26] *ibid.*, November 9, 1911.   [27] *ibid.*, December 5, 1911.

dent, lawyer, editor, and county prosecuting attorney. His first excursion into politics was as a member of the legislature of Missouri, where he had moved. Elected to the House of Representatives in 1892, he sat in that body until his death in 1921.[28] Long service in Congress inevitably gave Clark seniority among the Democratic members. For several years he was the lieutenant of John Sharp Williams, Democratic minority leader. During the Sixtieth Congress, 1907-1909, after Williams had been elected to the Senate, Clark succeeded to the leadership of his party in the House; when the Democratic Congress was organized in 1911 he was elected speaker.

During the high-tide of Bryanism, Clark was one of Bryan's most loyal disciples. He was a combination of Westerner and Southerner and had all the markings of an agrarian radical during the early Bryan period. On one occasion, for example, Clark condemned Cleveland for his stubborn stand against free silver, compared him to Judas and Benedict Arnold, and then apologized to these traitors for the infamy of the comparison![29] The Missourian was an old-fashioned Democrat, a strict party man, a free trader,[30] and of course an inveterate opponent of civil service reform;[31] on one occasion he had even advocated the abolition of the diplomatic corps.[32] He also had the dubious honor of being the only presidential candidate on record who had ever endorsed a patent medicine.[33] Even his habitual attire, his broad-brimmed black slouch hat and his long coat, bespoke the appearance of a country politician.

Clark's entrance into the presidential contest precipitated a bitter party struggle in Missouri. The Folk supporters, who claimed that the state Democracy was already committed to their candidate, charged that Clark was a "stalking horse" for Harmon, and that the Clark men would really vote for the Ohio governor at the Baltimore convention. "Joe Folk cannot lie in Missouri," Clark shot back.[34] Folk's managers, none the less, attempted to make the pre-convention contest in Missouri

[28] Except for the Fifty-fourth Congress (1895-1897), when he was defeated by a Republican landslide in his state in 1894.
[29] *Congressional Record*, 55th Cong., 2nd Sess. (May 3, 1898), 4539.
[30] *ibid.*, 53rd Cong., 2nd Sess. (January 15, 1894), 833.
[31] See *ibid.*, 53rd Cong., 2nd Sess. (July 14, 1894), 7499.
[32] *ibid.*, 55th Cong., 1st Sess. (March 31, 1897), 551.
[33] " 'At the end of the last campaign,' writes Champ Clark, Missouri's brilliant Congressman, 'from overwork, nervous tension, loss of sleep and constant speaking I had about utterly collapsed. It seemed that all the organs in my body were out of order, but three bottles of Electric Bitters made me all right. It's the best all-round medicine ever sold over a druggist's counter.' " Item in *Garland* (Tex.) *News*, April 5, 1901.
[34] *St. Louis Republic*, December 16, 1911.

a straight-out progressive-reactionary campaign. Clark, they asserted, was a reactionary and the candidate of reactionaries and machine politicians; Wilson, they admitted, was their second choice for president, and they declared that they would vote for him if Folk's nomination appeared impossible.[35]

The bitter struggle in Missouri was acutely embarrassing to Clark's managers, who were anxious to get a broad national movement started. Clark, however, obviously had first to demonstrate that he could command the support of his own state before organization politicians in the country at large would give him their support. Some immediate solution of the problem was necessary, for the Oklahoma state convention was to meet on February 22 and the Clark managers in that state were demanding that the speaker have the united support of the Missouri Democracy.

Bryan journeyed on a peace mission from Lincoln to St. Louis in January 1912, with the proposal that the Missouri delegation be evenly divided between the two contestants. The Clark managers, now certain of victory, unceremoniously rejected the olive branch.[36] The situation in St. Louis and Kansas City, where the city machines were solidly behind Clark, appeared so hopeless that Folk refused to enter the Democratic primaries in those cities.[37] He expected the rural voters to rally to his support, but when Clark carried the primaries in Hannibal and Palmyra, both rural counties, by decisive majorities on February 9, Folk withdrew from the contest altogether. Consequently, Clark had no opposition in the presidential primaries in Missouri on February 11, 1912.[38]

Early in February, national Clark headquarters had been established in Washington, with former Senator Fred T. DuBois of Idaho in command;[39] by the time Folk withdrew from the race in Missouri, efficient Clark organizations were already at work in Oklahoma, Kansas, Illinois, South Dakota, Colorado, Michigan, California, and Idaho. A month later Clark headquarters were established in Chicago and Arkansas.[40] It was largely a congressional movement; Clark's numerous friends in Congress over the years loyally rallied to his support and were leading his campaign in almost every state. Clark's managers were all seasoned, veteran politicians who had no hesitation in making bargains with machine leaders in the cities and states. Clark was first of all a

[35] *Kansas City Star,* January 25, 1912.
[37] *ibid.,* February 11, 1912.
[39] *St. Louis Republic,* February 14, 1912.
[40] *ibid.,* February 11, March 17, 1912.

[36] *St. Louis Republic,* January 29, 1912.
[38] *Kansas City Star,* February 11, 1912.

politician accustomed to dealing with his friends on a *quid pro quo* basis; it was not surprising, therefore, that machine leaders for the most part supported Clark rather than Wilson, the party bolter and machine smasher. As will be demonstrated later, this was true because Wilson had little to offer the organization men, not because the Wilson managers were any more scrupulous than the Clark managers.

Probably the most important factor in Clark's success as a presidential candidate was the support he received from William R. Hearst and his newspapers and magazines. There is no definite proof that the Clark-Hearst alliance was the result of a "deal" between the two men, but the evidence points strongly in the direction of some sort of agreement between them. Clark, after all, recognized Hearst as a leading Democratic spokesman; Hearst replied by contributing the support of his powerful newspapers and his personal fortune to the Clark movement.[41]

One other element of strength in Clark's candidacy has usually been ignored: he had the advantage of a consistent progressive record both in the Missouri legislature and in Congress. During his long public career he had never wavered in his opposition to railroad malpractices, monopolies, and tariff protection;[42] and if he was something of a party hack, if his name was not associated with any of the leading issues of 1912, if he was neither an aggressive leader nor an original thinker, he could at least point to a more consistent progressive record than Wilson or any other Democratic candidate could claim.[43]

[41] Hearst allegedly contributed $8,500 to the Clark pre-convention campaign fund, which totaled $45,948.98. Senator Clarence Watson of West Virginia, who contributed $10,000, was the chief contributor. Senator Stone contributed $5,200; Edward L. Doheny, afterwards implicated in the oil scandals of the Harding administration, gave $2,500. See *Campaign Contributions,* p. 774, testimony of Fred T. DuBois. DuBois' testimony is undoubtedly grossly inaccurate and incomplete, and for that reason we shall probably never know the total amount of contributions to the Clark fund. The *St. Louis Republic,* for example, raised $20,017 by popular subscriptions, and this amount was simply not reported by DuBois. There must have been many similar cases.

[42] See John E. Lathrop, "The Views of Champ Clark," *Outlook,* CI (May 11, 1912), 72; John T. Graves, "Speaker Champ Clark," *Independent,* LXXI (November 2, 1911), 959-962, for sympathetic examinations of Clark's record.

[43] cf., however, the following description by F. P. Stockbridge: "A human, likeable old gentleman, this member from Missouri—pleasant to talk with or to listen to, popular, magnetic, devoted to his books and his home and his family. . . . An interesting personality, that of Champ Clark—and if he has any conception of the vital, burning questions the American people are asking, any grasp on the issues and problems on which the voters of the nation are sharply divided . . . , any comprehension of the great readjustments that are going on across party lines as the Progressives and Conservatives are reclassifying themselves, one finds no evidence of it in his conversation or recorded speeches." "Champ Clark of Pike County," *World's Work,* XXIV (May, 1912), 36.

Clark was the surprise of the pre-convention campaign. Few political observers at first believed that he would even make a creditable showing in the primaries; at first Wilson's managers were inclined to laugh at his candidacy. What, then, is the explanation of Clark's success? First, he made the campaign upon a platform fully as progressive as Wilson's;[44] secondly, he succeeded in identifying himself in the West so completely with the Bryan tradition that he, not Wilson, became the legatee of the Bryan heritage in most states in the West. This was not the result of any commitment on Bryan's part; Bryan consistently declared that he believed Clark and Wilson were equally progressive and equally worthy of progressive support. It was, rather, the logical result of Clark's long association with and leadership of the Bryan wing of the party.

The rise of Clark's candidacy was an ominous sign of the hard struggle ahead for the Wilson managers. McCombs redoubled his efforts and attempted to draw closer the thinly scattered Wilson organizations throughout the country. In March he made a long tour through the South and conferred with Democratic leaders in Georgia, South Carolina, Florida, Louisiana, Mississippi, and Arkansas. From Little Rock he went to Chicago, where he conferred with Roger Sullivan, boss of the Illinois Democracy.[45] Shortly afterward he went to Kansas and again to Chicago and met with Wilson leaders in the Midwest. By April he had established close relations with the state Wilson organizations already in existence and had established organizations in many of the states in which there were no Wilson organizations.

During the early months of 1912 McCombs's chief concern was the problem of maintaining a full campaign larder; it was a difficult job because of his extravagance. During the course of the campaign he and the other Wilson leaders in the national organization expended slightly over $193,000: $22,000 for office expenses; almost $18,000 for printing expenses; over $12,000 for advertising and publicity; and $15,000 for the maintenance of the Washington headquarters. In addition, McCombs distributed some $67,000 to various state leaders—for example, $10,000 each in Wisconsin and South Dakota.[46]

Although McCombs was a prodigal spender, he was also unusually adept at the business of raising campaign funds. He contributed $11,000

---

[44] For a summary of Clark's program, see the *St. Louis Republic*, February 14, 1912.

[45] W. F. McCombs, *Making Woodrow Wilson President*, pp. 107-109.

[46] From McCombs's testimony before the Clapp Committee of the United States Senate, 1912, *Campaign Contributions*, p. 870.

himself to the Wilson movement. Wilson's friend on the Princeton Board of Trustees, Cleveland H. Dodge, New York banker and merchant, contributed $51,300 and collected $21,000 from Thomas D. and David B. Jones of Chicago, $1,000 from Edward W. Sheldon of New York, and $12,500 from Cyrus H. McCormick of Chicago, head of the International Harvester Company, commonly known as the "harvester trust." Wilson's old Princeton friends and supporters, therefore, contributed $85,000, or almost half of the money McCombs spent before the Baltimore convention. Henry Morgenthau loyally gave $5,000 a month for four months, while McCombs persuaded Frederick C. Penfield, wealthy Philadelphia landlord, to contribute $12,000. Samuel Untermeyer and Abram I. Elkus, wealthy New York philanthropists, contributed $7,000 and $12,500 respectively. Charles R. Crane, plumbing fixtures manufacturer and La Follette's chief financial supporter, was converted by McCombs and contributed $10,000.[47] McAdoo, for his part, contributed and collected $6,575.[48]

The income that kept the Wilson machine functioning was so unpredictable, however, that more often than not McCombs was heavily in debt. Around the first of March 1912, for example, he was personally committed for campaign debts of $42,000; a month later the outlook was more encouraging, yet he was still indebted to the amount of $14,000. It was little wonder that he was more interested in obtaining the contribution than in scrutinizing the contributor! Not a single contribution was refused by McCombs, and Wilson, as a general rule, did not bother to examine the list of contributors to his campaign fund.[49] On one occasion he told reporters that the bulk of his campaign fund had come from men who made small contributions; of course this was not true and Wilson would have been exceedingly embarrassed had the Senate forced McCombs to publish the contributors' list in June rather than in October 1912.

Perhaps it was good campaign tactics for McCombs to cry "Wall Street" every time Wilson was attacked, but the fact is that McCombs was just as anxious to have the support of "Wall Street," even the support of the notorious Thomas F. Ryan, as any other manager. The fact remains, furthermore, that the Wilson pre-convention campaign was financed by a few leading bankers and manufacturers. It is fantastic, however, to·assume that there is any sinister implication in this fact; Wilson, it should be emphasized, did insist upon drawing a line be-

[47] *ibid.*, pp. 867-868.   [48] *ibid.*, p. 910.
[49] See Wilson's statement in the *Baltimore Sun,* April 30, 1912.

tween the wealthy men from whom he would and would not accept support. He accepted money from Dodge, McCormick, and his other trustee friends because he knew and respected these men who had stood by him so loyally in the Princeton controversies. He accepted the support of Crane, Morgenthau, Elkus, Penfield, and Untermeyer as evidence that these men, who had supported worth while endeavors in the past, were anxious to underwrite another worthy cause. On the other hand, Wilson would not accept the contributions of Ryan and Hearst; to be sure, he rejected Ryan's proffered contribution chiefly because he thought that it would injure his chances for the nomination if it became known that he had accepted Ryan money, but he did at least reject it, while Harmon and Underwood did not. There is not the slightest evidence to indicate that either Wilson or McCombs made any political commitments in exchange for financial contributions, or that Wilson was subsequently influenced by his financial backers.[50]

Publicity and propaganda, speechmaking and "swings around the circuit" all serve a vital function in political campaigns, but campaigns are won by the methods of organization, by obtaining the support of state organizations, and by working through the regular channels of party politics. For obvious reasons McCombs and the other Wilson leaders could not establish and direct campaign organizations in more than a

---

[50] The fact that Wilson was unpurchasable, however, did not gainsay the widespread adverse comment that McCombs's spending evoked. Bryan was disturbed by the charges that Wilson had a large "slush" fund and wrote to Wilson, suggesting that he join with the other candidates in publishing the sources of their campaign funds. Wilson's reply to Bryan was plaintive. He agreed with Bryan that the publication of pre-nomination subscriptions should be made obligatory by law, and complained that signs were multiplying that the nomination would be made by money. He feared, however, that publishing the list of campaign contributors would discourage men who had come by their money cleanly and honestly, because they would be squeezed and put out of business by the system if they supported progressive causes. W. W. to W. J. Bryan, March 15, 1912, copy in Baker Papers.

When Bryan reiterated his conviction that campaign contributions should be made public, Wilson assured him that he, Wilson, was anxious to follow the Commoner's wishes in the matter. His conviction, Wilson added, was clear as to what ought to be done. The full disclosure of pre-nomination (as of all other) campaign funds ought to be made obligatory by law. W. W. to W. J. Bryan, April 3, 1912, copy in Baker Papers. Simple matter that it was, Wilson never gave the list of his campaign contributors to the newspapers, and it was not until a senatorial investigating committee forced the information from McCombs in the fall of 1912 that the facts became known. Wilson, of course, was not the only candidate who would have been embarrassed by such a disclosure. The knowledge, for example, that Ryan had largely financed the Harmon and Underwood pre-convention campaigns would not have increased the popularity of these candidates.

few states. The plain necessity, therefore, was for the Wilson managers to secure the support of powerful state and city organizations that were already established and that could swing the votes to Wilson in the state primaries or conventions.

The cause of truth is badly served if historians continue to insist that Wilson refused to accept the support of political machines within the states, that no agreements were made between the Wilson managers and local Democratic leaders during the pre-convention campaign, and that it was McCombs alone who saw the practical necessities of the campaign and was willing to bargain for support. On the contrary, the truth is that Wilson and his managers accepted support where they found it. For the most part the alliances that they made were generally with the progressive factions within the states, and this was indeed a natural consequence of Wilson's record as a progressive leader. In Delaware and Kentucky, at least, the Wilson movement was led by conservative Democrats, while McCombs, with Wilson's approval, assiduously wooed the reactionary Democratic boss of Illinois, Roger Sullivan.

The failure of Wilson's managers to win the support of the dominant organizations in most of the states was a result neither of diffidence nor of inactivity on McCombs's or Wilson's part, but rather of the fact that Wilson simply had little to offer machine politicians. McCombs realized that this was the reason why the Wilson movement was not receiving the support of most of the organization politicians. Thus, he wrote to Wilson early in April:

"It is an old story at this time to tell you that the popular sentiment of the country favors your nomination, but unfortunately that is entirely inadequate. The great difficulty with your campaign is the aloofness of a great many of the men in the various districts who do things. These are the men the people follow and are the men who in the main select the delegates. They have an impression of you in a large degree that you are austere and dictatorial and that you will not have a due appreciation of what is to be done for you. It is hard to convince the hundreds of men who really control things that this is not so. It is hard to see them and tell them. Another thing I hear much of, particularly throughout the East, is that you are unreliable. All these things the Smiths, Wattersons, Pynes, etc., have accomplished.

"There is no use disguising the fact. I have suggested that you have your strong friends in Congress and elsewhere as far as possible come and see you. I think it is vital. The human contact is more valuable than anything I know. These people will be greatly pleased to come and see you. It is a valuable thing to give people attention and notice whether you take their advice or not. Furthermore, I regard it as of the essence of things at this time that a strong group be organized to further your candidacy. This group should include eight or ten strong men in Washington. They are easy to select. You alone can get them to work.

"I have been exerting every ounce of energy and influence for almost a year in furthering the idea of your nomination. I have abandoned my practice entirely. These sacrifices I have been quite willing to make. I have sought cooperation in all quarters. I have raised $122,500 and have spent most of it. At present I don't know where I am going to get much more, although I am personally obligated to the extent of $30,000 for future expenses. The foundation is well laid. We must go further." [51]

The pre-convention struggle for delegates had already got into full swing when McCombs wrote this melancholy letter. In Oklahoma the first real test of strength between Wilson and Clark was made, and the outcome was altogether encouraging to the Wilson leaders. Oklahoma had been thoroughly organized for Wilson by blind Senator Thomas P. Gore and William H. ("Alfalfa Bill") Murray; throughout the length and breadth of the state, at Oklahoma City, Tulsa, Enid, Guymon, Shawnee, Ardmore, and Muskogee, Wilson supporters had organized Wilson clubs; progressive newspapers, led by the *Daily Oklahoman* of Oklahoma City, had broadcast the Wilson appeal. [52] Progressive Democratic politicians in the state, however, were about evenly divided as between Wilson and Clark, and the dominant Democratic organization, headed by Governor Charles N. Haskell, was supporting the speaker. Threatened with political annihilation by the organization should he speak for Wilson in Oklahoma, [53] Gore nevertheless came to the state and carried on a vigorous undercover campaign for his candidate. The result was that a comfortable majority of the delegates at the state convention that met at Oklahoma City on February 22 were Wilson supporters. Total victory was easily within Gore's reach, but for some un-

[51] W. F. McCombs to W. W., April —, 1912, published in J. Kerney, *The Political Education of Woodrow Wilson,* pp. 156-157.

[52] Straw ballots conducted by half a dozen newspapers in Oklahoma revealed that Wilson was the choice of a majority of the Democratic voters there. In a poll of at least one-seventh of the total voters of the state taken by the *Daily Oklahoman,* for example, Wilson received three times the number of votes that Clark received, and thirty times Harmon's number. *Daily Oklahoman* of Oklahoma City, February 14, 1912.

[53] See the letters from the Clark managers to T. P. Gore, printed in the *Muskogee Daily Phoenix,* February 13, 1912.

known reason he generously divided the state's delegation to Baltimore evenly with the Clark managers.[54]

The outcome of the pre-convention campaign in Kansas was plainly indicative of what was bound to happen in states where Wilson sentiment was strong but unorganized. There was little doubt that Wilson was the presidential choice of a large majority of Kansas Democrats. There had been publicity enough for Wilson in the state; McCombs had poured $5,000 into the Kansas campaign;[55] yet the Wilson leaders in the state had apparently not bothered to effect a state-wide organization.[56] The inevitable happened; although Wilson supporters in the congressional district conventions elected 14 out of the 20 delegates to Baltimore, the Clark men succeeded in electing a majority of the delegates to the state convention, which met at Hutchinson on March 15 and instructed the Kansas delegation to vote first for Clark. It was a hollow victory for the Clark managers; the convention also decreed that "Whenever in the opinion of two-thirds of the delegation it is deemed expedient to do so," the delegates shall vote for Wilson.[57] Thus it appeared, as the *Kansas City Star* observed on March 15, "The results of the Kansas Democratic convention seem to be that Speaker Clark got all the delegates except two-thirds of them, and that the delegates were instructed to vote for Mr. Clark until Gov. Woodrow Wilson wants them to vote for him."

Wisconsin was the pivot of the Midwest, McCombs thought, the watershed of progressivism in the entire nation, and he determined to carry the presidential primary in that state on April 2 for Wilson. It would have been embarrassing, to say the least, if the leading progressive candidate could not win the support of Democrats in the most publicized progressive state in the country! Fortunately for Wilson, the progressive Democratic faction in Wisconsin, led by Joseph E. Davies, the national committeeman, had come out in support of his candidacy in the fall of 1911. The state organization, moreover, was given mighty support during the campaign by McCombs and the national Wilson headquarters. "Tons of literature" were sent from New York to Wisconsin Democrats;[58] McCombs supported the Wilson organization more generously in Wisconsin than in any other state;[59] Senator Gore

---

[54] *ibid.*, February 23-24, 1912.

[56] *Kansas City Star*, March 14, 1912.

[58] W. F. McCombs, *Making Woodrow Wilson President*, p. 95.

[55] *Campaign Contributions*, p. 870.

[57] *ibid.*, March 15, 1912.

[59] McCombs tells us in *ibid.*, p. 95, that he gave Davies $15,000 for the campaign in Wisconsin; he testified in 1912, however, that he had contributed $10,000 to the support of the Wisconsin organization. See *Campaign Contributions*, p. 870.

hurried to Milwaukee and "organized a campaign down to the precincts in Wisconsin." [60] Pressure applied in the right places usually brings results in political contests; on April 2 the Wilson men succeeded in electing twenty of the twenty-four Wisconsin delegates to the Baltimore convention. [61]

Meanwhile, nothing disturbed Wilson more than the disquieting political situation in the South, where the rise of Oscar W. Underwood's candidacy threatened to blast Wilson's confident expectations of carrying his native region. Underwood's candidacy was unique in that it represented the only attempt since 1860 of a resident Southerner to win the Democratic nomination. By his thwarting of Bryan's attempt to dictate to the Democratic Congress in the summer of 1911 and by virtue of his successful leadership in tariff reform, Underwood was catapulted into the presidential campaign. [62] Although the Underwood movement began as a "favorite son" movement in Alabama, it rapidly spread through the South, and national headquarters were established in Washington early in 1912, with Senator John H. Bankhead of Alabama in command. [63] The encouraging beginnings of a strong Wilson movement in Alabama were wrecked when Wilson Democrats decided that it would be ill-advised to campaign against Underwood in his own state. [64] Consequently, 100,000 Democrats gave their endorsement to Underwood at a presidential primary in April 1912, and the state convention a few weeks later instructed its delegation to vote "first, last, and all the time" for Alabama's favorite son. [65]

The turning point of the Democratic pre-convention campaign was the presidential primary in Illinois on April 9. Before the Illinois contest had ended it had been impossible for political observers to measure the relative strength of Wilson and Clark; certainly the outcome of the campaigns in Oklahoma, Kansas, Maine, and Wisconsin revealed no decided trend toward either candidate. The Underwood campaign had got off to a booming start in the Southeast, but it was impossible yet to judge whether it would make any appreciable headway outside Ala-

[60] McCombs, *Making Woodrow Wilson President*, p. 96.

[61] *New York Times*, April 3, 1912. The vote in the Wisconsin primary was Wilson, 45,945; Clark, 36,464. *World Almanac, 1914*, p. 727.

[62] A. S. Link, "The Underwood Presidential Campaign of 1912," *Journal of Southern History*, XI (May, 1945), 230-234.

[63] *Montgomery Advertiser*, July 28, October 1, 1911; *Birmingham Age-Herald*, February 20, 1912.

[64] *Charlotte Daily Observer*, March 11, 1912, quoting *Birmingham News*.

[65] *Montgomery Advertiser*, April 2, 18, 1912; *Birmingham Age-Herald*, April 20, 1912.

bama. The Harmon presidential movement had already signally failed. Bryan's relentless attacks upon the Ohio governor, his charges that Harmon was the "Wall Street" candidate and a reactionary unacceptable to progressive Democrats, had done as much as anything else to deflate the Harmon boom.[66]

In Illinois the Wilson managers were confronted with a well-nigh hopeless situation. The Democratic party in the state had been completely wrecked by factionalism and personal politics; even the progressives were divided between the faction headed by Chicago's mayor, Carter H. Harrison, who was supported by the Hearst newspapers, and the Democrats led by Edward F. Dunne, a "radical liberal" of the Windy City.[67] The conservatives, on the other hand, were organized into a well-oiled machine that was engineered by Roger Sullivan of Chicago.

Wilson's supporters naturally attempted to obtain Harrison's support in the pre-convention campaign; but Harrison had "an instinctive repugnance both to Wilson and to his candidacy," and, in cooperation with the Hearst editors of Chicago, espoused Clark's candidacy instead. Soon the Dunne faction fell into line behind Clark, and no other faction of organized Democrats remained in the field save the notorious Sullivan organization. McCombs labored hard, consequently, to win Sullivan's support for the Wilson movement; Sullivan, however, was fighting for his political life against the Harrison-Hearst-Dunne forces and concentrated all his resources on the struggle for control of the state party machinery. Sullivan waged a bitter fight for his nominees and spent between $40,000 and $50,000 in the primary campaign; but he refused to take sides in the presidential contest. The presidential candidates, he later recalled, were not "considered in the contest at all." [68]

Thus thwarted in his efforts to obtain the support of some Illinois Democratic organization for Wilson's candidacy, McCombs set about the hopeless task of forming, *de novo*, a Wilson organization. A little group of faithful Wilson men, headed by Representative Lawrence B. Stringer, established an impromptu state Wilson headquarters; McCombs had no illusions about the Illinois situation, yet he gave the

---

[66] See *The Commoner*, December 29, 1911, April 5, 1912; also W. J. Bryan to E. H. Moore, March 25, 1912, published in *ibid.*, April 5, 1912.

[67] Carter H. Harrison, II, *Stormy Years, The Autobiography of Carter H. Harrison, Five Times Mayor of Chicago*, p. 319.

[68] Sullivan has told the story of the Democratic primary campaign in Illinois in *Campaign Contributions*, pp. 918-925; cf. Harrison's account in his *Stormy Years*, pp. 315-330.

Wilson leaders there $3,000[69]—"more of a reward for the loyalty of their services," he later wrote, "than anything else."[70]

The Clark managers, on the other hand, were fully aware of their tremendous opportunity; by carrying Illinois by a decisive majority they could catapult Clark into the first place in the pre-convention campaign. The outcome of the contest hinged, of course, upon the results in Chicago, and a host of Clark speakers invaded the city. On April 4 Senator Stone led the Clark campaigners in their attack upon Wilson. He charged that Wilson had voted against Bryan in 1896 and that he had refused to vote in 1908; he asserted that Wilson was not a sincere progressive and quoted the Joline letter and several of Wilson's conservative declarations to prove his point; and he rang the changes upon Wilson's derogatory reflections upon southern and eastern European immigrants.[71]

The Harrison and Hearst leaders, however, had the situation well in hand in Chicago, and it is doubtful whether they needed the support of Missouri Democrats. The Hearst newspapers had a field day in their constant attacks, day in and day out, upon Wilson. The entire might of the city organization was thrown into the fight for Clark by Mayor Harrison, while appeals were sent over the state to progressive Democratic leaders to "go the limit" for Clark.[72] On April 8, the day before the primary, Harrison gave out a ringing statement supporting Clark and urging progressive Democrats to vote for him. "I will vote for Champ Clark at the Presidential preferential primary to-morrow," Harrison announced, "and I urge all Progressive Democrats to give him their votes. We can win with Clark, but it is doubtful whether we could win with Wilson."[73]

In a vain attempt to stem the rising Clark enthusiasm, Wilson made a hurried, last-ditch barnstorming campaign tour in Illinois on April 5 and 6. On April 5 he spoke at Bloomington, Peoria, Joliet, Dwight, Pontiac, Lincoln, Petersburg, Mason City, and Jacksonville. At Jacksonville, Bryan's birthplace, he paused to pay tribute to Bryan; at Bloomington he appealed to the progressive Republicans of Illinois to come to his aid in the struggle; at Peoria he called Hearst a "character assas-

---

[69] *Campaign Contributions*, p. 870.

[70] McCombs, *Making Woodrow Wilson President*, p. 101.

[71] *St. Louis Republic*, April 5, 1912. Clark enthusiasm was spreading like wildfire in Chicago. On April 6 Clark speakers from Missouri, Stone, David R. Francis, James H. Whitecotton, and Perl D. Decker, and the ubiquitous Massachusetts radical, George Fred Williams, harangued Chicago audiences. *ibid.*, April 7, 1912.

[72] *ibid.*, April 9, 1912.   [73] *New York American*, April 9, 1912.

sin" and scored Senator Stone for serving as an agent of the great demagogue. At Joliet he answered the Clark campaigners who had declared
that he was the candidate of Wall Street. "If I knew the money for the
expenses of my campaign were coming from such sources I'd be
ashamed to show my face," he said. With each successive speech, Wilson's anger increased; at Springfield, for example, he lashed out again
at Hearst and Stone:

"I have heard within the last thirty minutes that in Springfield I am
to be considered a dangerous man. I am told that since the announcement of my coming it has been deemed necessary to telegraph a United
States senator from Missouri to come here tonight to furnish an antidote for the poison I will spread.

"The one who has compounded this happens to own newspapers in
several sections of the country. It has been his particular pleasure to
seek to destroy every man who speaks for the Democratic party. I am
sorry a United States senator will distribute his wares." [74]

The following day Wilson renewed his attacks upon Hearst and the
Clark spokesmen. After speaking in a general way about progressive
democracy at Galesburg and Moline, at Sterling he made a thinly veiled
allusion to the charge of "presidential combination." "There are all sorts
of rumors floating around," he asserted, "rumors of combinations; rumors of understandings; rumors that make me feel very lonely. I don't
much care if these rumors are true or not . . . but there is a very strong
suspicion in the minds of a great part of the voters of the country that
there is a game being framed up." After speaking at De Kalb and
Rochelle, Wilson went next to Chicago, where he addressed several
audiences of foreign-born voters. [75]

From almost every aspect, Wilson's Illinois tour was a tactical blunder of the first magnitude. He should have known, as McCombs certainly knew, that he could not carry the state. It is doubtful whether his
defensive, almost apologetic, last-minute appeal won him any appreciable new support; and by going to Illinois in the heat of the campaign,
he inevitably created the impression that he expected to carry the primaries there. All of which emphasized and high-lighted the defeat that
was bound to come.

[74] *Chicago Daily Tribune,* April 6, 1912.

[75] *ibid.,* April 7, 1912. While Wilson was in Chicago, his hotel room was entered, his
luggage was rifled, and a suitcase, containing only letters, was taken. Nothing of value,
which might have caught the eye of a common thief, was disturbed. Those persons
acquainted with Hearst's methods were sure that the incident was another of his ex-
ploits. See Ferdinand Lundberg, *Imperial Hearst,* p. 212.

Defeat was certain, but no casual observer, probably not even the Clark managers themselves, had anticipated the amazing Clark landslide that swept the Illinois primaries on April 9. Wilson carried only the sixteenth, the Peoria, district and lost the state to Clark by the staggering vote of 75,527 to 218,483.[76] Wilson's managers were dismayed by the crushing blow, yet McCombs attempted to rationalize the defeat, even capitalize upon it. "The defeat in Illinois simply means that we must fight the harder," he declared in New York, the morning after the primary election. "It ought to show plainly enough for anybody to understand that a vote for Clark means a vote for Hearst. Does the Democratic party want to name as its choice a marionette of Hearst? . . . This is not the end of the fight by any means. It is going to solidify the Wilson sentiment and bring the issues to a point." Then McCombs added a damaging remark that he later vainly tried to repudiate and disavow. "I would wear my hands to the bone in the Republican party," he continued, "rather than work for Champ Clark as Democratic candidate for the Presidency, with the possibility of William Randolph Hearst as Secretary of State.[77] I know a thousand other good Democrats that would do the same." [78] To old-line Democratic regulars, this was about the most immoral thing McCombs could have said!

Clark and his spokesmen were of course jubilant over their victory. "From this day forward every person of intelligence cannot fail to recognize the fact that the Speaker's campaign is neither visionary nor foredoomed," asserted, prophetically, the leading Clark spokesman in the Midwest. "It is the lustiest of them all. . . . The Illinois verdict takes Champ Clark out of the favorite son class and places him at once in the lead." [79] When Clark entered the House of Representatives on the morning after the Illinois primary he was wildly cheered by Democratic representatives as the "next President." [80]

Clark's victory in Illinois was the most important single event of the pre-convention campaign. Before the Illinois primary it had been generally assumed that Wilson would enter the Baltimore convention with

[76] *World Almanac, 1914,* p. 727.

[77] "I am profoundly grateful to all who aided in carrying Illinois for me," Clark telegraphed to the editor of the *New York American* on April 9. "Among them was the powerful influence of the Hearst newspapers, which have stood by me loyally, manfully and unselfishly from the beginning from Massachusetts to California." Published in the *New York American,* April 10, 1912.

[78] *Trenton True American,* April 11, 1912. For the official statement from the Wilson headquarters in New York on the Illinois primary results, see the *New York Times,* April 11, 1912.

[79] *St. Louis Republic,* April 10, 1912.   [80] *Baltimore Sun,* April 11, 1912.

at least a majority of the delegates.[81] The shock was all the more severe, therefore, when it became suddenly apparent after April 9 that it was Clark, not Wilson, who was the most formidable Democratic candidate; that Clark could now probably command the support of a majority of the Democratic voters. Only six states had selected their delegates to the Baltimore convention before April 9, and the lesson of the Illinois primary was not lost upon the Democratic politicians in the other forty-one states, many of whom were waiting for some such indication of popular sentiment as the Illinois primary afforded. The anti-Wilson editors took new hope for the future and now predicted that the Wilson movement had received its death-blow. "The back of the Wilson movement was broken yesterday in Illinois . . . ," James Smith's newspaper taunted. "Gov. Wilson will serve out his term." [82]

The Wilson spokesmen were at a loss to find some way to counteract the growing conviction among Democrats that Clark's nomination was inevitable. One Wilson editor endeavored to find comfort in the thought that Wilson had been defeated in Illinois by "a gang that Sir John Falstaff would not be seen in Coventry with";[83] but that was a hopeless sort of rationalization. Several Wilson spokesmen attempted to make McCombs the scapegoat of the affair. It had been apparent for weeks, wrote a Charleston editor, that McCombs was ill-fitted for the management of the Wilson campaign. "With practical management the nomination of Governor Wilson at Baltimore ought to have been a certainty," the editor asserted. "He was the best advertised of all the candidates. He was conceded by every one to have a long lead in the race. There was no excuse for the Wilson forces having lost Illinois to Clark by such an overwhelming vote." [84]

Several days after the Illinois primary the New York state Democratic convention met in New York City; it was dominated completely by the boss of Tammany Hall, Charles F. Murphy, who dictated the election of eighty-six district delegates and four delegates-at-large. It was also a defeat for the Wilson progressives, led by O'Gorman and Franklin D. Roosevelt, for Murphy was openly hostile to Wilson's candidacy.[85]

The one bright spot on the pre-convention map in mid-April was Pennsylvania, where both the progressive and conservative factions of the Democratic party had come out in support of Wilson's candidacy.

[81] *New York Times,* April 11, 1912.   [82] *Newark Evening Star,* April 10, 1912.
[83] *Nashville Banner,* May 2, 1912.
[84] *Charleston* (S. C.) *News and Courier,* April 13, 1912.
[85] *New York World,* April 12, 1912.

Two days before the presidential primary in that state, Wilson went to Pittsburgh to put the finishing touches upon his campaign in Pennsylvania. National Committeeman Joseph F. Guffey, old-guard leader of the conservative Democratic faction, ostentatiously presided at the gathering that Wilson addressed on April 10. His speech was a repetition of his old stock-in-trade encomiums on popular government;[86] yet it was

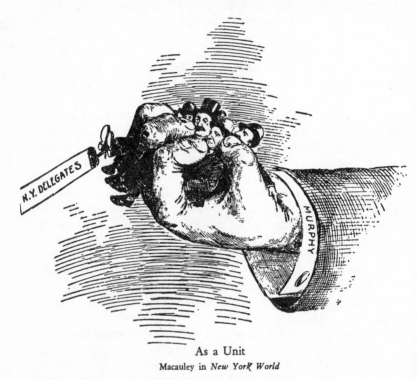

As a Unit

Macauley in *New York World*

apparently enthusiastically received by his listeners. "I spoke in Pittsburgh last night and had a very gratifying reception from a splendid audience," he wrote to one of his Pennsylvania managers. He felt a good deal cheered by what his friends there told him of the situation, and he was looking forward with a certain amount of confidence to results the next Saturday.[87] The Pennsylvania primaries on April 13 went so overwhelmingly in Wilson's favor that his candidacy was for

[86] For which see the *Pittsburgh Post,* April 11, 1912.

[87] W. W. to A. M. Palmer, April 11, 1912, photostat in Wilson Papers.

a time given new life. The Pennsylvania state Democratic convention met in early May and instructed its seventy-six delegates to "vote for the nomination of Woodrow Wilson for President, and to use all honorable means to accomplish his nomination." [88]

Meanwhile, Wilson had again invaded the South in an effort to head off the dangerous Underwood movement that was sweeping through the region. The Underwood managers were making a strong campaign largely upon the issues of sectional pride and tariff reform. They reiterated again and again that the sacred honor of the South was involved in the Alabaman's candidacy; the North was ready to accept Underwood, they declared, if the South would first rally to his support. For half a century Southerners had constituted the backbone of the Democratic party, had "hewn the wood and drawn the water," and "eaten the husks that fell from the table." "The South for a Southerner" thus became the Underwood campaign cry.[89] The "southern" issue was of course a two-edged sword that might be used against Underwood's candidacy by northern Republicans; his supporters, on the other hand, were on surer ground when they advocated his nomination because of his leadership in tariff reform and his skill in uniting the divergent elements of the Democratic party in Congress into a solid, working group, undisturbed by party rebellion or antagonism.

Generally speaking, the Underwood campaign united conservative southern Democrats into a counter-movement against the flood-tide of progressivism that was then sweeping the South.[90] The truth of this generalization is revealed by the nature of the support Underwood received. In every state in which the contest was fought between Underwood and Wilson, the conservative state organization was the body and substance of Underwood's strength. In Virginia the Martin-Swanson organization, in Georgia the Joseph M. Brown-Clark Howell-Tom Watson coalition, and in Florida the conservative faction led by Governor Albert W. Gilchrist and the *Florida Times-Union* of Jacksonville were arrayed in the vanguard of the movement to make Underwood president. The same general conservatism was apparent in Underwood's newspaper support, for the preeminent conservative journals of the

[88] A. M. Palmer to W. W., May 11, 1912, *ibid.*, relates an account of the Pennsylvania convention.

[89] See, e.g., *Atlanta Constitution*, May 1 and 12, 1912; *Memphis Commercial Appeal*, April 18, 1912; *Jacksonville Florida Times-Union*, February 16, April 30, 1912; *Mobile Register*, January 2, 1912; *Birmingham Age-Herald*, February 3, May 1, 1912.

[90] For an amplification of this point, see A. S. Link, "The Progressive Movement in the South, 1870-1914," *North Carolina Historical Review*, xxiii (April 1946).

Southeast—the *Charlotte Daily Observer*, the *Atlanta Constitution*, the *Augusta Chronicle*, the *Savannah Morning News*, the *Macon Telegraph*, the *Montgomery Advertiser*, the *Vicksburg Herald*, and the *Memphis Commercial Appeal*—were the chief spokesmen of the Underwood cause. Moreover, this identical conservative faction quite naturally was opposed to Bryan and his brand of progressive Democracy. It

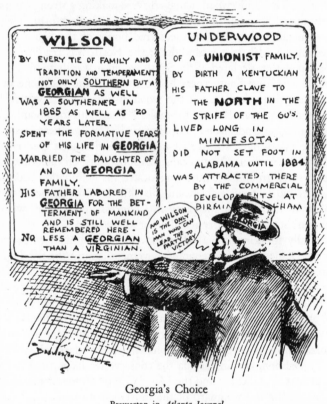

Georgia's Choice
Brewerton in *Atlanta Journal*

was not uncommon in the South, therefore, to read that Underwood was the "safe and sane candidate," that he stood in opposition to destructive socialism, that he was the man destined to safeguard American institutions from the ravages of the mob.

Wilson, his wife, and McAdoo went to Georgia in mid-April in a full-fledged effort to win the support of the state in which Mrs. Wilson had been born and in which Wilson himself had begun his public career. He opened his Georgia campaign on April 16, with a flamboyant address before an audience of some 9,000 persons in Atlanta. The following day he began a speaking tour through Georgia that took him to Forsyth, Jonesboro, Waycross, and Albany. On April 17 he went to Jacksonville and appealed for the support of Florida Democrats in the coming presidential primary. On April 18 he went to Savannah, the alleged center of Georgia conservatism, and found there a very receptive audience. He concluded his Georgia tour in Macon on April 20, full of confidence and hope because of the mighty cheering of the crowds, the warm greetings of old friends, and the enthusiasm of the people that was everywhere evident.[91]

Yet, as was so often the case in the pre-convention campaign, the outward, visible signs of southern enthusiasm for Wilson's candidacy was deceiving. Florida's presidential primary on April 30 resulted in a victory for Underwood; Georgia fell into the Underwood column on May 1, and Mississippi followed Georgia six days later. The Wilson managers in South Carolina managed to survive the Underwood onslaught and carried their state for Wilson on May 15; but the Wilson leaders in Tennessee were able to salvage only one-fourth of the state's delegates from the wreckage of the faction-split Democratic party in that state. Wilson sentiment in Virginia was strong, but the arduous work of Byrd, Harry St. George Tucker, and the other Wilson leaders in the state could not overcome the opposition of the Martin-Swanson organization, and Virginia fell to Underwood on May 23.[92]

If the success of the Underwood movement was not enough to dismay the Wilson managers, the virtual tidal wave of Clark enthusiasm that swept the country after the Illinois primaries assuredly was. It threatened to engulf even Nebraska, Bryan's home state, where the Wilson forces were well organized and united.[93] All Democratic eyes were on Bryan; observers were wondering whom he would support in the Nebraska contest. The canny Nebraskan steadfastly refused to deviate from his announced position of neutrality as between Clark and Wilson;[94] but he warned these two progressives that, in order to prevent

---

[91] *Atlanta Journal*, April 17-21, 1912.

[92] The Wilson men, however, did succeed in electing almost a third of the delegates in the Virginia delegation.

[93] See the *Kansas City Star*, December 14, 1911; *New York Times*, January 20, March 2, 1912, for accounts of the Wilson pre-convention campaign in Nebraska.

[94] Arthur F. Mullen, Clark's manager in Nebraska, writes that Bryan was covertly working for Wilson during the pre-convention contest in the state. A. F. Mullen, *Western Democrat*, pp. 164-166.

Harmon's endorsement in the presidential primary by a minority of the voters, the weaker progressive candidate should withdraw from the contest and support the stronger.[95] Although he refused to name the progressive whom he thought a majority of Nebraska progressives favored, there is some evidence that he was secretly supporting Wilson.[96] Three weeks before the Nebraska primary, however, Bryan reiterated that "as between Mr. Wilson and Mr. Clark" he did not "care to express a preference, regarding them both as progressive." On the other hand, he wanted Nebraska Democrats to know that should Harmon receive a plurality of the votes at the presidential primary he would resign his commission as a delegate to the Baltimore convention. Under no circumstances would he vote for Harmon, "a reactionary and the choice of the predatory interests of the country." [97] Bryan's fears, however, were groundless; on April 17 the Democrats gave Clark 21,027, Wilson 14,289, and Harmon 12,454 votes, and Clark captured the entire Nebraska delegation, Bryan and all.

There were a few encouraging signs on the political horizon for the Wilson men during the latter part of April and the first three weeks of May. The Oregon Democracy, led by William S. U'Ren, gave its votes to Wilson on April 20; Willard Saulsbury, Democratic master of Delaware, swung his state into the Wilson column on April 30. Then came defeat again. The Wilson leaders in Michigan, liberally financed by McCombs, had organized the state thoroughly for their candidate; yet the Clark and Harmon managers defeated Wilson instructions at the state convention at Bay City on May 15, and the Wilson men elected only twelve out of the state's thirty delegates to the national convention.[98] Ohio, where the progressive Democratic faction in opposition to Governor Harmon had come out strongly in support of Wilson, went to Harmon on May 21.[99] Harmon's victory in Ohio, however, was of such a

[95] *The Commoner,* March 12, 1912, p. 1.
[96] A. F. Mullen, *Western Democrat,* p. 166.
[97] *The Commoner,* March 29, 1912.   [98] *St. Louis Republic,* May 13-15, 1912.
[99] The Ohio pre-convention campaign is worthy of further comment. The progressive Bryan Democrats in that state, led by W. W. Durbin, Harvey C. Garber, John J. Lentz, and Newton D. Baker, mayor of Cleveland, determined in 1911 to prevent Harmon's endorsement at the presidential primary in the state in 1912. Garber and Durbin conferred with Bryan, who agreed to support them in their fight against Harmon. In December 1911, Durbin conferred with Clark and "came away feeling sure that he was in with Harmon, and . . . felt that the interests were using Clark to tie up with the various delegations only to turn them over in the end to Harmon." Durbin subsequently conferred with Alexander of the *Trenton True American,* McCombs, and Wilson; soon afterwards he and his colleagues in Ohio decided to support Wilson. W. W. Durbin to

dubious character that it ended by giving the death-blow to his presidential candidacy. In the state-wide primary Wilson won nineteen out of the forty-two district delegates to the national convention, while Harmon's popular plurality was less than 10,000.[100] As the *New York World* pointed out on May 22, if Harmon was to be nominated at Baltimore, he had to demonstrate conclusively that he had the undivided support of the Ohio Democrats and could carry his state in a national election. Of course he had failed to do this.

Notwithstanding these few signs of encouragement, the over-all picture was exceedingly gloomy for Wilson. Following Nebraska, one state after another fell into line behind Clark's candidacy. Colorado on April 29 voted to instruct its delegates for Clark; a combination of the supporters of Clark and Governor Eugene N. Foss swept Massachusetts safely into the Clark column on April 30.[101] The Wilson managers in

R. S. Baker, March 20, 1926, Baker Papers. McCombs subsequently gave the Ohio Wilson men $4,500 with which to finance the state campaign. *Campaign Contributions,* p. 870.

On January 2, 1912, Durbin and Garber organized the Progressive Democratic League of Ohio and came out openly in support of Wilson's candidacy. Bryan made a campaign tour through the state several weeks before the presidential primary and urged progressive Democrats to vote *against* Harmon by voting for Wilson. "In advising the progressive Democrats of Ohio to vote for Governor Wilson," he explained in his newspaper, "Mr. Bryan has repeatedly explained that he is for any progressive as against any reactionary and that he would earnestly urge the support of Speaker Clark if Clark were the candidate against Mr. Harmon in Ohio." *The Commoner,* May 17, 1912.

However, the spearhead of the Wilson movement in Ohio was the progressive citywide organization headed by Newton D. Baker in Cleveland. Baker organized Cleveland and carried the city for Wilson in the Democratic primary. For further information on the Ohio campaign, see the debates in the Baltimore convention over the question of the voting of the Wilson delegates from Ohio, *Official Report of the Proceedings of the Democratic National Convention . . . 1912,* pp. 59-75.

[100] The vote in the Ohio primary was as follows: Harmon, 100,099; Wilson, 89,116; Clark, 2,489; Bryan, 2,490. *World Almanac, 1914,* p. 727.

[101] The Wilson managers made a hard fight for Massachusetts. The Wilson movement in the state was formally organized under the auspices of the Boston Wilson Club, of which Robert Treat Paine was president. For the most part, however, the campaign for Wilson's endorsement was carried forward by former Congressman William F. McNary of Boston, who was designated as the manager of the Wilson headquarters in Boston. McCombs gave the Massachusetts leaders $4,100 with which to carry on the fight, and they expended a total of $4,536.60 during the primary campaign. See McCombs's testimony in *Campaign Contributions,* p. 870; also the testimony of Josiah Quincy in *ibid.,* pp. 915-917. Quincy, an old-time reformer, was one of Wilson's managers in Massachusetts.

Two weeks before the primary was held, Joseph E. Davies and Dudley Field Malone, representing the national Wilson headquarters, went to Massachusetts in an effort to organize a systematic campaign. See *ibid.,* pp. 915-916; also D. F. Malone to Richard

Maryland made a tremendous effort to carry that state; but the Clark managers won the support of the state Democratic organization and the Baltimore city machine, and carried the county primaries on April 30.[102]

Wyoming, on May 13, followed Maryland into the Clark ranks. A day later Clark swept the Democratic primaries in California, where the Hearst interests dominated the Democratic party, by a vote of 46,163 to 17,214 and also won the Democratic delegation in New Hampshire. On May 16 Iowa, after a hard fight by the Wilson men, fell into the Clark column; Kentucky, Rhode Island, West Virginia, Vermont, Louisiana, Arkansas, Idaho, Montana, Nevada, New Mexico, Arizona, and Washington followed in quick succession. Connecticut and Indiana, in the meantime, had pledged their support to "local son" candidates, Governor Simeon E. Baldwin and Governor Thomas R. Marshall.

The alarming realization, toward the end of the pre-convention campaign, that Clark would enter the Baltimore convention with almost a majority of the delegates frightened the spokesmen of progressive Democracy in the Northeast as much as it alarmed Wilson and his managers. As early as April 1912, newspapers like the *New York Times,* the *New York World,* the *Cleveland Plain Dealer,* the *New York Evening Post,* the *Springfield Republican,* and the *Indianapolis News;* magazines like *Collier's Weekly, American Magazine, World's Work,* and the *Nation* began a tremendous campaign of scorn, ridicule, and reasoned argument to prove that Clark's nomination would spell disaster for the Democratic party. Several of these journals were conservative in outlook and had liberally criticized Wilson's campaign appeals; but the spectacular progress of the Clark movement had the effect of driving

Olney, April 26, 1912, Richard Olney Papers, Library of Congress; hereinafter cited as Olney Papers.

Wilson, too, went to Boston four days before the Massachusetts primary in a last-ditch attempt to rally his supporters. He made a hard-hitting speech, attacking the campaign of misrepresentation that Hearst and G. F. Williams had been waging against his candidacy. See *Trenton True American,* April 27, 1912.

Clark's managers, Congressman James M. Curley and G. F. Williams, meanwhile had thoroughly canvassed the state for the speaker. In addition to obtaining the support of the state machine for Clark, they also persuaded Governor Foss, who was making a half-hearted effort to obtain a "favorite son" endorsement, to retire from the primary contest, presumably in Clark's favor. *New York American,* April 5, 1912; *New York Times,* April 11, 1912. In the presidential primary on April 30, practically the entire Clark-Foss slate of delegates was elected; the popular vote was Clark, 34,575; Wilson, 15,002.

[102] The popular vote in Maryland was Clark, 35,510; Wilson, 22,816; Harmon, 7,157. For a discussion of the pre-convention campaign in Maryland, see A. S. Link, "The South and the Democratic Campaign of 1910-1912." pp. 321-330.

them all into a position of unreserved support of Wilson's candidacy.

Let us examine a few examples of the anti-Clark editorial attack: One writer in the *American Magazine* asserted that Clark had won the support of a majority of the Democrats because most people hesitated to take the plunge into constructive reform; Clark was no standpatter, the author continued, yet he stood for nothing new or surprising or strange.[103] The Washington correspondent of the *New York Times,* on the other hand, charged that the Clark campaign was being financed by the liquor interests.[104] *Collier's Weekly,* under the aggressive editorship of Norman Hapgood, waged a relentless fight against Clark's nomination. Hapgood poured ridicule and contempt upon the Missourian by quoting from his many erratic outbursts;[105] he called Clark a "patent medicine statesman" because he had once endorsed Electric Bitters[106] and charged that Clark was the candidate of reactionaries.[107] "The menace of Champ Clark as the Democratic candidate for the Presidency daily grows greater," cried the *Nation,* as it saw one state after another fall to the speaker. ". . . Plainly, the man to beat Clark is Wilson. . . . It is high time for those Democrats who do not wish to concede the election to the Republicans in advance to do their utmost to check the drift to Speaker Clark—a drift due chiefly to popular ignorance of his complete unfitness for the Presidency." [108] Walter H. Page warned that Clark was "perhaps the only Democrat whose nomination would make Republican success certain whoever be the Republican nominee." [109]

Of all the newspapers in the East the *New York World* spoke most authoritatively; it had come to be regarded as the high priest of the eastern Democracy. In the latter part of April the *World* joined hands with the anti-Clark forces by asserting that Clark's nomination would be "equivalent to a certificate of election for his Republican opponent." The editor concluded:

"The World is not seeking to force a candidate of its own upon the Democratic party. It is merely dealing with the political situation as it exists. We had hoped that it would not be necessary to treat Mr. Clark's candidacy seriously. That was a compliment we had paid to the intel-

[103] R. S. Baker, "Our Next President and Some Others," *American Magazine,* LXXIV (June 1912), 132.

[104] *New York Times,* May 1, 1912.

[105] *Collier's Weekly,* XLIX (June 1, 1912), 8.

[106] *ibid.,* XLIX (June 22, 1912), 10.   [107] *ibid.,* XLVIII (March 9, 1912), 9.

[108] *The Nation,* XCIV (May 9, 1912), 451.

[109] *World's Work,* XXIV (June 1912), 130.

ligence of Western and Southern Democrats, but it was a compliment which we now find was undeserved. The sooner, then, that the plain, blunt truth is stated in the frankest possible fashion the better.

"Champ Clark's nomination would be Democratic suicide!" [110]

There were indications, too, that the Old Guard Republican managers were boosting Clark's candidacy because they thought he would be a weaker candidate than Wilson. "It is the hope of Republicans here," wrote the venerable Richard Olney from Boston, "that Clark will be nominated—they think him the most vulnerable of the Democratic possibilities named." [111] "I have observed that the Republican members of the press here in Washington," wrote Hilary A. Herbert from the national capital, "are doing all they can to set up Clark, in order that they may knock him down easily." [112] Josephus Daniels later recalled that Franklin D. Roosevelt came to Baltimore in June with the report that Kermit Roosevelt had declared, "Pop is praying for the nomination of Champ Clark." [113]

To all intents and purposes, the Wilson movement had collapsed by the latter part of May 1912. McCombs's organization was practically bankrupt; Wilson himself fell ill in May[114] and there were rumors that he was suffering from a nervous breakdown. McCombs's office and the headquarters at 42 Broadway were deserted. "Mr. McAdoo, Senator Saulsbury, Mr. Elkus, Mr. Morgenthau, and a few other staunch friends were about all that called and conferred." [115] McCombs, though utterly discouraged, tried to believe that Wilson had "a chance to be nominated." Colonel House on the other hand, lost heart and doubted that Wilson could be nominated. He thought that the opposing candidates in November might again be Bryan and Roosevelt,[116] and wrote to Mary Baird Bryan, pledging his support to the Commoner if he

---

[110] *New York World,* April 25, 1912.

[111] R. Olney to Hilary A. Herbert, April 13, 1912, Olney Papers. Interestingly enough, Olney, the arch-conservative, the anti-labor, big business attorney-general and secretary of state in Cleveland's second administration, confessed that he had voted twice for Bryan; and "as between him and Clark," he wrote, "I should much prefer to vote a third time for Mr. Bryan." R. Olney to H. A. Herbert, April 18, 1912, *ibid.*

[112] H. A. Herbert to R. Olney, April 17, 1912, *ibid.*

[113] J. Daniels, "Wilson and Bryan," *Saturday Evening Post,* cxcviii (September 5, 1925), 48.

[114] *Jersey Journal* of Jersey City, May 3, 1912.

[115] M. F. Lyons, *William F. McCombs, The President Maker,* pp. 75-76.

[116] E. M. House to C. A. Culberson, April 23, 1912, House Papers.

were again the Democratic nominee.[117] House also turned to his old friend, Senator Charles A. Culberson of Texas. "Do you feel that your health would permit you to accept the nomination if it were tendered to you?" he wrote. "In the event of a deadlock, which seems likely to occur, I can think of no one excepting you that would be satisfactory to all factions." [118]

With all the conflicting reports that were pouring into headquarters, the confusing editorials in the newspapers, and the optimistic statements McCombs was still giving out, Wilson at times revealed an unfounded confidence in the probability of his nomination. He wrote on May 13, for example:

"I am all right again and the reports about my 'breakdown' were absurd. I simply had to go to bed to cure a severe cold. . . .

"I think that, politically, things are in a fairly satisfactory shape. As a matter of fact most of the support of Clark and Underwood is perfunctory and on the surface, and underneath, if I am correctly informed, the purpose to nominate me is as strong as it ever was. These things cannot be depended upon, of course, but this is what is reported to me by men who ought to know.

"The combination against me has certainly done wonders, and yet my chief disappointment in the primaries of various states is not that they did not result in my favor, but that they were so small in respect to the numbers who voted. The people did not take any interest in them. They were about equivalent to caucuses held through the polling places. Possibly the people will wake up later to the significance of the whole thing, but for the present there seems to be extraordinary lethargy and indifference." [119]

While the accuracy of Wilson's statement might very well be disputed, there was no doubt whatever that his movement would disintegrate utterly and completely should he fail to carry the presidential primary in his own state on May 28. For that reason, therefore, the pre-convention struggle in New Jersey was of tremendous importance and merits detailed attention.

A few days after the Democratic defeat in the legislative elections of 1911, the members of the Democratic state committee, led by Chairman Edward E. Grosscup and National Committeeman Robert S.

---

[117] E. M. House to M. B. Bryan, June 22, 1912, *ibid.*
[118] E. M. House to C. A. Culberson, April 23, 1912, *ibid.*
[119] W. W. to R. H. Dabney, May 13, 1912, Dabney Papers.

Hudspeth, met in Trenton and resolved to undertake a campaign to secure New Jersey's endorsement for Wilson's candidacy.[120] With the exception of Essex County, the Wilson progressive machine was in complete control of the party machinery in the counties of New Jersey. A survey made by the *Jersey Journal* of Jersey City in March 1912, revealed that nineteen of the twenty-one county committees were solidly behind Wilson; that in one county, Atlantic, every member of the county committee save two were on the Wilson bandwagon; and that Essex alone was definitely controlled by the Smith-Nugent machine.[121]

Smith and Nugent had entered the lists against Wilson by the beginning of 1912, to be sure, but no one was surprised. Nugent, for example, met Democratic leaders from Camden, Gloucester, Burlington, Cumberland, Salem, Atlantic, and Cape May counties in Camden in early March and endeavored to win the support of South Jersey for his campaign against Wilson's candidacy;[122] but he made absolutely no headway among these politicians.[123] When Grosscup officially entered Wilson's name in the primary contest on March 20, he and the other Wilson managers apparently had the political situation firmly in hand.[124]

Not that there was not considerable dangerous and well organized opposition to Wilson's candidacy in New Jersey. All the disappointed office-seekers, all the Democratic politicians discontented with Wilson's leadership of the party joined with James Smith, Jr., and James R. Nugent to prevent Wilson's endorsement at the polls and wreck forever the chances of his nomination at Baltimore. Smith came out in open support of Champ Clark in the early spring of 1912 and even entered Clark's name on the presidential primary ballot.[125] When Clark, in protest, immediately withdrew his name from the New Jersey contest, Smith was forced to file a slate of delegates who would, if elected, go to Baltimore uninstructed, as pawns of the Newark boss. At least he made no secret of his intentions. "The issue is plainly Wilson and anti-Wilson," Smith's newspaper declared. "Sober-thinking Democrats, who are not actuated by personal interest and who are

[120] *Trenton True American,* November 10, 1911; also *Trenton Evening Times,* December 16, 1911.
[121] *Jersey Journal* of Jersey City, March 2, 1912.
[122] *Newark Evening News,* March 1, 1912.
[123] *Trenton Evening Times,* March 4, 1912.
[124] *Trenton True American,* March 20, 1912.
[125] *Newark Evening News,* April 1, 1912; *Trenton True American,* April 2, 1912.

looking for a presidential candidate to win in the November election, favor a Western candidate, Speaker Clark preferred." [126]

As in all Democratic contests in New Jersey, Hudson County, the cornerstone of the state Democracy, was the center and pivot of the struggle. The political situation in Hudson was no less confused in the spring of 1912 than it had been in the fall of 1911; but to all surface appearances Mayor H. Otto Wittpenn, the Wilson leader in the county, was still the dominant power in the county Democratic committee. Revolt against Wittpenn's leadership had been brewing for several months, however, and when the mayor's lieutenant, Frank Hague, bolted the Wittpenn organization and became the avowed Smith leader in Hudson County the pre-convention campaign took an exceedingly dangerous turn. By the middle of April it had become apparent that Hague had taken the anti-Wilson campaign in hand and had succeeded in luring a majority of the Hudson politicians away from Wilson's support. Hague had a clear majority at a meeting of the county committee on April 12, for example, when he attempted to secure the adoption of an anti-Wilson resolution; and he was thwarted only by a clever bit of trickery on the part of County Chairman James Hennessy, a Wilson supporter. [127]

Actually what was taking place was fairly clear. Hague, amply supplied with money by Smith (so the *Jersey Journal* charged) [128] was using the fight over the endorsement of Wilson as a means of obtaining personal control of the county Democracy. He delivered what might well have been a fatal blow to the Wilson movement: he split the Hudson legislative delegation, the faithful nine who had stood by Wilson loyally in his legislative fights. At an anti-Wilson rally in Jersey City on May 17, Assemblymen Thomas F. Martin, Charles M. Egan, Thomas Donnelly, Thomas Griffin, and William Davidson announced their opposition to Wilson's candidacy. [129]

Thus encouraged by the defection of a majority of the Democratic leaders in Hudson County from the Wilson-progressive coalition, Smith, Nugent, and Hague redoubled their campaign efforts. George A. Young, Jersey City banker, also entered the anti-Wilson ranks and

---

[126] *Newark Evening Star,* May 3, 1912. The causes for Smith's opposition to Wilson are obvious. Aside from the purely local political issues involved, it should also be remembered that Smith supported Clark, the strongest anti-Wilson presidential candidate, with an eye to the control of the federal patronage in New Jersey. If Wilson were president, Smith could not expect to control a single appointment in the state.

[127] *Jersey Journal* of Jersey City, April 13, 1912.

[128] *ibid.,* June 12, 1912.   [129] *ibid.,* May 18, 1912.

stumped the state for the election of an uninstructed-Smith delegation. Italian-American voters were numerous in Jersey City and in other North Jersey cities, and Hague assiduously broadcast pamphlets emphasizing Wilson's alleged contempt for the "new" immigrants from southern and eastern Europe.[130] In fact, he overlooked none of the devices that anti-Wilson men were using everywhere.

For the most part, Wilson refused to join in the campaign for his endorsement at the presidential primary. An active campaign for support from members of his own party in his own state would have been undignified on his part, he thought, and a confession of weakness besides. On May 9 he conferred at Trenton with the candidates who were running for election as delegates on the Wilson ticket, and expressed his gratification at the campaign his supporters were making.[131] When Senator John Sharp Williams of Mississippi and Senator Martine came to New Jersey to advocate his nomination, Wilson agreed to speak with them at a Democratic rally in Burlington on May 20. His speech was short and tart, and he lost no time in indulging in his favorite New Jersey sport of lambasting Jim Smith. "The chief purveyor of office in this state was a man who was the chief conspirator in the party's ruin in the Democratic councils," Wilson declared. "I am not here to mince words; I have found some of these gentlemen out. They have handed me the credentials of their characters." [132]

Three days before the New Jersey primaries, Wilson gave to the newspapers his final statement in the pre-convention contest in the state. It was a long statement, an appeal for support, recounting his services to the people of New Jersey; more important, however, was Wilson's warning that Smith was making "one last desperate attempt" again to secure control of the state Democracy and to destroy and supplant the new progressive Democratic regime. Thus he continued:

"What, therefore, is the present situation? What is happening now? What is happening within the Republican party is obvious to the whole country, and a very unedifying spectacle it is. But what is happening in this State within the Democratic party is not so obvious. It is, indeed, being done very quietly and very secretly, because it is being done by Mr. James Smith, Jr., who knows no other way of acting in politics and who has no suggestion to make to the voters of the State which he can quite venture to make in public. He does not, I understand, avow himself as in favor of any particular candidate for the Democratic

[130] *New York Sun*, May 27, 1912.   [131] *Trenton Evening Times*, May 9, 1912.
[132] *Trenton True American*, May 21, 1912.

nomination; he is only opposed to me; and the men he has induced to offer themselves as candidates to represent New Jersey in the National Democratic Convention wish to be sent 'without instructions.' [133]

"It is interesting to note how large a proportion of them are men who were candidates for appointment to office, and whom I did not appoint. There are one or two very conspicuous instances and a great many minor ones of petty spite and disappointment. But that is not the important side of the matter; that is cause for contempt rather than for concern. What concerns us and makes the matter very much larger and more serious than the mere incidental question of whether I am to be nominated at Baltimore or not, is the fact that this is Mr. Smith's attempt to reestablish his control over the Democratic party and put himself once more in a position to make the Democratic machine an adjunct and partner of the old Republican machine in serving the special interests in New Jersey. It is the last desperate attempt of the discredited old regime to destroy and supplant the new.

"Shall the Democrats of New Jersey send delegates to Baltimore who are free men, or are the special interests again to name men to represent them? The representatives of special interests will be in a helpless, intriguing minority at Baltimore. Is the progressive Democracy of New Jersey to contribute to that minority?

"We are speaking of very practical matters now and ought not to mince words. The question is, Do you wish to sustain the new regime; do you wish to support government conducted by public opinion, rather than by private understanding and management, or do you wish to slip back into the slough of the old despair and disgrace? . . .

"The choice in such a matter is so plain and obvious to every man who cares for principle and honor and free government that you will be apt to take it for granted that the result at the polls next Tuesday is a matter of course. But it cannot be. You dare not run the risk. The forces of the other side are marshaled and will be got to the voting places to the last man of them. If you stay away from the polls they will beat and laugh at you. You can win only by voting and by voting your full strength. Every man who stays away from the polls on Tuesday deliberately deserts a great cause and hands his State over to be plundered of even her good name." [134]

Wilson, therefore, made his leadership of the Democratic party in

---

[133] This accusation was hardly fair. Smith, through his newspapers, had made it perfectly evident that he was supporting Clark.

[134] *Trenton True American*, May 25, 1912.

New Jersey the chief issue of the campaign. His leadership and services to the state were overwhelmingly endorsed by the Democratic voters in the presidential primary on May 28. He carried twenty out of the twenty-one counties in the state by enormous majorities; the Smith-Nugent machine narrowly elected four anti-Wilson delegates from Essex county.[135] Jersey City, despite all the efforts of Hague and his cohorts, gave Wilson a remarkable majority, while his majorities were so large in some South Jersey counties that election officials did not bother to count all the votes.[136] Thus twenty-four of the state's twenty-eight delegates would go to Baltimore with ironclad instructions to vote for their governor.[137]

Perhaps it was entirely coincidental that the pre-convention situation in the nation at large improved measurably for Wilson after his victory in New Jersey. On May 28 the Texas Democratic convention instructed its forty delegates to vote for Wilson at Baltimore. North Dakota soon afterward gave her support to a favorite son, Governor John Burke; but it was apparent that the delegation would vote for Wilson. Utah, for some unknown reason, fell into line behind the Wilson movement. The Democrats in South Dakota, after a bitter primary campaign in which McCombs spent some $10,000, voted for Wilson on June 4; and the North Carolina Democratic convention on the same day elected a delegation that was composed largely of Wilson supporters. Minnesota and West Virginia were the last two states to vote in the pre-nomination campaign. West Virginia went to Clark, but Fred B. Lynch, former Governor John Lind, and the other Wilson men in Minnesota wound up the battle on June 6 by electing a full slate of twenty-four Wilson supporters as delegates to the national convention.

Wilson's decisive victory in New Jersey and the marked revival of what most observers had thought was the corpse of the Wilson movement gave new hope to progressive leaders in the East and South, most of whom had staked their political fortunes on Wilson's candidacy. Most encouraging of the late pre-convention developments was the conversion of the *New York World* to the Wilson cause. The

---

[135] They were Smith, Nugent, Arthur B. Seymour, and Harry F. Backus.

[136] *Trenton Evening Times,* May 29, 1912; *Trenton True American,* May 30, 1912.

[137] On May 29 Wilson wrote to Judge John W. Wescott: "Now that there is no doubt about the willingness of New Jersey to support me, I am writing to ask if you will do me the honour of placing my name in nomination before the Baltimore Convention. I know of no one who could do it more impressively or convincingly, and it would give me great personal gratification to have you do so."

World, it will be recalled, had been one of Wilson's severest critics in the East, and the long editorial of May 30, which was far and away the most persuasive editorial plea for his nomination, was reprinted in many Democratic newspapers and provoked widespread discussion in Democratic circles. The *World* advocated Wilson's nomination on the ground that only he among the Democratic candidates could defeat Theodore Roosevelt, the "most cunning and adroit demagogue that modern civilization had produced since Napoleon III." The editorial continued:

"During Gov. Wilson's public career, the World has been compelled to take issue with him on many questions. We regarded with grave misgivings his sudden conversion to the initiative and referendum, reversing the principles of a lifetime. We regretted his apparent disposition to imitate Mr. Bryan's sweeping charges against the so-called Money Trust. . . . We regretted his long campaign tours, his too eager chase after the nomination, and certain symptoms of instability which threatened to weaken his public usefulness. We have not hesitated to warn him when we thought he was going astray, and shall not hesitate to do so again in the future.

"But Gov. Wilson's elements of weakness are vastly overbalanced by his elements of strength. He has proved his political courage and his fearlessness. He has proved himself sound on the Sherman law. He has proved himself sound on corporation control. He has proved himself sound on trust prosecutions and personal guilt. He has proved himself sound against government by Wall street plutocracy. He has proved himself sound on the independence of the judiciary. He has proved himself sound on the fundamental principles of constitutional government. He has proved that he is instinctively and temperamentally a Democrat. He has proved himself a free man who cannot be bulldozed by bosses or influenced against his convictions even by his personal friends. That is the sort of man who ought to be President."

If the Wilson movement, at the end of the pre-convention campaign, had elements of great strength, it was nevertheless an open question whether the Wilson forces were strong enough to prevent Clark's nomination. Certainly the balance sheet of the campaign afforded a discouraging reckoning. Some 436 delegates were instructed to vote for Clark's nomination; while this number fell short of a majority (545), 224 votes were controlled by various bosses and leaders and the support of the Tammany-controlled ninety votes from New York would alone be almost sufficient to give Clark a majority; and a majority vote, at least since 1844, had been tantamount to nomination in Democratic conventions. Wilson, on the other hand, could count only 248 delegates definitely instructed in his favor; and the best the Wilson managers could hope for was that the support of the uninstructed Wilson delegates would give him control of at least one-third of the convention vote.

Apparently the Wilson men at Baltimore would have at the outside nothing more than a veto power over the nomination. As for Wilson's being nominated—well, who believed in miracles? Wilson had struggled hard to maintain a brave front; but he, too, at last was convinced by the compelling argument of reality. At last he was forced to admit that the Wilson movement had collapsed. Thus he wrote at the conclusion of the pre-convention campaign: "We go to the shore, to Sea Girt, on Friday, the 14th,—at least the family goes. I never know from hour to hour where sudden calls, for political conferences and the like, will take me on any given date. It is of great service to me just now to be able to look on at the political game as if I had no part in it at the same time that I am actively enlisted, and my own personal career involved. And it gives me, I think, a clearer vision and a steadier hand. Just between you and me, I have not the least idea of being nominated, because the make of the convention is such, the balance and confusion of forces, that the outcome is in the hands of the professional, case-hardened politicians who serve only their own interests and who know that I will not serve them except as I might serve the party in general. I am well and in the best of spirits. I have no deep stakes involved in this game." [138]

[138] W. W. to M. A. Hulbert, June 9, 1912, published in R. S. Baker, *Woodrow Wilson*, III, 321.

W[CHAPTER XIII]W

The Baltimore Convention[1]

"WHAT we now look forward to with not a little dread are the possibilities of the next fortnight in politics," Woodrow Wilson wrote to Mary Allen Hulbert on June 17. Two days before, Wilson and his family had moved from Princeton to the Governor's Cottage at Sea Girt, New Jersey.

"I was saying at breakfast this morning, 'Two weeks from to-day we shall either have this sweet Sunday calm again or an army of reporters camped on the lawn and an all-day reception. . . .' Now that the *possibility* is immediately at hand (it is no more than a possibility, as things stand) I find myself dreading it and wishing most devoutly that I may escape. Not that I dread what would be really big and essential and worth while in the whole thing, but all that would go with [it]—all that is *non*-essential, *not* of the *business,* merely distracting and exhausting and hateful without counting,—the excessive *personal* tax of a campaign. May the Lord have mercy on me! My heart is not faint, but my taste and my preference for what is genuine and at the opposite pole from mere personal notoriety revolts at the thought of what I may be in for! . . .

"I am well . . . and underneath, deep down, my soul is quiet." [2]

The peaceful family scene at the Governor's Cottage was destined to be short lived. To begin with, the reverberations of the Republican national convention, which was then meeting in Chicago, were enough to shatter the calm at Sea Girt. The fight between Taft and Roosevelt for the Republican presidential nomination had finally culminated in the disruption of the party; and Roosevelt and his angry followers had left the Chicago convention, vowing to organize a new third party. From Wilson's point of view, it was a dangerous development, for it further weakened his chances for the Democratic nomination.

[1] Portions of this chapter have been previously published in the *American Historical Review*, L (July 1945), 691-713; they are reprinted by permission of Mr. Guy Stanton Ford, managing editor.
[2] Published in R. S. Baker, *Woodrow Wilson*, III, 332-333.

The schism in the Republican party led many Democrats to conclude that it really made no difference whom they nominated; certainly the argument of Wilson's supporters that only he could win the presidency, because he alone among the Democrats could divide the insurgents from the Republicans, was vitiated now that Roosevelt had accomplished that division for them.

More than anyone else, however, William J. Bryan disturbed the peaceful scene at Sea Girt in the spring of 1912. Bryan was deeply concerned over the Democratic national committee's decision to select Alton B. Parker, Democratic standard-bearer in 1904, as the temporary chairman at Baltimore.[3] The committee on arrangements of the national committee, meeting at Baltimore on June 20, supported Chairman Norman E. Mack in his campaign to make Parker temporary chairman.[4] Bryan, who was in Chicago gleefully observing the great struggle between Taft and Roosevelt, was convinced that the same conservative forces that controlled the Republican convention were making ready to move to Baltimore. "What on earth does anybody want Parker for?" he asked Josephus Daniels, national committeeman from North Carolina. "He would start us off on a reactionary basis that would give the lie to all our progressive declarations." It would be "suicidal to have a reactionary for chairman when four-fifths of the country is radically progressive," Bryan protested to Mack; he could not believe that such "criminal folly" was possible.[5] Undismayed by the rebuff he had received from the committee on arrangements, Bryan next determined to carry his fight against Parker into the convention itself. Ignoring Harmon and Underwood, whom he considered "reactionaries" and therefore outside the progressive pale, he immediately sent identical telegrams to Wilson, Clark, and several "favorite son" can-

[3] It is interesting that Norman E. Mack, Democratic national chairman, several months before the convention met, had suggested to Bryan that the national committee would gladly name him for the temporary chairmanship. Bryan, however, declined to serve as the Democratic keynoter and wrote Mack: ". . . the committee should ask the two leading candidates—I suppose they will be Clark and Wilson—to agree upon the temporary chairman. I believe it would be conducive to harmony if we could get a man who would be agreeable to both of these candidates. I neglected to add that I do not desire the position myself. *I think that under the circumstances it is better for me not to take a prominent part in the organization of the convention.*" W. J. Bryan to N. E. Mack, May —, 1912, published in N. E. Mack, "Wilson and Marshall—Mr. Bryan and New York," *National Monthly*, IV (August 1912), 65; italics mine.

[4] *Official Report of the Proceedings of the Democratic National Convention . . . 1912*, p. 473; hereinafter cited as *Proceedings of the Convention*.

[5] Josephus Daniels, *The Wilson Era*, p. 50.

didates, asking if they would stand by him in his fight against Parker.[6]

At the Wilson headquarters in the Hotel Emerson in Baltimore, McCombs was terror-stricken by Bryan's move. He feared that an unequivocal answer from Wilson supporting Bryan's stand would alienate Charles F. Murphy and his Tammany cohorts and forestall any chance Wilson might have of obtaining the support of the New York delegation.[7] McCombs therefore immediately forwarded to Wilson a suggested reply to Bryan's letter that embodied the essence of a straddling statement Wilson had already made to the editor of the *Baltimore Evening Sun*.[8] At the insistence of Tumulty and Mrs. Wilson, however, Wilson gave a straightforward answer to Bryan's appeal. "You are quite right," he began. "The Baltimore convention is to be a convention of progressives—of men who are progressive in principle and by conviction," which must, moreover, "express its convictions in its organization and in its choice of the men who are to speak for it." [9] McCombs was heart-broken; "All my work has gone for nothing," he told McAdoo.[10] In fact, however, Wilson's clear-cut statement on the temporary chairmanship issue was a masterful stroke, for it marked him at the outset of the convention as one progressive leader with backbone. Champ Clark, on the other hand, who had everything to lose by discord within the convention, attempted to hedge by making a noncommittal appeal to Bryan for party harmony. The "supreme consideration," Clark wrote, "should be to prevent any discord in the convention." [11]

On Sunday and Monday, June 23 and 24, the Democratic hosts descended on Baltimore, traditional scene of Democratic gatherings. "It is of good augury that once more we meet in the glorious metropolis of Maryland," "Marse Henry" Watterson wrote. "Noble city! In deep

[6] Mary B. Bryan (ed.), *Memoirs of William Jennings Bryan,* pp. 161-166, has an interesting account of Bryan's activities during this period.

[7] W. G. McAdoo, *Crowded Years,* pp. 137-141, gives an interesting account of McCombs's attitude.

[8] Before Bryan sent his appeal to the candidates, J. H. Adams, editor of the *Evening Sun,* had asked Wilson to make a statement on the temporary chairmanship contest. Wilson replied instantly: "My friends in Baltimore, who are on the ground, will know how to act in the interest of the people's cause in everything that affects the organization of the Convention. They are certain not to forget their standards, as they have already shown. It is not necessary that I should remind them of those standards from Sea Girt; and I have neither the right nor the desire to direct the organization of a convention of which I am not even a member." Undated letter in Wilson Papers.

[9] *New York World,* June 23, 1912.

[10] W. G. McAdoo, *Crowded Years,* p. 141.

[11] C. Clark to W. J. Bryan, June —, 1912, published in *The Commoner,* June 28, 1912.

reflection the spirit of democracy walks thy streets this day; broods amid thy solitudes." [12] The solitude within the historic city, however, was rudely shattered by the incoming Democrats. Tammany Hall, led by Murphy and August Belmont, came in a special train. Thomas F. Ryan, delegate from Virginia, arrived under cover of night and quietly slipped into his rooms. Bryan had of course come from Chicago; Clark had established convention headquarters in the Speaker's Office in the Capitol at Washington. The New Jersey delegation, with the exception of the Essex delegates, came to Baltimore in a body with a great array of banners, pictures, and several brass bands, and occupied the entire fifth floor of the Stafford Hotel. There were no more enthusiastic Wilson men in Baltimore than the New Jersey delegates. [13]

The arrival of the Democrats in Baltimore was the signal for the traditional bargaining among the presidential managers to begin, or rather to become intensified. The temporary chairmanship became the outstanding issue of the day when, in a plenary session of the national committee, the Clark representatives combined with Tammany Hall and the conservatives to defeat the nomination of Ollie M. James of Kentucky[14] in favor of Parker for the temporary chairmanship. [15] This seemingly unnatural and, to Bryan's friends, immoral alliance between Clark's managers and Tammany gave rise to suspicions that the speaker's managers had concluded a bargain with Murphy by which the Clark delegations would support Parker for the temporary chairmanship and New York's ninety votes would come to Clark at some propitious moment in the balloting. [16]

The leading Clark newspaper spokesman, in fact, admitted as much. Clark's managers and Murphy, the newspaper reported, had reached "common ground" on the temporary chairmanship issue; William R. Hearst, moreover, had been brought into the Clark-Tammany coalition, and Hearst and Murphy had agreed to bury their political hatchets. [17] The Clark forces, it should be emphasized, held the key to the

---

[12] *Louisville Courier-Journal*, cited in *Pensacola Journal*, July 4, 1912.

[13] See *Trenton True American*, June 25, 1912, for a description of the activities of the New Jersey delegates in Baltimore. On June 11 the New Jersey delegation had drafted a long letter setting forth the arguments for Wilson's nomination, and sent it to all the delegates to the national convention. See *ibid.*, June 11, 1912.

[14] James was a Clark supporter and had Bryan's full approval.

[15] *Proceedings of the Convention*, p. 490.

[16] *Dallas Morning News*, June 25, 1912; Robert Latham in *Charleston News and Courier*, June 25, 1912; W. E. Gonzales in *Columbia* (S. C.) *State*, June 25, 1912.

[17] *St. Louis Republic*, June 25, 1912.

election of a temporary chairman. They could either defeat Bryan or they could aid him in smashing the plan of a few conservatives to control the convention. Yet Murphy and his allies controlled enough votes to give Clark a majority of the delegates in the convention, while Bryan did not.[18] The Clark men, besides, had a very real dread that should Bryan win his fight against Parker by an overwhelming vote he would be unbeatable as a presidential candidate himself.[19]

The tremendous crowd in Convention Hall, gathered for the first session of the convention on the afternoon of June 25, became hushed as the venerable Cardinal Gibbons invoked the blessings of God upon the deliberations of the body. The prayer was the lull before the storm. Chairman Mack rapped his gavel for order; he had been instructed by the national committee, he declared, to nominate Alton B. Parker for temporary chairman.[20] Bryan was immediately on his feet; he stood high on the speakers' platform. "He looked older than a few days ago at Chicago, pale and very grim. His heavy black brows were contracted over his piercing eyes. His hawk nose had an extra downward twist. His lipless mouth was like a thin dagger-slit across his broad face. He held his head erect, the magnificent dome of his brow contrasting with the curious lack of back to his head. The grizzled fringe of his dark hair was ruffled and moist with perspiration. He made a fine figure, standing up there, in an old dark sack suit, with a low collar and white string tie, holding his right hand up to quell the applause." [21] Bryan nominated Senator John W. Kern of Indiana, his running mate in 1908, as the man most worthy of the confidence of the convention. Now that the hour of Democratic triumph had

[18] Senator-elect James K. Vardaman of Mississippi was selected by the Parker forces to offer the olive branch of compromise to Bryan. It was a wise selection, for Vardaman had for years been an intimate friend and loyal follower of the Nebraskan. He offered Bryan the permanent chairmanship of the convention if he would accept Parker as temporary chairman. Bryan became so "frigid," according to one report, that Vardaman picked up his hat and started to leave the room. Turning again to Bryan, he said, "I thought our personal and political relations were intimate enough to permit me to talk about the matter to you." Bryan, smiling sadly, put his hand on Vardaman's shoulder and told him that he had not meant to hurt him, but that he could not possibly consent to such an agreement. Louis Seibold in *New York World*, June 24, 1912.

[19] Arthur Krock in *Louisville Times*, June 25, 1912. The *New York World*, June 25, 1912, called upon Bryan to make it plain that under no circumstances would he accept the nomination. Bryan was fighting for a great principle, the editor of the *World* asserted, and the only thing that stood in the way of a progressive victory was the growing suspicion that Bryan was secretly planning his own nomination.

[20] *Proceedings of the Convention*, pp. 2-3.

[21] *New York World*, June 26, 1912.

arrived, he asserted, a true progressive should lead the convention in the keynote address. The Democrats were announcing to the country whether they would take up the challenge thrown down at Chicago by a convention controlled by "predatory wealth," or answer it by giving themselves over to the same sinister forces.[22]

As he thundered the phrase, "He never sold the truth to serve the hour," he seemed the old Bryan, and the old spell seemed to be weaving as the hall rang with cheers. Bryan told how he had been offered the temporary chairmanship and had refused the offer, and how he had worked to secure the selection of a progressive compromise candidate. But it was not the old Bryan of '96, not the same spell of the Cross of Gold. The palm leaf fan in his right hand trembled. He went on and reviewed the fights for progressive Democracy that he had made at Kern's side. Then came the crisis. In the name of progressive Democracy, Bryan cried, "You cannot frighten it with your Ryans nor buy it with your Belmonts." This palpable defiance electrified the convention; men were on their feet all over the hall, waving their hats and shouting for Bryan. This was his natural climax; the old Bryan would have seized the opportunity and sat down. Too many lecture platforms had dulled the edge of the spell-binder's art, however, and he went on in an anticlimactic excoriation of Parker. The convention was now getting tired of Bryan: the cries of "Parker, Parker" grew louder; every other phrase of Bryan's was being interrupted by the impatient mob. "And so, with a last metaphor about a cloud of smoke by day, poor Bryan who had begun as a prophet, concluded as a bore and sat down amid a roar one-quarter of enthusiasm, three-quarters of relief." [23]

Before the noise had subsided, Senator Kern went to the speakers' platform. He was a small man in a brown sack suit, with a long, narrow, hatchet face, small eyes deeply set close together, a long, thin nose, and a grizzled mustache and beard. Kern made a dramatic appeal to Parker to withdraw from the contest and declared that if the New York delegation would agree to support either O'Gorman, Culberson, Henry D. Clayton of Alabama, Luke Lea, or Joseph W. Folk, all discord would cease. When there was no answer from the New York delegation, the Indiana senator withdrew from the contest and nominated Bryan himself.[24] The convention was in an uproar. Theodore Bell of California, who rose to answer Kern, was overwhelmed by a

[22] *Proceedings of the Convention*, pp. 5-6.
[23] *New York World*, June 26, 1912.   [24] *Proceedings of the Convention*, pp. 7-9.

torrent of noise from the Wilson delegates. Representative John J. Fitzgerald of New York seemed to have arrested the confusion and was delivering some telling blows for Parker when Cullen F. Thomas of Texas climbed into his chair and yelled, "Are you the distinguished New York Congressman who supported Joe Cannon?" This pointed interpellation ended Fitzgerald's speech.[25] The convention was anxious to vote, but Bryan pleaded for five additional minutes of debate before the roll call. Cone Johnson of Texas pushed to the front of the speakers' platform and with a voice as loud as a "human fog-horn," quieted the mob. The contest was not between men, he declared, and he did not pause to inquire who caused the fight. "This one thing I know—the fight is on and Bryan is on one side and Wall Street is on the other."[26]

The convention then proceeded to endorse the national committee, and elected Parker temporary chairman by a vote of 579 to 508. The Clark managers delivered enough of their delegates to insure Bryan's defeat, although most of the Clark men on the western delegations refused to deal what they considered was a treacherous blow against their old leader.[27] They accordingly stood by the Nebraskan, while the Wilson delegates almost to a man voted for him. Champ Clark himself had remained neutral during the fight but, as Bryan noted, his managers were "working like beavers for Judge Parker."[28]

The dramatic conflict between Bryan and Parker was a fitting introduction to the struggles at the Baltimore convention. It convinced thousands of progressive Democrats that the fight was on between Wilson and Bryan on the one hand, and Clark, Wall Street, and Tammany on the other.[29] Bryan had failed simply because 228 Clark delegates voted for Parker; Missouri, for example, had given 22 votes to Parker and 14 to Bryan. "Stated in terms of cold politics," commented the leading Clark spokesman, "Senator Stone, by thus casting nearly two-thirds of the State's 36 votes for the conservative candidate, made a deliberate 'bid' for New York's support for Clark in the later stages of the convention."[30] The Clark-Tammany "deal," moreover, convinced Bryan that Clark would not hesitate to desert him for the forbidden fruits of New York. "You see how Clark . . . threw his influence against you,"

[25] *Dallas Morning News*, June 26, 1912.
[26] *Proceedings of the Convention*, p. 13.   [27] *ibid.*, pp. 17-19.
[28] W. J. Bryan, *A Tale of Two Conventions*, p. 192.
[29] It stirred the people at home to action, and a flood of telegrams—from 100,000 to 120,000—poured in upon the delegates from their constituents, who urged their representatives to support Bryan. Mary B. Bryan (ed.), *Memoirs*, p. 170.
[30] *St. Louis Republic*, June 26, 1912.

Senator Martine told Bryan. "Now come out in the open and help swing every Progressive to the only real Progressive candidate, Woodrow Wilson." "I know what has happened," Bryan replied. "I am with you." [31]

The Wilson newspapers rose up in arms. The *New York World*, the *New York Evening Post*, the *Baltimore Sun*, and even the staid *New York Times* published militant editorials declaring that Bryan's defeat had emphasized the progressive-reactionary nature of the conflict at Baltimore. Wilson journals elsewhere of course praised Bryan's action. Conservative newspapers, on the other hand, jubilantly announced the Nebraskan's demise. One editor called him a "bawling and brawling political bully." [32] "At least, Mr. Bryan's fangs have been drawn," another exclaimed. [33]

The reaction of the convention was indicative of public feeling. When Parker began reading his keynote address, "the galleries rose . . . and left a rather dazed old gentleman reading a long manuscript, nervously looking over his glasses occasionally at the vanishing crowd." [34] The disturbance became so noisy that the reading was suspended and the convention adjourned until the evening. Bryan interpreted the rude treatment accorded Parker as proof that "as Mr. Parker's speech was written in the language of Wall Street, only two or three hundred of the delegates could understand it." [35]

The victory of the Clark-Tammany coalition was a Pyrrhic one. A move by the Murphy organization to retain Parker as permanent chairman was quickly detected and blocked by former Governor Thomas M. Campbell of Texas. [36] At the insistence of the Wilson men, Ollie M. James was chosen permanent chairman of the convention, [37] and Bryan was delighted. [38] Urey Woodson was ousted as secretary of the convention and Edward E. Britton, city editor of the *Raleigh News and Observer*, was chosen in his stead. [39]

Progressive sentiment was rising in the convention; and the first im-

[31] Julius Grunow in the *Jersey Journal* of Jersey City, June 26, 1912.
[32] *Houston Post*, June 26, 1912.
[33] *Chattanooga Daily Times*, June 26, 1912.
[34] William A. White, *Woodrow Wilson*, p. 254.
[35] Quoted in Morris R. Werner, *Bryan*, p. 185.
[36] *Dallas Morning News*, June 27, 1912.
[37] Vance McCormick later recalled that the Wilson managers decided to support James for the permanent chairmanship because they thought it was good strategy to have him as presiding officer rather than floor leader for the Clark forces. V. McCormick to R. S. Baker, September 17, 1928, Baker Papers.
[38] W. J. Bryan, *A Tale of Two Conventions*, p. 153.
[39] *Proceedings of the Convention*, p. 120.

portant progressive victory occurred in the abrogation of the ironclad unit rule in the voting of several state delegations. The fight developed when the convention committee on rules decreed that nineteen Wilson delegates from Ohio had to vote for Harmon because the state Democratic convention had thus instructed. The chairman of the rules committee, J. Harry Covington of Maryland, argued that the traditional Democratic usage should not be altered, that the national convention had no right to interfere in the internal party affairs of the states.[40]

Robert L. Henry of Texas presented the minority report of the committee,[41] but the foremost champion of the abrogation of the unit rule was Newton D. Baker, mayor of Cleveland. In an impassioned appeal to the convention, Baker insisted that the law of Ohio had taken from the state convention the authority to select delegates to national conventions and had vested it in the people. He had given a sacred pledge to his constituents that he would vote for Wilson; would the convention force him to betray the trust the people had confided in him?[42] Senator John Sharp Williams of Mississippi lost his temper for the benefit of the Wilson cause. If the convention adopted the majority report, he declared, it would do "the most dangerous and the most damnable thing" in its power. And "when you get through with it," he shouted, "you can quit your talk about 'popular government.'"[43]

When John W. Peck of Ohio attempted to defend the majority report he mentioned Wilson's name and set off a wild demonstration by the Wilson delegates. The New Jersey delegation began the uproar. A dozen pictures of Wilson appeared and were carried through the hall; on the platform, John Sharp Williams swung his hat above his head as he led cheers for Wilson. A large white Texas banner inscribed "40 for Wilson" was flung forth by the Texas men, while an enormous orange and black banner over thirty feet long was carried through the galleries by Wilson supporters from Staunton, Virginia. "Give us Wilson and we'll give you Pennsylvania" was unfurled over the Pennsylvania delegation. Deafening waves of sound crashed through the huge auditorium; the band struck up the "Star Spangled Banner," and from the galleries the bearers of the Staunton banner came down on to the convention floor. Hurrying to the press stand, the little band of Staunton men attempted to scale the platform; one of them reached the press stand, but he was seized by an irate reporter and thrown back into the melee. The monotonous chant of the galleries—"We want Wilson; we

[40] *ibid.*, pp. 59-60.
[41] *ibid.*
[42] *ibid.*, pp. 65-68.
[43] *ibid.*, p. 72.

want Wilson"—was lost in the roar of the crowd. Half an hour passed; finally the temporary chairman was able to quiet the mob.[44]

Robert L. Henry, Wilson's floor leader, sensed the rising Wilson sentiment, and after the demonstration had subsided announced that Virginia, "the mother of the doctrine of State sovereignty," had signed the minority report.[45] Largely because of the support the Wilson managers received from Mississippi, Virginia, Florida, and Alabama they succeeded in turning the tables on the Clark forces; the convention, by a vote of 565½ to 492⅓, adopted the minority report.[46] This important Wilson victory served as an effective antidote to the growing belief that Clark was certain to be nominated; more important, it added nineteen precious votes to the feeble Wilson numbers.

Another important episode in the struggle at Baltimore concerned the disposition of the South Dakota delegation. Two delegations from that state, one representing Wilson, the other Clark, presented their claims as the rightful delegation to the credentials committee on June 26. Clark supporters, who controlled the committee, voted to seat the Clark delegation. In the meantime another contest had come before the credentials committee. Two delegations from Cook County, Illinois, claimed to be the lawful representatives from Chicago; one group represented Roger Sullivan, the Illinois Democratic boss, the other represented the Hearst-Carter Harrison Chicago coalition. The Wilson managers, one of them afterward wrote, "lined up with Sullivan, knowing that we could never hope for anything from Hearst and that he absolutely dominated the contesting delegation." [47] Luke Lea, spokesman for the Wilson forces in the credentials committee, made a bargain with Sullivan that affected the outcome of the convention as greatly as any other single event at Baltimore. The Wilson representatives on the credentials committee agreed to support Sullivan in the Illinois contest; Sullivan in turn agreed to throw the weight of the Illinois delegation behind the Wilson men when they forced the South Dakota contest on the floor of the convention.[48] Consequently the Sullivan delegates were

[44] *Montgomery Advertiser*, June 27, 1912.

[45] *Proceedings of the Convention*, p. 75; see also *Richmond Times-Dispatch*, June 27, 1912 for an explanation of the action of the Virginia delegates.

[46] *Proceedings of the Convention*, p. 77.

[47] T. W. Gregory to E. M. House, July 9, 1912, House Papers. The present author has edited Gregory's letter, under the title, "A Letter from One of Wilson's Managers," *American Historical Review*, L (July, 1945), 768-775.

[48] *Charlotte Daily Observer*, June 27, 1912; *Houston Post*, June 28, 1912.

seated by the credentials committee;[49] and when the South Dakota issue was considered by the convention, Sullivan threw Illinois's fifty-eight votes to the Wilson delegation and they were seated.[50]

The importance of the shrewd Sullivan-Lea bargain has not been generally recognized. First of all, it added ten votes to the growing number of Wilson delegates; but more important, it assured Sullivan's dominance in the Illinois delegation and enabled him to cast the fifty-eight Illinois votes for Wilson at a crucial moment in the balloting.

As a result of the Wilson successes in the struggle for the abrogation of the unit rule and for the control of the South Dakota delegation, a decided reaction in the convention against the Clark-Tammany alliance set in. It was apparent that the Wilson delegates had taken a new lease on life. Bryan on the other hand, suspected that the conservatives were only biding their time and waiting for the propitious moment to strike. "I found that the representatives of Morgan, Belmont, and Ryan were at work," he later recalled.[51]

The fact that Thomas F. Ryan, one of the czars of Wall Street, was sitting as a delegate from Virginia was a cause of severe embarrassment to Senator Claude A. Swanson and other leaders in the Virginia delegation.[52] In the first place, Ryan had secured membership in the Virginia delegation through trickery;[53] his activities, moreover, were of a

[49] This was one of the most unconscionable "deals" made at the convention and compares strikingly with the Clark-Tammany bargain over the temporary chairmanship. From the evidence the author has gathered, it appears that there was no validity in Sullivan's argument that his henchmen were the legally elected delegates from Chicago; the evidence, on the contrary, reveals that the Hearst-Harrison delegates were deprived of their seats in an indefensible manner. Before the Illinois contest was considered by the credentials committee, Joseph E. Davies, one of Wilson's managers, intimated to Harrison that the Wilson delegates would support him if he would agree to swing the Illinois delegation to Wilson. When Harrison replied that he was bound to support Clark, the Wilson men made their bargain with Sullivan. See Carter H. Harrison, *Stormy Years*, pp. 319-328, for a full account of the Illinois struggle, from Chicago to Baltimore.

[50] *Proceedings of the Convention*, pp. 93-94.

[51] Mary B. Bryan (ed.), *Memoirs*, p. 173.

[52] *Richmond News Leader*, June 28, 1912.

[53] At a meeting of the tenth district committee at the Democratic state convention in Norfolk in May 1912, the anti-Wilson men, led by Hal D. Flood, greatly outnumbered the Wilson supporters. Flood, who was regarded as Ryan's chief lieutenant, suggested to the Wilson men that the Underwood and Wilson forces divide evenly the district's delegates to the national convention. There would be no election, as the offer went, but each group would choose its own man. Astonished at this seeming liberality, the Wilson men hastily accepted the offer. The organization faction then announced they had selected Ryan to represent them. At the time, Ryan's son was present, and the Wilson men supposed it was he who had been chosen as delegate. The secret was well kept and it was

suspicious character. One reporter charged that the Virginia financier was the "captain-general of the plutocrats" who were in Baltimore to depose Bryan as Democratic leader and to prevent Wilson's nomination.[54]

At three o'clock on Thursday morning, June 27, Charles W. Bryan told his brother that Clark's managers had concluded an agreement with Tammany whereby New York's ninety votes would be delivered to Clark at some time early in the balloting. This agreement, Charles W. Bryan insisted, would place the party under obligation to Wall Street and would prevent Clark from carrying out a progressive program were he elected president. In order to determine if the Clark organization would stand by Wall Street instead of the Commoner, he would have one of the progressive leaders introduce a resolution to expel Ryan and August Belmont from the convention. Charles W. Bryan told his brother that he would call together the Wilson leaders and endeavor to persuade one of them to introduce the resolution. William J. Bryan approved of the plan.

Charles W. Bryan soon afterward called together Thomas P. Gore, Luke Lea, Cone Johnson, Jerry B. Sullivan, Harvey Garber, and Henderson Martin, all of them ardent Bryan men. These Wilson leaders unanimously agreed that the proposed resolution demanding Ryan's and Belmont's expulsion from the convention was too harsh and furthermore unwise. None volunteered to introduce it.[55] Charles W. Bryan was discouraged when he saw his brother at his hotel Thursday evening. At Charles W.'s suggestion, W. J. Bryan wrote out a resolution specifically naming Belmont, Morgan, and Ryan as conspirators of Wall Street. He was not certain that he would introduce the resolution when he started to the evening session on June 27; but on the way he decided to take the fateful step.[56]

In the convention, therefore, Bryan rose and asked unanimous consent to introduce a resolution. Several delegates objected, but the rules were suspended, and the following words fell upon the ears of the astounded delegates:

Resolved, That in this crisis in our party's career and in our country's history this convention sends greeting to the people of the United

no little surprise to the Wilson delegates from Virginia to discover that the financier himself was a member of their delegation. Carter W. Wormley in *ibid.,* June 27, 1912.

[54] Samuel G. Blythe, in *New Orleans Times-Democrat,* June 27, 1912.

[55] Charles W. Bryan, in *New York Times,* March 6, 1921.

[56] Mary B. Bryan (ed.), *Memoirs,* pp. 175-176.

States, and assures them that the party of Jefferson and of Jackson is still the champion of popular government and equality before the law. As proof of our fidelity to the people, we hereby declare ourselves opposed to the nomination of any candidate for president who is the representative of or under obligation to J. Pierpont Morgan, Thomas F. Ryan, August Belmont, or any other member of the privilege-hunting and favor-seeking class.

Be it further resolved, That we demand the withdrawal from this convention of any delegate or delegates constituting or representing the above-named interest.[57]

It seemed as if all the furies of hell had broken loose on the convention floor. Scores of delegates leaped to their feet, demanding recognition. "My God, Josephus, what is the matter with Bryan?" Ollie James exclaimed. "Does he want to destroy the Democratic Party?"[58] One man rushed at Bryan and denounced him until he "frothed at the mouth" and had to be carried away by his friends.[59] The convention sergeant-at-arms and the police were unable to quiet the disturbance. Bryan, slightly pale, stood immovable before the howling mob. When the uproar finally subsided, he defended his resolution. It was an extraordinary measure, he admitted, but extraordinary conditions required severe remedies. "There is not a delegate in this convention who does not know that an effort is being made right now to sell the Democratic party into bondage to the predatory interests of this nation," he shouted. "It is the most brazen, the most insolent, the most impudent attempt that has been made in the history of American politics . . . to make the nominee the bond-slave of the men who exploit the people of this country." Bryan, now quite red in the face, said that if the New York and Virginia delegates would take an "honest poll" of their delegations, and if a majority of both states did not ask for Ryan's and Belmont's withdrawal, he would expunge the latter part of his resolution.[60]

As Bryan concluded, Hal Flood of the Virginia delegation, a short, stocky man with a deep olive complexion, a sharp nose, a head of bushy black hair, and eyes that blazed with indignation, forced his way up the steps to the speakers' platform. As he came up to Bryan's side the Commoner turned and held out his hand. Flood looked squarely at Bryan,

[57] *Proceedings of the Convention,* p. 129.
[58] Josephus Daniels, *The Wilson Era,* p. 57.
[59] Mary B. Bryan (ed.), *Memoirs,* p. 177.
[60] *Proceedings of the Convention,* pp. 131-132.

made an angry rejoinder with a vigorous shake of his head, and rejected the proffered hand. He stepped nearer to Bryan and in a ringing voice shouted that Virginia accepted "the insolent proposition" made by the only man who wanted "to destroy the prospect of Democratic success." [61] A tumultuous roar from the delegates followed this clear statement. When the delegates looked for Bryan he was surrounded by the crowd of people on the platform. He did not appear again until Senator-elect James K. Vardaman, in a long, drab frock coat, "his hair as long as a patent medicine man's," came forward and pleaded for silence. Then Bryan was greeted by a storm of hisses and catcalls. He declared that Virginia had notified him that she wanted the expulsion resolution withdrawn. Then, looking squarely at Murphy, Bryan, who was now very much excited, declared, "If a delegate authorized to speak for New York will rise and ask that the last part of the resolution be withdrawn—" [62]

Before the New York delegation could reply, the hisses and boos of the crowd again drowned out Bryan's stentorian voice. Former Governor W. A. McCorkle of West Virginia took a place beside Bryan on the platform and was given the nearest thing to a respectful hearing accorded any previous speaker. Bryan looked hopefully at McCorkle, but his face revealed his disappointment when McCorkle declared that Bryan's resolution was "senseless and foolish." Flood was back on the platform; the Virginia delegation asked nothing of Bryan, he declared. If Bryan withdrew the second part of his resolution, it was not at Virginia's request.[63] Then the crowd began to shout to Bryan, "Sit down! down! down! sit down!" He flushed at this rebuke and started to sit down; but he changed his mind and returned to the fight.[64]

Bryan was in an exceedingly difficult position. Obviously he wished to withdraw the expulsion resolution, for if it remained the entire resolution would probably be defeated; when Vardaman suggested that he withdraw the second part himself, Bryan hastily did so.[65] He then hurriedly demanded a roll call. While the vote was being recorded, Vardaman rushed over to Murphy and urged him to vote for the resolution. "If you do, Murphy, we will make Bryan look like a fool," he declared.[66] After consulting with Sullivan and Thomas Taggart, Murphy cast New

[61] *ibid.*, p. 132; *New York World*, June 28, 1912.
[62] *Proceedings of the Convention*, p. 133.
[63] *ibid.*, pp. 133-135. [64] *New York World*, June 28, 1912.
[65] *Proceedings of the Convention*, p. 135.
[66] *New York World*, June 28, 1912.

York's vote for the resolution. As the Tammany leader cast New York's "Aye" for the resolution he turned to Belmont and with a sly grin on his face said, "Now Auggie, listen to yourself vote yourself out of the convention."[67] The emasculated anti-Wall Street resolution was endorsed by a vote of 883 to 201½.[68]

Back of the scenes at Baltimore the Wilson and Clark men were working furiously. The Wilson leaders realized that only by shrewd strategy could they overcome the power of the forces arrayed against them and nominate their candidate. The general outline of the strategy, however, was clear. The Wilson men had to hold at least a loyal third of the delegates in order to block the first major threat, which was Clark's nomination. Several weeks before the convention assembled, Wilson had designated McCombs as leader of his forces at Baltimore, and A. Mitchell Palmer and Albert S. Burleson as official floor leaders in the convention.[69] At a meeting of the "General Staff" in McCombs's apartment in the Hotel Emerson preceding the balloting for the nomination, the Wilson managers counseled together and pledged to one another their loyalty.[70] Immediately afterward, Thomas W. Gregory and Thomas B. Love of Texas went to the Hotel Stafford and sought out the members of the Pennsylvania delegation. The Texans and Pennsylvanians agreed that they, the two strongest Wilson delegations, should work hand in hand in the convention and that the individual delegates should set to work at once to persuade the Clark delegates to swing over to Wilson.[71]

During the night and early morning of June 27 and 28 the nominations for president were made. It was nearly midnight and the teeming auditorium was sultry and hot; the riotous disturbance over Bryan's inflammable anti-Wall Street resolution had scarcely been quieted when Chairman Ollie James called for the presidential nominations.

Alabama was the first state to be called and made the first nomination. Senator John H. Bankhead yielded to his son, William B. Bank-

---

[67] Josephus Daniels, *The Wilson Era*, p. 57.

[68] *Proceedings of the Convention*, pp. 137-138.

[69] R. S. Baker, "Memorandum of a Conversation with Albert S. Burleson, March 17-19, 1927," Baker Papers.

[70] Present at the conference were McCombs, Burleson, Palmer, McAdoo, Willard Saulsbury, Thomas B. Love, Gregory, Davies, Robert Ewing of Louisiana, "Alfalfa Bill" Murray of Oklahoma, A. C. Weiss of Minnesota, John Gary Evans of South Carolina, Luke Lea, and Charles F. Johnson of Maine.

[71] T. W. Gregory to E. M. House, July 9, 1912, House Papers.

head,[72] the privilege of nominating Alabama's favorite son, Oscar W. Underwood. Young Bankhead presented Underwood as the chief exponent of tariff reform and attempted to persuade the convention that since there was no North, no South, the Alabaman was "available" as a presidential candidate.[73] When Bankhead finally mentioned Underwood's name the Alabama delegation rose to its feet. Then the Georgia, Florida, and Mississippi delegations joined in the brave demonstration; there was tumult of noise and cheering, and above the roar of the crowd the strains of "Dixie" were faintly heard. The demonstration continued for at least half an hour before Chairman James restored order.[74] Underwood's nomination was later seconded by Jefferson R. Anderson for Georgia, Governor Earl Brewer for Mississippi, and Hal D. Flood for Virginia.[75]

When Arkansas was called she yielded to Missouri. Senator James A. Reed rose gravely and went to the speakers' platform. His first utterances were an indictment of the Republican party, which he liberally blamed for all the ills of the nation; he then made a sly, underhand reference to Wilson that provoked great cheers from the Clark delegates. "Give me no political dilettante," he declared, "who comes into camp when honors are most ripe to pluck. I want no half fledge chanticleer who is only just beginning to acquire a Democratic crow." After recounting Clark's political labors during the past quarter of a century, Reed nominated the man "whose breast is covered with the scars of honor; who leads today and who should lead tomorrow—the Lion of Democracy, Champ Clark, of Missouri." [76]

At exactly twenty-five minutes after midnight Reed sat down and the demonstration for Clark began. In the crowd of delegates that surged through the aisles were half a dozen disheveled women. The Clark forces made their way toward the speakers' platform and quickly took possession of it. One Clark man stood on the convention secretary's table and led the excited crowd in a series of disorganized cheers. Another Clark enthusiast climbed upon the platform and moved that Clark be nominated by acclamation. He put the question himself and declared that it had carried. While the tumult was at its height a large, elderly Southerner managed to reach the platform with an old-fash-

[72] Afterwards speaker of the House of Representatives during the administration of Franklin D. Roosevelt.

[73] *Proceedings of the Convention*, p. 143.

[74] *Birmingham Age-Herald*, June 28, 1912.

[75] *Proceedings of the Convention*, pp. 162-164; 175; 190-192.

[76] *ibid.*, pp. 144-151.

Great Commoner in an Alpaca Coat

The Baltimore Convention

Harris & Ewin

Acceptance Speech at Sea Girt

McCombs and Presidential Candidate

President-Elect

ioned hunting horn. His mournful call, "Off Hounds," set off a new burst of enthusiasm. At 1:30, one hour and five minutes after the demonstration began, the tumult subsided.[77]

After the nomination of Governor Simeon E. Baldwin of Connecticut by Henry Wade Rogers, dean of the Yale Law School, the call of the states was resumed. At eight minutes after two Delaware yielded to New Jersey, and Judge John W. Wescott went forward to nominate Wilson. The lateness of the hour and the weariness of the delegates did not dampen the enthusiasm of the Wilson men. In fact, they did not give Wescott a chance to speak before they began their demonstration. From a side entrance, a line of Wilson men filed into the hall; the Texas and Pennsylvania standards swung into the procession. Huge Wilson banners were unfurled over the edge of the gallery; one of them announced that Wilson was the "Yankee Doodle Dixie Candidate." Meanwhile, the convention hall resounded with the terrific din of shouts, whistling, and horn-blowing. The Wilson men were determined to out-shout the Clark supporters; and at 3:15 the Wilson noise had exceeded the length of the Clark demonstration. At 3:20 Chairman James had almost brought order out of the chaos when some Wilson man sounded an electric horn and the bedlam broke out again.[78]

At 3:25 on Friday morning, June 28, one hour and fifteen minutes after the Wilson demonstration began, Wescott again arose. In a flamboyant, but truly eloquent, address he nominated his friend Woodrow Wilson. On the wreck of a bipartisan machine, Wescott declared, Wilson had erected an ideal commonwealth. Therefore a free New Jersey was commissioned to present Democracy's triumphant leader, "the ultimate Democrat, the genius of liberty and the very incarnation of progress." Wilson was the "national instinct." He had been in politics less than two years; he had no organization of the usual sort; he had only the practical ideal of the reestablishment of equality. New Jersey, Wescott concluded, had the honor of presenting to the convention "the seer and philosopher of Princeton, the Princeton schoolmaster, Woodrow Wilson." [79] There was a volley of speeches seconding Wilson's nomination by North Dakota's governor, John Burke, Senator Gore, Senator Ellison D. ("Cotton Ed") Smith of South Carolina, P. H. O'Brien of Michigan, Palmer of Pennsylvania, John Walsh of Wisconsin, and Alfred Jacques of Minnesota.

Day was breaking when Governor Marshall of Indiana and Gover-

[77] *Montgomery Advertiser*, June 28, 1912.
[78] *ibid.*   [79] *Proceedings of the Convention*, pp. 157-161.

nor Harmon were nominated; it was about 7:00 o'clock in the morning when the first ballot was taken. The ballot stood:[80]

Clark	440½	Marshall	31
Wilson	324	Baldwin	22
Harmon	148	Sulzer[81]	2
Underwood	117½	Bryan	1

The convention, having set the stage for the great struggle, then adjourned.

When the delegates assembled in the afternoon of June 28, the lines were tightly drawn for the coming battle. McCombs, nervous and excited, was in charge of the Wilson forces. On the speakers' platform A. Mitchell Palmer, who had the reputation of an excellent parliamentarian, stood by the chairman's side and bespoke Wilson's interests. On the convention floor, Burleson was in command of the Wilson delegates. Blind Senator Gore and McAdoo were constantly at Burleson's side, while Representative William Hughes of New Jersey and Thomas J. Pence of North Carolina gave aid to Palmer.[82]

During the first nine ballots little change in the voting occurred. Clark gained some fourteen votes, and Wilson picked up twenty-eight; but the managers were only sparring. The Wilson men knew that the knockout blow was yet to come. They expected that New York's ninety votes would be delivered to Clark on the third or fourth ballot but were forewarned by their friends in the New York delegation when Murphy decided to transfer the votes to Clark at a later time.[83] The expected transfer came on the tenth ballot when the Tammany boss electrified the convention by shifting his state's votes from Harmon to Clark.[84] It

[80] *Proceedings of the Convention*, p. 196.

[81] Representative William Sulzer, afterward governor of New York.

[82] Otto Praeger, "How Winning Fight for Wilson Was Made," *Dallas Morning News,* July 3, 1912.

[83] W. G. McAdoo to R. S. Baker, October 15, 1928, Baker Papers.

[84] *Proceedings of the Convention*, p. 221. One of the leaders of the New York delegation afterward wrote: "New York, after the ninth ballot, turned to Clark in preference to Wilson because many of the friends of the Missouri statesman had given their support to New York's candidate for temporary chairman in the meeting of the sub-committee, again in the National Committee and on the floor of the convention, and had put the New York delegation under an obligation to him which New York—in full recognition of the highest party welfare—could honorably repay." N. E. Mack, "Wilson and Marshall—Mr. Bryan and New York," *National Monthly,* iv (August 1912), 65.

was the signal for the Clark landslide, for New York's votes gave Clark 556 votes, well over a majority of the convention. Clark, who was in the Speaker's Office in the Capitol, had already prepared a telegram of acceptance which he expected to send to the convention; he told George W. Norris that he would be nominated on the next ballot.[85] Not since 1844 had a Democrat obtained a majority in a national convention and then failed of nomination by the necessary two-thirds! At Sea Girt, Wilson lost his nerve and was anxious to quit the fight. He sent a message to McCombs releasing his delegates "and asking him to tell them that they were not to vote for him any longer if they thought they ought to vote for someone else."[86] Fortunately for Wilson and his followers, McCombs refused to release the Wilson delegates.[87]

Clark's managers fully expected that the powerful tradition of nominating a candidate after he had obtained a majority, in addition to the irresistible momentum generated by New York's action, would bring about Clark's nomination on the tenth or eleventh ballot. The Clark delegates were naturally beside themselves with joy; they shouted, sang, and marched for almost an hour. It was a discouraging hour for the Wilson managers—McCombs, Palmer, McAdoo, and Burleson—who scurried over the convention hall, pleading with the Underwood delegates not to go over to Clark. What would the states following New York do? As soon as the Clark demonstration had subsided, North Dakota was called. An expectant silence fell over the great crowd. When the steady response, "Ten for Wilson," followed, the Wilson delegates let out a wild yell. Chairman James then called Oklahoma. One Oklahoman was on his feet; he had voted for Wilson, he declared, but since it seemed that Clark was the convention's choice he demanded a poll of his delegation. "Alfalfa Bill" Murray, collarless and wiping his face with a red bandana handkerchief, roared out that he did not object to a poll of the delegation; but, he declared, "we do insist that we shall not join Tammany in making the nomination!"[88] Oklahoma stood firm and the Wilson men began a wild counter-demonstration that lasted fully fifty-five minutes.

The tenth ballot continued without any further material change in the voting. When, on the eleventh ballot, the Underwood delegations

[85] Alfred Lief, *Democracy's Norris*, p. 135.
[86] Statement of Mrs. Wilson in an interview published in *Baltimore Sun*, July 3, 1912. "Mr. Wilson," she added, "thought that it was all over, and we tried to pretend to think we were glad that it was over."
[87] W. F. McCombs, *Making Woodrow Wilson President*, pp. 143-144.
[88] *Proceedings of the Convention*, p. 220.

stood firm, it became suddenly apparent that Clark's expected landslide had failed to materialize. Finally, at 4:03 in the morning of June 29, the convention adjourned.

Manifestly, the Underwood delegates, by standing firm against the Clark onslaught, prevented Clark's nomination. The hundred-odd votes Bankhead might have added to Clark's majority would not have given him the requisite two-thirds; but it would have made his nomination inevitable. Why, then, if the Underwood men had the power to decide the contest, did they not effect Clark's nomination? Certainly they were under heavy pressure from Clark's managers, who had assured Murphy that they would rally to Clark's standard once the speaker obtained a majority.[89] Why did not the Underwood leaders accept the vice-presidential nomination the Clark managers probably offered them? In the first place, Wilson, not Clark, was the second choice of a majority of the Underwood delegates.[90] In the second place, Underwood and his managers were after nothing less than the presidency; under no circumstances would Underwood have accepted the vice-presidential nomination.[91] The Underwood leaders, moreover, believed that the opposition of the Clark and Wilson supporters would result in a deadlock that could be broken only by a compromise candidate, and that the nomination would eventually fall to Underwood in this manner.

The skillful bargaining of Wilson's managers, however, was probably the decisive factor in effecting Clark's defeat. Since the Underwood delegations constituted the balance of power in the convention, they decided early in the balloting that it was "absolutely essential" that some arrangement should be made with Underwood's managers by which they could "supplement the Wilson forces with enough votes to block the convention." [92] Gregory, McCombs, and Gore had long conferences with leaders in the Underwood delegations and promised that if Wilson should be "put out of the race at any stage of the game," they would use their influence to deliver the Wilson delegates to Underwood. In return the Underwood men agreed to remain loyal to their candidate.[93]

[89] For an account of the negotiations between the Clark and Underwood managers, see *Trenton Evening Times*, June 29, 1912.

[90] This was certainly true of the Alabama delegation, in which at least fifteen and probably nineteen of the twenty-four delegates favored Wilson after Underwood. See "Memorandum for Governor Wilson of Delegates Who Are Favorable to Him," MS in Wilson Papers.

[91] See Bankhead's statement to this effect in *Baltimore Sun*, July 1, 1912.

[92] T. W. Gregory to E. M. House, July 9, 1912, House Papers.

[93] *ibid.;* also Thomas P. Gore to the author, August 15, 1942.

Thus a vote for Underwood was as good as a vote for Wilson and a solid anti-Clark bloc was formed, which effectually prevented the speaker's nomination.[94]

There yet remained the danger that McCombs, often nervous and panic-stricken, might take a fatal step that would ruin Wilson's chances for the nomination. Senator William J. Stone, Clark's manager at Baltimore, sent a telegram to Wilson, Underwood, Harmon, and Marshall on Saturday, June 29, urging them to withdraw and asserting that party tradition demanded that Clark be nominated.[95] Wilson had previously expressed his opposition to the two-thirds rule on the ground that it was undemocratic,[96] but that was at a time when it appeared that it would militate against his chances for the nomination. Early Saturday morning McCombs called Wilson on the telephone. He was very discouraged and suggested that Wilson authorize him to withdraw his name from the balloting; Wilson accordingly sent a telegram to that effect and considered sending Clark a message of congratulations.[97] The Wilsons even began to make plans for a visit to the lake country of England as soon as Wilson's gubernatorial term had expired. "Now we can see Rydal again," Mrs. Wilson told her husband.[98]

Later in the morning, when McAdoo discovered that Wilson had authorized McCombs to release his delegates, he immediately telephoned Wilson and urged him by no means to consider withdrawing because he was steadily gaining in strength and would eventually be nominated. Wilson authorized McAdoo to countermand the withdrawal authorization he had given McCombs and the danger was averted.[99]

---

[94] "I have no criticism to offer of anything that the Alabama delegation did," Wilson wrote to Frank P. Glass on July 31, 1912. "As you point out, they were extremely serviceable in resisting the break that might have been made when it looked as if things were going against us." Copy in Baker Papers. Hearst's newspaper in New York complained that the Underwood leaders prevented Clark's nomination by refusing to vote for him on the eleventh or twelfth ballots. *New York American*, July 3, 1912.

[95] See *ibid.*, June 30, 1912, for a copy of the telegram.

[96] W. W. to E. M. House, October 24, 1911, House Papers.

[97] J. P. Tumulty, *Woodrow Wilson As I Know Him*, pp. 120-121.

[98] Interview in *Baltimore Sun*, July 3, 1912.

[99] An acrimonious controversy has developed over the question of Wilson's withdrawal telegrams. It seems fairly clear that Wilson sent the first withdrawal message on his own initiative on June 28, after Clark had secured a majority vote. McCombs, unfortunately, has confused matters by connecting the sending of this telegram to Stone's message requesting that Wilson withdraw. It is also apparent that McCombs lost his nerve on Saturday, June 29, and *asked* Wilson for specific authorization to release his delegates. See W. G. McAdoo, *Crowded Years*, pp. 153-154; J. P. Tumulty, *Woodrow*

The convention assembled on Saturday, June 29, the fifth day, to take up again the laborious task of balloting for the nomination. The air was still charged with the excitement of the preceding day. Had Clark's managers secured the 200 votes that Clark needed for the nomination? On the twelfth ballot Clark lost seven votes; Wilson lost half a vote. On the thirteenth ballot the speaker gained seven and a half; Wilson gained two.[100]

In the meantime Wilson made a deliberate bid for Bryan's open support and, at the same time, endeavored to undermine Clark's chief source of strength. While the thirteenth ballot was being taken he called McCombs and dictated a statement that he wished delivered immediately to Bryan. "It has become evident that the present deadlock is being maintained for the purpose of enabling New York, a delegation controlled by a single group of men, to control the nomination and tie the candidate to itself," the statement read. It was the imperative duty of each candidate, Wilson continued, to guarantee that his own personal independence was beyond question. "I can see no other way to do this than to declare that he will not accept a nomination if it cannot be secured without the aid of that delegation. For myself, I have no hesitation in making that declaration. The freedom of the party and its candidate and the security of the government against private control constitute the supreme consideration."[101] McCombs received the message, but refused to give it to Bryan;[102] and fortunately for Wilson it was never published. It was easy enough for Wilson to give away something he never had, or to refuse to accept something he probably never would receive. Such questionable tactics would undoubtedly have caused an unfortunate reaction among several of the boss-controlled delegations that later helped to nominate him.

Bryan had been profoundly disturbed when Murphy threw New York's votes to Clark on the tenth ballot. Did not this confirm the charge made by his brother that there had been a bargain between Clark's managers and Tammany?[103] Moreover, a number of Nebras-

Wilson As I Know Him, pp. 121-122; R. S. Hudspeth to R. S. B., November 11, 1927, Baker Papers; Josephus Daniels to the author, January 24, 1942. McCombs, however, insists (*Making Woodrow Wilson President*, pp. 143-144) that on both occasions the initiative came from Wilson himself and that he, McCombs, prevented Wilson from withdrawing.

[100] *Proceedings of the Convention*, pp. 226-227; 230-231.

[101] Published in R. S. Baker, *Woodrow Wilson*, III, 353-354.

[102] W. F. McCombs, *Making Woodrow Wilson President*, p. 146.

[103] Bryan states that he "never heard anything other than circumstantial evidence to support this charge," and, he says, he never made it himself. Mary B. Bryan (ed.), *Memoirs*, p. 179.

kans were demanding that their delegation cease supporting Clark and go to Wilson's aid. Bryan, spokesman and chairman of the Nebraska delegation, hesitated; he thought New York would go to Underwood and that Clark would then be nominated by the progressives. On the other hand, he had promised the voters of Nebraska that he would not support a Tammany candidate; consequently he prepared a written statement explaining his change from Clark to Wilson, which he planned to use if it became necessary for him to desert Clark.[104] On the thirteenth ballot Senator Gilbert M. Hitchcock demanded that Bryan take a poll of the delegation. The poll revealed that Wilson had the support of thirteen of the delegates, Clark six. Bryan counseled against a change in his state's vote, but when the poll was taken he cast in his lot with Wilson.[105]

On the fourteenth ballot Hitchcock went to the speakers' platform and demanded that Chairman James take an official poll of the Nebraska delegation. When Bryan's name was called, he rose and asked permission to explain the reason for casting his vote as he was about to cast it. An expectant convention became silent. Bryan assured the delegates that Nebraska was a progressive state and that she had instructed her delegates to vote for Clark "with the distinct understanding that Mr. Clark stood for progressive democracy." By the anti-Wall Street resolution, the convention had pledged that it would support no candidate who was obligated to the sinister influences of Tammany Hall and Wall Street; Nebraska was unwilling to participate in the nomination of any man who was "willing to violate the resolution . . . and to accept the high honor of the presidential nomination at the hands of Mr. Murphy." Bryan declared that he would withhold his vote from Clark so long as New York's vote was recorded for him. He was about to announce his vote when he was interrupted by a terrific outburst of applause and hisses. One delegate shouted, "Are you a Democrat?" This made Bryan angry. A delegate from Alabama yelled, "There are a thousand delegates here, and we have something else to do besides listening to Mr. Bryan make his fourth or fifth speech." Senator Stone interceded for Bryan and asked the convention to listen to what he had to say. When the tempest subsided, Bryan declared that although he cast his vote for Wilson, he stood ready to withdraw it should New York vote for him.[106]

---

[104] *ibid.*, p. 182.
[105] *ibid.*, p. 183; Josephus Daniels in *Raleigh News and Observer*, July 7, 1912.
[106] *Proceedings of the Convention*, pp. 233-237.

The Wilson delegates broke into wild applause. In their excitement however, they did not pause to consider that Bryan had given no endorsement at all to their candidate; he had not voted for Wilson because of conviction, but because a reactionary group had voted for Clark. Moreover, he even threatened to withdraw his support from Wilson should New York ever vote for him! The Clark delegates, on the other hand, joined in a terrific onslaught of boos, hisses, and jeers at Bryan. John B. Stanchfield of New York said outright what many delegates were thinking when he declared, "no man can go forth from this Convention stigmatized and branded with Bryanism, and come within half a million votes of carrying the State of New York." Bryan, he added, was "a money-grabbing, selfish, office-seeking, favor-hunting, publicity-loving marplot," whose whole energies had been directed toward creating a deadlock by which he himself might be nominated.[107]

In Washington, Champ Clark was furious. After a conference with his managers and Hearst, he gave out a statement declaring that Bryan's charge that he was under obligation to Wall Street was "an outrageous aspersion" on his political character and demanded immediate "proof or retraction" of Bryan's charges.[108] Clark also went in haste to Baltimore to answer personally Bryan's challenge. Perhaps he might have stampeded the convention in his favor had he reached Baltimore in time. He never got the chance, however, for the convention adjourned just as he was arriving. But his fighting blood was aroused and he took personal command of his delegates in Baltimore; his chief object now was to prevent Wilson's nomination.[109] Clark's managers who were just as outspoken as Clark himself, let it be known that they still had a veto power over the nomination and that they were prepared to stay in Baltimore all summer and disrupt the Democratic party should that be

[107] *ibid.*, pp. 281-282.

[108] *St. Louis Republic,* July 1, 1912. Bryan answered Clark's demand for proof or retraction in a long public statement on June 30. He declared that the only criticism he had made of Clark was not that he had acted wrongfully, but that he had failed to act. Clark, Bryan continued, had declared his neutrality in the fight over the temporary chairmanship, "a contest between progressive Democracy on the one side and reactionary Democracy on the other." It had been Clark's duty to take one side or the other. "But the activity of Mr. Clark's managers," Bryan added, "is as objectionable as his own inactivity. They have been in constant co-operation with the reactionaries. If Mr. Clark did not authorize them to act, he has so far as I know failed to rebuke them for acting." *Baltimore Sun,* July 1, 1912.

[109] *ibid.* Clark never forgave Bryan for his action on the fourteenth ballot. Years later he wrote that the Nebraskan, dishonestly and hypocritically, had endeavored to cause a deadlock "and grab off the nomination for himself." *My Quarter Century of American Politics,* II, 424.

necessary to effect Clark's nomination.[110] Hearst worked himself into a terrible rage against Bryan and declared, "From the moment . . . that Mr. Bryan injected his selfish ambitions and ruthless methods into this convention Democratic prospects have diminished until to-day I feel, and every reasoning human being must feel, that a nomination delivered to any Democrat by this convention would be of but little value." [111]

The balloting continued throughout Saturday, June 29. Bryan's spectacular denunciation of Clark did Wilson slight immediate good; although Wilson gained twelve votes from Nebraska, he lost several votes from various delegations. Clark's lines held firmly; he lost only one and a half votes. On the twentieth ballot Kansas threw its twenty votes, which had hitherto been given to Clark, to Wilson; but the change can hardly be ascribed to Bryan's influence. Wilson was already the first choice of two-thirds of the Kansas delegation, which had been instructed to vote for Clark until his nomination appeared impossible. The balloting was tedious and monotonous, but Wilson slowly gained strength. His gains were so slight as to appear imperceptible; yet when the convention adjourned on Saturday at the end of a hectic and exhausting week, Wilson had gained some 83 votes and Clark had lost Massachusetts to Foss and Kansas to Wilson. The vote on the twenty-sixth ballot stood: Clark 463½, Wilson 407½, Underwood 112½, Harmon 29, Marshall 30, Foss 43, Bryan 1.[112]

June 30 was Sunday and although the rank and file of the delegates enjoyed a much-needed rest the political managers redoubled their efforts at the manipulation of bargains and trades. Interestingly enough, Wilson's managers at Baltimore had been greatly incensed when Bryan virtually outlawed New York's vote, for they had their eyes on Murphy's delegation themselves.[113] Several of Wilson's managers also dreaded lest Bryan might, at some dramatic moment, rally the progressives and capture the nomination for himself; and the charge was made and repeated many times that Bryan was really trying to prevent Wilson's nomination. Bryan's very actions throughout the pre-convention campaign had given rise to such suspicions; many observers thought that his policy of neutrality as between Clark and Wilson had been an ill-disguised plan to prevent either candidate from securing a decisive majority of the

[110] *St. Louis Republic,* July 1, 1912.   [111] *New York American,* July 1, 1912.
[112] *Proceedings of the Convention,* p. 277.
[113] *New York World,* June 30, 1912.

convention vote.[114] On June 30, at a time when Wilson was gaining steadily in strength, Bryan angered Wilson's managers by declaring that there was no reason why the delegates should not conclude their work the following day by nominating a president and vice-president. "There is every reason why the progressives should get together and select a ticket," he asserted, adding that either John W. Kern, Ollie James, James A. O'Gorman, Charles A. Culberson, or Senator Isidor Rayner of Maryland would be an acceptable candidate.[115] Bryan's selection of such political lightweights naturally infuriated the Wilson men who were sure that he meant, by implication, to put his own name at the head of the list.[116]

The Wilson leaders, moreover, resented the fact that not once during the convention did Bryan publicly advocate Wilson's nomination. While it is still a controversial question whether Bryan was seeking a fourth nomination, the evidence leans heavily in the negative direction. Certainly Bryan, experienced politician that he was, must have realized that his action in the temporary chairmanship fight, the anti-Wall Street resolution, and his vote against Clark had alienated so many delegates and powerful leaders that his nomination was impossible. Only on the condition that the convention were hopelessly deadlocked, Bryan told his wife, and only if he could unite the party, would he accept a fourth nomination.[117]

One thing, at least, is certain, that McCombs was not happy when Bryan voted for Wilson with the reservation that he would withdraw his support should New York vote for Wilson. McCombs, too, had been flirting with Murphy and expected the Tammany boss to desert Clark when he became convinced that the speaker's nomination was impossible.[118] It was Bryan, of course, who now stood in McCombs's way. On

---

[114] Carter Glass afterward wrote that several weeks before the convention Bryan endeavored to persuade him that Wilson's nomination would mean suicide for the Democratic party. By the facility with which he eliminated all other Democratic candidates but himself, Glass concluded that Bryan wanted the nomination for himself. C. Glass to M. F. Lyons, October 27, 1925, Baker Papers.

Colonel Harvey was at the convention and later wrote a friend that Bryan was terribly disappointed because he did not think he could be nominated. E. S. Martin to E. M. House, July 24, 1912, House Papers.

[115] *New York World*, July 1, 1912. Gregory afterward wrote: "I feel quite sure that Kern, of Indiana, was Mr. Bryan's personal preference for the nomination." T. W. Gregory to E. M. House, July 9, 1912, House Papers.

[116] Julius Grunow in the *Jersey Journal* of Jersey City, July 1, 1912.

[117] Mary B. Bryan (ed.), *Memoirs*, pp. 334-335.

[118] *New York World*, June 30, 1912.

Sunday, June 30, McCombs called Wilson on the telephone and told him that feeling against Bryan was so bitter that he could not secure the support from the conservatives that was necessary for Wilson's nomination unless Wilson gave assurances that he would not, as president, appoint Bryan secretary of state.[119] Wilson, however, refused categorically to make any such promise. "I will not bargain for this office," he allegedly told McCombs. "It would be foolish for me at this time to decide upon a Cabinet officer, and it would be outrageous to eliminate anybody from consideration now, particularly Mr. Bryan, who has rendered such fine service to the party in all seasons." [120]

Wilson's opponents charged that his managers were making promises of patronage in order to secure blocs of delegates. According to Tumulty, the only time during the convention that Wilson betrayed feelings of irritation was when he read these charges in the press.[121] He wanted it understood that he would not be bound by any agreements. "There cannot by any possibility be any trading done in my name; not a single vote can or will be obtained by means of any promise," he declared in a public statement.[122] His protests were undoubtedly well-meant, but McCombs, Burleson, and the other Wilson managers were on the ground at Baltimore and knew a great deal more about the exigencies of the situation than he did. Already they had concluded important agreements with Roger Sullivan and the Underwood delegations; other important bargains and "promises" would follow.

In the meantime, the Tammany bosses and other conservative leaders, seeing that they could not defeat Wilson by direct assault, endeavored to undermine his strength by drawing away from him his supporters. John J. Fitzgerald and Murphy of Tammany, Roger Sullivan of Illinois, and Thomas Taggart of Indiana attempted to persuade Burleson and Palmer to withdraw Wilson's name from the balloting. If they could persuade Wilson to withdraw, Murphy promised, "we will nominate Palmer for President." [123] When this offer was rejected by Palmer himself, the Tammany group turned next to the Texas delegation. If they could draw the Texans, "the faithful forty," from the Wilson ranks, they thought, Wilson's candidacy would collapse. The Tammany men

---

[119] Josephus Daniels, *The Wilson Era*, p. 62; J. P. Tumulty, *Woodrow Wilson As I Know Him*, p. 118.

[120] J. P. Tumulty, *Woodrow Wilson As I Know Him*, p. 118.

[121] *ibid.*, p. 117.   [122] *New York World*, July 1, 1912.

[123] R. S. Baker, "Memorandum of Conversation with A. S. Burleson, March 17-19, 1927," MS in Baker Papers.

promised to support Culberson for president if the Texas delegation would lead the way by voting for him; but the entire delegation, including Culberson himself, indignantly rejected the suggestion.[124]

"It is too late to talk compromise at Baltimore," warned the *New York World* on July 1, when rumors of these proposed compromises became known. "Ryanism and Murphyism have created an issue that makes the nomination of Woodrow Wilson a matter of Democratic life or death. . . . To compromise now is to send a Democratic ticket into the campaign shackled to bossism and plutocracy." [125] The other great metropolitan newspapers that were advocating Wilson's nomination also took advantage of the Sunday interlude to pound home the argument that Wilson's nomination was essential for the preservation of the Democratic party. The *Baltimore Sun* was the journal that most delegates read; on July 1 Grasty came out squarely and demanded Wilson's nomination.[126] The *New York Times* insisted that Wilson "should and must be nominated." [127]

On Monday, July 1, the balloting for the presidential nomination was resumed. On the second ballot of the day, Thomas Taggart, Democratic boss of Indiana, startled the convention by casting twenty-nine votes, hitherto given to Marshall, to Wilson. When Iowa took fourteen of her twenty-six votes from Clark and cast them for Wilson on the thirtieth ballot, Wilson for the first time had a greater vote than Clark.[128] In quick succession the delegations from Vermont, Wyoming, and Michigan left the Clark ranks and joined the growing Wilson forces. In spite

[124] *ibid.; San Antonio Express,* July 1, 1912.

[125] "Compromise was possible," the editorial continued, "until the Ryan-Murphy conspiracy was fully revealed and the Tammany boss carried out the terms of his bargain with the Clark managers by throwing New York's ninety votes to Champ Clark. Compromise was possible until Mr. Bryan was compelled by the inexorable logic of events to repudiate Champ Clark's candidacy and vote for Woodrow Wilson. Compromise was possible until it became apparent to every intelligent man that the Ryan-Murphy-Belmont-Hearst coalition had set out to strangle progressive Democracy, destroy Mr. Bryan politically and prevent the nomination of Woodrow Wilson at any cost."

[126] *Baltimore Sun,* July 1, 1912. "The Sun has tried to be wary as well as loyal," Charles H. Grasty wrote to Wilson on July 1, "and to avoid anything that might produce reaction. We sent the paper to all delegates for four weeks before they came to Baltimore and when they came they kept on reading it. We gave all candidates a fair show and this kept the minds of delegates open to our 'poison.' Our support has warmed up crescendo fashion, our editorial this morning striking the top key up to date." Copy in Baker Papers.

[127] *New York Times,* June 30, 1912.

[128] The vote on the thirtieth ballot was: Wilson 460, Clark 455, Underwood 121½, Harmon 19, Kern 2, Foss 30. *Proceedings of the Convention,* p. 302.

of these impressive gains made during the day, however, the Wilson leaders were still uncertain of success. True it was that Wilson had almost 500 votes and was definitely in the lead; yet he did not have even a majority, and his managers knew very well that they had come to the end of their rope, that they had corralled practically every vote they could possibly hope to secure, and that unless either Roger Sullivan or John H. Bankhead would commit his delegation to Wilson their cause would fail as inexorably as Clark's had failed—and for the same reasons.

Roger Sullivan was the chief enigma of the convention. He was so secretive and calculating in his political activities that none of the political reporters knew whom he favored for the nomination. He was, most observers thought, opposed to Clark and probably preferred Underwood to Wilson. His wife and son, however, were both ardent Wilson supporters and had argued Wilson's cause with Sullivan;[129] consequently Sullivan promised McCombs that when the Wilson men had secured sufficient strength to make Wilson's nomination appear probable, he would come to their aid.[130] Something besides simple altruism motivated this veteran politician. First, the Hearst-Harrison faction of the Illinois Democracy, Sullivan's arch-enemies, had first claims on Champ Clark, and Sullivan knew that if Clark were elected president he would receive few favors from the White House.[131] It was wiser to support Wilson who was not particularly his friend, Sullivan must have reasoned, than to give aid and comfort to his enemies. Moreover, the Illinois boss had not forgotten that the support he received from the Wilson delegates in the contest over the Chicago delegation had enabled him to obtain control of the entire Illinois group. Sullivan was not a man who forgot his "friends" or "obligations." The belief, furthermore, that Bryan was manipulating to achieve his own nomination caused Sullivan to be more favorably disposed toward Wilson. Better Wilson than Bryan any day.

As early as June 30 it was reported that forty-six of the fifty-eight Illinois delegates were anxious to support Wilson when Sullivan gave the word. After the adjournment of the convention at the end of the forty-

[129] The *Trenton True American,* July 6, 1912, has an interesting discussion of this point.

[130] T. P. Gore to the author, August 15, 1942.

[131] There was one report to the effect that Sullivan had been irritated because Clark had studiously ignored him during the convention proceedings. Clark came to Baltimore on Sunday, June 30, for example, and conferred with Hearst, Stone, and Murphy; not once did Clark confer with the man who had been casting 58 votes from Illinois for his candidacy. *New York Sun,* July 1, 1912.

second ballot on the morning of July 2 the Illinois delegation held an official caucus and voted, 45 to 13, to vote for Wilson when the convention met the following day.[132] On the first ballot taken in the convention on Tuesday, July 2, Sullivan accordingly fulfilled the promise he had made to the Wilson men on the preceding day and cast Illinois' fifty-eight votes for Wilson, thus giving him a majority of the convention vote.[133] A wild shout went up from the forty Texans; Sullivan was hugged and kissed by the Wilson delegates. "What did you get for it, Roger?" the angry Clark men shouted. "The choice of this convention, that's all!" Sullivan retorted.[134]

Meanwhile, Willard Saulsbury of Delaware had been assiduously pleading with the Democratic leaders from Kentucky, West Virginia, Maryland, and Virginia to cast in their lot with Wilson. McCombs, Saulsbury, and Senator John Walter Smith of Maryland met on the evening of June 30 with representatives from these states. These leaders, practically all Clark men, agreed that when the most favorable opportunity to nominate Wilson arose they would transfer their delegations to him.[135] Senator Clarence W. Watson, one of Wilson's most powerful antagonists, cast in his lot with the Wilson men,[136] while Senator Thomas S. Martin startled the Virginia delegation by suggesting that they vote as a unit for Wilson. The Virginia Wilson men, who had opposed the application of the unit rule, objected; it would be unfair, they argued, to force the Underwood supporters to vote for Wilson. Martin, however, was adamant and insisted that Virginia give its undivided support to its native son.[137]

The dramatic swing-over of Illinois to Wilson on the forty-third ballot was the signal for Watson and Martin to act. When Virginia was called Martin arose and delivered Virginia's twenty-four votes (including the vote of Thomas F. Ryan!) to Wilson. Immediately afterward, Watson, one of the original anti-Wilson men, made his peace with the progressives and cast West Virginia's sixteen votes for Wilson. Wilson now had over 600 votes; would he fail as Clark had failed? Since New York's votes were proscribed by Bryan they could not come

[132] Louis Seibold in *New York World*, July 2, 1912.

[133] *Proceedings of the Convention*, p. 337.

[134] W. F. McCombs, *Making Woodrow Wilson President*, pp. 173-174.

[135] M. F. Lyons, *William F. McCombs*, pp. 98-100.

[136] Memorandum of Charles H. Grasty in Baker Papers. Watson agreed to support Wilson if Grasty would give him adequate credit in the *Baltimore Sun* for his action. Grasty, of course, was happy to publicize Watson's swing-over to Wilson.

[137] *Richmond Times-Dispatch*, July 3, 1912.

to Wilson without creating a major disturbance. The loyal Clark and Underwood delegates, together with New York's ninety, could maintain a deadlock and prevent Wilson's nomination forever.

The Underwood leaders were even yet hopeful that the Alabaman would be nominated. Sullivan, according to several accounts, promised Bankhead that he would deliver the Illinois delegation to Underwood sometime during July 2. When the forty-fifth ballot passed, however, and Sullivan did not fulfill his promise, Bankhead, J. Thomas Heflin, and Henry D. Clayton decided that it was time to call his hand. When they asked Sullivan what he intended to do, the old veteran replied that he was going to swing Illinois back to Clark on the forty-sixth ballot.[138]

The forty-fifth ballot marked the major crisis for Woodrow Wilson at Baltimore. Burleson and McCombs were convinced that, if he could not gain the support of the Underwood delegations, Wilson would surely be defeated. Burleson was greatly excited and pleaded with Bankhead to release the Underwood following.[139] Bankhead, Heflin, and Clayton finally decided to withdraw Underwood's name; this, they believed, would break the deadlock and result in Wilson's nomination.[140]

When Alabama was called on the forty-sixth ballot, Bankhead went quickly to the platform. Underwood would gladly forego the nomination, he declared, if he could believe that he had succeeded in eradicating "for all time" any remaining vestige of sectional antagonism; then he withdrew Underwood's name. The convention was by this time in wild confusion. Senator Stone released the Clark delegates, but announced that Missouri would cast her last vote for "old Champ Clark."[141] John J. Fitzgerald of New York moved that Wilson be nomi-

---

[138] *Birmingham Age-Herald*, July 4, 5, 7, 1912. The following is a story that the reader may take for what it is worth. Clark, who was following the events of the convention in Washington, so the story runs, made a hurried visit to Baltimore when he learned that Sullivan had deserted him. Seated in a cab outside the convention hall, Clark pleaded with Sullivan to return to his standard. Sullivan declared that he had promised the Wilson leaders to vote for Wilson for a certain number of ballots, but that he would bring Illinois back to the Clark fold on the 46th or 47th ballot. T. P. Gore to the author, August 15, 1942. If the story is correct, Clark had probably agreed to recognize Sullivan as leader of the Illinois Democracy in the distribution of the federal patronage.

[139] *New Orleans Times-Democrat*, July 3, 1912.

[140] C. E. Stewart in *Birmingham Age-Herald*, July 4, 1912.

[141] Stone had conceded defeat the day before. On July 1 Clark met with Stone and several other supporters in Baltimore, who advised him to release his delegates and swing their support to some progressive Democrat who could be nominated. "The Speaker came over at my request," Stone explained afterward. "I felt that it was urgent that we should discuss the situation frankly, and I could not possibly arrange to leave this city long enough to go to Washington. Speaker Clark was told that the intriguing

nated by acclamation. Senator Reed objected; Missouri had no resentment toward Wilson, but she must insist upon casting her last vote for Clark. The Harmon delegates were released and Wilson received 990 votes. Amid the wildest confusion and tumult of joy the governor of New Jersey, at 3:30 in the afternoon of July 2, was made the Democratic nominee for President of the United States.

The delegates were completely exhausted and wanted to go home as quickly as possible. The Wilson managers were almost physical wrecks; McCombs had had hardly an hour's sound sleep for more than a week. But two important tasks had yet to be completed: the nomination of a vice-president and the adoption of a platform.

Wilson called Burleson on the telephone immediately after his nomination. "I want you to go to Washington," he said, "and see Underwood, and ask if he will not be Vice President. He is my candidate." Burleson went to Washington and learned from Underwood that he would not accept the nomination. On his return to Baltimore, the doughty Texan telephoned Wilson that Underwood had refused the nomination and that the convention was leaning toward Thomas R. Marshall. "But, Burleson," Wilson protested, "he is a very small calibre man." Burleson agreed, but argued that since Marshall was from the Midwest and from a doubtful state, his candidacy would supplement Wilson's. "All right, go ahead," Wilson agreed.[142] He did not know

of Mr. Bryan had made his (the Speaker's) nomination impossible and that Mr. Bryan was now engaged in an effort to kill off Woodrow Wilson." *New York Times*, July 2, 1912.

Clark spent the greater part of July 2 in Baltimore. He was too restless to remain in Washington and hurried to Baltimore immediately after breakfast in order to take charge personally of rallying his supporters. He was haggard and nervous, and when his friends urged him to take a nap after an early luncheon, he declared that he meant to "see the thing through fully awake." Clark desperately wanted to go to the convention hall and make one last effort to stampede the delegates in his favor, but his managers strenuously objected and he remained throughout the day locked in a room in the Baltimore Club. *Baltimore Sun*, July 3, 1912.

The news of Wilson's nomination was received by Clark by telephone. Soon afterward he departed for Washington, where he issued a final statement. "No set of men ever made a better or braver fight for any man in this world than my friends all over the country made for me," Clark declared. "They have my heartfelt thanks.

"We never had money enough even to pay for an adequate supply of postage stamps and literature. I was tied down here by my duties of the speakership. I could, therefore, aid my friends very little. They made the fight, gave me 200,000 majority in the States where Gov. Wilson and I competed in the primaries and caused me to lead on thirty ballots in the convention, in nine of which I had a clear majority. Nevertheless, the nomination was bestowed upon Gov. Wilson." *St. Louis Republic*, July 3, 1912.

[142] R. S. Baker, "Memorandum of Conversation with A. S. Burleson, March 17-19, 1927," MS in Baker Papers.

that McCombs had traded the vice-presidential nomination to Indiana in return for her votes![143] McCombs accordingly delivered the nomination to Marshall.

The platform was a progressive document, in the best Bryan tradition. It attacked the Republican protective tariff policy and promised that the Democrats would enact legislation to destroy the trusts and regulate business activities; it commended the proposed amendments for the adoption of the income tax and direct election of senators; it pledged the Democratic candidate to the principle of a single term (to which Wilson definitely did not agree); and it voiced Democratic opposition to the Aldrich bill or the establishment of a centralized banking system. With the blessing of Samuel Gompers, president of the American Federation of Labor, the Democrats adopted a plank that demanded jury trials in cases of criminal contempt of court and declared that labor organizations should be encouraged by exempting them from the provisions of the Sherman Anti-Trust law. The platform further declared that it was Democratic policy to recognize the independence of the Philippine Islands as soon as a stable government might be established, and commended to the nation numerous other reforms.[144]

Historians have for some reason or other written that Bryan's decision to vote for Wilson caused the latter's nomination,[145] and now a motion picture has given popularity to this interpretation. Certainly no person acquainted with the events of the Baltimore convention would underestimate the important work done by Bryan during the first struggles in the convention, during which he undoubtedly forced a more or less clear-cut alignment between conservatives and progressives before the balloting had begun.

It is not the purpose of this discussion to imply that Bryan did not have a considerable share in achieving Wilson's nomination; it should be emphatically reiterated, however, that there were other influences

---

[143] W. F. McCombs, *Making Woodrow Wilson President*, p. 177.

[144] *Proceedings of the Convention*, pp. 365-376.

[145] See, for example, Harry E. Barnes, *The Genesis of the World War*, pp. 628-629, in which America's entry into the first World War is accounted for by Bryan's action on the fourteenth ballot; Charles Seymour, *The Intimate Papers of Colonel House*, I, 66-67; Arthur D. Howden Smith, *Mr. House of Texas*, pp. 52-53; Matthew Josephson, *The President Makers*, pp. 445-446; Gerald Johnson, *Woodrow Wilson*, p. 66; Samuel E. Morison and Henry S. Commager, *The Growth of the American Republic*, II, 422-423; Louis M. Hacker and Benjamin B. Kendrick, *The United States since 1865*, p. 452; Jeanette P. Nichols, *Twentieth Century United States*, pp. 161-162.

and persons at work at Baltimore that were just as important. It should be remembered, first, that by voting for Wilson, Bryan did not deal the death blow to Clark's candidacy; by the fourteenth ballot it had become apparent that Clark, even with the impelling impetus of a majority behind him, could not be nominated. Clark, in short, had already demonstrated that he could not, under the best possible circumstances, win two-thirds of the convention. Clark's landslide was headed off, therefore, not by Bryan's belated action, but by virtue of the fact that the Wilson and Underwood delegates cooperated and held their ground in the face of the onslaught on the tenth and eleventh ballots. Consequently the threat of Clark's nomination had measurably passed when Bryan announced his vote for Wilson. If Bryan had been intent upon destroying Clark's chances for the nomination, it appears logical that he would have come out against him on the eleventh, not the fourteenth ballot.

In the second place, the balloting that followed Bryan's shift to Wilson further revealed that Bryan's action had only an inconsequential effect upon the subsequent voting. The reason for this is clear: Bryan's influence among the various delegations from the Underwood states and from the Northeast was practically nonexistent; his influence was strongest among the Clark delegations of the West, whom he alienated by his desertion of Clark. As a result of Bryan's voting for Wilson, Wilson eventually gained, by a liberal estimate, thirteen votes from Nebraska, fourteen from Iowa, one from Colorado, five and one-half from Idaho, and seven from Montana[146]—in all forty and one-half votes and certainly not of sufficient importance to warrant the statement of a distinguished historian that "Bryan gave the word at last and Wilson was nominated." [147] As a matter of fact, Bryan was really on the periphery during the convention in so far as the Wilson managers were concerned. He never once identified himself with the Wilson leaders and never participated in their deliberations. The truth of the matter is that after his action on the fourteenth ballot, Bryan played a role of inconsequential importance in the convention.

[146] This computation is based upon the results of the forty-second ballot, before the landslide to Wilson caused by Illinois's change developed. It is a liberal estimate and represents the outside number of votes that Bryan's influence might have brought to Wilson. It should not be forgotten, either, that most of the western Clark delegations remained loyal to Clark until it became evident that Wilson's nomination could not be prevented.

[147] William E. Dodd, "The Social and Economic Background of Wilson," *Journal of Political Economy*, xxv (March 1917), 279.

It is a part of the general irony of history that the nomination of Woodrow Wilson was made possible by the very men who had been his bitterest antagonists and who represented the forces against which he was struggling. Assuredly it must be clear that without the support of the master politicians and political bosses, Roger Sullivan, Tom Taggart, Clarence W. Watson, Thomas S. Martin, and John H. Bankhead, Wilson would not have received the Democratic nomination. It can be said with certainty that Wilson's nomination was not the result of the work or influence of any single man or group of men. It is a long story from Harvey's Lotos Club speech in 1906 to the Baltimore convention. Wilson's own political activities brought him first into the public consciousness; the labors of the little group of men in the headquarters at 42 Broadway in New York furthered his presidential movement; the important work of state politicians and editors won him support among the people; Bryan's fight at Baltimore emphasized the progressive character of Wilson's leadership and generated a widespread popular agitation for his nomination; the Underwood delegates helped prevent Clark's nomination at a critical time and, later during the balloting, definitely turned the tide in Wilson's favor; and, finally, the support of machine politicians brought over the votes without which Wilson could never have been nominated.

CHAPTER XIV

The Presidential Campaign of 1912

BY THE time the Baltimore convention had adjourned, the actual campaign to make Woodrow Wilson president of the United States was not quite eighteen months old. Its progress from 42 Broadway to Baltimore had been next to miraculous; the energies and money of scores of devoted Wilson supporters had been spent achieving the nomination, yet they had only started upon the road to the White House, and the entire summer campaign was before them. Needless to say, Wilson's managers were physically exhausted; poor McCombs was literally a physical wreck by the last day of the convention, and, if we may believe an observant Texan, looked something like a "skinned snipe." [1]

It was difficult, moreover, for Democrats, who had grown accustomed to Bryan's domination of the party since 1896, to realize that Bryan had actually surrendered his leadership into Wilson's hands. Yet, at the last session of the convention he had declared: "Tonight I come with joy to surrender into the hands of the one chosen by this Convention a standard which I have carried in three campaigns, and I challenge my enemies to declare that it has ever been lowered in the face of the enemy." [2]

Political observers naturally began at once to speculate as to the effect Wilson's nomination would have upon the political fortunes of Theodore Roosevelt. They wondered whether Roosevelt and his followers would carry out their threat to organize a third party now that the Democrats had nominated a candidate allegedly free from entangling political alliances and corporation control. It was not at all certain in the early part of July whether the third party would be organized. One of the seven Republican governors who, in February 1912, had called upon Roosevelt to seek the Republican nomination, asserted in a public statement that there was now no reason for a new party. "The issue is clearly joined for the people," declared Governor Chase S. Osborn of Michigan. "It is Wall Street vs. Wilson. It is even more than that. All of the evil forces of America will finally line up with Wall Street and Mr. Taft." [3]

[1] T. W. Gregory to E. M. House, July 9, 1912, House Papers.
[2] *Proceedings of the Convention,* pp. 382-383.
[3] *New York Times,* July 4, 1912.

There were, moreover, other indications early in July of what might easily have developed into a wholesale swing-over of progressive Republicans into the Democratic camp had not Roosevelt succeeded in stopping the movement. Mark M. Fagan, former reform mayor of Jersey City and one of the original New Idea leaders in New Jersey, for example, refused to join with George L. Record in the Roosevelt movement and announced on July 3 that he would support Wilson.[4] Senator Robert M. La Follette of Wisconsin, perhaps the greatest progressive of the era, advised his followers to remain within the Republican party, to ignore Roosevelt's siren call, and to vote against Taft.[5] La Follette's position during the campaign must have appeared incongruous to the average voter; he strenuously fought Roosevelt's candidacy and during the summer published several scathing attacks upon the former president; yet he would not leave the Republican party and come out openly for Wilson, although he was secretly supporting him.[6]

Even before the Progressive party was formally organized in August, therefore, it was necessary that Roosevelt convince his followers that although Wilson might be a sincere progressive, he could accomplish no constructive reforms because the Democratic party was boss-controlled and rotten to the core. "Cleveland was a stronger man than Wilson is," he wrote on July 16, "and yet during the eight years that he was President, Hill and Tammany absolutely dominated Cleveland's own State of New York. The same thing would be true now of Murphy, of Sullivan, of Taggart and of all the others."[7] The bosses, he added later, were

[4] *Jersey Journal* of Jersey City, July 3, 1912.

[5] R. M. La Follette, "A Call to Service," *La Follette's Weekly Magazine,* IV (July 27, 1912), 3-4.

[6] Soon after the Baltimore convention Senator Luke Lea sent Wilson the following letter which clarifies considerably La Follette's position in the campaign of 1912: "Yesterday I had a long talk with Senator La Follette about your candidacy and it was at his urgent request that I determined finally to make certain suggestions to you in regard to your campaign. He wanted his position made clear that under no circumstances does he now expect to give you active support. On the other hand he does not want any condition to arise that will cause him to attack you or your candidacy. He called attention to the active support that is being given to you by the President of the University of Wisconsin [Charles R. Van Hise]—a close personal friend of his—and The Journal, the most influential paper in Milwaukee which is edited by a devoted friend of his. He said he believed you would carry Wisconsin if your presidential campaign impressed the country as quite as progressive as your pre-convention campaign. La Follette expressed the belief that the real fight would be between you and Roosevelt. . . . He stated further that he was most anxious for you to make no mistakes that would result in Roosevelt's election." L. Lea to W. W., July 13, 1912, Wilson Papers.

[7] Theodore Roosevelt to Eugene Thwing, July 16, 1912, Theodore Roosevelt Papers, Library of Congress; hereinafter cited as Roosevelt Papers.

just as powerful in the Democratic as in the Republican party.[8] Moreover, Roosevelt's opinion of the Democratic platform convinced him that he could not support the Democratic ticket. It was "as vicious as any platform well could be," he charged;[9] it was a model of "dangerous insincerity and of bad faith," and offered "perhaps as good an example as any platform of the last thirty years of what has become a typical vice of American politics—the avoidance of saying anything real on real issues." [10]

Although there were a few exceptions, for the most part Roosevelt succeeded in stopping the drift of his personal followers to Wilson and in holding the new Progressive movement together until it could be formally organized. Governor Osborn soon qualified his support of Wilson,[11] and when Roosevelt formally entered the presidential contest joined the Progressive movement. Newspapers like the *Kansas City Star* and the *Philadelphia North American,* and magazines like the *Outlook,* which had supported Wilson throughout the pre-convention campaign, professed that they admired him no less than before, but now asserted that the Democratic party was not a free agent to serve the people and they would, perforce, support Roosevelt.[12] The point of view of the Roosevelt men was perhaps best expressed by Eugene Thwing, who wrote: "Perhaps Woodrow Wilson is a true Progressive. I am not sure. Opinions differ. I am willing to believe he is. But I know that the majority of his party is not. I know that the bosses of the state machines, and the district leaders, and the rank and file of the politicians scurrying eagerly at his heels are not. I know that a party which in many states is as reactionary and corrupt as the Democratic Party is cannot suddenly be made progressive by the nomination, still less by the election, of a progressive national ticket on a *partially progressive* and *partially retrogressive* platform. Woodrow Wilson has a respectable name, but his name cannot be made safely to cover such a multitude of sins." [13]

Wilson, meanwhile, was at Sea Girt, overwhelmed by a flood of letters and an unrelenting stream of callers and well-wishers. "You cannot . . . *imagine* such days . . . an invasion by the people of the United

[8] T. Roosevelt, "Platform Insincerity," *Outlook,* CI (July 27, 1912), 660.

[9] T. Roosevelt to W. O. Lynch, July 6, 1912, Roosevelt Papers.

[10] "Platform Insincerity," *loc. cit.*

[11] C. S. Osborn to W. W., July 6, 1912, Wilson Papers.

[12] See, e.g., *Kansas City Star,* July 3, 1912; *Outlook,* CI (July 13, 20, 1912), 567-568, 608-610.

[13] E. Thwing to C. S. Osborn, July 10, 1912, copy in Roosevelt Papers.

States!" he wrote soon after he was nominated. "I had read of the like, and *dreaded* it, but of course had never *realized* what it was to be the principal victim." [14] On July 4, thirty-five members of the Democratic national committee called at Sea Girt to pay their respects to the new leader. They came with their hats in their hands, the old bosses and leaders of the party, although many of them were still sulking over Wilson's nomination. One reporter noted, however, that they left Sea Girt, after a three hours' visit, enthusiastic and ready to undertake the presidential campaign in earnest. The leadership of the party, furthermore, was surrendered completely to Wilson. "We're here to see the new boss," was the way Tom Taggart put it. "All depends on him." [15]

They left Sea Girt with an outward show of harmony, and Democratic leaders elsewhere were determined to prove that all was sweetness and light within the camp. On July 4, Jim Nugent and Charles H. Gallagher, two anti-Wilson leaders in New Jersey, announced that they would support Wilson for the presidency.[16] Senator O'Gorman and Dudley Field Malone came to Sea Girt from New York the following day and declared that Tammany and the Murphy state organization had accepted Wilson's nomination with enthusiastic approval; John H. Bankhead, Jr., assured Wilson that all Underwood men were now supporting him as loyally as they had once supported the Alabaman. For his part, Wilson was ready to accept the olive branch the bosses had offered him, and he made it clear at the beginning of the campaign that he would undertake no assault upon Democratic bossdom. He had ended boss rule for a time in New Jersey, it is true, but New Jersey was not the nation, and he announced that he did not consider the old leaders as banished from the party.[17] After all, many of them had helped to nominate him; "I can never forget Illinois," Wilson had told Roger Sullivan.[18]

Except for one brief interlude, Wilson devoted most of his energies from July 9 until he delivered his speech of acceptance on August 7 to conferring with various Democratic and other national leaders. On July 9, for example, he had an hour's conference in Trenton with Samuel Gompers and other officials of the American Federation of Labor. Gompers had been deeply suspicious of the former conservative president of Princeton, but one meeting with Wilson was sufficient to win

[14] W. W. to M. A. Hulbert, July 6, 1912, published in R. S. Baker, *Woodrow Wilson*, III, 367.

[15] *New York World*, July 5, 1912.

[16] *Trenton True American*, July 5, 1912.

[17] *New York World*, July 6, 1912.

[18] *ibid.*, July 5, 1912.

him over. "In that meeting I felt my prejudices disappearing before the sincerity and obvious humanitarianism of the man," Gompers afterward wrote. ". . . I left Trenton feeling very much relieved."[19] Several days later Champ Clark came reluctantly to Sea Girt to make unpleasant obeisance to his new chieftain. He arrived an hour ahead of schedule and there was no one to welcome him at the station. Wilson was conferring with President Charles R. Van Hise of the University of Wisconsin and Charles R. Crane of Chicago, two leading progressive Republicans, when Clark, carrying a large black umbrella, walked up the gravel path leading to the Governor's Cottage. The meeting was superficially cordial, but the atmosphere was icy and Clark took no pains to conceal the fact that he had found his task exceedingly unpleasant. "I do not care to talk about national politics," he told reporters sharply after the interview, "unless they relate directly to the Ninth Congressional District of Missouri."[20]

The frigidity of the Clark-Wilson meeting was in sharp contrast to the warmth and friendship of the conference between Wilson and Underwood on July 16. Underwood spoke in glowing terms of the Democratic nominee, and Wilson publicly acknowledged his admiration for the Democratic House leader.[21] Four days later, on July 20, Clark returned to Sea Girt, shepherding the Democratic members of the House of Representatives.[22] On July 22 Wilson conferred with Representative Robert L. Henry of Texas and Clark's pre-convention managers, William J. Stone and James A. Reed. "We went over the campaign plans, of course," Stone later declared, "reporting particularly on the situations in doubtful states."[23]

The burden of working out the details of organization for the campaign—a problem with which Wilson had to deal during July—bore heavily upon his mind. When one considers the countless demands upon his time and his slight resources of physical energy, it is no wonder that he found it impossible to think through the outlines of his acceptance speech. "The life I am leading now *can't* keep up," he wrote in protest on July 14. "It is inconceivable that it should. I wish I could describe it to you, but I fear it is as indescribable as it is inconceivable. Not a moment am I left free to do what I would. I thought last night that I should go crazy with the strain and confusion of it."[24] When he

[19] S. Gompers, *Seventy Years of Life and Labor*, I, 544.
[20] *St. Louis Republic*, July 14, 1912.   [21] *Trenton True American*, July 17, 1912.
[22] *St. Louis Republic*, July 21, 1912.   [23] *Trenton Evening Times*, July 23, 1912.
[24] W. W. to M. A. Hulbert, July 14, 1912, published in R. S. Baker, *Woodrow Wilson*, III, 371-372.

could delay no longer writing the speech, he, Mrs. Wilson, Margaret Wilson, and Dudley Field Malone slipped away quietly to a friend's country home at Atlantic Highlands, near Sandy Hook. A short time later, on July 23, they boarded Cleveland H. Dodge's yacht, *Corona,* and sailed through New York harbor and into Long Island Sound. There Wilson at last found peace. He had brought with him only an official copy of the Democratic platform and several newspaper clippings relating to the political situation; but when he returned to Sea Girt on July 30, he had finished a shorthand draft of a 6,000-word speech.[25]

Wilson formally began his campaign for the presidency with this speech accepting the Democratic nomination on August 7. The spacious grounds surrounding the Governor's Cottage at Sea Girt were crowded with throngs of Democratic politicians and onlookers when the Kentucky veteran, Ollie M. James, delivered the notification address. The nomination came to Wilson, James asserted, as the free voice and will of the people's representatives in convention assembled. "I hand you this formal letter of notification . . . ," he added. "I have the honor to request your acceptance of a tendered nomination. And upon behalf of the Democrats of the whole Republic . . . we pledge you their united and earnest support, and may God guide you to a glorious victory in November."[26]

Standing on the porch of the Governor's Cottage, Wilson accepted the nomination "with a deep sense of its unusual significance and of the great honor" done him by the party. Then he proceeded to discuss the Democratic platform, with two notable exceptions, plank by plank.[27] He regarded tariff reform as the dominant issue of the campaign and discussed it at length; but he also promised that a Democratic administration would deal effectively with the problem of trust regulation.[28] Be-

[25] *Trenton True American,* July 30, 1912.

[26] *Proceedings of the Convention,* p. 399.

[27] Wilson avoided almost any mention of the platform declarations favoring a single term for the president and the exemption from tolls of American ships engaged in coastwise traffic passing through the Panama Canal. He was opposed to both declarations. He said in one speech of the Tolls plank: "This is not molasses to catch flies with."

[28] Wilson, however, did not cater to the popular demand for destruction of the trusts. The Democrats, he declared, were not opposed to mere bigness in business and industry; and he did not think that competition could be established by laws set against "the drift of a world-wide economic tendency." Neither did he believe that because a corporation was large, it was necessarily dangerous to economic freedom. "I dare say," he continued, "we shall never return to the old order of individual competition, and that the organization of business upon a great scale of co-operation is, up to a certain point, itself normal and inevitable." Unfortunately, he did not define the "certain point." Wil-

cause the Sherman Anti-Trust law had proved totally ineffective in halting monopolistic growth, Wilson insisted, the Democrats would supplement it with more stringent measures. Not only were there great trusts and combinations to be controlled, he continued, there were things more difficult, more subtle, more evasive. There were vast combinations of banks, railways, mining corporations, and the like, bound together by a small group of men who controlled the nation's credit and enterprise. He discussed also the necessity for legislation to protect and encourage organized labor, to protect the health of the workingmen, to promote agricultural, industrial, and vocational education, and to conserve and develop the nation's physical resources. He concluded:

"We represent the desire to set up an unentangled government, a government that cannot be used for private purposes, either in the field of business or in the field of politics; a government that will not tolerate the use of the organization of a great party to serve the personal aims and ambitions of any individual, and that will not permit legislation to be employed to further any private interests. . . .

"To be free is not necessarily to be wise. But wisdom comes with counsel, with the frank and free conference of untrammeled men united in the common interest. Should I be intrusted with the great office of President, I would seek counsel wherever it could be had upon free terms. I know the temper of the great convention which nominated me; I know the temper of the country that lay back of that convention and spoke through it. I heed with deep thankfulness the message you bring me from it. I feel that I am surrounded by men whose principles and ambitions are those of true servants of the people. I thank God and take courage." [29]

Confining himself at first closely to his manuscript, Wilson spoke with impressive seriousness. But the address was too dull, too grave, and much too long for a restless crowd on a summer's afternoon, and Wilson's listeners soon grew bored. It made good reading, however, and Democratic editors hailed it as the most important political pronouncement of the century. "Woodrow Wilson's speech of acceptance is the ablest, clearest, sanest statement of high public purpose this country has known in a generation," asserted the *New York World*.[30] "The domi-

---

son was at this time vague, uninformed, and superficial when dealing with this problem. His New Freedom ideal of regulated and free competition was to come later in the campaign and will be discussed in subsequent pages.

[29] The address is printed in *ibid.*, pp. 400-414.

[30] *New York World*, August 8, 1912.

nant thought," commented the *New York Times,* "the very soul of his discourse, is the common interest of all the people, their partnership in our activities and our prosperity. . . . It is a proclamation that will satisfy all save those who are determined not to be satisfied." [31] Even "Marse Henry" was pleased, and wrote in glowing words his praise of his erstwhile enemy. [32]

The presidential campaign got off to a roaring start, certainly not because of Wilson's mild and slightly academic acceptance speech, but because of Theodore Roosevelt's nomination for president by the Progressive national convention in Chicago on August 6. The Progressive convention was one of the most remarkable gatherings the country had ever witnessed. Social and economic reformers, disgruntled politicians and bosses, representatives of big business, idealists, suffragettes, and sundry others made up the motley crowd that nominated Roosevelt and then launched the new party upon its short-lived career. In his "Confession of Faith," his acceptance speech, Roosevelt championed every social and economic reform that he had proposed during his presidency and since 1909. He emphasized the necessity for a federal government powerful enough to regulate trusts and interstate corporations, determine fair minimum wages and maximum hours for women and children in industry, and in every way possible exert its influences to safeguard the welfare of the people. Social justice, political reform, a quasi-state socialism, and moral regeneration were Roosevelt's chief themes. "We stand at Armageddon, and we battle for the Lord," shouted the Bull Moose[33] candidate as he concluded his address to a convention that resembled an old-fashioned religious revival more than a political convention.

There was a great deal about Roosevelt's passionate enthusiasm for reform and social justice that appealed to the mentality of the professional reformer and social worker. "Mr. Roosevelt's 'Confession' is very exciting and made us feel as if the Social Reformers' Creed was about to become the religion of the politician," wrote Lillian D. Wald of New York's Henry Street Settlement. Wilson's pronouncement, on the other hand, was too intellectual, too deliberate to strike such an emotional response. "I read it with a cold chilly feeling of disappointment," Miss Wald added. "It is an essay of lofty sentiments, in my judgment, but

[31] *New York Times,* August 8, 1912.

[32] *Louisville Courier-Journal,* August 8, 1912.

[33] Roosevelt came to Chicago, he declared, feeling like a bull moose. The name stuck and the bull moose became the symbol of the Progressive party.

might be construed as a political hedge and an evasion of the sturdy things Bryan practised in Baltimore." [34] The reaction was characteristic of many professional reformers who were demanding that Wilson strike hard at corruption and privilege on all sides. "Wilson seems to be piping a very low note; or trying to conciliate the reactionaries in his party," Brand Whitlock, reform mayor of Toledo, confided to a friend, "when he ought to know that you can conciliate privilege only by surrendering abjectly to it." [35] Lincoln Steffens, too, was convinced that the bosses and vested interest groups were supporting Wilson in order to defeat Roosevelt. [36]

It was obvious by the middle of August that Taft simply was not in the running. "I think I might as well give up so far being a candidate," he had written as early as July 22. "There are so many people in the country who don't like me." [37] Except for his acceptance speech, the president refused to join in the campaign at all. Wilson realized early in the campaign that Taft was out of the running and that the fight was between himself and Roosevelt. To Mrs. Hulbert he wrote on August 25: "I feel that Roosevelt's strength is altogether incalculable. The contest is between him and me, not between Taft and me. I think Taft will run third,—at any rate in the popular, if not in the electoral, vote. The country will have none of him. But just what will happen, as between Roosevelt and me, with party lines utterly confused and broken, is all guesswork. It depends upon what the people are thinking and purposing whose opinions do not get into the newspapers,—and I am by no means confident. He appeals to their imagination; I do not. He is a real, vivid person, whom they have seen and shouted themselves hoarse over and voted for, millions strong; I am a vague, conjectural personality, more made up of opinions and academic prepossessions than of human traits and red corpuscles. We shall see what will happen!" [38]

As the contest narrowed down to a battle between Roosevelt and Wilson, the Bull Moose leader seemed to redouble the intensity and zeal

[34] L. D. Wald to Jane Addams, August 12, 1912, Jane Addams Papers, Library of Congress; hereinafter cited as Addams Papers.
[35] B. Whitlock to A. J. Nock, August 17, 1912, published in Allan Nevins (ed.), *The Letters and Journal of Brand Whitlock, The Letters,* p. 152.
[36] L. Steffens to A. H. Suggett, September 12, 1912, published in Ella Winter and Granville Hicks (eds.), *The Letters of Lincoln Steffens,* I, 308.
[37] W. H. Taft to Helen Taft, July 22, 1912, quoted in Henry F. Pringle, *The Life and Times of William Howard Taft,* p. 817.
[38] Published in R. S. Baker, *Woodrow Wilson,* III, 390.

of his campaign. Soon he had nominated Wilson for membership in his famous Ananias Club and was charging right and left that Wilson's trust program was so innocuous that "the enormous majority" of trust managers were supporting him for the presidency. Roosevelt was not surprised, therefore, that "every big crooked financier is against us and in favor of either Mr. Wilson or Mr. Taft." [39] By the end of the campaign, Roosevelt was grossly misrepresenting Wilson's solution for the monopoly problem and was savagely attacking him for his failure to obtain the repeal of New Jersey's notorious corporation laws, under the provisions of which most of the great holding companies had been incorporated.[40]

Most historians agree that the campaign of 1912 was largely a contest of personalities; they have portrayed in vivid colors the inevitable contrast between the emotional and impulsive Roosevelt, the deliberate and rational Wilson, and the obtuse and genial Taft. All of which, to some extent, is true. Roosevelt's vote in November, to be sure, represented the bulk of his personal following; Wilson's plurality represented the votes of the Democratic regulars and the independent progressives and conservatives who supported him; while Taft's following consisted of the faithful and, for the most part, conservative remnants of the once proud G.O.P. William Allen White has epitomized in Roosevelt's own phrase the similarity between the Wilson and Roosevelt programs in his famous epigram: "Between the New Nationalism and the New Freedom was that fantastic imaginary gulf that always has existed between tweedle-dum and tweedle-dee." [41]

Certainly Wilson and Roosevelt essentially agreed that there were gross economic maladjustments that could be remedied by means of the legislative process, and their economic and social objectives were practically identical. On the other hand, there was a wide ideological gulf separating the New Freedom and the New Nationalism, a gulf much broader than that caused by mere personal and temperamental differences. Roosevelt believed that trusts and monopolies were economically efficient and socially desirable, and he sought to apply the Bismarckian remedies of legalization and strict federal control to make them socially useful. He proposed, in addition, to apply the Bismarckian

[39] T. Roosevelt, "The Taft-Wilson Trust Programme," *Outlook*, CII (September 21, 1912), 106-107.

[40] See, e.g., T. Roosevelt to G. L. Record, published in the *Jersey Journal* of Jersey City, November 2, 1912.

[41] W. A. White, *Woodrow Wilson*, p. 264.

social code to ameliorate the lot of the workers.[42] Wilson, on the contrary, was yet too much imbued with the British tradition of free, competitive enterprise to admit of the necessity for its abandonment. There

And He Smote the Rock Time and Again—But Nothing Doing

Blessington in *Houston Post*

were, of course, other differences between the Roosevelt and Wilson programs of economic reform—the contrast in their approach to the tariff question, for example—but they were incidental to the larger issue of monopoly control.

[42] For a convenient summary of Roosevelt's proposals for social legislation, see his "The Minimum Wage," *Outlook*, CII (September 28, 1912), 159-160.

Notwithstanding the fact that Wilson could not make the warm, emotional appeal to his followers that was so characteristic of Roosevelt, there is plenty of evidence to prove that Wilson did receive the support of as many prominent reformers and progressive leaders as did Roosevelt. In the first place, the dragon seeds of imperialism, big-navyism, protectionism, and militarism that Roosevelt had sown so wildly during the years rose up in 1912 to challenge his claim to the leadership of the moral and social reform movement. "It seems strange," wrote the secretary of the Anti-Imperialist League, "that a demagogue who with no new practical suggestions who has merely embellished every catch-word with vigorous and eloquent language has been able to blind any of the elect." [43] Because of Roosevelt's imperialistic and jingo-istic record, the director of the World Peace Foundation favored Wilson over Roosevelt.[44] Roosevelt's past policy of opportunism, moreover, had convinced many progressives that he was intellectually dishonest. "I wish I could believe he intended to do a single honest thing," wrote Anna Howard Shaw, "or that he would carry out a single plank in the platform if he were to be elected. . . . I cannot." [45]

When Roosevelt sounded the battle cry for the rallying of all progres-sives behind his banner, therefore, many reformers ignored the call and turned to Wilson instead. They admired Wilson's courage, his frank-ness in refusing to claim omniscience and to promise the millennium within a single presidential term; they admired his moderation and his calm, rational approach to the evils he was attacking. "At last we have a leader of the 'New Thought,' a spokesman of the prevailing opinion of the great mass of the citizenship," wrote one supporter to Wilson. ". . . To say that your words have created enthusiasm is not all, for many of us believe that the programme outlined by you will be the means of hope, of stimulus and of encouragement in the work for what you aptly call the 'rule of right and of justice.' " [46] Brand Whitlock, who had been offered the Progressive nomination for governor in Ohio and who had wavered in his support of Wilson, best expressed the enthusi-asm that many of the middle-of-the-road progressives felt for Wilson's candidacy when he wrote to Newton D. Baker:

"When I came home the other day I found your letter awaiting me. I have written to McAdoo and to Brandeis, and to my old friend Frank

[43] Erving Winslow to J. Addams, August 7, 1912, Addams Papers.
[44] D. S. Jordan to J. Addams, November 25, 1912, *ibid.*
[45] A. H. Shaw to J. Addams, August 16, 1912, *ibid.*
[46] J. L. Davis to W. W., August 8, 1912, Wilson Papers.

Walsh, the Kansas City lawyer who is so deep in the Wilson campaign, and I have told them, as I told you, that I am of course supporting Governor Wilson. . . . I was of course impressed by the enthusiasm with which the Progressive cause was launched, and I like the social program which it put forth; to that extent the movement gave expression to a beautiful sentiment in this land, which you and I have been trying to make concrete in our cities for many years. But that sentiment did not get itself fully, or adequately, expressed in the movement, and now it seems to have fallen back into the old partisan spirit, which is the very antithesis of that sentiment. If Governor Wilson had not been nominated at Baltimore, we should have had a new liberal party in this country, and the alignment at last would have been clear. But in his personality Governor Wilson himself wholly satisfies and sums up that democratic spirit which means everything to you and me, and it is personality that counts, that tells, more than creeds or platforms. Governor Wilson's ability, his services, his mastery of himself and of affairs, his imagination, his literary ability, his sense of humor, all those combine to endow him with a rare culture, and his character is his best platform." [47]

It is not surprising, therefore, that Roosevelt had no monopoly on the progressive leadership of the country, or that such independent progressives as Rabbi Stephen S. Wise and Alexander J. McKelway, secretary of the National Child Labor Committee, supported Wilson instead of following the Progressive standard.[48] Louis D. Brandeis, Rudolph Spreckels, whose war on graft and civic corruption in San Francisco had made him a national figure,[49] Senator John D. Works of California, Jacob Schiff, the banker-philanthropist of Kuhn, Loeb & Company,[50] Dr. Harvey W. Wiley, former chief chemist of the Department of Agriculture and the leading champion of pure food legislation, Charles R. Crane of Chicago, Raymond B. Fosdick and the Reverend Madison C. Peters of New York, and Erman J. Ridgway, publisher of *Everybody's Magazine*—these were among the more than 40,000 members of the Wilson Progressive Republican League.[51]

[47] September 28, 1912, published in A. Nevins (ed.), *The Letters of Brand Whitlock*, p. 154.

[48] S. S. Wise to J. Addams, September 16, 1912; A. J. McKelway to J. Addams, October 5, 1912, both in Addams Papers.

[49] For Spreckels' reasons for supporting Wilson, see his "The Presidential Candidates," *La Follette's Weekly Magazine*, IV (August 31, 1912), 7; also his *Why Republicans Should Vote for Wilson* (Democratic campaign pamphlet, 1912).

[50] For Schiff's statement, see the *New York Times*, August 17, 1912.

[51] "Republican Progressives for Wilson," *National Monthly*, IV (November 1912), 138.

Meanwhile, during the confusion and heat of July, when Democratic politicians were making daily visits to Sea Girt and Wilson was desperately trying to find time to write his acceptance speech, the problem of the organization of the presidential campaign demanded the harried candidate's urgent attention. The most difficult task on hand was the selection of a chairman for the national committee. Wilson's position was delicate and trying; he plainly distrusted McCombs, the obvious candidate for the job, and probably would have preferred McAdoo as national chairman.[52] McCombs was regarded by many progressive Democrats as a conservative, ill-suited to manage the campaign; Bryan did not regard him with favor;[53] yet any other course than naming McCombs would have been sheer stupidity on Wilson's part. McCombs had been his manager during the pre-convention campaign and expected to retain the leadership of the Wilson forces. He had given unstintingly of his time and money for the cause. He had alienated some prominent Democrats, to be sure, but he had accomplished a near-miracle at Baltimore. If, as contemporary writers agree, his health was ruined, it should be remembered that he was a casualty of the pre-convention battle.

Democratic leaders like Burleson, Daniels, Hudspeth, and Robert Ewing, national committeeman from Louisiana, realized this perhaps better than Wilson, and they warned him that he would do the worst possible thing if he failed to show public appreciation of McCombs's services. Wilson, consequently, gave in and announced from Sea Girt that he had selected his old manager to direct the presidential campaign.[54] On July 14 he gave to Hudspeth, national committeeman from New Jersey, a long memorandum embodying his plans for the campaign, which Hudspeth was to use as a basis for his discussions with the national committee. Hudspeth, Grosscup, McCombs, Daniels, Ewing, and Thomas J. Pence left Sea Girt for Chicago, where the national committee was to meet the following day, "loaded and locked," as Wilson put it, with the Wilson master plan for the campaign.[55]

The Democratic veterans officially surrendered their leadership of the party at Chicago, on July 15. Some of them did not like Wilson's campaign plan, and a few of them muttered protests in the corridors of the Congress Hotel before the national committee met; but there were no

[52] Josephus Daniels, *The Wilson Era*, p. 68.
[53] See L. Lea to W. W., July 13, 1912, Wilson Papers, for a summary of the anti-McCombs argument.
[54] *New York World*, July 13, 1912.　　　　[55] *New York Times*, July 15, 1912.

dissenting voices when Hudspeth outlined Wilson's campaign plans and nominated McCombs for national chairman.[56] McCombs was on hand and, leaning on a cane, limped into the committee room to receive the chairman's gavel from Norman E. Mack.[57]

After a five hours' conference with McCombs, Burleson, Daniels, and other progressive Democrats, Wilson on July 18 announced the names of the Democratic campaign committee. Most of the men were original Wilson supporters who had been active in the pre-convention campaign: McCombs, Hudspeth, Daniels, Saulsbury, Ewing, Palmer, Davies, Gore, O'Gorman, Representative Daniel J. McGillicuddy of Maine, Burleson, and McAdoo. At Burleson's insistence, however, Wilson added Senator Reed of Missouri as a representative of the Clark forces and Judge Will R. King of Oregon as a representative of the Pacific Coast area.[58] It was a matter of considerable comment that Wilson ignored almost altogether the old guard politicians, who had heretofore taken an active part in the management of Democratic presidential campaigns, in selecting what the *New York Times* described as his "verandah cabinet." Thus Senator Isidor Rayner of Maryland wrote: "The Committee you have appointed is a most admirable one, is free from 'entangling alliances' and represents in its membership the highest ideals of party policy." [59]

Early in August, Democratic organization headquarters were established in New York City. There were ugly rumors to the effect that friction between McCombs and McAdoo had already developed in the campaign committee;[60] Wilson went to New York on August 3 to iron out the differences. He conferred for several hours with McCombs and soon afterward announced the appointment of Morgenthau as chairman of the finance committee, Davies as vice-chairman in charge of the headquarters that would soon be established in Chicago, and McAdoo as vice-chairman in charge of the New York headquarters.[61] When Wilson announced three days later that Rolla Wells of St. Louis and Charles R. Crane had accepted positions in the campaign organization

[56] *New York World,* July 16, 1912.

[57] The official account of the Chicago meeting is printed in the *Proceedings of the Convention,* pp. 492-521.

[58] *New York World,* July 19, 1912; A. S. Burleson to D. F. Houston, February 6, 1926, Burleson Papers.

[59] I. Rayner to W. W., July 30, 1912, Wilson Papers.

[60] *Trenton Evening Times,* August 3, 1912.

[61] *New York World,* August 4, 1912.

as treasurer and vice-chairman of the finance committee, the organization of the presidential campaign was largely completed.[62]

The work of organizing the Democratic campaign was gigantic, and for the most part Wilson parceled it out to the members of the campaign committee and did not concern himself with bothersome details. Senator Gore, for example, headed the organization bureau where he perfected the business of campaign organization to an extraordinary degree; Gore also took the lead in organizing Wilson and Marshall clubs throughout the country and supplied them liberally with campaign literature and Wilson buttons.[63] Josephus Daniels, one of the leading Democratic editors in the South, was named by Wilson to head the publicity bureau at the New York headquarters. Daniels' staff compiled and published the *Democratic Text-Book,* distributed thousands of campaign articles and editorials to newspapers and magazines, and covered the nation's sign-boards with posters. In addition, hundreds of thousands of Democratic handbills and pamphlets[64] were scattered throughout the country.[65] Burleson, head of the speakers' bureau, was given the task of rounding up the leather-lunged Democratic orators and sending them to reinforce the weak spots on the Democratic map with their rhetoric. During the campaign there was a wholesale emigration of southern spellbinders to the North and West to campaign for the Democratic ticket.

In an effort to counteract the rising tide of Roosevelt sentiment in the Midwest, where the Progressive party was strongest, the Wilson managers divided their campaign headquarters and established a co-ordinate branch in Chicago. Davies, Wilson leader from Wisconsin, headed the Chicago group; Frank B. Lord, Washington press correspondent, managed the publicity bureau; and Burleson and Gore moved their staffs from New York to Chicago. Ewing established a press contributions bureau, which successfully used Democratic newspapers as collectors of campaign contributions. A young Chicago millionaire,

[62] *St. Louis Republic,* August 7, 1912.

[63] Gore's bureau distributed 760,000 packages of campaign materials to approximately 360,000 different individuals. About 3,300,000 pieces of printed matter were sent directly from Gore's office, while about 2,500,000 were sent from the general supply room by order of the bureau. W. D. Jamieson to T. P. Gregory, November 7, 1912, copy in House Papers.

[64] For a complete list of the publications of the publicity bureau, see the Bibliography at the end of this volume.

[65] Daniels has written about the work of his organization during the summer and fall of 1912 in his *The Wilson Era,* pp. 69-70, 76-77; see also M. F. Lyons, *William F. McCombs,* p. 114.

John Borden, organized a college men's bureau in order to unite college students behind the former Princeton president; Judge Martin Wade of Iowa directed the labor bureau; James A. Reed headed the senatorial

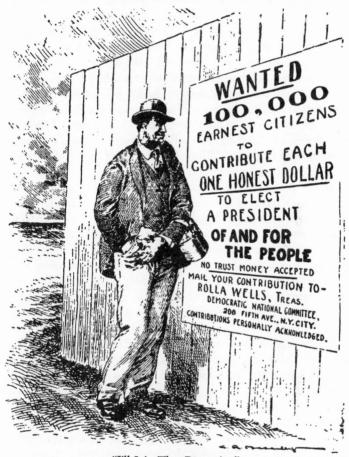

"I'll Join That Procession"
Macauley in *New York World*

campaign committee; and Jerry South, a former Clark manager in Arkansas, was chief of a mysterious special organization that worked to bring the foreign-born voters within the Democratic fold.[66]

[66] The best description of the Chicago headquarters is Arthur Krock's article in the *Louisville Times*, September 13, 1912.

The strain and excitement of the campaign soon proved too great a tax upon McCombs; he collapsed on August 12 and left soon afterward, "yellow-skinned, hollow-eyed and emaciated," [67] for an extended rest in the Adirondacks. McAdoo immediately assumed the generalship of the campaign, and under his direction Morgenthau, Ewing, and Wells set to work to raise the money for the campaign. Ewing worked through the newspaper editors, and by November some 210 daily and 800 weekly newspapers were collecting campaign contributions from their readers. Morgenthau and McAdoo persuaded the banks and trust companies to receive contributions to the campaign funds of the three major parties, and the system worked remarkably well. [68] For the first time in an American political campaign, Morgenthau instituted a budget system for campaign expenditures; the system was so successful that by January 1, 1913, all bills had been paid and there was a balance of $25,000 in the national committee's treasury. [69]

At the very outset of the campaign, Wilson insisted that Morgenthau and McAdoo should not solicit contributions from corporations, that no money should be accepted from men who expected to receive political compensation for their gifts, that special attention should be paid to small contributors, and in particular that three wealthy Democrats (presumably Morgan, Belmont, and Ryan) should not be allowed to contribute to the campaign fund. [70] Wilson's dictum was generally adhered to by the campaign committee: no contributions from corporations were received; Morgan, Belmont, and Ryan did not besmirch the Democratic fund with their fortunes; and the campaign committee tried sincerely to win the financial support of the great mass of Democratic voters. There were great "dollar drives," and time and again appeals were sent out to the voters, reminding them that as Wilson was the people's candidate, they stood obligated to support his campaign with their own small contributions.

When one considers the really tremendous effort made by the Democratic newspapers to make the campaign fund drive a truly popular affair, it must be concluded that the mass appeal was a disappointing failure. The campaign of 1912, in short, was not financed by small contributors; and had the campaign committee depended upon "the

[67] M. F. Lyons, *William F. McCombs,* p. 124.

[68] *Houston Post,* August 19, 1912.

[69] Rolla Wells, *Report of the Treasurer of the Democratic National Committee* (1913), p. 171; hereinafter cited as *Treasurer's Report.*

[70] Henry Morgenthau, *All In a Life-Time,* pp. 152-153; *New York Times,* August 10, 1912.

people" for financial support, the party would have been bankrupt indeed in November. A total of 89,854 persons contributed to the national fund. Some 88,229 contributors gave less than $100, while 1,625 contributed in amounts greater than $100. Of the total sum subscribed, $1,110,952.25, less than one-third, $318,909.50, came from the small contributors.[71] The 1,625 persons who gave over $100 contributed a total of $729,042.75;[72] 155 contributors gave $508,708, or almost half of the entire campaign fund. The forty contributors giving $5,000 or over contributed $364,950 to the fund, considerably more than the total given by 88,229 contributors!

It was largely the same old story, therefore, of a few rich men financing a presidential campaign, except that in 1912 the ogres of Wall Street—Morgan, Belmont, and Ryan—were outlawed by the candidate and the burden fell upon other and perhaps more progressive men of wealth. The inscrutable Charles R. Crane, who had largely financed La Follette's pre-convention campaign, gave $40,000 and was the largest contributor. Cleveland H. Dodge sank $35,000 more into the political future of his friend; Jacob H. Schiff contributed $12,500, while Samuel Untermeyer gave $10,000. One of the nation's leading brewers, Jacob Ruppert, gave $10,000; Bernard M. Baruch, wealthy stockbroker, contributed $12,500. The Jones brothers, Thomas D. and David B., of the "Harvester Trust" in Chicago, gave $20,000, while Cyrus H. McCormick, president of the trust, contributed $12,500.[73] It is perhaps coincidental but nevertheless interesting that Wilson never once denounced the harvester trust in his campaign speeches, although he criticized freely several of the other leading trusts. Morgenthau gave $10,000, making a total of $30,000 he had invested in Wilson's political career; John Barton Payne of Chicago, $15,000; James W. Gerard of New York, afterward Wilson's ambassador to Germany, $13,000. The bosses of the reactionary Democratic machine in Kentucky invested $12,500 in future federal patronage, while the conservative leader

---

[71] Rolla Wells, *Treasurer's Report*, p. 3.

[72] See *ibid.*, pp. 3-34, for the list of contributors who gave $100 or more.

[73] When Bryan heard of McCormick's contribution, however, he strongly urged the Democratic managers to return the contribution. W. J. Bryan, MS memorandum on the McCormick contribution, dictated October 16, 1912, in the William Jennings Bryan Papers, Library of Congress.

The report of the McCormick contribution evoked considerable criticism elsewhere and, at the initiative of Cleveland H. Dodge and McCormick himself, was returned on October 22. See C. H. Dodge to C. H. McCormick, October 22, 1912, Bryan Papers; also Wilson's statement on the matter in the *Baltimore Sun,* October 26, 1912.

of the West Virginia Democracy, Senator Clarence W. Watson, contributed $7,500.[74]

In the campaign headquarters in New York there was a great deal of petty discord and jealousy. McCombs was ill, irritable, and bitterly jealous of McAdoo; McAdoo was ambitious and chafed at the necessity of working under McCombs, whose wretched health from the outset of the campaign prevented him from assuming active leadership of the organization. After his physical collapse in August, McCombs seemed to grow suspicious of almost everyone in any way connected with the campaign, and in his abnormal mental state concluded that McAdoo was secretively endeavoring to undermine him in Wilson's favor;[75] it was a suspicion, incidentally, that probably was well-founded. McCombs recovered sufficiently to return to New York by the middle of October, but of course by then most of the campaign work had already been done. McCombs in his memoirs tells us that he found McAdoo sitting at his desk, and that he ordered him out of his office![76]

In spite of the hopeless confusion and discord in the leadership of the campaign, the various bureaus in New York and Chicago did an efficient job, and it is difficult to see that the McCombs-McAdoo feud interfered with the progress of the campaign which, after all, was being carried on largely by the Democratic organizations within the states. The Democrats, moreover, were not hamstrung by a lack of funds necessary to the prosecution of an effective campaign, as had so often been the case when Bryan was the nominee. The New York headquarters spent and distributed the lion's share, $828,122.79, of the $1,110,952 fund. Some $236,178 was distributed among the various local Democratic leaders, for the state campaigns; Daniels' publicity bureau expended almost $95,000, while an additional $116,174 was

[74] Rolla Wells, *Treasurer's Report, passim.*

[75] M. F. Lyons, *William F. McCombs,* p. 129.

[76] W. F. McCombs, *Making Woodrow Wilson President,* p. 193. McAdoo saw the root of McCombs's trouble as a psychological maladjustment resulting from a split personality. *Crowded Years,* pp. 114-117. Tumulty thought sheer personal jealousy of McAdoo actuated McCombs to "every contemptible and underhand method." *Woodrow Wilson As I Know Him,* p. 136. Baker saw McCombs as the symbol of the patronage-hungry Democrats. *Woodrow Wilson,* III, 413. Lyons knew the man better than any other person and has left a fitting commentary on the McCombs-McAdoo controversy: "Poor McCombs—few seemed to understand his condition." Because he gave the best that he had during the pre-convention and presidential campaigns, he had become desperately ill, and all his actions must be judged in light of this fact. *William F. McCombs,* pp. 146-147.

spent for "shipping and documents." Nearly $133,000 was lavished, and for the most part wasted, on the foreign-born and Negro voters.[77] The total expenditures of the Chicago headquarters, $206,273, were slight as compared to the expenses of the New York organization, chiefly because the latter carried the heavy burden of publication and local campaign expenses. In Chicago another $13,000 was expended to corral the foreign-born vote; almost $38,000 was spent to convert labor to the Wilson cause; the senatorial campaign committee spent almost $22,000.[78]

Early in August Wilson confidently announced that he would not engage in "swings around the circle" through the country, and above all that he would not speak from the rear platforms of railroad cars. "I intend to discuss principles and not men," he declared, "and I will make speeches only in such debatable States where I accept invitations from the party leaders." [79] Long stumping tours he now thought were neither dignified nor impressive; he hoped, however, that Bryan would stump the country for him. Wilson's naive expectation that he could escape the rigors of a national campaign evoked strong protests from his managers and from Democratic newspapers, who warned that 1912 was no time for front-porch campaigns and that he, too, must share the burden of carrying the Democratic appeal to the voters.[80]

During the latter part of August, Wilson made three speeches in New Jersey, but it was actually not until September that he really opened the speaking phase of his campaign. He delivered a diatribe against tariff protection—one of the worst speeches of his public career—at Washington Park, on August 15.[81] Four days later, at Schutzen Park, in Union Hill, he spoke before an uproarious crowd of German-Americans who drank beer and consumed huge quantities of food while he spoke; he had just begun an inspiring address when the noise of four German brass bands drove him off the speaker's platform.[82] On August 20 he told a gathering of Mercer County Democrats that there was no man who could say that "the representatives of privilege made the nomination at Baltimore." [83]

Certainly there was no indication in either of these three New Jersey addresses of the kind of campaign Wilson would make, or of the great

[77] Rolla Wells, *Treasurer's Report*, p. 172.
[78] *ibid.*, p. 173. [79] *New York World*, August 4, 1912.
[80] *Jersey Journal* of Jersey City, August 12, 1912.
[81] *New York Times*, August 16, 1912. [82] *ibid.*, August 20, 1912.
[83] *Trenton True American*, August 21, 1912.

issues he would emphasize most heavily. He had declared at Trenton that the chief issue of the campaign was privilege versus equal rights; but this was a threadbare and vague theme and he wisely decided not to repeat his mistakes of the pre-convention campaign by basing his appeal upon a demand that the government be returned to the people, whatever that might mean. He seemed undecided, searching about for some great issue to carry to the people.

On August 28 occurred a meeting at Sea Girt that was to have momentous consequences for the presidential campaign and for the whole course of domestic reform during the Wilson administration. Louis D. Brandeis and Wilson met for the first time. Brandeis, one of the leading progressive lawyers in the country, was also probably the outstanding authority on monopoly control and railroad regulation; he was, besides, the chief spokesman of the philosophy of regulated competition, unhampered enterprise, and economic freedom for the small businessman. "The record of Mr. Louis D. Brandeis as a defender of the public welfare against the aggressions of the special interests," admitted Roosevelt's leading editorial spokesman, "has been such as to entitle anything that he may say concerning the trusts to a considerate hearing." [84]

Brandeis came for lunch and remained to confer with Wilson for three hours. It was an altogether delightful meeting; Brandeis at once converted Wilson to the proposition that he make his campaign upon the issue of the restoration of competition and free enterprise by means of the regulation and control of competition itself. "I found Gov. Wilson a man capable of broad, constructive statesmanship," Brandeis afterward declared, "and I found him to be entirely in accord with my own views of what we need to do to accomplish industrial freedom." [85]

No one would assert that it was Brandeis who first stirred Wilson's interest in the trust problem; as early as 1906, in his Jamestown speech, Wilson had indicated his growing concern over the problem. The important fact about his relationship with Brandeis is the fundamental

[84] *Outlook,* cii (September 28, 1912), 146.

[85] *New York Times,* August 29, 1912. When a reporter asked why he had left the La Follette ranks and joined the Wilson movement, Brandeis declared that he believed the Democratic party offered the best hope of legislation for industrial freedom. The Roosevelt party, he continued, would fail because it proposed to regulate monopoly and thus make legal that which was illegal. "We must undertake to regulate competition instead of monopoly, for our industrial freedom and our civic freedom go hand in hand and there is no such thing as civic freedom in a state of industrial absolutism."

change in Wilson's attitude that occurred as a result of the association. In 1906—indeed until his conferences with Brandeis—Wilson insisted that only by making corporation officials personally responsible for their monopolistic practices could the problem of trust control be met. It was a simple and totally innocuous approach to the problem, a carry-over from Wilson's reactionary phase; the truth was that he was dismally ignorant on the subject until Brandeis outlined his program for the regulation of competition to him. It was, moreover, a happy coincidence that Wilson's and Brandeis's fundamental objectives, the establishment of unhampered competition and the liberation of economic enterprise in the United States, were the same. It is not surprising, therefore, that Wilson time and again went to him for advice with regard to the specific ways of regulating competition. He was an avid student and rapidly absorbed all that Brandeis taught him.

During the pre-convention campaign Wilson had approached the problem of monopoly regulation with singular timidity. He had denounced the trusts often enough; he had warned his listeners of the impelling necessity of doing something effective to restore competition; he had declared that the protective tariff had spawned the trusts. Yet his total effort of the pre-convention campaign had been merely to describe the conditions of American economic life, and progressive leaders had been doing exactly this for many years. The core of the problem was the method by which monopoly could be prevented and free competition might be restored—and this was where Wilson had demonstrated his most appalling ignorance. Because Brandeis understood the problem thoroughly, because he was ready with a definite plan for the bridling of monopoly, he became the chief architect of Wilson's New Freedom. After his first interview with Brandeis, for example, Wilson spoke with new confidence on the subject. "Both of us have as an object the prevention of monopoly," he declared. "Monopoly is created by unregulated competition, by competition that overwhelms all other competitions, and the only way to enjoy industrial freedom is to destroy that condition." New words, these, for Woodrow Wilson!

In his first important speech of the campaign, after the acceptance speech, Wilson sounded the keynote of his new appeal. He spoke on Labor Day to 10,000 workers at Buffalo, and for the first time he dealt with specific issues and proposals. Roosevelt, he asserted, was "a self-appointed divinity," whose proposal to legalize and regulate the trusts by a "Board of Experts," which would inevitably be controlled by the trust leaders themselves, offered nothing but slavery for the "wage slaves" (he used the term) of the United States. Thus, he continued:

"As to the monopolies, which Mr. Roosevelt proposes to legalize and to welcome, I know that they are so many cars of juggernaut, and I do not look forward with pleasure to the time when the juggernauts are licensed and driven by commissioners of the United States. . . .

"And what has created these monopolies? Unregulated competition. It has permitted these men to do anything they choose to do to squeeze their rivals out and crush their rivals to the earth. We know the processes by which they have done those things. We can prevent these processes through remedial legislation, and so restrict the wrong use of competition that the right use of competition will destroy monopoly. Ours is a programme of liberty; theirs a programme of regulation.

"I want you workingmen to grasp that point, because I want to say to you right now that the programme I propose does not look quite so much like acting as a Providence for you as the other programme looks. I want frankly to say to you that I am not big enough to play Providence, and my objection to the other plan is that I do not believe there is any man who is big enough to play Providence. . . . If you want a great struggle for liberty, that will cost you blood, adopt the Roosevelt regulation programme, put yourself at the disposal of a Providence resident at Washington, and then see what will come of it."

Those sections of the Progressive platform demanding social justice and a square deal for the common man, Wilson admitted, expressed warm sympathy for "practically every project of social betterment to which men and women of broad sympathies are now turning with generous purpose." On the other hand, the proposals in the platform to retain the protective tariff and to license and regulate monopolies were so dangerous, so fraught with dreadful implications, that they completely overshadowed the commendable features of the Progressive program.

He objected to Roosevelt's trust and labor program, Wilson continued, because it was paternalistic, because it would inevitably mean that workingmen would become wards of the federal government. "My kind of leading will not be telling other people what they have got to do," he added. "By leading I mean finding out what the interests of the community are agreed to be, and then trying my level best to find the methods of solution by common counsel. That is the only feasible programme of social uplift that I can imagine."

"When you have thought the whole thing out, therefore," he continued, "you will find that the programme of the new party legalizes
monopolies and systematically subordinates workingmen to them and
to plans made by the Government, both with regard to employment
and with regard to wages. By what means, except open revolt, could
we ever break the crust of our life again and become free men, breath-
ing an air of our own, choosing and living lives that we wrought out
for ourselves? Perhaps this new and all-conquering combination between money and government would be benevolent to us, perhaps
it would carry out the noble programme of social betterment, which
so many credulously expect of it, but who can assure us of that? Who
will give bond that it will be general and gracious and pitiful and
righteous? What man or set of men can make us secure under it by
their empty promise and assurance that it will take care of us and be
good?" [86]

Thus, in his first major campaign address, Wilson indicated the
path he was to follow throughout the summer and fall of 1912. His
education in monopoly control, however, had just begun. He understood clearly enough now that monopoly was the result of unregulated
competition, but what exactly, he wondered, did Brandeis mean by
"unregulated competition"? More specifically, he asked, how could
the federal government regulate competition so as to prevent monopoly? On September 27 he conferred with Brandeis in Boston and
discussed these problems at length. After the meeting Wilson sent a
telegram to Brandeis, requesting him to "set forth as explicitly as possible the actual measures by which competition can be effectively regulated." "The more explicit we are on this point," he added, "the
more completely will the enemies' guns be spiked." [87]

Brandeis replied on September 28 by sending Wilson copies of two
articles he had written for *Collier's Weekly*.[88] Two days later he sent
Wilson a large quantity of material that embodied his own researches
and ideas on the trust problem. One item was entitled "Memo on La
Follette Anti-Trust Bill," which proposed a number of specific amendments to the Sherman law in order to make federal control really
effective. Another item, entitled "Suggestions for letter of Governor
Wilson on Trusts," summarized all of Brandeis's proposals and ideas
with regard to trust control. From this lengthy statement Wilson

[86] *ibid.,* September 3, 1912.
[87] W. W. to L. D. Brandeis, September 27, 1912, copy in Baker Papers.
[88] L. D. Brandeis to W. W., September 28, 1912, copy in *ibid.*

drew all of his ideas that he expressed during the presidential campaign, although in certain important respects he did not go as far as Brandeis had suggested. Brandeis's approach to the question is revealed in the following opening paragraphs:

"You have asked me to state what the essential difference is between the Democratic Party's solution of the Trust Problem and that of the New Party; and how to propose to 'regulate competition.' My answer is this:

"The two parties differ fundamentally regarding the economic policy which the country should pursue. The Democratic Party insists that competition can be and should be maintained in every branch of private industry; that competition can be and should be restored in those branches of industry in which it has been suppressed by the trusts; and that, if at any future time monopoly should appear to be desirable in any branch of industry, the monopoly should be a public one—a monopoly owned by the people and not by the capitalists. The New Party, on the other hand, insists that private monopoly may be desirable in some branches of industry, or at all events, is inevitable; and that existing trusts should not be dismembered or forcibly dislodged from those branches of industry in which they have already acquired a monopoly, but should be made 'good' by regulation. In other words, the New Party declares that private monopoly in industry is not necessarily evil, but may do evil; and that legislation should be limited to such laws and regulations as should attempt merely to prevent the doing of evil. The New Party does not fear commercial power, however great, if only methods for regulation are provided. We believe that no methods of regulation ever have been or can be devised to remove the menace inherent in private monopoly and overweening commercial power.

"This difference in the economic policy of the two parties is fundamental and irreconcilable. It is the difference between industrial liberty and industrial absolutism, tempered by governmental (that is, party) supervision." [89]

After his Labor Day speech at Buffalo, Wilson became the leading political spokesman of Brandeis's program for the regulation of competition. On the other hand, it was Norman Hapgood, progressive crusader, Hearst's chief editorial antagonist, exposer of patent medicine

[89] L. D. Brandeis, "Suggestions for letter of Governor Wilson on Trusts," MS in Baker Papers; also L. D. Brandeis, "Memo on La Follette Anti-Trust Bill," MS in *ibid.*, and L. D. Brandeis to W. W., September 30, 1912, *ibid.*

frauds, and editor of *Collier's Weekly,* who became Brandeis's chief journalistic mouthpiece. Hapgood had supported Wilson's candidacy since the beginning of the pre-convention campaign; during the summer of 1912 he invited Brandeis to write a series of articles on the monopoly question for the *Weekly.* What a remarkable combination it was, this Brandeis-Hapgood team! Not only did Brandeis write the articles[90] that furnished Wilson with much of his campaign ammunition; he also wrote the editorials that Hapgood published in his editorial columns.[91] The ideas embodied in many of Wilson's campaign utterances, therefore, can also be traced directly to the pages of *Collier's Weekly,* which became for a time the leading Democratic spokesman in the fall of 1912.[92]

Wilson's address to the workers of Buffalo was the opening blast of a full-fledged campaign to win the forty-five electoral votes of New York State. On September 4 he went to New York City, where he spoke before a group of foreign language newspaper editors and proclaimed a new standard for immigration legislation. "If we can hit upon a standard which admits every voluntary immigrant," he

[90] They are as follows: "Trusts, Efficiency, and the New Party," *Collier's Weekly,* XLIX (September 14, 1912), 14-15; "Trusts, the Export Trade, and the New Party," *ibid.,* L (September 21, 1912), 10-11; see also L. D. Brandeis, "Labor and the New Party Trust Program," *La Follette's Weekly Magazine,* IV (October 12, 1912), 6-8, 19-22. Spatial limitations prohibit a discussion of Brandeis's views in this study; his articles, however, have been published in two volumes, *Business a Profession,* and *Other People's Money.*

[91] See, e. g., L. D. Brandeis to N. Hapgood, October 2, 1912, copy in Baker Papers; also L. D. Brandeis to R. S. Baker, July 23, 1928, *ibid.* The editorials written by Brandeis were "Monopoly," *Collier's Weekly,* September 7, 1912; "Labor and the Trusts," *ibid.,* September 14, 1912; "The Wastes of Monopoly," *ibid.,* September 21, 1912; "Concentration," *ibid.,* October 5, 1912; and "The Method," *ibid.,* October 19, 1912.

[92] Robert J. Collier, publisher of *Collier's Weekly,* was an ardent supporter and intimate friend of Roosevelt. Collier finally lost patience with Hapgood's campaign for Wilson's election, ousted him from the editorship of the *Weekly,* assumed the editorship himself, and converted the magazine into a leading Roosevelt sheet. The issue of October 19, 1912, was the last that Hapgood edited. Collier explained the reason for his break with Hapgood in the issue of November 2: "He [Collier] believes that Collier's attitude in the campaign just closing has not been true to its own best traditions. It has been captious, unresponsive, even sneering. Since the owner's opinion did not coincide with the former editor's, he has decided to edit his own paper according to his own convictions." *Collier's Weekly,* L (November 2, 1912), 10. Hapgood contended, however, that political differences had not caused the rupture. He had resigned from the editorship of the magazine, he asserted, because Collier had allowed the advertising manager to dictate the editorial policy of the *Weekly.* "When I saw Mr. Collier break the custom of years by seeking occasions to interfere with me," Hapgood continued, "I knew its meaning and acted at once." *New York Times,* October 19, 1912.

declared, "and excludes those who have not come of their own motion, with their own purpose of making a home and career for themselves, but have been induced by steamship companies or others to come in order to get the passage money, then we will have what we will all agree upon." [93] Later in the day he spoke before a group of plainly dressed members of the Woodrow Wilson Working Men's League.[94] On September 9 he returned to New York, where he participated in three conferences at the campaign headquarters, made four speeches, helped to organize a Pure Food League, and visited McCombs, who was convalescing in Flushing.[95]

Meanwhile, an alarming rupture in the Democratic party in New York had developed soon after the Baltimore convention. It threatened to split the state party wide open and endanger Wilson's prospects of carrying the state in November. The difficulty was caused by the rebellion of a group of progressive Democratic leaders against Murphy's inexorable dominance of the state party through his control of the Tammany machine. A small group of progressive Democratic legislators in the spring of 1911 had successfully thwarted Murphy's efforts to obtain the election of William F. Sheehan to the United States Senate, and had forced the election of James A. O'Gorman. After Wilson's nomination they gathered in New York on July 17 and, under the leadership of State Senator Franklin D. Roosevelt, bolted the regular Democratic organization, organized the Empire State Democratic party, and promised to nominate a full slate of candidates for the election of state officials in November and to rid the state of Tammany control.[96]

The chief newspaper spokesman of the anti-Tammany rebels was the *New York World,* which began a tremendous pressure campaign in September to discredit the Murphy machine and drive it from power. On September 11 the *World* let go with the following blast:

"A political party that permits itself to be bossed by a Murphy is corrupt. A political party that permits itself to be bossed by Murphy is unfit to govern. A political party that permits itself to be bossed by Murphy gives the lie to the Democratic National Convention. It gives the lie to the platform adopted at Baltimore. It gives the lie to the ticket nominated at Baltimore. There is no common ground for men who

[93] *New York World,* September 5, 1912.
[94] *New York Times,* September 5, 1912.
[95] *ibid.,* September 10, 1912.   [96] *New York World,* July 18, 1912.

believe in the Woodrow Wilson kind of Democracy and for men who believe in the Charles F. Murphy kind of Democracy.

"All that The World said in its Declaration of Independence editorial Saturday (September 7) it wishes to repeat with the utmost emphasis. Not only shall we refuse to support a candidate for Governor . . . who does not measure up to the political standards of Woodrow Wilson, but we shall use every honorable effort to defeat such a ticket.

"Murphy must go. So far as The World is concerned, he has already gone. If there is a Democratic machine in this State that is determined to retain him, it must take the consequences of its own folly and corruption."

When it became apparent that Murphy was determined to renominate Governor John A. Dix, the *World* announced that it would oppose his election; a group of up-state progressive Democratic newspapers, including the *Rochester Herald, Knickerbocker Press* of Albany, *Syracuse Post-Standard,* and *Troy Times* announced that they, too, would support the anti-Tammany Democrats.

Such was the political situation in the state when Wilson went to Syracuse on September 12 as the guest of the New York state fair committee. Actually he walked into a trap set for him by the state fair commissioner, George W. Driscoll, and by Murphy and Dix. He had accepted the invitation to go to Syracuse, expecting to meet only Driscoll and to make a non-partisan speech at the state fair grounds; on his arrival in the city, however, he found that he was the guest also of Murphy, Dix, the entire state Democratic committee, and the association of Democratic county chairmen.

The whole affair at Syracuse resembled more an *opéra bouffe* than a serious political gathering. Driscoll, for example, paraded Wilson in company with Murphy to the grandstand in the fair grounds. When Wilson mounted the open-air stand to make his speech, Murphy remained in the crowd below; but he and several other Tammany bosses surreptitiously climbed to the platform after Wilson had begun his speech. When the Democratic politicians afterward went to the Democratic clubhouse in Syracuse, Murphy, who had already arrived, hid in the bushes until Wilson passed; after the 200 politicians had sat down with Wilson at the tables on the porch for lunch, Driscoll went outside, brought Murphy in, and seated him close to Wilson. There were deviled crabs and mutton in plenty, but Wilson ate only a piece of bread and left the table before Murphy had begun to eat. After lunch, Wilson was taken to the auditorium where he was to address the state and county politicians. The doors were locked behind him and he found himself alone with Dix; an ex-prize fighter stood guard at the door. For ten minutes Dix and Wilson were alone in the room; Dix talked and Wilson, sitting grim and silent, listened. When the Democratic committeemen were finally admitted, they found Wilson sitting by himself in a corner of the room.

Wilson's address before the New York leaders was brief, but it was packed with political dynamite. He mentioned neither Dix's nor Murphy's name, yet he intimated bluntly that the New York Democrats should rid themselves of the incubus of Murphy. "The example of New York State," he declared, "is marked as perhaps the example of no other State is marked, and the people are waiting to see—I mean the people of the Nation are waiting to see—if we have our eyes open and see the lesson and the duty, or I should prefer to say, the privileges of the time." [97]

After Wilson's snubbing of Murphy and Dix at Syracuse, the progressive Democratic leaders in the state took new courage and were soon demanding that Wilson openly repudiate Murphy and the entire Tammany gang.[98] Certainly Wilson understood the gravity of the situation; yet he had promised soon after the Baltimore convention that he would not interfere with the affairs of the various state organizations, and how could he repudiate Murphy and Dix without breaking his pledge? Such interference on Wilson's part might be dangerous, besides, for it might cause Murphy to knife the Wilson-Marshall ticket in November, as David B. Hill had betrayed Cleveland in 1892.

Wilson, on the other hand, was being driven irresistibly by his own convictions and by his progressive New York advisers, O'Gorman and McAdoo, to a repudiation, evasive though it was, of the Tammany machine. On September 23 he conferred with McAdoo and announced his determination to enter the fight against Murphy. "I will put my foot down and put it down hard," he was reported to have said, "against boss control of the New York State situation." McAdoo hastened to Democratic headquarters in New York with a warning from Wilson that he would not tolerate Dix's renomination.[99] A week later, Wilson gave to the New York newspapers a statement that left no doubt as to where he stood. The country, he declared, expected the New York

[97] *New York Times,* September 13, 1912.
[98] *New York World,* September 23, 1912.
[99] *ibid.,* September 24, 1912.

Democrats to be free in making their choice for governor; he believed they were "ready to choose a progressive man of a kind to be his own master and to adopt a platform to which men of progressive principles everywhere can heartily subscribe, if only . . . [the party] be left free from personal control of any sort." The entire country would feel a chill of disappointment should the New York Democracy fail to subscribe to the progressive principles of the party.[100]

On the afternoon of October 3, the Democrats of New York gathered in state convention in Syracuse. O'Gorman was there as Wilson's personal representative and informed Murphy that the entire national organization was opposed to Dix's renomination. Murphy, much to everyone's surprise, decided to capitulate; consequently, on the fourth ballot Representative William Sulzer of New York City was nominated for governor.[101] The progressives were enormously pleased by their seeming victory over the Tammany Tiger. The *New York World* and the *New York Times* immediately declared that Sulzer was the choice of a majority of the New York Democrats and that they would support him heartily, while F. D. Roosevelt's protest party, the Empire State Democrats, which had already nominated a full slate of state candidates ten days before, withdrew its ticket and pledged support to Sulzer and the regular Democratic nominees.[102] Of course it was only a superficial victory that Wilson had won over Murphy, for Tammany's control of the Democratic party in the state had hardly been jarred, much less ended. Yet it was a spectacular demonstration of Wilson's commanding influence in party councils; moreover, it gave an effective reply to Theodore Roosevelt's oft-repeated charge that the Democratic party was boss-ridden and boss-controlled.

In the meantime, Wilson had been forced again to play the role of a chastiser of bosses when his old antagonist, James Smith, announced that he would be a candidate for the Democratic senatorial nomination in New Jersey.[103] The difficulty was not so much that Smith was a candidate, but that three of Wilson's close friends and supporters, John W. Wescott, William Hughes, and William C. Gebhardt, had entered the contest, and each was stoutly contending that he was the Wilson candidate. If all three progressives insisted upon making the canvass, Smith would inevitably be nominated because

[100] *New York Times,* September 30, 1912.
[101] *New York World,* October 3, 1912.
[102] *ibid.,* October 4-5, 1912; *New York Times,* October 4, 1912.
[103] *Trenton True American.* August 15, September 4, 1912.

of the division in the progressive vote. Wilson conferred with Wescott, Hughes, and Gebhardt on August 30 and warned them that there could be only one Wilson-progressive candidate; he could not, however, choose among the three men who had been among his most consistent supporters in his New Jersey battles.[104] On September 11, Gebhardt withdrew from the contest; Hughes and Wescott several days later agreed to submit their respective claims to an arbitration committee from the Democratic national headquarters in New York. And when McAdoo, O'Gorman, and Daniels decided in Hughes's favor, Wescott retired from the race and threw his support to Hughes.[105] "Governor Wilson had no knowledge of these conferences," McAdoo declared later. "They resulted wholly from the initiative of the National Campaign Committee." [106]

In spite of the heavy burden of the presidential campaign, Wilson threw himself wholeheartedly into the fight to defeat his indefatigable rival. On September 8, five days after Smith formally announced his senatorial candidacy, Wilson gave to the newspapers a ringing declaration demanding Smith's defeat: "Mr. Smith's selection as the Democratic candidate for the Senate would be the most fatal step backwards that the Democrats of the State could possibly take. It would mean his restoration to political leadership in New Jersey the moment my service as Governor ended, and, with his restoration, a return to the machine rule which so long kept every active Democrat in the State in subordination to him, and prevented every progressive program conceived in the interest of the people from being put into effect." [107]

No unhappy Orestes was pursued by the Fates more relentlessly than was Smith by the implacable Wilson, who insisted that New Jersey Democrats declare finally that they would not submit to the domination of the Newark boss. On September 21 Wilson paused in his campaign and went to Jersey City and Hoboken, where he pleaded for Hughes's nomination and Smith's final repudiation by the voters.[108] Once more the Democrats of the state heeded Wilson's plea and nominated Hughes by so resounding a majority that Smith retired for good from the political field.[109]

[104] *Trenton Evening Times,* August 30, 1912; *Jersey Journal* of Jersey City, August 30, 1912.
[105] *Trenton True American,* September 19, 1912.
[106] J. Daniels, *The Wilson Era,* pp. 73-76, has an account of the negotiations leading to Wescott's withdrawal.
[107] *Trenton True American,* September 9, 1912.
[108] *Trenton Evening Times,* September 23, 1912.
[109] *Trenton True American,* September 26, 1912.

As if the job of proving that the bosses did not control the Democratic party was not troublesome enough, the old matter of Wilson's derogatory writings about the "new" immigrants again arose to plague him. Hearst had nearly defeated his nomination on the same issue, and certainly it was a no less dangerous threat during the presidential campaign. Although Taft and Roosevelt did not drag in the immigration issue, their spokesmen did. The president of the American Association of Foreign Language Newspapers, for example, which served some 20,000,000 readers, was working hand in glove with the Republican managers.[110] Typical of the anti-Wilson propaganda was the broadside he published in the entire foreign language press. This reviewed the matter of Wilson's writings and concluded: "No man who has an iron heart like Woodrow Wilson, and who slanders his fellowmen, because they are poor and many of them without friends when they come to this country seeking honest work and wishing to become good citizens, is fit to be President of the United States." [111]

Special bureaus in the Democratic headquarters in New York and Chicago made herculean efforts to prove to foreign-born voters that the charges of certain Democratic leaders during the pre-convention campaign were slanders and lies. Henry Green, director of the American Immigration and Distribution League labored to convince the foreign-born voters that Wilson was "sound" on the question of immigration legislation.[112] For his part, Wilson again wrote dozens of letters to prominent Italian-, Polish-, Hungarian-, and Jewish-American leaders, repeating for the most part what he had said during the pre-convention campaign.[113]

While is it impossible to determine whether Wilson's efforts to win the support of the foreign-born voters from Eastern Europe was successful, there is some evidence that it was not. A poll of 2,313 Catholic priests and brothers in New York, Massachusetts, Connecticut, Ohio, Indiana, and in St. Louis, Louisville, Chicago, Milwaukee, Detroit, and several counties in Oklahoma revealed the following significant results: 60 per cent of the Irish priests and 80 per cent of the German priests

---

[110] L. N. Hammerling (?) to W. H. Taft, August 29, 1912, Taft Papers.

[111] "Woodrow Wilson's Latest Letter. It Shows Him to Be Still Unfriendly to the Immigrant from Europe," undated MS in *ibid*.

[112] H. Green to W. W., July 5, 1912, Wilson Papers.

[113] See, e.g., W. W. to L. E. Miller, editor of the *Jewish Daily Warheit*, August 28, 1912, published in the *New York Times*, August 29, 1912; W. W. to a group of Hungarian-Americans at Sea Girt, August 10, 1912, *St. Louis Republic*, August 11, 1912; W. W. to Anthony Geronimo, August 16, 1912, Wilson Papers.

were supporting Wilson; on the other hand, 90 per cent of the Italian priests and 70 per cent of the Polish priests were supporting Roosevelt.[114]

Rumors were also set afoot that Wilson was bigoted and narrow in his attitude toward Roman Catholics, and a prominent Catholic layman, James Charles Monoghan, was commissioned by the Democratic headquarters to write a pamphlet, *Is Woodrow Wilson A Bigot?*, to prove that Wilson had been kindly disposed toward Catholics in New Jersey. On the other hand, an anti-Catholic rumor was circulated about the Westinghouse plants at East Pittsburgh to the effect that Wilson had accepted with warm appreciation honorary membership in the Knights of Columbus, an organization of Catholic men.[115] This evoked from Wilson a reply, which he hoped would silence the attacks from both sides: "I am a normal man, following my own natural course of thought, playing no favorites, and trying to treat every creed and class with impartiality and respect."[116]

Wilson's campaign to win the support of organized labor has been briefly reviewed and will be discussed more fully in subsequent pages. Gompers, it will be recalled, had been converted to Wilson at their first meeting; at the beginning of the campaign, however, he and the American Federation of Labor leaders cautiously refused to endorse outright either of the presidential candidates. As the campaign progressed, however, it was plain that Gompers and the executive committee of the A. F. of L. were supporting Wilson as they had supported Bryan in 1908. In the October issue of the official publication of the Federation, for example, Gompers condemned the Republican platform and nominee, praised Wilson and the Democratic platform plank on labor, which he, Gompers, had written in 1908,[117] and declared that although the Progressive platform and Roosevelt's labor pronouncements were highly gratifying, labor had found it impossible to obtain legislative protection while Roosevelt was president.[118] In November, Gompers endorsed Wilson's candidacy almost to the exclusion of approval of Roosevelt.[119]

[114] J. K. McGuire to J. A. O'Gorman, October 12, 1912, *ibid.*
[115] L. C. Woods to W. W., October 22, 1912, *ibid.*
[116] W. W. to W. G. McAdoo, October 22, 1912, leaflet in *ibid.*
[117] The plank in the Democratic platform of 1912, entitled "Rights of Labor," was a literal repetition of the declaration in the 1908 platform.
[118] *American Federationist*, xix (October 1912), 801-804.
[119] S. Gompers, "The Presidency in the Pending Campaign," *ibid.*, xix (November 1912), 889-894.

A more delicate and troublesome issue was Wilson's and the Democratic party's attitude with regard to the Negro question. The day had not yet arrived when the Democratic party openly courted the Negro vote, or when the Negroes held the balance of power in the large northern states; yet the Democratic managers in 1912 were at least anxious not to offend the Negroes in the North.

The chief fear of the intellectual Negro leaders concerned the Democratic party itself, which in the past had not been friendly to the black race. With good cause the militant Negroes feared that a Democratic Congress and administration controlled by southern white men might enact legislation hostile to their interests. They knew, for example, that James K. Vardaman of Mississippi had been elected to the United States Senate in 1911 on a platform demanding the repeal of the Fourteenth and Fifteenth amendments. What, except hostility and an attitude of scorn and contempt, could the Negroes expect from the Democratic party when a responsible Democratic spokesman and Wilson manager, Josephus Daniels, published such an editorial as this during the fall of 1912, which is paraphrased in part and quoted in part:

> The attitude of the South regarding the Negro in politics is unalterable and uncompromising. We take no risks. We abhor a northern policy of catering to Negroes politically just as we abhor a northern policy of social equality.
>
> Out of bitter experience the South has evolved certain paramount convictions. Southerners are not seeking merely a sectional policy, but also a national policy on this subject of the race question, for they know that short of a national policy they will never be secure. The South is solidly Democratic because of "the realization that the subjection of the negro, politically, and the separation of the negro, socially, are paramount to all other considerations in the South short of the preservation of the Republic itself. And we shall recognize no emancipation, nor shall we proclaim any deliverer, that falls short of these essentials to the peace and the welfare of our part of the country." [120]

The Negroes feared, moreover, that Wilson was a Southerner who had inherited the usual baggage of southern prejudices against Negroes. As one Negro editor put it, "The NEW YORK AGE does not see how it will be possible for a single self-respecting Negro in the United States to vote for Woodrow Wilson. . . . Both by inheritance and absorption, he has most of the prejudices of the narrowest type of Southern white

[120] *Raleigh News and Observer*, October 1, 1912.

people against the Negro." [121] W. E. Burghardt Du Bois, the most responsible spokesman of militant Negro opinion, expressed the same foreboding more temperately when he wrote, "On the whole, we do not believe that Woodrow Wilson admires Negroes." [122] And of course the Negro bosses feared that Wilson as president would place them beyond the pale of federal patronage.

Although he never shared the extreme anti-Negro sentiments of many of his contemporaries, there is no doubt that Wilson remained largely a Southerner on the race question. It was true, as Negro spokesmen charged, that Wilson had by evasion prevented Negroes from enrolling at Princeton University.[123] Actually, Mrs. Wilson felt much more strongly about the necessity of drawing the color line than did her husband, but both were opposed to social relations between the races.[124]

The Negro question was one of those problems, like the liquor question and woman suffrage, that Wilson would have preferred to ignore. He was badgered so constantly by his reformer friends and by the Negroes themselves, however, that soon after the Baltimore convention he was forced to deal with the spokesmen of the race. On July 16 he conferred with the Reverend J. Milton Waldron and William Monroe Trotter, representatives of the National Independent Political League of Washington, a Negro Democratic organization.[125] Two weeks later he spoke to a delegation from the United Negro Democracy of New Jersey, who had called at Sea Girt. "I was born and raised in the South," he declared. "There is no place where it is easier to cement friendship between the two races than there. They understand each other better there than elsewhere. You may feel assured of my entire comprehension of the ambitions of the negro race and my willingness and desire to deal with that race fairly and justly." [126]

This, of course, sounded like the apologies for racial discrimination that any southern Bourbon might make; something more definite and assuring was necessary before Negro leaders would give Wilson their approval. Oswald Garrison Villard, grandson of William Lloyd Gar-

[121] *New York Age,* July 11, 1912.   [122] *Crisis,* IV (August 1912), 181.

[123] See S. Axson to R. S. Baker, October 31, 1928, Baker Papers, for a discussion of this point.

[124] R. S. Baker, "Memorandum of an interview with Jessie W. Sayre, December 1, 1925," MS in Baker Papers.

[125] See J. M. Waldron and J. D. Harkless, *The Political Situation in a Nut-Shell. Some Un-Colored Truths for Colored Voters* (Washington, 1912), for a discussion of the program of the National Independent Political League.

[126] *Trenton Evening Times,* July 31, 1912.

rison, crusading editor of the *New York Evening Post,* and one of the founders of the National Association for the Advancement of Colored People, was in 1912 unquestionably the leading white champion of Negro rights in the United States. He was, moreover, on fairly intimate terms with Wilson, because he had given Wilson his own and his newspaper's enthusiastic support in the gubernatorial contest in 1910 and in the hotly disputed battle for the presidential nomination. It was natural, therefore, that he should become Wilson's chief adviser on the race question in the summer of 1912.

On August 13, a month after the Baltimore convention, Villard went to Trenton for a three hours' conference with the Democratic nominee. Their conversation centered about four subjects in which Villard was particularly interested: woman suffrage, the navy question, the New York political situation, and the general question of the Negro. Villard was not entirely satisfied with Wilson's attitude on the first three issues, but he was delighted by Wilson pronouncements on the race question. Among other things, Wilson told him that of course he would attempt to be president of all the people and that, in the matter of appointments, merit, and not race or creed, would be the deciding factor.[127] He said, furthermore, that he would gladly speak out against lynching—"every honest man must do so"—but he did not want the Negro people to form the impression that he, as president, could help them in this matter. Finally, Wilson promised to send to Villard a statement of his attitude toward the problem for publication in the *Crisis* and the *New York Evening Post*.[128] The day following the Trenton meeting, Villard wrote to Wilson, strongly urging him to go as far as he consistently could in assuring the Negroes that they would have equal treatment before the law and that he also would not discriminate against them, either in the matter of appointments, or in other ways.[129]

Meanwhile, as has been briefly noted, Wilson conferred at Trenton on July 16 with the Reverend J. Milton Waldron and William Monroe Trotter. After the meeting Waldron apparently attempted to set down from memory the details of Wilson's conversation. The result was an unauthorized statement that was printed in the September issue of the

[127] "The only place," Wilson said, "where you and I will differ is as to where the entering wedge should be driven." Wilson stated that he would not make an appointment like that of Crum at Charleston, because he felt such appointments resulted in great injury to the Negro people and increased racial antipathies.

[128] Oswald Garrison Villard, memorandum, dated August 14, 1912, of an interview with Wilson on August 13, 1912, MS in the Villard Papers.

[129] O. G. Villard to W. W., August 14, 1912, *ibid.*

Crisis, in which Wilson was quoted as having said that he needed and sought Negro support in the campaign and pledged himself to deal with Negroes, if he were elected president, as he would deal with other citizens, both in executing the laws and in making appointments. Wilson, moreover, allegedly assured Waldron and Trotter that Negroes had nothing to fear from a Democratic Congress and promised that if, by some accident, Congress should enact legislation inimical to the Negro's interest, he would veto such laws.[130]

The publication of the Waldron statement caught Wilson off balance; he apparently had not seen a copy of what Waldron published until Villard sent him one on August 14, and he was irritated and alarmed. On August 23 he wrote Villard that he had just read with amazement the Waldron statement. He of course had said that he would seek to be president of the whole country, and he had declared that the Negroes had nothing to fear from a Democratic Congress. On the other hand, he had not promised to veto legislation inimical to the Negro's interest, for he would make no such promise to any man; he had not said that he felt himself in need of Negro votes; and he had not given his listeners any assurances about appointments, "except that they need not fear unfair discrimination." Without bothering to define "unfair discrimination," Wilson concluded with an urgent plea that Villard prepare a general statement along the lines of what he, Wilson, had just written, which might be issued as Wilson's own statement.[131]

A few days later Villard replied to this appeal by sending to Wilson a statement that Du Bois had drawn up. Villard was obviously disturbed by Wilson's refusal to commit himself to the Waldron statement. Thus he wrote: "So far as your proposed statement is concerned, I feel very strongly that nothing important can be accomplished among the colored people until we have an utterance from you which we can quote. They not unnaturally mistrust you because they have been told that Princeton University closed its doors to the colored man (and was about the only Northern institution to do so) during your presidency. They know that besides yourself, both Mr. McAdoo and Mr. McCombs are of Southern birth, and they fear that the policy of injustice and disfranchisement which prevails not only in the Southern states, but in many of the Northern as well, will receive a great impetus by your presence in the White House." [132]

[130] For which see the *Crisis,* IV (September 1912), 216-217.
[131] W. W. to Villard, August 23, 1912, Villard Papers.
[132] Villard to W. W., August 28, 1912, *ibid.*

The conclusion is inevitable that the Du Bois statement, although it was exceedingly moderate in tone, went entirely farther than Wilson was willing to go. Obviously, he was not willing to assure the Negroes, as Du Bois had suggested, that the Democratic party sought and would welcome their support as American citizens, and that the Democrats were opposed to disfranchisement on account of race.[133]

The limit to which Wilson was willing to go was made evident in October. Bishop Alexander Walters of the African Zion church, who had joined the Democratic party in 1909 and who was in 1912 president of the National Colored Democratic League, invited Wilson to speak before a mass meeting of the League in New York City. Wilson replied that he could not attend the meeting; on the other hand, there were certain things that he did want to say to the colored people: that he earnestly desired to see justice done them in every matter, "justice executed with liberality and cordial good feeling," and that his sympathy for the Negroes in their struggle for advancement was of long standing. "I want to assure them through you," Wilson concluded, "that should I become President of the United States, they may count upon me for absolute fair dealing and for everything by which I could assist in advancing the interests of their race in the United States." [134]

Apparently this unequivocal promise of fair dealing, although stated in vague and general terms, had the effect of swinging Du Bois and many other leaders of militant Negro opinion in the North to the Wilson ranks. Although Du Bois had profound misgivings about supporting Wilson, he distrusted Taft and Roosevelt[135] even more, and resigned his membership in the Socialist party in order to support the Wilson cause. It was better, he concluded, "to elect Woodrow Wilson President . . . and prove once for all if the Democratic party dares to be Democratic when it comes to the black man." [136]

On September 15 Wilson began his first campaign tour, a tour that took him through Ohio, Indiana, Illinois, and deep into the heart of the

[133] The Du Bois statement is printed in A. S. Link, "The Negro as a Factor in the Campaign of 1912," *Journal of Negro History*, January 1947.

[134] Letter published in Alexander Walters, *My Life and Work*, pp. 194-195.

[135] Roosevelt had alienated the Negro intellectuals by excluding southern Negroes from membership in the Progressive party. See A. S. Link, "Correspondence Relating to the Progressive Party's 'Lily White' Policy in 1912," *Journal of Southern History*, x (November 1944), 480-490; also A. S. Link, "Theodore Roosevelt and the South in 1912," *North Carolina Historical Review*, xxiii (July 1946), 313-324.

[136] *Crisis*, v (November 1912), 29.

Midwest. Wilson's train followed a tortuous route over side tracks and dusty freight lines from New York to Chicago, and because it was always behind schedule Wilson could make only impromptu speeches from the rear platform of his car. He spoke at Columbus, Ohio, Union City, Marion, and Logansport, Indiana, and in all of his speeches made attacks on the protective tariff and the trusts the leading issues of the campaign.[137] On September 17 he reached Sioux City, Iowa, the first major stop in his journey, where he spoke at the grounds of the Interstate Live Stock Fair.[138] From there Wilson went to Sioux Falls, South Dakota, where he spoke before two audiences during the evening. Roosevelt's proposal to legalize and regulate the trusts, he charged, had come directly from the fertile minds of Elbert H. Gary, president of the United States Steel Corporation, and George W. Perkins, erstwhile Morgan partner now turned social reformer. He continued:

"They have thought this thing out. It may be, for all I know, that they honestly think that is the way to safeguard the business of the country. But whatever they think, this they know, that it will save the United States Steel Corporation from the necessity of doing its business better than its competitors. For if you will look into the statistics of the United States Steel Corporation you will find that wherever it has competitors the amount of the product which it controls is decreasing; in other words, that it is less efficient than its competitors, and its control of product is increasing only in those branches of the business where, by purchase and otherwise, they have a practical monopoly." [139]

The special train carrying Wilson and his party arrived in Minneapolis on September 18. On the whole, the tour through Iowa and South Dakota had not been notably successful. Wilson had failed to make "contact" with the people; his speeches had been too scholarly, too restrained, too much concerned with the facts and figures of the tariff and trusts to have any considerable popular appeal. In Minnesota, however, he seemed deliberately to make an effort to reach the mass of his listeners, and the effort sometimes resulted in undignified outbursts. He told a crowd of 8,000 persons in Minneapolis, for example, that "Rats" was the best answer to Roosevelt's proposal for trust control; and later he added "Let Roosevelt tell it to the Marines."

Wilson never enjoyed the billingsgate of a campaign and was always

[137] *New York Times*, September 17, 1912.

[138] *Sioux City Journal*, September 18, 1912.

[139] cf. L. D. Brandeis, "Trusts, Efficiency, and the New Party," *Collier's Weekly*, XLIX (September 14, 1912), 14-15.

exceedingly awkward in using it. He recognized this fact when he told the members of the Minneapolis Commercial Club: "Now, the difficulty of a popular campaign is that the most successful thing is association, and the most difficult thing is argument, and that argument is considered academic, that every intellectual process is under suspicion, that if you happen to know the facts, and happen to know how to reason from them, you are supposed to have gotten all you know from books." [140]

From Minneapolis Wilson went next to Detroit, on September 19, where he made an impassioned plea for popular government, the destruction of the partnership between vested interests and the national government, an honest tariff, the bridling of monopolies, and public control of the nation's credit resources. It was, on the whole, a vague presentation of the issues, reminiscent of the speeches of the pre-convention period. [141]

The following day he arrived in Columbus, Ohio, where he helped to open the Democratic presidential and gubernatorial campaigns in the state. He was greeted at the station by a brass band and the entire slate of state Democratic candidates, headed by Representative James M. Cox, the gubernatorial nominee. After a luncheon at which he was the guest of the Democratic candidates, Wilson spoke before a gathering of Ohio Democratic politicians. It was the first time, he said, that he had ever seen a political organization in the flesh. "And," he added, "I must say it looks very good to me."

Shortly afterward, Wilson spoke before an assemblage of businessmen and quoted extensively from Brandeis's articles on monopoly regulation. During the evening he spoke with Governor Harmon and Cox before a huge crowd in Memorial Hall; he was in a confident, jaunty mood and flung out to Roosevelt and Taft a challenge to explain why they had abandoned to him "the two great issues of the tariff and the trusts." The Democrats alone, he asserted, were "bold enough and far-sighted enough to see that they must tackle frankly and directly this question: Upon what principle shall tariff duties be laid, and by what means shall monopoly be prevented?" [142]

His first great tour of the presidential campaign completed, Wilson returned to Sea Girt for a brief interlude in September. Two days later he went to Scranton, Pennsylvania, to participate in the opening of the Democratic campaign in that state. He lashed out savagely at Roose-

---

[140] *New York Times,* September 19, 1912.
[141] *Detroit Free Press,* September 20, 1912.
[142] *New York Times,* September 21, 1912.

velt's protective tariff and trust legalization program; and when he declared that the people were not deceived "by a colossal bluff any longer," the 10,000 persons who had jammed their way into the city's largest auditorium cheered wildly. Wilson then launched into a fierce attack against the protective tariff and industrial monopolies; "I want to fight for the liberation of America," he shouted. Thus he continued:

"I am fighting, not for the man who has made good, but for the man who is going to make good—the man who is knocking and fighting at the closed doors of opportunity. There is no group of men big enough or wise enough to take care of a free people. The small classes that are trying to govern us are finding that we are kicking over the traces. . . . And having once got the blood in my eye of the lust for the scalps of those who resist the liberties of the people, I don't care whether I am elected President or not. I'll find some way to keep fighting." [143]

In spite of the fumbling and hesitancy that were characteristic of Wilson's early campaign speeches; in spite of his awkward efforts on certain unhappy occasions to speak down to the people; in spite of the fact that the campaign itself had not yet really got into high gear, there can be no doubt that Wilson was striking a responsive chord with many voters. As the campaign progressed from September into October, and as Wilson increased the tempo of his campaign addresses, Democratic editors reviewed his campaign with delight and approval. Wilson, of course, had vociferous editorial supporters in every city and state in the country, and it would be futile to review here the campaign editorials that appeared in the various Democratic newspapers.[144] Even Hearst, who refused to commend Wilson's candidacy personally,[145] finally committed his newspapers to the Wilson cause in the middle of October.[146]

In the last week of September, Wilson set out upon a political invasion of New England. He seemed anxious to emphasize that he had come to the region of rock-ribbed conservatism as the chief conservative candidate, that his economic program would strengthen legitimate

---

[143] *ibid.*, September 24, 1912.

[144] The following journals might be listed as the leading Wilson newspapers during the campaign of 1912: *New York World, New York Times, New York Evening Post, Baltimore Sun, Springfield Republican, Boston Globe, Boston Herald, Philadelphia Public Ledger, Cleveland Plain Dealer, Cincinnati Enquirer, Milwaukee Journal, Madison Wisconsin State Journal, St. Louis Globe-Democrat, St. Louis Republic, Detroit Free Press, Daily Oklahoman* of Oklahoma City, *Rocky Mountain News* of Denver, *San Francisco Chronicle*, and all of the leading southern newspapers.

[145] See Hearst's statement in the *London Daily Express*, September 13, 1912.

[146] See, e.g., *New York American*, October 14, 1912.

business enterprise, and that his program of political reform would preserve, not destroy, America's cherished institutions. "We ought to go very slowly and very carefully about the task of altering the institutions we have been a long time in building up," he told a Hartford audience on September 25. "I believe that the ancient traditions of a people are its ballast." [147]

Wilson spoke at Springfield and Barre, Massachusetts, during the afternoon of September 26; in the evening he addressed a large audience of factory workers at Fall River and spoke straight from the shoulder about the labor question. "The right to organize on the part of labor is not recognized even by the laws of the United States," he declared, "and nowhere in the third-term platform is it promised that that right will be granted. Any employer can dismiss all of his workmen for no other reason than that they belong to a union. So the thing is absolutely one-sided. I believe we ought to hold a brief for the legal right of labor to organize." [148]

It was at Boston, however, on September 27, that Wilson received his tumultuous welcome in New England. He spoke at the Tremont Temple in downtown Boston at noon, and aristocrats from Back Bay cheered just as loudly as the plebeians from South Boston and the waterfront. Richard Olney called it a "Boston welcome." "We are not fighting the trusts," Wilson asserted, "we are trying to put them upon an equality with everybody else." He jeered at Roosevelt's warning that the dominance of the trusts in industry was inevitable and probed the Bull Moose's weakest spot when he condemned Roosevelt's approval of the absorption of the Tennessee Coal, Iron & Railroad Company by United States Steel in 1907. "He thought that it was inevitable," Wilson charged, "that the Chief Executive should consent to an illegal thing in order to build up an irresistible power." Wilson also made a significant departure from his previous campaign declarations. Heretofore he had sneered at Roosevelt's proposal for the establishment of an industrial commission to regulate the trusts and had scorned what he called "government by experts." Meanwhile, Brandeis had proposed that a federal trade commission be established to regulate competition; [149] Wilson now admitted that it might be necessary to set up an industrial commission to regulate business enterprise. [150]

---

[147] *New York Times*, September 26, 1912.
[148] *New York Times*, September 27, 1912.
[149] "Monopoly," *Collier's Weekly*, XLIX (September 7, 1912), 8.
[150] *New York Times*, September 28, 1912.

Wilson left Boston in an exceedingly happy humor. All the way from Boston to Bridgeport he addressed crowds from the rear platform of his train; he often reached the platform before the audiences had gathered, threw campaign buttons to bystanders, and waved to men and women who stood at windows and on the sidewalks in towns where his train did not stop. At Willimantic, Connecticut, he found a large crowd in the railroad yard and on the tops of boxcars. "Fellow-citizens and gentlemen in the pit, and ladies and gentlemen in the boxes," he began playfully. During the evening he ended his three days' tour with a rousing address in Bridgeport. Shortly afterward he left for New York and a meeting with McCombs.[151]

On this optimistic and confident note Wilson thus concluded the first phase of his presidential campaign. He had begun haltingly in August; he had searched about for a great issue upon which to make the fight. Finally, he had found that issue in the restoration of free and competitive enterprise. Brandeis had given him a program and he had given the nation a slogan, the New Freedom. If he had not yet swept the country by his campaign appeal, if he had somehow generally failed to make that electric contact with his audiences that was so characteristic of the later phase of the campaign, he had at least charted his course, found his bearings, and made an auspicious beginning. And if that course required that he relegate to second place the old political issues that he had discussed in the pre-convention campaign; if it resulted in Wilson's engrossment in economic matters almost to the exclusion of political questions, it was perhaps an indication of the dawning realization in his mind that economics and politics go hand in hand and that the establishment of the political millennium must await the full growth of economic democracy in the United States.

[151] *ibid.*

Campaign Climax and Election

Woodrow Wilson had campaigned at length before the summer and fall of 1912, but never before had he experienced the rigors of anything like this presidential campaign. The demands from Democratic leaders that he make speaking tours through their states increased as the months passed from summer into autumn. When a friend insisted that he make a campaign tour through the South, however, he protested: "Alas! it seems a physical impossibility for me to get into the South during the campaign. I haven't a Bull Moose's strength, as Roosevelt seems to have, and it seems imperative both to the Committee and myself, that I should devote the few remaining weeks of the campaign to the debatable parts of the country." [1] Yet, he actually seemed to thrive under the heavy strain of speaking and traveling. He wrote to Mrs. Hulbert, for example: "I keep singularly well. I've gained seven pounds and a half since I was nominated. I weigh 177½ pounds. I am obviously becoming a person of some weight,—at any rate on the scales. If my days are trying and so full of—everything that fatigues and distracts—as to make them quite overwhelming, they at least fly fast with satisfactory rapidity, and it will not be long before I am either elected or bidden to stay quietly at home." [2]

Early in October Wilson set himself again to the wheel when he embarked upon the longest and most important tour of his presidential canvass. At Indianapolis, on October 3, he spoke before a riotous crowd of some 25,000 persons at the Washington ball park; Tom Taggart, Democratic boss of Indiana, tried four times to introduce Wilson, but the crowd cheered more wildly each time he tried. Such mass enthusiasm intoxicated Wilson immeasurably, and when the noise finally subsided he launched into a scathing attack upon his chief antagonist, Theodore Roosevelt. [3] The following day he campaigned through northern Indiana; it was a glorious October day, crisp and clear, and he was in high spirits. At Kokomo, the home of Senator Kern, he spoke briefly

---

[1] W. W. to F. P. Glass, September 6, 1912, copy in Baker Papers.
[2] September 1, 1912, published in R. S. Baker, *Woodrow Wilson*, III, 400-401.
[3] *Indianapolis News*, October 4, 1912.

on the monopoly question; shortly afterward he spoke at Peru, before an audience of industrial workers, and promised that a Democratic administration would safeguard labor's right to organize.

At the climax of a day's hard campaigning in a dozen Indiana towns, Wilson went to Gary, the United States Steel city in the northern part of the state, and, before a great audience of steel workers, denounced the corporation's unlawful methods and what he termed its alliance with the leaders of the Progressive party. Had the blessings of the protective tariff extended as far as the pay envelopes of the workers, he shouted. "No! Never!" chorused a thousand voices in the auditorium. He next discussed the history of the steel trust and asserted that the corporation's gross overcapitalization had prevented efficiency in management and honest prices for steel products.[4]

During the overnight trip from Gary to Omaha Wilson narrowly escaped death at Cedar Rapids, Iowa, when a freight car ran into his Pullman, tore the guard rail off, smashed the observation platform, and broke the windows. He arrived in Omaha unharmed, however, on October 5, and was greeted by Mayor James C. Dahlman, Senator Hitchcock, and Charles W. Bryan. Although Dahlman and Hitchcock had refused to have anything to do with the Bryans because the Commoner had been largely responsible for Dahlman's defeat in the gubernatorial campaign in Nebraska in 1910, they agreed to bury the political hatchet. They joined with their enemies in a love feast in Wilson's honor. Wilson made six speeches in seven hours in Omaha. After his chief address at the city auditorium in the afternoon he was nearly mobbed by a crowd of several thousand persons who surrounded his automobile and endeavored to shake his hand or touch his arm.[5]

The reception at Omaha had been cordial enough, to be sure, but the warmth of the welcome Wilson received at Lincoln far exceeded anything he had thus far experienced in the campaign. Greeted at the station by nine brass bands, a dozen marching clubs, and thousands of Democrats from all over the South Platte territory, Wilson stepped from the end of his car virtually into the arms of William J. Bryan. The demonstration that followed lasted for half an hour and recalled the tumultuous days of the campaign of 1896. Wilson later declared that he had never seen or imagined its like.

With the sound of whistles blowing in the factories, the noise of automobile horns, and the music of the bands providing a cacophonous

---

[4] *New York Times*, October 5, 1912.   [5] *Omaha World-Herald*, October 6, 1912.

undertone of confusion, Wilson and Bryan rode together to the Lindell Hotel. The two Democratic leaders seemed to vie with one another in expressing their mutual affection and confidence. "We are free to serve the people of the United States," Wilson declared at a banquet of the Democratic state committee, "and in my opinion it was Mr. Bryan who set us free." To which Bryan replied:

"I want to express my deep gratitude to Gov. Wilson for the masterly manner in which he has led our forces in this campaign. We had reason to expect much of him; he has done better than we could have expected. He has shown wisdom and discretion in the choosing of the men who are to be around him, and upon whom he is to rely for counsel and advice, and he has shown a courage that not one man in a million has shown.

"And now let me use this occasion to speak to those who are the workers of our party. When I have been a candidate you have worked for me. No man has ever run for office who has had a more loyal band of workers than I have had, and nowhere have they been more loyal than in Nebraska. . . . Let me ask you to do twice as much for Wilson as you ever did for Bryan. For I have as much at stake in this fight as he has, and you have as much as I have." [6]

After the banquet, Wilson and Bryan went together to the city auditorium and complimented one another again before a large audience. Wilson was supremely happy. That was obvious from the gleam in his eyes and the broad smile on his face. But he was also utterly exhausted. It was, after all, the tenth speech he had made that day; he was hoarse and spoke so ineffectively that the audience did not realize that he had completed his address until they saw that he was shaking hands with Bryan.[7]

Refreshed by a day's rest at the Bryan home on Sunday, Wilson arrived in Pueblo on the following day, October 7, to open his campaign in Colorado. The climax in his campaign in that state came with his triumphal entry into Denver in the late afternoon of October 7. Thousands of persons had gathered at the railroad station to welcome him, and thousands more lined the streets of Denver as the Democratic procession moved slowly through the city. The convention auditorium, where Wilson had delivered his memorable address on the Bible a year

[6] *New York Times,* October 6, 1912.
[7] *Lincoln State Journal,* October 6, 1912. Bryan, it might be added, was a tower of strength to Wilson during the campaign. He spoke every day, averaging almost ten speeches a day, for seven weeks.

and a half before, was packed with some 15,000 persons when Wilson began to speak.

After a short introduction, he turned abruptly to the fundamental economic problem that most politicians ignored, the existence of marked economic inequalities in the nation. There were, he declared, distinct economic classes in the country, but the chief cause for the great disparity in the distribution of incomes was that great monopolistic combinations had succeeded in engrossing a considerable part of the national wealth and resources. Was there not any peaceful political process that the people could use to free themselves and to provide a sound economic basis for political democracy?

Wilson then proceeded to discuss the monopoly problem in the most specific terms he had yet used during the campaign. He enumerated the processes by which monopolies had been created: price fixing, tying contracts between manufacturers and retailers, control of the sources of raw materials, espionage, cutthroat competition, and so forth—all of which was what unregulated competition consisted of. When the federal government had prevented these practices, he asserted, it would have prevented the existence of monopoly. Under a system of regulated competition, he continued, the over-capitalized trusts would be forced either to reorganize their industries on a more efficient basis or else to surrender the field to competitive rivals who were honestly capitalized and efficiently managed. It was not a campaign against individuals that he was making, Wilson continued; it was a "crusade against powers that have governed us—that have limited our development—that have determined our lives—that have set us in a straitjacket to do as they please." "This," he added in a supreme outburst, "is a second struggle for emancipation. . . . If America is not to have free enterprise, then she can have freedom of no sort whatever." [8]

The tremendous enthusiasm of the western people, the brass bands, cheering crowds, and the triumphal entries into Lincoln and Denver had all made a remarkable impression on Wilson. The West succored and strengthened him by its ebullience and outpouring of good will, and there he at last discovered the true meaning of his anti-monopoly appeal. He had emphasized the tariff and trust questions before he set out upon this western tour, to be sure; yet somehow he had failed to translate the meaning of these issues into the language of the people. It was all very well to talk interminably about the processes by which monopolies had been created, and to recount the history of the organi-

[8] *Rocky Mountain News* of Denver, October 8, 1912.

zation of the steel trust. It was more satisfactory still to crusade for economic freedom for the small producer, but even this appeal lacked reality for the average voter. It was Wilson's discovery that he was battling for the traditional American way of life, for a kind of economic democracy, and that this economic equality of opportunity was absolutely necessary for the preservation of political liberty that gave life and depth and meaning to the words "New Freedom."

From Colorado, Wilson campaigned his way through the small towns of Kansas on October 8, and arrived in hostile Kansas City, Missouri, in the evening. The Missouri Democrats were still sulking over Clark's defeat, but they tried hard to prove themselves good Democrats and good losers. Clark and Attorney-General Elliott W. Major, Democratic gubernatorial nominee, had come to Kansas City to attend a "peace dinner" at the Hotel Baltimore given by the Democratic politicians of the city. After the dinner, Wilson, Clark, and Senator Reed spoke before an audience of 15,000 persons in Convention Hall. Wilson was exhausted and hoarse, and probably not more than half the audience heard him reply to Roosevelt's challenge, made at Albany, New York, on October 7, that the Democratic nominee "prove or retract" his accusation that the steel trust was supporting the Progressive nominees. Wilson's reply was vague. He had not meant to imply that the corporation's directors were financing the Roosevelt campaign, he declared. "What I meant was that they are supporting him with their thought, and their thought is not our thought. I meant, and I say again, that the kind of control which he proposes is the kind of control that the United States Steel Corporation wants." [9]

The following day, October 9, Wilson went to Springfield, Illinois, where he claimed for the Democratic party the heritage of Abraham Lincoln. During the afternoon he went to St. Louis, where his reception was decidedly more encouraging than had been the chilly welcome he received in Kansas City or Springfield. It was truly a western welcome that he received; throngs of people crowded the sidewalks, and there were bands, the blare of horns, and a torchlight procession four miles long. Wilson spoke first at the City Club to a group of businessmen; he went next to East St. Louis, where he spoke before a gathering of workingmen; at a banquet given in Wilson's honor by the Democratic editors of Missouri shortly afterward, former Governor A. M. Dockery promised that the Missouri Democrats would be "as loyal to Woodrow

Wilson and the principles upon which he stands as . . . [they] were to Champ Clark." [10]

It was nearly ten o'clock before Wilson, surrounded by a crowd of Democratic politicians, reached the huge Coliseum, where more than 15,000 persons had been waiting nearly two hours to hear him speak. As he stepped upon the stage a terrifying bedlam broke loose in the auditorium. Policemen stationed at the doors were overrun by hundreds of persons outside who were fighting to break in, and a large band of men carrying lighted torches managed to force their way into the building. When the noise of the crowd finally subsided, Wilson began to speak. He was visibly affected by this demonstration of confidence and began: "I want to express to you the very proud feeling within me when I face such a great company as this, but I cannot do so." But he made no effort to make himself heard at a distance, and cries of "Louder" went up from the audience. [11]

The following morning, October 10, the Democratic campaign reached its peak in the Midwest when Wilson made a triumphal entry into Chicago. Some 100,000 persons stood on the sidewalks in a cold rain to greet the Democratic nominee; streams of ticker tape floated down from office buildings as the Wilson procession passed along La-Salle Street; business was suspended in the offices, and street car traffic was completely blocked for a time. The bitter factional warfare between the Harrison and Sullivan Democratic groups had required that the Democratic national committee manage all arrangements for the celebration, yet the Sullivan men somehow managed to secure seats in Wilson's automobile. Wilson made three speeches in the city, but none of them was particularly notable. [12]

On October 11 the Democratic nominee wound up his western tour with a whirlwind campaign through northern Ohio. He spoke first at Canton, in the early afternoon, and paid a gracious tribute to the memory of President McKinley. A short time later, at Orrville, he unloosed a scathing attack upon the late Mark Hanna. All along the route of the Pennsylvania Railroad from Canton to Cleveland—at Canton, Orrville, Barberton, Akron, and Hudson—enthusiastic crowds gathered to greet Wilson. There was little left of his voice when he arrived in Cleveland in the late afternoon; and when he tried to speak before an immense audience in the evening the result was an inaudible and rambling

[10] *St. Louis Republic,* October 10, 1912.

[11] *ibid.; St. Louis Globe-Democrat,* October 10, 1912.

[12] *Chicago Daily News,* October 10; *Chicago Daily Tribune,* October 11, 1912.

speech. In the end he returned to the monopoly question with something of the old fire that was characteristic of his western speeches: "If I did not believe monopoly could be restrained and destroyed I would come to doubt that liberty could be preserved in the United States. It is a choice of life and death—whether we shall allow this country to be controlled by small groups of men or whether we shall return to the form of government contemplated by the fathers." [13]

By October 12 Wilson was back in Princeton. During his western tour he had spoken over thirty times in seven states to at least 175,000 people. He was exhausted, more tired than he had been at any time during the campaign, and for several days he did nothing but sleep and rest at home. The peaceful interlude was short-lived, however. On October 14 Roosevelt was shot by an insane anti-third-term fanatic at Milwaukee, and for a time it appeared that the wound was serious. At once Wilson sent a message of sympathy to the wounded Bull Moose leader and announced a day later that he would cut short his active campaigning until Roosevelt could go on the stump again. He had, however, already promised to make a campaign tour through Delaware, West Virginia, and Pennsylvania, and he could not cancel these engagements "without subjecting those who have arranged them to a very serious embarrassment and great unnecessary expense." [14]

On October 16 Wilson left Princeton on what was to be his last extensive campaign tour. His train went first to Harrington, Milford, Ellendale, and Georgetown in southern Delaware, and all along the way he insisted upon speaking only on state issues. "I came out to fulfill the engagements of this week with a very great reluctance," he declared at Georgetown, "because my thought is constantly of that gallant gentleman lying in the hospital at Chicago." Since he could not with propriety attack Roosevelt, he was more or less compelled to center his attention on Taft and the Republicans. [15]

Wilson's return from Georgetown to Wilmington during the afternoon of October 17 was, as one newspaper observed, "like the march of a triumphant army." Tremendous crowds greeted him at Dover, and the reception at New Castle was even more enthusiastic. In Wilmington, an anonymous and elusive Italian had threatened to "shoot Wilson the same as Roosevelt was shot," and a large number of policemen were

---

[13] *Cleveland Plain Dealer*, October 12, 1912.
[14] *New York World*, October 16, 1912.
[15] *Baltimore Sun*, October 18, 1912; *Wilmington* (Del.) *Every Evening*, October 17, 1912.

scattered among the audience in the Wilmington opera house. Wilson's voice had once again given way after a hard day's campaigning, and he spoke with considerable effort. He had come to Delaware, he began, to speak not for himself, but for the state Democratic candidates. It was impossible for him to ignore the national issues, however, and by a circuitous route he came to the monopoly problem and the progressive movement in general. It was in this connection that he paid a memorable tribute to La Follette, who was by now throwing the full weight of his influence to the Democratic cause.[16]

The following day Wilson campaigned through northern West Virginia, along the route of the Baltimore & Ohio Railroad to Pittsburgh. At Clarksburg he spoke from a temporary stand in front of the courthouse and scorned the assertions of the Republican spokesmen that wages increased with tariff protection and that the factories would close should the Democrats control the national government. In the early afternoon he arrived at Wheeling, where he spoke briefly. A short time later he was greeted by a tremendous crowd at the railroad station in Pittsburgh, and a guard of honor accompanied him to a banquet given in his honor by the Woodrow Wilson Club of Allegheny County. Shortly afterward he made an important address on the tariff and trust questions before some 12,000 persons in the Duquesne Garden auditorium. He discussed in general terms the iniquities of the protective system and then came to the relation of the Democratic party to the progressive movement. The Democrats, he declared, had been a "chilly minority of a great nation" because they had stood firm in the progressive tradition during the long years when privilege and vested interests were firmly entrenched in power. Thus, he continued:

"Don't you think that the steadfastness of a minority looks very much like the steadfastness of absolute faith? The Democratic party has stood steadfast in a deep-rooted faith which they could not deny, and it is a faith as old as human liberty. It is a faith—the only faith that has ever made the intolerable burden of life possible to bear, namely, the faith that every man ought to have the interest of every other man at his heart. The faith that would set up a government in the world where the average man, the plain man, the common man, the ignorant man, the unaccomplished man, the poor man had a voice equal to the voice of anybody else in the settlement of the common affairs, an ideal never before realized in the history of the world."

[16] *Wilmington Every Evening*, October 18, 1912.

The economic future of America, he continued, depended upon the decision of the voters in November. A Democratic administration would seek to end unregulated and piratical competition and the monopolistic control of raw materials; it would endeavor to establish a New Freedom of economic opportunity for the sons of the United States. The opportunity, therefore, was at hand; the road was open for the voters to inaugurate a regime of right and of freedom. His chief ambition, he concluded, was "to be, so far as is possible, with the gifts that God has given me, the spokesman, the interpreter, the servant of the people of the United States." [17]

From Pittsburgh Wilson went to New York on October 19 and delivered addresses at the Academy of Music in Brooklyn and at Carnegie Hall. First he spoke to an uproarious gathering of German-Americans at Carnegie Hall. Then Wilson and Sulzer, the Democratic gubernatorial nominee, spoke from the same platform at the Academy of Music in Brooklyn. The meeting got off to a roaring start, but no sooner had Wilson veered around to the monopoly question than an embarrassing incident occurred. Miss Maude Malone, a militant suffragette, whose chief diversion seemed to be disrupting political meetings, arose in the balcony and demanded to know Wilson's opinion of the male monopoly of the right to vote. Luckily, Wilson had not been confronted before during the presidential campaign with such a direct challenge; on this occasion he hedged by replying that woman suffrage was "not a question that is dealt with by the National Government at all," and that he was only the representative of the national party. Miss Malone, however, demanded a straightforward answer; "I am speaking to you as an American, Mr. Wilson," she said. The unfortunate woman had to be carried off to jail while Wilson concluded his discourse on freedom and competitive enterprise.[18]

Within a week after Wilson's New York addresses on October 19, Roosevelt had recovered sufficiently for Wilson to return to the stump.[19] He entered the contest again on October 28, enthusiastic and confident as he brought his campaign to a magnificent climax. In southeastern Pennsylvania he made a whirlwind speaking tour; going from West Chester and Media to Philadelphia, he made his greatest addresses of the campaign in the latter city. First he spoke before a gathering of progressive Republicans at the Academy of Music. It was entirely a

[17] *Pittsburgh Post,* October 19, 1912.   [18] *New York Times,* October 20, 1912.
[19] Roosevelt had announced that he would speak in New York on October 30.

Republican conclave, but the audience cheered wildly for over five minutes when Wilson entered the auditorium.

No personal issues were involved in the campaign, Wilson began; it was a contest of programs and of purposes. What, therefore, were the great economic issues at stake in the campaign? First of all, the government had to concern itself with the plight of the middle class, from which came the new enterprises, the initiative, and the vigor of America's economic life, and which was being ground down by "the processes of prosperity."

"This great middle class," he continued, ". . . is being crushed between the upper and the nether millstone. There is a weight above them, a weight of concentrated capital and of organized control, against which they are throwing themselves in vain; and beneath them the great body of working people, the great majority of people in this country upon whom that control is directly exercised by the determination of the industries of the country and the determination of the share that the working people shall have in the industries of the country."

The alarming fact, Wilson continued, was that the middle class no longer originated economic activity or controlled the American economy. Domestic competition, which formerly quickened the country with life and beckoned men on to new enterprise, had been stifled by the processes of monopoly. He was no disciple of Marx, yet he feared that the socialist prophet of doom had forecast correctly the development of American capitalism unless the stranglehold of a few monopolists could be forever broken. Thus he explained the Democratic mission:

"We have entered the lists in order to free the average man of enterprise in America, and make ourselves masters of our own fortunes once again, because what I want to impress upon every thoughtful voter is this: The Trusts lie like a great incubus on the productive part of American brains. . . . The sap of manhood may never be allowed to express itself in action in America if we do not see to it that the places where the sap produces the fruit are kept free for its beneficent action. We are in danger of this taking place in the upper strata, the great financiers, the organizers of combinations of industry, the masters of monopoly bearing down with their great intolerable burden of controlled enterprise until this originative class is absolutely squeezed out and America consists of masters and employees."

The processes of modern society were not individualistic, he continued; they were processes of association, and the danger was great that private association would become stronger than public association and that there would be combinations of men and of money more powerful than the government itself. Therefore, Americans were literally at the parting of the ways; it was a time when common thought must determine the destiny of a nation.[20]

Wilson had poured out his heart in this, his greatest campaign speech; he had explained the "faith that was in him," not so much by discussing the intricate details of the economic issues, but rather by translating their meaning into language the people could understand. He had sacrificed specific details to generalizations, but it was high time for him to be doing exactly that. After his address at the Academy of Music, Wilson went to the Convention Hall where he and the Democratic leaders of the state addressed a gigantic throng of 15,000 enthusiastic Democrats. It was the largest political gathering Philadelphia had yet witnessed, and the crowd was full of confidence and hailed the Democratic nominee as the "next President of the United States."

By the end of October it was evident that Wilson would be elected by a sweeping plurality. All the newspaper polls indicated as much, and gamblers in New York were offering 6-to-1 odds that he would win. He realized, however, that he would be powerless in the White House without a Democratic majority in Congress and pleaded time and again in his speeches for the election of a Democratic Congress. On October 27 he resorted to an unusual expedient by issuing a special message to the voters of the several states and appealing for their support in the congressional and senatorial elections.[21]

In so far as the enthusiasm of the voters was concerned, the climax of the Democratic campaign was Wilson's address before an immense audience at Madison Square Garden on October 31. Roosevelt had returned to the campaign in the same auditorium the night before and had been given an extraordinary demonstration lasting forty-five minutes by a throng of shouting and singing Bull Moosers. The Democratic enthusiasts, however, were determined to outdo the Progressive shouters. A whole array of prominent Democratic leaders, state and national, sat upon the speakers' platform at this last rally of the national Democracy. The first great outburst of the crowd came when the preliminary speakers, Cleveland H. Dodge, Sulzer, Underwood, Martin H. Glynn, and Augustus Thomas, the playwright, entered. After Sulzer and Glynn had spoken, Thomas introduced Underwood; the crowd leapt to its

[20] *Philadelphia Record*, October 29, 1912.
[21] *New York World*, October 28, 1912.

feet, and the band did its best to make "Dixie" heard above the roar of shouts and applause. Underwood, however, was soon interrupted by Wilson's entrance into the auditorium. The great crowd was on its feet, cheering madly. Wilson had turned a regular old-fashioned political meeting into a "wild, waving, cheering, yelling, roaring, stamping mob of enthusiasts that needed no songs and no hymns and no encouragement to keep it at high pitch." He looked about over the flag-covered hall; Mrs. Wilson was seated in a box directly in front of him, and once or twice he gazed in her direction. In spite of Wilson's efforts to stop the demonstration, the cheering, whistling, and yelling lasted for an hour and four minutes. It was no longer a political rally; it was a mob of emotional people, confident of victory.

When Wilson was finally able to make himself heard, he was so overcome by the demonstration that he completely forgot the speech he had "thought out" and planned to make. "It simply was bewildering," he later declared.[22]

Of course it did not matter what Wilson said upon such an occasion. His speech was relatively short and he rambled considerably in an attempt to summarize all the issues he had been emphasizing during the campaign. Thus, he concluded, the case was made up and before the jury. He did not doubt the verdict.[23]

The presidential campaign might now be over as far as the voters were concerned, but Wilson would not rest, would not sit out the last four days before the election. On November 1 he went to Rochester, spoke before two large audiences, and probed deeper into the monopoly problem than he had yet done. He was now chiefly concerned about the monopoly of certain vital raw materials that a few corporations held, and he advocated in a vague way legislation designed to set uniform prices for the sale of raw materials. He did not want the federal government to fix prices, he explained, but he did want to see "some government step in and say you can sell that raw material at any price you please, but you have got to sell it to everybody at the same price."

During the last few days before the election Wilson campaigned northern New Jersey, pleading for the election of a Democratic legislature. On October 31 he spoke at Burlington and appealed for the election of the Democratic senatorial and congressional candidates; on November 2 he reiterated this appeal at Long Branch and Red Bank. The following day he narrowly escaped serious injury at Hightstown

[22] *New York Herald,* November 1, 1912.
[23] *New York Times,* November 1, 1912.

when the automobile in which he was riding struck a rut in the road and threw him against the top of the car; he received an ugly scalp wound four inches long.[24]

November 5 was election day. The shouting and tumult of the campaign had ended; Wilson was at home, in the Elizabethan cottage on Cleveland Lane, with his wife and daughters. Also part of the family circle were his brother Joseph, from Nashville, his cousins James and Fitz William Woodrow, his brother-in-law and old companion in arms Stockton Axson, and his faithful friend Dudley Field Malone. Wilson slept soundly and ate a late breakfast. At ten o'clock he walked to the firehouse on Chambers Street to vote. Captain Bill McDonald, the Texas Ranger whom Colonel House had sent to guard Wilson after the shooting of Roosevelt, and Walter Measday accompanied him on the walk up Bayard Lane and down Nassau Street. He stopped to point out to Captain McDonald and Measday the house on Nassau Street in which he had boarded when he was a freshman many years before.

In the afternoon McAdoo and Daniels came from New York and joined the intimate group at the Wilson home. Wilson took several of his friends on a long walk through the countryside surrounding Princeton; they came back through the campus and visited several of the University buildings. After supper they settled down to await the election returns. The final announcement of what everyone knew would happen came at about ten o'clock, when the telegraph operator brought the message of Wilson's election to Mrs. Wilson.

When the news of Wilson's election was publicly announced, President Hibben ordered the bell in Nassau Hall rung and announced that November 6 would be a University holiday. A great crowd of students soon gathered on the campus and went to "Prospect," where Hibben greeted them. Then, armed with flags and torches, they marched to Cleveland Lane. The cheers of the students brought Wilson to the front porch; he stood there, bareheaded, while the shouts of the undergraduates mingled with the sound of the bell ringing in old Nassau. "Gentlemen, I am sincerely glad to see you," he began; there were tears in his eyes as he continued:

"I can't help thinking this evening that something has only begun which you will have a great part in carrying forward. There is so much to reconstruct and the reconstruction must be undertaken so justly

[24] *New York Herald*, November 3-4, 1912; *Trenton Evening True American*, October 31, 1912.

and by slow process of common counsel, that a generation or two must work out the result to be achieved. . . . I summon you for the rest of your lives to work to set this government forward by processes of justice, equity and fairness. I myself have no feeling of triumph to-night. I have a feeling of solemn responsibility." [25]

Since the middle of October there had not been much doubt as to the outcome of the contest. Roosevelt had made a spectacular, even a magnificent campaign; he had the support of the rank and file of the Republican progressives, especially in the Midwest. He had failed, however, to demoralize the Republicans and had drawn few progressive votes away from Wilson. More important, he and his colleagues had failed to establish their party on a well-organized basis; as George E. Mowry has shown, Roosevelt ran far ahead of the local Progressive candidates. [26]

What the result would have been had the Democrats nominated Clark or a conservative at Baltimore no one can know. Clark would have succeeded in holding the Democratic party together and in winning the minimum Democratic vote; that would have been sufficient for election in 1912. Had an avowed conservative been nominated by the Democrats, on the other hand, Bryan and most of the Democratic progressives undoubtedly would have joined forces with Roosevelt and a genuine progressive party, combining the progressive elements of the two major parties, might have been launched in 1912. At any rate, it is a safe assumption that Wilson's nomination precluded the success of the Progressive ticket. [27]

The results of the election demonstrated at least one fact clearly, that the country, judged by the popular vote for the candidates, was overwhelmingly progressive in temper, for Wilson's 6,293,019, Roosevelt's 4,119,507, and Socialist Eugene V. Debs's 901,873 votes constituted most of the votes cast. This generalization, however, should be accompanied by important reservations: there were many Bull Moose

---

[25] *Princeton Alumni Weekly*, xiii (November 6, 1912), 31-32.

[26] *Theodore Roosevelt and the Progressive Movement*, pp. 281-282.

[27] In this connection, Governor Herbert S. Hadley of Missouri, who had originally supported Roosevelt in the pre-convention campaign but who had refused to join the Progressive movement, wrote Wilson the following letter: "Ever since the Baltimore convention I have had in mind writing you to convey my sincere congratulations upon your nomination. . . . Any other nomination would have unquestionably brought about the result of three national parties with neither of sufficient strength to control and be responsible for the conduct of our national government." September 2, 1912, Wilson Papers.

enthusiasts who were only superficially progressive; many conservative Republicans voted for Wilson in order to defeat Roosevelt; not all of the votes Wilson received from the South or from the boss-controlled city machines in the North and Midwest were progressive. Taft, the candidate of the Republican conservatives, received only 3,484,956 votes and ran a poor third.[28] The results in the electoral college were even more startling. Taft carried Vermont and Utah and received 8 electoral votes; Roosevelt won 11 of California's 13 votes, Michigan, Minnesota, Pennsylvania, South Dakota, and Washington, for a total of 88 electoral votes; Wilson won all the rest, 435 electoral votes. Almost as important as Wilson's victory was the election of a Democratic House and Senate.

Sweeping though the victory was for the Democrats, the bare facts of the election returns could scarcely have elated the president-elect. He had not polled as many popular votes as had Bryan in 1908;[29] he had not succeeded in establishing the Democratic party as the majority party in the country; and he and the Democrats had only a tenuous two years' control of the House of Representatives. Outside the former Confederate states and Kentucky, Wilson polled a majority of the popular votes only in Arizona. It is a safe assumption, however, that neither Roosevelt nor Taft was responsible for the decrease in the Democratic vote in 1912, for the combined popular vote given Wilson's two chief opponents in 1912 was also slightly less than was Taft's vote in 1908. Apparently what happened was that about half a million progressives refused to follow either Roosevelt or Wilson in 1912 and voted for Debs, who increased his popular vote almost half a million from 1908.

All during the day following the election, messages of congratulation and personal friends poured in upon Wilson at Princeton. Democrats throughout the land hailed the results with joy and, in many cases, with riotous celebrations. The two great progressives who never reached the White House seemed genuinely exuberant at Wilson's triumph. For Bryan, the Democratic victory also had its pathos; he who had carried the standard three times unsuccessfully must stand on the sidelines and see a newcomer win the presidency at a time when he himself probably could have won. But there was no trace of envy or bitterness in the Commoner's great heart; Clark might sulk over opportunities lost, but not Bryan. "It is a great triumph and means much to the country," Bryan wrote. ". . . Let every Democratic heart

[28] Figures given in the *World Almanac, 1914*, p. 725.
[29] Bryan polled 6,393,182 votes in 1908; Wilson, 6,293,019 in 1912.

rejoice. If hope deferred maketh the heart sick, Democratic hopes at last realized ought to make us all happy." [30]

La Follette's reaction was perhaps more significant than Bryan's for Wilson's election meant nothing by way of party preferment and patronage to him as it did to the Nebraskan. La Follette interpreted the meaning of the election thus:

". . . Oppressed and heartsick, a nation of ninety million people, demanding plain, simple justice, striving for educational, political and industrial democracy, turned to Woodrow Wilson as the only present hope. . . .

"The meaning of Mr. Wilson's election is plain. The people have been mere pawns in the political game. They had Roosevelt as President. They had Taft as President. And during the seven years' administration of the one and four years' administration of the other, they had seen Special Privilege fastening its grip upon the country, each year with firmer hold. They had seen the trust grow and multiply, and the gigantic mergers and combinations welding Business into a Plutocracy, under Roosevelt. They had seen the special interests wax arrogant and the tariff wall raised by the hands of its pampered beneficiaries, under Taft. They demanded a change. And they forged their demand into a call for Wilson." [31]

There were, in short, few editorial dissidents on the morning of November 6. Even the Negro editors seemed certain that, as one Negro editor put it, Wilson would be the "champion of equal rights, friend of the colored American and President of all the people of every section, and of every race." [32] Most Democratic spokesmen interpreted the election results as a sign that the people demanded emancipation from professional politicians, boss rule, special privilege, and the trusts; and most agreed that Wilson's administration would bring better government, honest tariff legislation, financial and monopoly reform, and an end to class conflict and antagonism. The South, especially, felt a thrill of pride when it recalled that once again, after sixty-four long years, a Southerner had been elected president. There were also manifestations of local pride in Virginia and in the southern cities where Wilson had lived.

Some of the more sober minds pointed out that the Democratic victory had come as a result of Republican suicide and that the mil-

[30] *The Commoner*, November 8, 1912.
[31] *La Follette's Weekly Magazine*, iv (November 9, 1912), 3.
[32] *Boston Guardian*, cited in *Crisis*, v (December 1912), 69.

lennium, which the starry-eyed Democrats were forecasting so glibly, might be difficult to achieve. But a realization of the responsibilities that came with victory could not dampen the unmitigated joy that Democrats felt. Even old "Marse Henry" was reconciled at last. "God give him wisdom and grace and send prosperous gales to the ship of state about to be entrusted to his keeping," was his salutation to the president-elect.[33]

What was the fundamental meaning of Wilson's election; what did it portend for the future of the country? Certainly it was as much a political revolution as was Jefferson's triumph over the Federalists in 1800. As in 1800, the election of 1912 resulted in an important shift in geographical control of the federal government, as well as a change of parties. The government since the Civil War, whether under the control of the Republicans or the pseudo-Democratic Cleveland Democrats, had been consistently representative of the interests of industry, business, and finance. Even Roosevelt and Taft had not been able to dislodge the Old Guard Republican leaders from their seats of power in Congress, and neither had accomplished any really thoroughgoing reforms with regard to the tariff and trusts.

In spite of Wilson's conservative past, his rapid conversion to progressivism, and all his vagaries and hedges, he had emerged as the present heir of the great populist-Bryan tradition, which was in turn the child of a deep-rooted American faith in democracy, equality of opportunity, humanitarian reform, and fair play. Wilson was a more cautious liberal than the populist reformers had been; he was perhaps a little more concerned about preserving certain property rights. Yet no man could now doubt that his concern for the general welfare was profound, and that regardless of how he came by his progressive principles he would see them through as leader of the American people. He could honestly say at the end of the campaign, "Nobody owns me." He could begin his administration with no binding commitments or promises to special interest groups. He could stand as the impartial representative of all the people.

Wilson's triumph determined also that for the next four years the southern Democracy would literally be in the saddle of the federal government. Southern representatives and senators, firmly entrenched by an undisturbed tenure of office, would assume the headship of almost all the congressional committees; southern Democrats would take over

[33] *Louisville Courier-Journal*, November 9, 1912.

half the cabinet posts. Southerners, at last, were "back in the house of their fathers." The oft-dreamed-of alliance between the South and the West had not yet come, but a government progressive in point of view and sympathetic to farmer and labor demands would assume the reins of power on March 4, 1913.

What the results of the next four years ahead were to be, no man could foresee, but the lonely man at Princeton had not forgotten his promises to the people or ceased to dream of a new birth of freedom for America.

Bibliography of Sources and Works Cited[1]

THE author wishes to acknowledge his indebtedness to the following publishers:

To Charles Scribner's Sons, for permission to quote from *The Confessions of a Reformer*, by Frederick C. Howe; *Memoirs of An Editor*, by Edward P. Mitchell; *An Old Master and Other Political Essays*, by Woodrow Wilson.

To Columbia University Press, for permission to quote from *Constitutional Government in the United States*, by Woodrow Wilson.

To D. Appleton-Century Company, for permission to quote from *The Letters and Journal of Brand Whitlock*, edited by Allan Nevins; *The Political Education of Woodrow Wilson*, by James Kerney.

To D. C. Heath and Company, for permission to quote from *The State*, by Woodrow Wilson.

To Doubleday and Company, for permission to quote from *The True Story of Woodrow Wilson*, by David Lawrence; *Woodrow Wilson As I Know Him*, by Joseph P. Tumulty; *Woodrow Wilson: Life and Letters*, Vol. III, by Ray Stannard Baker.

To Houghton Mifflin Company, for permission to quote from *Congressional Government* and *Mere Literature & Other Essays*, by Woodrow Wilson.

To the Johns Hopkins Press, for permission to quote from *The Economic Thought of Woodrow Wilson*, by William Diamond.

And to the following persons and libraries, for permission to quote from hitherto unpublished letters:

Mrs. Warren W. Bailey, letter of Warren Worth Bailey; Mr. Walter Brown, letter of Thomas E. Watson; Mr. J. Lionberger Davis, personal letter; Duke University Library, letters of William Garrot Brown; Mr. Charles M. Egan, personal letter; Mr. James F. Fielder, personal

---

[1] This bibliography makes no attempt to offer a complete list of the sources and published works that were used in the writing of this book. For a more complete bibliography, see A. S. Link, "The South and the Democratic Campaign of 1910-1912" (unpublished Ph.D. dissertation, now in the Library of the University of North Carolina), pp. 489-542.

letter; Mrs. Corinne McCombs Hardy, letters of William F. McCombs; Mrs. Mary Hemphill Greene, letters of James C. Hemphill; Mrs. Ronald Hudson, letters of Moses T. Pyne; Mr. Melancthon W. Jacobus, Jr., letter of Melancthon W. Jacobus; Captain Luke Lea, Jr., letter of Luke Lea; Mr. Isaac H. Lionberger, personal letter, Messrs. Cyrus McCormick and Gordon McCormick, letter of Cyrus H. McCormick; Mrs. E. E. McCoy and Mrs. Pettersen Marzoni, letter of Frank P. Glass; Mrs. Isabella O. Osgood, letters of Edward W. Sheldon; Mr. Clarence Poe, personal letter; Princeton University Library, restricted collections; Mr. Henry B. Thompson, Jr., letters of Henry B. Thompson; Mrs. Margaret Farrand Thorp, memorandum of Wilson Farrand; Dr. C.-E. A. Winslow, letter of Irving Winslow; Mr. Oswald G. Villard, personal letters and memoranda; Dr. Randolph West, letter and memorandum of Andrew F. West; Mr. Lawrence C. Woods, Jr., letter of Lawrence C. Woods; Yale University Library, letters of Edward M. House.

MANUSCRIPTS

In the Library of Congress:
  Jane Addams Papers.
  Ray Stannard Baker Papers.
  William Jennings Bryan Papers.
  Albert S. Burleson Papers.
  Richard Olney Papers.
  Theodore Roosevelt Papers.
  William Howard Taft Papers.
  Daniel Augustus Tompkins Papers.
  Henry Watterson Papers.
  Woodrow Wilson Papers.
In the Library of Duke University:
  William Garrot Brown Papers.
In the Library of Harvard University:
  Walter H. Page Papers.
In the Library of Princeton University:
  Joline, John F., Jr. "A Footnote to the Campaign of 1912. The 'Joline Letter.'"
  West, Andrew F. "A Narrative of the Graduate College of Princeton University From Its Proposal in 1896 Until Its Dedication in 1913."
  Gilbert Close File of Wilson Speeches.
  Wilson Farrand Papers.

Moses Taylor Pyne Papers.
Edward W. Sheldon Papers.
Woodrow Wilson-Robert Bridges Correspondence.
Woodrow Wilson-J. Maxwell Gordon Correspondence.
Woodrow Wilson-Henry S. McClure Correspondence.
In the Library of the University of North Carolina:
Daniel Augustus Tompkins Papers.
Thomas E. Watson Papers.
In the Library of the University of Virginia:
Richard Heath Dabney Papers.
In the Library of Yale University:
Edward M. House Papers.
In the possession of Oswald Garrison Villard, New York City:
Oswald Garrison Villard Papers.

PUBLIC DOCUMENTS

Publications of the United States Government.
Congressional Record. Fifty-Third Congress, Second Session, through Sixty-Second Congress, First Session, xxvi-xlvii. Washington, 1894-1911.
United States Senate. *Campaign Contributions. Testimony before a Subcommittee of the Committee on Privileges and Elections. United States Senate, Sixty-Second Congress, Third Session,* 2 v. Washington, 1913.
Publications of the State of New Jersey.
Journal of the Sixty-Seventh Senate of the State of New Jersey. Trenton, 1911.
Journal of the Sixty-Eighth Senate of the State of New Jersey. Trenton, 1912.
Laws of New Jersey, 1893, 1896, 1903-1911.
Minutes of Votes and Proceedings of the One Hundred and Thirty-Fifth General Assembly of the State of New Jersey. Trenton, 1911.
Minutes of Votes and Proceedings of the One Hundred and Thirty-Sixth General Assembly of the State of New Jersey. Trenton, 1912.

CORRESPONDENCE AND COLLECTED WORKS

Baker, Ray Stannard. *Woodrow Wilson, Life and Letters,* 8 v. Garden City: Doubleday, Page, 1927-1939.
Elderkin, John, et al. (eds.). *After Dinner Speeches at the Lotos Club.* New York: Printed for the Lotos Club, 1911.

Nevins, Allan (ed.). *The Letters and Journal of Brand Whitlock,* 2 v. New York and London: D. Appleton-Century, 1936.

Seymour, Charles (ed.). *The Intimate Papers of Colonel House,* 4 v. Boston and New York: Houghton, Mifflin, 1926-1928.

Winter, Ella and Granville Hicks (eds.). *The Letters of Lincoln Steffens,* 2 v. New York: Harcourt, Brace, 1938.

AUTOBIOGRAPHIES AND MEMOIRS

Bryan, Mary Baird (ed.). *The Memoirs of William Jennings Bryan.* Philadelphia and Chicago: John C. Winston, 1925.

Clark, Champ. *My Quarter Century of American Politics.* New York and London: Harper and Bros., 1920.

Daniels, Josephus. *The Wilson Era. Years of Peace.* Chapel Hill: University of North Carolina Press, 1944.

Elliott, Margaret Axson. *My Aunt Louisa and Woodrow Wilson.* Chapel Hill: University of North Carolina Press, 1944.

Gompers, Samuel. *Seventy Years of Life and Labor,* 2 v. New York: Dutton, 1925.

Harrison, Carter H., II. *Stormy Years, The Autobiography of Carter H. Harrison, Five Times Mayor of Chicago.* Indianapolis: Bobbs-Merrill, 1935.

Houston, David F. *Eight Years with Wilson's Cabinet, 1913 to 1920.* Garden City: Doubleday, Page, 1926.

Howe, Frederick C. *The Confessions of a Reformer.* New York: Charles Scribner's Sons, 1925.

Hurley, Edward N. *The Bridge to France.* Philadelphia and London: Lippincott, 1927.

Lyons, Maurice F. *William F. McCombs, The President Maker.* Cincinnati: Bancroft Co., 1922.

McAdoo, Eleanor R. W. *The Woodrow Wilsons.* New York: Macmillan, 1937.

McAdoo, William G. *Crowded Years.* Boston and New York: Houghton Mifflin, 1931.

McCombs, William F. *Making Woodrow Wilson President.* New York: Fairview Publishing Co., 1921.

Mitchell, Edward P. *Memoirs of An Editor.* New York: Scribner's, 1924.

Morgenthau, Henry. *All In a Life-Time.* Garden City: Doubleday, Page, 1922.

Mullen, Arthur F. *Western Democrat.* New York: Wilfred Funk, 1940.

Scott, William B. *Some Memories of a Palaeontologist.* Princeton: Princeton University Press, 1939.

Tumulty, Joseph P. *Woodrow Wilson As I Know Him.* Garden City: Doubleday, Page, 1921.

Walters, Alexander. *My Life and Work.* New York: Revel, 1917.

Watterson, Henry. *"Marse Henry,"* 2 v. New York: George H. Doran, 1919.

Wister, Owen. *Roosevelt, the Story of a Friendship, 1880-1919.* New York: Macmillan, 1930.

CAMPAIGN AND POLITICAL LITERATURE

Bacon, Alexander S. *The Enemies of Woodrow Wilson.* New York: n. p., 1912.

Published by the Democratic National Committee, New York, 1912:

Eliot, Charles W. "Why Dr. Eliot Will Vote for Wilson and Marshall."

Rogers, Henry Wade. "Why I Shall Vote for Wilson."

Spreckels, Rudolph. "Why Republicans Should Vote for Woodrow Wilson."

Wilson, William B. "What Democrats Have Done for Labor."

"Democracy's Case in a Nutshell."

Democratic Text-Book, 1912.

"Gov. Wilson a Friend of Immigration."

"Gov. Wilson and the Farmer."

"Gov. Wilson's Labor Day Speech."

"Governor Wilson's Position toward Labor."

"High Tariff Primer."

"Scheme to Deceive Labor Exposed by Louis D. Brandeis."

"Thomas R. Marshall. Story of His Life Record as Governor."

"Twelve Reasons Why I Should Vote for Woodrow Wilson."

"What High Tariff *Sugar* Means to You, Mr. and Mrs. Consumer."

"Which Party Can Labor Trust?"

"Why Railroad Men Should Vote for Wilson."

"Wilson and Labor. 'Proof of the Pudding Is the Eating Thereof.'"

"Woman's Opportunity."

"Woodrow Wilson, Friend of the Railroad Employee."

"Woodrow Wilson Places Human Rights Above Property Rights."

"Woodrow Wilson's Promise and Performance."

"Would You Trust the Steel Trust to Regulate the Trusts?"

McCombs, William F. *Some Reasons Why Woodrow Wilson Should be the Democratic Nominee.* New York: Editorial Review Co., 1912.

Monaghan, James Charles. *Is Woodrow Wilson a Bigot?* New York: n. p., 1912.

Waldron, J. Milton and J. D. Harkless. *The Political Situation in a Nut-Shell. Some Un-Colored Truths for Colored Voters.* Washington: National Independent Political League, 1912.

Wells, Rolla. *Report of the Treasurer, Democratic National Committee. Presidential Campaign 1912.* New York: Democratic National Committee, 1913.

Woodson, Urey (ed.). *Official Report of the Proceedings of the Democratic National Convention of 1912.* Chicago: Peterson Linotyping Co., 1912.

MISCELLANEOUS CONTEMPORARY WORKS

Bacon, Charles Reade. *The People Awakened.* Garden City: Doubleday, Page, 1912.

Bridges, Robert. *Woodrow Wilson, a Personal Tribute.* New York: Privately Printed, 1924.

Bryan, William Jennings. *A Tale of Two Conventions.* New York: Funk and Wagnalls, 1912.

Hale, William Bayard. *Woodrow Wilson, the Story of His Life.* Garden City: Doubleday, Page, 1912.

House, Edward M. *Philip Dru: Administrator.* New York: B. W. Huebsch, 1912.

West, Andrew F. *The Proposed Graduate College of Princeton University.* Princeton: Printed for the University, 1903.

Legislative Manual, State of New Jersey, 1911, 1912. Trenton, 1911, 1912.

World Almanac, 1914. New York: The Press Publishing Co., 1913.

WORKS BY WOODROW WILSON

Baker, Ray Stannard, and William Edward Dodd (eds.). *The Public Papers of Woodrow Wilson,* 6 v. New York and London: Harper and Bros., 1925-1927.

Congressional Government. Boston: Houghton, Mifflin, 1885, 1900.

Constitutional Government in the United States. New York: Columbia University Press, 1908.

Division and Reunion. New York and London: Longmans, Green, 1893.

George Washington. New York and London: Harper and Bros., 1896.

A History of the American People, 5 v. New York and London: Harper and Bros., 1902.

Mere Literature, and Other Essays. Boston and New York: Houghton, Mifflin, 1896.

An Old Master, and Other Political Essays. New York: Charles Scribner's Sons, 1893.

Robert E. Lee: an Interpretation. Chapel Hill: University of North Carolina Press, 1924.

The State. Boston: D. C. Heath, 1889.

"Cabinet Government in the United States," *International Review,* VII (August, 1879), 146-163.

"Civic Problems," published in *Civic League Annual Report, 1909.* St. Louis, 1909.

"Committee or Cabinet Government?" *Overland Monthly,* III (January 1884), 17-33.

"Democracy and Efficiency," *Atlantic Monthly,* LXXXVII (March 1901), 289-299.

"Hide and Seek Politics," *North American Review,* CXCI (May 1910), 585-601.

"The Ideals of America," *Atlantic Monthly,* XC (December 1902), 721-734.

"Leaderless Government," published in *Report of the Ninth Annual Meeting of the Virginia State Bar Association.* Richmond, 1897.

"The Making of the Nation," *Atlantic Monthly,* LXXX (July 1897), 1-14.

"Mr. Cleveland as President," *Atlantic Monthly,* LXXIX (March 1897), 289-300.

"Prince Bismarck," *Nassau Literary Magazine,* XXXIII (November 1877), 118-127.

"The Reconstruction of the Southern States," *Atlantic Monthly,* LXXXVII (January 1901), 1-15.

Review of James Bryce's *The American Commonwealth,* in *Political Science Quarterly,* IV (March 1889), 153-169.

"The Study of Administration," *Political Science Quarterly,* II (June 1887), 197-222.

"The Tariff Make-Believe," *North American Review,* CXC (October 1909), 535-556.

"University Training and Citizenship," *The Forum,* XVIII (September 1894), 107-116.

"When a Man Comes to Himself," *Century Magazine,* LXII (June 1901), 268-273.

"William Earl Chatham," *Nassau Literary Magazine,* xxxiv (October
1878), 99-105.

NEWSPAPERS CITED

Atlanta Constitution, 1902, 1912.
Atlanta Georgian, 1911-1912.
Atlanta Journal, 1911-1912.
Augusta (Ga.) *Chronicle,* 1902, 1912.
Baltimore American, 1902.
Baltimore Sun, 1910-1912.
Birmingham Age-Herald, 1910-1912.
Boston Evening Transcript, 1912.
Boston Globe, 1912.
Boston Herald, 1902.
Boston Post, 1912.
Brooklyn Daily Eagle, 1912.
Brooklyn Times, 1910.
Charleston (S. C.) *News and Courier,* 1911-1912.
Charlotte (N. C.) *Daily Observer,* 1902, 1912.
Chattanooga Daily Times, 1910-1912.
Chicago Daily News, 1912.
Chicago Daily Tribune, 1910, 1912.
Chicago Evening Post, 1911.
Chicago Examiner, 1911.
Cincinnati Enquirer, 1912.
Cleveland Plain Dealer, 1912.
Columbia (S. C.) *State,* 1910-1912.
Dallas Morning News, 1911-1912.
Denver Rocky Mountain News, 1911-1912.
Des Moines Register and Leader, 1912.
Detroit Free Press, 1911-1912.
Galveston Daily News, 1912.
Garland (Tex.) *News,* 1901.
Harrisburg (Penna.) *Patriot,* 1911.
Hoboken Hudson Observer, 1910.
Houston Post, 1911-1912.
Indianapolis News, 1910, 1912.
Jacksonville Florida Times-Union, 1911-1912.
Jersey City Jersey Journal, 1910-1912.
Kansas City Journal, 1911.

Kansas City Star, 1911-1912.
Lincoln Nebraska State Journal, 1911-1912.
Little Rock Arkansas Democrat, 1912.
London Daily Express, 1912.
Louisville Courier-Journal, 1910-1912.
Louisville Times, 1912.
Los Angeles Times, 1911.
Madison (Wisc.) *Democrat*, 1911-1912.
Madison Wisconsin State Journal, 1912.
Memphis Commercial Appeal, 1912.
Minneapolis Evening Tribune, 1911.
Minneapolis Journal, 1911.
Mobile Register, 1912.
Montgomery Advertiser, 1912.
Muskogee (Okla.) *Daily Phoenix*, 1912.
Nashville American, 1902.
Nashville Banner, 1911-1912.
Nashville Tennessean and American, 1911-1912.
Natchez Daily Democrat, 1911.
Newark Evening News, 1902, 1910-1912.
Newark Evening Star, 1910-1912.
Newark Morning Star, 1911.
Newark Sunday Call, 1910.
New Orleans Times-Democrat, 1910, 1912.
New York Age, 1912.
New York American, 1910-1912.
New York Daily Tribune, 1902.
New York Evening Journal, 1910, 1912.
New York Evening Post, 1902, 1906, 1910, 1912.
New York Evening World, 1910-1911.
New York Globe, 1912.
New York Herald, 1912.
New York Mail and Express, 1902.
New York Sun, 1904, 1910-1912.
New York Times, 1902, 1907, 1910-1912, 1921.
New York World, 1904, 1908, 1910-1912.
Norfolk Virginian-Pilot, 1910-1912.
Oklahoma City Daily Oklahoman, 1910, 1912.
Omaha World-Herald, 1911-1912.
Pasadena (Cal.) *Star*, 1911.

Passaic (N. J.) *Daily News,* 1910-1911.
Pensacola Evening News, 1912.
Pensacola Journal, 1912.
Philadelphia North American, 1910, 1912.
Philadelphia Public Ledger, 1912.
Philadelphia Record, 1912.
Pittsburgh Dispatch, 1910.
Pittsburgh Post, 1912.
Portland Evening Telegram, 1911.
Portland Oregon Daily Journal, 1911.
Raleigh News and Observer, 1911-1912.
Richmond News Leader, 1912.
Richmond Times-Dispatch, 1902, 1910-1912.
Richmond Virginian, 1911.
Roanoke (Va.) *Times,* 1912.
Sacramento Bee, 1911.
St. Louis Globe-Democrat, 1912.
St. Louis Republic, 1910-1912.
St. Paul Dispatch, 1911.
St. Paul Pioneer Press, 1911.
San Antonio Express, 1912.
San Francisco Bulletin, 1911.
San Francisco Chronicle, 1911.
Seattle Times, 1911.
Sioux City (Ia.) *Journal,* 1912.
Springfield (Mass.) *Republican,* 1912.
Staunton News-Dispatch, 1912.
Topeka State Journal, 1912.
Trenton Evening Times, 1910-1912.
Trenton State Gazette, 1910.
Trenton True American, 1909-1912.
Washington Post, 1912.
Waterbury (Conn.) *American,* 1900.
Wilmington (Del.) *Every Evening,* 1912.
Wilmington (N. C.) *Messenger,* 1902.
Wilmington (N. C.) *Morning Star,* 1911-1912.

PERIODICALS CITED FOR EDITORIAL OPINION

American Federationist, 1912.
Christian Advocate (Nashville, Tenn.), 1912.

Collier's Weekly, 1911-1912.
The Commoner (Lincoln, Neb.), 1910-1912.
Crisis, 1912.
Harper's Weekly, 1906, 1909-1910.
Independent, 1910.
The Jeffersonian (Thomson, Ga.), 1912.
La Follette's Weekly Magazine (Madison, Wisc.), 1911-1912.
The Nation, 1873, 1878, 1879, 1882, 1885, 1887, 1910-1912.
Outlook, 1910-1912.
Presbyterian of the South (Richmond, Va.), 1911.
Presbyterian Standard (Charlotte, N. C.), 1911-1912.
Review of Reviews, 1910.
World's Work, 1912.

CONTEMPORARY ARTICLES

Baker, Ray Stannard, "Our Next President and Some Others," *American Magazine*, LXXIV (June 1912), 131-143.

Baker, R. S., "Wilson," *Collier's Weekly*, LVIII (October 1916), 6.

Barton, George, "Woodrow Wilson: His Human Side," *Current History*, XXII (April 1925), 6.

Bradford, Gamaliel, "The Progress of Civil Service Reform," *International Review*, III (September 1882), 266-267.

Brandeis, Louis D., "Labor and the New Party Trust Program," *La Follette's Weekly Magazine*, IV (October 12, 1912), 5-8.

Brandeis, L. D., "Trusts, the Export Trade, and the New Party," *Collier's Weekly*, L (September 21, 1912), 10-11.

Brandeis, L. D., "Trusts, Efficiency, and the New Party," *Collier's Weekly*, XLIX (September 14, 1912), 14-15.

Daniels, Josephus, "Wilson and Bryan," *Saturday Evening Post*, CXCVIII (September 5, 1925), 6-7.

Daniels, Winthrop More, "Woodrow Wilson: An Appraisal," *Independent*, LXXIII (November 14, 1912), 1111-1114.

Ewing, Robert, "To the Citizens of Tennessee," *Nashville Banner*, January 19, 1912.

Ford, Henry Jones, "Woodrow Wilson,—A Character Sketch," *Review of Reviews*, XLVI (August 1912), 177-184.

Gompers, Samuel, "The Presidency in the Pending Campaign," *American Federationist*, XIX (November 1912), 889-894.

Graves, John Temple, "Speaker Champ Clark," *Independent*, LXXI (November 2, 1911), 959-963.

Hazeltine, Mayo W., "Whom Will the Democrats Next Nominate for President?" *North American Review,* cxcii (April 1906), 481-491.

Hendrick, Burton J., "Judson Harmon, Progressive Candidate," *McClure's Magazine,* xxxviii (April 1912), 619-624.

Hendrick, B. J., "Woodrow Wilson: Political Leader," *McClure's Magazine,* xxxviii (December 1911), 217-231.

Inglis, William O., "Helping to Make a President," *Collier's Weekly,* lviii (October 7, 14, and 21, 1916).

Kerney, James, "Woodrow Wilson, Governor," *Independent,* lxx (May 11, 1911), 986-989.

La Follette, Robert M., "A Call to Service," *La Follette's Weekly Magazine,* iv (July 27, 1912), 3-4.

Lathrop, John E., "The Views of Champ Clark," *Outlook,* ci (May 11, 1912), 65-73.

Lewis, Alfred Henry, "The Real Woodrow Wilson," *Hearst's Magazine,* xxi (May 1912), 2265-2274.

Link, Arthur S. (ed.), "Correspondence Relating to the Progressive Party's 'Lily White' Policy in 1912," *Journal of Southern History,* x (November 1944), 480-490.

Link, A. S., "A Letter from One of Wilson's Managers," *American Historical Review,* l (July 1945), 768-775.

Mack, Norman E., "Wilson and Marshall—Mr. Bryan and New York," *National Monthly,* iv (August 1912), 65.

Malone, Dudley F., "Woodrow Wilson—The Man," *National Monthly,* iv (September 1912), 91.

Needham, Henry Beach, "Woodrow Wilson's Views," *Outlook,* xcviii (August 26, 1911), 939-951.

Praeger, Otto, "How Winning Fight for Wilson Was Made," *Dallas Morning News,* July 3, 1912.

Roosevelt, Theodore, "The Minimum Wage," *Outlook,* cii (September 28, 1912), 159-160.

Roosevelt, T., "Platform Insincerity," *Outlook,* ci (July 27, 1912), 659-663.

Roosevelt, T., "The Taft-Wilson Trust Programme," *Outlook,* cii (September 21, 1912), 105-107.

Steffens, Lincoln, "A Servant of God and the People. The Story of Mark Fagan, Mayor of Jersey City," *McClure's Magazine,* xxvi (January 1906), 297-308.

Steffens, L., "The Gentleman from Essex," *McClure's Magazine,* xxvi (February 1906), 421-433.

Stockbridge, Frank Parker, "Champ Clark, of Pike County," *World's Work,* xxiv (May 1912), 27-36.

Stockbridge, F. P., "How Woodrow Wilson Won His Nomination," *Current History,* xx (July 1924).

Thomas, Norman, "Mr. Wilson's Tragedy and Ours," *The World Tomorrow,* March 1921.

UNSIGNED ARTICLES

"Concentration," *Collier's Weekly,* L (October 5, 1912), 8. By Louis D. Brandeis.

"The Farmer Orator," *Saturday Evening Post,* CLXXXIII (April 8, 1911), 27.

"Labor and the Trusts," *Collier's Weekly,* XLIX (September 14, 1912), 8. By L. D. Brandeis.

"The Method," *Collier's Weekly,* L (October 19, 1912), 8. By L. D. Brandeis.

"Monopoly," *Collier's Weekly,* XLIX (September 7, 1912), 8. By L. D. Brandeis.

"Republican Progressives for Wilson," *National Monthly,* IV (November 1912), 138.

"The Wastes of Monopoly," *Collier's Weekly,* L (September 21, 1912), 8. By L. D. Brandeis.

"Woodrow Wilson and the New Jersey Governorship," *Review of Reviews,* XLII (November 1910), 555-562.

SECONDARY WORKS

Bagehot, Walter. *The English Constitution.* Boston: Little, Brown, 1873.

Barnes, Harry Elmer. *The Genesis of the World War.* New York: Knopf, 1926.

Carlson, Oliver, and Ernest Sutherland Bates. *Hearst, Lord of San Simeon.* New York: Viking Press, 1936.

Diamond, William. *The Economic Thought of Woodrow Wilson.* Baltimore: Johns Hopkins University Press, 1943.

Eaton, Allen H. *The Oregon System.* Chicago: A. C. McClurg, 1912.

Hacker, Louis M., and Benjamin B. Kendrick. *The United States Since 1865.* New York: F. S. Crofts, 1940.

Hendrick, Burton J. *The Life and Letters of Walter H. Page,* 3 v. Garden City: Doubleday, Page, 1922-1925.

Hendrick, B. J. *The Training of an American. The Earlier Life and*

Letters of Walter H. Page, 1855-1913. Boston and New York: Houghton Mifflin, 1928.

Hollingsworth, William W. *Woodrow Wilson's Ideals as Interpreted from His Works.* Princeton: Princeton University Press, 1918.

Hutchinson, William T. (ed.). *The Marcus W. Jernegan Essays in American Historiography.* Chicago: University of Chicago Press, 1937.

Johnson, Gerald. *Woodrow Wilson.* New York and London: Harpers, 1944.

Johnson, Willis Fletcher. *George Harvey, "A Passionate Patriot,"* Boston and New York: Houghton Mifflin, 1929.

Josephson, Matthew. *The President Makers.* New York: Harcourt, Brace, 1940.

Kerney, James. *The Political Education of Woodrow Wilson.* New York and London: The Century Co., 1926.

Kraus, Michael. *A History of American History.* New York: Farrar and Rinehart, 1937.

Kull, Irving Stoddard (ed.). *New Jersey, a History,* 6 v. New York: American Historical Society, 1930-1932.

Lawrence, David. *The True Story of Woodrow Wilson.* New York: George H. Doran, 1924.

Lief, Alfred. *Democracy's Norris.* New York: Stackpole Sons, 1939.

Lundburg, Ferdinand. *Imperial Hearst, a Social Biography.* New York: Equinox Cooperative Press, 1936.

Morison, Samuel E., and Henry S. Commager. *The Growth of the American Republic,* 2 v. New York: Oxford, 1937.

Mowry, George E. *Theodore Roosevelt and the Progressive Movement.* Madison: University of Wisconsin Press, 1946.

Nichols, Jeanette P. *Twentieth Century United States.* New York: D. Appleton-Century, 1943.

Noble, Ransome E., Jr. *New Jersey Progressivism before Wilson.* Princeton: Princeton University Press, 1946.

Notter, Harley. *The Origins of the Foreign Policy of Woodrow Wilson.* Baltimore: Johns Hopkins University Press, 1937.

O'Brien, Frank M. *The Story of the Sun.* New York and London: D. Appleton and Co., 1928.

Pringle, Henry F. *The Life and Times of William Howard Taft.* New York and Toronto: Farrar and Rinehart, 1939.

Sackett, William E. *Modern Battles of Trenton,* 2 v. Trenton: J. L. Murphy, 1914.

Smith, Arthur D. H., *Mr. House of Texas.* New York and London: Funk and Wagnalls, 1940.

Synon, Mary. *McAdoo.* Indianapolis: Bobbs-Merrill, 1924.

Wallas, Graham. *The Life of Francis Place.* London: George Allen and Unwin, 1918.

Waltersdorf, M. C. *Regulation of Public Utilities in New Jersey.* Baltimore: Waverly Press, 1936.

Werner, Morris R. *Bryan.* New York: Harcourt, Brace, 1929.

White, William Allen. *Woodrow Wilson.* Boston and New York: Houghton Mifflin, 1924.

Woodward, C. Vann. *Tom Watson: Agrarian Rebel.* New York: Macmillan, 1938.

SECONDARY ARTICLES

Baker, Paul, "Woodrow Wilson's Political Philosophy," *Texas Christian University Quarterly,* i (January 1925), 2-39.

Bradford, Gamaliel, "Brains Win and Lose. Woodrow Wilson," *Atlantic Monthly,* cxlvii (February 1931), 152-164.

Daniel, Marjorie L., "Woodrow Wilson—Historian," *Mississippi Valley Historical Review,* xxi (December 1934), 361-374.

Dodd, William Edward, "The Social and Economic Background of Woodrow Wilson," *Journal of Political Economy,* xxv (March 1917).

Link, A. S., "The Baltimore Convention of 1912," *American Historical Review,* l (July 1945), 691-713.

Link, A. S., "The Democratic Pre-Convention Campaign of 1912 in Georgia," *Georgia Historical Quarterly,* xxix (September 1945), 143-158.

Link, A. S., "The Negro as a Factor in the Campaign of 1912," *Journal of Negro History,* January, 1947.

Link, A. S., "The Progressive Movement in the South, 1870-1914," *North Carolina Historical Review,* xxiii (April 1946), 172-195.

Link, A. S., "Tennessee Politics and the Presidential Campaign of 1912," *East Tennessee Historical Society's Proceedings,* 1946.

Link, A. S., "Theodore Roosevelt and the South in 1912," *North Carolina Historical Review,* xxiii (July 1946), 313-324.

Link, A. S., "The Underwood Presidential Movement of 1912," *Journal of Southern History,* xi (May 1945), 230-245.

Link, A. S., "The Wilson Movement in Texas, 1910-1912," *Southwestern Historical Quarterly,* xlviii (October 1944), 169-185.

fore 1909, 263; revision of laws governing relationship between employer and employee, 263; appointment of commission to study problem, 263; introduction of bill, 263; passage and provisions of, 263-264.

Works, John D., 479.

World Peace Foundation, 478.

World To-Day, the, a Hearst anti-Wilson journal, x.

World's Work, an early journalistic supporter of Wilson presidential movement, x; Wilson edition of, 318.

Wyeth, John A., 110-111.

Wyman, Isaac C., 88.

Yoakum, Benjamin F., 187, n. 37.

Young, George H., 187, n. 37; 425-426.